THE
HOMOSEXUAL
NETWORK

THE

HOMOSEXUAL

NETWORK

PRIVATE LIVES AND

PUBLIC POLICY

ENRIQUE RUEDA

The Free Congress Research & Education Foundation

THE DEVIN ADAIR COMPANY

OLD GREENWICH, CONNECTICUT

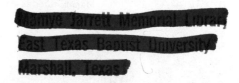

Copyright © 1982 by the Free Congress Research
and Education Foundation, Inc.
721 Second Street, N.E.
Washington, D.C. 20002

Permission to quote from this volume must be obtained in writing from the Free Congress Research and Education Foundation, Inc., and from the publisher, The Devin Adair Company,
Old Greenwich, Connecticut 06870.

Library of Congress Cataloging in Publication Data

Rueda, Enrique, 1939–
The homosexual network.

Includes bibliographical references and index.
1. Gay liberation movement—United States.
I. Title.
HQ76.8.U5R83   1983   306.7′66′0973   82–71936
ISBN 0–8159–5714–9
ISBN 0–8159–5715–7 (pbk.)
Second Printing, 1983

Manufactured in the United States of America

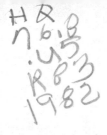

The Devin Adair Company
143 Sound Beach Ave.
P.O. Box A
Old Greenwich, Connecticut 06870

EXCELLENCE SINCE 1911

131868

The Free Congress Research and Education Foundation is a tax-exempt research organization engaged in a variety of educational projects in two separate areas of concentration. The Political Division of the foundation analyzes U.S. House and Senate elections and studies current political trends which are of national significance.

Its two regular publications are the *Political Report,* a weekly newsletter, and the *Initiative and Referendum Report,* a monthly. The *Political Report* gives completely original, up-to-date information about key congressional elections. The *Initiative and Referendum Report* analyzes important local and state ballot measures. It provides readers with hard to obtain information about citizen-initiated measures and places them in the context of their national significance.

The foundation's second major area of concentration focuses on trends affecting the stability and well-being of American family life. At a time when abortion, homosexual rights, euthanasia, and children's liberation are under active discussion in the news media, the Family Policy Division seeks to give balance to the debate by presenting traditional alternatives.

The Family Policy Division publishes a monthly newsletter, the *Family Protection Report,* which covers such topics as: adoption laws, education, sex education, judicial nominations, domestic violence, abortion, homosexuality, and *in vitro* fertilization, among others. It covers legislation of importance to the family at the state and national levels.

Besides the regular publications, both divisions of the foundation sponsor conferences, conduct survey research, and publish monographs and shorter studies.

ABOUT THE AUTHOR

The Reverend Enrique Rueda is Director of the Catholic Center at the Free Congress Research and Education Foundation, where he holds a research fellowship. A native of Cuba, he was imprisoned by the Communists during the Bay of Pigs invasion. Father Rueda has done extensive research and writing on Latin America in general and the current situation in Central America in particular. His several degrees include a Master of Arts in Political Science from Fordham University and advanced degrees in Divinity and Theology from St. Joseph's Seminary. He has served as a chaplain to migrant workers and college students, directed a drug abuse education center, and done pastoral work in the South Bronx, New York. Father Rueda's previous publications include numerous monographs and a book-length work on drug abuse education. He writes a weekly column of analysis on public policy issues.

CONTENTS

Contents

Contents

Contents

Contents

INTRODUCTION

In April 1981, Paul Weyrich, President of the Free Congress Research and Education Foundation, came to my desk and asked me to research the social and political impact of the homosexual movement in America and to write a monograph about the subject. Being an avid newspaper reader, I was aware of the movement, and as a priest, I had had the opportunity of helping homosexuals with their spiritual and psychological problems. However, I was neither very interested nor enthusiastic at the prospect of dedicating any substantial amount of time to such a subject.

Over the next three weeks, though, I read all I could and visited the local homosexual bookstore, where I acquired several homosexual newspapers and magazines. This served to increase my awareness of the importance of the homosexual movement and the extent to which it has infiltrated many national institutions, becoming an integral part of the liberal establishment that dominated American social and political life for the past few decades. At this point, I realized that a monograph would not be adequate to the scope of these issues. Thus I have invested most of this past year researching the homosexual movement. I have visited a number of homosexual organizations and have gathered thousands of pages of documentation on the social and political activities of homosexual leaders and their allies. The result of these efforts, with the help of my colleagues, is this book.

A few words of explanation will help place its contents in their proper context. This is not a book about the ethics or psychology of homosexuality or homosexual behavior. Only to the extent that religious, philosophical, or psychological considerations have a bearing on the sociopolitical process have they been included. No judgment, then, is made on the correctness of the various positions advanced by theologians, philosophers, or psychologists. If the reader is seeking enlightenment on the value of homosexual behavior, he will not find it here. This is not a work about the way things *ought to be,* but about the way things *are.* As a Bible-believing Christian steeped in the traditions of the Roman Catholic Church, I believe that homosexuality is a manifestation of the sinful condition that affects mankind and each man, and that homosexual behavior is gravely sinful by the very nature of reality. This same commitment, however, leads me to accept homosexuals completely as human beings and as children of God. Homosexuals are entitled to our love and concern. They are loved by God as much as anyone else. This I believe while affirming the evil nature of their sexual condition and while fully committed to the proposition that homosexuals should not be entitled to special treatment under the law. That would be tantamount to rewarding evil. Personally, of course, I do not advocate the persecution of homosexuals or their condemnation on account of their condition. In this book, however, I do not advocate anything. Rather I have endeavored to be objective and to abstain from proposing solutions to the problems described. In selecting materials and areas for study, all researchers must proceed inevitably from a frame of reference, which may appear as biased to others. I have no reason to believe that in my case it is any different. This I freely acknowledge. I do not believe, however, that this is a negative feature but one which, if exploited with honesty, will stimulate further analysis. No inquiry is possible without a viewpoint from which to start and a heuristic structure to guide the process. This must also be freely accepted, lest the debate degenerate into a shouting match wherein there is much noise while egos are exalted and smashed, but where little light is found. The reader is invited to examine this work in this spirit.

I have written not about individual homosexuals or their practices, but about the homosexual movement. This is an important distinction. As soon as it became known that I was studying the subject, I was approached by many with "horror stories" about the alleged homosexual behavior of prominent individuals, in many cases apparently a matter of common knowledge. I firmly rejected any suggestions that such material be included in this book. If in any case an individual is identified as a homosexual in this book, this is because he has publicly identified himself as such, usually in a homosexual publication, and his sexual preferences were judged important to illustrate a point. Although many participants in the homosexual movement are themselves homosexuals, this is not necessarily the case. The reader should not conclude that an individual mentioned in connection with a homosexual organization is a homosexual. As a matter of fact, it is not very important whether such an individual is or is not a homosexual, except to the extent that his affiliation indicates the degree to which the homosexual ideology has become accepted in America. A concept that must be clarified is that of "prohomosexual." By this I do not mean that the individual, theory, legislation, institution, etc. to which it is applied explicitly favors or promotes the practice of homosexuality. "Prohomosexual" in the context of this work means promoting conditions that favor the practice of homosexuality, or a principle of the homosexual ideology, as proposed by various homosexual sources. This is a crucial distinction which is rooted in the sociopolitical nature of the homosexual movement and its goal of creating a society in which the practice of homosexuality is widely accepted. The term is used in keeping with the broad perspective of my research.

The approach I used in structuring this book is inductive. The opening chapter examines the degree to which homosexuality and its attendant behavior have been accepted in contemporary American society. Although some examples are given which indicate that American elites have

Introduction

begun to consider homosexual behavior as acceptable, the ultimate conclusion of this analysis is that the vast majority of Americans reject homosexuality as normative, morally acceptable, or worthy of protection by
custom or legislation. Like other groups which have established a basis
for self-identity, certain homosexuals in the United States have developed
peculiar ways and institutions. By their nature, they constitute a subculture with defined boundaries, at both the individual and collective
levels. The various institutions and identifying characteristics of the homosexual subculture are examined next, with emphasis on two important
aspects of the homosexual subculture. First, the effects of the homosexual
lifestyle on the physical wellbeing of active homosexuals and the relevance
of this phenomenon to the rest of society are analyzed. This is followed
by a presentation of various aspects of the language of the homosexual
movement and the value of this language for the movement. All political
movements require an ideological infrastructure that provides a rationale
for its members. This is also true of religious and social movements. The
homosexual movement is no exception; as a movement rather than a
cohesive party, it does not possess a universally accepted standard for
validating its ideology.

The ideology presented in chapter III is the result of analyzing a number
of writings of movement leaders, as well as the homosexual press. It should
be read as a tentative formulation, subject to revisions. Some of the
statements offered in this synthesis could perhaps be expressed in more
felicitous propositions. This is the inevitable result of the nonexistence
of generally accepted theoretical foundations for the homosexual movement's ideology. The core concept of this chapter is the notion that the
various statements by which the homosexual movement justifies its actions
and program are ideological rather than objective in nature. The evidence
offered in this regard serves to justify the assertion that the homosexual
movement is, in fact, a political movement, with all the characteristics,
advantages, and limitations that political movements offer their constituencies. Like all political movements, the homosexual movement possesses a structure through which it carries out its activities and attempts
to implement its program.

Chapter IV presents the various components of the movement. This
presentation, however, is not exhaustive. In order to avoid repetition,
religious organizations, for example, have been excluded from this chapter. Throughout the work, other components of the movement are also
examined. Chapter V outlines the program or objectives of the homosexual
movement. Once again, the broad basis of the movement and its lack of
over-all coordination limit its ability to develop a consistent program. In
many instances, homosexual organizations are single-issue groups (e.g.,
organizations which promote intergenerational sexuality). I have attempted to synthesize the goals and objectives of the movement. The

categories into which the various goals have been organized could perhaps have been different from the ones employed here. I believe, however, that the framework used is fair to the objectives themselves.

At this point, I could have stopped writing; chapters I through V are a logical whole. It seemed to me, however, that there were other aspects of the homosexual movement that could not be ignored. In order to carry out its activities, the movement needs supporters and financial backing. Among the supporters of the homosexual movement, I could find none more important than religious and political institutions and leaders. They not only validate the ideological claims of the homosexual movement, but also provide much of the financial support the movement requires. Chapters VI and VII are devoted to examining the relationships between religion and the homosexual movement. While the former portrays the manner in which various religious traditions have dealt with homosexuality, the latter shows how specific religious organizations have related to the homosexual movement and the manner in which the homosexual movement has used various religious institutions for its own political advantage. Originally I intended to examine a large number of religious bodies, but the amount of data collected was so large that it became obvious that I would have to limit myself to one or two case studies. For reasons which I explain in the body of the work, I selected the Roman Catholic Church and the Jewish community for this purpose. The reader should not conclude that they were chosen because they represent extremes in the various possibilities for infiltration of a religious body by the homosexual movement. As a matter of fact, neither one is a case of extreme infiltration, as I point out. As a Catholic, it was not easy to publicize information about my Church which is not only embarrassing but could open the Church to attack. I finally judged that my total commitment to the Catholic Church would not only increase the credibility of my findings, but would also preclude any interpretation that anti-Catholic feelings motivated their publication. My commitment to truth, my belief that knowledge of truth—although sometimes painful—usually works for the ultimate good of all concerned, and my hope that this knowledge will serve to remedy any deficiencies within the Church, eventually compelled me to make these findings public. All that I have reported is either readily available information, or was obtained in institutions that operate with the pretense that they are Catholic, presumably with the knowledge of Church authorities. I hope that animosity against Catholicism will not lead some to use this information against the Church. They are reminded here of the Lord's injunction concerning the speck in one's neighbor's eye and the plank in one's own (Mt 7 : 3–5) and St. Paul's advice to those of us who yield to the temptation of being judgmental (Rom 2 : 1).

Chapter VIII shows the close connections between American liberalism

Introduction

and the homosexual movement. The conclusion that the homosexual movement is a subset of the spectrum of American liberal movements is inescapable. Chapter IX is an analysis of the various funding sources of the homosexual movement. This chapter culminates the book in a dual sense. Because of the effectiveness of the homosexual organizations in creating a subculture which has become acceptable to important segments of American society (religious bodies, political institutions and actors, and other significant elements) funds have been made available to them. These funds, and the legitimacy they imply, have generated activities which, by implementing the goals of the movement, result in a further acceptance of the various principles of the homosexual ideology. The funding of the homosexual movement is the ultimate evidence that this movement is not only alive, but quite effective as well.

In conducting this study, I have relied mainly on sources within the homosexual movement itself. An examination of the footnotes at the end of each chapter clearly indicates that I have based most of my conclusions on the evidence provided by the homosexual movement in its own publications. Valuable information was also obtained in a survey conducted during the summer months of 1981. A universe of 394 nonprofit homosexual organizations was assembled from a variety of sources: the *Gayellow Pages*, *The Advocate* (a national homosexual newspaper), and the representative homosexual papers in New York, San Francisco, and Washington, D.C. A random sample of 125 organizations was drawn and telephone interviews were conducted which yielded 80 valid questionnaires. The interview protocol was designed to ensure that interviewees would be as truthful as possible by not disclosing any possible bias concerning the subject of homosexuality on the part of the interviewer. The interviewer did not indicate that the purpose of the study was to ascertain the characteristics of homosexual organizations or that only homosexual organizations were being contacted. The questions asked covered numerous other subjects. Only officials of the organizations contacted were accepted as interviewees.

A final word of caution is due at this point. Some of the material in this work will probably be offensive to some persons, for which I apologize. If we are to understand the true nature of the homosexual movement, however, we must look at it as it is. I assure the reader that all quotations herein are from materials received through the mail upon simple request, purchased in public establishments, or made available to me at public institutions. For those who object to some of this material, I must point out that killing the bearer of bad news was of no help to the king.

I am grateful to those who helped me complete this work. First of all to Paul Weyrich, who constantly encouraged me to seek information in complete freedom and to come to my own conclusions. To Connie Marshner, for reviewing the manuscript and making many valuable suggestions. To Julie Hajjar, who acted as an interviewer for the survey and, to Brenda Davis, a Christendom College intern who helped me collect valuable data. To the many on the staff of the Free Congress Research and Education Foundation who provided much-appreciated advice. The statistical part of my study could not have been possible without the help of Fernando Troncoso and especially Maria Carbonell, who sat with me for hours painstakingly revising my conclusions. To many individuals and organizations who made it their business to provide me with data I could not have collected on my own. I am especially grateful to sources within the Roman Catholic Church and to JLS and JAB of New York City who provided data and documents otherwise unavailable. Eric Licht, who managed the production of this book for the Foundation, was particularly patient with me. A special word of gratitude must go to Susan Arico, who typed a voluminous manuscript written in almost illegible script. She was not only an excellent typist, but a good editor as well. While they all helped, and I am grateful to them, I must confess that all errors are mine.

ENRIQUE T. RUEDA

April 1982

THE
HOMOSEXUAL
NETWORK

CHAPTER

I

Acceptability of Homosexuality in the United States

One of the most striking phenomena of the past few years is what appears to be a massive increase in the acceptability of homosexual behavior in America. Parallel to, although slightly behind, the civil rights movement and militant feminism, the homosexual movement has tried to make a claim, frequently successful, to 1) the acceptance of homosexuality as a normal expression of human sexuality, and 2) the full participation in the homosexual subculture as a legitimate lifestyle.

America's traditional religious beliefs have always condemned the practice of homosexuality, and social convention has systematically reduced even the mention of the subject to a minimum, and then in roundabout ways. When one considers the historical background in which this phenomenon has arisen, it is clear that a veritable revolution has taken place in the last thirty years. There are now thousands of "gay bars" where homosexuals congregate; most cities have "baths" where they seek relief from their sexual urges; respectable newspapers advertise homosexual establishments that feature pornographic movies; churches ordain homosexual ministers and lend their facilities to "religious" groups that promote homosexual behavior; homosexual churches as such have been established; homosexual groups have enjoyed the support of the White House, and the practice of homosexuality has been declared "normal" by the psychiatric establishment. The Bible has been reinterpreted so as to make the old condemnation "unbiblical," while in homosexual newspapers, male prostitutes freely advertise their availability.

Still, this is not sufficient for the homosexual movement. Full acceptability of homosexuality is its final goal, although this is not really expected. At best, the fundamental abandonment of the Judeo-Christian beliefs required for such acceptance will occur—in the estimation of some of their theoreticians—over a long period of time. Psychologist Charles A. Tripp has described well this state of affairs:

> Q. *Can you foresee a time when homosexuality will be fully accepted in the United States?*
> A. If you mean accepted openly and generally, certainly not. In the first place, we know from cross-cultural studies that minority sexual practices are never fully accepted. Homosexuality has been fully sanctioned only in those times and places where it has predominated. Examples of predominantly homosexual cultures are found in 64 percent of the tribes catalogued by Ford and Beach in *Patterns of Sexual Behavior* and in ancient Greece, recently shown in K. J. Dover's *Greek Homosexuality*. Our society will probably go only a small distance toward accepting homosexuality. The great middle class will gradually adopt the attitudes that now prevail at the upper social levels—a tacit acceptance of homosexuality and an embarrassment in appearing prudish about it, yet a disdain for it whenever disdain is socially useful. Even this will take time. Remember, Judeo-Christian mores are fundamentally ascetic and still don't approve even heterosexual sex without love and "responsibility."[1]

For people interested in preserving traditional American values and culture, this position is unacceptable and must be rejected. Their perception of homosexuality as a threat to the family and the very nation is bound to cause a reaction. At the same time, it is entirely possible that the present flurry of openly homosexual behavior and the prominence that the homosexual subculture currently enjoys is a social aberration, the product of the philosophical confusion of the times and the abandonment of Judeo-Christian values by our elites. The acceptance of homosexuality may be only skin-deep, and, in a few years, the present trends may be viewed as an oddity. Even if this were to be the case, however, it is necessary to examine the current situation if homosexuality is to be kept in its proper perspective. In a sense, this whole work is a study on the acceptance of homosexuality. This chapter may thus be viewed as an introduction to the homosexual movement.

Homosexuality in the Polls

Numerous polls have been conducted, purporting to show a slow but steady increase in the acceptability of homosexuality. Paul Siegel, in an

Acceptability of Homosexuality in the U.S.

openly prohomosexual article published in *Christianity and Crisis,* has indicated what appears to be a clear increase in acceptability for homosexuality.[2] He points out that as late as 1970 a Gallup poll revealed that 84% of respondents believed that homosexuality is a "social corruption that can cause the downfall of a civilization." Moreover, three-quarters were of the opinion that homosexuals should be barred from the ministry, the judiciary, and the teaching profession, while two-thirds objected to homosexuals being physicians or government workers. By 1977 56% affirmed "equal rights in terms of job opportunities," although substantial numbers still objected to homosexuals in certain key professions: 66% to homosexual teachers, 54% to homosexual clergymen, and 44% to homosexual doctors. Different and at times contradictory results have been reported by other researchers. For example:

> In a survey of public attitudes towards homosexuality, published in *Sociology and Social Research,* the authors found that only 29 percent of the sample believed homosexuality should be against the law; only 17 percent believed citizens should report suspected homosexuals to the police; only 19 percent believed the police should revoke the licenses of gay bars; and only 37 percent believed homosexuals should not be allowed to teach in school.[3]

Political events have undoubtedly influenced the results of the polls. Simply in measuring the opinions of interviewees *when they are asked,* it is questionable whether they accurately reflect the underlying sentiment of the population. Nevertheless, poll results have been used in America for political propaganda by movements and individuals of all ideological shades. This is no less true of the homosexual movement than it is of other political actors. It is thus important to understand the effects that the adoption or repeal of prohomosexual legislation have on public opinion concerning this issue. Some polls are conducted whenever such legislation is being debated merely because homosexuality at that point becomes "news." The data thus obtained are highly suspicious since, even if impeccable statistical methodology has been used, it measures public opinion under the stressful conditions of public debate.

Shortly after the 1977 vote to repeal the Dade County, Florida, prohomosexual legislation, the Gallup and Harris organizations conducted polls in this area, resulting in the following data:[4]

Gallup

Issue	Yes	No
Legalization of homosexual relations	43%	43%
Homosexuality today more prevalent than 25 years ago	68%	24%
Equal employment rights for homosexuals	56%	33%
Right for homosexuals to adopt children	14%	77%

5

THE HOMOSEXUAL NETWORK

Harris

Issue	Yes	No
Right of homosexuals to work as:		
Counselors for young people in camps	27%	63%
Policemen	48%	42%
Artists	86%	7%
Factory Workers	85%	7%
TV News Commentators	72%	19%
Congressmen	53%	37%
Equal employment opportunity for homosexuals	48%	41%

A similar poll was also conducted in 1977 by the *Minneapolis Tribune*, while prohomosexual legislation in Minnesota was pending. The following table summarizes the results of this poll.[5]

Nature of Homosexuality:			
Abnormal Condition	56%		
Alternate Lifestyle	22%		
Neither/Other	22%		

	Yes	No	Don't know
Homosexuality a sin according to the Bible	46%	24%	30%
Homosexuality a sin according to the interviewee	47%	42%	11%
Homosexuals are a threat to children	47%	42%	11%
Equal housing opportunity for homosexuals	49%	42%	9%
Equal employment opportunity for homosexuals	45%	46%	9%

In terms of traditional values, the results of these polls are disturbing, since they indicate that a substantial proportion of our population has opinions which, if translated to public policy, would result in wide toleration for the open practice of homosexuality. There are strong reasons to believe, however, that these results can be looked at with great suspicion.

The phrasing of the questions asked interviewees alters the results, as exemplified in the above-mentioned Miami polls by Gallup and Harris. Moreover, if the interviewees had really believed that there should be equal employment opportunity for homosexuals by a margin of 48 percent over 41 percent (Harris Poll), there would not have been such diversity in the answers to the questions on various fields of employment. That is, many of those in the 63 percent who denied, for example, the right of homosexuals to be counselors for children *cannot* also hold the view that there should be equality of opportunity for homosexuals.

6

Acceptability of Homosexuality in the U.S.

There is an eight-point difference in both "yes" and "no" responses between the Harris and Gallup polls in the area of equal employment opportunity. While Gallup asked, "In general, do you think homosexuals should have equal rights in terms of job opportunities," Harris's question was, "Should homosexuals be barred from certain jobs even if they are qualified?". Strictly speaking, these questions are identical. However, the use of such code words as "equal rights" and "job opportunities" with which people easily identify, as well as the differences between Gallup's "in general" and Harris's "certain jobs," could well account for the difference.

The motivation of individuals becomes important when one realizes that in the implementation of policy, proactive persons are more likely to have an influence than those who are merely reactive. When this is taken into consideration, the results vary dramatically. An advertisement was placed by the Moral Majority in the one hundred largest newspapers nationwide (combined readership over one hundred million) in 1979. This advertisement requested responses (by means of a coupon) to several questions, among them, "Do you approve of known practicing homosexuals teaching in public schools?". Of some 723,300 valid responses received, 689,700 were negative (95.4 percent) and 33,600 were affirmative (4.6 percent). Considering that those who answered represent the part of the population that reads newspapers, tends to live in urban areas, would be interested enough in this issue to read an advertisement, and would be motivated sufficiently to fill in the coupon and then mail it, the results are quite impressive. Acceptance of homosexuality, by this indicator, is "soft."

The very purpose of the poll is perhaps an important factor. Polls taken for the purpose of addressing various questions related to homosexuality are probably inherently biased by the liberal ideology of the social sciences in which their designers have usually been trained. This bias does not have to be conscious, and the errors it generates are very difficult to address in practice. An interesting case in which no bias of this nature was present was a report prepared for the Connecticut Mutual Life Insurance Company by Research and Forecasts, Inc.[6] Prepared by organizations without a vested interest in this question, the results were surprising to all concerned. According to this study, opposition to homosexuality is widespread among all groups in the population and is based on ethical grounds. The following tables illustrate our point. The only group that comes close to "splitting its vote" on the question is that of persons with the lowest index of religiosity. This was to be expected. It is also interesting that the least mature segment of the population, agewise, is the most likely to approve of homosexuality. Tables 1 and 2 present the various factors affecting acceptance of homosexuality.

TABLE 1

Factors Affecting Perceived Morality of Male Homosexuality[7]

Question: Do you believe male homosexuality is morally wrong, or do you believe it is not a moral issue?

	Morally Wrong %	Not a Moral Issue %
General Public	71	29
Level of Religious Commitment		
Lowest	54	46
Low	67	33
Moderate	78	22
High	83	17
Highest	87	13
Age		
14–20	70	30
21–24	63	37
25–34	64	36
35–49	70	30
50–64	79	21
65 and over	81	19
Gender		
Male	72	28
Female	72	28
Region		
Northeast	63	37
West	69	31
Midwest	73	27
South	79	21
Place of Residence		
Large City	66	34
Small City	72	28
Suburb	67	33
Rural	82	18
Race		
White	72	28
Black	73	27
Income		
Under $12,000.	76	24
$12,000. to $25,000.	73	27
Above $25,000.	64	36
Education		
11th grade or less	79	21
High school graduate	75	25
Some college or more	60	40
Political orientation		
Liberal	62	38

TABLE 1 (*cont.*)

	Morally Wrong %	Not a Moral Issue %
Moderate	72	28
Conservative	80	20
Party Affiliation		
Republican	77	23
Democrat	74	26
Independent/Other	66	34

This table reveals that level of religious commitment has the greatest impact on whether Americans believe homosexuality is morally wrong. Age, region, place of residence, income, education, and political orientation have a lesser, but still significant, impact. There is comparatively little, or virtually no difference between men and women, Whites and Blacks, and between those with different party affiliations.

TABLE 2
Factors Affecting Perceived Morality of Female Homosexuality[8]
Question: Do you believe female homosexuality is morally wrong, or is it not a moral issue?

	Morally Wrong %	Not a Moral Issue %
General Public	70	30
Level of		
Religious Commitment		
Lowest	52	48
Low	65	35
Moderate	75	25
High	83	17
Highest	88	12
Age		
14–20	70	30
21–24	62	38
25–34	62	38
35–49	69	31
50–64	75	25
65 and over	81	19
Gender		
Male	69	31
Female	72	28
Region		
Northeast	62	38
West	67	33
Midwest	71	29
South	77	23

TABLE 2 (*cont.*)

	Morally Wrong %	Not a Moral Issue %
Place of Residence		
Large City	63	37
Small City	73	27
Suburb	65	35
Rural	77	23
Race		
White	70	30
Black	74	26
Income		
Under $12,000.	75	25
$12,000 to $25,000.	71	29
Above $25,000.	63	37
Education		
11th grade or less	77	23
High school graduate	75	25
Some college or more	57	43
Political orientation		
Liberal	60	40
Moderate	70	30
Conservative	80	20
Party Affiliation		
Republican	76	24
Democrat	71	29
Independent/Other	66	34

This table reveals that level of religious commitment has the greatest impact on whether Americans believe lesbianism is morally wrong. Age, region, place of residence, income, education, and political orientation have a lesser, but still significant, impact. There is comparatively little, or virtually no, difference between men and women, Whites and Blacks, and Republicans and Democrats.

Probably one of the most serious problems involved in this issue is the gap that exists between the general public and our leaders. According to the Connecticut Mutual Life Report, there is basic disagreement between the leadership of American society and the public at large, not only in the area of homosexuality but in other value-laden questions. The study included a sample representative of leaders including such groups as public officials, clergymen, our leadership takes positions on specific value-issues in substantial disagreement with the rest of the population.

This reveals a consistent pattern according to which national leadership systematically falls short of the moral standards of the public at large. This is bound to create social conflicts, since leaders will often propose solutions for existing problems—and at times will even try to implement them utilizing the coercive powers of the State—which are in conflict

Acceptability of Homosexuality in the U.S.

TABLE 3

Leaders and the Public on the Moral Issues [9]

Issues Considered Morally Wrong	Public	Leaders
Abortion	65%	36%
Homosexuality	71%	42%
Lesbianism	70%	42%
Smoking marijuana	57%	33%
Sex before age 16	71%	55%
Living with someone of the opposite sex before marriage	47%	32%
Adultery	85%	71%
Pornographic movies	68%	56%
Hard drugs	84%	73%
Sex between two single people	40%	31%
(Number of Respondents)	(1610)	(1762)

with values cherished by the citizenry. Teachers might promote abortion or homosexuality against the beliefs of the parents, certain government officials might tolerate prostitution or pornography—which they consider acceptable—against the feelings of their community, judges might free pornographers, for many of them feel that pornography is legitimate, while most people think it is wrong.

The differences of opinion are also considerable where family issues are concerned. Since homosexuality is by its nature unproductive of children, the homosexual movement has traditionally striven to change the definition of family in order to include homosexual partners as "family." Table 4 illustrates the gap between leaders and the public concerning certain family issues.

On the specific question of homosexuality, the differences of opinion become most marked when the opinions of various types of leaders are compared. As Tables 5 and 6 reveal, leaders who are most likely to form public opinion and policy are least opposed to homosexuality.

Thus it appears that the ostensibly widespread support for homosexuality is really the approval of this condition as a legitimate lifestyle by the nation's elites. It is only to be expected that public officials will advocate prohomosexual policies, that the educational establishment will teach ideas sympathetic to homosexuality, that judges will render decisions favorable to the movement, and that the media will present homosexuality in a positive fashion when two-thirds or more of the leadership of these professional groups sees nothing wrong with homosexual behavior. It is clear how the activities of these leaders will in fact give the impression that homosexuality is accepted beyond what is actually the case.

TABLE 4
Leaders and the Public on the Family[10]

	Percent Saying "Very Important"	
	Public	Leaders
Making new friends	56%	33%
Playing with children	69%	50%
Going out of your way to help a friend	83%	70%
Talking to older members of your family	67%	54%
Being with friends	69%	59%
Having a rewarding sexual relationship	61%	53%
Doing things as a family	74%	71%
Sharing personal feelings with a spouse or intimate companion	79%	77%

TABLE 5
Leadership Groups on Male Homosexuality[11]

Is homosexuality morally wrong, or is it not a moral issue?		
	Morally Wrong	Not A Moral Issue
General Public	71%	29%
Leaders	42%	58%
Religion	73%	27%
Military	58%	42%
Business	51%	49%
Voluntary Associations	41%	59%
News Media	38%	62%
Government	36%	64%
Education	30%	70%
Law & Justice	30%	70%
Science	27%	73%

Acceptability of Homosexuality in the U.S.

TABLE 6

Leadership Groups on Female
Homosexuality[12]

Is lesbianism morally wrong, or is it not a moral issue?		
	Morally Wrong	Not A Moral Issue
General Public	70%	30%
Leaders	42%	58%
Religion	74%	26%
Military	60%	40%
Business	53%	47%
Voluntary Associations	45%	55%
News Media	37%	63%
Government	35%	65%
Law & Justice	30%	70%
Education	28%	72%
Science	26%	74%

Rejection of Homosexuality

There is little question that the overwhelming majority of the American public rejects the practice of homosexuality. Leaders of the homosexual movement undoubtedly know this and, although little is said about it, behave accordingly. The National Gay Task Force, for example, has published a monograph designed to convince politicians that they have nothing to lose by supporting the homosexual cause.[13] The argument used is not that the public supports homosexuality or is "neutral" on the question, but that the rejection of homosexuality, when translated into votes, is not sufficient to offset the support of the homosexuals themselves. Moreover, although it is true that a certain number of individuals have admitted publicly that they practice homosexuality, the number is miniscule when compared with the total number of homosexuals. Homosexual physician Howard J. Brown complained in a 1976 article that only 20 out of some 39,000 American homosexual physicians (Brown's estimate) had then manifested the nature of their sexual preferences.[14] Another indication that homosexual leaders are aware that their sexual practices are abhorred by most Americans is their standard practice of keeping their mailing lists in strict confidence.

The widespread rejection of homosexuality is manifested in various ways. One of them is the systematic exclusion of homosexuals from certain jobs. This is especially true in occupations in which the individual has close contact with or supervises children. Parents and heterosexual managers are obviously concerned that the children will be seduced. In the case of positions in which the incumbents are expected to live up to high ethical standards, the danger of blackmail makes homosexuals undesirable. This is also true of occupations in which persons of the same sex have to maintain close physical contact and share showers and sleeping quarters (e.g., the military, policemen, firemen). The navy has a policy of discharging homosexuals, probably for this reason. This policy is enforced, although its constitutionality has been challenged.[15] The rationale for this policy is not difficult to appreciate, since males, for instance, would probably find it objectionable to be forced to live with other males for whom they would be objects of sexual attraction.

Another form that the rejection of homosexuality takes is the commission of acts of personal violence or vandalism against homosexual persons or establishments. At times murders have been committed, for no apparent reason. In other instances, homosexual bars have been "invaded" and widespread acts of violence have been committed against patrons, employees, and the physical plant. The case of the "gay bar" Equus in the District of Columbia is notorious.[16] Located near the Marine Barracks, it has been attacked a number of times, allegedly by members of the Marine Corps. Violence is also not unknown to the Iwo Jima Memorial in Arlington, Virginia, where homosexuals are also said to congregate in search of quick sex or night-long partners. It would be difficult to justify the violation of the law in the commission of violence against homosexuals. However, it is obvious that these are clear indicators of the rejection of homosexuality by perpetrators who are acting, in some sense, as social agents of the majority of the population, which is frustrated by the seeming incapability of the political system to control homosexual behavior. Still, this majority of the American public rejects homosexuality without condoning the violence against homosexuals.

A clearer example of the nonacceptance of homosexuality by American society is the case of tennis player Billie Jean King, who allegedly had homosexual relations with another woman. Mrs. King is one of the top female tennis players in history, and the alleged incident had taken place several years before it was publicized. She is also married. It was subsequently reported that a contract she had to help promote vitamins would not be renewed.[17] The reason could not have been that taking a certain vitamin would turn a person into a homosexual, but it would seem logical to assume that the advertiser concluded that the assets Mrs. King could offer were more than offset by the liabilities of a long-past alleged homosexual affair.

There are prohomosexual associations of relatives of homosexuals who affirm the acceptability of the practice *after* they have found out that their son, brother, or friend is a homosexual. There are no associations, however, of parents who would *like* their sons to be one. Under political pressure, employers have been known to seek homosexuals. However, only homosexual organizations (baths, bars, etc.) are known to prefer homosexuals as employees. The very existence of the movement committed to bringing about social acceptability for homosexuality is the best indicator that this form of human sexuality is generally rejected. The great intensity of the movement's leaders in their efforts clearly reveals their perception that they are far from their goals.

Acceptance of Homosexuality: Significant Examples

There are multiple forces and practices encouraging the increased acceptability of homosexuality. It is impossible here to do more than to provide a few representative examples. In a sense, the activities of the homosexual movement and its supporters described throughout this work constitute efforts to increase the acceptability of homosexuality. Examples offered in this chapter are meant to be illustrative and in no way pretend to exhaust the question.

TEENAGE HOMOSEXUALITY

Under traditional concepts, a child suspected of homosexual tendencies would have been referred to a practitioner in a helping profession to try to arrest the condition. Under the present climate, this is not always done. As a matter of fact, measures that would tend to foster the child's tendencies might be undertaken. It has been reported that the State of New Jersey Department of Human Services has placed a number of homosexual teenagers in foster homes headed by female homosexuals.[18] According to a spokesman for the department, only "sexually experienced" children were considered for placement; in a number of instances, children so classified have been placed with a homosexual couple. Since one of the roles of the foster parent is to serve as role model for the child, it is only logical that such a practice will tend to eliminate any possibility of the child developing heterosexually. The fact that the children are sexually experienced might increase the possibility of seduction.

Another indication of acceptance of teenage homosexuality is the willingness of schools to accept—sometimes under the compulsion of prohomosexual court orders—the participation of homosexual couples in school affairs. In 1979 Paul Gilbert, a member of the prohomosexual Catholic organization Dignity, tried to bring a male date to his prom at Cumberland High School in Rhode Island. Rejected by the school, he was unable to sue (although he had the support of the American Civil Liberties Union) because his parents would not authorize it and he was a minor.[19] At the

1980 prom, he became the date of Aaron Fricke. Since Fricke was then eighteen, he was able to bring suit. Under the guise of protecting his First Amendment rights to free expression, the courts forced the school to accept two homosexual teenagers as companions at the prom. Subsequently, Fricke wrote a book about his experience, having been acclaimed by the homosexual movement as a pioneer.[20]

Actually, there was a precedent for Cumberland High to follow. In the 1979 prom season, Lincoln High School in Sioux Falls, South Dakota, had accepted Randy Rohl, a seventeen-year-old senior, and Brady Quinn, his twenty-year-old date, as a "gay couple" attending the senior prom.[21] The school in this case accepted the participation of the homosexual couple without any opposition. It is interesting to note that, printed next to the report of the homosexual incident at Lincoln High, there appeared a story of efforts by the American Civil Liberties Union and the United Presbyterian Church to stop the use of any songs with religious motifs at Sioux Falls schools. Although no direct connection can be claimed for the two events, given the fact that religion is the major force in opposition to homosexuality, it is probable that there is a relation between the climate of opinion that made both events possible.

Since then, there have been other incidents in which homosexual teenagers have attended school dances with same-sex partners (e.g., an incident has been reported at Skyline High School in Los Angeles, California). It is predictable that if the moral climate of the nation does not change, incidents like these are bound to continue. It is difficult to imagine, however, that high school dances will become publicly sponsored versions of the classical "gay disco." Even judges with prohomosexual biases realize that they must be responsive to public opinion; neither parents nor students are likely to accept passively wholesale orders to force heterosexual teenagers to accept homosexual couples at school dances.

There is little question that teenage homosexuality, although not generally endorsed by responsible individuals, does enjoy the "understanding" tolerance of certain legislators. In the District of Columbia, a bill legalizing homosexual relations between consenting children was headed for approval until a local newspaper reported the nature of its provisions.[22] The bill eliminated references to gender and lowered the age of consent to twelve, legalizing sex between children, provided the age spread between the partners was four years or less. According to council member David A. Clarke (D-Ward 1), author of the bill and chairman of the judiciary committee, "Teenaged sexual activity that is consensual is not an area for criminal law." The widespread opposition to this bill motivated even its proponents to eliminate some of its most offensive provisions—including the legalization of teenage homosexuality. However, the intentions of its framers reveal a state of mind in which homosexual relations among teenagers ought to be legally acceptable, so long as there is no

Acceptability of Homosexuality in the U.S.

force involved. Reasonable persons, though, might argue that the issues of "consent" and "force" are not clear when a twelve-year-old "boy" is approached by a nearly seventeen-year-old "man."

HOMOSEXUAL COUPLES

A clear indication of the increasing acceptance of homosexuality is the openness with which more or less permanent homosexual partners declare publicly the existence of their relationships. The status such relationships are accorded by significant social structures is also indicative that homosexuality enjoys an unprecedented degree of recognition. Since the practice of homosexuality has been traditionally rejected as sinful, irrational, and criminal by the dominant segments of our society, the idea of homosexuals living together in marriage-like unions has been particularly abhorrent. For a society that considers the nuclear family its basic cell, homosexual "couples" appear to be a form of cancer.

Still, for the homosexual movement, the existence and acceptance of such arrangements is most important. This explains the relentless campaign waged during the White House Conference on Families to have "alternative" families (including a variety of homosexual liaisons) recognized as legitimate. It also explains the existence of "gay union" rituals, parallel to wedding ceremonies, which take place in homosexual and mainline churches alike. For the homosexual movement, any rejection of the legitimacy of same-sex couple relationships is tantamount to oppression. For Jennie Boyd Bull, writing in *The Gay Christian*, a homosexual theological journal, such oppression is similar to the slavery to which black people were subjected in the past:

> A particularly instructive comparison between the black community and the gay community is the manner of inculcation of self-hatred by the dominant society. Slaves were brainwashed into accepting their inhumanity through separation from their past culture and in particular through destroying much of the family structure. Thus, many black people were deprived of basic social and economic institutions, as well as a source of identity and strength. In this same sense, society has systematically denied to gays the right to any form of legal relationship and through economic and social discrimination does not recognize the existence of same-sex couple relationships. The result is similar to that of slavery: loss of social cohesion and self-identity.[23]

Consistent with these ideas, the Universal Fellowship of Metropolitan Community Churches has introduced the rite of "holy union" among its homosexual members. The status of these homosexual couples is well illustrated by the manner in which a new staff person assigned to the church's international headquarters was introduced in the denomination's official publication.[24] The biographical description of Phil Gallinitz reads,

"Originally from Detroit, Michigan, Gallinitz moved to Los Angeles in July with his spouse, Richard O'Dell."

The article also features a photograph of the two men sitting very close to one another in what appears to be a love seat. The caption reads: "Phil Gallinitz (left), new UFMCC office manager, relaxes at home with his spouse, Richard O'Dell."

Although marriage licenses are not granted to same-sex couples, in at least one instance two homosexuals obtained such a document in Boulder, Colorado.[25] In a move that also amounts to a recognition of homosexual couples, it has been reported that the Boston City Hospital's Intensive Care Unit allows homosexual lovers visitation rights.[26] The excuse offered by the hospital apparently is that these are "significant others."

This acceptance of homosexual "marriages" extends to the behavioral sciences, having obvious consequences in the realm of therapeutic praxis. A newly produced treatise titled *Principles and Practice of Sex Therapy* provides a good example of the extent to which same-sex couples have become accepted in this field.[27] Chapter XI of this work is titled "Treatment of Sexual Dysfunction in Homosexual Male Couples." Obviously, the principle utilized is that the function of therapy, when homosexuals find their practices dissatisfying, is to help make these practices satisfactory. The intrinsic propriety of this behavior, which according to traditional principles is the very source of the dissatisfaction, is systematically ignored. Homosexuality is thus deemed normal and acceptable, at least by a significant segment of the behavioral science establishment.

The tacit acceptance of homosexual "marriages" is apparent in the discussion of what happens to the "widow(er)" [*sic*] when a homosexual dies. The problem was discussed in *Behavior Today*.[28]

> "The gay world, or at least a part of it, celebrates the couples who have been together for endless numbers of years, then hopes just as fervently that they will go right back into their homes lest one get sick and die—die in public, thus disturbing *our* equilibrium." Speaking is Dr. Charles Silverstein, psychologist, founder, and former director of a number of clinics for gay men in New York City.

The article also discusses the specific problems of female homosexual couples as well as the role of other homosexuals. The promiscuous nature of homosexual relations is revealed by the following comments, which remind the reader of the situation of a harem facing the death of the Sultan:

> The gay community usually takes on the responsibilities of family at times like these. But there are differences, warn Moses and Hawkins. For example, within a close group of lesbian friends, there may be others who have been involved

Acceptability of Homosexuality in the U.S.

in a love relationship with the deceased and who are also grieving. This may make it difficult for them to have the kind of semidetachment that is true of in-laws and friends of the family where a non-gay married couple is concerned. The helping professional may need to take an advocacy role in intervening in institutional policies and procedures so that the lovers may spend time together in an intensive care setting, for example.

It must be pointed out that *Behavior Today* is *not* a homosexual publication, nor does it deal primarily with sexual questions. The casual and matter-of-fact manner with which it deals with homosexual couples is but an indication that homosexuality has reached a status that would have been unimaginable just a short generation ago.

THE EDUCATIONAL SYSTEM

Although not basically oriented toward homosexuality, the goals and outcomes of sex education also reveal the degree to which homosexuality has been accepted in our society. The practice of nonsexist education, where gender differences are minimized or even obliterated, also reflects the acceptance of homosexuality in the United States.

A massive evaluation of sex education was undertaken on behalf of the former Department of Health, Education, and Welfare by Mantech, Inc., a consulting firm.[29] This study revealed that the acceptance of homosexuality and masturbation is a projected outcome of a substantial number of sex education programs. Not only in terms of interviews with sex educators, but also in reviewing the literature descriptive of other sex education programs, the researchers discovered that students participating in these programs tended to become more accepting of homosexuality and masturbation.

Sex education classes probably have the effect of making promiscuity in general and homosexuality in particular more acceptable to the student population. In support of these courses, a number of textbooks totally identified with the homosexual movement, or highly sympathetic to it, have been developed. The following section is taken from a grammar school textbook of sex education:

> However, many homosexuals—more every year—are happy and satisfied. They hold good jobs and live successful lives. They are found in all walks of life—sports, business, the arts, science, government, and labor, to mention a few. And each year, more people feel that homosexuals have the right to live the kind of sexual lives they want to as long as they do not harm or bother others. They are no more likely to be harmful to others than people who are not gay.[30]

Professional associations which are obviously in sympathy with homosexuals actively cooperate in these endeavors. It is, however, surprising

19

that an organization with the prestige of the American Library Association endorsed the book from which the above quote is taken: "*Sex: Telling It Straight* is being marketed by the publisher as a sex education guide for adolescents. A review in *Booklist*, the reviewing journal of the American Library Association (June 1, 1979), recommends it for grades 5–8 and notes that this edition changes homosexuality from 'another problem of sex' to a matter of choice between consenting adults."[31]

The elimination of gender-assigned roles is bound to increase the acceptance of homosexuality, since it is by identification with these roles that the sexual identities which by nature are correlated with members of each gender become confirmed. It is thus that in all cultures some actions and items are "masculine" while others are "feminine." In spite of the phenomenon of camp, people are not normally attracted to members of the same sex. Nonsexist education, with its emphasis on the elimination of sex-related roles, is thus bound to increase the acceptance of homosexuality. Conversely, the homosexual movement has a stake in and strongly supports nonsexist and sex education, as promulgated by secular humanism and backed largely by political power. (Religious organizations have traditionally provided sex education in the context of morality. This discussion refers to secular humanist sex education, mostly, though not exclusively, promoted by the coercive power of political authority.) It is also clear why nonsexist education organizations are in general supportive of the homosexual movement. An example of such an organization is New York City's Women's Action Alliance, the publisher of *Non-Sexist Education for Young Children* and sponsor of the federally funded Non-Sexist Child Development Project.[32] In a June 10, 1981, letter, the information services staff person of the Alliance indicated that "We have and will again lend our name in support of gay and lesbian struggles such as petitions, demonstrations, and other protests."[33]

Although schools frown on the idea of openly homosexual teachers in the classroom, there are instances in which they can maintain their positions. A homosexual pastor at the New Orleans Metropolitan Community Church is reportedly also employed by the local public school system.[34] The *Washington Blade*, a homosexual newspaper, printed an article by a male homosexual teacher who analyzed the contributions he thought he could make to his students as a "gay male teacher."[35] The influence of these and similar individuals as role models for their students cannot be ignored. The fact that they are accepted by school administrators is another indicator that homosexuality is viewed with indulgence in certain circles.

RELIGIOUS BODIES

It is difficult to ascertain the degree of support for the homosexual movement by religious bodies across the board. It is, however, so im-

Acceptability of Homosexuality in the U.S.

portant that a complete section of this work has been dedicated to this purpose. Because of the normative character of religion, it is clear that any support for this practice by churches and synagogues is bound to have a profound effect on public acceptance of homosexuality. However, the participation of religious bodies in the acceptance of homosexuality is as diverse as the nature of these institutions. Such support is seen in the existence of:

- Homosexual churches and synagogues
- "Gay" organizations within most mainline churches
- Developments of new theories in Biblical exegesis, speculative theology, and moral theology which fit perfectly the ideology of the homosexual movement
- Participation of homosexual divinity students preparing for the ministry in prohomosexual churches in seminaries of mainline denominations
- Policies which view leniently the admission and maintenance of open homosexuals in the ordained clergy
- Religious rituals currently in use for the establishment of gay unions (homosexual marriages)
- Underground organizational systems (retreats, publications, religious orders) for the "support" of homosexually oriented clergymen and nuns, sometimes tolerated, if not encouraged, by officials in their churches

The few examples offered at this point serve merely to illustrate the current situation and are neither exhaustive nor completely representative. They have been chosen to illustrate patterns rather than as complete descriptions.

On March 28 and 29, 1980, a meeting of homosexual seminarians took place in New York City. The following announcement appeared in *A New Day,* a publication of the Universal Fellowship of Metropolitan Community Churches.

GAY SEMINARIANS TO MEET IN MARCH
The Third Lesbian and Gay Seminarians Conference has been scheduled for March 28 and 29, 1980, at Union Theological Seminary in New York City.
The second gathering of Gay seminarians was held last fall in Cambridge, Massachusetts and was a significant success.
Lesbians and Gay men who are in seminary are welcome to join the third conference at Union this spring. If you are interested, write Allen Grooms, 527 Riverside Drive, Van Dusen Hall, Apt. #3-C, New York, N.Y. 10027.[36]

Homosexual seminarians eventually become homosexual ministers. The fact that they are organized and that one of the most prestigious institutions of higher theological learning in the country has been placed at their disposal can only be interpreted as acceptance of them *as homosexuals* by the religious authorities of this institution.

Utilizing speakers who are prohomosexual or "friends" of homosexual organizations is another way in which the virtual endorsement of the movement is effected by religious bodies. An added advantage of this practice is that it allows the building of networks of sympathetic individuals. *RECord*, the official newsletter of Evangelicals Concerned (the homosexual group within evangelical churches) has reported the appearance of two "good friends" of the movement as guest lecturers at the annual Finch Symposium. This event took place at the prestigious Fuller Theological Seminary.[37] The persons named were J. Harold Ellens, a Christian Reformed theologian who is a member of the Board of Evangelicals Concerned, and psychologist and Hope College professor Dr. David G. Myers, described as "also a good friend of the EC ministry."

Cross-seminary registration to aspirants for the ministry at the Metropolitan Community Churches is available at one of the foremost centers of theological scholarship, the Chicago Cluster of Theological Schools. This has been accomplished through an arrangement between the prohomosexual denomination and the United Presbyterians' McCormick Theological Seminary. The official publication of the UFMCC published an advertisement inviting candidates to apply.[38] Among other advantages, the ad mentioned cross-registration opportunities at seminaries of various denominations, including Catholic, Lutheran, Baptist, Unitarian, and others. Widespread use of this opportunity can only result in the deeper participation of churches in the progressive acceptance of homosexuality. At the same time, it reflects the current level of acceptability of this practice by religious bodies which, a few short years ago, would have considered it unthinkable.

PUBLIC OFFICIALS

The superb organization of thousands of homosexual groups throughout the nation accounts for the support homosexuality has received from public officials at all levels of government. The leadership of the movement has been received at the White House, and the strategy for the passage of prohomosexual legislation has been formulated at the Capitol itself. Judges have rendered prohomosexual decisions, and a religious institution has been forced to use part of its funds to avoid being forced to employ a homosexual, as the result of a prohomosexual ordinance currently in force.

Police departments now recruit homosexuals, both male and female. The San Francisco Police Department advertises in one of the local homosexual papers as part of its "Gay Outreach Program."[39] These ads appear near the Models/Escorts section where male prostitutes openly promote their services. The police chiefs of Portland and San Diego have reportedly invited homosexuals to become policemen,[40] and the Minneapolis Police

Acceptability of Homosexuality in the U.S.

Department has also advertised in the local homosexual papers as part of its efforts to recruit "clerical help."[41]

The decisions of certain judges reveal that the traditional attitude of rejection of homosexuality has, in many instances, given way to a much more tolerant—if not approving—viewpoint on this practice. The 4th Circuit Court of Appeals in Richmond, Virginia, forced the United States to accept a homosexual as a citizen,[42] and in June 1980 the courts also forced the public transportation system in the District of Columbia to display prohomosexual propaganda designed to change public opinion on homosexuality.[43] In Milwaukee, U. S. District Judge Terence T. Evans forced the U.S. Army to reinstate a homosexual female discharged on account of her homosexual condition.[44] The judge ruled that the U.S. Constitution made it illegal for the U.S. Army to discharge soldiers on account of homosexuality. It is difficult to understand how the Constitution addresses the question of homosexuality in the Armed Forces, or whether the judge could appreciate the potential morale problems should the army become a haven for homosexuals.

Judges can act with impunity in making decisions which deeply offend the moral sense of the citizens, since they are, to a large extent, insulated from the political process. It is also possible for individuals who would otherwise have very little opportunity to become judges to reach the highest levels of the federal judiciary as appointees. It is probably for this reason that homosexuals have been appointed justices in California. Appointed a Superior Court judge by Governor Jerry Brown in 1979, self-acknowledged homosexual Stephen M. Lachs was asked in 1981 by Chief Justice Rose Bird to sit temporarily on the California Supreme Court.[45] A prominent advocate of "gay rights," and herself a homosexual, Mary Morgan was also appointed a judge of the San Francisco Municipal Court.[46] The value of this appointment as a tool to increase the acceptability of homosexuality by the rest of the population did not escape Morgan. She did not seem to view the appointment as a normal exercise by which a qualified attorney is elevated to the bench, but as a political triumph for the homosexual movement: "I think it's absolutely a step forward for the gay and lesbian community. I think it's important to have more lesbians and gays visible in our society so people can see there's not an enormous difference between us and we don't have anything to fear from each other."[46]

Regulatory and other administrative agencies have also reflected the current climate of acceptability of homosexual practices. Many instances can be cited; for our present purposes, two will suffice. On January 11, 1980, the Veterans Administration issued a regulation (38CFR Part 3, Sec. 3.12 [d] [5]) which had the effect of making most persons discharged from the service for homosexual behavior eligible for VA benefits.[47] Only individuals who had been involved in homosexual acts that included prostitution or coercion remained ineligible. In the eyes of servicemen and even the public at large, the abrogation of such penalties is bound to imply that the Armed Forces in some sense condone, or at least have a more tolerant attitude toward, the practice of homosexuality. In response to a request by the National Gay Task Force (RM-2937), the Federal Communications Commission adopted a ruling which implied a requirement for broadcasters to include homosexual organizations among those consulted pursuant to the renewal of their licenses.[48] This ruling was adopted on March 12, 1980, and released on April 4, 1980. The "Memorandum Opinion and Order" and the "Notice of Proposed Rule Making" were generally favorable to the homosexual organizations and their allies, which filed friendly comment.[49] The FCC, even under the pressure of a Freedom of Information Act request, refused to disclose materials that would reveal the specific arguments used in arriving at their final decision. It is thus very difficult to show the possible prejudices of staff and/or commissioners. However, the bias of the FCC was glaring: "We have carefully considered NGTF's arguments and find merit in much of what is stated."[50] The same document rejected a petition by the tradition-oriented Eagle Forum and Stop ERA Committee which would have ensured that nonfeminist women's organizations be consulted in license renewal ascertainments.[51] The FCC deemed it important to be responsive to the homosexual movement but rejected the proponents of traditional values.

Two other instances which reveal the depth of acceptance of homosexuality by governmental agencies will be cited. Both cases show not mere responsiveness to the movement, but the stated judgment that homosexuality is a positive feature. Harrison V. Goldin, New York City Comptroller, is reported to have proposed that the large homosexual community there be listed as one of New York's attractions when the city is promoted nationwide.[52] The fact that many homosexuals have tended to move to large metropolitan areas—New York among them—is a demographic fact. To say that the presence of many homosexuals constitutes a tourist attraction is debatable, unless the promotion is addressed to other homosexuals seeking sexual relief. Homosexuals were glorified in a Jamestown, Virginia, exhibit prepared by the National Park Service until a flood of complaints from irate citizens led incoming Park Service Directors to remove the offensive items, which alleged that homosexuals had been involved in founding Jamestown.[53] Careful research of the issue revealed that "the primary reference to homosexuality during the colonial period . . . is the chronicle of a ship's captain who was executed in 1620 for raping a cabin boy."[54]

OTHER INSTANCES
Other significant forces in our society have displayed support for the homosexual movement and/or the implied practice of homosexuality. At

times, these are powerful agents in the formation of public opinion or policy and cannot be discounted. The media have been traditionally supportive of the homosexual movement. Both the printed and broadcast means of social communication have virtually adopted the language of the movement and are very careful not to use expressions to which homosexual leaders object. By the very use of language, they contribute substantially to frame issues in a direction favorable to their own biases. From Anchorage to Georgia and from California to Massachusetts, there are some thirty "gay and lesbian" radio programs.[55] One of the two most influential newspapers in the country, the *New York Times*, is on the record as favoring the employment of homosexuals as teachers.[56]

The acceptability of homosexual organizations as legitimate service providers is not enhanced solely by the reception of large federal and local grants (in some instances amounting to several hundred thousand dollars), but in the willingness of other "already respectable" organizations to use them for referral purposes. The American Social Health Association, for example, has indicated in reference to its VD National Hotline project:

> The VD National Hotline has access to phone numbers of gay crisis intervention services, gay information and resources services, gay community centers, gay coalition groups, "rap" lines, and numerous switchboards which have been brought to our attention by a wide variety of gay organizations. These phone numbers are referred to gay people when requested. We are also in touch with the National Gay Coalition out of Virginia who assist us with keeping our referrals up-to-date.[57]

Publishers sometimes provide for the support and acceptance of homosexuality by their willingness to utilize openly prohomosexual authors in their publications. There is a difference between scholars or researchers who are engaged in the search for truth and from whom the whole spectrum of opinions is to be expected, and well-educated prohomosexual activists who *by definition* have something at stake in the acceptance of their opinions. It is not reasonable to expect that a "liberated" homosexual will be capable of addressing the question of homosexuality with any degree of objectivity or scientific detachment. One can easily call into question the use of Dr. Ralph Blair, president of the prohomosexual group Evangelicals Concerned, as author of the chapter on homosexuality for a new medical textbook.[58] For many years, the overwhelming majority of therapists believed that homosexuality is an illness, thus a fitting subject for a medical textbook. A chapter in a medical textbook written by an activist who believes that homosexuality is *not* an illness can only reflect a degree of acceptance for homosexuality hitherto unknown.

THE HOMOSEXUAL NETWORK

Conclusion: Is Homosexuality Really Accepted?

A number of instances pertaining to acceptance of homosexuality in our society have been presented. The issue has not been the incidents as isolated events, but the pattern they reveal. None of the instances cited would mean much *by itself*. When considered as a group representative of many other items presented throughout this work, they reveal the unprecedented degree of support which homosexuality enjoys today.

Yet, invariably, the support for homosexuality comes from social leaders out of touch with the feelings or self-defined interests of the public. The results of the Connecticut Mutual Life Report have thus been confirmed: American leaders are out of touch with their constituents. Seminaries train homosexual ministers for congregations who reject them. The *New York Times* advocates homosexual school teachers for children whose parents do not want them. The Governor of California names homosexual judges over people who view their condition as a sign of perversion. Homosexual couples are presented as "families" to a people who consider them as violating the canons of decency. Sex educators seek to change the values of students so that they will become accepting of masturbation and homosexuality, when the children's parents loathe these practices.

If the public remains out of synchrony with its leadership, the results will be a change in leadership, or an increase in cynicism based on the inability to trust the established institutions. Of course, it is always possible that the people will come to believe the prohomosexual ideas accepted by the leadership. Should the public at large come to believe the homosexual ideology, we will have not only a "unisex" society, but one in which our traditional sexual ethics will have been totally obliterated.

Notes

In order to simplify the following notes, several sources which are used a number of times have been abbreviated as follows throughout the book:

SHORTENED VERSION	SOURCE
Marotta	Toby Marotta, *The Politics of Homosexuality* (Boston: Houghton Mifflin Co., 1981).
Blade	*Washington* (D.C.) *Blade*
Advocate	*Advocate* (San Mateo, CA: Liberation Publications, Inc.).
Bondings	*Bondings* (Mt. Ranier, MD: New Ways Ministry).
Tripp	C. A. Tripp, *The Homosexual Matrix* (New York: New American Library, Inc. Times Mirror, 1976).

Acceptability of Homosexuality in the U.S.

SHORTENED VERSION   SOURCE

In Unity   *In Unity* (Los Angeles, CA: Universal Fellowship of Metropol-
                              itan Community Churches).

A Time to Speak   C. Robert Nugent, S.D.S. and Jeannine Gramick, S.S.N.D.,
                              eds., *A Time to Speak* (Mt. Ranier, MD: New Ways Ministry,
                              n.d.).

Hearing   U.S. Congress, House, Committee on Education and Labor,
                              *To Prohibit Discrimination on the Basis of Affectional or Sexual
                              Orientation, and for Other Purposes, Hearing before the Sub-
                              committee on Employment Opportunities on H.R. 2074,* 96th
                              Cong., 2nd sess. San Francisco, CA, October 10, 1980.

Gays on the Hill   *Gays on the Hill* (Washington, D.C.: Washington Office, Uni-
                              versal Fellowship of Metropolitan Community Churches).

A New Day   *A New Day* (Washington, D.C: Washington Office, Universal
                              Fellowship of Metropolitan Community Churches).

It's Time   *It's Time* (New York, N.Y.: National Gay Task Force).

1. Philip Nobile, "The Meaning of Gay: An Interview with Dr. C. A. Tripp," *New York*, June 25, 1979, p. 41.

2. Paul Siegel, "Homophobia: Types, Origins, Remedies," *Christianity and Crisis*, November 12, 1979, p. 284.

3. C. R. Ruff and J. E. Scott, "Deviance and Cognitive Consistency: Patterns in Public Attitudes Toward Deviance," *Sociology and Social Research*, July 1975, pp. 330–343, quoted in Pennsylvania Department of Education, *What is a Sexual Minority, Anyway?* (1980), p. 7.

4. The following tables are the result of data provided in two sources: *Lesbian Tide* 7 (Los Angeles, CA: Tide Publications, September/October, 1977): 12; and *New York Times*, July 19, 1977, p. 17.

5. *Minneapolis Tribune*, August 28, 1977, p. 1.

6. Research and Forecasts, Inc., *The Connecticut Mutual Life Report on American Values in the 80's: The Impact of Belief* (Hartford, CT: Connecticut Mutual Life Insurance Co., 1981).

7. Ibid., p. 96.

8. Ibid., p. 94.

9. Ibid., p. 201.

10. Ibid., p. 208.

11. Ibid., p. 220.

12. Ibid., p. 221.

13. *Does Support for Gay Rights Spell Political Suicide?* (Washington, D.C.: The Gay Rights National Lobby and the National Gay Task Force, 1981).

14. Howard J. Brown, "In Secret, In Public," *New York Times*, October 21, 1976.

15. *Washington Star*, April 12, 1981.

16. *Washington Post*, June 14, 1981.

17. Richard Cohen, "Billy Jean King Pays for America's Fantasy," *Washington Post*, May 7, 1981.

18. *New York Times*, November 27, 1979.

19. *Calendar* (New York: Dignity/New York), July 1980, p. 8.

20. Aaron Fricke, *Confessions of a Rock Lobster: A Story of Growing Up Gay* (Boston: Alyson, 1981).

21. *Washington Post*, May 24, 1979.

22. Ibid., June 25, 1981.

23. Jennie Boyd Bull, "UFMCC: Our Theological Task for the 80s," *The Gay Christian*

(Chicago: Universal Fellowship of Metropolitan Community Churches), Fourth Quarter 1980–First Quarter 1981, p. 4.

24. *In Unity*, December 1979–January 1980, p. 14.

25. Personal communication.

26. *In Unity*, December 1979–January 1980, p. 11.

27. Sandra R. Leiblum and Lawrence A. Pervin, *Principles and Practice of Sex Therapy* (New York: Atlantic Institute, 1981).

28. "Death of a Lover Creates Complex Problems for Surviving Homosexual Mate," *Behavior Today* 12 (New York, N.Y.: ADCOM, February 9, 1981): 6.

29. U.S. Department of Health, Education, and Welfare, Public Health Service, *An Analysis of U.S. Sex Education Programs and Evaluation Methods*, by Douglas Kirby et al., Contract No. 200-78-0804, Report No. CDC-2021-79-DK-FR (Atlanta), July 1979. See especially vol. 1, chapters 2, 3, and 4.

30. Eric W. Johnson, *Sex: Telling It Straight* (Lippincott, 1979), quoted in *Gay Teachers Association Newsletter* 4 (New York: Gay Teachers Association, June 1981): 2.

31. Ibid.

32. Women's Action Alliance, Inc., *Catalog and Order Form*, (New York).

33. Letter to the author, June 10, 1981.

34. *In Unity*, January/February 1981, p. 19.

35. Bill Springmann, "What a Gay Male Teacher Offers Children," *Blade*, March 20, 1981, p. A–15.

36. *A New Day* 4 (January 1980): 1.

37. *REcord* (New York: Evangelicals Concerned), Spring 1981, p. 1.

38. *In Unity*, October/November 1979, p. 29.

39. *Sentinel* (San Francisco), August 7, 1981, pp. 18, 19.

40. *In Unity*, February/March 1980, p. 14.

41. Ibid., April/May 1980, p. 12.

42. *Washington Star*, February 28, 1981.

43. Ibid., April 9, 1981.

44. *In Unity*, September/October 1980, p. 12.

45. *Moral Majority Report* (Lynchburg, VA: Moral Majority), July 20, 1981.

46. *Washington Post*, August 28, 1981.

47. *Federal Register* 45, no. 8, January 11, 1980, pp. 2318–19.

48. Federal Communications Commission, 80–134 (15526) BC Docket No. 78–237.

49. Federal Communications Commission, 78–583 (95792) BC Docket No. 78–237.

50. Ibid., p. 7.

51. Ibid., pp. 2, 8.

52. *In Unity*, December 1979/January 1980, p. 10.

53. *Washington Star*, June 24, 1981.

54. Ibid.

55. Information furnished by Lambda Resource Center for the Blind, 3225 N. Sheffield Avenue, Chicago, IL 60657.

56. *New York Times*, May 24, 1977, p. 34.

57. Letter to the author, June 15, 1981.

58. *Record* (New York: Evangelicals Concerned), Spring 1981, p. 1.

CHAPTER

II

The Homosexual Subculture

The Subculture

It is apparent even to a casual observer that in every sizable city—and even in many small communities—not only are there homosexuals, but many of these individuals have acquired certain social traits and developed behaviors not directly attributable to their sexual propensities. Not all homosexuals, not even all those who have publicly "celebrated" their condition by "coming out" (see chapter III), exhibit all these traits and behaviors. However, there is a sufficient correlation between the individuals and the traits and behaviors that one can often reasonably assert that a person is homosexual without being positive about his sexual desires. These traits and behaviors also serve as reinforcers of the homosexual's identity.

As a counterpart to these traits and behaviors, a host of social institutions has developed which homosexuals utilize in "acting out" their homosexuality vis-à-vis their peers, or even themselves. These institutions include *bars* and *discos* where homosexuals drink, dance, relax, and find sex partners; homosexual *churches* and mainline-church-related groups, where they socialize while confirming their homosexual identity from the ethical, theological, and cultic standpoints; *baths,* which are essentially places for engaging in one-to-one or group sex, either publicly or privately; *publications* in which homosexuals find information they need from their particular perspective, stimulation for their sexual fantasies in pornographic stories and photographs, and, when needed, the services of male prostitutes; *professional associations* (gay caucuses) where homosexuals meet

29

their professional peers while advancing the interests of their cause; homo-sexual *prostitution* of young people who satisfy the desires of older in-dividuals for an appropriate fee; homosexual *"marriage,"* where homosexuals find companionship and mutual acceptability in the context of their sexual needs.

These and many other institutions, together with the traits and behav-iors mentioned, constitute a peculiar subculture of contemporary Amer-ican society. Like all subcultures, it is a superstructure only intentionally related to the trait held in common by its participants. The homosexual subculture is fluid and alive, having arisen in a dynamic relationship with the predominant culture and other subcultures (e.g., the "feminist" sub-culture). From its remote antecedents in the nineteenth century,[1] the homosexual subculture has been strengthened at a logarithmic rate since the late 1950s. At this point it is so vast and complex that it probably defies detailed analysis. Although virtually distinct in its lack of direction, the homosexual subculture is in fact coextensive with the homosexual movement. The homosexual subculture provides the movement with its "flavor" and "distinctiveness," while receiving from it the ideology which provides it with intellectual solidity. In a sense, subculture and movement are two ways of looking at one and the same phenomenon. Conducted under different aspects, analysis thus provides a better understanding of the same reality.

The homosexual subculture is also coextensive with the homosexual community. The self-defined needs of homosexuals and the social bound-aries which separate them from the rest of society are normally operative only insofar as the individuals are homosexual (i.e., insofar as they have the compulsion or desire to have sexual relations with members of their own sex) or insofar as they have acquired other needs connected with the traits and behaviors mentioned above (i.e., insofar as they are members of the homosexual subculture). The homosexual community, however, is not identical with all homosexuals, but only with those homosexuals who have "affirmed" their condition and have "come out." (See chapter III.) The political needs of the movement have encouraged its leaders to dis-seminate the notion that the homosexual community is widespread. It would be more proper, however, to speak of the homosexual community as comprising those homosexuals who, by deed, word, or thought, have made the conscious choice to become part of the community.

Manifestations of the Homosexual Subculture

The social expressions of the homosexual subculture are multiple. They range from the various institutions which have already been mentioned to artistic and cultural events which are meant to advance the homosexual ideology while cementing the various components of the homosexual community. Several examples of manifestations of the homosexual subculture will serve to illustrate its characteristics. In no way do they exhaust the vast complex by which the homosexual community expresses itself.

OBJECTS AND SYMBOLS

There are hundreds of objects by which the homosexual can identify himself as a member of the subculture. A number of these objects are directly related to sexual practices, ranging from artificial electric masturbators—Accujacs—to such chemical products as butyl nitrite (poppers), a substance similar to the illegal drug amyl nitrite, which increases peripheral blood circulation and induces tachycardia, giving the user the illusion of a prolonged and more pleasurable orgasm. They include other items such as metal rings to be placed around the genitals; metal clips to cause pain in the male nipples; chains, whips, and leather straps with which sexual partners are ritually "punished"; dog collars and other gadgets designed to convey the feeling of inferiority and degradation on sexual partners; artificial male organs, etc. Pornographic material is available at almost all prices and in a variety that would surprise the inexperienced. There are inexpensive pornographic "novels," including some with illustrations, comic books, magazine-size publications featuring photographs of naked youths and pornographic stories, and tabloid papers featuring nude pictures, stories, and lewd advertisements. The only feature common to these publications seems to be the overwhelming preoccupation with sexuality. Homosexual printed matter is designed to satisfy the specific needs of the user. There are items that concentrate on children having sex with one another, adults having sex with children, multiethnic and one-race publications, items which portray only individuals who have overdeveloped muscles, using leather articles or motorcycles. In some cases the sexual activities depicted are of only one variety; other items depict a wide variety of sexual behavior. The purpose of these items is to provide sexual stimulation to the users, who might either be polyfacetic or perhaps prefer only a narrow selection of sexual practices.

Other objects which do not directly relate to sexual acts but which are indirectly—sometimes rather remotely—associated with homosexual practices include such items as greeting cards with homosexual themes (some with enormous genitals), naked attractive youth, or crude phrases descriptive of homosexual behavior; chocolates in the shapes of genitals; earrings for one ear, which many homosexuals use; sets of colored handkerchiefs which serve as a code by which homosexuals announce to each other their preferred practice (i.e., each color corresponds to a certain sexual activity, while the side of the body where displayed indicates whether the person prefers to be active or passive); magnetic attachments

THE HOMOSEXUAL NETWORK

for cars and refrigerators in the shape of individuals with over-developed genitals; "gay dolls" complete with fully stimulated genitals and a "closet"; purses, pocket books, change holders, book markers, key rings, and bumperstickers, all centered around the issue of homosexuality. There are pins that identify the users as homosexuals, utilizing one of the various insignia of the movement. The Washington office of the UFMCC, for example, has sold "Pink Triangle pins." The following description of these pins, which appears in a handout, illustrates the powerful effect of symbols in the formation of the homosexual identity. The reader will easily notice the value of these symbols in terms of stimulating pride in the homosexual condition, a sense of historical continuity and the establishment of solidarity among "liberated" homosexuals.

The Washington Office of the Universal Fellowship of Metropolitan Community Churches is proud to announce that it has in stock a quantity of beautiful enamel Pink Triangle pins for $2.00 each.

The pins are hand-made by Judy Stone, a well-known California craftswoman, and are three-quarters of an inch on each side. The pin is triangular in shape, metal with a pink enamel front, and has a locking pin.

The Pink Triangle is part of our history as Lesbians and Gay men. In Nazi Germany, as most people know, Jews were required to wear yellow Stars of David sewn conspicuously to their clothing. Jews throughout Nazi Europe had to wear the yellow Star of David at all times. Over six million European Jews went to their deaths in Nazi concentration camps wearing the yellow six-pointed star patch on their clothes.

What is much less well-known is that the Nazis forced homosexuals to wear Pink Triangle patches in the same way. The Pink Triangles were seen throughout Nazi-dominated Europe, and many thousands of Lesbians and Gay men were sent to the death camps. Between 250,000 and 500,000 of our brothers and sisters were murdered in concentration camps by the Nazis because they were Gay.

We wear the Pink Triangle today, though we do not live in a Nazi regime and our people do not face concentration camps, as a symbol of solidarity with our brothers and sisters in the past who were martyrs to Nazi homophobic oppression. We wear the Pink Triangle to demonstrate that we have not forgotten our martyred sisters and brothers. We wear the Pink Triangle because we know that so long as homophobia exists, we are not safe from a recurrence of the kind of horror Lesbians and Gay men faced in Nazi Germany. We wear the Pink Triangle because we know that hatred, bigotry, intolerance, oppression, and homophobia do not belong to any one time or place or society in history. We wear the Pink Triangle because of our commitment to educate people about homophobia and Gay civil and human rights.

These pins are beautiful examples of craftwork and can be worn with pride as an understated piece of jewelry that also serves as an educational device. Wear the Pink Triangle and be ready to tell people who ask about it this terrible part of *our* history as Lesbians and Gay men.[2]

The Homosexual Subculture

Another powerful device which the homosexual movement has developed as the international symbol for homosexuality is the Greek letter lambda (λ). Since the early 1970s, λ has signified liberation for homosexuals, and it is now the acknowledged "logo" of the homosexual movement. It appears in publications and on bumperstickers; ties with the lambda motiff are sold by mail and in homosexual shops; tie tacks, pendants, brooches, and other jewelry advertise the sexual interests of the wearer; six lambdas making up a "mogen David" constitute the symbol of Jewish homosexuality; Christian homosexual ministers have incorporated lambda in their sacred vestments and vessels. Lambda has indeed become the sign of homosexuality.

All these objects, from those closely connected with the most violent and purposefully degrading forms of sexual behavior to the lofty vestments by which homosexual ministers share with their congregations—in a cultic and highly symbolic fashion—their theological conviction that the homosexual condition is a God-given avenue toward personal integration and sanctification, in fact constitute powerful socializing agents for homosexuals who have chosen to affirm their sexual peculiarity. In this process, they also become part of and help embody the subculture of homosexuality as we know it today.

HOMOSEXUAL BARS

Among all the social institutions within the homosexual subculture, none has been more influential than the "gay bar," of which there are no fewer than 2,000 nationwide. (The *Gayellow Pages* list 1,913 homosexual bars; undoubtedly, the number is much larger.) These bars are *the* meeting place for homosexuals. From the earliest times of the movement they have been at the center of the effort to enshrine homosexuality as a legitimate lifestyle. Table 7 shows the distribution of homosexual bars nationwide. They range from small "sleazy" places in dark and dangerous alleys to plush establishments which compete favorably with the best discoteques. Some bars cater to a conventional-looking clientele. Others specialize in sadomasochists or transvestites. There are bars which purposely attract young people, prostitutes who serve to attract older homosexuals who in turn purchase drinks for the youngsters while sexual deals are arranged. Printed guides for traveling homosexuals or for newcomers usually specify what they can find at the various bars. This includes the ethnic composition of the patrons, whether the bar caters to homosexual males, females or a "mixed crowd," whether heterosexuals are normally in attendance or not, the availability of prostitutes or "rough trade" (i.e., homosexuals who enjoy appearing violent or who actually behave violently).

Without the "gay bar," it would be impossible to conceive of the homosexual movement as it exists today. Homosexuals in fact trace the event

THE HOMOSEXUAL NETWORK

TABLE 7

Homosexual Bars

Jurisdiction	Number	Jurisdiction	Number
Alabama	13	Montana	5
Alaska	4	Nebraska	10
Arizona	28	Nevada	10
Arkansas	8	New Hampshire	3
California	381	New Jersey	39
Colorado	16	New Mexico	7
Connecticut	15	New York	264
Delaware	5	North Carolina	19
District of Columbia	34	Ohio	65
Florida	130	Oklahoma	21
Georgia	32	Oregon	25
Hawaii	12	Pennsylvania	95
Idaho	2	Rhode Island	11
Illinois	82	South Carolina	8
Indiana	22	South Dakota	2
Iowa	9	Tennessee	26
Kansas	11	Texas	111
Kentucky	8	Utah	6
Louisiana	55	Vermont	2
Maine	13	Virginia	13
Maryland	22	Washington	33
Massachusetts	70	West Virginia	7
Michigan	48	Wisconsin	32
Minnesota	16	Wyoming	6
Mississippi	5	Puerto Rico	19
Missouri	26	Virgin Islands (US)	7
		Total	1913

SOURCE: *Gayellow Pages*, Renaissance House, New York, N.Y., 1981 edition.

which brought the movement into the open, the Stonewall riot, to an attempt by the New York City police to curtail homosexual activity at a bar. Today, politicians who court the homosexual vote campaign in bars and derive some of their funds from bar owners and activities (dinners, parties, etc. at bars). The importance of the bar for the homosexual community has not escaped its leaders. As Adam DeBaugh has pointed out, the success of the movement can only result in increasing economic benefits for bar owners since "with the continued success of the gay rights movement, more and more people are coming out, and some of the places they are coming out to are bars."[3]

Inasmuch as the main product consumed at bars is at the center of what is generally acknowledged to be an illness, alcoholism, the fact that bars are the central institution of the homosexual movement presents obvious dangers for its members. Since homosexuals form the only subculture in

The Homosexual Subculture

which one of the basic institutions is the bar, it is to be expected that a high rate of alcoholism will develop among them. Moreover, although alcoholism is also present among heterosexuals, the very fact that no children are produced by homosexual couples increases their opportunity to spend considerable time at bars. This fact probably also contributes to alcoholism among homosexuals.

THE BATHS

Another institution central to the homosexual subculture is the "gay bathhouse" or simply "the baths." There are no fewer than 168 homosexual baths, located in most major cities. Table 8 shows the distribution of baths in various American cities. This listing is not complete, since the *Gayellow Pages* from which it was taken does not list all establishments. The total number of baths is thus certainly larger than 168. Although they are officially labeled "health clubs," the baths are really places where homosexuals find sexual partners. They make it possible for homosexuals to seek relief from their sexual urges without the need to establish personal relationships and to be burdened by the responsibilities these relationships imply. As Morton Hunt—hardly an unfriendly author—points out: "Cruising in the baths is even more impersonal and nonsocial than in the bars: there is practically no conversation, and sex acts take place right on the premises, often in front of onlookers."[4] Baths provide their customers with a locker for storing clothing or small cabins where homosexuals get together to have sex. There are also large rooms called "orgy rooms" or "mazes" where large numbers can congregate for group sex. The "better" baths also have screening rooms for the showing of pornographic films. In general there is little or no conversation except what is required for the establishment of a sexual liaison. The homosexuals simply wait, in poses that reflect their favorite sexual practices. In specialized establishments there are "dungeons" or "torture rooms" where homosexuals who wish to be degraded submit to sadists whose expertise is to inflict punishment or humiliation. Special events to satisfy the specific needs of customers are also held. An example of such an event is the regular "slave auction" held at the Bulldog Baths in San Francisco the second Wednesday of every month (Figure 1). Other features of baths, such as exercise rooms, showers, steam rooms, lounges, and snack bars are merely added attractions to the fundamental purpose of the establishment.

There is no question that baths are completely accepted by the homosexual community. In fact, the baths are probably the single most typical establishment of the homosexual subculture and certainly one that is exclusive to this subculture. Should the homosexual ideology become an integral part of our beliefs, we could very well see the organization of sex establishments similar to baths, but perhaps specializing in particular groups: sadomasochists, boy lovers, transvestites, lovers of overweight or

TABLE 8
Homosexual Baths

Jurisdiction	Locality	
Arizona	Phoenix	2
	Tuscon	1
California	Alameda	1
	Fresno	1
	Long Beach	3
	Los Angeles	20
	Monterey	1
	Oakland	2
	Sacramento	2
	San Diego	4
	San Francisco	8
	San Jose	1
Colorado	Denver	5
Connecticut	Hartford	1
Florida	Fort Lauderdale	3
	Hollywood	1
	Jacksonville	1
	Key West	1
	Miami	2
	Tampa	1
Georgia	Atlanta	2
Hawaii	Honolulu	3
Illinois	Chicago	6
Indiana	Hammond	1
	Indianapolis	2
Iowa	Council Bluffs	1
Louisiana	New Orleans	4
Maryland	Baltimore	4
Massachusetts	Boston	2
Michigan	Detroit	5
Minnesota	Minneapolis	2
	St. Paul	1
Missouri	Kansas City	2
	St. Louis	2
Montana	Great Falls	1
Nebraska	Omaha	1
Nevada	Las Vegas	2
New Jersey	Asbury Park	1
	Atlantic City	1
	Newark	1
New Mexico	Albuquerque	1
New York	Albany	1
	Buffalo	1
	New York City	16
	Rochester	2
	Syracuse	1
North Carolina	Charlotte	1

TABLE 8 (*cont.*)

Jurisdiction	Locality	
Ohio	Akron	2
	Cleveland	3
	Columbus	1
	Dayton	1
	Toledo	1
Oklahoma	Oklahoma City	1
Oregon	Portland	4
Pennsylvania	Philadelphia	3
	Pittsburgh	3
Rhode Island	Providence	1
Texas	Austin	2
	Dallas	2
	Houston	3
	San Antonio	1
Utah	Salt Lake City	1
Washington	Seattle	4
Wisconsin	Milwaukee	2
Washington, DC		4
Puerto Rico		1
	Total	168

SOURCE: *Gayellow Pages*, Renaissance House, New York, N.Y., 1981 edition.

elderly persons, etc. Not only openly pornographic publications, but also "respectable" newspapers like *The Advocate* (San Mateo, California), *The Sentinel* (San Francisco), and the *New York Native* advertise baths, with material well designed to attract customers. Whenever they show human bodies, inevitably they are nude (or seminude), attractive, and muscular young men. They are probably designed for lonely homosexuals, especially older ones.

The degree of promiscuity in the baths defies the imagination of those not familiar with homosexuality. From the point of view of traditional values, they are probably some of the most destructive and degrading institutions in America today. There is no indication, however, that any of the homosexual organizations has opposed or in any way showed interest in counteracting the effects of the baths. From the medical point of view, the baths probably constitute a major focus for the transmission of disease. Psychologically, they constitute the antithesis of mental health. Ethically, it is difficult to justify the impersonality and degradation they institutionalize. However, as Hunt points out:

As peculiar or even "sick" as this may seem to most straight people, it seems perfectly reasonable to a good many gays. The baths are second in popularity

Figure 1
SOURCE: *The* (San Francisco) *Sentinel*, August 7, 1981.

only to bars as places to cruise (some cities have a dozen or more of them), and there are so many in the United States that the owners and managers of gay baths recently held a week-long convention, like other businessmen, to discuss their business problems and methods of dealing with them.[5]

MUSIC AND THE ARTS
In addition to bars and baths, there are innumerable organizations and institutions which define and express the homosexual subculture. Most of them will be presented elsewhere in this work. It is important, however, for the reader to avoid the mistaken assumption that the only activities of liberated homosexuals with their community is to socialize, drink, and seek sexual partners in bars, or to participate in orgies at baths. Although it is in fact the sexual attraction for same-sex partners and the behavior which originates therein that constitutes the least common de-

nominator of homosexuals, there are many other activities within the homosexual community which have much in common with cultural activities of the rest of society. It must be noted, nevertheless, that there is an erotic component to most—if not all—activities identified as "gay."

One of the most viable, successful ventures of the homosexual movement is the San Francisco Gay Men's Chorus, one of several homosexual bands and choral groups that exist in major U.S. cities. This group travels throughout the country, hosted by the most prestigious cultural centers. During the 1981 tour, the Chorus was scheduled to perform at such places as the Dallas Convention Center, the Boston and Seattle Opera Houses, New York City's Beacon Theatre, and the national center of American culture, Washington's Kennedy Center.[6] While visiting Washington, the Chorus performed on the steps of the Capitol. The group has cut a commercial record and is reviewed by the regular media. The following letter was written to the *Washington Post* by Joseph A. Izzo, a member of the Xaverian Brothers, a Roman Catholic teaching order, in appreciation for a positive review. It was published by the *Washington Blade* on June 26, 1981, with an introduction by Izzo which reads in part: "I feel it is very important to thank those who give us good media coverage. They deserve to be commended for their courage and ought to be affirmed for being honest, fair, and non-discriminatory."[7]

This letter illustrates not only the role of the Chorus in the homosexual subculture, but how its activities are appreciated by the leadership of the movement.[8]

Dear Mr. Hume,

Like yourself, I had the treasured opportunity to attend the Kennedy Center concert by the San Francisco Gay Men's Chorus. I, too, was overwhelmed by the beauty and precision of their performance. The whole experience, however, including your laudatory review of the concert, moved me emotionally and spiritually.

As a Gay man myself and a minister/counselor to Gay men and Lesbians, I am most frequently in touch with the hurt and pain which we Gay people experience because of the homophobic attitudes and behavior of the larger society. We are very often reduced as people to our sexual orientation alone. We often do that to ourselves and allow the churches and society to do the same to us.

For me, the real triumph of the Gay Men's Chorus was not so much its musical brilliance, but the pride and self-esteem that the Chorus projected and instilled into its audience of predominantly Gay people. For once, all of us could stand and be proud of our many gifts and talents without being reduced simply to our sexual orientation. The standing ovations which you noted occurred about ten times were our way of saying, "We are somebody, we are good and whole people!" It was a personal and political statement made through the medium of beautiful music.

THE HOMOSEXUAL NETWORK

I hope that your wish for some recording companies to pick up this unique chorus will materialize. For me, and I hope, for my other Lesbian and Gay brothers and sisters, the San Francisco Gay Men's Chorus can be the "Good Will Ambassadors" of the Gay community to the larger society. By the beauty of their music they can bridge the gap of misunderstanding, heal the wounds that have been inflicted on us for many centuries, and demonstrate to the Jerry Falwells and the Moral Majority types that we are real human beings, not moral misfits.

By simply doing what they are doing as musical artists and without making a single political statement, they can do as much for the Lesbian and Gay Community as the Gay Rights National Lobby or the National Gay Task Force now do through political action.

Being used to criticism, discrimination, and persecution because of my Gayness, I really didn't expect the concert to receive much of a review. We are so often slighted or ignored by the mainline press and media. So it is a special word of thanks that I offer to you for treating the San Francisco Gay Men's Chorus with the respect and acclaim they so rightly deserved. Thank you for allowing them and all Lesbian and Gay people to rightfully hold our heads a little higher with genuine pride and self-worth.

I am grateful, too, to the *Washington Post* for its positive coverage of the Gay Men's Chorus. It is that type of media publicity that will help to change some of the misunderstanding and homophobia that still exists.

BROTHER JOSEPH A. IZZO, C.F.X.
Catholic University of America
Washington, D.C.

The inextricable connection between the homosexual community and its subculture is apparent in this letter. Whether the Chorus's music is good or not from an artistic point of view is largely irrelevant. The important points are that the Chorus exists and that it has been accepted by such institutions of the dominant culture as the *Washington Post* and the Kennedy Center. Izzo's hope that recording companies will produce a record of the Chorus expresses the need for acceptance by yet another social institution. This evidences the intrinsic flaw of the homosexual subculture. If homosexuality is not an important factor (the "without being reduced simply to our sexual orientation" of Izzo's letter) as the basis of discrimination, the very legitimacy of a "Gay Men's Chorus" can be called into question. After all, the desire to engage in sexual activities with people of one's own sex cannot be rationally related to the capability for making music, and there is no evidence that homosexuals have been excluded from any such groups. The rejection of homosexuality by most Americans is not based on any implication that homosexuals are incapable of reason or artistic intuition, but on the fact that their sexual inclinations lead to a behavior which is in conflict with human nature from the biological, psychological, and sociopolitical viewpoints.

The production of works of art by the homosexual community qua

The Homosexual Subculture

homosexual is well illustrated by the Great American Lesbian Art Show (GALAS) held in May 1980.[9] GALAS was actually a series of cultural events held by homosexual females throughout the United States. In large and small cities alike, homosexuals involved themselves in "honoring the creative contributions made by lesbians to culture." Represented were visual art, film, poetry, and other performances. It was reported by *In Unity* that 300 artists were represented.

Another case of homosexual art which had considerable public repercussions is the Gay Pride Sculpture in New York City. Created by George Segal, it constitutes a glorification of homosexuality, having the appropriate erotic undertones that characterize the homosexual subculture. The sculpture is made up of two homosexual couples, two males and two females. It became something of a cause célèbre when attempts were made to install it in Sheridan Square, at the heart of Greenwich Village's homosexual neighborhood. The opposition of community groups was utilized by homosexual leaders as a conscientizing point for their constituency. The list of supporters provided by the Mariposa Foundation, funder of the project, comprises what can only be described as New York City's liberal establishment.[10] The commentaries cited by the foundation illustrate the cultural value of this sculpture for the homosexual community:

> I've looked down from my window onto Christopher Park for years in dismay at the desolation. The prospect of seeing George Segal's Gay Pride Sculpture there is wonderful. As a resident who lives there and raised a family there, I couldn't be more pleased.
>
> ARYAH NEIER
> (Former Executive Director,
> American Civil Liberties Union)

> The George Segal sculpture appropriately belongs in Sheridan Square as a symbol, tribute, and celebration of our population. As a long-time resident of the Square, I am thrilled by the prospect of such a statue.
>
> DAVID ROTHENBERG
> (New York City
> Human Rights Commissioner)

> The roots of our movement are in Sheridan Square and Christopher Park. It is entirely appropriate and wonderful that George Segal has created a splendid Gay Pride Sculpture to go there.
>
> GINNY APUZZO
> [Homosexual Activist]

It is interesting to note that, as in the case of the Gay Men's Chorus, the aesthetic value of the statue is not mentioned. The cultural value of

41

the piece is, in a sense, identical with its political significance. From a cultural standpoint, this makes the homosexual movement suspicious. The question is not whether homosexuals are capable of creating a work of art. It is, in fact, known that in the past artists have been homosexuals, and their productions have achieved a level of excellence no different from that of heterosexuals. The question is not whether the homosexuality of an artist can have an impact on the artist's production. A person cannot be separated from his sexuality, and it is reasonable to assume that the social and psychological pressures which a homosexual person must endure in our society may bring out a depth of perception for suffering, loneliness, and angst which, when combined with the required artistic skills, enables the homosexual to become a good artist. What seems clear is that the homosexual qua homosexual, from either an individual or a collective point of view (i.e., insofar as he desires to engage in certain sexual practices, or insofar as he considers himself to be a member of the homosexual community) is no better an artist, even if he possesses the required skills to paint, compose poetry, or write music. In other words, homosexuality as such has no cultural value or meaning. Homosexual art and the "gay culture" are merely political devices designed to impress the heterosexual world with what might otherwise be genuine works of art and to provide the homosexual with feelings of self-worth and belonging.

HOMOSEXUAL LITERATURE

The homosexual literature is crucial for the movement; some of the most important homosexual professional organizations are the Discussion Group for Gay Studies in Language and Literature, an official body of the Modern Language Association (MLA), the Gay Caucus for the Modern Languages, and the Gay Task Force of the American Library Assocation (ALA). This is not difficult to understand, since literature is the ideal means for the transmittal of ideas. These organizations have, if not a high profile, a profound influence on the homosexual subculture. The ALA Gay Task Force publishes and disseminates widely bibliographies centered on homosexuality from various viewpoints (religious, political, sociological, etc.). These bibliographies, in turn, are used by librarians, teachers, scholars, and sociopolitical activists to propagate the homosexual ideology while perpetuating the subculture.[11] The Gay Caucus for the Modern Languages sponsors, among other activities, scholarly sessions at MLA conventions with such titles as "Interpretative Problems in Nondeclared Lesbian Writers," "Feminist Science Fiction: Utopian and Alternative Societies," and "Homosexuality, Literature, and Society: Voltaire, Beckford, Bentham."[12] In 1977 it was reported that fifty-three homosexual titles (exclusive of hard-core pornography) had been published "recently."[13] Since then, many others have followed. A casual visit to a homo-

The Homosexual Subculture

sexual bookstore will convince the reader that, even excluding self-defined pornographic works, this figure is far too low. It is difficult to ascertain how many books can be categorized as products of the homosexual subculture, since there are no defined boundaries or clear-cut ways of identifying them, but the annual production of prohomosexual literary works certainly numbers in the hundreds.

An organization which promotes the homosexual movement through literature is the Gay Theatre Alliance, founded in 1978. Its statement of purpose reads: "Recognizing the need for communication and support among gay theatre artists, a group of lesbians and gay men have joined together to form the Gay Theatre Alliance (GTA) to foster and promote the development of Gay Theatre. The Alliance is open to all people who seek to expand awareness and understanding of gay lifestyles through theatre."[14] Activities of GTA include (or are planned to include) publications, cultural exchanges, regional/national conferences, and the Gay Theatre Archive, which is charged with "preserving gay theatre for future generations through the creation of a gay theatre archive at a major New York City cultural institution."[15] In addition to the Archive, GTA has undertaken two projects of great value for the promotion of homosexuality. The *Directory of Gay Plays* features comprehensive information on "over 400 plays, including title, playwright, character and set requirements, plot description, royalties, date of first production, date of first publication and other information."[16] The plays included are those having "lesbian and gay themes." A yearly International Gay Playwriting Contest also serves to promote the production of plays having "a major gay character or major gay theme."[17] Although none of the materials available from the GTA directly indicates a prohomosexual bias, the language used makes it difficult to conceive that the GTA would sponsor works of a neutral or traditional position on the homosexual question. One can safely assume, for example, that a play portraying homosexuality from the point of view of the traditional Judeo-Christian ethic (e.g., casting homosexuality in a negative light, pointing out that it is curable or that it is a sin) would not find an approving reception from the GTA.

The GTA is organized into six regions with a coordinator in Australia. Its members include writers, actors, directors, musicians, technicians, etc. Theatre companies are also members of GTA. This allows the organization to facilitate the production of plays which receive awards in its yearly contests.

One of the fundamental components of any subculture is its intelligentsia. The Gay Academic Union (GAU) is the focal point of the homosexual intelligentsia. Together with "gay archives" and the "gay caucuses" of professional associations, the GAU promotes homosexuality from an intellectual platform. The by-laws of the Washington Chapter of the Gay Academic Union state the following as the purpose of the organization:

THE HOMOSEXUAL NETWORK

"The Gay Academic Union is a voluntary organization of individuals who have a scholarly interest in homosexuality and the gay/lesbian subculture. The purpose of the organization is to increase the knowledge of the members, to provide opportunities for professional and social contacts, and to serve as a resource for the gay community."[18]

Although apparently the organization is "somewhat in a state of disarray at the moment,"[19] the GAU sponsors programs which, in the long run, are bound to result in the strengthening of the homosexual subculture. Its award program includes the granting of Literary, Fine Arts, and the Evelyn Hooker Research awards.[20] Such activities as a lecture on homosexuals' participation in World War II,[21] Lesbian History, and Sexual Politics in the '80s[22] indicate the existence of the intellectual substratum in the homosexual subculture.

The Liberated Homosexual and the Dominant Culture

The various institutions of the homosexual subculture—those described in this chapter and others presented elsewhere—resocialize liberated homosexuals, providing the support they need to survive in heterosexual America, both socially and psychologically. The homosexual who chooses to be resocialized into this subculture does not have to interact with heterosexuals, or nonhomosexual institutions, in any meaningful way in order to feel part of society. He can find religion, culture, recreation, education, and many other needs in institutions that are supportive of his sexual choices. These homosexual institutions create a total environment for their members. Consider the case of the 1980 Gay Book Award to *Now the Volcano: An Anthology of Latin American Gay Literature* and the presentation of two prohomosexual films, *World of Light: A Portrait of May Sarton* and *Christopher Isherwood: Over There on a Visit*, as arranged by the Gay Teachers Association. The event took place at the Gay Synagogue on July 2, 1980. An announcement for it appeared in the program for the meeting of the Gay Task Force of the American Library Association (ALA) and it was scheduled to coincide with the 1980 Annual Conference of the ALA.[23]

In a different field, another example of the way in which the homosexual subculture satisfies its members' needs is FOLKS (Friends of Little Kids), a "big brother/big sister" program for homosexuals who want to establish close relationships with the children of female homosexuals. An invitation to attend a New York City informational meeting on FOLKS, sponsored by Integrity (homosexual Episcopalians), was circulated by Dignity (homosexual Catholics).[24] Apparently, FOLKS relieves homosexual mothers of the need to seek role models for their children in non-homosexually

The Homosexual Subculture

oriented social services like Big Brothers, Boy Scouts, and Campfire Girls. The homosexual movement can meet this need as well.

The perception of nonacceptance by the dominant culture is fostered by the homosexual subculture in its members for two obvious reasons. First, this feeling makes the homosexual participate in activities of institutions that form an integral part of the homosexual subculture. After all, it is in those institutions that he perceives himself to be accepted in terms of what the subculture—sometimes against some of its own ideological principles—fosters as the dominant feature of his self: the desire to engage in sexual relations with members of his own sex. This is vital for the subculture, since it guarantees the existence of those institutions that embody and ensure historical continuity. The participation of homosexuals in the activities of these institutions is thus a matter of sheer survival for the homosexual subculture. Secondly, this dynamic opposition between the "liberated" homosexual and the dominant culture is precisely the raison d'être of the homosexual movement. The moment a homosexual becomes convinced that there is no radical opposition between his *objective* interests (i.e., those rooted in his human dignity and biological make-up rather than in a psychosocial superstructure) and the interests of the dominant culture, the psychological barrier hindering the participation of the homosexual in institutions available to the population at large will disappear. This would, however, require of the homosexual: 1) the acceptance of homosexuality as a disorder of human nature and of homosexual behavior as inimical to his own best interests; 2) the active desire to become heterosexual or, if this were shown to be impossible on account of the condition being too deeply ingrained, the cessation of homosexual practices; and 3) the intellectual abandonment of the basic principles of the homosexual ideology and of all sociopolitical activities in support of the homosexual movement. Naturally, such requirements can be expected to meet with the total and fierce opposition of the movement.

As a result of the perception of nonacceptance by ordinary institutions, certain homosexuals will avoid them whenever possible. A typical example of this is the apparent failure of "The Alternate Lifestyle VD Clinic" at Pima County (Tucson), Arizona.[25] This failure occurred although the county staffed the clinic with "persons who are sympathetic to the needs of gay people"[26] and the institution was meant to serve approximately 40,000 homosexuals. The clinic was opened to replace the apparently successful "Gay Community Services of Tucson VD Testing Center," clearly identifiable as part of the homosexual subculture. The moment the similar institution opened—this time under a sponsorship not clearly identifiable as homosexual—the flow of clients ceased.

There is very little question that homosexual institutions have as one of their purposes the strengthening of the "homosexual component" of the personality of their clients and participants. This is the positive side of the fostering of rejection of heterosexual institutions by the homosexual subculture mentioned above. At times, this purpose is not stated explicitly. In many instances, however, it is openly acknowledged. For example, the Gay and Lesbian Christian Alliance (GLCA) was formed at North Carolina State University in 1979, having as a faculty advisor Willie White—also a "campus minister" at the University and pastor of the Raleigh Metropolitan Community Church. According to the organization's first president, Junior Todd Ellis, the group would promote "feelings of self-acceptance among gay and lesbian students."[27]

It would be accurate to describe the homosexual subculture as a complex web of interlocking organizations and institutions which, while re-socializing its members, provides them with political, social, psychological (and at times even economic) support. Once a person becomes involved in this subculture, he has little or no reason to leave it; immersion in the subculture may become total. Some of the elements of the subculture even facilitate the relief from sexual needs which undoubtedly assail every homosexual. Strange as it may appear, becoming a full-fledged member of the homosexual subculture entails centering one's life on one's sexual peculiarities. It constitutes an ever-stronger bonding of the homosexual to others like himself, objectively decreasing the individual's freedom even as it provides him with a sense of liberation. From a traditional point of view, this is no liberation at all, but rather enslavement to an all-consuming passion. In short, "gay liberation" is not merely the acquisition of social and political privileges as a "legitimate minority," but a freeing of the homosexual to seek the complete satisfaction of his sexual appetites without the restrictions which children, family responsibility, and the tenets of the Judeo-Christian ethic impose on heterosexuals. In this way, the homosexual subculture is solidly anchored in the psycho-sexual needs of its members which, in turn, it heightens. The more deeply the homosexual participates in "his" subculture, the stronger is his condition. Conversely, the deeper the homosexuality, the stronger the subculture in which he subsists.

There are two aspects of the homosexual subculture which, although not related to each other, reflect the nature of the subculture and its interactions with the dominant culture. On the one hand, the possibility that homosexuality is an illness and thus a sexual disorder makes the subculture unique. This is especially true when it is considered that homosexuality involves the will and human consciousness, i.e., it is not just a physical condition. There are certain other illnesses which, while not physically the result of the homosexual condition, are clearly related to the practice of homosexuality. Since many of these illnesses are infectious, and their treatment at times utilizes public monies, their existence is important for the society at large.

On the other hand, one of the factors which has created the homosexual

The Homosexual Subculture

subculture, and a tool widely used by the movement in the accomplishment of its objectives, is language. The use of language by the homosexual subculture must be examined in some detail if an appropriate understanding of this subculture is to be reached.

Illness and the Homosexual Subculture

Whether homosexuality is or is not an illness is, as we will see, a much debated question among those interested in this subject. Part of the problem could lie in the very definitions of "illness" and "homosexual." There is no difficulty when homosexuality is defined in terms of sexual attraction for members of one's own sex, but ascertaining whether or not a particular individual belongs to this category can be very difficult, if not impossible.

In 1948 Alfred Kinsey published a statistical study in which he classified men in terms of the heterosexual-homosexual continuum. On a 0–6 scale, 0 meant exclusive heterosexuality and 6 exclusive homosexuality. (For a concise description of Kinsey's work, see Ronald Bayer, *Homosexuality and American Psychiatry*.) In fact, the usual ways in which sociologists and statisticians (including Kinsey) define homosexual are quite arbitrary, although they are useful in organizing the data obtained from surveys. For the purpose of this analysis, however, these definitions are meaningless. The problem we confront is typical of all efforts to categorize and should not be surprising.

With this in mind, it must be said that the acceptance that the sociobiological substratum of human life demands heterosexuality—both affective and physical—as normative implies that homosexuality is an illness, since this condition interferes with the proper operations of those affected. Within the frame of traditional morality, if affection for spouse and children does not result in the structuring of a family in which the children can develop physically and psychologically, that which makes it impossible for such a family to exist can be deemed an illness. In this context, illness would be understood as any condition interfering with an organism's ability to function properly (and "properly," the key word here, implicitly involves value judgment). This concept naturally assumes a teleological frame of reference without which the definition of illness (and probably all discourse) must be totally subjective or it will become meaningless. That the definition of homosexuality as an illness is preceded by a set of values cannot be questioned. This is true of all conditions which have behaviors as their sole symptoms. If values are deemed to be the result only of the free decision of men, then there is no way of ascertaining whether homosexuality (or any other psychological condition) is an illness.

47

If certain values are accepted as part of the *philosophia perennis*, there is very little question that, from a psychological viewpoint, homosexuality is a mental disorder. (The counterparts to this statement are that 1) from a theological viewpoint, homosexuality is an indication of the sinful condition of mankind, and 2) from a sociopolitical viewpoint, homosexuality is a social disorder.)

As we will see hereafter, the notions that homosexuality is an illness or that it can be remedied are tenaciously denied by the homosexual movement. These denials, as we will show, have an ideological value only, inasmuch as they describe the needs and aspirations of the movement rather than the nature of homosexuality itself. As an ideological expression, they have served the movement well. However, they have little or no validity per se and should be ignored. Similar definitions made by the professional associations (e.g., the American Psychological Association or the American Psychiatric Association), academicians, political leaders, and other institutions should also be discounted, inasmuch as they purport to describe reality whenever their context indicates that they are made for the purpose of supporting the homosexual movement. In the intellectual environment of scientism—i.e., empiricism—which dominates post-Kantian thought, the only way of avoiding this logical trap is to maintain a fundamental trust in our ability to know and express our nature in teleological terms by means of epistemological processes founded in immediate evidence.

The ultimate answer to the question of the nature of homosexuality in terms of the health/illness polarity is thus a metaphysical problem. However, there is another sense in which homosexuality can be understood in terms of the same health/illness pair which goes beyond the concerns of each individual homosexual qua homosexual. Within a Western frame of mind, individuals have a meaning in themselves and are well-defined in terms of ego boundaries. An Eastern viewpoint tends to be holistic. Although one does not have to accept in toto the Oriental mind set, it is an extremely useful alternative point of view for examining such issues as the one that concerns us. Health and sickness acquire a different though related meaning when analyzed holistically, since the behavior of an organism is viewed not solely in terms of the "interests" of that organism but with reference to other organisms to which it is inextricably connected. The implications of homosexuality for the rest of the community in terms of the health/illness continuum acquire a significance that goes far beyond the interests of the individual homosexual or his subculture. The status of homosexuality as an illness cannot be ascertained only in terms of the opinions of individual homosexuals or their collective expression by the homosexual movement. It is necessary to analyze the movement's effects on the larger society in terms of the mutual dependence of its various parts.

The Homosexual Subculture

Given the fundamental unproductiveness of homosexual acts, it is nearly impossible to establish the value of this practice for the species from the point of view of the continuing existence of the human race. The biological nature of sex in reference to procreation is negated by homosexuality. Individual homosexuals may claim that the feelings of "love" and "affection" between partners generated by their practices, and the relief from sexual tension experienced through engagement in these practices, are positive contributions to society (making for "happier" or "more satisfied" people—i.e., themselves—who are thus more productive). This, however, is based purely on subjective affirmations that have no value beyond the fact that they are made. It can be as easily argued that a homosexual who ceases to believe in the homosexual ideology can find relief (and become just as happy) in religion, psychotherapy, or the sublimation of his tendencies in the pursuit of goals. (The reader is reminded that many homosexuals "put up" with their condition, resigning themselves to unfulfilled desires, or find in their sufferings a sense of strength and growth. They reject the notion that homosexuality is "normal" and refuse to consider acceptance and affirmation of their sexual desires as a form of liberation.) In short, while there are, in fact, homosexual writers, musicians, teachers, ministers, and politicians, their accomplishments are not traceable to their condition (beyond, perhaps, their need to cope with it in a nonhomosexual environment). In other words, such institutions as "gay baths," "gay unions" of homosexual partners, and homosexual pornography are the only distinct contributions of the homosexual movement to our culture.

A holistic view of society reveals the homosexual community qua community as a sick portion of the social body. There is little question that some members of the homosexual subculture do contribute to society: they hold jobs and pay taxes; they are at times productive and increase the efficiency of social, economic, and political processes; homosexual artists and writers are capable of producing works of beauty and social worth. In no way, however, are these contributions made by these homosexuals in terms of their condition, nor insofar as they partake of the homosexual subculture. When this subculture is examined in its own terms, and inasmuch as it embodies homosexuals as individuals who are attracted to and engage in sexual acts with people of their own gender, it can only be described as a sick component of American society. This is true not only from the strictly medical but also from the social viewpoint.

There is considerable documentation for identifying the homosexual community as a reservoir of disease for the rest of society. Although the homosexual movement resists these allegations, which are inimical to its interests, not only is the homosexual community a medically diseased portion of the social body but their strictly physical ailments—most of them transmissible—are easily linked with the practice of homosexuality.

There is little question that the homosexual community is very much aware of this. Many homosexual periodicals have medical advice columns which provide information and/or answer questions. The medical information provided consists basically of advice on the nature, treatment, and prevention of illnesses directly related to homosexual practices. Writers of these columns include physicians who specialize in the treatment of homosexuals affected by these maladies. Not only are there services available to treat homosexuals thus affected, but there is a national organization representing the interests of these services, the National Coalition of Gay Sexually Transmitted Disease Services, located in Arlington, Virginia.

The degree to which the homosexual community is affected by Sexually Transmitted Diseases (STDs) and the promiscuity prevalent among homosexuals are revealed in some of the advice given by this coalition to homosexuals who want to engage in "healthful sexual activity":

> Always exchange your name and telephone number to facilitate contact in case signs or symptoms of an STD are later discovered or recognized. It is also best to tactfully bring up health before sexual activity begins. If the person just got over hepatitis, make it a friend's encounter without sex, since you may be susceptible. When you do go to bed with someone, undress in a lighted area and casually inspect for growths, sores, or rashes, especially around the genitals. If no reasonable explaination [sic] is given, postpone the encounter![28]

Homosexual baths owners are advised "to print cards and/or matchbook covers to enable patrons to exchange their names and phone numbers . . . (to encourage) showering after each sexual encounter . . . to exchange all soiled towels for free to allow for frequent showering and washing."[29] The impression given is certainly one of ceaseless and quite impersonal sexual activity which creates the ever-present danger of STDs.

The NCGSTDS has also devised a measuring scale to enable the homosexual to ascertain his relative probability of contracting an STD. At the risk of being offensive to some readers, it is printed below as it has been issued (except for the deletion of one word) because it is helpful to comprehend the relationship between the homosexual subculture as a focus of infection for the community and the sexual practices of its members:

> Many factors must be considered when determining a person's risk for acquiring or transmitting an STD. Seven major categories are listed below, describing the relative risk factors as high, medium, or low:
>
> 1) Frequency of sexual contact.
> High risk: More than 10 different sexual partners per month.
> Medium risk: Between 3–10 different sexual partners per month.
> Low risk: Less than 3 different sexual partners per month.
> 2) Type of sexual encounter.
> High: Primarily one-night-only encounters; group sex.

The Homosexual Subculture

Medium: Dating, or several nights with the same person; sex within a small group of friends.

Low: Primarily monogamous sexual activity for both you and your partner.

3) Place of sexual encounter.

High: Bathhouses; bookstores

Medium: Public restrooms; parks; bars; motor vehicles

Low: Private homes

4) Hygiene. Answer these questions as Always (low risk), Occasionally (medium risk), or Rarely (high risk):

Do you wash with soap and water before and after having sex?

Do you urinate after having sex?

Do you gargle with hydrogen peroxide, glyoxide, or another mouthwash before and after sex?

5) Drug Use. Indicate frequency of use before, during, or after sex with any of the following agents (Frequent = high risk; Occasionally = medium risk; Rarely = low risk):

"Poppers" (amyl/butyl nitrite, Rush, etc.)

Marijuana

Alcohol (beer, wine, or hard liquor)

Cocaine or amphetamines

Barbiturates

Hallucinogenics (LSD, mescaline, etc.)

PCP ("angel dust")

Others (specify)

(It is thought that use of mood or consciousness altering drugs or medicines before, during, or after sex may effect [sic] decision-making abilities that may contribute to less awareness about the sexual activities practiced, having sex with more people, etc.)

6) Geographical area where you and your sex partner live and have sexual encounters.

High: New York City, Los Angeles, San Francisco, Chicago, foreign countries

Medium: Other large urban areas

Low: Small cities and towns, or rural areas

7) Types of sexual activities practiced since last VD examination.

High: Active or passive rectal; rimming-(oral-fecal/rectal); "scat"; fist/f——— [fornication]. Major surgery may be required to repair injuries sustained from fist f———; any type of oral-fecal contact carries a high risk for contracting hepatitis, pinworms, giardiasis, amebiasis, shigellosis, etc.

Medium: Active or passive oral (fellatio; passive has greater risk than active)

Low: Masturbation only (J/O, mutual etc.); body rubbing, water sports; touching only. (It should be stressed that any type of anal contact, but especially oral-anal/fecal contact ("rimming," or "scat") is definitely associated with increased risk for acquiring and transmitting diseases such as amebiasis, giardiasis, hepatitis, and others.[30]

The following review appeared in another issue of the same newsletter:

Intestinal Parasites

The September 1980 issue of the New York-based magazine *Christopher Street* (volume 4:12, pp. 16–23) has an outstanding review of the intestinal parasite epidemic in an article entitled "Guess what's hit the fan." An accompanying article entitled "A visit to the parasite lab" describes the reporter's visit to the laboratory to donate a laxative-induced purged specimen of stool. Although the causitive organism for amebiasis (Entamoeba histolytica) is a major focus, other parasites are mentioned—Giardia lamblia, Dientamoeba fragilis, and others. Most importantly, the article describes the mode of transmission and the difficulty of diagnosis and treatment, especially with the popularity of certain forms of sexual expression (especially oral-rectal). Parasitologist Asa Chandler, and Drs. Lawrence Downs and Dan William were interviewed for the article. (Dr. William is an active member of the NCGSTDS, and works with the New York Gay Men's Health Project). Readers are urged to obtain this issue.[31]

The *New York Native* has published a list of diseases and infestations by which the homosexual community threatens the community at large.[32] They include the following maladies:

Gonorrhea
Non-gonococcal or non-specific Urethritis (NGU, NSU)
Syphilis
Genital herpes
Venereal warts
Pubic lice
Scabies
Viral hepatitis, (Types A, B, and Non-A/Non-B)
Intestinal parasites (amebiasis and giardiasis).

Dr. King Holmes of the University of Washington, also head of the infectious diseases section of the Public Health Service Hospital in Seattle, has identified twenty separate "disease agents" transmissible by sexual relations.[33] They include nine bacteria, five viruses, three protozoa, one fungus, and two parasites. Although Dr. Holmes did not identify homosexuals specifically as vectors for these diseases—homosexuality was not the focus of his study—there is little doubt that the extreme promiscuity associated with the homosexual condition, particularly in men, guarantees that in fact they are such vectors. There is considerable evidence that active homosexuals are a high-risk population for these diseases. *The Sentinel*, a well-established and respected homosexual newspaper in San Francisco, has admitted that the "risk of contracting disease among gay persons is approximately ten times that of persons in the general population."[34] It has also been reported that homosexuals have a risk of developing hepatitis B ten times greater than that of other persons.[35]

These conclusions were confirmed by a survey reported in the official publication of the American Public Health Association.[36] Although the sample used was not selected on a random basis, its source (1,800 organizations listed by the National Gay Task Force and an advertisement in a homosexual publication), and the structure of the questionnaire, ensure no bias on account of medical condition. A lengthy questionnaire in which only 4 out of 692 questions pertained to medical data yielded the following results.

78% had been affected at least once by an STD.
60% had been affected at least once by an STD other than infestations.

Proportions Affected

24% by urethritis
18% by venereal growths
13% by syphilis
10% by hepatitis
9.4% by herpes (a viral disease)
66% by pediculosis (an infestation)

The same survey indicated an average of 49 different sexual partners per homosexual (over a lifetime). It was also reported that between 8 and 12 percent of homosexuals have more than 500 sexual partners during their lifetimes.

The high rate of illness in the homosexual community has been repeatedly linked to the promiscuity of its members. San Francisco—"gay capital of the United States"—has a VD rate almost 22 times the national average (240 cases per 100,000 persons vs. the national average of 11 cases per 100,000).[37] The connection between the promiscuous lifestyle of homosexuals and their tendency toward infection is clear. Commenting about the high incidence of VD in San Francisco, Dr. Irvin Braff, director of the City Clinic, indicated that "the problem is due to generally active people having multiple sex partners," mostly single people, attributing it to the large homosexual population of the city.[38] Dr. Merv Silverman, director of public health for San Francisco, has indicated that San Francisco is "a tolerant city, so there's a great many lifestyles. . . . We see a very large rate of venereal disease in the homosexual community."[39] In explaining San Francisco's explosive VD rates for the first quarter of 1980, Dr. Irene Heindl, a public health medical officer with the state Department of Health's Venereal Disease Control Unit, has pointed out that "When you get crowded into situations such as San Francisco, that creates problems. You have the gay communities. They tend to have more sexual partners, they're not particular about their partners, and they tend not to take precautions."[40]

In 1979 there was a sharp increase in certain diseases prevalent in the homosexual community. The following report was published by the *San Francisco Chronicle/Examiner*:

A substantial rise in the incidence of hepatitis among males . . . reported by the San Francisco Health Department. The Bureau of Disease Control had received reports of 744 cases of hepatitis up to mid-November (1979). The average number of cases for the past three years was 400–500 a year. Amoebic dysentery is also on the sharp increase; for the past three years it was about 130 cases annually while this year 220 cases. Although both sexes are equally susceptible, the incidence of the disease was 8 to 10 times greater in males between 20 to 40 years of age than the rest of the population.[41]

The homosexual community provides employment for a certain number of people who are in contact mostly with other homosexuals, posing no direct health threat to the rest of the population. For example, homosexuals who work in pornographic movie houses, "gay bars," baths, homosexual publications/bookstores, and similar establishments may very rarely come in contact with heterosexuals. However, most homosexuals do work in establishments where they come in close contact with nonhomosexuals (e.g., nurses, teachers, counselors, doctors, food handlers). It is reasonable to assume that these homosexuals as a group pose a health threat to the rest of the community. If the "ten percent of the population is gay" principle of the homosexual movement is accepted (see chapter III), and a substantial number of them are infected at a particular time, then the risk is real. This issue was raised in hearings on H.R. 2074, a prohomosexual law proposed in the U.S. House of Representatives in 1980:

> It might be a realistic situation. I read in today's paper, the *San Francisco Chronicle*, October 10, 1980, an article on page 3 on an ice cream establishment which apparently sent out a number of containers of contaminated ice cream, contaminated with hepatitis.

> There was this little side article, which makes the comment on hepatitis:

> "Homosexual communities, where hepatitis is widely transmitted by sexual conduct, are considered high-risk groups for both the common types of disease. In San Francisco the hepatitis rate has been soaring. Dr. Selma Kretz, assistant director of the city's Bureau of Communicable Disease, said that about five percent of all hepatitis A cases are food handlers and two-thirds of those food handlers are gay men."[42]

There are other diseases which affect homosexuals, with no apparent relationship to homosexual acts. In July 1981, the Center for Disease Control (part of the U.S. Department of Health and Human Services) announced that a large number of cases were being reported of Pneumocystic Pneumonia and Kaposi's Sarcoma—a form of cancer among homosexuals.[43] These diseases were hitherto relatively rare and not specifically associated with homosexuality. Other rare infections have begun to make their appearance among homosexuals, especially young homosexuals who were not considered particularly prone to them. By December 1981, it had been reported that new cases were being found at the rate of five or six each week, with a total count of 180 cases nationwide.[44] Reporting on studies made by thirty-two researchers in California and New York and published in the *New England Journal of Medicine* in December 1981, the *Washington Post* indicated that a breakdown of the homosexuals' immune system (i.e., capacity to fight disease) could explain this phenomenon:

> The cancer and pneumonia have previously been known to occur more frequently in patients with damaged immune systems, the result of drug treatment—cancer drugs or drugs administered to those undergoing kidney transplants—or underlying disease. But scientists are puzzled as to why these ailments should appear in an even more virulent form in young homosexuals.

> Most of the 19 described in the New England Journal had pneumoscystis pneumonia as well as other infections, three had the cancer as well, and four had severe skin ulcers. Prior to getting the life-threatening diseases, many were reported to have suffered for several months from undiagnosed illness, including fatigue, fever, and weight loss. In all, the infection-fighting white blood cell counts fell below normal. . . .[45]

> The diseases were marked by strange infections of the mouth and windpipe, dry coughs, fever, labored breathing, white spots on the skin near the mouth or genitals, fatigue, and weight loss. Several patients suffered severe and rare skin ulcers.[46]

Although most people are normally exposed to some of these viruses, it was reported that they attacked the homosexuals selectively.[47] However, it was also reported by the *Washington Blade* that male homosexuals were found to be affected by a virus which is transmitted by semen and/or urine (ingestion of which are common homosexual practices):

> In addition to these ailments, CDC researchers say Gay men have been found to harbor antibodies, or traces, of cytomegalovirus, a condition thought to contribute to suppressed immune functioning but which rarely causes overt symptoms. Recent random tests in San Francisco, according to CDC officials, show that as many as 90 percent of the Gay men tested showed evidence that they once harbored the cytomegalovirus. About 15% of those tested had the virus itself at a given time.

> However, officials are quick to note that about 45 percent of a heterosexual male sample also was found to have the cytomegalovirus antibodies and that the condition itself cannot be shown to cause Pneumocystis or Kaposi's. Nevertheless, almost all of those stricken with the two diseases also tested positively

for the cytomegalovirus antibody. Cytomegalovirus is commonly found in semen and urine, researchers say.[48]

The *Blade* also quoted a New York City physician, Dr. Daniel C. Williams, whose words can only make the rest of the population aware of what a risk the homosexual community presents for the rest of America: "Williams said the increasing incidence of sexually transmitted diseases among Gay men may be reaching a 'threshhold level' in some cities that could be causing a sudden outbreak of seriously damaged immune systems. 'I hope I'm wrong,' Williams told the *Medical World News* journal recently. 'If I'm right, we're seeing only the beginning.' "[49]

In addition to the strictly medical viewpoint, there is another aspect under which the homosexual community should be considered a diseased portion of the body politic. From a social viewpoint, the homosexual community is affected by and is a source of dysfunctions which make society less efficient and productive. There are three examples of such antisocial activities which are intrinsic (i.e., related to homosexuality itself) to the homosexual community.

1) By the advocacy of homosexuality as a legitimate alternative lifestyle, this community disrupts the rest of society. This advocacy is reflected not only in the presentation of prohomosexual ideas, but in the various attempts—sometimes successful—to enshrine the homosexual ideology as law and custom. On the one hand, our tradition rejects homosexuality as a destructive perversion. Attempts to modify this tradition in an unreasonably forceful manner interfere with social processes, in some cases violently. Attempts by society at large to neutralize prohomosexual activities—necessary in the opinion of most people to ensure the survival of our value system and even of society itself—consume vital social energy which could be better employed in more positive pursuits.

2) Besides posing the danger of transmitting infectious diseases, certain sexual practices themselves are life-threatening. Sadomasochism (S & M) is intrinsically violent, and homosexual prostitution very often involves violence. In some cases, the death of the masochistic partner in an S & M relationship is not at all accidental. Reporting on homocides, a publication of the Universal Fellowship of Metropolitan Community Churches observed that "of the reported homocides, two were considered 'lover quarrels,' three were 'S & M'-related, where one of the partners, willingly or unwillingly, met with death at the hands of his sexual partner."[50] Moreover, during the past few years several instances of mass murders of young people by homosexuals have been reported. Obviously, the overwhelming majority of homosexuals does not desire sexual pleasure from the association of physical death with sexual practices. Nevertheless, there is no question that it does happen in some instances. And there are many homosexuals who do associate pain, degradation, and/or humiliation

The Homosexual Subculture

with sexual pleasure. The number of sadomasochistic-oriented establishments is sufficient evidence of this fact.

3) Prostitution, an integral part of the homosexual subculture, constitutes another such dysfunctional contribution to the rest of society. Homosexuals do gravitate toward places where young people sell themselves to them for a variety of reasons; this inevitably engenders criminal activities that consume resources potentially available for other purposes. (While prostitution is itself a crime in most jurisdictions, the controversy about its status as a so-called victimless crime makes it expedient to leave its criminal nature out of account.)

Both the prostitutes themselves and their partners can be victims of crime. Reporting on the murders of several homosexuals in Washington, the local homosexual paper indicated that some of them "invited young hustler types" to their homes.[51] The young people who make a living as prostitutes also run the risk of being assaulted while "working." The dangers involved, however, do not seem to interfere with the "business." An article in the leading homosexual publication, *The Advocate*, describes this vividly:

> Driving off with the wrong customer can have even more serious consequences, however. It is not uncommon on the street to hear stories of hustlers being robbed and then summarily dropped off in a remote area of Los Angeles, usually somewhere in the nearby Santa Monica Mountains—with or without being violently raped.
>
> And sometimes more serious things happen. Rumors circulate of boys being picked up on the boulevard, only to end up at the bottom of someone's trash can—in little pieces. Last month a regular Santa Monica hustler, a somewhat seasoned 17-year-old from a Los Angeles suburb, known simply as "Jason," drove off one night with "a kind of cute guy with lots of tattoos." Jason came back with more than a dozen cigarette burns on his face and neck. Although Jason's face is starting to heal, he still doesn't get through the night without waking from an anguished nightmare about the ordeal.
>
> Seemingly undaunted, though, by either the threat of arrest or worse, literally hundreds of hustlers flock to the "S and M" boulevard every week. Sometimes the atmosphere is tense with competition, and fights among hustlers over potential clients are not uncommon. But for the most part an air of camaraderie prevails, assisted by the widespread belief that however plentiful the supply of hustlers, the demand is almost always greater.[52]

Law enforcement agencies are well aware of the deleterious effects of prostitution from the point of view of both individual and social morality. Commenting on the situation, Lieutenant Ed Washington of the Hollywood Police Department has indicated that "I can't give you a direct quote from the Bible or anything, but prostitution is wrong; and besides, it is against the law. Prostitutes attract crime-related activities, like trafficking in illegal drugs, burglary, and robbery. By getting rid of the prostitutes, you cut the crime rate by 30 per cent."[53]

At least eight murders of Black male homosexuals occurred in the Washington, D.C., metropolitan area during the first half of 1981.[54] In response to this "mini–crime wave," the D.C. Police Department formed a special team of detectives and supervisors to deal exclusively with these murders. Members of the team met with the D.C. Coalition of Black Gays. The intimate connection between the murders and the homosexual lifestyle seemed to be accepted. In the words of a team member, Detective F. G. Michael Helwig, "Most of the victims were in the habit of inviting home persons they had never met before."

Thus it appears that, on the surface, the homosexual subculture features religion, art, social service institutions, camaraderie, and social support for its members. Under this appearance, however, there is a world of social and individual dysfunctions, a focus of infectious diseases and, in some instances, crime and even murder. If we look at society as an organism and emphasize the interdependence of its members and subordinated structures, it is fair to assert that the homosexual community is a diseased portion of this body.

This is, of course, only one way of looking at the question. From the point of view of the "liberated" members of the homosexual community— i.e., those who accept, live, and celebrate the ideology and their own sexual orientation—the reality is quite different. Any dysfunction in the homosexual community is seen as a manifestation of society's refusal to recognize the value of homosexuality for those who practice it. This rejection of the homosexual from his earliest years by the most significant individuals (i.e., parents, close relatives, and friends) and institutions (church, school, society) is depicted as engendering self-hate or homophobia in the homosexual himself. The damage inflicted by the homosexual community on the rest of society can thus perhaps be seen as the way in which society receives back the damage it tries to inflict on homosexuals by rejecting them in what is most cherished to them. While from a traditional point of view the solution (if any) is for homosexuals to renounce their condition in itself or in its behavioral manifestations, the homosexual community would propose as the only solution the acceptance of homosexuality.

Arthur Evans, one of the founders of the Gay Activists Alliance in the early days of the homosexual movement, has said of the present situation of the movement: "There is a great deal of conformity, resignation, alcoholism, and suicide."[55] The answer, from a homosexual perspective, is to reject the identity provided each homosexual by society: "We need to find a gay identity and we need to be able to live it. In the past the gay identity that's been given to us has been given to us by people in institutions that hate us: by psychiatrists, by priests, and by the Mafia. Now we're creating a new gay identity for ourselves."

While traditional thinking would call for a heterosexually oriented society, Evans's aspirations are quite different: "I want a gay world where I can live. Me, as a person . . . where I can live and feel some kind of decency as a human being."[56]

Language and the Homosexual Subculture

Any subculture is characterized by the development of its own language, a set of oral and/or written symbols that express its nature, contributes to the integration of its members into the subculture, and satisfies certain sociopolitical needs of the group. The characteristics and uses of these languages vary with the subcultures in which they flourish, since they are not only the medium through which the subculture expresses itself, both within and without its boundaries, but also the very message which the subculture tries to express. The language of a subculture is thus the embodiment of the subculture in thought, feeling, and action. The reason why these languages develop is not only the relative isolation in which members of the subculture live, but also their need to create a vehicle through which they can express their desires and aspirations. These languages are not merely collections of new words which correspond univocally with the vocabulary of the prevalent culture; they have a power of their own to articulate the sociopolitical needs of the subculture and fashion a setting in which people who share certain values and beliefs can function while serving the needs of the subculture.

Before we examine how this generalized sociological statement applies to the homosexual subculture, we turn to the nature and functions of language, emphasizing those elements which best apply to the language that has been developed by this specific subculture. The dictionary offers two definitions of language which are the first analogs of the concept we are discussing here. Language is defined as "the words, the pronunciation, and the methods of combining them used and understood by a considerable community," and as "a systematic means of communicating ideas or feelings by the use of conventionalized signs, sounds, gestures, or marks having understood meanings."[57]

The obvious implication is that language is an agreed-upon system of arbitrary symbols by which reality is expressed and communicated. Yet, this is a naive view of language, for its assumes that reality is "out there," quite independent of the mind that observes it or the language by which the observer expresses its nature. The deeper and far more active function of language was realized by Eastern thinkers (both Hindus and Buddhists) hundreds of years before the advent of language philosophy in the West a few decades ago. In his discussion of Kriyātantra (an action-tantra closely related to the Mantrayoga), Herbert V. Guenther points out that language has several other functions applicable to our discussion: Language is creative, it hides from view features of the very reality it creates, and it is essentially evaluative.[58] These and other features, as Guenther points out, give language a tremendous power: "This myth-making tendency (of language) then leads to all sorts of fictional systems, philosophical, religious, and political."[59]

Ken Wilber points out that, as with other sets of relations of the Biosocial Band (defined as the largely unconscious "pool of introjective sets" or "internalized society" transferred from society into the biological organism), language is characterized by being, above all else, a matrix of distinctions.[60] In Whorf's conception moreover, "Segmentation of nature is an aspect of grammar," and "we dissect nature along the lines laid down by our native languages."[61]

This creative aspect of language has also been pointed out by Postman and Weingartner. Concerning the work of Sapir and Whorf, they observe that:

> their studies of the language systems of different cultures led them to the conclusion (Whorf more than Sapir) that each language—including both its structure and its lexicon—represents a unique way of perceiving reality. They believed that we are imprisoned, so to speak, in a house of language. We try to assess what is outside the house from our position within it. However, the house is "oddly" shaped (and no one knows precisely what a "normal" shape would be). There is a limited number of windows. The windows are tinted and are at odd angles. We have no choice but to see what the structure of the house permits us to see.[62]

They quote a number of authors, from Shakespeare to Albert Einstein, all of whom in some way accept the notion that "language is not merely a vehicle of expression, it is also the driver; and what we perceive, and therefore can learn, is a function of our languaging processes."[63] The creative aspect of language allows for what Postman and Weingartner refer to as "blurring," which occurs when names are applied to entire classes without allowing for individual distinctions.[64] This is the foundation of prejudice and allows for immediate action either in favor of certain individuals with whom one identifies, or against other "types" which are "obviously" inimical to one's interests.

Inextricably connected with its "naive" function as vehicle for "plain" or "objective" communications, language has other equally important functions which are summarized below. The reader must take into consideration, however, that these functions are neither independent nor

The Homosexual Subculture

properly distinguishable from one another. They exist in dynamic inter-action and formal mutual interpentration within themselves:

Function:	Examples: Application in the Homosexual Subculture
Creativity	• Definition of American culture as oppressive • Segregation and isolation of the homosexual subculture by the development of the language itself.
Ability to Hide the Reality it Creates	• Definition of homosexuality as a "normal" and/or "creative" lifestyle • Reference to homosexual acts as "loving" or "nonviolent." (This is especially shocking in the case of sadomasochism, bondage and discipline, and/or dominance and submission styles of sexuality.)
Evaluation	• The language of the homosexual subculture is essentially judg-mental of the dominant culture.
Myth-Making	• Development of homosexual ideology.
Blurring/Segregation	• Designation of homosexual or gay as classes of people, in con-tradistinction to other people. There's a weakening of person-hood within the homosexual subculture. • Bias in favor of liberated homosexuals in terms of credibility, artistic abilities, honesty, contributions to society, etc.
Subcultural Nucleation	• Identification of liberated homosexuals with themselves as a special kind of person and with their peers through their pe-culiar way of communicating with one another.

All these characteristics of language are apparent in the homosexual subculture. Even a cursory examination of the way in which the homo-sexual movement makes use of language for its own benefit, and of its attempts to impose the homosexual ideology on the rest of society, will enable us to comprehend the nature of this subculture and thus deal with it better, as it attempts to play an increasingly important sociopolitical role in America.

A visit to any homosexual bookstore reveals the existence of a number of glossaries, some of them quite extensive, which provide the uninitiated with thousands of words by which homosexuals describe themselves, the world, and especially their sexual activities. The appendices of modern books on homosexuality usually provide more or less comprehensive glos-saries without which the reader could make little or no sense of many quotes from homosexuals or even the very text of these works. There is no question that the homosexual subculture has developed its own lan-guage. As promoted (and accepted) within the homosexual community, this language has created a perception of homosexuality that is social and political by its nature. To be homosexual is a political act, an affirmation of power: "To call onself a lesbian is a political act."[65] One of the values of language for the homosexual movement originates in the homosexual's perception that the rejection of his condition by society has its source in the descriptions by which he has been identified. Van Fossen points out how "the move from sin to crime to illness caused lesbians and gay men to be classified for the first time. Focusing on lesbians and gay men as an 'effected' group created a climate whereby class consciousness became possible."[66] Homosexuals are what they are (i.e., members of a class with consciousness, power needs, awareness of their conditions) by virtue of the fact that they are so called. The language used creates the homosexuals as a class and, if fashioned properly, empowers them to seek control of the manner in which society at large deals with homosexuals as a class. The leadership of the movement is conscious of the role of language as used by both homosexuals and heterosexuals. Expressions of concern about the use of language presumably not in line with the ideological tenets of the movement are constant. They descend even to the use of cultic phrases enshrined by centuries of use in a religious setting. The homosexual publication *In Unity* announced that Sister Mary O'Keefe of the National Association of Women Religious (a Roman Catholic organization) would refuse to attend Mass or take Communion where the expression "all men" was used to refer to those for whom Jesus died.[67] In much the same way, the well-known codirector of the Catholic homosexual organization New Ways Ministry, Sister Jeannine Gramick, SSND, complained about the "wrong" language in this fashion:

> I was particularly appalled by Monsignor Richard Malone's cold, legalistic jargon. Typical, typical! Last Sunday I attended a parish liturgy which he celebrated; he consistently addressed the congregation as "brothers" and used the now legally outmoded "for all men" at the consecration!
> When will the men of our church who hold the power begin to listen and try to feel the powerlessness of women?[68]

The sensitivity to the nature of language as a social institution laden with power for its users is evident. Sister Gramick is merely echoing two related themes within the homosexual movement, especially among female homosexuals: that inclusive language (in which there are no gender distinctions) must be imposed on all members of society, and that this must be done as a matter of redressing the balance of power. This is a subject to which we will return.

Homosexual organizations try to sensitize their members to the power of language. During the 1979 convention of the National Council of Teachers of English, the homosexual caucus within this organization sponsored a program entitled "Panel on the language of heterosexism." Aside from two homosexual poetry readings, this was their only substantive activity at the convention.

One of the most important contributions of the homosexual movement to contemporary English usage is the word "gay." In the next chapter we will see its ideological significance and the centrality of this concept. "Gay" is utilized to create the sexual class consciousness of members of the movement, to create the social environment in which new members of the subculture feel welcome, supported, and proud by providing members with pride and self-acceptance. "Gay" is used to distinguish the person who merely feels sexually attracted to members of his own sex from those who also *celebrate* this attraction, define this attraction as "good," and identify those who suffer from this attraction with others who are like them. Adam DeBaugh has pointed out that this distinction between "gay" and "homosexual" is rooted in language and culture.[69] "Gay" serves to create and point to the supportive environment and the services a homosexual can find in bars, baths, churches, bookstores, health clinics, beauty parlors, radio programs, and restaurants. "Gay" has a function not unlike that of a Tantric mantra, a magical word that has a creative power of its own. In the minds and perception of its users, it is the key indicator for today's liberated homosexual that he has nothing to fear from that to which it is pegged. He is "gay," "all-gay," and anything "gay" is part of him.

The importance of using the word "gay" as opposed to such better-suited words as "homosexual" or "queer" is universally acknowledged throughout the homosexual community. Sister Jeannine Gramick, SSND, in a prohomosexual workshop for religious personnel, has emphasized this concept.[70] In fact, "homosexual" (homo = equal) is a far better word to describe those who feel sexually attracted to persons of the *same* sex. *Queer,* which has as its first meaning "deviating from the expected or normal; strange,"[71] corresponds with the facts that homosexuals are a small minority of the population and that their practices are considered by most people to be in disharmony with the natural order. The difficulty in the usage of "queer" is that it has become a derogatory term; thus we have avoided it studiously. Similarly, the words "faggot" and "dyke" are usually used in a derogatory sense.

The collective decision to use "gay" as a code word for the promotion of the movement's interests took place over a decade ago. Although there is not one person, place, or instance with which this decision can be identified, the process by which the term was adopted and the purpose of its usage have been aptly expressed by Marotta in his discussion of the founding of New York's Gay Liberation Front (GLF):

> Simply by settling on a name, the radicals who met at Alternate U acknowledged that any persisting collectivity had to have an identity. Gay Liberation Front— each word in that name was selected with organizational as well as political considerations in mind. Unlike *homosexual*, the clinical term bestowed by heterosexuals, and *homophile*, the euphemism coined by cautious political

forerunners, *gay*, which homosexuals called each other, was thought to be the word that would most appeal to homosexuals who were thirsting to be known as they knew themselves. Hence also *liberation*, intended to suggest freedom from constraint. *Front* implied a militant vanguard or coalition; it suggested that GLF was the crest of a swelling wave destined to force people to recognize and respect the openly gay population.[72]

The sociopolitical significance of "gay" is thus apparent. If anything, the homosexual movement needs its acceptance as a matter of sheer survival. Naturally, should "gay" cease to be used, many people would still be attracted to members of their own sex, homosexuality would still be practiced, and some parts of the subculture would still be fully in place. However, like God, if "gay" ceased to exist it would have to be invented. In acquiescing without any resistance to the use of "gay," American society and government have, in fact, bought into the homosexual movement. By the same token, profamily and other traditional-value-oriented activists can wage a most effective campaign against homosexuality simply by insisting on the abolition of "gay" as an accepted word. In fact, there are indications that, without any conscious decision of specific individuals, "society" is taking care of this problem. Parents and young people alike have reported to the author that in schools across the nation "gay" is starting to be used by young people as a derogatory remark, as "faggot," "pansy," or "sissy" have been employed in the past. Should this usage become widespread, the implications for the homosexual movement would be ominous, since this would indicate a societal refusal to acknowledge homosexuality as an acceptable lifestyle and homosexual practices as normal.

The preoccupation of the homosexual movement in general and of the homosexual religious leadership in particular with the question of inclusive language is also indicative of the overwhelming importance attributed to language by the homosexual subculture. This preoccupation is not exclusive to the homosexual movement, being shared by feminists of various persuasions, including homosexual feminists. In fact, one of the common agenda items between both movements is precisely the imposition of inclusive language throughout society. (The formal objects of the feminist and homosexual movements are distinct; thus they are referred to as separate entities. However, there is considerable overlap in terms of membership, activities, tactics, and ideology. In many respects, they are one and the same.)

Speech and the authority it engenders are rooted in religious practices. This is due to the fact that, scientism notwithstanding, societies are invariably religious. In thoroughly secularized societies—even in formally atheistic states—the prevalent ideologies take on the role that traditional religion has played in the United States. The languages which originate in religion, and the patterns of thought they generate, are then transposed to the more mundane day-to-day affairs of men. This is why the homosexual and the feminist movements have joined forces to provoke a change in the language by which religion is fashioned and expressed. The proposed change consists in the usage of inclusive or nonsexist language, wherein all references to God or persons in general by the use of "masculine" words is eliminated (i.e., elimination of the generic masculine). One of the obvious effects of this change is to blur the distinction between genders and the attribution of specific roles according to gender. Naturally, anything that contributes to the dissolution of gender-related distinctions is propounded by the homosexual movement. (This can be interpreted as an indication that homosexuality is a form of confused or arrested gender identification.) The homosexually oriented Universal Fellowship of Metropolitan Community Churches has been at the forefront of these efforts:

> One of the most significant actions of General Conference IX was to approve the establishment of a Special Elders' Taskforce on Inclusive Language, chaired by Rev. Brent Hawkes of MCC-Toronto, which has the awesome responsibility of creating a definition of, and guidelines for usage of, inclusive language in our Statement of Faith and in the worship and life of MCC congregations. These initial proposals will be circulated to all MCC congregations in 1980 for final action at General Conference X in 1981. By-law proposals 1 through 8 dealing with language change were referred to this Taskforce.[73]

During the Seventh General Conference of the UFMCC (Washington, D.C., 1976), the Task Force on Women presented the following resolution (number 5 on its agenda):

> RESOLVED THAT UFMCC, at this General Conference, reaffirming the recommendation of the UFMCC 1975 General Conference, direct its member churches to continue to change the language used during worship services (including hymns, liturgy, scripture and sermons) and that each church use inclusive (nonsexist) language therein, as informed by guidelines supplied by the Task Force on Women and the Commission on Faith, Fellowship and Order.[74]

Two women leaders of the UFMCC, Marge Ragona and Jennie Bull, have, the group reports, "put together an excellent manual called 'DeSexing Your Local Hymnal,' which provides a guide to language problems in over 700 of our favorite hymns."[75]

The ultimate source of religious language in America is the Bible; thus the UFMCC announced (with obvious glee) the attempts of the National Council of Churches (NCC) to reinterpret the Scriptures according to the dictates of the homosexual and feminist movements:

The National Council of Churches' task force on biblical translation is recommending that the NCC prepare a new lectionary with an emphasis on inclusive and nonsexist language. The task force also suggested to the RSV Bible Committee, who is presently working on an updated version to be published in the mid-1980s, that they consider studying the possibility of a separate inclusive language New Testament building on the new lectionary.

The task force has recommended using the word "children" for "sons" and "ancestors" for "patriarchs."[76]

In fact, the incorporation of inclusive language in the Bible or other sacred writings amounts to a reinterpretation of the text. By imposing the newly found categories on the original language, the message intended by the authors is twisted to serve the ideological—and thus political—aims of homosexuals and feminists alike. The following parallel passages will allow the reader to see the effect of utilizing inclusive language in reinterpreting the Scriptures:[77]

Passage	King James Version of the Bible	Inclusive Language
Mark 14:62	And Jesus said, "I am; and ye shall see the Son of man sitting on the right hand of power, and coming in the clouds of heaven."	Then Jesus said, "I am. And you will see Humanity's Child sitting at the right hand of power, and coming with the clouds of heaven."
Mark 14:36	And he said, "Abba, Father, all things are possible unto thee; take away this cup from me: nevertheless not what I will, but what thou wilt."	And he said, "Holy source of my being, all things are possible to you; remove this cup from me. Yet, not what I desire, but what you will."
John 1:51	And he saith unto him, "Verily, verily, I say unto you, hereafter ye shall see heaven open, and the angels of God ascending and descending upon the Son of man."	And Jesus continued, "Thus truly I tell you, you will see heaven opened, and the angels of God going up and coming down upon the Child of Humanity."

The enshrinement of inclusive or nonsexist language in religion is expected to further the acceptance of the homosexual and feminist ideologies. Thus organizations representing them spend considerable efforts in ensuring that not only the Bible but hymns and other elements in worship are reinterpreted to suit their sociopolitical needs. We already saw some of the efforts in this regard by the UFMCC. Other churches not specifically homosexual, have gone a long way to satisfy the demands of their homosexual and/or feminist leaders. The largest single church in America, the Roman Catholic Church, is the last to accede to these efforts. A petition has been forwarded to the central authorities in Rome by the Church's Conference of Bishops requesting authorization to make the language of the Mass—even the most sacred parts at the very core of the service—conform with the ideology of the homosexual and feminist movements. No evidence exists that the leaders of homosexual organizations within the Church had a direct participation in this decision, or that the bishops made their decision as the result of pressure from the homosexuals, although Catholic radical feminists—traditionally allies of the homosexuals—have been demanding these changes, as noted earlier, for several years. There is no evidence that the bishops were aware that their petition, if granted, would in fact result in a practice which strengthens the contentions of the homosexual movement. In practice, of course, the intentions of the bishops would not alter the prohomosexual and feminist results of the widespread usage of inclusive language in Catholic services. In addition to the power of language itself, the impression that the bishops "buckled" under pressure from the homosexuals and feminists could damage considerably their credibility with the overwhelming majority of Catholics.

Not only the church, but also the media, businesses, and the government have accepted the use of inclusive language, both for their internal affairs and for their dealings with the public. The reader is familiar with the constant use of spokesperson and chairperson for hitherto accepted expressions, a form of "newspeak" reminiscent of George Orwell's *1984*. Other, more subtle forms of language modification are apparent in the usages of "police officer" and "fire fighter" for the "policeman" and "fireman" which remain in general use outside the media and official business. Even the 1980 Census forms were carefully designed to conform with homosexual-feminist orthodoxy. The Bureau of the Census noted that "The 1980 Census Questionaire [*sic*] will no longer refer to 'head of household.' Instead, the categories 'partner' and 'roommate' have been added and the pronoun 'he' has been substituted with 'person.' "[78]

The efforts to institute inclusive language can backfire, since language has the characters of creator and mirror, driver and vehicle, message and medium. As Virginia Mollenkott has indicated, the design of nonsexist language must be taken into consideration, or the result will be a semantic rather than a substantial change:

> The moment one speaks of a chairwoman, because of social conditioning the imagination pictures garden clubs and theater parties. The word chairperson was invented to allow both males and females to imagine themselves in such leadership roles. But in actual practice chairperson has not been used when men chaired (they remained chairmen) but only when women were chairing. The end result was not an advance for women, but a wipeout of our bodily nature, our femaleness. Chairperson has therefore only made matters worse. The solution would be either to use the neutral word chair as a noun as well as a verb, or to view the word chairman as a designation of office or role rather than as sexually differentiated. In this case I think the word chair is clearly the more satisfactory solution, since it focuses on work to be done (chairing) without designating the sex of the doer.[79]

From a traditional point of view, the problem Mollenkott points out is due rather to the natural resistance of the world to being "mislabeled." Those who assert the objective nature of reality would understand that no amount of language manipulation can hide the fact that the differences between men and women, cultural as well as biological, are not arbitrary, but rooted in nature. Language can only try "to change" these facts at its own peril. Either it will become meaningless, or users will redefine its terms so as to express reality as it is.

There is yet another way in which the homosexual subculture utilizes language. As is common with other political movements, the homosexual movement "frames issues" in its own favor when articulating its understanding of society. The very use of "gay" and "homophobia" are examples of such a valuing process. Since "gay" is by definition a word of celebration and affirmation, while "homophobia" implies a negative quality (i.e., "irrational fear"), their use makes it difficult (if not impossible) for the user—unless he has a basic value system formed by traditional principles—to reject the values implied by gay (= good) and homophobia (= bad). Even in very specific instances, and the homosexual literature is full of examples, the use of language by the homosexual movement inevitably involves this framing of issues.

Cassano has pointed out a number of instances in which the clever use of language by proponents of the morality of homosexual behavior within the churches biases the discussion of various issues.[80] Examples:

Expression	Meaning	Effect
Compassionate	Homosexual behavior must be accepted.	Places opponents on the defensive by making them feel guilty and unloving.
Stable, loving relationship with one partner.	"Gay unions" are equivalent to marriage among heterosexuals.	People come to accept the premises that: 1) Many homosexuals live in such "good" relationships. 2) Homosexuality is not a psychological disorder. 3) A permanent homosexual relationship is better than a temporary one.
Stereotyping homosexuals.	It is irrational to assume that all homosexual practices are radically wrong.	Makes an ethical judgment concerning the nature of homosexuality impossible for fear of being prejudiced.
Sexual minority, oppression, rights, disenfranchisement and other political terms injected in the controversy over homosexuality.	Homosexuals qua homosexuals are a legitimate minority.	Frames the question of homosexuality in political terms. The code words used (from the civil rights movement) arouse feelings of sympathy in friends and paralysis in foes.

The Homosexual Subculture

Code words designed to evoke a certain response from the listener have often been used to frame the issue of homosexuality, not unlike the use of such phrases as "popular democracy," "democratic centralism," and the "vanguard of the working class" by Marxist-Leninist parties. Raymond Hartman, "cochairperson" of the Gay Rights National Lobby, has alleged that the majority of Americans sympathize with "gay rights" by citing an NBC/AP survey in which most respondents who took a position responded affirmatively to the question, "Should fair employment and fair housing laws be extended to cover homosexuals?"[81] The answer is not surprising since "fair employment" and "fair housing" are considered by most Americans to be rights all persons have as persons. In this case, of course, the question referred not to (all) persons, but exclusively to homosexuals; this was not made clear. In any case, it is difficult to be against anything "fair." The results might have been different if the questions had taken this form: "Should an employer be forced to hire homosexuals?"; "Should you be forced to work (or sleep) next to an openly homosexual person?"; "Would you have the right to object to a homosexual couple moving next to you, if you have small children?"; "Should a school be forced to hire an openly homosexual teacher?" (Cf. chap. I, "Homosexuality in the Polls.")

Words taken from the civil rights movement vocabulary are used by the homosexual movement precisely because they have already been enshrined in the American political jargon and can be expected to yield certain results for the movement, namely, a substantial increase in the movement's political power and in the ability of homosexuals to satisfy more openly their sexual desires. If the present tendency of America to return to its constitutional roots continues, it is questionable whether the homosexual movement will succeed in this exercise in wordsmanship. The basis for questioning this approach has been laid by J. M. Sobran:

Everyone senses that "civil rights" has become a code-word for government favoritism.

The bad semantics, unfortunately, aren't confined to the gay rights movement. It was the prototype of that movement, the Negro civil rights movement, that introduced a serious verbal corruption into our public discourse. The phrase "civil rights" used to mean legal protections of the citizen against the state. The Bill of Rights, for instance, enumerates limitations on the (Federal) Government's power over the citizen. But more recently the term has been used to mean protection of citizen against citizen; guarantees not against oppressive political action, but against free social action; guarantees secured—above all—by an actual increase in state jurisdiction. In what sense can we be said to have more "civil" rights than before, when the government in fact has more authority over us than ever?[82]

In yet another way, the homosexual movement creates a nurturing environment by the use of language and other forms of communication. Practically any homosexual publication contains references to sexual practices and suggestive photographs or drawings which just a few years ago would have been considered pornographic, or at least grossly improper outside hard-core pornography. The use of what most people consider vulgar language pervades the homosexual literature and even otherwise "serious" publications. Likewise, the practice of "camp" by a large number of homosexuals constitutes an almost distinctive feature of the homosexual culture. This is another form of communication which, as we will see shortly, is related to the use of vulgarity in homosexual publications. Hunt describes camp this way:

> The words "camp" and "camping" were first used to mean gay male behavior of a deliberately super-swishy and humorous kind. If a gay man is somewhat effeminate by nature, that isn't camping, but if a gay man puts on an exaggerated and ridiculous feminine manner, that *is*. When gay men speak in lisping voices, bat their eyelashes at each other, mince around with limp-wristed, hip-wiggling movements, and call each other "Mary" and "Alice," that's camp. When a gay actor in a Broadway show plays the part of a gay man who flits around on tiptoe, throws tantrums, and bursts into tears whenever he's frustrated, that's camp. When gays come to a party gotten up as angels with wings or as peacocks with huge feathered tails, that's camp.[83]

There seem to be several ways in which these two features in the communication of the homosexual subculture contribute to its goals. First, by camp and the use of vulgarity the homosexual subculture desensitizes nonhomosexuals to its existence and needs. This is not unlike what occurs with other social issues such as abortion, euthanasia, and incest. Those interested in promoting these practices must first bring them out into the open. By the constant use of their peculiar terms, people become accustomed to them and eventually come to accept these practices as natural. Second, both camp and vulgarities are probably an aggressive reaction by liberated homosexuals to the rejection of homosexual practices by society at large. The homosexual subculture, by utilizing these forms of aggressive communication, in fact creates the boundaries that define itself socially and protect itself from the encroachment of the rest of society. This manifests the dynamic instability of the homosexual subculture. On the one hand, it strives to show its members to be "like everyone else." On the other hand, it must assert the obvious differences between its members and the rest of society, lest it cease to exist by lack of differentiation.

There is no doubt that the homosexual subculture has not only developed a peculiar language, but that this language is structured and functions

The Homosexual Subculture

in a manner conceived to satisfy the needs of the homosexual movement and its members. Their needs are both identificational and political. If our discussion of the language of the homosexual subculture were not sufficient, even a cursory examination of an official glossary prepared by the State of California shows the ideological function of the language of homosexuality.[84] Practically every element of the homosexual ideology is enshrined in this document. Produced under the aegis of the Sexual Orientation Project of the State Personnel Board, and purporting to represent "the current state of social scientific research in the area of sexual orientation," the glossary is in fact a political tool for the promotion of the homosexual ideology within the California State government.

It seems evident that its peculiar language is not just a means of communication for the homosexual subculture. It is fundamentally a political tool by which the movement seeks to increase its political power, impose its ideology, and thus provoke a fundamental change in our thought and social practices. Although it would be naive to assume that if this language should cease to be utilized the homosexual movement would disappear, it is probable that a well-organized campaign within schools, professional and religious bodies, economic institutions, and the media would contribute, by exposing the true character of the homosexual language, to a substantial check on the acceptance of the homosexual ideology. Such a move would be fiercely resisted, since it would spell the intellectual demise of the homosexual subculture.

Should the homosexual language and ideology prevail, society would have no way of speaking—or thinking—in traditional terms. Conversely, should the profamily forces prevail, homosexuality would come to be viewed as a manifestation of sinfulness, an illness, or a potential and/or actual source of crime. In any case, it would be seen as a form of psychosocial disruption. Once it was viewed this way—even by the homosexuals themselves—the movement would cease to exist.

Notes

1. Charles H. Whittier, *Gay Rights in Perspective: Religious Aspects, Past and Present* (Washington, D.C.: Congressional Research Service, The Library of Congress, April 18, 1980).

2. "Pink Triangle Pins" are distributed by the Washington Office, Universal Fellowship of Metropolitan Community Churches.

3. Adam DeBaugh, "Bar Owners Supportive of Gay Rights Struggle," *Gays on the Hill* (August–September 1974): 2.

4. Morton Hunt, *Gay: What You Should Know About Homosexuality* (New York: Farrar, Straus & Giroux, 1977), p. 153. The description of baths which follows is taken largely from this source.

5. Ibid., p. 154.

6. *It's Time* 8 (March–April 1981): 3.

7. *Blade,* June 26, 1981, p. A-14.

8. Brother Izzo is a member of the Board of Directors of New Ways Ministry, a homosexual national center. See *Bondings,* (Winter 1980–81).

9. *In Unity,* September/October 1980, p. 13.

10. Undated memorandum from the Mariposa Foundation, n.p.

11. Stuart R. Mill et al., *Censored, Ignored, Overlooked, Too Expensive? How to Get Gay Materials into Libraries* (Philadelphia: Gay Task Force, American Library Association, 1979).

12. Programs of the 1979 and 1980 meetings of the Gay Caucus, Modern Language Association.

13. *Publisher's Weekly,* August 8, 1977, quoted in Clarke Taylor, "Gay Power," *New York,* August 29, 1977, p. 46.

14. Organizational brochure (San Francisco: Gay Theatre Alliance, n.d.).

15. Ibid.

16. Ibid.

17. News release (New York: Gay Theatre Alliance, Northeast Region, January 12, 1981).

18. By-laws, Gay Academic Union, Washington D.C. Chapter.

19. Letter to the author from Kay Loveland, Secretary, Lesbian and Gay Academic Union, Los Angeles Chapter, June 1981.

20. Gay Academic Union Interim Newsletter, n.p., Spring 1981.

21. Gay Academic Union Announcement/Newsletter, San Francisco Bay Area, n.d. (probably July or August, 1981.)

22. Ibid., January–June 1981.

23. Leaflet announcing the activities of the Gay Task Force, American Library Association (Social Responsibility Round Table), Philadelphia, PA, during the 1980 Annual Conference of the American Library Association.

24. *Calendar* 4 (New York: Dignity/New York, April 1978): 3.

25. *Official Newsletter of the National Coalition of Gay STD Services* 2 (Arlington, VA: National Coalition of Gay Sexually Transmitted Disease Services, May 1981): 9.

26. Ibid.

27. *In Unity,* February–March 1979, p. 24.

28. National Coalition of Gay STD Services, "Guidelines and Recommendations for Healthful Sexual Activity," 4th revision, (Arlington, VA: National Coalition of Gay Sexually Transmitted Disease Services, 1980). Reprinted in the *Official Newsletter of the National Coalition of Gay STD Services* 2 (Arlington, VA: National Coalition of Gay STD Services, January 1981).

29. Ibid., p. 4.

30. Ibid., p. 3.

31. Ibid., 2:7.

32. Dr. Harold S. Ross, M.D., "The Ross Report: All About STDs," *New York Native* (May 18–31, 1981), p. 32.

33. *San Francisco Examiner,* January 15, 1980, p. 14.

34. *Sentinel* (San Francisco), October 3, 1980, p. 9, quoted in "Statement of Grant Mickins," *Hearing,* p. 57.

35. *San Francisco Chronicle,* September 29, 1980.

36. *Washington Post,* September 1, 1981, p. A3.

37. *San Jose Mercury,* April 24, 1980.

38. Ibid.

39. Ibid.

The Homosexual Subculture

40. Ibid.

41. "Sharp Increase in Hepatitis and Dysentery in San Francisco," *San Francisco Chronicle/Examiner*, 1979, quoted in "Prepared Statement of Rev. Charles A. McIlhenny," *Hearing*, p. 27.

42. "Statement of Grant Mickins," *Hearing*, p. 56.

43. U.S. Department of Health and Human Services, Public Health Service, Center for Disease Control, *Morbidity and Mortality Weekly Reports*, vol. 30, no. 25, Atlanta, GA, July 3, 1981.

44. Christine Russell, "Immunity Systems Linked to Ailment Afflicting Gay Men," *Washington Post*, December 11, 1981.

45. Ibid.

46. "Homosexuals Found Particularly Liable to Common Viruses," *New York Times*, December 12, 1981.

47. Ibid.

48. Lou Chibbaro, Jr., "Incidence of Rare Cancer Is Rising: First D.C. Victim Is Reported," *Blade*, December 18, 1981.

49. Ibid.

50. *In Unity*, January/February 1981, p. 14.

51. *Blade*, June 12, 1981, p. 1.

52. William Franklin, "Hustlers in Hollywood," *Advocate*, September 20, 1979, p. 30.

53. Ibid.

54. *Blade*, September 11, 1981.

55. Brandon Judell, Interview with Arthur Evans, "I Want A Gay World I Can Live In," *New York Native*, June 29–July 12, 1981, p. 19.

56. Ibid., p. 40.

57. *Webster's New Collegiate Dictionary*, 1981 ed., s.v. "Language."

58. Herbert V. Guenther, *Buddhist Philosophy in Theory and Practice* (Boulder, CO: Shambala, 1976), pp. 174–175.

59. Ibid., p. 175.

60. Ken Wilber, *The Spectrum of Consciousness* (Wheaton, IL: Theosophical Publishing House, 1977), p. 135.

61. J. Krishnamurti, *First and Last Freedom* (Wheaton, IL: Quest, 1954), pp. 170–171, quoted in Wilber, p. 134.

62. Neil Postman and Charles Weingartner, *Teaching as a Subversive Activity* (New York: Dell Publishing Co., 1969), p. 101.

63. Ibid.

64. Ibid., p. 108.

65. Marianne Van Fossen, "Beyond Cliches: A History of Lesbian Oppression," *The Gay Christian* (Chicago: Universal Fellowship of Metropolitan Community Churches, Third Quarter, 1980), p. 6.

66. Ibid.

67. *In Unity*, February/March 1980, p. 13.

68. Letters to the Editor, *National Catholic Reporter* (Kansas City), August 14, 1981, p. 12.

69. Personal communication.

70. *Catholic Observer* (Springfield, MA), October 17, 1980.

71. *The American Heritage Dictionary of the English Language*, 1976 ed., s.v. "queer."

72. Marotta, p. 91.

73. *In Unity*, October/November 1979, p. 31.

74. *Workbook on Christian Social Action*, (Washington, D.C.: The Commission on Christian Social Action, Universal Fellowship of Metropolitan Community Churches, 1978), p. 30.

75. Ibid.

76. *In Unity*, September/October 1980, p. 12.

77. Brochure, (Arlington, VA: The Roundtable, n.d.). The changes reported in the above brochure are proposed by the Coalition on Women and Religion.

78. *In Unity*, February/March 1980, p. 12.

79. Virginia Mollenkott, "Imagining God Inclusively," *In Unity*, October/November, 1979, p. 21.

80. Anthony Cassano, "Coming Out in the Churches," Pastoral Renewal, March 1981, pp. 71–72.

81. Testimony of Raymond W. Hartman, *Hearing*, p. 63.

82. J. M. Sobran, "Capital M" (second in a two-part series entitled "Gay Rights and Conservative Politics"), *National Review*, March 17, 1978, reprinted in *Hearing*, p. 105.

83. Hunt, p. 130.

84. Ellen Lewin et al., *A Glossary of Terms Commonly Associated with Sexual Orientation* (Sacramento, CA: California State Personnel Board, 1980).

CHAPTER

I I I

Ideology of the Homosexual Movement

Homosexuality and Ideology

Although homosexuality in individuals seems to be related to deep-seated and often not fully conscious needs, the homosexual movement as a social phenomenon requires a set of ideas to give it intellectual cohesiveness. The development of such an ideology seems to be a precondition for the survival of social movements and nations alike. Prior to examining the content of the ideology of the homosexual movement, it is useful to discuss the nature and function of ideology in general.

The dictionary definition of ideology serves as a good point of departure for analysis. The *American Heritage Dictionary of the English Language* defines it as "the body of ideas reflecting the social needs and aspirations of an individual, class, or culture."[1] Thus ideology is not defined in terms of the objective truthfulness of the ideas it encompasses, but in terms of its ability to reflect and satisfy the needs of its proponents. The value of an ideology lies not so much in its veracity as in its functionality. In philosophical terms, ideology has been made possible by the Kantian distinction between *noumenon* and *phenomenon*.[2] While difficult to express in easily understood terms, this concept can be described as the difference between "reality as it is" *(noumenon)* and "reality as it is experienced" *(phenomenon)*. This characteristic of ideology must be kept in mind in examining the homosexual movement, since approaching its principles in a frame of mind acceptant of the objective nature of reality might lead to the adoption of doctrines designed to alter the behavior of homosexuals and heterosexuals alike. This is particularly true in that this ideology is expressed in concepts acceptable to the society at large. It is very difficult for modern man to resist the appeal of such code words as human rights, privacy, minority rights, discrimination, dignity, and freedom. These words shroud the core concepts which provide the homosexual movement with a consistent intellectual frame of reference.

Theorists do not agree on a definition of ideology. We will utilize elements from various authors in arriving at a working concept. This will not be merely an abstract definition, but will serve to illustrate the manner in which ideology serves the homosexual movement.

Von Mises distinguishes between World View and Ideology.[3] The former is "as a theory, an interpretation of all things, and as a precept for action, an opinion concerning the best means for removing uneasiness as much as possible. A world view is thus, on the one hand, an explanation of all phenomena and, on the other hand, a technology, both these terms being taken in their broadest sense." On the other hand, according to von Mises, "In speaking of ideology we have in view only human action and social cooperation and disregard the problems of metaphysics, religious dogma, the natural sciences, and the technologies derived from them." As will become evident, the ideology of the homosexual movement partakes of some of the characteristics of von Mises's World View and Ideology alike. In most instances, the homosexual movement's ideology is not all-encompassing. However, within the areas with which it is concerned, the ideas offered are presented in a comprehensive and coherent fashion. For example, when homosexuality is presented as determined before a child attains the use of reason, *no exceptions* or deviations are allowed. Similarly, *all* questioning of the validity of homosexual-sponsored legislation or ideas are attributed to homophobia,[4] and *no* instance of a person changing from homosexual to heterosexual is accepted. Testimonies of individuals reporting such changes in themselves are rejected as prima facie false.

In addition to being a coherent explanation aimed at dealing with human action and social cooperation, the homosexual movement's ideology partakes of the normative nature of both world view and ideology as described by von Mises. It goes "beyond the limits imposed upon a purely neutral and academic study of things as they are." It is "not only scientific theory, but also a doctrine about the ought." The need for such a normative ideology—as opposed to a purely scientific study of the question—was first articulated by Donald W. Cory [pseud.], an early intellectual pillar of the contemporary American homosexual movement. In his book *The Homosexual in America*, he attributed the woes of homosexuals to the fact that their condition was "without a spokesman, without a leader, without a publication, without a philosophy of life, without an accepted

Ideology of the Homosexual Movement

justification for its own existence."[5] This is not the statement of a detached observer, but the passionate cry of a man in search of a truth he can use.

The ideology of homosexuality also has the characteristics of both *ideology* and *utopia* as defined by Lasswell and Kaplan.[6] Both are defined as political myths, i.e., patterns of basic political symbols utilized to preserve certain social structures and practices and to modify or eliminate others. While there are a multitude of tactics which the homosexual movement employs in its efforts to enforce such symbols, their ultimate aim remains the creation of certain sociopolitical conditions favorable to the acceptance of homosexual behavior as normal.

The mythical character of modern homosexual ideology is evident in the creation of new concepts (e.g., homophobia) which are suited to its peculiar needs, as well as in the construction of elaborate theological explanations which have become commonplace among "feminist" theoreticians.[7] As noted before, the homosexual movement expresses its core ideas in terms found universally acceptable (e.g., human dignity, liberation, etc.). This points out the basic instability in which homosexual leaders find themselves vis-à-vis the society at large. In the homosexual ideology words are given new meaning, often contradictory to what has been accepted heretofore. For example, certain sexual practices traditionally deemed to be distasteful and destructive begin to be characterized as dignified and loving. Behaviors considered to be the manifestation of deep-seated neurosis suddenly become indicators of normal variants. What had been considered the natural rejection of antinatural behavior becomes an illness (homophobia). The ultimate purpose of these and other modifications of "normal" speech and the implied utilization of newly fashioned myths has the natural purpose of all ideologies: the exercise of political power by their formulators.

The ideology of the homosexual movement, however, does not have significance only for an anonymous mass of individuals whose interest in this movement is due to their sexual peculiarities. As Dahl points out, "Leaders in a political system usually espouse a set of more or less persistent integrated doctrines that purport to explain and justify their leadership in the system."[8]

Mutatis mutandis, it is not difficult to understand how leaders in a multibillion dollar movement with access to the White House, congressional offices, and the sympathetic pages of the nation's largest newspapers acquire a vested interest in their leadership. What originally was a band of nonconformists during the 1960s has been transformed into a well-managed and well-financed operation. The ideology manages not only to explain the inner workings of the homosexual movement and the aspirations of homosexuals who are identified with it, but also to confer legitimacy on the leadership of dozens of individuals. Eventually, allegiance to the movement and its leaders overcomes loyalty to the churches, the armed forces, the various professions, and even the families to which the homosexual belongs. The identification of a homosexual with the movement can become so intense—via his homosexuality—that in case after case even the normally stronger bonds of religious affiliation are functionally dissolved. It is relatively common to find clerics who have not only become dissenters within their churches in the matter of sexual ethics, but who actively use their churches as vehicles to spread the teachings of the homosexual movement. In view of the traditional role of the church in the area of morality, this is a most remarkable phenomenon.

Formulation of the Homosexual Ideology

With these ideas in mind, we can now proceed to a detailed examination of the ideology of the homosexual movement. As is the case with any living political movement, the ideology of the homosexual movement is not static. Representing the needs of the movement, the ideology must be adapted to geographic and temporal conditions. Moreover, it must also satisfy the needs of a multitude of individuals and organizations which integrate the movement. Still, there is a remarkable degree of consistency and uniformity in the ideological presuppositions of homosexual movement theorizers and practitioners alike.

Contemporary homosexual ideology was not formulated without much controversy in the movement. As a matter of fact, the history of the homosexual movement and the development of its ideology from the early Mattachine Society to the current homosexually oriented churches and religious organizations, are practically coextensive. One of the necessary conditions for the development of the homosexual ideology was a thorough critique of "old style homosexuals" who accepted traditional values and customs and their replacement by newly liberated "gays." Up to a point in the late sixties, "it was difficult to specify what it meant for homosexuals to express themselves naturally, if only because it was impossible to know just what it meant to be homosexual and whether traditional gay styles of self-expression were eternally dictated, happily embraced, or the result of a combination of conditioning and choice."[9] In other words, there was no such thing as a homosexual-generated matrix in which homosexuals could find self-expression according to their nature.[10]

The need to reject the "old" homosexual lifestyle, and certainly the traditional values in which it developed, was a characteristic of the early prohomosexual theoreticians of the late sixties. In the first issue of *Come Out!*, a publication of New York's Gay Liberation Front, Leo Martello "argued that liberation required homosexuals to discover unwarranted guilt and inferiority and to learn to feel good about themselves." He was

Ideology of the Homosexual Movement

then "expressing sentiments shared by all the early gay liberationists." Moreover, "Martello carefully equated liberation with the elimination of negative feelings about homosexuality and portrayed voyages of homosexual self-discovery as open-ended and diverse. With subtlety, he urged homosexuals to reject cultural conditioning and to be true to their own selves without suggesting that this would result in specific conclusions or choices."[11] It is thus clear that the homosexual ideology has resulted from the subjective experience of homosexuals prodded by a continuing process in which they are the main participants. It is definitely not the result of objective analysis. We can also surmise that the various components of the ideology will have the intended result of eliminating guilt or sorrow and promoting a positive appreciation of their sexual proclivities and practices in the homosexuals themselves.

In addition to the experience of homosexuals, religious thought has become a source of the homosexual ideology. F. Jay Deacon, a minister in the homosexually oriented Metropolitan Community Church, explains this process in a dialectical fashion. According to Deacon, the original inhabitants of Canaan were peaceful believers in God as a female; there most of the priests were women, who also enjoyed a privileged position in the conduct of government and business. Then "during the period of the Levite conquest, tribes of new, male-dominated cultures invaded country after country, proclaiming . . . that God was male and replacing matriarchy with patriarchy. You might say that a second phase of world history had begun—the era of masculine domination."[12] The coming of Jesus represented then a synthesis which transcended both positions:

> In the first century of our era, Jesus arrived on the scene, and he died in the crush between the dying age, dominated by the exclusive masculine God, and the new age he brought, the age of androgynous wholeness and balance. In his death, the opposites of life and death come together, reconciled by the power of the Eternal Love that created all of us and fully embraces every one of us. In his life, the so-called masculine qualities of bold strength and clear thought are joined with the so-called feminine qualities of nurturing, caring, and receptive sensitivity (to people and to the Spirit).
>
> In the light of Christ's salvation we can learn the healing truth of androgyny— that the opposites of life are really one. . . . speaking the truth that God is not just a God of maleness, but a God whose being includes male and female, straight and gay, black and white, and every condition known to people.[13]

The Christian era is thus the era of homosexuality. Although Christians for almost 2,000 years have not been aware of it, the age of homosexuality has dawned, and in Christ it is possible to transcend the "limitations" imposed by maleness and femaleness. Once more, it is clear that from such a frame of mind it is possible to develop a set of propositions which explain and promote the sexual and social behavior of homosexuals qua homosexuals in positive and supportive ways.

In many instances, though without reaching the extremes of openly prohomosexual theorists, religious leaders of various persuasions have accepted and thus promoted the homosexual ideology. The example of the Roman Catholic Church comes easily to mind. A prohomosexual organization of Roman Catholics, New Ways Ministry, has published *A Time To Speak,* a collection of statements by Catholic leaders and publications which reflect elements of the homosexual ideology.

Although not having the same value as theological or philosophical statements, the importance of empirical science in contemporary society has encouraged the development of such institutions as the Center for Research in Education and Sexuality (CERES, formerly Center for Homosexual Education, Evaluation, and Research) at San Francisco State University. In this institution, sociological and psychological research designed to validate "scientifically" various aspects of the homosexual ideology are undertaken and disseminated.[14] It is thus that apparently "objective" centers engaged in "scientific research" also contribute to the formulation of the homosexual ideology.

Homosexual Ideology: An Example

David Thorstad, spokesman for the North American Man/Boy Love Association, has attempted to articulate an ideology of homosexuality which reflects the needs not only of pederasts but of all homosexuals.[15] Thorstad's system is consistent, including the following components:

1) *Sex.* In all its forms, sex is good so long as it is consensual. Specifically, homosexuality is good for those who practice it: "NAMBLA takes the view that sex is good, that homosexuality is good not only for adults, but for young people as well. We support all consensual sexual relationships regardless of age. As long as the relationship is mutually pleasurable, and no one's rights are violated, sex should be no one else's business."[16]

The concept of right immediately introduces legal, political, and, ultimately, moral considerations. Are rights definable in terms of individuals without reference to society at large? Who decides who has which rights? Should the purpose of human functions vis-à-vis society at large be taken into consideration? Is it proper to speak of and to demand natural obligations and rights which go beyond the free desires of individuals? What is the rational basis for discerning responsibilities and rights? These questions are crucial for a proper evaluation of NAMBLA's argument.

2) *Children's Liberation.* The concept of liberation is central to the homosexual ideology. A popular notion, having roots in both Eastern and

Ideology of the Homosexual Movement

Western religions, it has been appropriated by contemporary revolutionary ideologies. For the homosexual movement, liberation entails the ability of all homosexuals and their partners to be free of all external and internal constraints in the pursuit of sexual pleasure. According to NAMBLA:

> Sexual liberation cannot be achieved without the liberation of children. This means many things. Children need to gain control over their lives, a control which they are denied on all sides. They need to break the yoke of "protection" which alienates them from themselves, a "protection" imposed on them by adults—their family, the schools, the state, and prevailing sexual and social mores.

3) *Motherhood.* At the center of the homosexual ideology seems to be the need or desire to challenge the traditional family centered on a loving relationship between a man and a woman for the purpose of begetting children. Biologically, homosexual activities are nonprocreative; thus a homosexual "family" stands in sharp contrast to the traditional family. NAMBLA, which represents the ideological edge of the homosexual movement, challenges the traditional family:

> With the decline of the extended family and traditional church influence, the state has increased its investment in maintaining a preferred family structure, i.e., male-dominated, heterosexual, nuclear variety. The state continues to have a vested interest in regulating and channeling sexual activity into the type it can best control. The greatest threat to this hierarchical and repressive system is presented by sexual and affectionate personal relations outside the approved mode. Specifically, this means the freedom of those over whom the state still has greatest control (minors) and those with whom they would create their own lives.[17]

The alienating influence of the family is presented by Thorstadt in terms of motherhood:

> Parents often fear the sexuality of their children, because once the child begins to have sex, they feel they have lost an important measure of control over the child. The best mother (or father) for a boy is one who gives him the freedom he needs to explore himself and the world around him. . . .

> The child himself should have the right to decide whom to live with, whether a lesbian mother or a gay father, the "natural" parents, a boy-lover, or someone else. . . .

> Mothering the young is a role imposed on women, frequently against their will. This role can have a profoundly negative character when it is internalized, as it often has been, by feminists and even by lesbians who are not themselves mothers. It is destructive of the interests of boys when it is invoked as a way

of restricting their freedom of action. Insofar as it manifests a belief in the biological abilities of the female to nurture the young—abilities allegedly absent in the male of the species—the family, and religion, oppress young people.

The liquidation of the traditional family as normative requires the elimination of sex-ascribed roles. Far from a merely theoretical statement, this position has had profound influence on the activities espoused by the homosexual movement and is responsible for its close relationship with feminism and the contemporary practice of nonsexist education.

4) *Age of consent.* The concept of the ability of people to decide for themselves—without regard for a norm which limits their peculiar propensities—is central to the homosexual ideology. While moral limitations have traditionally been accepted as enhancing freedom, the homosexual movement separates the sexual practices of the consensual partners from moral considerations. This is crucial for NAMBLA:

> There is no age at which a person becomes capable of consenting to sex. The age of sexual consent is just one of many ways in which adults impose their system of control on children. . . .

> The state is the enemy of freedom, not its guarantor. The best evidence against the argument that children cannot consent to sex, including with adults, is the fact that millions of them do it anyway.

5) *Homosexuals a minority.* One of the characteristics of a minority is the ability of its members to identify themselves with what makes them part of the minority in such a way that only they know what it means to be this kind of person. The depth of this experience, with its obvious emotional overtones, serves as the source for the cohesion of the movement. In NAMBLA's words:

> Just as homosexuals are the best qualified to interpret and explain what homosexuality is like, so man/boy lovers are the most qualified to explain what our relationships are like.
> Ours is a struggle to speak the truth. There will be some who do not wish to be confused by the facts. But others will refuse to put on the blinders offered in the name of traditional morality, respectability, or feminism.

Homosexual Ideology: A Synthesis

Up to this point, no one has articulated systematically the ideology of the homosexual movement. It is possible to isolate its various components by

Ideology of the Homosexual Movement

an analysis of existing documentation, but no complete or overall statement has been made. The following description of an attempt to produce a more or less complete statement of homosexual ideology is offered by way of example. It constitutes an approach to the same question: the self-actualization of homosexuals "homosexually" in society.

An analysis of the vast literature produced by the homosexual movement enables us to discern ideological elements which can be assembled in a logical system. The following scheme provides the structure of this system:

			Ideological Statement
Homosexual Ideology	Homosexuality in Itself	What homosexuality Is	• Distinction between gay and homosexual • Gay is good
		What Homosexuality Is Not	• Homosexuality is not a matter of choice • Homosexuality is not changeable • Homosexuality is not an illness
	Response to Homosexuality	Individual	• "Coming out" is a desirable action • Homosexuality in itself has no moral implications • Homophobia is an undesirable condition
		Collective	• Homosexuals constitute a legitimate minority • There are large numbers of homosexuals. • The homosexual ideology is revolutionary in nature

We now proceed to discuss and document each one of these eleven ideological statements. There is an interdependence and a logical progression among them which will become evident as they are examined.

Although composed of seemingly diverse components with homosexuality as its sole focal point, the homosexual ideology is, in fact, a well-constructed and coherent intellectual structure designed to satisfy the individual and social needs of the movement's members. Not all homosexuals can be said to accept each individual statement, even among those who are identified with the movement. However, there seems to be nearly universal agreement on the statements discussed below.

I HOMOSEXUALITY IN ITSELF

The first category to be examined is the nature of homosexuality in view of the contemporary homosexual movement. As mentioned before, this perception goes beyond the strictly scientific realm. Although presented in language chosen from the behavioral sciences, careful analysis reveals that the statements are in fact sociopolitical in nature, intended to serve the needs of the movement. No reference is made to the various psychological theories on the origin of homosexuality, inasmuch as there is little agreement within the movement about their usefulness. So long as a theory is consistent with the sociopolitical requirements of the movement, it usually evokes little interest beyond that of academics. Otherwise, it elicits considerable negative response. Opinions or theories which contradict elements of the homosexual ideology, whether expressed by theologians, sociologists, or psychologists, normally result in attacks on their proponents.

A. What Homosexuality Is

The significance of homosexuality for the movement goes far beyond the attraction between persons of the same sex and the practices that follow this attraction. One of the leaders of the homosexual movement, Sister Jeannine Gramick, defines "homosexual orientation" as "the combination of erotic feelings, fantasies, and activity regarding the members of one's own sex."[18] This definition, however, does not satisfy the psychosocial needs of members of the movement or the political needs of the movement. Any of the "standard" definitions of homosexuality is used as a basis and then transcended in the interest of the movement. The definition of homosexuality from the movement's point of view involves an evaluation of homosexuality and a distinction between unregenerated or traditional homosexuality and its transformation by the conscientization of homosexuals.

The homosexual movement has thus arrived at two propositions which frame the character of homosexuality:

- There is a distinction between Gay and Homosexual.
- Gay is good.

These two propositions help clarify the homosexual movement's conception of homosexuality and its value.

1) *Distinction Between Gay and Homosexual.* Traditionally, the word "gay" has signified cheerful or happy. In many countries, it is still used in this sense. In America, however, for the past twenty-five years, it has increasingly come to mean homosexual. Within the movement, however,

Ideology of the Homosexual Movement

this complete identification is rejected. Early in the development of New York's Gay Liberation Movement, the concept of a "liberated" homosexual, as opposed to traditional homosexuals, became entrenched. As Marotta points out:

> Reform-minded gay liberationists believed further that individuals with homosexual feelings were better off if they expressed them fully and freely, and that others had an obligation to recognize and respect homosexual paths to personal fulfillment. In their view, a "liberated" homosexual was one who was comfortable with his sexuality and his subculture and successful at integrating his homosexuality into his life instead of denying, concealing, or compartmentalizing it. A "liberated" homosexual was one who felt free to explore homosexual as well as heterosexual feelings, was comfortable with homosexuals, and saw gay life as valid, even if it was personally unappealing.[19]

A recent letter to the *Wall Street Journal* clearly expressed the nature of the distinction between "gay" and "homosexual":

> Contrary to Edward H. Seagraves [letter, July 8], "gay" is no synonym—hence no "euphemism"—for "homosexual." Not every person engaging in a homosexual act is gay. As the term is knowledgeably used nowadays, a gay is a person who recognizes and accepts the homosexual component of his or her makeup with some measure of self-respect, dignity, and pride.
> Contrary to Mr. Seagraves, the term gay is not intended to conceal the fact of same-sex activity. It is, rather, a forthright challenge to knee-jerk homoerotophobia which decries such activity as "repulsive, disgusting, repugnant" and which masks an antipathy to sex in any form. All sex, gay or straight, is physical.[20]

The transition from plain homosexual to gay thus implies a profound reappraisal of the self and its relationships to others. In this context, a gay person is a "liberated" homosexual. The process by which a homosexual becomes gay (described below as "coming out") is conceived as a form of liberation. (The theme of "liberation" has acquired considerable importance in the twentieth century, although it is rooted in the sixth-century B.C. philosophical movement that produced Plato and the Buddha. It has been received in the modern West mediated by Christianity and ultimately appropriated by Marxism. Adam DeBaugh, Director of the Social Justice Field Office for the Universal Fellowship of Metropolitan Community Churches, sees the distinction between gay and homosexual as rooted in the language and ideology of the homosexual movement.[21] According to DeBaugh, gay speaks of culture, pride, celebration, and affirmation of who a person is. It is thus a political, social, economic, and cultural term. A homosexual himself, Mr. DeBaugh identifies homosexual with engaging in sexual relations: ("I act like a homosexual when I am having sex with another man"). To be gay, however, has entirely different implications: "I live in a gay family. This means people living together, not necessarily having sex with one another. I live as a single gay man with two couples, two gay men and two lesbians. If I go to a gay restaurant, I am demonstrating my gayness, but I am not having sex." In the ultimate analysis, DeBaugh conceives of "gay" as going beyond sexuality: "Gay actually transcends sexuality." Clearly, it is possible to be homosexual and not gay. However, there is no clear answer as to whether a person can be heterosexual *and* gay. The distinction between homosexual and gay breaks down at this point.

This distinction is instilled in the socialization of young homosexuals advocated by the movement. In the homosexual education textbook *Young, Gay and Proud*, the process is reversed: "Some gay men, after years of marriage, find that they really prefer other men and become homosexuals."[22] It is thus possible to be gay while behaving heterosexually and afterward "become" homosexual.

The distinction between gay and homosexual, when actualized at the existential level, implies the personal identification of the individual with his sexuality at the deepest level. This total identification with being homosexual among "gay persons" implies that homosexuality among "gays" stands at the core of their existence and totally defines them. In his review of John Reid's *The Best Little Boy in the World,* an account of Reid's experience as a homosexual, Michael England presents the following dialogue with approval: " 'Would *you* take that pill and make yourself straight?' "[23] And we can all joyfully learn, " 'That would be like killing myself.' "[24]

This total identification of the homosexual with his homosexuality in the process of becoming gay presents serious dangers to the movement. While gaining the loyalty of many individuals, it runs the risk of closing itself off to other sympathetic organizations. In the case of female homosexuals with their natural interest in the feminist movement, this danger is particularly acute. This was understood from the very early days of the movement by such leaders as Dorothy DelMartin, who advised female homosexuals, in the editorial "The Lesbian's Majority Status" (June 1967 issue of *The Ladder*) to "involve themselves in organizations like the [then] newly formed National Organization for Women (NOW), the League of Women Voters, and the Business and Professional Women's Club."[25] This strategy, as will be seen later on, paid off handsomely for the movement.

2) *Gay is Good.* We have already surmised that homosexuality is not perceived by the movement as a liability. As a matter of fact, when transmuted to *gay*, homosexuality becomes an asset. The proposition *Gay is Good* constitutes one of the most challenging statements of the homosexual ideology. In frank opposition to the *philosophia perennis* that has constituted the backbone of traditional sexual morality, this is the central statement of the homosexual ideology.

Ideology of the Homosexual Movement

From the early days of the movement, this notion has had a therapeutic role for individuals and has been a source of political power for the organization. Arnie Kantrowitz, an early leader, reports the profound effect that chanting "Two-four-six-eight: Gay is just as good as straight" had on him.[26] Although firmly committed to the anti–Viet Nam War movement, Kantrowitz reveals how he sang the homosexual mantra "with a feeling I'd never had when I'd yelled 'Peace! Now!' "[27]

Frank Kameny, the elder statesman of the homosexual movement, instituted a suit in the early sixties upon being fired by the Army Map Service on account of his homosexual condition. After losing repeatedly in lesser courts, he filed a petition to the Supreme Court. In this petition, he indicated his belief that homosexuality "is good, right, and desirable for those who choose to engage in it."[28]

The political value of this statement was well understood by Kameny. One of the earliest disputes within the homosexual movement occurred between such moderates as Dick Leitsch and militants like Kameny. In a reply to Leitsch after serious clashes which took place in a May 1968 United Church of Christ meeting, Kameny wrote:

> The ONLY people in this entire country—in the entire world—that I know of, who are standing up and telling the homosexual person that he IS equal, and that his homosexuality is NOT a badge of inferiority, etc., and who are doing it without reservation, without excuse, not as a "crumb of pity from the table, for those poor psychologically maimed people who can't help themselves," who is saying NOT merely grudgingly, "Homosexuality is a valid way of life for some people," but, in parallel to Carmichael, "Homosexuality is GOOD"—positively and without reservation—the ONLY people in all the world who are doing this are the pitifully small handful of us in the homophile movement. And our people are very sensitive to any squeamishness and half-heartedness on our part.[29]

Kameny's understanding was adopted by the North American Conference of Homophile Organizations (NACHO) in a 1968 resolution presented by him. This resolution, printed below in its entirety, reveals the ideological nature and ultimate purpose of the statement "gay is good":[30]

> BECAUSE many individual homosexuals, like many of the members of many other minority groups, suffer from diminished self-esteem, doubts and uncertainties as to their personal worth, and from a pervasive false and unwarranted sense of an inferiority and undesirability of their homosexual condition, and from a negative approach to that condition; *and*
>
> BECAUSE, therefore, many individual homosexuals, like many of the members of many other minority groups, are in need of psychological sustenance to bolster and to support a positive and affirmative attitude toward themselves and their homosexuality and to have instilled into them a confident sense of the positive good and value of themselves and of their condition; *and*

BECAUSE it would seem to be very much a function of the North American Homophile Conference to attempt to replace a wishy-washy negativism toward homosexuality with a firm no-nonsense positivism, to attempt to establish in the homosexual community and its members feelings of pride, self-esteem, self-confidence, and self-worth, in being the homosexuals that they are and have a moral right to be (these feelings being essential to true human dignity), and to attempt to bring to bear a countervailing influence against negative attitudes toward homosexuality prevalent in the heterosexual community; *and*

BECAUSE the Negro community has approached similar problems and goals with some success by the adoption of the motto or slogan: *Black is Beautiful*

RESOLVED: that it be hereby adopted as a slogan or motto for NACHO that

GAY IS GOOD

The message comes across from every quarter of the movement. Ellen Barnett, a female homosexual ordained an Episcopal priest in 1977, not only indicated that homosexuality was an "alternative life-style," but referred to it as a "good and creative thing."[31]

A further specification of the meaning of "gay" as good has been offered by Father John McNeill, S. J., a Roman Catholic priest and also a noted leader of the homosexual movement. In a lecture held at the Harvard Divinity School on April 12, 1980, Father McNeill broke a two-year silence on the subject of homosexuality. (He had been ordered by his Jesuit superiors to refrain from speaking on homosexuality or sexual ethics.) Father McNeill "urged his audience to appreciate the unique sexual identity of every person and, in addition, called attention to the unique and positive role which the gay community must perform in the building of a more human society."[32]

According to Father McNeill, this contribution, which makes "gay" good, occurs in three areas leading to "true liberation." First, "homosexual relationships based on equality and dignity should be a positive and alternate model to the paternalistic sexual roles of male-female relationships and to the traditional basis of the family." To accept homosexuality in any form as a model for family relationships implies the destruction of the traditional family unit. This understanding that heretofore the relationship between men and women has been based on power rather than love is further reinforced by McNeill in his second area, in which "he noted the connection between the male 'macho' identity and the high frequency of violence," further suggesting that "homosexuals are potentially free from the psychological need to establish their identity by means of violence," and pointing out "the near absence of violence among self-accepting gays." McNeill seems to be ignoring here the existence of sadomasochistic practices among homosexuals. "S & M" (sadomasochism) is based precisely on violence. The rather large number of homosexuals who are devoted to S & M is evident from the number of deaths resulting from this practice, sometimes reported by the homosexual press.[33] (Cf. chapter II.) Homosexual publications regularly publish advertisements for establishments which sell S & M "toys" (whips, chains, bondage equipment, etc.), bars that cater to S & M devotees, and similar resources. Moreover, in San Francisco a workshop has been offered for instructing homosexuals in how to practice sadomasochism without causing each other real harm.[34]

The third area in which the positive aspect of homosexuality is manifested, according to McNeill, is the supernatural or spiritual. Published reports state that Father McNeill also "noted the special sensitivity that many homosexuals feel for the value of human life and compared that way of living with the nonviolence, service, and sensitivity of Jesus." This implication that Jesus was somehow affected with homosexuality, however indirectly, is bound to raise serious objections from traditional believers. It is obvious, however, that if to be homosexual is good, and Jesus (or any other religious leader) is considered "all good," somehow He would in some sense partake of that homosexuality.

The positive nature of homosexuality is proclaimed by the homosexual movement. Organized pederasts, for example, insist that homosexuality is good not only for individuals but for society at large:

> There may be a valuable contribution in man-boy intimacy (when it is naturally entered into by two people who want each other) which heretofore has been bludgeoned into the underground without a fair appraisal of its possibilities as a positive social force. Eglinton (*Greek Love*, 1971) asked for this fair appraisal, and predicted as early as 1964 (U.S. edition of *Greek Love*) that pederasty could well be the solution to some of the social problems involving today's youth, instead of being itself a social problem as seen by Victorian moralists in today's society.[35]

The consequences of accepting such a position seem evident. If homosexuality is seen as good, no real objections can be made to pornography— the First Amendment question being a separate issue—for adults or for children. Thus on May 12, 1981, the New York State Court of Appeals, by a 5–2 decision, declared the 1977 State "kiddie porn" law unconstitutional.[36] This law was not based on the concept of obscenity as accepted by the U.S. Supreme Court (i.e., that obscenity is to be judged by community standards), but "made it illegal to produce, promote, or sell materials that showed children in sexual activity whether the materials had been judged obscene or not."[37]

The liberation of children from constraints in the area of sexuality— other than those imposed by the rule of consensuality—is at the root of the homosexual ideology. Consonant with this ideology, David Clark, the District of Columbia Councilman representing one of the areas where most homosexuals reside, nearly succeeded in lifting almost all restrictions for consensual sex between children, homosexual or heterosexual.[38]

Homosexual sex education aimed at making children experts in the various techniques of homosexual sex—in case they "discover" that they are homosexuals—also becomes a given. The textbook already mentioned, *Young, Gay and Proud*, provides children of both sexes with vivid and detailed descriptions of the various acts by which homosexuals satisfy their sexual needs. The promotional value of sex education has been amply documented. According to Jacqueline Kasun of Humboldt State University, for example, sex education has demonstrably resulted in an increase in sexual activity.[39] It is only to be expected that homosexual sex education will result in an increase in homosexual activity among young people.

The acceptance of the principle that to be a homosexual is good is particularly significant in the case of homosexual teachers. Bill Springmann, a homosexual teacher writing in a popular publication, makes this connection explicit:

> Then there are my favorite boys. I don't know that they will be Gay when they grow up, but at this point they need and seek my affection rather than that of the women teachers. They trust me, turn to me, and are more dependent on me. They even seek physical intimacy, caressing my arms or unbuttoning my shirt. I realize that sexual orientation is determined by the age of three or four. Since I feel that Gay is good, I'm a little biased in imagining that these boys might turn out to be healthily Gay identified.[40]

It can be easily seen that the concept "gay is good" has not just theoretical implications. In the case of this teacher, his behavior—based on this ideological principle—results in what amounts to a form of recruitment of children to become homosexuals themselves.

It is difficult to ascertain the reason why "gay is good" in the minds of homosexual theorists beyond the physical and psychological satisfactions that the fulfillment of "gayness" seems to engender in certain homosexuals (i.e., those who have "come out," an idea that will be discussed later on in this chapter). The fact that homosexual sex is incompatible with reproduction seems to be the key. Whereas traditional morality has always considered the procreative aspect of sexual intercourse to be the ultimate explanation for its existence and dignity, this explanation is obviously inadequate for homosexuals. The connection between the goodness of homosexuality and the separation of the unitive and procreative aspects of human sexuality has been presented by Father Robert Nugent and Sister Jeannine Gramick, Catholic leaders of the homosexual movement. After attempting to show apparent discrepancies between the positions of the Vatican and the American Catholic bishops, they assert:

Ideology of the Homosexual Movement

This has led some theologians to question whether homosexual behavior that falls within some kind of relationship comparable to marriage would also be judged as morally wrong if the Church were to separate, for any reason, the procreative from the unitive aspect of sexual intercourse. In doing this they have in mind those heterosexual, nonprocreative (for physiological reasons) relationships such as the valid marriage of a sterile couple, which has always been accepted and blessed by the Church. They draw a parallel between such homosexual activity and heterosexual nonprocreative behavior of a sterile couple beyond the procreative years, which has always been approved.[41]

This relationship between the homosexual ideology and the antireproductive mentality was also evidenced in a statement issued by the Public Morals Committee of the Quakers (Wilmington Yearly Meeting), as the result of a 1978 directive to make a study concerning the issue of homosexuality and Friends (i.e., Quaker) meetings. The statement in question read in part: "Two major sins in the world in 1979 are the overproduction of human beings, and the overconsumption of resources. . . . Homosexuality does not create overproduction of humans. I do not advocate homosexuality, but it is not as great a sin as cigarette smoking."[42]

The nature and consequences of such positions have been pointed out by other less sympathetic writers. Professor Charles Rice of Notre Dame University indicates that:

> The legitimization of homosexual activity, of course, is a predictable consequence of the separation of the unitive and procreative aspects of sex. So are promiscuity, pornography, divorce, abortion, etc. We have sunk to extraordinary depths in our contraceptive society. And it may be that we will bottom out only when the natural consequences of depravity become so intolerable as to remind us of the Lawgiver whose Law we are flouting. ". . . men with men doing shameless things and receiving in themselves the fitting recompense of their perversity" (Romans 1:27).[43]

From a Jewish perspective, homosexual behavior has also been contested for much the same reason by Hershel J. Matt, acting director of the B'nai B'rith Hillel Foundation at Princeton University. After introducing relevant Biblical passages (Genesis 1:27, 1:31, 2:23–28; Isaiah 45:18; Genesis 17:7), he asserts that:

> In light of such Scriptural passages, some of the reasons for the Torah's prohibition of homosexuality become discernible. One reason must be that in the Order of Creation the sexual "nature" and "structure" of the human male and female—including what we refer to as their anatomy, physiology, and psyche—call for mutual complementation, completion, and fulfillment through a heterosexual relationship. Another implied reason is that only through such a

relationship, using the organs of generation in a manner conducive to generation, can a new generation appear to populate the earth.[44]

In the political and legal arenas, the contention that homosexuality is right and proper has important consequences. Naturally, all prohomosexual legislation is ultimately based on the idea that "gay is good," at least for those who are homosexuals (See Kameny's statement above). In an attack on New York City's proposed homosexual "rights" legislation, Adam Walinsky contended that this bill would not only result in the protection of homosexuals, but would force school administrators, landlords, employers, and others to "accept" homosexuals. The worst feature, according to Walinsky, is that "the bill amounts to a formal declaration that homosexuality is morally or socially equal to heterosexuality. This would be wrong."[45] The assumption here is that heterosexuality is good, but that homosexuality is not. The importance of the challenge to the fundamental tenet of the homosexual movement implicit in Walinsky's statement did not pass unnoticed to the movement's activists. The Gay Activists Alliance reportedly organized a demonstration in which some fifty homosexuals armed with baseball bats and bullhorns threatened to burn his home.[46]

B. What Homosexuality Is Not

From an ideological standpoint, the homosexual movement basically completes its *positive* description of homosexuality in terms of affirmation and acceptance. However, this movement is in essence reactive against the traditional thinking, which it perceives as having resulted in the "oppression" of homosexuals. Therefore, homosexual theoreticians and activists alike are forced to deny the traditional views which are the "sources of their oppression." Homosexuality is thus presented as not a matter of choice, as irreversible, and as a "normal variant" of human sexuality rather than an illness.

1) *Homosexuality Is Not a Matter of Choice.* An almost universal theme within the homosexual movement is the idea that homosexuals are in no way responsible for being the way they are. In the process of growing up, homosexual movement writers assert, a person "discovers" that he is homosexual. The acquisition of a homosexual consciousness is, therefore, seen as a process of self-discovery and maturation rather than as involving conscious choices on the part of the homosexual. It must be kept in mind, however, that this statement is ideological rather than scientific in nature, i.e., that it has been formulated for the purpose of serving the goals and objectives of the homosexual movement.

One of the clearest exponents of the principle that homosexuality per se does not include a personal choice is Dr. Clarence A. Tripp, who as early as 1966 was a member of the Mattachine Society's Board of Psychiatric Advisers.[47] Tripp presents the development of homosexuality not

Ideology of the Homosexual Movement

only as a very complex phenomenon, but as one in which the individual's will plays almost no role. In chapter 6 of his classic, *The Homosexual Matrix*, he asserts that homosexual actions result from an already established homosexual value system, rather than the other way around. After discussing the origin of "beginning" homosexual experiences, he states:

> But when one takes a closer look at the examples, the homosexual motives usually turn out to have far more specificity and more importance to the individuals than can be accounted for by "loose morals," money, or mere sex pressure. Often there is more than enough picking and choosing of partners, even an idealization (if not of the partner, then of maleness itself), to indicate the presence of a quite definite sexual value system. In particular instances, this value system stems most directly from repeated early experiences. But since the cultures and social levels at which loosely begun homosexual practices are the most prevalent are also the ones which laud male values to the sky, we are again faced with the probability that values more often lead to experiences than vice versa.[48]

It appears that in this context "values" refers not to intellectual ethical categories but rather to deeply ingrained attitudes. Unrelated to experiences, and as extrinsic causes relate to effect, these "values" serve as the root causes—efficient and final—of homosexual behavior. Although early homosexual experiences are significant in the eventual establishment of the homosexual orientation, Tripp seems to indicate that homosexuality in an incipient form actually precedes *any* form of voluntary homosexual behavior:

> At any rate, there is a note of irony in the fact that regardless of how easy or hard it may be for a homosexual pattern to become established by overt experiences, its least effective starting sources are precisely those about which the public is most anxious and on guard: Neither "child seduction" nor the kinds of instances law courts describe as "impairing the morals of a minor" seem to have much effect. Child seduction, though it can be traumatic when parents make an issue of it, is virtually powerless to start a sexual pattern.[49]

This whole question, as we will see shortly, is a particularly sensitive point for the homosexual movement. If it could be shown that homosexuality can be the result of "seduction" or "recruitment," the homosexual movement would certainly lose the support of many liberal heterosexuals. If homosexuality is determined before the age of reason, and its establishment is not dependent on early sexual experiences, the homosexual movement can count on the support of many heterosexuals who have come to believe that it is unavoidable.

Even in the case of older individuals, e.g., teenagers, homosexual experiences are seen as a manifestation that people are *already* homosexuals:

> Sexual experiences around the time of puberty can be more influential, but even so, it is hard to find instances of people having developed homosexual tastes through casual or "accidental" experiences. On close examination, it usually turns out that the die was already cast by then and often that the "victim" was the provocateur. This latter detail is of more than passing significance when it is realized that a person who merely participates in a sexual activity is much less subject to being conditioned by it than is the instigator.[50]

Once the principle that the teenage "victim" of homosexual seduction is really the "instigator" has been established, it is very difficult to condemn or criticize in any way an adult involved in such a seduction.

Tripp describes the process of self-realization that one is homosexual in terms of the appearance in a boy of "an intense personal attraction to a particular male—often a stranger or near-stranger with whom he has no thought of sex. He may have a fierce urge to know and to be close to a particular teacher, a young policeman, or one of his father's friends, or an older boy in another class at school whom he has not yet met."[51] Tripp describes the case of a fourteen-year-old boy who literally pursues an older man without knowing why he is interested in the man. Commenting on his example, Tripp concludes, "In this example, as in so many others, it is as if the young, inexperienced homosexual has a ready-made appetite, a worked-out value system which is neither fully eroticized nor consciously realized until an appropriately complementary partner is suddenly encountered."[52]

The experience of discovering one's homosexuality is thus akin to a quasi-mystical experience in which an individual finds himself "fixed" on a person of the same sex. This obsessional interest is, for Tripp, not unlike a religious conversion:

> . . . an obsessional interest . . . What it does do—often impressively for the homosexual—is to define a person's bailiwick and, in the process, give his ship a certain gyroscopic directionality, no matter how rough the seas. Undoubtedly, this is why religious conversion (or a more personalized neurotic symptom) tends to hold a person together, often as well as does a fervent interest in being an artist or artisan.[53]

This function of homosexuality as an "obsession" is, for Tripp, a source of psychological stability for the homosexual. In yet another way, "gay is good":

> Intuitively, it is easy to understand how having an obsessional focus of some kind reduces a person's vulnerability to hysterical scatter or to a breakdown.

Ideology of the Homosexual Movement

But exactly how does having a commitment to virtually anything manage to immunize him against depression and against the sting of personal rejection? When one asks the person who manages to stay secure in the face of adversity exactly how he does it, he usually grants all the credit to the obsession itself.[54]

The idea that the constitution of one's personality and the desires and activity derived therefrom are a matter of unconscious determination are, as the result of Freud's contribution to psychology, accepted as a matter of course by a substantial number of contemporary psychologists. Even psychologists who can in no way be described as apologists for homosexuality agree on this point. Charles Socarides, a psychiatrist with considerable expertise on the subject, but who is definitely not a supporter of the movement, readily accepts that "contrary to popular belief, this is not a sexual *preference* as there is no *choice*."[55] In Socarides's case, however, this is an expression of his perception of the process rather than an ideological expression designed to support the homosexual movement. As will be seen later, he concludes that homosexuality is indeed a psychic condition.

From a behavioral point of view, people's sexual activities would indicate that some individuals are 100 percent heterosexual, others 100 percent homosexual, and the balance take all the middle positions. Ideologically, if it is taken to reflect the way people *are*, this is not an acceptable notion, since it implies a degree of choice which is incompatible with the interests of the homosexual movement. Thus, against Leitsch, who used Kinsey's statistics to show that the number of people exclusively homosexual is relatively small, Frank Kameny "insisted that 'homosexuality and heterosexuality are not really a continuum,' that 'people are always either one or the other,' and that 'those who engage in sexual acts with men and women both are simply 'closet queens' who use their heterosexual acts as a facade to hide their homosexual behavior.' "[56]

The homosexual movement has tried for years to make prohomosexual legislation conform to its ideological presuppositions. Andy Humm, a New York City Catholic homosexual leader, speaking about the 1981 version of the New York City homosexual rights bill, points this out:

What makes this bill new is a simplification of its language. The bill which has been defeated for ten years adds the category of "sexual orientation" to the list of bases on which one may not discriminate, and defines sexual orientation as "the choice of sexual orientation according to gender." This definition is thought to be limiting, inaccurate, and uninstructive. It introduces the concept of choice when we are trying to establish sexual orientation as an innate part of human personality. Thus, the definition will be dropped. . . .[57]

95

A similar change was introduced in the 1979 Weiss-Waxman prohomo-sexual bill (H.R. 2074). The participation of the homosexual leadership in the drafting of this bill and the incorporation of the homosexual ideology in its language and intent are evident:

> . . . Major changes have been made in the bill, after consultation between the UFMCC Washington Office, the Gay Rights National Lobby, other Gay organizations, and Members of Congress and their aides. First, the old term "affectional or sexual preference," has been changed to "affectional or sexual orientation." The reason for this is that it was felt "orientation" best expresses the nature of human sexuality, while "preference" raises the possibility that we believe sexuality is a matter of choice.
>
> Secondly, the definition of terms section has been considerably cleaned up. The new definition of "affectional or sexual orientation" will be "male or female homosexuality, heterosexuality and bisexuality by orientation or practice."[58]

The concept "orientation" does not by itself denote any behavior. The homosexual movement, however, would not be responsive to the needs of practicing homosexuals should it accept such a definition. Thus this very orientation which exists in homosexuals by no choice of their own is normally linked with homosexual acts as part of its definition. We have already seen that Sister Jeannine Gramick's definition of homosexuality involves sexual activity as one of its elements.

If homosexuals are necessarily thus, and if homoerotic behavior is part of their definition, it is difficult to believe that homosexuals—given the opportunity—will not engage in sexual relations with children. However, this conclusion, a logical sequel to the homosexual ideology, is system-atically rejected by the homosexual leaders and their sympathizers: "The assumption that males [sic] homosexuals constitute a significant threat to young children is totally unfounded. In actuality the seeking of children as sexual objects is much less common among homosexuals than among heterosexuals."[59] Father Andrew Greeley, the noted Catholic sociologist, advanced a similar idea in support of homosexual rights:

> I'm opposed to discrimination for any reason—be it against women who want to be jet pilots or homosexuals who want to teach in high schools. . . . Despite Anita Bryant they are not interested in "corrupting" or "recruiting" young people. Mostly, they would like to be left alone, a not unreasonable request. They do not want to hurt others and they wish others would stop hurting them. To ask for freedom from discrimination does not mean for them to advocate a revolution.[60]

These assertions, however, cannot stand in the face of evidence provided by spokesmen of the homosexual movement. During a NAMBLA con-ference in Boston:

Ideology of the Homosexual Movement

Tom Reeves, who had come out as a boy-lover a year ago, said over 500 men had spoken with him since then, most of whom were struggling with their attraction to boys. "Sex is everywhere between men and boys," Reeves asserted. The men with whom he spoke "are not open at all . . . and who are they? Almost to a man, they are teachers and boy scout leaders and boys' club leaders!" he shouted, pounding the podium with both hands. "The men who work with boys—many of them, and this obviously can be used against everybody, but I think we have to say it—the motivation behind that work [has] a sexual and erotic element."[61]

According to Reeves, moreover, for a man to have homosexual relations with a child is "healthy and good," provided a man behaves "ethically and responsibly."[62] It would be extremely difficult to accept Reeves's estimate that one-third of the men who work with boys are either sexually attracted to these children or, in fact, act out these feelings.[63] However, the perception that there is substantial interest in boys by homosexuals is undeniable.

Another example of homosexual interest in young people is that of the "Country Experience for Young Womyn" [sic], a feminist camp for girls between seven and fourteen years of age. Planned and staffed entirely by female homosexuals, the camp featured activities in which "nothing was deleted because of age. At the workshop on self-help, every woman [sic] was given a speculum and the opportunity to examine the vaginas and cervixes of two adult women."[64] The person responsible for collecting funds for this operation was the head of the Recreation Department of the City of Willits, California. The ultimate effect of these practices on young girls is difficult to ascertain precisely. It is reasonable to expect, however, that, at a minimum, a reinforcement of tendencies toward homosexuality would take place.

Instances in which college-age women have started homosexual practices as the result of peer pressure and the systematic application of the feminist ideology have been reported. In a long and well-documented article which appeared in the *New York Times Magazine*, Anne Roiphe related the effect of peer pressure on hitherto heterosexual women. Commenting on conflicts created by administrative efforts to make Sarah Lawrence College coeducational, and the subsequent reaction by feminists, she reported:

The lesbian faction of this women's movement makes its appeal on two planes. The first is biological. Lonely and loveless students who cannot find heterosexual partners for the love dramas that form the closing phase of adolescence are forced, by the proud and open talk of the bisexual alternative, to question and justify their own sexual orientation. The second plane is political. The lesbian choice is presented as an expression of radical political and social thought, and often it is difficult for the young student to reject these claims without seeming to be a reactionary coward. . . .

The very existence of a cohesive, open homosexual group and its vocal political philosophy presents each student with the need to take some attitude toward it; in a sense, to make an active choice that never entered most people's heads in more covert days. At a time of life when sexual feelings run high, and in a community with little opportunity to meet with the opposite sex, there comes to be a kind of pull toward homosexual experimentation. . . .

Given the feminist mandate for the right of women to make their own choices, few would conclude—or, at least, state openly—that such experimentation is wrong. In a recent self-rating test, only 6 percent of the female freshmen thought homosexual relations at the college should be prohibited—compared with 46 percent of students nationwide.

I would suspect that many girls who feel threatened and upset by the open homosexual behavior accepted by the Sarah Lawrence community are, at the same time, ashamed of their reaction. A freshman from the Middle West told me: "It's really weird here. Girls check you out. I don't know where to look. It makes me feel so creepy. My roommate and I went to this party, and girls were making out together on the couch. There were only five boys there, and they were all taken. This girl asked me to dance. I didn't want to say no, but afterward I went back to my room and cried."[65]

It might be argued that this form of "recruitment" is the result of social forces rather than the decisions of particular individuals, and certainly not the result of the conscious motivation of homosexual leaders. Undoubtedly, this is true in many instances. However, there are documented cases in which this is not so. According to the *Davis* (California) *Enterprise*, the 1980 celebration of Eleanor Roosevelt's birthday by female homosexuals of Davis City included an appearance by Kathy McDevitt before the Davis City Council. Having noted with approval the fact that National Lesbian Day coincides with National Sex Education Week, Miss McDevitt is reported to have said, "we finally realize that recruitment is the only answer," adding that "lesbian goals must be to recruit more lesbians."[66]

Controversies over whether the appropriate word is "seduction," "recruitment," or "allurement" are not very fruitful. What is important is that there is evidence for the case that people—especially young people— are influenced by a variety of social institutions to become homosexuals. The testimony of Bill Springmann, the homosexual teacher mentioned previously, is particularly revealing:

I've since discovered I'm generally more affectionate than my female team members. Finally I've eased up and kiss and hug whenever it's appropriate in the class routine. The boys respond particularly well, because they are the ones who lack male affection the most, especially when there is an absent father. My coteachers have even encouraged my affection.

I tend to be more naturally and easily affectionate with boys and prefer them to the girls. There's nothing particularly wrong with taking advantage of my natural affection, since the boys stand to benefit from it. In fact, the best teachers are those who most effectively tap and express that something that is unique to them. I feel affection for men and boys. If I didn't take advantage of those feelings, I wouldn't be nearly as good a teacher as I could be. . . .

On the other hand, I have to invite the boys to be close to me, which makes me feel better about the affection I give them. I give it when I want and am offering them something special. I feel that I want to continue to *enjoy* giving affection to boys. . . .

One thing I dislike about being a Gay male teacher is that since I'm the only man in the classroom, the children occasionally call on me to be the example and embodiment of male behavior. I refuse to speak in favor of values I don't share, since those very values oppress me. I realize, however, that the boys need many different positive male role models. I insist that there are varieties of ways of behaving as men. In fact, I want to be a role model for them. However, there is a fine line I must tread. I can't be so different from all the other men they see that they conclude that I'm a "girl." However, I don't force myself to appear traditionally masculine when that's not comfortable, and I remain gentle when that's what's normal for me. When I talk to the children about my lover, whom I refer to as my friend, I don't switch pronouns. I occasionally kiss the little boy who claims that his father says boys and men don't kiss or hug—they shake hands. By now I know he likes to be kissed, he likes me, he likes to kiss me, and he can possibly like himself if he ever feels like kissing another boy or man.[67]

The utilization of schools to offer children "sexual alternatives" is neither an isolated phenomenon nor the opinion of a solitary eccentric homosexual teacher, but part and parcel of the homosexual ideology. Jean O'Leary and Bruce Voeller, then coexecutive directors of the National Gay Task Force, asserted in 1977 that "we believe it is immoral to pretend to children that they don't have a variety of loving options in their own lives, or to force them to believe that they are the only ones in the world to have loving or sexual feelings for their own sex."[68]

Thus it appears not only that people, including homosexuals, are in at least some sense responsible for who and what they are, but that other people share in the responsibility for who they come to be. There is an intrinsic tension which results when responsibility is abrogated, since it is a deeply ingrained principle that the value of a human action or condition is related to the freedom from which it originates. Even in the homosexual movement, this old principle asserts itself in the feminist principle that "every woman has the right to decide whether to be homosexual, heterosexual, or bisexual."[69]

Responding to a different need—their perceived oppression into play-ing roles attached to their biological condition as females—homosexual feminists sometimes opt for a principle which, while contradicting the notion that homosexuals are not responsible for being such, satisfies im-mediately a more pressing need. In either case, we have an expression of ideology rather than an attempt to be objective or scientific. For this reason, logical contradictions cease to have any importance.

2) *Homosexuality is Not Changeable.* The unchangeability of the homo-sexual condition is also a central ideological tenet of the movement. C. A. Tripp thus rejects any possibility of a homosexual becoming hetero-sexual:

> Q. *Why is the question of curing homosexuality so controversial? Surely you can either change homosexuals or you can't.*
>
> A. Not quite. The "cure" issue is seldom raised these days. Nobody could possibly cure homosexuality, because the phenomena it comprises are not illnesses in the first place. A number of moralists and psychiatrists still claim to be able to *change* homosexuality, but whether that is ever possible depends entirely on your criteria. If stopping the action is all that's meant, then joining a monastery or a nunnery might do it, or listening to Billy Graham and swearing off in the name of Jesus might work for a while. Or if "making a commitment to heterosexuality" is the criterion—Masters and Johnson demand this of their patients—then this sometimes "works," but only with people who have a degree of heterosexual response and who, by dint of will under the eyes of kindly authority figures, push their homosexual tastes aside. It all amounts to a brittle, desperate, tenuous hold on a forced heterosexuality.
>
> But if by change you mean getting a person to not want what he does want, and at the same time make him sexually want what he has never wanted, then forget it; there's never been a validated case on record, and I predict never will be. Just think how hard it would be to get the average heterosexual guy to be turned off by women *and* revved up by men—the same goes for the homosexual male in reverse. Hell, we can't even change a breast man into a leg man, let alone hurdle the heterosexual-homosexual divide. Sexual prefer-ences of all kinds tend to be as stable as they are sharp, especially in males.[70]

This is the "old" Tripp position already presented in *The Homosexual Matrix.* After rejecting the "few" instances of reported changes, he asserts that regardless of the techniques used, or the degree of cooperation a homosexual offers a "change-oriented" therapist, it is impossible for a homosexual to change his condition.[71]

Thus homosexuality is made an integral part of the homosexual as a person. In a sense, homosexuality is so identified with the person that it becomes his nature—in the traditional sense of this word. The conse-quences of homosexuality becoming part of the nature of the homosexual are apparent not only in the perception that it is unchangeable, but also in the notion that it is actually wrong for a homosexual to attempt such a change. In his controversy with Leitsch, Kameny asserted:

> To submit to the pressure of immoral societal prejudice is immoral. Self-respecting people do not submit. Self-respect is what *I* am trying to inculcate into my people, even if you are not. When you acquiesce to "therapy" and "change" in the manner which you do, you simply confirm (on a "gut" basis) all of the feelings of inferiority, wrongness, and self-contempt with which society has inculcated the homosexual. You harm the homosexual, and you harm the movement. [72]

The interests or desires of the individual, his perception of what his welfare means for him, clearly take a second place in the interest of the homosexual movement. Not only is he "locked" into being a homosexual, but even attempts to change are described as immoral. This should not be surprising, since a denial of the possibility of change implies the responsibility of the rest of society to accept homosexuality (including homosexual practices, which are part of the definition of being homosexual, as we have already seen). Moreover, legally it becomes impossible to demand that an individual attempt to change a condition in order to enjoy certain rights. Since change is impossible, and the individual is not responsible for his condition, no legal or moral guilt can be imputed.

This issue has practical consequences of great importance for the homosexual movement. In the case of James Gaylord, a homosexual teacher who admitted his condition to his principal, the Washington Supreme Court refused to force his readmission as a teacher on the basis—among others—that he " 'desired no change and has sought no psychiatric help' to change his sexual orientation, therefore, 'He has made a voluntary choice for which he must be held morally responsible.' "[73] It is thus vital for homosexuals to assert that they cannot change, lest they be forced to undergo such a conversion.

The perception that homosexuality is unchangeable is not universally shared outside the homosexual movement. Such traditional psychotherapists as Edmund Bergler[74] and Irving Bieber[75] are of the opinion that homosexuality is indeed changeable. According to the latter, out of seventy-two patients, 38 percent had become heterosexuals or bisexuals (19 percent each) and 27 percent had shifted from homosexuality and bisexuality to exclusive heterosexuality. The process is long and tedious, sometimes requiring over 350 hours of therapy.[76] Similarly, sex therapists William H. Masters and Virginia Johnson have indicated, on the basis of a 15-year study of more than 300 male and female homosexuals, that they were successful in helping two-thirds of the 54 men and 13 women who indicated a desire to become heterosexual.[77]

For homosexuals who are disinclined to invest the time and funds required to undergo psychotherapy, another avenue of change is offered by religion. Elsewhere it will become evident that among mainline churches, the homosexual ideology has made substantial inroads. Among fundamentalists and other evangelicals, however, traditional teaching is still accepted. Among the various human afflictions which evangelical healers claim to "cure," homosexuality is a prime example. Not only is it seen as a heavy psychological burden, incapacitating its victims for normal behavior, but in their view it involves the commission of serious sins. It is perceived as alienating man from the self and from God alike. The examples of religion-centered changes from homosexuality to heterosexuality abound. According to Marc Robertson—not his real name—a self-confessed ex-homosexual, "I knew I had to be born again, saved, and I knew once I made that decision, I had to give up a lot of things." Speaking of the difficulties involved in becoming heterosexual, Robertson says, "The force is so powerful. There is this drive, and you just can't stop on your own strength. It's like an undercurrent in the ocean that sweeps you out."[78]

Similar testimony has been offered by other individuals, sometimes resulting in demonstrations against churches harboring "offending alleged ex-homosexuals." The Neighborhood Church is a glaring example. Located in Greenwich Village, the church has aroused the anger of pro-homosexual New York City groups. According to a spokesman for the Committee Against Racism, Anti-Semitism, Sexism and Heterosexism (CRASH), "There is no reason we should tolerate their (i.e., the church's) presence here, and we are going to force them to leave."[79]

Writing in *Christianity Today*, an Evangelical magazine, Tom Minnery argues that homosexuality is reversible with God's help.[80] He cites the example of several men, homosexual for many years, who now minister to homosexuals after becoming heterosexual, and the witness of a woman who nine years after "accepting Christ" believes she has "conquered homosexuality." The condition for ceasing to be a homosexual within this religious model is that one must first accept that it is both possible and divinely mandated to stop the practice of homosexuality.

Minnery also cites the evidence offered by Mansell Pattison, Chairman of the Psychiatry and Health Behavior Department at Augusta's Medical College of Georgia, in an article published in the December 1980 issue of the *American Journal of Psychiatry:*

[Pattison] . . . documented 11 cases of men who claimed not only to have resisted successfully their homosexual drives, but changed their basic homosexual orientation to the point where they have developed satisfactory sexual attraction to females. Eight of them no longer have homosexual dreams, fantasies, or physical arousal.

In other words, these eight were cured—something gay activists often claim

Ideology of the Homosexual Movement

is impossible. The changes documented by Pattison came without psychotherapy, but by what he called "religiously mediated change." They sought help from a Christian ministry to gays.

Minnery concludes that "The fact is, many people are experiencing deliverance from homosexuality. The evidence is too great to deny it." The reaction of the homosexual movement was swift and uncompromising. Dr. Ralph Blair, himself a psychotherapist of ten years' experience, is also president of the prohomosexual Evangelicals Concerned. Blair devoted the Spring 1981 issue of *Review,* "a quarterly of Evangelicals Concerned," to criticism of Minnery's article.[81] According to Blair, this article "has succeeded in perpetuating hurtful falsehoods"; he accuses *Christianity Today* of using the article as an "instrument for the clobbering of homosexuals."

An attitude similar to Dr. Blair's is exhibited by the anonymous author of a monograph billed as "an examination of the Mormon attitude towards homosexuality."[82] Almost sixty pages of small print are nearly exclusively devoted to attacking attempts by the Church to change the condition of its homosexual members, especially when this involves the use of behavioral conditioning.

The question here is not whether, in fact, one or more persons have ceased to be homosexuals. Such a question is clearly beyond the scope of this work. It seems, however, unreasonable to discard the evidence provided by the therapists and pastors involved, or the testimony of those who claim to be ex-homosexuals. Their very existence constitutes a threat to the whole ideological structure of the homosexual movement. This explains the visceral and reflexive reaction elicited when the changeability of the homosexual condition is asserted.

Logically, such a reaction makes little sense. If one accepts as given that homosexuality is good and not a matter of choice (previous statements of homosexual ideology), what need is there to say that it is *also* unchangeable? Reason seems to dictate that it would be sufficient for the "liberated" homosexual to assert his refusal to change—whether possible or not—for the very simple reason that there is no motive for him to leave something good. It thus appears that the necessity to affirm the unchangeability of the homosexual condition is rooted in a basic fear within the homosexual movement that its members will be prodded to leave their lifestyle of choice, plus the reassuring value this has for people who *know* that they are different. This would support the notion that we are dealing with an ideological rather than a scientific or objective statement.

3) *Homosexuality is Not an Illness.* Traditionally, homosexuality has been considered a vice, a quality of the homosexual inducing him to engage in a certain negative kind of sexual behavior. Vice being the opposite of virtue, this view was based on the biblical teaching, accepted

103

for centuries, that homosexual behavior is sinful. Such behavior was viewed as having a voluntary component and, inasmuch as procreation was a responsibility of each generation to God and society, homosexual behavior was also defined as criminal. Although it was widely tolerated, there was always a strong condemnatory component in the traditional view of homosexuality.

The advent of Freud and other psychologists in the early part of this century provoked a veritable Copernican revolution in the understanding of human behavior. No longer was the free human will to be the center of behavior, but in its place an array of unconscious motivators were said to be "responsible" for behavior. At best, individual consciousness could be said to be aware of the behavior. In no way, however, could it comprehend—let alone be the cause of—the process by which decisions were made. Underneath the level of self-consciousness, it was said, there existed a murky world of which the individual was not and could not possibly be aware. It was in this world of unconscious—and at times brutal—forces that significant behavior originated. Faith and love, hate and despair, likes and dislikes, petty preferences, and the grandiose plans of genius; all originated in the bowels of the unconscious. This unconscious realm was, moreover, basically structured before consciousness acquired sufficient solidity to provide the continuity required for the existence of a durable self. In regard to sex, both homosexuality and heterosexuality were found to be rooted in these unconscious structures. The point is not that the person is unconscious of being homo- or heterosexual (final cause), or that he must be aware of the factors involved in his coming to be one or the other (efficient cause), but that he cannot be aware of the inner nature of his condition (formal and material causes).

Even then, however, homosexuality was considered to be something less than desirable. Although not a vice or a sin, outside the category of criminality—a realm determined by positive law rather than reason—it became a pathological condition, that is, an illness. Heterosexuality represented the norm, while homosexuality represented a deviation or arrest. With varying degrees of optimism in terms of outcome, homosexuality was considered to be a proper subject for therapy. Irving Bieber and Edmund Bergler represent this school of thought, and so does Charles Socarides:

> Study of a large number of psychoanalytic references demonstrates through numerous clinical examples and case histories that homosexuality is a form of arrested psychosexual development whose etiology is childhood fear (anxiety). This developmental failure results in disturbed gender identity, produces associated infantile fears, and becomes the basis for the later development of homosexuality. The sexual arousal pattern in homosexuality is fear-based, unconscious, and very often completely beyond the awareness of those so afflicted.

Ideology of the Homosexual Movement

The repetitive quest for homosexual contacts is thus not motivated solely by the desire for sexual pleasure; relief from and avoidance of anxiety is of paramount importance. In some homosexuals the anxiety is chronic, sometimes conscious and other times unconscious. It is this anxiety which the homosexual attempts to neutralize through homosexual activities. This clinically validated construct forms an important basis for the understanding of homosexuality. Any attempt at approaching a female sexually results in an increase in anxiety due to the fact that his basic conflict is inextricably tied to the fear of women. Consequently, even if a marriage has been attempted, these individuals will be unable to initiate or sustain a loving, tender attachment to the female partner without therapy. These two considerations—fear-based homosexual arousal patterns, and an inability to form an emotionally meaningful and gratifying attachment to the opposite sex—are but two of the criteria which clearly place homosexuality in the category of a pathological sexual adaptation.[83]

Socarides attributes homosexuality to "severe disturbances in the early child-parent relationship when critical maturational changes are taking place." He distinguishes between episodic and obligatory homosexuality. While the former is "due to conscious, deliberate choice" motivated by such goals as "personal gain, power, self-defeating behavior, search for variational experience (an extra sexual thrill), preferred status and position," the latter is described as "a mental disorder whose only effective treatment is psychotherapy." For Socarides there is a definite distinction in quality between homosexuality and heterosexuality. "Although psychosis and neurosis exist, of course, in heterosexuality, the heterosexual orientation is not of itself an indication of pathological condition, while obligatory homosexuality always is."[84] Such negative categories as sin, crime, or sickness, nevertheless, are not only objective descriptors of the human condition, but tools which enable society to protect itself and define acceptable forms of behavior. Modern sociologists have incorporated this understanding in the concept of "deviance," as much a descriptor of social attitudes as it is of behaviors themselves.

Ronald Bayer, an Associate for Policy Studies at the Hastings Center, Institute of Society, Ethics and the Life Sciences, has written a carefully researched study on the process by which homosexuality "lost" its character as an illness and "became" a way of life; we have drawn extensively from his study, *Homosexuality and American Psychiatry,* in this section. Bayer describes the role of Talcott Parsons in laying the sociological basis for incorporating social values into the concepts of illness, especially mental illness.[85]

The view that homosexuality is an illness not only constitutes an attack upon the very core of the homosexual ideology—i.e., that "gay is good"— but is also utilized by society to "brand" and "control" homosexual behavior. Leaders in the homosexual movement thus realized early that a frontal attack had to be launched against this view. In the one-hundredth lecture to the New York Mattachine Society (1964), Kameny asserted:

> There seems to be no valid evidence to show that homosexuality, per se, is a sickness. In view of the absence of such valid evidence, the simple fact that the suggestion of sickness has been made is no reason for entertaining it seriously, or for abandoning the view that homosexuality is not a sickness, but merely a liking or preference similar to and fully on a par with heterosexuality. Accordingly, I take the position unequivocally that, until and unless valid, positive evidence shows otherwise, homosexuality, per se, is neither a sickness, a defect, a disturbance, a neurosis, a psychosis, nor a malfunction of any sort.[86]

The homosexual movement found support within the psychiatric establishment. For example, the theories of a Syracuse University professor, Dr. Thomas Szasz, denied the very existence of mental illness outside the perceptions of those who did not label themselves as mentally ill. R. D. Laing in England propounded similar views which dissented from accepted psychiatric doctrines. As Bayer points out, the professional support for the ideological view that homosexuality is not an illness was offered by Evelyn Hook and Judd Marmor.[87] The problem with homosexuality came to be presented more as a question of society's way of dealing with homosexuals than with anything they did.

As the representative of the psychiatric establishment, the American Psychiatric Association was given the responsibility of proclaiming the new orthodoxy. Prodded by homosexual organizations, homosexuality was deleted from the official listing of pathologies in the *Diagnostic and Statistical Manual of Psychiatric Disorders* (DSM-II). The process by which this came about, described in detail by Bayer, is a classical example of the politicization of science and illustrates well the ideological nature of the homosexuals' contention that their condition is not an illness.

On December 15, 1973, the board of trustees of the American Psychiatric Association voted to declare homosexuality not an illness. This vote followed a year of political maneuvers engineered by the National Gay Task Force. This vote was not the result of scientific analysis after years of painstaking research. Neither was it a purely objective choice following the accumulation of incontrovertible data. The very fact that the vote was taken reveals the nature of the process involved, since the existence of an orthodoxy in itself contradicts the essence of science. Nevertheless, the board acted unanimously, theoretically in the name of some 25,000 American psychiatrists.

The response to this vote was even more astonishing. The psychiatric defenders of the view that homosexuality is an illness demanded and obtained a mail referendum on the question. The National Gay Task Force panicked at the prospect of the referendum. Under its leadership, a letter recommending approval of the board's decision was mailed to the members of the APA. This letter was signed by all three candidates for the presidency of the APA, including Judd Marmor. In Bayer's words:

> The National Gay Task Force orchestrated the process of obtaining signed copies of the letter, purchased the necessary address labels from the American Psychiatric Association, and underwrote the full cost of the mailing. In order to raise the required funds ($2,500), the NGTF sent an urgent request to its supporters:
> "It is essential that this referendum be defeated, and the best guess is that the vote will be close. We are convinced that this mailing could be the deciding factor in that vote. Now is the time for gay people to show that they care about their own lives. Now is the time for anyone who cares about civil rights and human dignity to show that they care."
> Though the NGTF played a central role in this effort, a decision was made not to indicate on the letter that it was written, at least in part, by the Gay Task Force, nor to reveal that its distribution was funded by contributions the Task Force had raised. Indeed, the letter gave every indication of having been conceived and mailed by those who signed it.[88]

Some 10,000 psychiatrists voted on the referendum, almost 6,000 favoring the board's action. If it is considered that there are almost 25,000 psychiatrists, the affirmative vote constituted less than 25% of the total number of psychiatrists. Nevertheless, the board's action stood approved.

The objective validity of the decision—as opposed to its symbolic or political value—can be called into question. It is obviously absurd that the pathological nature of a condition should be decided by majority vote, or that what was an illness yesterday ceases to be one today because "experts" decide that it is not. Most psychiatrists, of course, are fully aware of this. It has been widely reported that the majority of psychiatrists hold to the notion that homosexuality is an illness and that homosexuals are sick.[89]

Ideologically, however, the value of the notion that homosexuality is not an illness is immeasurable. It would be impossible to list the occasions on which prohomosexual apologists have invoked the authority of the American Psychiatric Association in support of their views. What most people do not know, however, is that such a decision has no scientific value, expressing merely the wishes of the homosexuals themselves.

Still, the homosexual movement lays claim to its principle. In the words of the North American Man/Boy Love Association, "Homosexuality is no sicker than heterosexuality. What is sick is society's efforts to supress [sic] and persecute it."[90]

II   RESPONSE TO HOMOSEXUALITY

The phenomenon of homosexuality demands a response, not only from homosexuals but also from heterosexual people. Human sexuality is such an ingrained component of personality, it exercises such a pervasive influence on all that a person is or does, that the very existence of persons who claim to be unresponsive to the demands of the natural sexual condition (men feeling attraction for women and vice versa) constitutes a challenge to that condition. This response to homosexuality exists not only in individuals qua individuals but also in society. The distinction between individual and societal response is not altogether clear and distinct, a necessary reflection of the interpenetration between persons and the groups to which they belong. The homosexual movement, however, has formulated ideological statements which pertain to both areas of response.

A. Individual Response

As an individual homosexual comes to perceive fully the implications of his condition, it becomes necessary to ascertain how he is going to relate to his condition and what is the (ethical) value of the sexual behavior to which he is inclined. Moreover, for the homosexual and heterosexual alike, the possibility of rejection of homosexuality remains open. This analysis yields three ideological principles which describe the homosexual movement's perception of the individual's response to homosexuality. The following constitutes an analysis of these positions.

1) *"Coming Out" is a Desirable Action.* In the homosexual movement, coming to terms with the homosexual condition requires undergoing a process not unlike a religious conversion. This is a process "leading toward self-understanding and acceptance: what we call 'coming out' "[91] It is important to understand that coming out is not just becoming aware that one is homosexual and accepting this as a fact. Anyone with a modicum of psychic stability, upon realizing that he is a homosexual, will come to accept that he is affected by this condition. As a matter of fact, the precondition for any attempt to change from homosexual to heterosexual is the acceptance that homosexuality is present. Coming out (a shortened version of "coming out of the closet") implies an appreciation and acceptance that the homosexuality that is part of one's self-definition is good. Coming out is the existential counterpart of "gay is good." The implication of such an understanding is a rejoicing in the homosexual condition, hence the word "gay" by which "liberated" or "out" homosexuals describe their sexual propensity. It also demands the communication of this feeling and self-knowledge to others. Hence Adam DeBaugh says that " 'coming out' is a bit of verbal shorthand for the concept of 'coming out of the closet.' It means, for most gay people, accepting, celebrating, and sharing the truth about who they are sexually."[92]

Coming out is not a singular event, although at times a homosexual "comes out *to*" one or another person. In some instances, telling significant others in his life (e.g., parents, teachers, a trusted friend or minister) is spoken of as a homosexual's coming out. However, coming out is best described as a *process* by which a homosexual becomes a fully actualized person. In the final analysis it could be said that a homosexual never stops "coming out," since new levels of self-awareness are always possible, and new forms of discrimination always remain to be conquered.

DeBaugh distinguishes four steps in the process of coming out. The first step is described as *acceptance* of the fact that one is homosexual. It includes a surrender to that notion once the fact of being homosexual is recognized. It requires the intellectual understanding that homosexuality is unchangeable—at least in this particular instance. The second step involves *celebration* of homosexuality in the self. This requires the internalization of the principle that "gay is good." It obviously implies a confrontation with the rest of the world—perhaps one's own family—which denies the value of the homosexual condition and a willingness to enjoy having sexual relations with persons of one's own sex. Celebration requires the elimination of guilt and "self-hatred." In the first issue of *Come Out!*, Lois Hart (a Gay Liberation Front leader) expressed the nature and value of celebration of gayness for her:

> There is no question that you will feel more whole and happier when you can be who you are all of the time. This is no easy thing, I know. It took me until age 32 to finally give in to myself, and though it felt at the time that I was losing everything (the good opinion and sanction of this society from my family right on up to any career dreams I have had), I have in truth gained the whole world. I feel at a loss to convey to you right now what that means. I can just say that I have never felt better in my life. I know now in retrospect that I only began to be really alive when I was able to take that step.[93]

A third step in coming out is *sharing* the fact that a person is homosexual with other people. DeBaugh further distinguishes in this step categories of people to whom a homosexual comes out. The most important person is the self. This is, of course, identical with the acceptance and celebration steps and it requires finding out how to act out the role of being a homosexual in a "liberated" sense. This means breaking the "traditional mold" to which homosexuals have been "confined by society." It seems that this step is crucial in establishing the homosexual identity in that it implies that homosexuality is unchangeable and that it is acceptable for the self to be homosexual.

Afterward, the homosexual comes out to other homosexuals. This is also a very important step, in that the homosexual acquires the support he needs to strengthen his homosexual identity from the relationships he establishes and for his increasing participation in the "gay culture." This might mean affiliating himself with homosexual organizations, attending bars or baths, purchasing homosexual publications, wearing homosexually oriented jewelry, etc. It also provides the opportunity for finding sexual partners without having to resort to paying prostitutes or having "impersonal" sex. Next, the homosexual may come out to his heterosexual friends or relatives, eventually to his parents or the people who are most significant in his life. As DeBaugh points out, this might never happen because the person might be incapable of handling the negative reaction that such revelation would entail. On the other hand, it might happen as an act of defiance, punishment, or hatred toward those who should have been closest to him.

Coming out is a progressive form of self-identification with the homosexual condition, a continuing and increasing commitment to homosexuality as a positive and creative thing. By coming out, the homosexual creates around himself a web of relationships and situations from which he finds it virtually impossible to break free. The initial perception that homosexuality is unchangeable is strengthened when the person brands himself as "different" on account of his sexual proclivities. The people to whom the homosexual comes out also begin to perceive the homosexual not only as someone who *now* likes people of his own sex, but as someone who cannot help but feel this way and who acts on his feelings in the practice of homosexuality. The homosexual, while coming out, might acquire one or more sexual partners who are introduced to others as "lovers." In cases where the homosexual becomes a member of a homosexually oriented church, or a homosexual group within one of the established churches, the partners might have undergone the rite of "holy gay union," similar to marriage.

For the movement, the importance of homosexuals coming out lies precisely in the effect this process has in raising the consciousness of the homosexual. In a sense, it is coming out that makes a homosexual part of the movement. The political consequences of coming out are clear; indeed, DeBaugh has identified *political* and *communal* action as the last step in this process: "The last step is coming out politically. When we begin to understand the depth of our oppression as gay people, and we begin to act on that understanding, we are coming out in political ways."[94] This means lobbying Congress and other legislative bodies on behalf of homosexuality, being willing to serve as plaintiff in court cases, pressuring the administrative and executive branches of the government, contacting businesses and private organizations on behalf of the movement, and similar activities. This is what, in fact, constitutes the homosexual movement. Without coming out, there would be no movement. Homosexuals who come out thus transcend their individuality; while remaining homosexual and actively following up their sexual inclinations, their political devotion to their community becomes paramount in their lives. As DeBaugh puts it: "The political coming out is also important because it helps us to focus our community. We need to remember that all gay people share in the oppression of our community. We are all threatened, and we all share in the responsibility of combating that threat."[95]

Ideology of the Homosexual Movement

One can legitimately question whether the politicization of the homosexual's self-identity is anything but a convenient cover for the "legitimate" procurement of sexual partners by sex-starved individuals. By becoming part of the movement, homosexuals have the opportunity to contact many other homosexuals in the context of being socially and politically useful to themselves and the "gay community." It cannot be denied, however, that in fact the movement benefits greatly when large numbers of homosexuals come out. This is probably one of the central functions of the marches and parades for which the homosexual movement has become noted; these activities give homosexuals the opportunity of coming out, thereby identifying themselves with their condition and with each other in the context of changing the objective sociopolitical conditions in their favor.

The political importance of coming out was perceived by the "Red Butterfly Cell," a homosexual Marxist study group. They reprinted an earlier (1970) "Gay Manifesto" written in San Francisco by an activist of the radical Students for a Democratic Society (Carl Wittman) which described coming out as "the polarity between personal head-freeing and the need for collective, social action to change institutions . . . two distinct and in some ways opposed actions."[96] The importance of coming out not only individually but politically is expressed in clear terms: "Emphasis on personal liberation, the experience of feeling free, which is the meaning often given to 'coming out,' can and often does lead to a kind of escapism or . . . detachment from the actual conditions confronting us."

Not only politically oriented groups or leaders are aware of the political nature of coming out. Brian McNaught, the Catholic homosexual leader, expressed his perception of the political nature of coming out in his interview with the influential left-leaning publication *U.S. Catholic:* "That's why the coming-out process is important politically as well as personally. Studies have shown that in those areas where people have had to vote on gay rights, those who knew a gay person were more likely to vote affirmatively than a person who didn't. It's difficult to vote against the rights of someone you know."[97]

The political importance of homosexuals who have come out seems to be, in McNaught's opinion, their ability to "make friends and influence people." This is a different view from that of Adam DeBaugh or the Red Butterfly, probably complementary rather than contradictory to the opinions of the other homosexual leaders.

One of the founders of the National Gay Task Force, and New York City's Health Services Administrator under Mayor John Lindsay, the late Dr. Howard J. Brown assessed the political value of coming out in terms of the influence that important homosexuals "still in the closet" would have after they openly declared the nature of their sexual inclinations. He praised the decisions of a number of noted homosexuals to "come out" and indicated the positive effect this had in favor of homosexuality: "In the fields of law and religion, probably no more than a dozen men have helped—by publicly announcing their homosexuality—to shatter stereotypes and provide role models for young homosexuals."[98] Coming out is, for the homosexual movement, not only desirable but vital to its existence. Should homosexuals stop coming out, and those who are open somehow be forced to "go back in the closet," the homosexual movement will disappear. Homosexuality itself would continue to exist, as it is part of the human condition. But the marches and parades, the public praise of the "gay lifestyle," the gay businesses and culture, the promotion of homosexuality by public and private funding, all that which makes the homosexual movement a powerful social and political force, would suddenly become a thing of the past. This is so much the case that it appears that a strategy of choice in combating the homosexual movement would be the creation of social conditions that would impede or even reverse the coming out process.

2) *Homosexuality in Itself Has No Moral Implications.* Morality is not only an expression of the ethical value of human behavior and social structures, but one of the strongest forces in shaping and controlling them. When homosexuality per se is seen as having ethical connotations, these can be used to curb the sexual behavior of homosexuals. Since much of the movement's support has its roots in its ability to satisfy (or justify the satisfaction of) the needs of its members—including the perceived need to have sexual relations with persons of the same sex—an ideological statement that denies the attachment of any ethical value to homosexuality itself must logically be part of the movement's belief system. This does not mean that homosexuals will affirm ethical nonvalue of any and every action in the practice of their preferred form of sexual activity, but that homosexuality in itself has no ethical connotations. Those homosexuals who profess to be religious, and who have integrated their "gay is good" ideology with their sexual practices and religious beliefs, will, in fact, affirm that homosexual actions are morally good. However, there is never the implication that homosexuality per se has moral significance. The ethics of the homosexual action are seen as coming from the intention of the homosexuals rather than from the actions themselves.

In responding to an article by William Bennett in *American Educator* (Fall 1978) that mentioned some of the potentially deleterious effects of having self-acknowledged homosexuals as teachers, Meryl Friedman and Marc Rubin of the Gay Teachers Association of New York indicated that homosexuality implies no particular set of moral values that a homosexual could communicate to his students:

> . . . Bennett offers us more specious argumentation about the "values particularly associated with homosexuality." He knows there are no such values.

Ideology of the Homosexual Movement

Where is there any evidence that proves that a set of values springs from any sexual orientation? Values do arise from economic status, religious training, peer pressure, and cultural demands. Even getting married and having children is not a value of being heterosexually inclined. It is a societal value imposed through societal conditioning.[99]

Dr. Judd Marmor, past president of the American Psychiatric Association, whom we have seen as an exponent of principles which harmonize with the homosexual ideology, indicated much the same in his testimony on behalf of prohomosexual federal legislation (H.R. 2074). According to Marmor, "Moral character is not determined by sexual preference, and individual homosexuals should be evaluated on their own merits and not on the basis of stereotyped behavior."[100] Sexual preference is thus divorced from morality.

Ideologically, this divorce is a very convenient device, since it precludes the possibility of evaluating homosexual behavior from an ethical point of view. From a financial point of view, homosexual behavior may be quite lucrative—for example, for male prostitutes, homosexual bar and bath owners, manufacturers of homosexual paraphernalia, and the pornography industry. From a hedonistic point of view, homosexual behavior is pleasurable. Psychologically, once values are removed from the scene, homosexual behavior can be advocated as helpful in providing homosexuals with self-identification. Politically, homosexuality is said to be an asset, since the "homosexual community" constitutes a powerful voting bloc. It is the question of morality that remains a barrier for homosexuals as individuals and for the movement as a social force. Thus the movement clears the way toward "total sexual freedom" by declaring that homosexuality and morality are, in reality, unrelated items.

This is a question that is of great interest to the "religious" leaders of the homosexual movement. For many years, the Archdiocese of New York has been the main obstacle to the passage of prohomosexual legislation in New York City. On July 18, 1977, Father Kenneth Jadoff, a spokesman for the Archdiocese, published a letter which, among other things, questioned the ethical value of homosexuality. In a strongly worded response, three prohomosexual priests (among them the president of Dignity/New York) and a layman pointed out their view of this question:

Father Jadoff is concerned about the morality of homosexuality from a religious point of view, but seems to miss the point of what the Bible says about human fulfillment. He questions whether "being gay is as fulfilling and rewarding as heterosexuality." In our view, Scripture implies that what is fulfilling is person-centeredness, service, and love, into which sexual orientation, as well as all other aspects of the human personality, are to be integrated.[101]

According to this view, biblical morality, the basis of Christian ethics,

113

is not incompatible with homosexuality, since it is presumably devoid of any objective foundation. Thus there is no way of deciding whether a specific form of sexual behavior is *not* morally correct through objective analysis, since the determining factors for moral rectitude have become "person-centeredness, service, and love," all of which are (unless further specifications are provided) purely subjective categories.

This idea underlies the kind of sexual relationship maintained by the Catholic homosexual leader, Brian McNaught, with his sexual partner of choice, a man identified only as "Ray." In an interview with the editors of *U.S. Catholic*, McNaught was asked, "Do you think the moral code you live with in your relationship should be the norm for the gay community?"[102] The subject was the apparently promiscuous lifestyles of some of McNaught's friends who maintained, in his words, "open relationships" (a euphemism derived from the feminist concept of "open marriage," meaning a pattern of sexual activity in which both parties are free to engage in various practices with an unlimited number of partners). McNaught contrasts this pattern with the apparently "monogamous" relationship between himself and "Ray," revealing in his answer a completely subjective understanding of ethics, at least in terms of homosexual affairs: "I'm nervous about stating a gay ethic or morality. My strongest voice says, 'Don't force us to mimic heterosexuals. We are not heterosexuals. We have different experiences, different obstacles, different insights.' Another voice states, 'If we seek to be accepted by the church and society, our code of conduct needs to encourage monogamy.' "

McNaught went on to describe the application of this subjective view to his own case: "Personally, I find it hard to condemn people's behavior. I can condemn my own behavior if it's inconsistent with my life's guidelines. If I believe that the purpose of my life is reaching a level of selflessness, in communication with Christ, then I have to put my relationship within that framework. If I have sex outside my relationship with Ray, I confront myself with whether that is consistent with my goal."[103]

The following question elicited a fuller exposition of his position: "What does the Gospel have to say? Do you find a standard there that is not only good for you, but for all—heterosexual or homosexual? Surely there's something the church could present as an ideal":

I have difficulty with that because I'm confused. For one thing, when people talk about sex, they're generally talking about totally different things. . . . I've heard hundreds of stories about relationships that were meaningful for individuals which didn't happen to fit my very neat packaging of what made a relationship meaningful. Many told me about their previous monogamous relationships where they spent most of their time worrying about where the other person was and whether he or she was having sex with another. Now they don't throw up and they enjoy the time they have together. I'm not defending their relationships; I'm just saying that is what they find meaningful.

Ideology of the Homosexual Movement

If my relationship has any meaning, I would like it to be something that other gay people can look to as a model of what is possible. If what I'm doing is right, then the example itself will be enough. [104]

The problem here lies with the definition of "meaningful." If *meaningful* is taken to mean that which is rooted in the nature of the act itself (i.e., whether the act agrees with the biological order as evidenced by the disposition and purpose of the genital organs and the distinction between the sexes), the ontological basis of morality is preserved, since intelligibility is rooted in reality. The evident meaning of the word as used by McNaught precludes this interpretation.

McNaught ends by rejecting both alternatives in order to avoid "judging" fellow homosexuals. If he had avoided judging these apparently promiscuous individuals on account of their "invincible ignorance" or "compulsiveness," moral objectivity would have been preserved. In fact, however, what we find in McNaught is a strong hedonistic component ("Now they don't throw up, and they enjoy the time they have together."). Morality seems to have been reduced to pleasure, the quintessential subjective category.

This idea appears in Tripp under a different guise. Asceticism, the self-denial of raw impulses for the sake of higher values, is of the essence of rational sexual behavior. While pleasure is not denounced as evil within an ascetical conception of life, it is certainly frowned upon when pursued as the ultimate or even as an autonomous positive value. The typical "free-style" homosexual relations, in which there are rarely objections to extremely promiscuous sex, thus constitute a threat to the traditional ethical values. The basis of opposition between our ethical views on heterosexuality and homosexuality are presented by Tripp in this way:

Finally, there is a more important set of reasons for homosexuality's arousing as much opposition as it does—reasons which have less to do with anything in this kind of sex than with the ogres it can raise near the philosophic base of heterosexuality. Not that heterosexuality needs the particular basis our society happens to rest it on, for it is and always will be the preference of most people. But in our society, it is hemmed in by a multitude of restraints that dampen the dignity of sex in all but a few forms. Even in the most conventional heterosexual settings, one violates basic codes by pursuing sex for fun, for variety, for conquest, and for still other "purely" erotic and personal desires. To do so is to hear charges of shallowness and adulteration—if not the adulteration of one's marriage then of love itself, frequently with lectures on what constitutes "mature" relationships. In short, the philosophic basis of our heterosexuality is still essentially ascetic, with the curse fully lifted off sex when, and only when, it is transcended by affection and social commitments. [105]

The acceptability of promiscuity in the practice and expression of homosexuality is evidenced in two courses taught at the homosexual "Lavender University of the Rockies," sponsored by the Gay and Lesbian Community Center of Colorado. Course #121, "Support Group for Married Gay Men or Gay Men Going with Gay Married Men," is described in explicit terms. "To discuss and share problems and concerns about being a married gay, or going with one—what you do at three in the morning when you have to leave your lover and go home to your wife, and how do both lovers cope with it? How do you cope with children involved in the marriage? Can gay married men have meaningful lover relationships, or should they, and so on?" Course #120 is titled the "Androgynous Alternative." The following course description reveals a conscious attempt to divorce sex roles at their root from ethical value and the creation of a way of living in which masculinity and feminity disappear, although not sexual practices in all possible combinations. "Having masculine and feminine values/ roles . . . expressing gender-free values (androgyny) openly . . . men friends and men as lovers . . . women as friends and women as lovers . . . men and women as friends and lovers (bi-intimacy) . . . living collectively with men and women, gay and straight . . . developing an androgynous lifestyle consciously in clothing, hairstyle, attitudes, politics, mannerisms, tastes . . . humanism, life without gender roles, and men's/ women's movements."[106] The implication is clear: "All sex is OK; it is up to you."

Such a purely subjective approach to sexual morality is logically dependent on two conditions, the first of which is a separation of physical sexuality and emotional considerations. It is thus that a homosexual can maintain a promiscuous lifestyle while professing to make deep personal commitments to a lover. Second, universal acceptance of heterosexual behavior as the only legitimate form of sexuality must be rejected. In this fashion, the objective basis of sexual morality is weakened. The former condition has been enunciated by Ken George in his article "Couples: Open Marriage?" as the foundation for the acceptability of multiple sexual partners among homosexuals:

> Is it within our nature to remain faithful to a single partner? Monogamy is a matter each couple has to decide upon, but few couples today regard an outside sexual relationship by itself as sufficient cause to separate. In fact, most people can better tolerate their partner's having a sexual encounter rather than having a significant emotional relationship without sex with someone else.[107]

The latter condition is fulfilled by the "findings" of anthropology.[108] When utilized in a purely descriptive sense, anthropology shares some of the characteristics of empirical science. Very often, however, normative conclusions are drawn from anthropological data. In certain instances, this is done because metaphysics is not available as a source of ethics and the behavioral sciences are left to explain human action by themselves. In other cases, social science data conclusions are used (ideologically) to justify preconceived notions. In both instances, empirical science ceases to provide epistemological models and is allowed to become the source of praxis.

In its divorce of homosexuality from ethics, the homosexual movement is, from an ideological standpoint, quite compatible with certain strands of contemporary thought which are rooted in Kantian subjectivism. One may question, however, whether homosexuality and/or homosexual actions are capable of satisfying the ultimate need of the homosexuals themselves. If in the objective order homosexuality is contrary to the natural order, the effects of its practice are bound to result in the moral destruction of homosexuals regardless of their beliefs. Moreover homosexual practices would also be deleterious to the social order due to the web of interpersonal relationships that defines society. Meanwhile, however, the homosexual movement and its adherents continue to reap the benefits of their ideology.

3) *Homophobia Is an Undesirable Condition.* One of the commonest terms in the homosexual literature is "homophobia." This newly coined word, always used in a negative context, constitutes the counterpart of "gay." All that has been said positively about "gay" is repeated, in a negative way, about "homophobia." If being "gay" is the condition of accepting and affirming joyfully the fact that one is a homosexual, "homophobia" means the rejection of such a condition. In its need to promote the value of homosexuality, the movement thus considers homophobia as a most undesirable condition. It is spoken of as an illness that has to be cured, a form of discrimination that has to be obliterated and, in the religious context, a sin that must be forgiven.

The simplest and most concise definition of homophobia is given by Ralph Blair, the psychotherapist director of the Homosexual Community Counseling Center and president of Evangelicals Concerned (a prohomosexual religious group). According to Blair, "homophobia is an expression of fear of homosexuality."[109]

A more elaborate, though similar, definition has been given by Adam DeBaugh, who attributed the term to Dr. Mark Friedman: "Homophobia is the irrational fear and hatred of homosexuality in oneself or in others."[110] DeBaugh has also indicated that homophobia is considered by "some therapists" to be a mental disease that affects both heterosexuals and homosexuals. The elimination of homophobia in a homosexual undoubtedly involves "coming out" and becoming "gay." These three concepts are thus linked in a dynamic and practical way designed to serve the needs of the liberated homosexual and the movement alike.

Paul Siegel, a communication professor at Northwestern University, limits homophobia to heterosexuals and relates it to fear of physical proximity to homosexuals, attributing the term to Dr. George Weinberg: "The term 'homophobia' was coined by Dr. George Weinberg and first appeared in his book *Society and the Healthy Homosexual.* By it he meant an irrational fear on the part of heterosexuals of being in close proximity to a homosexual."[111] He cites Jim Milham's work at the University of Houston on constructing a scientific scale to measure homophobia. This scale includes four dimensions by which homophobia is defined. The various dimensions are independent factors, with no implication that the appearance of homophobic manifestations in one factor demands the presence of similar manifestations in any of the other factors:

1) *Dangerous-repressive.* This is the belief that homosexuals are dangerous to society and that it is therefore society's right or obligation to repress them.
2) *Moral reprobation.* Here we find a strong feeling that homosexuals are sinful or immoral.
3) *Cross-sexed mannerisms.* This is the equating of homosexuality with "sex role inversion." That is, gay males are judged effeminate, while lesbians are seen as overly aggressive or masculine.
4) *Personal anxiety.* This is the subjective experience of discomfort in the presence of known homosexuals, or with the topic of homosexuality generally.[112]

Homophobia is thus said to cover not only societal values and preconceptions, but also individual feelings and deeply ingrained personality structures. Homophobia enables the homosexual movement to link arms with other "liberation movements." Joan Clark, fired in the late 1970s from the staff of the Women's Division, Board of Global Ministries of the United Methodist Church after she came out as a female homosexual, has clearly linked the "antihomophobia" struggle with other aspects of liberation theology (the reinterpretation of Christianity in Marxist categories). In an article that appeared in *Integrity Forum,* the official publication of Episcopalian homosexuals, she asserts: "I will focus on the struggle to eliminate homophobia as a commitment to justice with the depth, power, and intertwining of issues that characterize other liberation struggles, i.e. those to eliminate racism, sexism, classism, and imperialism."[113]

Homophobia is perceived as functioning to perpetuate the oppression of homosexuals. The following analysis of the definition and function of homophobia according to Clark stands in sharp contrast with the traditional view, which affirms the value of heterosexuality and the hierarchical distinction between the sexes for the purpose of constituting families through which the human species is perpetuated. This nature-centered and biologically oriented view contrasts with the society-centered approach offered by Clark:

Ideology of the Homosexual Movement

I will use *homophobia* to mean the fear of lesbians and gay men, or the fear of homosexuality that causes individuals and groups to act in irrational ways. Homophobia is characterized by the silencing and invisibility expressed in denial, misrepresentation, the perpetuation of ignorance, and the response of fear. Homophobia serves as a method of control for the purpose of exercising power over individuals and groups. It functions as a contemporary lavender herring, much like the red herring "communist menace" of the 1960s civil rights movement. Homophobia perpetuates a practice of victimization in which everyone is potentially vulnerable regardless of her or his orientation. Therefore, it is unnecessary to establish any gay-straight polarities for our purposes this morning.[114]

The concept of homophobia and the function of this notion will become clearer by examining the course on homosexuality offered by the Graduate School of Social Work of the University of Connecticut at West Hartford. This course is particularly significant because of the considerable participation by homosexual organizations in its preparation.[115] Far from a scientific examination of issues in an unbiased way, the course is presented as an exercise designed to alter the values and belief-systems of the students and develop in them prohomosexual attitudes. The complete description of the course, "New Perspectives on Lesbians and Gay Men," reads:

> This course will view the problems of America's homosexual minority. Homophobia (fear of homosexuals or homosexuality) will be presented as a prejudice held by all people, lesbian and gay men and straight, in a society which holds that heterosexuality is the "normal" and "acceptable" behavior and attitude. The intent of the course is to expand the students' awareness of how homophobic attitudes them [sic] and their relationships with other people in both professional and nonprofessional settings. This is an elective course offered for one semester for 2 credits. Registration will be limited to 15 students.[116]

The functions of the concept of homophobia in the furthering of homosexual movement objectives are evident in some of the goals of the course:

1. To develop an awareness and understanding of the pervasiveness of heterosexual biases.
2. To explore how homophobia:
    a. Obscures an objective awareness of special service needs of lesbians and gay men.
    b. Impairs the effective functioning of the social worker as an advocate and helper.
    c. Affects relationships among professional social workers.
    d. Creates feelings of discomfort for workers encountering lesbian and gay men clients and/or colleagues.[117]

After the students are sensitized by this course, be they heterosexuals or homosexuals, they are presumably able to conduct and apply analyses of society at large and their area of professional interest in terms of the homosexual ideology.

The activities of the Task Force on the Status of Lesbian and Gay Male Psychologists of the American Psychological Association (APA) are also helpful in illustrating the importance that the acceptance of the concept of homophobia has for the homosexual movement. In its effort to "reeducate" psychologists, the Task Force, with the full support of the Continuing Education Committee of the APA, has sponsored workshops which focus on homophobia ("Dealing with Homophobia": APA in San Francisco, 1977, and American Orthopsychiatric Association Convention, also in San Francisco, 1978).[118] Moreover, the first item on the research agenda of the Task Force is "Nature and Meaning of Homophobia." We can thus expect that a flow of "research" purporting to demonstrate the existence and negativity of homophobia will appear in the future.[119]

Within the movement, there is a multiplicity of views on the origin of homophobia. These views are not necessarily incompatible with one another, but rather complementary. They reveal not only the nature of homophobia as understood by the homosexual movement, but also the nature of the movement itself. F. Jay Deacon, a leader in the prohomosexual Universal Fellowship of Metropolitan Community Churches, alludes to homophobia as the natural extension of "sexism."[120] Any manifestation of complementarity—implying distinction—between the sexes is rejected in favor of "androgyny," the acceptance of masculinity and femininity in all people. Once a person is sexist, he must perforce be homophobic. Inasmuch as sexism is wrong, homophobia is also undesirable. From an ideological point of view, this opinion is extremely important, since it provides the linkage between the homosexual movement and contemporary feminism.

A different approach is followed by Ralph Blair. In his address to the Strategy Conference on Homophobia in the Churches, Dr. Blair presents five sources from which homophobia arises. For each of these sources, Dr. Blair prescribes a strategy to combat the problems and indicates pitfalls to be avoided. Table 9 summarizes Dr. Blair's exposition.[121]

Marxist homosexuals attribute homophobia to the rise of private property. It is interesting to note that in their interpretation, the rejection of homosexuality is also linked with its nonprocreative nature (In fact, the separation of sexuality's unitive and creative aspects is common to Christian, Marxist, and secularist homosexual ideologies.):

> Homosexual relations did not produce children. This fact by itself is enough to account for the fact that homosexuality came to be disparaged at the same time that private wealth began to be coveted.

TABLE 9

"Homophobia": Alleged Sources and Solutions Proposed

Source of Homophobia	Problem Statement	Prescribed Strategy	Pitfalls to be avoided
1) The Bible and Theology	*The Bible and biblical theology speak against homosexuality.* This is a proposition which some people use "to justify a priori sentiments, including homophobia." (p. 9)	"Patiently [to] present as clear an opportunity as possible to take the Bible seriously and to assist any who would wish to know better what the Bible does and does not say." (p. 10)	Calling "homophobes" those who sincerely believe that the Bible speaks against homosexuality. (p. 10)
2) Treatment and "Deliverance" Promises	*Homosexuality is sinful.* ". . . [I]f only homosexuals would 'get saved' they would be 'delivered' from homosexuality. This is not possible." (p. 11)	"To assist them—i.e., the homophobes—to realize that there is no cure for what is not a disease and there is no healing or deliverance from that which is not a spiritual affliction. (p. 12)	"Make fun of them and pretend that they constitute a small minority of backwater fundamentalists." (p. 11)
3) Prejudice	"Another way in which Christians might tend to be what we might call homophobic . . . is by way of preconceived notions of what homosexuality is." (p. 12)	Counter the thinking that all homosexuals are leftists, promiscuous, pro-abortion, etc. (p. 13)	None indicated.
4) Civil Religion and Americanism	"The following statement from Adolph Hitler is accepted throughout the Bible Belt and in other segments of American Christianity: 'We must seek firmly to protect Christianity as the basis of our entire morality, and the family as the nucleus of the life of our people.'" (p. 13)	Speak up when "politics or neurotic excesses" are presented as "homosexuality." (p. 15)	Knee-jerk reaction that results in the "gay community" speaking with one voice. (p. 15)
5) Defense Mechanism	"Some people use homosexuals and the gay rights issues, etc. to defend themselves against their own deep sense of guilt, inadequacy, and insecurity." (p. 16)	Assess whether one is dealing with a person who is "honestly misinformed" or is using "homophobia as a defense mechanism." Respond accordingly. If the homophobic person is insecure or feels inferior, provide the required reassurance. (p. 16)	Engage the homophobe in strenuous arguments in which the prohomosexual party presents very powerful reasons to support his position (pp. 16 and 18)

NOTE: All page numbers from Blair, *Homophobia in the Churches.*

Emotions and sexual feelings for the first time in history came under harsh social-class scrutiny and stringent sexual prohibitions were erected. Shame, guilt, and fear began to be connected with sex. What had been casual, spontaneous, and *natural* in the true sense of the word, became the source of conflict, and ultimately, persecution, when forced into the confines of patriarchal class society. With the rise of private property the natural became "unnatural."[122]

These various understandings of homophobia reveal that this is not a scientific but an ideological statement. What is important is not the source of homophobia, but the acceptance of this "condition" as a fact in describing society and the "oppression" of homosexuals. The religionist will discover religious reasons behind homophobia, and the Marxist will see dialectical materialism as the explanation for this phenomenon. From the point of view of the homosexual movement per se, these are irrelevant concerns. What is important is to acknowledge that homophobia exists and that it must be stamped out.

In the perception of homosexual leaders, this is a vital issue since homophobia does not merely pertain to the rejection of homosexuality in the abstract, but to the positive hatred and disgust that the homophobe feels for *individual* homosexuals. Bill Bogan, one of the producers of *Friends*—the Washington, D.C. homosexual radio program—points to the need to bring out these hitherto hidden aspects of the homophobic condition: "If we did such a show—i.e., one about antihomosexual activity—I'd like the callers or guests to talk about a homosexual they hate and name their first name. The one thing about people with homophobia is they always make their attitude into a class statement and avoid the specifics."[123]

The elimination of homophobia is an important goal of the homosexual movement, and the struggle against this condition is being waged on a continuing basis. As a matter of fact, one could conceive of the movement as a gigantic effort to end homophobia, thus allowing homosexuals to give free rein to their desires, however bizarre they would have been considered under homophobic conditions. We have already seen some of the strategies Dr. Ralph Blair has prescribed against homophobia. New Ways Ministry utilizes an "Index of Attitudes Toward Homosexual People" which enables those who use it to confront their own feelings toward homosexuality and thus have the opportunity to modify these feelings. The index is in the form of twenty-five questions scored on a five-point scale. The subject is confronted with twelve "prohomosexual" statements such as "I would feel comfortable if a member of my own sex made an advance toward me," and "if a member of my sex made an advance toward me I would feel flattered," and thirteen antihomosexual statements such as "I would feel uncomfortable if I learned that my spouse or partner was

Ideology of the Homosexual Movement

attracted to members of his/her own sex," and "I would feel disappointed if I learned that my child was homosexual." Such expressions of self-disclosure are bound to bring a confrontation with tradition-minded individuals who have otherwise accepted—intellectually only—the homosexual ideology, or who are struggling with this issue. As a result of this value conflict, and under the pressure of the "progressive" attitude that constitutes the framework in which the homosexual ideology is normally presented, the individual is forced to give up his homophobia and embrace the homosexual ideology.

An alternative approach to the "problem" of homophobia has been proposed by Allen Grooms. In an appeal for funds on behalf of the Washington Office of the Universal Fellowship of Metropolitan Community Churches, he pronounces education the cure for homophobia:

> Homophobia can be cured with education, if we are willing to accept the challenge of providing opportunities for Gays to learn more about their own potential and for our changing society to be allowed some valid opportunities to explore the roots of homophobia.
>
> The Washington office of the UFMCC has begun a major educational campaign to supply information to a wide audience covering a number of possibilities for "curing" homophobia. This effort includes educational items such as buttons, pamphlets, posters, audio-visual presentations, and also more in-depth materials such as support packets and books. [124]

Homophobia seems to have been demoted from mental illness to a case of "common ignorance" which public education and propaganda can eliminate.

In order to appreciate better the ideological usefulness of the concept of homophobia, it will be helpful to examine some of the benefits that the homosexual movement can expect to reap from its elimination. Religious homosexuals can expect, for example, that under nonhomophobic conditions, the Bible will be interpreted in a manner compatible with the satisfaction of their sexual proclivities. This is shown in the contention that it is not homophobia which is rooted in the Bible, but antihomosexual interpretations of the Bible that are caused by homophobic attitudes. This point is made by L. Robert Arthur, formerly of Bob Jones University, an ex-Baptist minister who is currently a minister and seminary professor of the prohomosexual Universal Fellowship of Metropolitan Community Churches. According to Arthur: [125]

> It was not until around 200–250 A.D. that marked homophobia, which is *fear of expressing love for persons of the same gender*, began creeping into theology. . . .
>
> Homophobic theologians jumped at this opportunity to prove that Paul was

anti-homosexual, even though in his own time his language would never have indicated this attitude. . . .

But, for homophobic reasons which are not justified by the language itself, they twist the meaning of the same word when it is used by Paul in 1 Corinthians 6:9.

Brian McNaught attributes to the homophobia that has been inculcated in homosexuals by the predominant heterosexual culture a number of personal and social problems including "alcoholism, drug abuse, frequent impersonal sexual encounters, an inability to establish long-lasting relationships."[126] To the extent that these problems are caused by homophobia, it can be safely assumed they will disappear when the homosexual movement is finally successful. Since it is difficult to be proalcoholism, drug abuse, or casual sex, this approach precludes the potential "homophobe" from asserting his feelings in the matter with complete liberty. From an ideological viewpoint, the issue has been framed for people who hold traditional values.

Another potential benefit from the elimination of homophobia, according to homosexual leaders, is an improvement in the treatment of children and adolescents who exhibit incipient symptoms of homosexuality. This subject was discussed during the Washington, D.C. hearing in preparation for the 1980 White House Conference on Families. Speaking on behalf of the National Gay Task Force, Carolyn Handy expressed the opinion that "a serious problem results from misinformed or antagonistic state government agencies that automatically refer gay youths to often homophobic psychiatrists."[127] In common English, this means that effeminate children and youth suspected of having homosexual tendencies should not be treated by therapists who do not accept the homosexual ideology. By implication, no effort should be made to arrest the condition, and/or they should be encouraged to actualize their homosexuality.

A clear example of the ideological political value of the concept of homophobia is evidenced by the denunciation against the Archdiocese of New York by Dignity—a prohomosexual Catholic organization—on the occasion of the 1979 anniversary of the Stonewall riot. Dignity protested "against the homophobia of the Archdiocese of New York."[128] The question here is neither ignorance nor a mental illness but a political opinion—albeit based on religious convictions—diametrically opposed to that of the homosexual movement. Dignity, as an integral part of the movement, responded with the typical political tactics of pressure, lobbying, demonstrations, and a well-orchestrated public relations effort.

The traditional vulnerability of churches to demands involving such categories as "human dignity," justice," "progress," and "civil rights," have made religious institutions powerless to resist the onslaught of the

Ideology of the Homosexual Movement

homosexual movement. The adoption of the concept of homophobia is a glaring example of this vulnerability. Homophobia is a concept most unlikely to be accepted by churches, since it involves no religious categories and is not found—even in a seminal way—in the doctrinal sources of the church or synagogue. Nevertheless, the following quotation from the (Roman Catholic) Justice and Peace Center newsletter (Milwaukee) illustrates our point well:

> The irrational and pervasive fear of homosexuality, rooted in centuries of ignorance and misunderstanding, is called homophobia. . . . This fear not only creates oppression for the homosexual, it illustrates the profound lack of understanding of human sexuality . . . justice demands every person be given the right to live authentic and full human lives. It also requires of us a corresponding responsibility: to create and energize opportunities whereby all people can enjoy that right. That includes the homosexual person.[129]

The importance of churches and their vulnerability to the concept of homophobia motivated the Quixote Center—a fringe Catholic radical organization located near Washington, D.C.—and two prohomosexual components of the Episcopal community, the Church and Society Network and *The Witness* magazine, to cosponsor a Strategy Conference on Homophobia in the Church.[130] Funding was provided by the National Organization for Women (Lesbian Rights Committee and Committee on Women and Religion) and New Ways Ministry. A representative of the District of Columbia's Metropolitan Community Church acted as Process Coordinator of the three-day affair on May 4–6, 1979. In addition to representatives of sixteen mainline churches, the conference was attended by representatives of the National Organization for Women, the Quixote Center, New Ways Ministry, the National Council of Churches (Commission on Women in Ministry), a pro-ERA organization of men, the Center for Women Religious of Berkeley, California, and the Women's Ordination Conference (also a Catholic group). The purpose of the conference was not merely to analyze the question of homophobia, but to develop an action plan. The existence of such a plan, currently being carried out by prohomosexual elements within the churches, is evidenced by the following conclusions of the conference:

> 4) that homophobia is part of the churches' politically expedient movement away from the whole Gospel along with racism, sexism, ageism, and classism, and is as contrary to the liberating Gospel of Jesus Christ as these other forms of oppression;
> 5) that as part of our strategy to combat homophobia we begin a process of inter-denominational network building for purposes of mutual support, ministry, and a sharing of resources and tactics;

6) and that we have developed a selection of strategies for exploration and implementation, where applicable, by May 6, 1982.[131]

Although appearing in this instance in a primarily religious setting, homophobia as a condition to be eradicated is basically a political concept, conceived to increase the power of "liberated" homosexuals. The churches in this case appear to have the role of convenient vehicles through which the movement is able to achieve its goals. In another setting, *Workers World* reported on the 1981 commemoration of the Stonewall riot, emphasizing the celebration of the first New England Lesbian and Gay Conference. One of the key issues discussed was, not surprisingly, homophobia.[132]

Through graduate school classes, professional meetings, church conferences, and grass roots gatherings, the homosexual movement is vigorously "marketing" the concept of homophobia and its undesirability. By thus framing the issue of attitudes toward homosexuality, it precludes the possibility of a reaction to its other efforts on behalf of its constituency. Here lies the ideological value of homophobia.

B. Collective Response

The concept of homophobia stands halfway between the individual and collective aspects of the response to homosexuality. Homosexual ideologues, in fact, refer to homophobia not only as a condition affecting individuals, but also as a general condition of society. The homosexual ideology is completed, however, by other statements which purport to reflect the manner in which liberated homosexuals constitute and act as a collectivity. These ideological statements do not exhaust the sense in which homosexuals constitute a collectivity. However, they do represent statements of the collective needs of the homosexual movement from the ideological point of view. By professing their belief in these principles, supporters of homosexuality as a legitimate lifestyle assert both the possibility and the methodology for achieving a substantial share of political power. This logically results in increasing the acceptability of homosexuality by individuals and society alike.

1) *Homosexuals Constitute a Legitimate Minority.* People can and do identify with each other and with their selves in terms of what they have in common: their human nature. It is on the fact that a man is a human being that traditional philosophy has predicated the dignity, duties, and rights that such a man possesses. Human nature is thus conceived as the universal source of solidarity among men. Existentially, however, the situation can be otherwise, especially in such complex societies as the United States. Without formally denying the fact that there is a common bond of humanity linking all persons, in many instances individuals derive their first source of self-identification from something other than the fact

Ideology of the Homosexual Movement

that they are persons. This can have serious repercussions by creating a tendency to then cease perceiving others as fully human.

There are many interpretations of the source of this phenomenon, undoubtedly a form of alienation. Religionists will see in it the mask of original sin; Marxists believe it is a manifestation of the unequal distribution of property and of the ownership of the means of production by capitalists; those who believe in certain forms of contemporary psychology understand it to be rooted in the existence of certain unconscious personality structures, or in peculiar quirks of the "superego"; believers in sociology's "conflict theory" will assert that it is nothing but a manifestation of the need of groups to establish "boundaries" by stressing differences; while devotees of behaviorism will insist that it is *in reality* a form of learned behavior perfectly modifiable by the right mix of reinforcements. These explanations are undoubtedly important for their proponents, and there is no intent to deny or affirm any of them. The explanations are, however, less important than the function which the phenomenon has in providing the ideological and emotional "fuel" which is the source of sociopolitical and economic changes.

The perception that such lack of appreciation for the common humanity of mankind was taking place is a root cause of the civil rights movement in the 1960s and 70s. This movement enshrined the concept of the "minority" in America's political and legal landscape. While individuals of various ethnic and cultural characteristics had always shared the nation— often under unequal conditions rooted in history and economics—the civil rights movement brought to the fore the concept of the minority as a group of individuals who, having suffered unjustly on account of a common trait, are entitled to special treatment involving a series of social, political, and economic privileges designed to alleviate their inferior status.

It is important to note that the concept of minority as used here requires more than the mere existence of a common trait among certain people, and that it does not require that its members constitute less than half the population. According to many statutes passed under the influence of the civil rights and feminist ideologies during the '60s and '70s, women are a recognized minority, although they constitute over 50 percent of the population. White males, while less than 50 percent of the population and sharing a common trait, are not a minority, nor are red-haired women, seafood lovers, or guitar players. What is essential to the definition is the allegation of injustice suffered by all members of the group on account of their common trait, absolute numbers or percentages notwithstanding.

The homosexual movement has struggled since the appearance of its "activist" component under Frank Kameny in the '60s to have its members recognized as a minority. Using as a model the example of ethnic minorities, Kameny asserted in the New York Mattachine Society's one-hundredth public lecture in July 1964:

> I do not see the NAACP and CORE worrying about which chromosome and gene produces [a] black skin or about the possibility of bleaching the Negro. I do not see any great interest on the part of the B'nai B'rith Anti-Defamation League in the possibility of solving problems of anti-Semitism by converting Jews to Christianity.
>
> In all of these minority groups, we are interested in obtaining rights for our respective minorities *as* Negroes, *as* Jews, and *as* homosexuals. Why we are Negroes, Jews, or homosexuals is totally irrelevant, and whether we can be changed to whites, Christians, or heterosexuals is equally irrelevant.[133]

Marotta points out Kameny's use of the "minority" theme throughout the lecture: "Kameny's references to blacks and Jews were deliberate and repeated. During the course of his speech, he cited the characteristics that made homosexuals a similar minority, likened the role he recommended for the homophile group to that of the civil rights organization, and argued that it was necessary to build a homophile movement analogous to the civil rights movement."[134]

Similar efforts aimed at identifying homosexuals with members of "legitimate" minorities have been undertaken throughout the movement. For example, Bill Katzenberg, a member of Students for a Democratic Society, expressed shortly after the Stonewall riot the belief that "minorities had to be mobilized around their own causes in order to create an 'alliance of the oppressed' powerful enough to overthrow the capitalist system. As a homosexual, he felt that he could contribute to the revolution by organizing the homosexuals. . . ."[135] Although the "revolutionary talk" has diminished considerably, the efforts to assert that homosexuals constitute a minority continue unabated. In his testimony on behalf of pro-homosexual bill H.R. 2074, Judd Marmor asserted:

> To discriminate against homosexuals as a class, therefore, is a manifest injustice and no different than it would be to discriminate against blacks, Hispanics, Orientals, Jews, or Catholics, simply on the basis of their group identity. An enlightened and civilized society must ultimately rid itself of its prejudice against homosexuals. The vast majority of homosexual men and women ask only to be accepted as human beings and allowed to live their own lives free of persecution or discrimination.[136]

Attraction to persons of one's own sex is identified with membership in an ethnic group or the sharing of a religious faith. This might be particularly repugnant to those groups or their members who consider homosexual practices to be repulsive or sinful, but from an ideological point of view it is quite useful. On the one hand, labeling homosexuals

Ideology of the Homosexual Movement

as a minority enables the movement to frame the issue in its own favor. Americans in general feel guilty about the conditions under which some of its minorities have lived. Words such as "minority" and "discrimination" conjure up images of a plantation with a slave driver whipping helpless women and children, or rat-infested ghettos where young people become narcotic addicts. The idea of protecting children from possible seduction by a homosexual teacher, or of a family being forced to rent their upstairs apartment to a "gay couple" who maintain an "open relationship" and thus feel free to bring in other homosexuals and to sponsor orgies, is not part of the imagery created by the call to consider homosexuals a legitimate minority. This, however, is a logical outcome of considering homosexuals in this light. Once it is accepted that homosexuals are a minority, the die is cast, and the legal existence of the same rights guaranteed to other minorities is inevitable.

The idea that homosexuals are a minority implicitly includes the granting of certain privileges afforded other groups. Although homosexuals have strenuously rejected the idea that they are seeking affirmative action—i.e., forcing employers, landlords, service providers, etc. to establish homosexual quotas—demands for such quotas have, in fact, been made. A glaring example is the Task Force on the Status of Lesbian and Gay Male Psychologists of the American Psychological Association. One of the demands made of the APA in 1973 by the Association of Gay Psychologists was that "all panels on homosexuality (at national and regional meetings) shall include at least one member of the Association of Gay Psychologists as a panel member, and all paper sessions (at national and regional meetings) shall include at least one member of the Association of Gay Psychologists to serve as a discussant."[137]

In much the same way, Dignity demanded of Baltimore's Archbishop William Borders of Baltimore that the "gay and lesbian" community be made part of a study committee to advise the Archbishop concerning homosexuality.[138] In neither case would it have been sufficient to include one or more homosexuals; the demands were that homosexuals sharing the "gay ideology" had to be the "representatives" of the homosexual minority.

An added advantage of considering homosexuals as a minority is the legitimacy it gives to the ideology of homosexuality. This legitimacy in turn makes it an allowable subject for the indoctrination of young people. We have seen the case of a prohomosexual course taught at the University of Connecticut. As a matter of fact, should homosexuals be accepted as a legitimate minority, prohomosexual sex education would follow as a logical consequence. The case of schools teaching black and Spanish culture courses and churches offering religious education courses comes to mind as a logical analogue. In their response to William Bennett, Meryl Friedman and Marc Rubin of the Gay Teachers Association of New York clearly indicate that prohomosexual activities in the school will take place under the guise of discussing the "legitimate interests" of the homosexual minority:

> Why should not gay people who know from experience what homosexuality is truly about educate in the same way as do members of other minority groups? Would Bennett oppose black teachers teaching black history or Jewish teachers teaching Jewish history? . . .

> Finally, Bennett's stand against what he calls proselytizing is implying that blacks should not discuss the black experience, and Italians should not speak of Italian culture and that Jews should hide in a Christian closet. Bennett must agree that these implications are nonsensical and violate free speech and academic freedom.[138]

From the point of view of the movement as a social force, its interests are served by acceptance of the principle that homosexuals do constitute a minority; they are thereby assured of members with a defined self-identity that stands in clear contrast with the larger society in which the homosexual movement exists. Marotta points out how this took place during the early years of the movement:

> Paradoxically, the preoccupation with assuring people that in important respects homosexuals resembled heterosexuals, because it encouraged homosexuals to think their sexuality insignificant and made them all the more reluctant to risk ostracism, was precisely what kept homophile leaders from rousing large numbers of people with homosexual feelings to identify themselves as gay and to support homophile efforts to secure rights and status for homosexuals. This situation persisted until homosexuals began to abandon conventional views and values and to reject liberal assumptions as the basis for their gay political thinking. These homosexuals were countercultural. The assumptions that shaped their political perspectives were those of the New Left. And their gay political outlooks were not homophile, but liberationist.[140]

This situation exists today. Its alternative represents the logical objective and operational goal for tradition-minded Americans, since the moment that liberated homosexuals go "back into the closet," cease to behave differently from other people, and thus abandon their self-defined minority status, the movement will come to an end. From the standpoint of traditional morality, this is a most desirable objective. In fact, while a dehomosexualized America will certainly not be the end of homosexuality as part of the human condition, no "gay" person could possibly exist in such an America.

It would be impossible to cite the multiple ways and sources in which *it is taken for granted* that homosexuals constitute a legitimate minority (bearing in mind that "minority" is not used here in a statistical sense).

Ideology of the Homosexual Movement

As an example of a nonhomosexual religious organization accepting such a principle, in 1978 the House of Delegates of the National Federation of Priests' Councils (a Roman Catholic organization) prefaced a formal resolution with the words "whereas together with the Church and the Nation, NFPC has addressed the issue of human rights as a legitimate issue in the struggle of many minorities, such as Blacks, Chicanos, women, homosexuals, and migrant workers; . . .".[141] Not only are homosexuals presented as a minority, but their condition is equated with the ethnic and social characteristics of legitimate minorities.

Where social conditions have made the homosexual ideology part of the creed of public officials, it is taken for granted that homosexuals are a legitimate minority. In his testimony in favor of H.R. 2074, Grant Mickins, Executive Director of the Human Rights Agency of San Francisco, made this point clear:

> Recently, members of the Governor's staff came to our office and asked about the procedure for investigating sexual orientation complaints, as it differed from the usual kind of complaint. I was a little surprised because it is felt by persons in the field that there is another approach you use for investigating this kind of complaint. . . . I would say you treat this type of complaint the same way you would a disability, racial complaint, or any other. The same kind of factors are involved. You need to do your investigative work thoroughly. Once your class is identified, the same investigative techniques come into play. So there is not really that much of a difference in that whole process.[142]

There is no doubt that acceptance of homosexuals as a "legitimate minority" is very advantageous to the movement, which is why it insists on the objective validity of this ideological principle. It also seems clear that homosexuals do qualify as a minority in terms of possessing a common trait. The issue of whether they have suffered unjustly on account of this trait can be called into question. Were it to be accepted that the practice of homosexuality is legitimate, or that the feelings underlying such a practice are consonant with the order of nature, the injustice of any suffering willfully inflicted on an individual due to his homosexuality would follow logically. If it were then shown that such injustice was the rule in society, homosexuals would qualify, within the accepted scheme of American social and legal practices, as a legitimate minority. However, these notions are specifically questioned by opponents of the homosexual movement, who tend to deny that such practices are a legitimate expression of human sexuality and that homosexual feelings are part of the natural order. To leave this question to the decision of each autonomous individual is tantamount to social chaos by the implied abrogation of objective morality. If we accept the objective validity of traditional social ethics, the limitations imposed on homosexuals with regard to the expression and acting out of their sexual propensities, or their participation in social institutions, do not constitute an injustice.

In practice, the problem is faced only by those who insist on flaunting their sexual predilections by word and deed. Any homosexual who is otherwise a productive member of society and whose inclinations are not known has nothing logically to fear; in no way could he be discriminated against or suffer as a result of his condition. The problem arises when individuals who are affected by what, in the estimation of the social majority, is a repugnant and potentially disruptive condition, contend openly and aggressively that this is not so. The problem centers in the insistence of certain homosexuals on disrupting the established social order, which most people consider to be founded in the very nature of things. Ironically, it is in the interest of the homosexual movement that homosexuality be flaunted by word and deed against the sensitivities of the rest of society. It is precisely in the ensuing clash (with its perceived injustice) that open homosexuals acquire the "gay identity," "come out," and constitute themselves a minority.

2) *Homosexuals Exist in Large Numbers.* Once it is accepted that homosexuals do, in fact, constitute a minority, the next logical question involves the size of this minority. Although the intrinsic value of each individual makes it unacceptable that an injustice be committed against even one person, we tend to react with greater concern—all other things being equal—when we are confronted with widespread injustice than when there are only isolated wrongs committed against a few individuals.

The homosexual movement has answered this question by the acceptance a prima facie of the 1948 and 1953 figures provided by the Kinsey Institute. In 1948 Alfred Kinsey published the result of a large-scale survey of American males.[143] His figures indicated that 37 percent of males had had at least one orgasmic experience with at least one other male. Moreover, ten percent of males between eleven and fifty-five were reported to have been "more or less" exclusively homosexual for at least three years. Four percent of males were found to be exclusively homosexual. The incidence of "exclusive homosexuality" among females was reported to be between one and three percent. On this basis, the homosexual movement repeats incessantly that ten percent of the population is homosexual. This assertion is basically an ideological statement designed to advance the goals of the movement. In this sense, it does not have any more scientific validity than the principle that "gay is good." In point of fact, the value of Kinsey's results can be legitimately questioned. For example, assuming that the sample utilized is representative of the population, how do we know that people do not lie when asked such intimate questions as those pertaining to their own sexuality? The idea that Kinsey merely measured the responses his sample produced rather than the actual sexual practices of his universe must always be considered. The

Ideology of the Homosexual Movement

fact that the homosexual movement has assented with little or no criticism, however, makes its embrace of Kinsey's conclusions suspicious. The reiteration of Kinsey's finding that ten percent of the population is homosexual is patently invalid. Even if homosexuality is accepted as an unchangeable condition, the fact that ten percent of a population whose life-span is four or five decades was "more or less" exclusively homosexual for three years in no way implies that they have *always* been homosexual or that they are *presently* homosexual.

The question here being discussed, however, is not whether ten percent of the American population is actually homosexual, but the insistence of the homosexual movement that this is true. Throughout America's prohomosexual literature, the ten percent figure is taken for granted. The reason is not difficult to understand. Besides appealing to the abovementioned sense that injustices against large groups tend to arouse greater sympathy, the sheer size of the claim implies, and is used as an assertion of, the power of the homosexual movement; hence its ideological character. In a denunciation of the American Federation of Teachers for publishing an article questioning the propriety of employing homosexual teachers in our schools, representatives of the Gay Teachers Association of New York protested: "That this article appeared when California's voters were to go to the polls and decide whether gay teachers and their supporters should be allowed to teach was a betrayal of the gay members of the AFT who constitute at least ten percent of its membership."[144] In an official publication, the Pennsylvania Department of Education proposed a series of openly prohomosexual principles, concluding: "None of this, of course, finally settles the question of how people become gay. But it may at least suggest that openly discussing the lifestyle of ten percent of our population will not cause anyone to become homosexual—and it may help us all to better understand our first question: What is a sexual minority, anyway?"[145] Here again, the ten percent figure is accepted without question.

The ideological nature of the statement becomes apparent in a monograph published by the Gay Rights National Lobby and the National Gay Task Force with the aim of convincing politicians that it makes political sense to favor homosexuality. The appeal for support based on the idea that there are large numbers of homosexuals is made at the outset: "This report is written for the practical politician. The moral claims that can be made about granting civil rights protection to some 20 million Americans may fall on deaf ears if our leaders believe that the idea's time has not yet come and that to embrace it now would constitute political suicide. This report should help lay those concerns to rest."[146]

The first section quotes approvingly from sources ostensibly not prohomosexual but which have believed this element of the homosexual ideology:

THE HOMOSEXUAL NETWORK

GROWTH OF GAY POLITICAL POWER

A December 13, 1979, issue of *Campaigning Reports* —a Washington-based practical politics newsletter—declared:

> The gay vote is now so important in national politics, and in some local races, that no serious politician can afford to ignore or ridicule it.

Using the estimated figure of 15 million gay Americans of voting age, the newsletter stated "the assumption can be made that as many as 10–12 million can be activated on specific issues or to support specific candidates," and concluded:

> This vote bloc has a series of documented victories behind it, and it can be expected to push harder for access to the political system. Gays have demonstrated ability to generate votes and raise money. This represents a resource modern candidates are tapping at every turn.

These conclusions were echoed in a column by *Washington Star* political editors Jack Germond and Jules Witcover, who reported:

> The gay community—which numbers by various estimates 10 to 20 million Americans—has proved to be a lode of political contributions now that it has become so much more socially acceptable for gays to surface and identify themselves individually and as a bona fide pressure group.

The legitimacy accorded gay political power by an establishment political newsletter and two respected political journalists needs no further elaboration.[147]

A similar argument was made by Tom Chorlton, president of Washington, D.C.'s Gertrude Stein Democratic Club, as reported in an article on homosexual participation in the District of Columbia's political life: "Gay leaders are concentrating more on watching 'the whole field,' says Chorlton, who estimates that gays represent 10 percent to 20 percent of the District population."[148] Homosexual leaders not only accept Kinsey's 10 percent figure at face value, but extend this proportion to any population. We have already seen the allegation that ten percent of Washingtonians and of members of the American Federation of Teachers are homosexual. The late Howard J. Brown—former New York City Health Services Administrator—affirmed that 10 percent of physicians are homosexual: "There are some 334,000 doctors in this country. According to Kinsey's percentages, this would mean that 13,000 American doctors are exclusively homosexual, and another 20,000 or so are predominantly, though not exclusively, homosexual."[149] A similar claim has been made by the Gay Task Caucus of the American Psychiatric Association. Inasmuch as there are some 25,000 psychiatrists, the Caucus has assumed that there are between 1,250 and 2,500 homosexual psychiatrists.[150] This ongoing assumption that in every group of Americans there is a substantial number ("at least ten percent") of "more or less" homosexual individuals has led to the well-publicized slogans by which the movement intends to enshrine its claim: "We are everywhere" and "There is someone gay in your life."

Although the ideological value of the claim is evident, and even assuming that Kinsey's conclusions are correct, the application of the ten percent proportion to all populations is obviously mistaken. There is no reason to think that ten percent of all blacks or Hispanics, Jews or Catholics, doctors or bird watchers, are homosexual *even if ten percent of Americans are.* The reason is that there is no proof that homosexuals are evenly distributed among *all* the strata of the population. The fact that the homosexual movement insists upon counting one homosexual among every ten human beings, no matter how the ten have been selected, is further evidence of the ideological character of the assertion. By holding on to this assumption, homosexual leaders in all groups (i.e., ethnic, religious, professional, geographic, etc.) can claim that ten percent of their memberships are homosexuals who are entitled to a share in the power of, and influence over, the group's affairs. In this way, potential antagonists of the movement are neutralized.

A variation of the theme that there are numerous homosexuals is the assertion that there have been and are many famous or exceptionally competent persons affected by homosexuality. The Mormon homosexual author of *Prologue: An Examination of the Mormon Attitude Towards Homosexuality* is a case in point. Although no names are mentioned, specific categories distinguished by features attractive to the reader in terms of physique, prowess, status, achievement, and so forth are emphasized in this work:

Many of the strikingly handsome and masculine men on this campus are homosexual. It would astound you to know how many student body officers, football players, branch officers, wrestlers, and outstanding students at BYU over the years have been homosexual. Some of these homosexual students are the sons of the very top administrators and faculty, administration, and staff, as well as many strong supporters of BYU among the alumni, who are homosexual. This will continue to be the case in spite of all your prohibitions, preachments, and inquistions [sic] against homosexuality. Over the past ten to fifteen years, this university has made a determined effort to exterminate and purge the homosexuals from this campus. As a first-hand observer both then and now, I simply conclude that, if anything, there are proportionally more homosexuals here now than before, and it appears that the number is steadily increasing. This observation is shared by the Church Authorities, who are alarmed at the wave of homosexuality rampant among the youth of the Church. It could be, however, that much of their alarm is more accurately due to their belated realization of how prevalent homosexuality has always been here at BYU. Likewise, we will expect to hear from your department of an increasing number of cured homosexuals, since there will be a proportional increase in the number coming to the counseling service for help. The security force will likely catch a few more indiscreet men, some of whom want to be caught. Perhaps they will step up their already extreme and questionable efforts to catch and expel the homosexuals. Together, you will think you are doing something about the problem. Your gestures could not be more futile.

Next fall, virtually hundreds of homosexuals will enter BYU for the first time. The vast majority of these young men will spend their years at BYU without ever coming to the attention of the university or the Church in any way. Is this not borne out in the experience of Dr. McBride, who found it difficult to find even a handful of men who wanted to undergo therapy?[151]

Famous men of antiquity and contemporary notables are presented as homosexuals. Frequently there are whole lists of such names: "What would Bennett do with non-gay teachers who teach that Socrates, Alexander the Great, Michelangelo, Willa Cather, Emily Dickinson, Rosa Bonheur, Tennessee Williams, as well as many politicians, scientists, and athletes, were and are gay?"[152] How it can be known that Socrates or Alexander the Great were homosexuals is difficult to ascertain. Neither their graves nor anything they wrote or possessed have been identified, and they lived thousands of years ago. There is very little evidence about Michelangelo's sexuality beyond the allegations of Aretino—a notorious blackmailer—and the fact that he was unmarried. Irving Stone, one of the foremost authorities on Michelangelo and author of *The Agony and the Ecstasy*, has said in this regard that "in no place did we find a scintilla of evidence to support the accusation that Michelangelo was a homosexual. . . . There are still a few people who continue to perpetuate this charge against Michelangelo, but they offer absolutely no proof except the Aretino slander."[153]

There is no logical reason to accept the assertions that there are massive numbers of homosexuals, or that famous and esteemed persons in history have been widely affected by homosexuality, though opponents of the homosexual ideology have never based their objections on a claim that homosexuality diminished intellectual or artistic ability, or that very few people were homosexual. As a matter of fact, it can more properly be said that certain writers, scientists, philosophers, and artists have been achievers in spite of, or independently of, their sexual propensities. The very struggle with an all-consuming and destructive sexual passion might have made some of these individuals more sensitive to the human condition by a process not dissimilar to that of a physically handicapped person who rises to high levels of heroism by overcoming his deficiencies. To date, however, no one has published any proof that sexual attraction to members of one's own sex increases intelligence or intuition. Objections to homosexuality are usually based on ethical or religious grounds, and even the most ardent moralists concede that a person can be humanly

Ideology of the Homosexual Movement

competent in the fields of art, science, or technology while being completely corrupt in his personal life.

In its insistence that there are numerous homosexuals, and that many of them are notable people, it seems that the movement not only strives for political and social power, but also satisfies a need of its members. Perhaps the security engendered by feeling part of a vast community, and one of the company of the famous, satisfies a deep-seated sense of inadequacy and inferiority. After all, a sound principle of counseling indicates that the best way to discover what a person is lacking consists in finding out what it is that he boasts about. Therefore, a person who insists on affirming that he is happy can be suspected of being unhappy, and he who insists on his own superiority is really exhibiting feelings of inferiority. In the case of homosexuals who claim continuity and identification with historical heroes, feelings of inferiority and inadequacy are to be expected. Tradition-minded thinkers would suggest that such feelings are the result of having violated the order of nature, and that the craving for notoriety is simply a manifestation of lack of self-worth.

3) *The Homosexual Ideology Is Revolutionary in Nature.* While homosexual organizations will seldom, if ever, describe themselves as revolutionary, a clear understanding of the movement's nature and of some statements made by homosexual leaders reveals that this is indeed the case. American society has traditionally been conservative, and throughout the 1970s public sentiment grew consistently more so. Therefore, it would be disruptive for the homosexual movement to proclaim its revolutionary nature openly; its leaders rarely mention this characteristic.

The word "revolutionary" is used here in two senses, and the homosexual ideology qualifies under both of them. On the one hand, revolutionary can mean the inversion of a way of living or thinking. Should the homosexual become the dominant force in American society, a change of such magnitude would become inevitable. Revolutionary can also be taken as identification with and profession of one or more principles held by other radical organizations which advocate total changes in our social, economic, or political structures outside our traditional constitutional framework. This identification exists across the board among homosexual leaders and organizations. In both instances, the revolutionary nature of the homosexual movement makes it a political phenomenon. That this character of the movement is ideological is indubitable. In being revolutionary, the movement satisfies not only its own needs but the needs of its members, who must perceive that the goals and activities of the movement will predictably create the social and political conditions in which they will be free to engage in their favorite sexual practices.

During the 1960s, the homosexual movement took on a revolutionary character. As Marotta has pointed out, the founders of the Gay Liberation Front in 1969 understood that the opposition between gay and homosexual reflected the radical nature of their choice.[154] While words like homosexual and homophile have the connotation of cautiousness, moderation, and reform, gay was always understood to be radical and revolutionary in nature. As a matter of fact, "the name Gay Liberation Front was also favored because it had the same ring as National Liberation Front, the alliance formed by the Viet Cong. Radicals and revolutionaries thought that this would help attract others with leftist perspectives and establish GLF's place in the Movement."[155]

From the earliest days of the movement, the notion that part of the homosexual ideology is the expression of homosexuality in terms of revolution has been very influential. Arnie Kantrowitz points out that one of the first slogans of the budding movement was "Two-four-six-eight; we don't want a fascist state,"[156] and how the homosexual marchers along New York City's Eighth Street in a demonstration of the sixties "became revolutionary streamers in the darkness . . . it feels as if we are before the Bastille in another time and place."[157] In effect, "we were a revolution."[158]

This extreme leftist rhetoric has to some extent been abandoned by certain segments of the movement. However, as we saw before, the homosexual organization of the Episcopal Church listed typically radical issues as some of the issues of the movement. This is not an exception, but the rule. A minister of the prohomosexual Metropolitan Community Church identified with sexism—against which the homosexual movement stands—typically leftist issues: "People must deal with the chains that destroy us. Wrapped up in this sexist issue is the key to freedom. Contained within the bondage of sexism is racism and classism, homophobia, and the rape and plunder of our earth."[159]

The final goal of the homosexual movement, named for lack of a better word "liberation," is basically a political concept; it is accomplished by bringing profound revolutionary changes to the self and society. To be a homosexual in a heterosexually oriented society is to be alienated and in need of a violent conscientization that turns all perceptions of the self and the social structures that "oppress" homosexuals. Such transformation—behaviorally expressed by "coming out" in its fullest sense—can only be understood in a political sense. It must inevitably result in political activity. In a sense, as DeBaugh has pointed out, to come out is *already* a political statement. In their invitation to the 1981 Lesbian Gay Freedom Week, the Gay and Lesbian Community Center of Colorado points this out:

> Ah Summer! And what better way to ease into long days than to celebrate our lesbian and gay identities with Lesbian and Gay Freedom Week. The week has been designated as "freedom" instead of "pride" in recognition of the fact that our lives as lesbians and gays have yet to be freed from both legal and

extra-legal discrimination and that we do have the power to change this injustice.

This is not to say that our status as outlaws in a heterosexually biased culture is not already being changed through the work, some of it visible and some of it invisible, of many gays, lesbians, feminists, and heterosexual supporters both locally, nationally and internationally. Calling this week "freedom" is also not saying that we should not have pride in our gay and lesbian identities or have fun and celebrate our lives and our sexuality. It is saying that we need to expand our celebrations to include serious political aspects of what we face on a daily basis.[160]

The acceptance of homosexual ideology would imply a fundamental change—best described by the word *revolutionary*—in our society. We would see an immediate rejection of such fundamental values as: the traditional distinction between male and female; the normative character of the heterosexual family; the ability of parents to be the main agents in the socialization of their children; the tenets of religion and rational ethics in the areas of human sexuality; the prohibition of prostitution, pornography, incest, free sex, adult/child sexual relationships, child pornography; etc. The principle of consensuality in sexual relations as the norm for their legitimacy is key to the homosexual ideology. This principle implies the fundamental independence and capacity for sexual self-definition in man, sex being a feature which pervades human nature. Traditionally, it has been understood that man is responsible to society in the area of human sexuality, since this is the natural and thus the only way by which the species is perpetuated. Homosexual behavior, unproductive by its nature, represents a complete departure from the satisfaction of the reproductive needs of the species. An acceptance of the separation of reproduction from human sexuality is indeed a revolutionary concept.

The public/private dualism in relation to homosexual sexuality introduces a tension for liberated homosexuals living in a heterosexually oriented society that can only be resolved—within the tenets of the "gay" ideology—by a radical transformation of society. Jeff Greenfield based his critique of the homosexual demand for special rights precisely on the idea that if the sexual practices of homosexuals are a private matter, they do not have any claim to special rights, since the government can in no way address itself to behavior that has no public consequences.[161] In fact, of course, many homosexuals have recognized that homosexual behavior *does have* a public dimension; hence the current penchant of homosexuals to achieve "liberation":

Finally, I would like to note that sexual orientation is not totally a private matter. Sexual activities may be, but one cannot compartmentalize sexual activity and keep it separate from one's total emotional life. I suggest that married heterosexuals try to imagine eliminating references to a spouse in all conver-

139

sations for the next week, especially with those to whom you wish to relate your true feelings. How does Bennett expect me to eliminate my lover in the same way? Suppose you could not mention a wife or husband in the classroom in the same way he expects me to eliminate mention of my lover. Why should I be expected to appear at social events alone? So many books have been written on the debilitating effects of such a double life that I will not mention all the arguments here. But to assume that sexual orientation is in any way related to rights of privacy is both foolish and devious.[162]

In a heterosexual society (i.e., in society as we have known it), it is assumed that people are heterosexuals—in fact, the overwhelming majority are—and their sexual preferences are then taken for granted. But this state of affairs makes the homosexual feel oppressed, and a subculture has been created by certain homosexuals who want to change this situation to their advantage. This subculture, the substratum of the homosexual movement, provides its members with support and constitutes the kernel of a different society, in which sexuality ceases to be identified with heterosexuality. Instead of being centered in the complementary relationship of men and women who wed each other to form a family, it is centered on the needs of each individual, whose sexual desires have a meaning only in terms of his own satisfaction. He can be homosexual, bisexual, heterosexual, or transsexual. He may enjoy bestiality, sadomasochism, or paedophilia. The only significance of his sexual desires involves his ability to find a suitable partner for their satisfaction. This is a profoundly revolutionary development since, as George Gilder has shown, the basis for social and economic progress is the heterosexual family in which the man is willing to work for the sake of his progeny.[163]

Conclusion

The homosexual movement, as we have shown, does have a fairly consistent and highly developed ideology. All homosexuals, even those who have come out, do not fully share every principle we have presented. These principles, however, do satisfy the needs of the movement and its members. They serve to frame the issues of importance to the movement, which are political by nature. Like all ideologies, the homosexual ideology is neither scientific nor objective. Its statements are "working principles" designed to increase the ability of liberated homosexuals to modify their social environment for their own benefit. Any denial of these principles, especially when such denial is enshrined in laws or public policy, is bound to elicit a strong and perhaps violent reaction by the homosexual movement. However, the preservation of traditional society and the values

Ideology of the Homosexual Movement

most Americans cherish does require the denial of the homosexual ideology. It is impossible to predict whether or not the homosexual movement will be successful. Were it to succeed, however, the nation we have known would cease to exist.

Notes

1. *The American Heritage Dictionary of the English Language,* 1976 ed., s.v. "ideology."

2. A popular anthology of post-Kantian philosophers has thus been entitled, *The Age of Ideology,* Henry D. Aiken, ed. (New York: The New American Library, 1956).

3. Ludwig von Mises, *Human Action* (Chicago: Henry Regnery Co., 1963), p. 168.

4. Homophobia is a central concept of the ideology of the homosexual movement. It will be discussed extensively below.

5. Quoted in Marotta, p. 5.

6. Harold D. Lasswell and Abraham Kaplan, *Power and Society: A Framework for Political Inquiry* (New London: Yale University Press, 1950), p. 123.

7. Andrea Dworkin, "Why So-Called Radical Men Love and Need Pornography," *Gay Community News* (Boston, MA), December 28, 1973, p. 10.

8. Robert Dahl, *Modern Political Analysis* (Englewood Cliffs, N.J.: Prentice Hall, 1963), p. 20.

9. Marotta, p. 108.

10. This assertion already has deep ideological implications, since it assumes that there is a "homosexual nature" independent of social conditioning. This is at variance with current orthodoxy, which attributes all sexual characteristics—except purely physical parts of the body—to social causes.

11. Marotta, p. 105.

12. F. Jay Deacon, "Is the Church Sexist? Is the Pope Catholic?," *In Unity,* February/March 1979, p. 10.

13. Ibid., p. 11.

14. Letter to the author from Michael Shively, Associate Director, Center for Research and Education and Sexuality (San Francisco), June 3, 1981. See also the Center's "Summary of Projects" (no date).

15. David Thorstad, "Man-Boy Love and Feminism," *NAMBLA News* (Boston, MA), issue #4, December 1980/January 1981, pp. 12–14.

16. Unless otherwise indicated, all quotes which pertain to NAMBLA's ideology are taken from the Thorstad article referred to in note 15.

17. "Editorial," *NAMBLA News* (Boston, MA), issue #4, December 1980/January 1981, p. 1.

18. Laurel Rowe," Symposium Points to Need for Ministry to Gay Catholics," *Catholic Observer* (Springfield, MA), October 17, 1980.

19. Marotta, p. 110.

20. James Lively, letter to the editor, *Wall Street Journal,* July 22, 1981.

21. Private communication.

22. *Young, Gay, and Proud* is published by an autonomous collective of the Melbourne Gay Teachers and Students Group, Melbourne, Australia, n.d., p. 14.

23. "Straight" is the antonym of "gay."

24. *In Unity,* August/September 1979, p. 4.

25. Marotta, p. 55.

26. Arnie Kantrowitz, *Under the Rainbow: Growing up Gay* (New York: Pocket Books, 1977), p. 131.

27. Ibid.

28. Donia Mills and Phil Gailey, "Kameny's Long Ordeal Personifies Wider Gay Struggle," *Washington Star*, April 10, 1981, p. A-8.

29. Letter from Frank Kameny to Dick Leitsch, June 19, 1968, quoted in Marotta, p. 63.

30. Quoted in Ronald Bayer, *Homosexuality and American Psychiatry: The Politics of Diagnosis* (New York: Basic Books, 1981), pp. 90–91.

31. *Time*, January 24, 1977, p. 58.

32. Gordon Duggins, "McNeill Breaks Self-Imposed Silence," *Gay Community News* (Boston, MA), April 26, 1980. Subsequent quotes from McNeill in this section are taken from the same source.

33. *In Unity*, January/February 1981, p. 14.

34. *The Journal* (Manitou Springs, CO), June 1, 1981, p. 5. See also the *Sacramento* (CA) *Bee*, March 13, 1981.

35. *NAMBLA Journal* (New York: North American Man/Boy Love Association), number 3, n.d., p. 11.

36. *Daily News* (New York City), May 13, 1981, p. 3.

37. *Courier Journal* (Rochester, N.Y.), May 20, 1981.

38. Fred Hiatt, "Proposed D.C. Law on Child Sex Backs Off Full Decriminalization," *Washington Star*, June 30, 1981, p. A-1.

39. Jacqueline Kasun, "Turning Children Into Sex Experts," *Public Interest*, Spring 1979, cited by Patrick J. Buchanan, "Sex Ed and Secretary Schweiker," *Washington Inquirer* (Washington, D.C.: Council for the Defense of Freedom), February 20, 1981.

40. Bill Springmann, "What a Gay Male Teacher Offers Children," *Blade*, March 20, 1981, p. A-15.

41. Robert Nugent et al., *Homosexual Catholics: A New Primer for Discussion* (Washington, D.C.: Dignity, 1980), p. 3.

42. *Friends for Lesbian and Gay Concerns Newsletter* 3 (Sumneytown, PA: Friends of Lesbians and Gays Concerned [Quakers], Autumn 1979): 2–3.

43. Charles E. Rice, "Nature's Intolerance of Abuse," *The Wanderer*, August 6, 1981.

44. Hershel J. Matt, "Sin, Crime, Sickness or Alternative Life Style?: A Jewish Approach to Homosexuality," *Judaism: A Quarterly Journal of Jewish Life and Thought* 24 (Winter, 1978): 15.

45. Adam Walinsky, "Homosexual rights—and the Duty of Privacy," *Daily News* (New York City), June 21, 1977, p. 44.

46. *New York Times*, August 16, 1977, p. 34.

47. Marotta, p. 35.

48. Tripp, p. 84.

49. Ibid.

50. Ibid.

51. Ibid., p. 79.

52. Ibid., p. 80.

53. Ibid., p. 247.

54. Ibid.

55. Charles W. Socarides, "Homosexuality Is Not Just an Alternative Life Style," in *Male and Female*, edited by Barnhouse/Holmes (New York: Seabury, 1976), p. 144.

56. Leitsch's account of the United Church of Christ Conference, cited in Marotta, pp. 60–61.

57. Andy Humm, "Gay Rights Bill," *New York City News*, March 10, 1981.

58. Adam DeBaugh, "Gay Rights Introduced," *Gays on the Hill* 3 (March 1979): 1.

59. Prepared statement by Judd Marmor, M.D., past president, American Psychiatric Association, *Hearing*, p. 67.

60. *Chicago Tribune*, July 7, 1977, cited in *A Time to Speak*, p. 6.

61. "Men and Boys: The Boston Conference," *Gaysweek*, February 12, 1979, p. 9.

62. Ibid.

63. Ibid.

64. Mimeographed sheet describing the camp, n.d.

65. Anne Roiphe, "The Trouble at Sarah Lawrence," *New York Times Magazine*, March 20, 1977, pp. 21 ff.

66. "Lesbians Invite City to Celebrate," *Davis Enterprise* (Davis City, CA), October 2, 1980, p. 1, reproduced in *Hearing*, p. 148.

67. Springmann.

68. Jean O'Leary and Bruce Voeller, "Anita Bryant's Crusade," *New York Times*, June 7, 1977.

69. "Workshops," *Quicksilver Times* (Washington, D.C.), November 24-December 4, 1970.

70. Philip Nobile, "The Meaning of Gay. An Interview with Dr. C.A. Tripp," *New York*, June 25, 1979, p. 41.

71. Tripp, pp. 236 ff.

72. Letter from Frank Kameny to Dick Leitsch, June 19, 1968, quoted in Marotta, p. 63.

73. 559 P.2d 1340(1977), quoted in David Stivison, "A Decade of Gay Teacher Cases," *Gay Community News* (Boston, MA), March 3, 1979, p. 10.

74. Edmund Bergler, *Homosexuality: Disease or Way of Life?* (New York: Hill and Wang, 1956).

75. Irving Bieber et al., *Homosexuality: A Psychoanalytic Study of Male Homosexuals* (New York: Basic Books, 1962).

76. Bayer, p. 33.

77. Victor Cohn, "Homosexuals Not Ill, Therapists Say," *Washington Post*, April 17, 1979, p. A-9.

78. Alice Murray, "Ex-Homosexual Claims He Was Saved by Jesus," *Atlanta Constitution*, June 10, 1978.

79. *Daily News* (New York City), May 26, 1981.

80. Tom Minnery, "Homosexuals CAN Change," *Christianity Today*, February 6, 1981, pp. 36ff.

81. *Review* 5 (Spring 1981).

82. *Prologue: An Examination of the Mormon Attitude Towards Homosexuality* (Salt Lake City: Prometheus Enterprises, 1978).

83. Socarides.

84. Ibid.

85. Bayer, p. 183.

86. Marotta, p. 24.

87. Bayer, Chapter 2.

88. Ibid., pp. 145–146.

89. "Homosexuality: Tolerance vs. Approval," *Time*, January 8, 1979, p. 48.

90. *NAMBLA Journal* (New York: North American Man/Boy Love Association), number 3, n.d., p. 1.

91. Allen Grooms, "Homophobia Can Be Cured," *Gays on the Hill* 3 (March 1979).

92. R. Adam DeBaugh, "Coming Out!" (Washington, D.C.: Universal Fellowship of Metropolitan Community Churches, n.d.).

93. Marotta, p. 10.

94. DeBaugh, "Coming Out!"

95. Ibid.

96. Marotta, p. 124.

97. "Is Our Church Big Enough for Gay Catholics? The Editors Interview Brian McNaught," *U.S. Catholic*, June, 1980, p. 10.

98. Howard J. Brown, "In Secret, in Public," *New York Times*, October 21, 1976.

99. Meryl Friedman and Marc Rubin, letter to the editor, *American Educator*, Winter 1978.

100. Prepared statement by Judd Marmor, M.D., past president, American Psychiatric Association, *Hearing*, p. 67.

101. James Hess, O. Carm., Robert Riley, Robert Carter, S.J., and Thomas Nolan, O.S.B., Letter of Reply to Rev. Kenneth G. Jadoff, July 21, 1977.

102. "Is Our Church Big Enough for Gay Catholics? The Editors Interview Brian McNaught," *U.S. Catholic*, June, 1980, p. 10.

103. Ibid.

104. Ibid.

105. Tripp, p. 227.

106. Lavender University of the Rockies, *Spring/Summer 1981 Catalog*, Denver.

107. Ken George, Ph.D., "Couples: Open Marriage?" (n.p., n.d.), taken from the "Gay Marriages" file at New Ways Ministry (Mt. Rainier, MD).

108. Cf. Tripp, p. 66 for various examples of anthropological research purporting to demonstrate that homosexuality is acceptable.

109. Ralph Blair, *Homophobia in the Churches* (New York: Dr. Ralph Blair, 1979).

110. Personal communication.

111. Paul Siegel, "Homophobia: Types, Origins and Remedies," *Christianity and Crisis*, November 12, 1979, p. 282.

112. Ibid.

113. Joan L. Clark, "Homophobia: Hysteria and Hypocrisy," *Integrity Forum* 7 (Oak Park, IL: Integrity, 1981): 1. This article is a reproduction of Clark's address at the Integrity Convention held in Boston during August 1980.

114. Ibid.

115. Course description distributed by the University of Connecticut, cover page.

116. Ibid.

117. Ibid.

118. "Removing the Stigma," Final Report of the Board of Social and Ethical Responsibility for Psychology's Task Force on the Status of Lesbian and Gay Male Psychologists, American Psychological Association, Washington, D.C., 1979, p. 15.

119. Ibid., p. 126.

120. Deacon.

121. Table extracted from Blair, pp. 8–18.

122. Bob McCubbin, *The Gay Question: A Marxist Appraisal* (New York: World View Publishers, 1976), pp. 13–14.

123. Dennis J. Lewis, "Friends' Focuses on Gay Issues," *Washington Star*, July 25, 1981.

124. Grooms, p. 2.

125. L. Robert Arthur, *Homosexuality in the Light of Biblical Language and Culture* (Los Angeles, CA: Universal Fellowship Press, 1977), pp. 6–7.

126. "Is Our Church Big Enough for Gay Catholics? The Editors Interview Brian McNaught," *U.S. Catholic*, June, 1980, p. 10.

127. "Redefining the Family," *It's Time* 7 (February-March 1980): 1.

128. Handbill passed out at a demonstration in front of St. Patrick's Cathedral, New York City, in June 1979.

129. *Justice and Peace Center Newsletter* (Milwaukee: Justice and Peace Center), July 1977. Reproduced in *A Time to Speak*, p. 7.

130. *In Unity,* April/May 1979, p. 5.

131. R. Adam DeBaugh, "Representatives of 16 Denominations Gather to Discuss Homophobia in the Churches," *A New Day* 3 (June 1979): 1.

132. Phil Allen and Heidi Silver, "12,000 Lesbians, Gays in Boston Commemorate Stonewall Rebellion," *Workers World* (New York, N.Y.), June 26, 1981.

133. Quoted in Marotta, p. 24.

134. Ibid., pp. 24–25.

135. Ibid., p. 80.

136. *Hearing,* p. 66.

137. "Removing the Stigma," Final Report of the Board of Social and Ethical Responsibility for Psychology's Task Force on the Status of Lesbian and Gay Male Psychologists, American Psychological Association, Washington, D.C., 1979, p. 15.

138. *Baltimore Sun,* April 12, 1981.

139. Friedman and Rubin.

140. Marotta, p. 68.

141. *A Time to Speak,* p. 3.

142. Statement of Grant Mickins, *Hearing,* pp. 50–51.

143. Alfred Kinsey et al., *Sexual Behavior in the Human Male* (Philadelphia: Saunders, 1948).

144. Friedman and Rubin, p. 67.

145. Pennsylvania Department of Education, *What is a Sexual Minority, Anyway?* (1980), p. 6.

146. *Does Support for Gay Rights Spell Political Suicide?* (Washington, D.C.: Gay Rights National Lobby and National Gay Task Force, 1981), p. 1.

147. Ibid., pp. 1–2.

148. Donia Mills and Phil Gailey, "D.C. Homosexuals Increase Influence by 'Using System,' " *Washington Star,* April 9, 1981.

149. Brown.

150. Bayer, p. 163.

151. *Prologue: An Examination of the Mormon Attitude Towards Homosexuality* (Salt Lake City: Prometheus Enterprises, 1978).

152. Friedman and Rubin, p. 65.

153. Letter from Irving Stone to Abigail Van Buren, *Washington Star,* April 20, 1981.

154. Marotta, p. 91.

155. Ibid., pp. 91–92.

156. Kantrowitz, p. 161.

157. Ibid.

158. Ibid., p. 158.

159. Shelley Hamilton, Letter to the Editor, *In Unity,* August/September 1979, p. 20.

160. *Gaynin'* 5 (Denver: Gay and Lesbian Community Center of Colorado, June 1981): 1.

161. Jeff Greenfield, "Why is Gay Rights Different from All Other Rights?" *Village Voice,* February 23, 1978, p. 23.

162. James Levin, Letter to the Editor, *American Educator,* Winter 1978, p. 69.

163. George Gilder, *Wealth and Poverty* (New York, N.Y.: Basic Books, 1981), pp. 68–74.

CHAPTER

IV

The Homosexual Movement

The multiplicity of organizations in which "liberated" homosexuals have chosen to express their interests is as varied as the human condition itself. Except for the most basic elements among them (i.e., sexual attraction for members of their own sex and the generalized acceptance of the homosexual ideology), there is nothing that *all* homosexual organizations have in common. Their variety is so great, moreover, that we cannot provide a description that will cover the whole field. Even a superficial examination of the *Gayellow Pages* reveals a plurality of organizations hitherto unsuspected by the uninitiated. Homosexuals have organized from every conceivable point of view and for almost any purpose imaginable. If one is willing to accept the imposition of the homosexual ideology as a goal, and a membership composed largely of homosexuals or their sympathizers, there is a homosexual group somewhere in America to fit the needs of the most discriminating individual.

The meteoric rise of the homosexual movement in America has rather obscure origins. It has been reported that "as early as 1924 an attempt was made to set up a homosexual organization in the United States modeled after the German Scientific Humanitarian Committee."[1] In 1951 Donald Webster Cory [pseud.] published his opus *The Homosexual in America,* which included a call for activities that would eventually result in the development of the homosexual movement. Cory pointed out (see chapter III) that the homosexual minority was more disadvantaged than others in that it lacked leadership, communication, philosophy, and self-justification:[2]

The Homosexual Movement

As a minority, we homosexuals are therefore caught in a particularly vicious circle. On the one hand, the shame of belonging and the social punishment of acknowledgement are so great that pretense is almost universal; on the other hand, only a leadership that would acknowledge would be able to break down the barriers of shame and resultant discrimination. Until the world is able to accept us on an equal basis as human beings entitled to the full rights of life, we are unlikely to have any great numbers willing to become martyrs by carrying the burden of the cross. But until we are willing to speak out openly and frankly in defense of our activities, and to identify ourselves with the millions pursuing these activities, we are unlikely to find the attitudes of the world undergoing any significant change.[3]

At about the same time, through the efforts of a homosexual Marxist named Henry Hay, the Mattachine Society was founded. As Marotta indicates, the political ambiance of those days impelled Hay to propose a "mode of organization [that] was similar to what he had found in the American Communist Party and among European Freemasons."[4] For female homosexuals, the Daughters of Bilitis came into existence in the 1950s. By the 1960s, the movement was well on its way. The reader can find a detailed history of the early days of the movement in Toby Marotta's *The Politics of Homosexuality*. Although centered in New York City, Marotta's work provides a good account of what was essentially the success of the more radical elements within the movement. The Stonewall riot (June 1969) marks the second phase of the homosexual movement; its anniversary has become the focal point of "Gay Pride Weeks" as celebrated in most American cities, representing the homosexual refusal to accept the judgment passed upon their practices by society. During the 1970s, the movement consolidated and proclaimed itself a permanent feature in the American cultural and political landscape. Homosexual churches have been formed; within most social bodies, formal groups of homosexuals have evolved to promote their ideology in the context of these larger organizations; a sense of history and of the existence of a homosexual subculture have developed; and actual pride in the homosexual condition has become conscious in countless individuals. One of the most important activities in the movement's formation has been the promotion of local, regional, and national conferences. It appears that homosexual organizations are constantly meeting, and it is in these meetings that acquaintances are made, ideas exchanged, and networks established. One such event at the regional level was the first New England Lesbian and Gay Conference which, according to *Workers World*, took place during the commemoration of the Stonewall riot.[5] A clue to the number and variety of homosexual-related conferences is provided by a list (no doubt partial) published by the Gay and Lesbian Community Center of Colorado:[6]

Title	Location	1981
National Call to Unity Conference	Los Angeles, Calif.	
Black and White Men Together International Convention	San Francisco, Calif.	
Sixth International Conference of Gay and Lesbian Jews	Philadelphia, Pa.	July 2–5
1981 Michigan Women's Music Festival	Mt. Pleasant, Mich.	August 13–16
1981 Midwest Lesbian-Feminist Conference	Lincoln, Neb.	September 4–6
Second Annual West Coast Women's Music and Cultural Conference	West Hollywood, Calif.	September 10–13

The result has been a multifaceted social organization, really a loose coalition of separate organizations held together by the homosexuality of its members. As we have seen, this coalition—or more properly movement—has a reasonably well-structured ideology, consonant with the activities required to accomplish its goals. As mentioned before, no attempt will be made to portray the movement comprehensively. The rest of this chapter will acquaint the reader with the movement and the economic power of its members, and will provide an idea of some of the political activities which explain its rapid accumulation of political influence, beyond what anyone would have thought possible even ten years ago.

Variety of Organizational Components

BACKGROUND

The homosexual movement exists at different levels. There are international, national, regional, and local organizations. Although its founders had from the beginning a broad vision which encompassed *all* homosexuals, the strength of the movement lies in the fact that it is basically a grassroots movement. The homosexual movement is the Wilde-Stein Club in Orono (Maine) and the Gay Nurses Alliance of Brownsville (Texas). The Alaska Gay Community Center, the Congregation Etz Chaim of Miami, and *The Community Voice* of the Wichita Gay Community Association are also the homosexual movement. The many congregations which make up the Universal Fellowship of Metropolitan Community Churches, the college-centered associations of homosexual students, the caucuses of professional homosexuals, the thousands of publications—from one-page newsletters to *The Advocate* and *The Sentinel*—are also the homosexual movement. At the national level there are organizations that promote the homosexual ideology forcefully and effectively. For each national organization, however, there are dozens of small groups that work (most of them quietly, some with noise and fanfare) to ensure that the pressure of the liberated homosexual is felt throughout the land. (The best single source of information on this subject is the *Gayellow Pages*, available for $6.95 from Renaissance House, Box 292, Village Station, New York, N.Y. 10014.)

Within the movement, there are businesses (bars, baths, bookstores, movie houses, etc.), services (doctors, dentists, realtors, movers, counselors, and others) and nonprofit organizations. The survey undertaken as part of the research which resulted in this book included, as previously mentioned, investigation of a random sample of 80 nonprofit homosexual organizations from a universe of 394 organizations. Table 10 presents the number of organizations employing staffs of various sizes. The average (mean) number of persons employed in nonprofit homosexual organizations during the summer of 1981 was 5, while the median was 2.5. A sizable number of organizations (31%) had no employees and 50% had two or fewer. However, 5% of the organizations had 20 or more employees. Assuming that the sample is representative of the universe, no fewer than 1,870 individuals were paid workers in nonprofit homosexual organizations nationwide. It is possible that the 1982 budget cuts have reduced this number considerably, but this has yet to be determined. There is no evidence of a concerted effort by the Reagan administration to defund the homosexual movement by depriving it of federal monies.

Table 11 shows the years in which the various organizations of the sample were founded. Given the climate that existed throughout the 1940s and '50s, it can be safely assumed that the organizations listed as having been founded in 1948 and 1952 must have had a different function then, or conducted their activities surreptitiously. The median year of the foundation of organizations in the sample is 1974 (i.e., 50% of the organizations were founded before 1974 and 50% in 1974 or afterward. Fifty-seven percent of the organizations were founded between 1971 and 1975. The number decreases markedly after 1978. The average age of a nonprofit homosexual organization is 7.68 years. (The reader is cautioned about possible bias due to our selection of the universe from, among other sources, the *Gayellow Pages*.) As Table 11 shows, 1971 was a crucial year, in which the number of nonprofit homosexual organizations increased dramatically. The possibility that other organizations (perhaps many more) founded before 1971 have not survived until today cannot be discounted. However, the very history of the homosexual movement does favor the notion that not many nonprofit organizations were started prior to 1971. Moreover, were we to assume that the rate of disappearance of these organizations is unrelated to their date of foundation or—what is more likely—that organizations tend to dissolve within the first two or three years of existence or to remain in business more or less "indefinitely,"

TABLE 10

Number of Organizations by Staff Size

Number of Paid Staff Persons Employed	Number of Organizations	Percentage
0	25	31
1	7	9
2	7	9
3	6	8
4	3	4
5	9	12
6	4	5
7	1	1
8	4	5
9	4	5
12	1	1
13	2	3
14	2	3
18	1	1
20	1	1
22	1	1
36	1	1
42	1	1
Totals	80	101*

*Rounding accounts for total over 100%

the fact that a very small number of such organizations reportedly founded during 1979 and 1980 (fewer in 1980 than in 1979) would indicate that no new organizations are being founded. Whether this is due to a saturation of the market or the existence of unfavorable conditions for the appearance of new homosexual organizations has yet to be determined. It would be interesting to explore the possibility that the apparent move of America toward conservatism explains this decrease in new nonprofit homosexual organizations. It is noteworthy that the Washington office of the UFMCC was closed during 1981.

NETWORKING: THE LOCAL LEVEL
Although the homosexual movement can be described as a set of institutions, such a description provides an incomplete view, since the interrelations among groups and the various ways in which individuals participate in the life of these institutions is as important as the institutions themselves. In a sense, the homosexual movement is nothing but a nationwide network of interested individuals who have associated with each other for the promotion of an ideology that satisfies their own interests, both theoretical and practical. When looking at the movement, therefore,

The Homosexual Movement

TABLE 11

*Date of Establishment of Nonprofit
Homosexual Organizations*

Year of Establishment	Number of Organizations	Percentage
1980	1	1
1979	3	4
1978	7	9
1977	10	13
1976	5	6
1975	7	9
1974	7	9
1973	12	15
1972	7	9
1971	12	15
1970	2	3
1969	2	3
1968	1	1
1967	1	1
1965	1	1
1952	1	1
1948	1	1
Totals	80	101*

*Rounding accounts for total over 100%

it is essential to consider its characteristic of network under two aspects: first, the leadership of the movement is made up of individuals who form a veritable network, usually acting in concert and often participating in various organizations. Second, homosexual organizations do act in concert, share information, and support one another. This is based on their shared interest (promotion of the homosexual ideology) and in the communality of their leadership. In many instances, moreover, the homosexual movement has successfully "infiltrated" other organizations. This provides additional platforms for the pursuit of common interests.

The chart below illustrates the affiliations of various members of the Board of Directors of the National Gay Task Force. This is a partial list, chosen from several boards of the NGTF. The network-like character of the movement is apparent.

One way in which this networking occurs is by the creation of "front organizations" such as the Fund for Human Dignity. Located at the address of the National Gay Task Force (NGTF) in New York City, the Fund appears to be an arm and a fundraising mechanism of the NGTF.

THE HOMOSEXUAL NETWORK

Name	Other Organization(s) in Which the Person Has a Leading Role
Steve Endean	Gay Rights National Lobby
Meryl Friedman	New York City Gay Teachers Association
Barbara Gittings	Gay Task Force, American Library Association
José Gómez	Boston Gay and Lesbian Advocates and Defenders
	United Farm Workers Union (former executive assistant to César Chávez)
Larry Bagneris	Houston Gay Political Caucus
	Texas Gay Task Force (former Regional coordinator)
	National Students Association (former vice president)
Richard Cash	United Methodist Church (Gay Caucus)
Kay Whitlock	National Organization for Women (Lesbian Rights Committee)
Kerry Woodward	Gay Rights National Lobby
Franklyn Kameny	Gay Activists Alliance (activist founder of the contemporary homosexual movement)
Mel Boozer	Gay Activists Alliance (Vice-Presidential nominee 1980 Democratic National Convention)
Carolyn Handy	Local Activist Leader, Member of the Reagan Transition Team/Department of Education

Its initial fundraising letter did not mention any affiliation with the NGTF and had no homosexual leaders as endorsers; rather it displayed conspicuously the endorsement of prominent individuals who have not identified themselves as homosexuals: Paul Moore, Episcopal Bishop of New York; Ira Glasser, Executive Director of the American Civil Liberties Union; U. S. Representative Shirley Chisholm (D-N.Y.); Karen DeCrow, former president of the National Organization for Women; and U.S. Senator Alan Cranston (D-Calif.). The Fund is referred to in the NGTF newsletter as "our foundation."[7] It appears that there is no *real* separation between the Fund for Human Dignity and the NGTF. The following excerpt from a speech by then coexecutive director of the NGTF, Charles Brydon, before the Mandamus Society of Norfolk, Virginia, corroborates this impression.

> Finally, we need a comprehensive five-year national public education program. Our target is the nongay public and the three major institutions that are basic to forming attitudes about gay people—organized religion, the education establishment, and the media. We have started such a program. Dr. Charles Hitchcock of Long Island University has begun research on the basic issues funded by a small grant from our foundation, the NGTF Fund for Human Dignity. Implementing the program will require the cooperation of local groups and a great deal of money. But this commitment is crucial if we are to get to the roots of homophobia in our society and break the cycle that perpetuates the lies, myths, and stereotypes that bedevil our cause.[8]

On the other hand, Dr. Hitchcock is referred to in the same issue of the newsletter as "NGTF Public Education Consultant." Whose work he is doing when he is spending tax-deductible funds is obviously not at all clear.

152

The Homosexual Movement

In the health field, there is also a network of individuals who have formed complementary organizations. Typical examples are the National Gay Health Education Foundation, Inc. (NGHEF) and the National Gay Health Coalition (NGHC). These organizations involve a multitude of health-related homosexual organizations (e.g., the National Coalition of Gay Sexually Transmitted Disease Services is a member of the NGHC). This rather complex network and its modus operandi have been well described in a homosexual newsletter:

> In other words, the NGHEF and the NGHC are independent organizations which by design have mutually exclusive responsibilities and close relationships and which are both accountable to the national gay health organizations and through them to all gay/lesbian health workers and the gay/lesbian community at large.
>
> The formal (legal) connection between the NGHC and the NGHEF is properly limited to the composition of the NGHEF's governing body and does not deal with the NGHEF's policies and functioning. Specifically, the NGHEF's By-Laws provide that its Board of Directors be comprised primarily of persons nominated by the national gay health organizations which comprise the NGHC.
>
> However, the functioning of both the NGHEF and the NGHC is enhanced by an active, extensive, but informal (nonlegal) connection which ensures full sharing of information and ample opportunity for consultation. This includes: a) the provision by each to the other of copies of policy and goal statements, minutes of meetings, work programs, literature, and similar basic written material, and b) the designation by each of a liaison person (and alternate) to the other who is expected to be a regular, nonvoting participant in the other's governing body meetings.[9]

Although there is considerable evidence of networking at the national level, the homosexual movement works best at the local level. Even if national leadership is not lacking, the movement is basically a grassroots operation. Especially in areas where there are large concentrations of homosexuals, in bars, baths and church groups, the practice of homosexuality and its perceived "value" for the psychosocial development of its devotees becomes entrenched in the minds of the "liberated" homosexual.

The importance of local groups and the need to recruit at the local level have not escaped the national leadership of the movement. Many associations of homosexual college students, as we shall see, have been formed with the help of the Gay Academic Union. The National Gay Task Force has a National Community Organizing Program with a full-time staff person responsible for developing new homosexual organizations.[10]

Efforts to organize homosexuals on the local level have resulted in the existence of some 3,000 organizations.[11] The NGTF is engaged in a project to computerize them. It is well beyond the task of this work to describe this array of groups, which are, by their nature, very diverse. As a matter of fact, probably no one individual or group possesses the information required for this task. San Francisco alone, for example, has a homosexual telephone directory listing some 600 businesses owned or managed by homosexuals, largely catering to a homosexual clientele. It has been reported that there are, among others:

11 legal services
10 medical services
40 organizations (social, etc.)
13 religious organizations
10 political organizations (both Democratic and Republican)
 9 organizations for homosexual youth
14 real estate businesses[12]

In New York, the Greater Gotham Business Council has 100 members, presumably all homosexual businesses. An accurate description of the homosexual movement, at least at the local level, appears to be impossible. However, its character as a well-established network is undeniable.

THE INTERNATIONAL GAY ASSOCIATION

The homosexual movement is not limited to the United States. In a world where communications bridge thousands of miles in seconds and millions of people travel across international borders, no social development of the magnitude of the homosexual movement can be isolated. Homosexuals exist in all societies. The homosexual ideology, on the other hand, seems to be limited to Western nations. The Socialist bloc holds fast to the belief that homosexuality is a perversion, destructive of society. Its totalitarian governments have not allowed the development of anything remotely similar to the American homosexual movement. Although Moslem societies have traditionally been alleged to tolerate widespread homosexuality, the prevailing Moslem faith would not allow the existence of homosexual organizations.

There are reasonably well-defined homosexual organizations in Western nations. Representing twenty-one countries, national homosexual organizations have formed the International Gay Association (IGA). The IGA was organized in Coventry, England in 1978 by representatives of twelve countries. Currently twenty-one nations are fully represented (see Table 12), with "associate" members in fifteen other countries (Austria, Brazil, Colombia, Costa Rica, Guatemala, Hong Kong, India, Indonesia, Japan, Mexico, Philippines, Poland, Portugal, South Africa, and Turkey).

Structurally, the IGA is divided into three sections: 1) the *Secretariat*, located in Dublin, "is responsible for dissemination of all information to member organizations, coordination of all political actions undertaken on IGA.'s behalf, and response to inquiries from members and associate

The Homosexual Movement

TABLE 12

I.G.A. Member Organizations

County	Member Organization
Australia	Camp Lobby
Belgium	Federatie Werkgroepen Homofilie (FWH)
Canada	Canadian Lesbians and Gay Rights Coalition
Denmark	Forbundet af 1948
England/Wales	Campaign for Homosexual Equality (CHE)
	Gay Activists Alliance (GAA)
Finland	Seksuaslinen Lasavertaisuus ry (SETA)
France	C.I.D.H.
	Centre du Christ Liberateur
Germany, Federal	AHA, Berlin
Republic of	NARGS, Heidelberg
	Ag Schwule in Kommunistischen Bund, Hamburg
	glf-AHB, Bonn
Greece	Apeleftherotiko Kinema Omofylogilon Elladas (AKOE)
Iceland	Samtokin '78 (Iceland Hospitality)
Ireland, Northern	Northern Ireland Gay Rights Association (NIGRA)
Ireland, Republic of	Campaign for Homosexual Law Reform (CHLR)
	National Gay Federation (NGF)
Italy	FUORI!
The Netherlands	N.V.I.H.—C.O.C.
	Stichting Vrije Relatierechten
New Zealand	National Gay Rights Coalition
Norway	Det Norske Forbundet av '48
	AHF, Oslo
Scotland	Scottish Homosexual Rights Group (SHRG)
Spain	Front d'Alliberament Gai de Catalunuya (FAGC)
	Institute Lambda
Sweden	Riksforbundet for Sexuellt Likaberattigande (FRSL)
Switzerland	SOH
United States of	Gay Community Center/District of Columbia
America	National Gay Task Force (NGTF)
	We Are Everywhere

SOURCE: International Gay Association, Organizational Brochure

members";[13] 2) the *Financial Center*, located in Amsterdam, "is responsible for IGA's financial planning and management"; and 3) the *Regional Liaison Office*, which "in conjunction with the Secretariat, inform[s] organizational members, individual members, and associate members of conditions of lesbians and gay men in other countries and respond[s] to the Secretariat's request for immediate and coordinated international action."

The main activities of the IGA are directed toward cooperation with the World Council of Churches (support for homosexual rights); Amnesty

International (status for homosexuals in jail as "prisoners of conscience"); the World Health Organization ("deletion of homosexuality from its list of diseases and mental defects"); and other international bodies such as the United Nations and the Council of Europe ("consultative" status for IGA). Some of the activities and concerns of the IGA are exemplified by the agenda of its First Annual Conference, held in the Netherlands in 1979. The topics discussed included "the status of lesbians and gay men around the world with respect to immigration and citizenship, child custody, persecution for engaging in homosexual acts, prison conditions, children's rights, education, and possible sources of support such as Amnesty International, the U.N., and the World Council of Churches."[14]

Subsequent meetings were held in Costa Brava, Spain in 1980 and Torino, Italy in 1981. Efforts made between these conferences to have the U.N. accept the IGA on a consultative status have been unsuccessful. The reason for this failure, however, has not been related to the homosexual affiliation of the organization but, according to the homosexual press, to the predominance of "first world" (i.e., white) countries in its membership and the lack of a constitution.[15]

There is little question that the international appeal for support by the homosexual movement will find a receptive ear among those who favor the demise of nations and the appearance of an international order. Tradition-oriented forces which affirm the values of family and nationhood have stood firm against the homosexual movement. Traditional values have stressed the distinction between genders and the maintenance of socioeconomic structures in which the hierarchical family can flourish and children develop within an orderly environment. These same values— and the principle of subsidiarity which they imply—have affirmed the need to preserve the nation-state against the forces of internationalism. It would not be surprising if the IGA sought support among the havens of internationalism.

THE NATIONAL GAY TASK FORCE

Within the homosexual movement in the United States, there are only three truly national organizations: the Gay Rights National Lobby (GRNL), the Universal Fellowship of Metropolitan Community Churches (UFMCC), and the National Gay Task Force (NGTF). There are other organizations which do not specifically relate to local issues and that, on this account, can also be called "national." However, they have neither the resources nor the influence to deserve this title with propriety. Of the other two, the NGTF is older, more respected, and far more influential; thus we have chosen it as a model national homosexual organization.

The NGTF was founded in 1973 as a successful attempt to synthesize the earlier dichotomy between moderate and radical homosexual leaders in New York City.[16] Among the original founders were Frank Kameny,

The Homosexual Movement

Ginny Vida, Barbara Gittings, Meryl Friedman, and David Rothenberg, all well-known leaders of the homosexual movement. The board of directors of the organization still includes some of the most influential persons in the movement.

The accomplishments of the NGTF on behalf of homosexuality in America have left a deep and not easily eradicable mark on our culture. It was due to the efforts of the NGTF that the American Psychiatric Association officially took homosexuality from its list of mental illnesses. The NGTF was also instrumental in making the White House accessible and willing to lend a favorable ear to the leadership of the homosexual movement during the Carter Administration. This and the introduction of several prohomosexual statutes in the U.S. Congress—to a great extent also the work of the NGTF—exemplify the high degree of acceptance of homosexuality by the U.S. government. The high visibility of homosexual issues and personalities at the White House Conference on Families and the International Women's Year Conference was also due to the efforts of the NGTF, as was the presence of prohomosexual individuals and agenda items at the 1980 Democratic Convention. The NGTF has been influential in causing a number of U.S. agencies (e.g., Internal Revenue Service, Bureau of Prisons, Federal Communications Commission) to make regulatory decisions which favor the acceptance of homosexuality as a legitimate lifestyle. Another area in which the NGTF has been active is the promotion of the homosexual ideology in corporations by the adoption of "homosexual rights" policies. The NGTF has secured support for the homosexual movement from dozens of organizations which could have been expected to remain "neutral" at best, among them the Young Women's Christian Association, the National Organization for Women, the American Civil Liberties Union, the National Council of Churches, and the National Federation of Priests Councils.[17]

The NGTF is basically a political organization. Its activities encompass three areas: 1) exertion of legal, legislative, and political pressure on the government, corporations, unions, and other organizations to "persuade" them to institute prohomosexual policies; 2) propaganda activities on behalf of the homosexual movement and in support of its ideology, especially in, but not limited to, the media; 3) grassroots organization, on both geographical and interest bases. The NGTF acts to initiate small groups of homosexuals within "straight" organizations, with the specific aim of using the resources of these organizations on behalf of the goals of the homosexual movement.

Although traditionally the NGTF has had male and female "codirectors," the female halves of these pairs have, in fact, overshadowed their male counterparts. The first two codirectors were Bruce Voeller and Jean O'Leary, who is acknowledged as the most influential female homosexual in the nation. A former Roman Catholic nun (in the order of the Humility of Mary) she was associated with the NGTF for five years. Subsequent to her election as a delegate to the 1976 Democratic National Convention, she was variously: "appointed by President Carter to the National Commission on the Observance of International Women's Year (IWY) and to the National Advisory Committee for Women, established in the wake of the IWY-sponsored National Women's Conference held in Houston in the fall of 1977; appointed by Ed Koch to the Mayor's Commission on the Status of Women in New York City; and elected an alternate delegate to the 1980 Democratic National Convention."[18] She is also the founder of Lesbian Feminist Liberation, an organization for female homosexuals, and has served on President Carter's "51.3% Committee for Women," the Advisory Board of the National Women's Political Caucus, the New York City Health Systems Agency, and the Board of Directors of the Gay Rights National Lobby.

Miss O'Leary can be reasonably presented as a model "organization man" of the homosexual movement. Her progress from the convent to national prominence as a female homosexual leader and advocate of what Catholic orthodoxy considers a form of perversion is astonishing.

In 1979 the top leadership of the NGTF changed and two new codirectors were named, Charles F. Brydon and Lucia Valeska. Once again, the female part of the duo was by far the stronger partner. A mother of three children, Mrs. Valeska is a former co-coordinator of the New Mexico Coalition of Lesbian and Gay Rights.[19] Like O'Leary, Valeska has been heavily involved in the feminist movement. "She was a founder and organizer of the University's Women's Center, Women's Studies Program, and Gay Student Union, as well as the Albuquerque Women's Center and the Albuquerque/Santa Fe chapter of the National Lesbian Feminist Organization."[20] A sociologist by profession, Lucia Valeska's academic expertise is the history of lesbian feminism.

One of the organizations spun off by the NGTF is the Gay Rights National Lobby (GRNL), created to promote the passage of the first prohomosexual bill ever to be introduced in the U.S. Congress.[21] Under the direction of Steve Endean, the GRNL has in effect become a rival to the NGTF. The old dichotomy of moderates vs. activists was not, in fact, transcended by the foundation of the NGTF. The pressure of Ronald Reagan's victory in 1980, an indication that the nation had embarked on a more conservative road, opened the old wounds. Apparently, Valeska and Brydon opted for a more moderate course, making several moves that proved near-fatal for the leadership of the NGTF. A congratulatory message sent to President Reagan "included the claim that gays had helped put him in office. Gay leaders who had worked hard to deliver precincts to Carter, and had the statistics to show they had succeeded, were offended."[22] Valeska and Brydon also took a much more moderate position than other homosexual leaders in the dispute between the Immigration and Naturalization Service and the homosexual community on the admissibility of homosexuals to the United States.[23] They also apparently refused to become involved with a proposed Federal Communications Commission decision to eliminate community ascertainments, which for the first time were to include homosexual groups—this despite appeals from a major supporter of the homosexual movement, the United Church of Christ.[24] The final action which caused a major scandal within the homosexual community was a letter sent by Valeska and Brydon to Representative Peter McCloskey (R-Calif.), a major advocate of the homosexual movement in the U.S. Congress, asking him not to introduce certain prohomosexual legislation affecting the U.S. Army.[25]

Valeska and Brydon were soundly condemned by such influential homosexual political organizations as the Harvey Milk and Stonewall Gay Democratic Clubs[26] and the Alice B. Toklas Memorial Democratic Club,[27] all of which demanded their resignation. The GRNL did not miss the opportunity to launch an attack on the NGTF and claim the exclusive right to lobby Congress. According to reports published in *The Sentinel,* the leading homosexual newspaper in San Francisco, the letter to McCloskey was "harshly condemned by Gay Rights National Lobby (GRNL) director Steve Endean as being contrary to GRNL advice to McCloskey and a matter out of the purview of NGTF."[28] The paper also made reference to an apparent agreement between the NGTF and the GRNL giving the latter the exclusive right to lobby the U.S. Congress. This problem only culminated what seems to be a history of difficulties between the two organizations: "Many other gay leaders concur that the recent squabbles between NGTF and GRNL are detracting from substantive progress toward gay rights. 'Our community cannot tolerate that our only two organizations are continually at each other's throats,' said Cleve Jones,"[29] (a noted activist).

The sequel to this dispute was a reaction typical of organizations under fire. Valeska emerged as the sole director, Brydon resigned, and six Board members decided not to seek reelection.[30] The Valeska/Brydon rivalry became apparent when Valeska declared after the shakeup that "this would have happened anyway at some point . . . but the heat of the press and among some community groups speeded up the process and accentuated the differences and difficulties we are experiencing as a result of the codirector structure."[31] It was also reported that Valeska took steps to dissociate herself from the policies that had resulted in the strong criticism of the NGTF.[32]

On October 23, 1981, the National Gay Task Force launched a campaign to combat the Family Protection Act at a press conference held at an official congressional office, under the sponsorship of two prohomosexual congressmen, S. William Greene (R-N.Y.) and Michael Lowry (D-Wash.). The absence of representatives of the GRNL and other major homosexual organizations indicated that the rift in the movement had not been completely healed even after the sacrifice of Brydon.

Part of the problem of the NGTF is that, while formally an agent of revolutionary change in America, it is, in fact and function, a middle-class organization. The codirectors earn $29,000 a year (up from $13,000 in 1977),[33] a salary that has been noted by the homosexual press. This is not the pay scale of the typical activist organization, wherein people generally pride themselves on their disinterest and willingness to sacrifice for the sake of the cause. The organization is overwhelmingly white (95%), male (85%), and concentrated in three states: New York (25%), California (19%), and Illinois (5%).[34] The organization has some 10,000 members in all 50 states and some foreign countries, 85% of them single (average age 38 years). Some 83% are college graduates and 45% have completed graduate or professional school. Consequently, income levels of the NGTF members tend to be much above average: 47% of the members earn more than $20,000 per year and 21% over $30,000. Except for the probable fact that there are large numbers of homosexuals among the members, the NGTF membership can only be described as part of the "establishment."

The future of the NGTF is very much in doubt. The leadership of Lucia Valeska may provide the stimulus it needs to continue as a viable institution. In the final analysis, however, the survival of the movement is contingent upon the acceptance of the homosexual ideology not by America's elites (to a great extent this has already been accomplished), but by the majority of the population. Other prohomosexual institutions—notably church-related organizations—may be far more important than the NGTF in reaching this goal.

ACADEMIC ORGANIZATIONS

The importance of schools in the promotion of ideas and social revolution is obvious. Education is not only the most powerful "business" from an economic point of view, but the educational establishment views itself as the depository of the national ethos and the privileged elite responsible for molding the future generations. As Ivan Illich has pointed out, in modern society the educational establishment believes it has the role, and acts in a manner similar to, the medieval church.[35] New ideas and practices are not "acceptable" until they are sanctioned by the intellectual establishment. Thus promoters of any new order must make their presence felt in academia if they hope to be successful. The alternative is relegation to the intellectual wilderness by the new gurus of secular humanism who make up the backbone of the educational elites. The homosexual movement has devoted considerable efforts to establishing an effective presence within academia. These efforts have paid off handsomely in terms of numbers, recognition, and influence.

The Homosexual Movement

We have already referred to the Gay Academic Union (GAU). The GAU, incorporated in New York for the "advancement of gay studies,"[36] is organized on the basis of local chapters. There are fully chartered units in Los Angeles, San Diego, San Francisco, Dallas, St. Louis, Chicago, Cincinnati, Greensboro, North Carolina, and Boston.[37] Three more chapters were in formation during the spring of 1981, in Minneapolis, Tempe, Arizona, and Washington, D.C.[38] These chapters seem to be well organized and active. The San Diego chapter, for example, has ten "semi-autonomous" special interest groups (SIGs), among them the Arts and Entertainment SIG, the Artists' SIG, Research and Education SIG, etc. It also maintains a scholarship fund.[39]

A central activity of the GAU is the promotion of the homosexual ideology on college campuses via university-based groups of homosexual students and faculty members. The very title of a publication of the GAU designed to accomplish this objective is quite revealing: "How to Infiltrate Your Own University: Organizing University and Para-University Gay Groups."[40] This manual was reportedly prepared with the advice of the American Civil Liberties Union.[41]

At the national level, the counterpart of the GAU is a project of the U.S. National Student Association—the National Gay Student Center in Washington, D.C.[42] Although the National Gay Student Center does not have the level of visibility the GAU enjoys, its influence cannot be underestimated. Nor can we ignore the influence of homosexual groups on college campuses. On the one hand, their very presence constitutes a source of confusion and pressure on certain students. In chapter III we saw this effect on the campus of Sarah Lawrence College. There is no reason to believe that a similar effect does not take place on other campuses, albeit on a reduced scale. Homosexual student organizations also channel student activism for the support of homosexuality. It has been pointed out that between one-half and one-third of local jurisdictions having prohomosexual legislation are college towns.[43] Funding is no problem for homosexual student organizations. As already stated, the National Gay Student Center is a project of the National Student Association. According to the former organization, "most homosexual groups have no problems with either recognition or funding."[44] The schools actually finance the prohomosexual activities of these groups from the student activity funds. It is doubtful that most students or their parents approve the use of their money for the promotion of sexual practices generally rejected as aberrant and destructive. Moreover, homosexual groups themselves admit that there is evidence of resistance to the funding of homosexual groups by colleges: "Furthermore, homophobia on campus is becoming more visible . . . and so homosexual groups don't always have clear sailing."[45]

There are many homosexual groups on American colleges and universities; they account for some twenty percent of all the homosexual organizations in the United States.[46] A listing of college-related homosexual organizations appears in the appendix, where it is apparent that almost every important campus features a homosexual group. The homosexual movement has thus succeeded in ensuring that the future American intellectual elite has been exposed to the homosexual ideology during its formative years.

At the elementary and secondary level, homosexuality is not promoted by the students themselves. However, homosexual teachers are well organized in certain areas of the country, including the following:[47]

Boston Area Gay and Lesbian School Workers	Boston, Mass.
Gay Educators Association	Denver, Colo.
Gay Teachers Coalition	San Francisco, Calif.
Gay Teachers of Los Angeles	Los Angeles, Calif.
Gay Teachers of Maryland	Baltimore, Md.
Gay Schoolworkers	Ann Arbor, Mich.
Gay Teachers Association	New York, N.Y.

According to the Gay Teachers Association of New York City, there are up to 10,000 homosexual teachers in New York City alone.[48] The following list of goals set forth by this organization reveals the way in which organized homosexual teachers promote their sexual proclivities.[49] (Cf. chap. III, section B(1).) Should these goals be accomplished, it would be much easier for homosexual actions and homosexuality itself to be accepted by students, administrations, and faculties alike:

1. To provide a setting in which gay teachers can meet, share problems and ideas, and give each other support.
2. To conduct continuous negotiations with the New York City Board of Education and the United Federation of Teachers to obtain contractual guarantees of the right of gay teachers to teach in the city's public schools.
3. To work for the retraining of school administrators, teachers, and guidance personnel to enable them to meet the needs of gay students for counseling and support.
4. To promote curriculum change in all subject areas to enable gay and nongay students to gain a realistic and positive concept of current gay lifestyles and the historic contributions of gay people.
5. To lobby as a teacher organization for the gay rights bill.

The reader is reminded that the "current gay lifestyles" mentioned in item 4 would logically involve transgenerational sex (i.e., child/adult sex), sadomasochism, homosexual prostitution, promiscuous sexual liaisons as seen in bars and baths, pornographic movie houses, and more. These practices not only seem to be intrinsic to the "current gay lifestyles" but

The Homosexual Movement

are verified by the most casual examination of the average homosexual newspaper. Thus it is reasonable to include these practices in the "current gay lifestyle." Item 4 basically proposes a revision of curricula across the board (i.e., in all subjects and grades) to make the schools promote homosexuality and clearly implies censorship of class materials to fit the ideology of the homosexual movement. It is at least questionable whether most parents would appreciate a curriculum that would help their children develop a "realistic and positive concept" of sadomasochism, homosexual prostitution, or man/boy love.

Although none of these goals has been fully achieved, some of what has been accomplished is encouraging from the viewpoint of the homosexual movement. For example, the United Federation of Teachers, the New York State United Teachers, and the Chancellor and the Office of Personnel of the New York City Board of Education have already made prohomosexual statements. The Gay Teachers Association has been recognized by *The New York Teacher,* "a newspaper received by every union-affiliated teacher in New York state."[50] Moreover, in its campaign to "educate" the public and promote the homosexual ideology, the Gay Teachers Association has formed a team of speakers "to talk to Parents' Associations, teacher-in-service courses, school boards," and others.

A parallel organization for librarians, who obviously have a great deal of influence on the intellectual formation of youth, is the Gay Task Force of the American Library Association (ALA), Social Responsibilities Round Table division. This organization "was launched in 1970 and was the first openly gay subgroup in a professional association."[51] The Task Force is quite active in promoting the homosexual ideology through libraries. By its own admission, GTA members "work to get more and better gay materials into libraries and out to users, and to deal with discrimination against gay people as librarians and library users."[52]

The preoccupation of the homosexual movement with the indoctrination of young people in the tenets of its ideology is evidenced by the activities of the Gay Task Force of the ALA. The program of the Task Force for the 1975 ALA conference, for example, was entitled "The Children's Hour: Must Gay Be Grim for Jane and Jim?" The subsequent publication of *Guidelines for Treatment of Gay Themes in Children and Young Adult Literature* is also significant. For the 1980 ALA Annual Conference, the following themes were scheduled in cooperation with the Gay Teachers Association of New York City:[54]

"Homophobe by Default? Examining Gay Information Deficiencies and Access in the Schools"
"Staff Support: Assisting Curriculum Areas and School Counseling Services"
"The Hidden Minority: Meeting the Needs of Lesbian and Gay Male Students"

"Anita Too? Intellectual Freedom Considerations in Providing Gay Materials in School Libraries."

The Task Force distributes bibliographies used by homosexual activists to ensure that publications favorable toward homosexuality are available in public libraries, including school libraries. Figure 2 is a reproduction of the "core collection list" recommended by the Task Force in 1980. As the reader can appreciate, none of the books presents homosexuality in a critical or objective fashion. Some of the publications, e.g., the *Gayellow Pages*, contain drawings which are highly sexually suggestive and would probably be found offensive by most library patrons. The Gay Task Force of the ALA is only one of several groups of homosexuals within professional associations, which maintain close relationships with academic institutions; that is why these so-called gay caucuses are mentioned here. In the strictly academic field, the Gay Caucus, National Council of Teachers of English, and the Gay Caucus for the Modern Languages have figured prominently in the affairs of their "parent organizations," from which they have gained official recognition. The collaboration offered to the homosexual movement by the National Council of Teachers of English (NCTE) has been much appreciated by the leadership of the homosexual group within the NCTE:

> In spite of a very narrow margin for approval of the Gay rights resolution passed at the 1976 NCTE convention, the organization—i.e., the NCTE and particularly its executive personnel, have cooperated very well with the Gay Caucus and the officially appointed Committee on the Concerns of Lesbians and Gay Males in the English Teaching Profession. We have had information booths and at least some space on the program at each of the last several conventions. An article on Homophobia in the Academy which I did the research for and Louie Crew wrote is soon to be published by *College English,* an official journal of the NCTE.[55]

This is probably a case of the leadership and bureaucracy of an organization ignoring the wishes and sensitivity of the membership.

The subject of the homosexual-sponsored session at the 1976 meeting of the NCTE reveals a preoccupation with the promotion of homosexuality through the schools not unlike that of previous organizations we have encountered: "Towards a Healthy Gay Presence in Textbooks and Classrooms in Secondary Schools and Colleges." The panelists who participated presented materials on "the unique and valuable perspective of lesbians as teachers," "ways in which teachers can work to correct the lack of information and the misinformation about Gay people in public school teaching and teaching materials," and "Greek pederastic values in education and the suppression of them in later educational systems."[56] A

Gay Materials Core Collection List
Revised 1980

Standard collection development tools such as H.W. Wilson's PUBLIC LIBRARY CATALOG have
failed to reflect publishing trends with respect to gay materials. So we offer this list
as a recommended core collection of non-fiction gay materials for small and medium size
public libraries. We think college libraries also will find this basic list useful.

BOOKS

Adair, Nancy and Casey Adair, editors. WORD IS OUT: STORIES OF SOME OF OUR LIVES. New
  Glide/Delta, 1978.
Berzon, Betty and Robert Leighton, editors. POSITIVELY GAY. Celestial Arts, 1979.
Brown, Howard. FAMILIAR FACES, HIDDEN LIVES: THE STORY OF HOMOSEXUAL MEN IN AMERICA TODAY.
  Harcourt Brace Jovanovich, 1976; Harvest.
Curry, Hayden and Denis Clifford. A LEGAL GUIDE FOR LESBIAN AND GAY COUPLES. Addison-
  Wesley, 1980.
Fairchild, Betty and Nancy Hayward. NOW THAT YOU KNOW: WHAT EVERY PARENT SHOULD KNOW ABOUT
  HOMOSEXUALITY. Harcourt Brace Jovanovich, 1979.
Hanckel, Frances and John Cunningham. A WAY OF LOVE, A WAY OF LIFE: A YOUNG PERSON'S
  INTRODUCTION TO WHAT IT MEANS TO BE GAY. Lothrop, Lee & Shepard (Morrow), 1979.
Jay, Karla and Allen Young, editors. AFTER YOU'RE OUT: PERSONAL EXPERIENCES OF GAY MEN AND
  LESBIAN WOMEN. Links, 1975; Pyramid.
Klaich, Dolores. WOMAN PLUS WOMAN: ATTITUDES TOWARD LESBIANISM. Simon and Schuster, 1974;
  Morrow.
Martin, Del and Phyllis Lyon. LESBIAN/WOMAN. Glide, 1972; Bantam.
McNeill, John J. THE CHURCH AND THE HOMOSEXUAL. Sheed Andrews & McMeel, 1976; Pocketbooks.
Richmond, Len with Gary Noguera, editors. THE NEW GAY LIBERATION BOOK. Ramparts, 1979.
Scanzoni, Letha and Virginia Ramey Mollenkott. IS THE HOMOSEXUAL MY NEIGHBOR? ANOTHER
  CHRISTIAN VIEW. Harper and Row, 1978.
Vida, Ginny, editor. OUR RIGHT TO LOVE: A LESBIAN RESOURCE BOOK. Prentice-Hall, 1978.
Weinberg, George. SOCIETY AND THE HEALTHY HOMOSEXUAL. St. Martins, 1972; Anchor.

PAMPHLETS AND DIRECTORIES

ABOUT COMING OUT. National Gay Task Force, 80 Fifth Ave., New York, N.Y. 10011, 25¢ plus
  SASE; also bulk rates.
A GAY BIBLIOGRAPHY. Gay Task Force, American Library Association, 6th edition March 1980.
  Selective non-fiction list of 563 books, articles, pamphlets, periodicals, directories,
  films. $1 prepaid from "Barbara Gittings--GTF" at address below; also quantity rates.
GAY CIVIL RIGHTS SUPPORT PACKET. Statements from groups in science, government, religion,
  health, etc. Natl. Gay Task Force, 80 Fifth Ave., New York, N.Y. 10011, $2.50 prepaid.
GAY RIGHTS PROTECTIONS IN U.S. AND CANADA. List of law changes, revised quarterly. Natl.
  Gay Task Force, 80 Fifth Ave., New York, N.Y. 10011, 25¢ plus SASE; also bulk rates.
GAYELLOW PAGES. Classified directory of gay/lesbian organizations, businesses and services
  in U.S. and Canada. Renaissance House, Box 292 Village Station, New York, N.Y. 10014,
  $8.50 prepaid. Also available, New York-New Jersey regional edition, $3.50 prepaid.
RELIGIOUS SUPPORT PACKET. List of churches, officials and groups in religion that support
  gay rights. Natl. Gay Task Force, 80 Fifth Ave., New York, N.Y. 10011, $3.00 prepaid.
TWENTY QUESTIONS ABOUT HOMOSEXUALITY. National Gay Task Force, 1978. National Gay Task
  Force, 80 Fifth Ave., New York, N.Y. 10011, $1.25 prepaid; also bulk rates.
WRITING TO CONGRESS. How to be effective in contacting representatives in Congress.
  Washington Office, Metropolitan Community Churches, 110 Maryland Ave. N.E., Suite 210,
  Washington, D.C. 20002, 1-4 copies, 25¢ each; 5-49 copies, 15¢ each; 50 copies $6.00.

**Gay Task Force, American Library Association (Social Responsibilities Round Table)
Box 2383, Philadelphia, PA 19103. Coordinator: Barbara Gittings (215) 471-3322.**

FIGURE 2
Collection of Pro-Homosexual Materials Recommended by a Unit of the
American Library Association.

Roman Catholic nun, Sister Diana Culbertson, O.P., of Kent State, presented a paper which "traced and explained misinterpretations of passages from Genesis and from Dante's *Inferno* which have been used to condemn homosexual people and homosexual behavior."[57]

Other organized groups of homosexuals within the various professional associations have been appearing as an integral part of the homosexual movement. The *Gayellow Pages* lists the Association of Gay Psychologists, the Caucus of Gay Public Health Workers, the Gay Nurses Alliance East, the Gay Nurses Alliance West, the Gay People in Medicine Task Force, the National Association of Gay Alcoholism Professionals, the National Caucus of Gay and Lesbian Counselors, and the National Lawyers Guild Gay Caucus. We have already encountered the National Coalition of Gay Sexually Transmitted Disease (STD) Services, and there are reports of organized groups of homosexuals among sociologists, anthropologists, historians, and the Gerontological Society.[58]

SERVICE ORGANIZATIONS

There are literally hundreds of organizations to satisfy the needs of homosexuals in a variety of service settings. Many are profit-making while others are nonprofit. In all major cities there are "dating services" of one sort or another which match homosexuals on the basis of their wishes and characteristics (including specific sexual needs) to maximize the probability of a "successful encounter." A very interesting and novel approach to the satisfaction of homosexual needs is that of the "Loving Brotherhood," "an international network of men interested in developing fulfilling relationships with other men."[59] The organization has some 500 members and was founded by Ralph Walker in August 1977. Mr. Walker is a New Jersey State educational institution professor (William Patterson College in Wayne, N.J.) who brings his "mate" Patrick to meet his students every semester "so he can also share openly with them in any way he wishes."[60] For a fee, members of the Loving Brotherhood receive a card, a button, a monthly newsletter with a membership list, and an invitation to attend a monthly male-only "Celebration of Life and Gathering" which takes place at the Barn, a facility located in rural northwestern New Jersey.[61]

This is just an example of a service provided to homosexuals for the satisfaction of one of their most basic needs: the wish to have intimate physical relations with persons of their own sex. There are many others. In some cases men are "matched" by computer. One interesting organization is San Francisco's "David the Matchmaker," which advertises "relationship-oriented personalized introductions" for homosexual males.[62]

The widespread promiscuity which characterizes the homosexual lifestyle results in physical and psychological maladies which require careful attention. In communities where there are substantial numbers of "lib-

The Homosexual Movement

erated" homosexuals, this need, and the increased self-consciousness which also characterizes the homosexual movement, has encouraged the formation of service organizations, switchboards, clinics, counseling centers, and so forth which specialize in serving homosexuals. Many of the organizations interviewed in our survey do offer these services. For example, typical self-descriptions of the services provided included:

> "Counseling, employment, legal services, sexually transmitted disease control, alcohol abuse prevention/treatment, information and referral."
> —Gay Center in California

> "Rehabilitation of lesbian drug addicts."
> —Gay Project in New York City

> "Mental health services, one-to-one counseling, group counseling, information, education."
> —Drug and Alcoholism Program, California

> "Counseling, referral, VD clinic."
> —Gay Community Center, Rhode Island

> "Referral, Counseling."
> —Gay Community Center, Ohio

> "Referrals."
> —Gay Switchboard, New York

> "Counseling, support groups, education, referrals, library."
> —Lesbian Alliance, Iowa

> "Resource Center, peer counseling."
> —Lesbian Resource Center, Washington

The number of services is so large that there are organizations of homosexual service providers. For example, the National Association of Gay Alcoholism Professionals (NAGAP) "is made up of counselors, nurses, social workers, psychologists, AA members, Al-Anon members, doctors, drug and alcohol agencies, organizations and institutes, as well as gay agencies and organizations all over the United States."[63] Organized on a local chapter basis, the NAGAP is nonprofit and tax-exempt. This organization has effectively infiltrated the most prestigious alcoholism education institution in the United States, the Rutgers Summer School of Alcohol Studies. In effect, the NAGAP has become part of the "Rutgers Team," responsible for a special program on homosexuality covering such issues as "homophobia, coming out and developing a positive identity, special problems of the gay or lesbian recovering alcoholic, clinical issues, and special issues of the gay and lesbian professional."[64] Through NAGAP, the homosexual movement has also been successful in penetrating a federal agency, the National Institute of Alcohol Abuse and Alcoholism (NIAAA).

THE HOMOSEXUAL NETWORK

In fact, a "homosexual seat" has been set aside for liaison between the NAGAP and the NIAAA's Advisory Council.[65] NAGAP serves homosexuals in other ways: it is also a network through which homosexuals can obtain both employment and sexual partners.[66]

There is no question that alcoholism is a major problem among homosexuals. This is borne out by the fact that there are countless groups of homosexual AA meetings across the United States. The numbers involved are so large that during Memorial Day weekend (1981), an International Advisory Council of Homosexual Men and Women in Alcoholics Anonymous was formally constituted in Boston.[67]

Alcoholism is a health problem within the homosexual community. However, it is probably much less serious than venereal diseases, the so-called STDs (sexually transmitted diseases). It has already been shown that the homosexual community can be accurately described as a reservoir of infection for the rest of society, and that there is an organization to represent the interests of the various centers providing services for the hundreds of thousands of homosexuals involved with venereal diseases or infestations (see in chapter II, "Illness and the Homosexual Subculture"). The National Coalition of Gay STD Services was established in 1979 in Chicago "by representatives from several of the nation's gay STD services and interested individuals: Chicago's Howard Brown Memorial Clinic, Milwaukee's Gay Peoples Union Venereal Disease Clinic, New York's Gay Men's Health Project and St. Mark's Clinic, Washington, D.C.'s Whitman-Walker Gay Men's Venereal Disease Clinic, and gay representatives (unaffiliated) from Denver and New Orleans."[68] This organization has established a very close relationship with the Center for Disease Control (CDC), a U.S. government agency.[69] This relationship is very beneficial to the homosexual movement in terms of recognition and funding. The coalition itself has reported that it serves as the vehicle through which the CDC receives information for the preparation of its VD research agenda. The control of this information is crucial in the allocation of public research funds. As happens in so many other areas of public funding, the recipients of the funds come to exercise a key role in the allocation of the funding. In this case, it is homosexual organizations that are involved in these activities.

In addition, the coalition provides educational services and propaganda in which the homosexual ideology is effectively promoted, makes available to its members technical information on VD and program management, and facilitates the process of funding by public funds for its members.

To provide a broader perspective on some of the services available within the homosexual communities, it is helpful to focus on two additional organizations: CALM, Inc. and the Lambda Resource Center for the Blind. A serious problem caused by the increased militancy of the homosexual movement and the progressive weakening of family structures is

168

the insistence of an increasing number of female homosexuals who have children to participate actively in the upbringing of their offspring and even to retain custody of them. (The factors behind this phenomenon are much too complicated to be discussed here, but probably include the decline of traditional religious values, the extreme mobility of American families, the change in expectations as they relate to economic reality, the interference of government at all levels in family life, and the acceptance of antifamily ideology by American elites, including the courts, feminist leaders, the educational establishment, etc.) For psychobiological reasons this problem is basically centered on female homosexuals, since the probability of male homosexuals having children is small when compared with that of their female counterparts. Inasmuch as children are presumed to be incapable of understanding the facts and making the distinctions which form the basis of guardianship decisions, the state has a paramount interest in deciding whether the home of a female homosexual is a fitting place for the rearing of her children. This is especially true whenever there is a promiscuous environment in the home, or even where the mother is engaged in a continuing relationship with only one other woman. Even in instances when the father (as the presumed normal partner) has abrogated his rights over the offspring, society is responsible for ensuring that the environment in which the children are reared is free from factors which result in permanent damage to their personalities. These concepts are hotly contested by the homosexual movement since its ideology presumes that the homosexual condition is not only not an illness but good and positive for those affected by it. Ideologically, this is an important battle, since one of the ways in which the "liberated" homosexual can assert his ideology is precisely by making society accept the concept that homosexual households are fit places for the rearing of children. From the point of view of traditional values and morality, this is absurd, since homosexual mothers are presumed to be unfit to take care of their children. The *Gayellow Pages* lists five "Parent Groups":

Custody Action for Lesbian Mothers (Philadelphia, Pa.)
Gay Parent Custody Fund (Denver, Colo.)
Gay Parents Legal and Research Group (Lynnwood, Wash.)
Gay Fathers Coalition (Washington, D.C.)
Lesbian Mothers National Defense Fund (Seattle, Wash.)

The first organization listed, CALM Inc., was founded in 1974 as the result of the experiences of a homosexual mother "threatened with the loss of her children. As the preparations for the case took place, she became aware that her story was not unique, and that her legal situation was extremely precarious."[70] The organization began as a center for collecting and disseminating information. Very soon, however, it started providing direct services, and it presently furnishes a volunteer (herself a homosexual mother) to clients with the specific purpose of ensuring that their children remain under the control of the homosexual mother. The organization has the following features:

> is a free legal counseling service,
> has volunteer lawyers who will argue your [i.e., the homosexual mother's] case,
> offers psychological support throughout the entire process,
> protects your [i.e., the homosexual mother's] privacy in and out of court.[71]

Probably the most important component of this service is the provision of moral support for the client. The concept of a "homosexual mother" is so alien to our culture and so repugnant to what most people have concluded to be the natural order—not only biological, but social as well—that a woman who starts practicing homosexuality and becomes involved with another woman to the point of rejecting her husband, or even one who rejects her husband without having a specific female sexual partner in mind, will find very little sympathy or support outside the homosexual movement or the circles in which its ideology has become fully accepted. The role of another person who supports the homosexual mother throughout the process can be crucial in ensuring that she pursues her goal to the very end: "The presence of another woman at the meetings between lawyer and client helps to reduce the tension at both ends. The issue of sexual orientation which must be discussed can leave the mother feeling exposed and embarrassed, and the attorney uncomfortable."[72]

Another case of an organization providing unique nationwide services on behalf of homosexuals is Chicago's Lambda Resource Center for the Blind (LRCB), an organization launched in 1980 with the active cooperation of the Catholic Guild for the Blind.[73] Affiliated with Gay Horizons, Inc., a homosexual counseling center, LRCB provides braille and radio materials of interest to blind homosexuals. A particular service is the reproduction of homosexual books on casettes for distribution at minimum cost. The organization has casettes of many books that promote the homosexual ideology, including John Boswell's *Christianity, Social Tolerance and Homosexuality;* K. J. Dover's *Greek Homosexuality;* Jay and Young's *Lavender Culture;* Don Clark's *Loving Someone Gay;* and Lande Humphreys' *Out of the Closet.* It is particularly revealing that both *The Joy of Gay Sex* and *The Joy of Lesbian Sex* have been recorded. In their printed versions, these are extremely detailed and profusely illustrated guides to homosexual love-making.[74]

The LRCB maintains close relationships with the Gay Task Force of the American Library Association and seems to enjoy the universal support of the various components of the homosexual movement. A little over a year old at this writing, its accomplishments are a witness to the strength and resourcefulness of the homosexual movement. The existence of such a specialized service and its ability to draw support from a wide variety of sources also indicate the sophistication of the movement.

The problem of custody rights for homosexual parents is only one of the many legal problems "liberated" homosexuals can encounter. Other organizations—some of them basically lawyers in private practice—aim to take care of such problems as "palimony" (legal consequences of the breakup of a "gay union"), homosexual couples desiring to hold property in common, legal consequences arising out of the discharge of homosexuals from the armed forces, and others. In areas where the homosexual movement is strong, organizations providing these services exist and freely advertise in the homosexual press.

OTHER ORGANIZATIONS

The homosexual movement is a complex phenomenon, and the organizations through which it acts reflect the almost infinite variety of human needs and concerns. Except for their common desire to satisfy their sexual appetites by entering into intimate physical relations with members of their own sex, homosexuals outwardly have little else in common. The ideology of the movement, to which liberated homosexuals subscribe essentially as a matter of sheer social and psychological survival, is an intellectual superstructure designed to satisfy the political needs of the movement while supporting its members. Such an ideology favors the multiplicity of groups within the movement, since it demands promotion within all structures of society which are not incompatible per se with homosexuality. (When an organization, e.g., churches and other religious groups, is incompatible with the practice of homosexuality, the ideology itself demands that such an organization be turned around and "converted" into a supporter of the practice.) The variety of homosexual organizations, even at the national level, is so great that it is not possible to describe or catalogue them all. Exclusive of religious organizations—to be examined elsewhere in this work—and the types of organizations we have already seen, there is a wide variety of other groups whose common aim is the promotion of homosexuality. Some of these will be described in order to provide a proper perspective on the true nature of the homosexual movement.

Some of the most important prohomosexual organizations are the more than 100 groups of parents and friends of homosexuals across the United States. These groups have their common origin in the Parents of Lesbians and Gay Men, Inc., founded in New York City in the early 1970s, which is at this writing a not-for-profit corporation.[75] In 1979 the National Federation of Parents of Gays was founded in Washington, D.C., during a convention of its member organizations; a second national convention was planned for Los Angeles in mid-1981.

The importance of these organizations cannot be underestimated, since their existence and activities strike at the very root of family life as it has been traditionally conceived in the United States. Together with religion, the family has been at the forefront in defending the value of male/female relations as part of the natural order and proclaiming the intrinsic disorder of all other relations as inimical to the good order of family and society. The parents of homosexuals traditionally deplored the condition that affected their children, expressing shame and disgust at their "perverse" choices. By its nature, this organization advocates the homosexual ideology by having some of these very parents support, applaud, and express pride in their children's heretofore evil tendencies.

There are three basic purposes for the group. First and foremost, it offers emotional support for parents and other relatives of homosexuals. It must be noted, however, that this is done in the context of the homosexual ideology. Any counselor or minister would help a person, in this case the relative of a homosexual, cope with the situation that causes pain and/or confusion. Parents of Gays does not limit itself to convincing the relatives of homosexuals that the condition of their loved ones is "natural to them," but insists that they support and be proud of them. The brochure of the Washington, D.C., group expresses it in this way: "In our group, we often speak (and we're only half-kidding) of the day when, instead of the parents' saying: 'Where did we go wrong?' they will say 'Where did we go right!' [sic] Once Mom and Dad begin to understand homosexuality, the feeling that it is a tragic condition that they are responsible for is rather quickly dispelled."[76] This is only a fancy way of getting parents to say "Gay is Good."

Second, Parents of Gays is also political and a lobbying organization which, in various degrees, works through the political process (e.g., voting, demonstrating) and by lobbying (writing letters to legislators, visiting them, contacting them by telephone) to modify our sociopolitical organization in a manner consonant with the homosexual ideology.[77] A third purpose of the organization is to influence public opinion by public speaking, the use of the media, and other communications aimed at making America more acceptant of homosexuality. This promotional component is most important for the movement, since the image of ostensibly heterosexual parents approving and showing pride in the homosexuality of their children is bound to create considerable anxiety and confusion among the rest of the population, especially among parents who accept traditional family values but are faced with the possibility that one of their children is affected by homosexuality.

That the goals of the National Federation of Parents and Friends of

The Homosexual Movement

Gays are identical with those of the homosexual movement in general is evident in a speech by Adele Starr, a representative of the organization and herself the mother of a homosexual, at the White House Conference on Families: "We ask for an Executive Order and Proclamation to prevent further discrimination in housing, employment, in government institutions like the Immigration and Naturalization Service and the branches of the armed services. We ask for sensitivity and understanding in educational programs wherever it is needed."[78] Thus the legal and educational systems must be made to conform with the homosexual ideology.

The activities of the various "Parents of Gays" groups are as varied as the talents and interests of their members will allow. They demonstrate, lecture, lobby, pressure public officials, write letters to newspaper editors, and talk to other parents when they are most vulnerable—i.e., at the height of their emotional turmoil—about "accepting and being proud" of their child's sexual proclivities. Their basic propaganda item is *About Our Children*, a short and attractive pamphlet summarizing the essence of the homosexual ideology. *About Our Children* is available in English, Spanish, Chinese, Japanese, and French.[79]

Homosexual organizations exist on a variety of bases: ethnic, age, professional, sexual proclivities, and others. The International Union of Gay Athletes, for example, purportedly represents homosexual college-level varsity athletes, claiming a membership of well over 1,000 in six countries.[80] The perception of the athlete as a heterosexual "jock" is clearly under attack by the existence of this organization. It is easy to see how members of such a group would create considerable confusion in the minds of male adolescents who have learned to identify their prowess in sports with their self-perception of heterosexuality.

Many homosexual organizations have been created around the peculiar sexual needs of their members; from these we have chosen Black and White Men Together, the Eulenspiegel Society, the North American Man/Boy Love Association, and the Rene Guyon Society as representative of the choices available to homosexuals with specialized sexual needs.

It is apparent that the racial disharmony affecting certain segments of American society has not escaped the homosexual community. To remedy this situation, Black and White Men Together (BWMT) was founded in San Francisco in January 1980, ostensibly "to promote interracial friendship and understanding."[81] The organization has grown at an accelerated rate, with thirty independent chapters in the United States, England, Canada, and Australia by mid-1981. The activities by which BWMT attracts members include those shown in Table 13, which in some instances appear to relate to the attraction certain homosexuals feel across ethnic boundaries.

The Eulenspiegel Society involves people whose interests are in the areas of sadomasochism and/or dominant/submissive sexuality. Founded

TABLE 13

Activities: "Black and White Men Together"

Type of Activity	Examples
Local	Events hosted by BWMT groups.
	Social: parties, dances, picnics, informal get-togethers, trips to BWMT groups in other cities.
	Support: rap groups, newsletters, interracial discussion.
	Special: theatre-going, music, book clubs, sports, outdoors.
Features	Annual Convention. Action Fund. Special news items, interviews.
Couples	Actual dialogues with interracial couples, exploring relationships.
Letters	Readers all over the world: Black men, White men, others, sharing feelings, ideas.
Newsletter Ads	Section for Black men, White men, others to meet, correspond, make new friends.
	• hundreds of personal ads
	• free for subscribers
	• direct contact; many with phone numbers

SOURCE: Promotional brochure of Black and White Men Together, San Francisco, undated.

in 1971, the organization accepts as members both heterosexuals and homosexuals provided they agree to, and act in a manner consistent with, the principles of the organization. The basic principle of the Eulenspiegel Society is "sexual liberation," meaning the acceptance of purely subjective standards in social conduct, provided that the principle of "mutual consent" is respected.

The society's creed, reprinted below in its entirety, is not only a theoretical statement of belief, but also a political program of sexual revolution and a code of behavior based on a comprehensive and consistent moral system. The basic *inconsistency* it manifests—and this flaw is common to all forms of subjectivism and scepticism—is its inability to answer the critical question: If each person is to determine his own standard of behavior according to his own way, what determines the propriety of this way when it interferes with someone else's way? Another way of posing the same question is by a radical critique of mutual consensuality as the exception to the rule of pure subjectivity. Is this a matter of principle or convenience? If principle, why is it to prevail over the "right" to pursue joy and happiness in one's own way? If convenience, there is obviously no basis for the principle of subjectivity. Rather than a principle, it becomes an excuse to justify the pursuit of one's inclinations and desires without reference to rationality.

The Eulenspiegel Society's "creed" speaks for itself:

The Eulenspiegel Society is a not-for-profit corporation which began as an informal association in the winter of 1971. We support sexual liberation as a

The Homosexual Movement

basic requirement of a truly free society. Our special concern is freedom for sexual minorities and particularly the rights of those whose sexuality embraces S/M, or dominant/submissive fantasies and urges. These rights have largely been denied through negative public attitudes, internalized to a great extent by those possessing such inclinations themselves. We assert the following rights for all:

1. The right to pursue joy and happiness in one's own way, according to one's evolving nature, as long as this doesn't infringe on the similar rights of others.
2. The right to define oneself, and not be defined by persons whose experiences have not provided them with the understanding to appreciate one's mystique, nor by those whose repressed urges may panic them into rigid hostility toward it.
3. The right freely to communicate and socialize with others of similar sexual orientation, and to explore together the deeper, positive meaning of our experiences.
4. The right to challenge established value systems which oppress by condemning and repressing sexual drives or practices of erotic minorities.
5. The right to publicize activities and views—freely, without fear of occupational or professional repercussion—thereby raising the consciousness of both the public and ourselves regarding sexual minorities and sexual freedom.

To realize these rights, we seek to foster consciousness-raising and understanding among our members and the public at large through public forums and workshops on S/M, advertising, dissemination of Society publications and literature, by providing speakers for all forms of media, colleges and other audiences, and by giving support to other sexual liberation movements.

Most of all, we extend to our brothers and sisters who may be, as we once were, isolated, repressed and frustrated, the word that they are not alone, that a Society exists for them—Straight, Gay and Bisexual, all working together, with understanding and warmth, against misunderstandings and stereotypes, for freedom and fulfillment.[82]

The subjects announced for discussion in several of the society's meetings during the first part of 1981 further clarify the interests of its members:[83]

April 27—Dominant/Submissive Sex and the Transsexual
May 4—Unique Problems of Male Masochists
May 18—Tatooing and Dominant/Submissive Sex
May 25—Monogamy and Polygamy in Dominant/Submissive Sex
June 1—Why is Humiliation a Turn On?
June 8—Transvestites and Dominant/Submissive Sex
June 29—How to Conduct a Scene with a Beginning Masochist.

On other occasions, there are film and exhibit nights, for which the following description is offered: "BONDAGE AND TOYS and the D/S [Dominant/Submissive Sex] FILM NIGHT AND ART EXHIBIT are programs for displaying, demonstrating and/or swapping your S/M toys, draw-ings, photographs or other items. No prior arrangements are required of exhibitors, but they should arrive early. We must stress that the program's success depends upon you."[84]

The rejection of traditional values by the society, expressed theoreti-cally in its creed, is apparent not only in the subject matters for discussion at its meetings, but even in the titles of some of its affairs. One of its newsletter columns is "Deviant Data." The same publication refers to another column titled "Perverse Perspectives." The society's tenth an-niversary party was announced as "Getting-Together-From-All-Over Perverts Party and D/S DecaDance."

Although for obvious reasons the homosexual movement rejects the notion that its organizations and "liberated" homosexuals are interested in children as sexual objects or are any sort of threat to their autonomous sexual development, we have already seen evidence that this is not en-tirely accurate. Although not all active homosexuals seem to have or want to have relations with children, the existence of child-centered pornog-raphy ("kiddie porn") and very young homosexual child prostitutes, as well as a number of instances in which homosexuals have been convicted of seducing children, are clear indications that for a substantial number of homosexuals, children are the sexual object of choice. In the language of homosexuality, *chicken* and *hawk* refer to the young people and their adult sexual partners. The existence of such terms—and probably others as well—is also a clear indication that homosexual pedophilia (also called pederasty) is a widespread phenomenon.

The promotion of sexuality for children is certainly not limited to the homosexual movement. The modern sexual liberation ideology in con-temporary America has reached the logical conclusion of its premises and advocated not only unrestricted sex, but also sex for children, pornog-raphy, and incest. Homosexuals who are attracted to children welcome these developments, since they provide a rationale for their sexual incli-nations and practices. "Sexual liberation" legitimizes pederasty.

The best-known organization of pederasts is the North American Man/ Boy Love Association (NAMBLA), which has been mentioned. NAMBLA was founded in 1978 at a Boston conference on Man/Boy Love And The Age of Consent.[85] The organization has held a number of conferences (New York City, March '79; Baltimore, October '79; New York City, June '80; Boston, December '80) for the purpose of exchanging information, providing support for pederasts, and enabling them to meet one another. NAMBLA is organized on a chapter basis with active groups in New York, Boston, Philadelphia, Toronto, New Jersey, Connecticut, and Portland. By May 1981 pederasts were also organizing in California (Los Angeles/ San Francisco), the Midwest (including Michigan, northern Ohio, and

Indiana), and Montreal.[86] Between conferences, there is a national steering committee that runs the organization.

NAMBLA's activities include the publication of three periodicals: the *NAMBLA Bulletin*, the *NAMBLA News*, and the NAMBLA *Journal*. The organization's Prisoner Support Committee supports imprisoned homosexuals who have been convicted of child molestation or other related crimes. The NAMBLA Emergency Defense Fund, to which all members are supposed to contribute 1% of their annual incomes, is utilized to defray the legal expenses of child molesters when they find themselves in trouble with the law.[87] In addition, NAMBLA is a regular participant in homosexual marches and other events having the active support of the movement. NAMBLA members, for example, marched on the Pentagon with other homosexuals in a March 3, 1981, demonstration against American support for the people of El Salvador in their struggle against Communism. The core issue for NAMBLA, however, is the homosexual affection of men for boys. This is clearly expressed in the official statement of its philosophy and goals.

The North American Man/Boy Love Association (NAMBLA) is an organization founded in response to the extreme oppression of men and boys involved in consensual sexual and other relationships with each other. Its membership is open to all individuals sympathetic to man/boy love in particular and sexual freedom in general. NAMBLA is strongly opposed to age of consent laws and other restrictions which deny adults and youth the full enjoyment of their bodies and control over their lives. NAMBLA's goal is to end the long-standing oppression of men and boys involved in any mutually consensual relationship by:

1) building a support network for such men and boys;
2) educating the public on the benevolent nature of man/boy love;
3) alligning [sic] with the lesbian, gay, and other movements for sexual liberation; and,
4) supporting the liberation of persons of all ages from sexual prejudice and oppression.

This statement concludes with NAMBLA's postal address, for use by those interested in finding out more about its activities.

The Rene Guyon Society concentrates on all aspects of child sexuality, advocating the most radical changes in our legal system to actually make it possible for adults to provide sexual stimulation for virtually all children. Founded in 1962 under the inspiration of Dr. Rene Guyon, a lawyer/psychologist associated with Sigmund Freud, the Society has some 5,000 sympathizers nationwide. The main purpose of the organization is to convince the public that all laws controlling nonconsensual sex must be abolished. By demystifying sexuality, the society argues, some of the effects of repressed sexuality will disappear. In a certain sense, the ideology of the Rene Guyon Society substitutes repressed sexuality for the traditional concept of original sin; thus it expects that a number of social ills will disappear with the unfettering of sexuality.

Table 14, extracted from the society's promotional package, is a summary of the revisions to the California Penal Code proposed by the Rene Guyon Society. *The reader is cautioned that this chart and the rest of this section include material which some people will find offensive.* It is reproduced here to allow readers to have a more complete understanding of the homosexual movement.

TABLE 14

Penal Code Revision Sought by The Rene Guyon Society

		Reasons	
		Particular	Overall
HOMOSEXUALITY Anal Copulation (PC 286)	*We suggest:* Allow child-child and child-adult if a male rubber is used when one male is under 18.	Makes child aware of anal V.D. and its prevention.	Part of the natural progress of development to heterosexuality
Oral Copulation (PC 288a)	Delete section.	Trains for heterosexuality. No data exists showing that any harm is done.	
HETEROSEXUALITY Penis-Vagina Copulation (PC 261.1)	Under 18, require a male rubber and a vaginal foam used simultaneously; allow child-child and child-adult.	Prevents VD and pregnancy. Older person passes on tender, loving mannerisms.	Lack of premarital sex leads to divorce, drug abuse, crime, and suicide.
Masturbation of Child (PC 288 & PC 288.1)	Delete sections	Parents and nonparents help a child toward good mental health by masterbating it or encouraging it to masturbate.	

The proposals in Table 14 are amplified by the following explanations for each of the items proposed, as provided by the Rene Guyon Society:

The Homosexual Movement

ANAL COPULATION

At age 4, and sometimes sooner, both male and female children *want*, can easily hold after massage, and will be allowed to have a teenager or older male's, condom-cover penis in their anus. Tiny children will be required to wear a small "finger stall" or "finger cot" (obtainable from a drug store) condom from age 4 or any earlier age that they start penetrating male and female anuses. 99% of the day there is no fecal matter in the anus. No enema is required.

ORAL COPULATION

At age 4, and sometimes sooner, both male and female children *want*, can easily hold, and will be allowed to have a tiny child, teenager, or older male's penis in their mouth. This will bring an end to thumbsucking. The child will at last get valuable hormones that appear in the mature male's ejaculate that have been denied children in the past. Very young, teenage and adult females will be allowed to provide sexual satisfaction with their mouths and tongues to the penis and clitoris of young children.

PENIS-VAGINA COPULATION

At age 10, 11 or 12, females *want*, can easily hold, and will be allowed to have a teenager or older male's condom-covered penis in their vagina. From the earliest age of desire, a very young female will be allowed to have a tiny male's penis in her vagina if the penis is covered with a "finger stall" or "finger cot" (obtainable from a drug store). At all ages prior to age 18 for the female, the female is required to have vaginal foam inserted before penetration of the covered penis.

MASTURBATION

No restrictions will be on the masturbation of a child so that such enjoyment will be provided by family, friends, or neighbors so that the child will no longer seek out strangers for this satisfaction (self-masturbation, from crib age on, not to be discouraged).

NUDITY ALONE WITH NO SEXUAL ACTIONS

No restrictions; thus freeing Law Enforcement to tackle disease-spreading and unwanted-pregnancy activity and photos. Almost all American children have seen an erect adult penis and an adult spread-eagle vagina or pictures thereof.[89]

It would be a mistake to think that this group is inconsequential. Undeniably, the specific goals and objectives of the group cannot be fully achieved until other more pressing objectives are reached (e.g., "gay rights," legal homosexual marriage, the general acceptance of the homosexual ideology, etc.); thus the group is not in the mainstream of the movement. On the other hand, the specific proposals and ideology of the Guyon Society (as well as those of NAMBLA and the Eulenspiegel Society) are perfectly compatible with the moral subjectivism and the pansexualism that characterize the homosexual movement. Once the initial objectives of the movement are implemented, more "refined" objectives like those of the Rene Guyon Society and NAMBLA would be the next in line for proposal. With acceptance of the main tenets of the homosexual ideology, what might now look like sheer lunacy and perversion would become merely "avant garde."

Economic Power

One aspect of the movement that is often ignored is the economic power at the disposal of homosexuals and homosexual-related businesses and organizations. In a sense, the homosexual community has locked itself into permeable social boundaries. While it provides practically every service (sexual and otherwise) that homosexuals need, its members in many cases enjoy the flexibility of obtaining certain services outside their own community. The tendency within the movement, however, is to stress the need for homosexuals to do business with homosexuals. According to a member of the National Gay Task Force, "I can get my windows washed by a gay person, get my television repaired, do anything, and never see a straight person again."[90] Dr. Kenneth Unger, a Greenwich Village physician, has reportedly asserted that "I speak the same language as my patients. . . . It is something I believe in. . . . The gay community can do best by buying gay."[91]

The economic power of the homosexual community can be measured by the purchasing power of the homosexuals and by the sales or income of homosexual businesses and organizations. In either case, the movement can be shown to have an enormous economic potential at its disposal. This has obvious repercussions in terms of the homosexual movement's ability to impose its ideology on the rest of the nation, and evidently it is a force to be reckoned with by people who believe in traditional family values.

For all the hue and cry that homosexuals are an oppressed minority, there is no sense in which they can be compared with ethnic minorities, which have traditionally been at the lowest end of the economic ladder. In 1977 a survey was conducted by Walker & Struman Research, Inc. of Los Angeles on behalf of *The Advocate*, sampling 73,000 readers. *Business Week*, summarizing the results of the survey, indicated "that income for the average gay household of 1.4 persons is $23,600, about 50% above the national average; that 79% of the readers use commercial airlines for an average of nearly four trips a year; that more than 80% own at least one car; and that 80% order drinks by brand names. Seventy percent are college graduates, 97% are employed, and 84% are regular voters—about double the national average."[92] Another study conducted by Walker and

The Homosexual Movement

Struman Research, on readers of the November 15, 1980, issue of *The Advocate* revealed a median annual household income of $30,000; 68% of the readers of this homosexual publication answering the survey questionnaire were professionals or managers. The level of education was also much above the national average (28% had completed graduate school and 64% were college graduates). Other data of the same study portray readers of *The Advocate* as economically affluent and financially more secure than the rest of the population by almost any index.[93] A Los Angeles study indicated the probability that 19% of all spendable income in the United States is in the hands of homosexuals.[94]

A travel agency that offers tours "for men" to places ranging from "the Grand Canyon to Machu Picchu" has some 20,000 names of homosexuals in its card file. It has been reported that 25% of its $1.5 million annual gross derives from these specialized services. In 1977 it was reported that the 5,000-member Club Gypsy Feet, founded in 1969, grossed $135,000 per year.[95] This club reportedly had an additional mailing list of 5,000 persons in the New York City metropolitan area alone. An annual homosexual cruise, the High Sea Islanders, reportedly grossed up to $300,000.[96]

There are several other indicators that homosexuals are a class with considerable clout:

- A wealthy New York homosexual—still "in the closet" when his opinions were recorded—has estimated that in New York City alone homosexuals control as much as $20 billion dollars (1977).[97] In 1981 dollars, the figure is probably closer to $30 billion.
- Neil Bogart, president of the company which owns Casablanca records, estimated that in 1977 homosexuals comprised 25% of the $4 billion disco market.[98]
- *Blueboy* magazine, which features pictures of nude men and articles—sometimes sexually explicit—of interest to homosexuals, possesses a list of 400,000 homosexuals. The readers of the magazine have been found to fit the following description:

  The *Blueboy* reader is a man between the ages of 25 and 40, with an annual income of between $15,000 and $24,949. He has a college degree and has completed some graduate work. He carries up to five major credit cards, owns a car (a Chevrolet or Ford), and takes two to three vacations yearly. He smokes, drinks beer, liquor, wine, and/or champagne, usually by brand. He spends between $500 and $1,000 on clothing each year, the same figure he spends to purchase his color television and high-fidelity, camera, and tape equipment. He is very well groomed, using skin toners, lotions, and hair rinses, as well as the usual toiletries.[99]

In 1977 *Blueboy* sold 135,000 copies nationally and readership was estimated to be over 800,000. At the present time, there are many magazines similar to *Blueboy*. The total readership is much larger.

- At the height of the prohomosexual campaign in Florida (1977), the movement raised over $300,000 to support the implementation of its ideology in that state alone.[100]
- In 1965 the Club Bath Chain was founded by an enterprising homosexual in Cleveland. The initial investment—in an already existing sauna-bath—was $15,000. Today Club Bath remains a model of homosexual entrepreneurship, a highly successful chain comprising over forty establishments where homosexuals go to satisfy their sexual appetites.[101]
- The *Blade*, Washington's homosexual newspaper, has grown from a one-page mimeographed handbill to a regular forty-page publication with 20,000-circulation editions.[102] Like other homosexual newspapers, it carries considerable advertising, including non–sex-related items.
- Major corporations advertise in homosexual periodicals. They include not only the entertainment industry, but also banks, beer manufacturers, travel concerns, etc.
- There are hundreds of members in the homosexually oriented Golden Gate Business Association. The nature and variety of the homosexual business community in San Francisco is revealed in the following report by Joe Flower in *San Francisco* magazine:

It is four o'clock on a Sunday afternoon. Trinity Place, a little side canyon among the financial canyons downtown, is blocked off. Halfway along, marked only by a lantern over the door, is Trinity Place, the cavernous, two-story gay hideaway watering hole. The tribes have already begun to gather. Pure Trash and the Bottom Line Dancers are setting up. It's party time for the GGBA 500. The Golden Gate Business Association, the City's gay Chamber of Commerce, is welcoming its 500th member. (Earlier, when I mention this to a skeptical neighbor, he asks, "Can there be 500 hair salons and antique stores in San Francisco?" We checked the most recent GGBA buying guide and found only six hair salons and three antique shops. On the other hand, we found 19 lawyers, 13 contractors, 11 printing firms, two dozen real estate firms, four savings and loan associations—Atlas, Continental, Fidelity, and United Federal—and such corporate members as Holiday Inn and United California Bank).[103]

Never does the truth of the expression "money talks" become more obvious than when banks and major hotel chains join ranks under an umbrella rejected by the rest of society.

The economic power of the homosexual community can also be analyzed from the perspective of the homosexual establishments. This presents serious difficulties, however, since there is not one comprehensive list of businesses who acknowledge their "sexual preference" in a way that places them unmistakably within the homosexual community. There are probably many degrees of self-identification with homosexuality in myriad commercial or service establishments, from the baths where only homosexuals are admitted, to a local laundromat managed and frequented by homosexuals but which other persons also utilize freely. The approach we will follow instead will be to analyze briefly four types of services which cater primarily to homosexuals and to try to develop a reasonable figure indicative of the total sales volume/income of the businesses involved. In some cases hard data have been utilized; in others, information has been sought from some of the individuals/businesses offering the services. Finally, estimates have been made when no data were available. Whenever 1977 data have been utilized, a factor of 1.46 has been applied to account for inflation (10% compounded for four years).

The first type of business we will examine is the *homosexual bar*. The *Gayellow Pages* lists 1,913 bars. There is no way of knowing exactly how many bar owners did not submit information to this publication, and there are a number of bars which are "gay" only part of the day (e.g., in Washington, D.C., there are a number of bar/restaurants which cater to the general population for lunch, but where only homosexuals congregate during evening hours). It is not unreasonable to assume that one bar is missing for each one listed, which would bring their total number to 3,826. According to the U.S. Bureau of the Census, in 1977 there were 70,886 bars in the United States with a total yearly sales volume of $6,901,388,000.[104] (This figure excludes bars "without payroll," where only family members work, and such membership clubs as the Knights of Columbus, Veterans of Foreign Wars, Elks, etc.)

The sales volume per bar in 1977 was thus $97,359. The comparable figure for 1981, after factoring inflation, is $142,144. Using this as the mean sales volume of homosexual bars, their total sales volume can be estimated at $543,843,000. Homosexual bars are 5.40% of the total number of bars in the United States. Considering that all homosexuals do not drink, that of those who drink many probably never go to homosexual bars, and that homosexual bars cater almost exclusively to homosexuals, the 5.40% figure is remarkably high. With a total take of over $500,000,000 for the homosexual bar business alone, there is much at stake in the preservation and encouragement of homosexuality as an open lifestyle.

Another business that appears to be very prosperous is that of the *homosexual bath*. The *Gayellow Pages* lists 168 homosexual baths nationwide. Assuming that some are not listed—and a comparison between actual advertisements in the homosexual press and the *Gayellow Pages* does show that some baths are missing from the latter—it is reasonable to assume some 200 baths nationwide. By calling various baths it has been established that their prices are ten dollars for rooms and five dollars for lockers. Assuming that three times as many clients rent lockers as rent rooms, and that on the average there are fifty clients per day (a very conservative figure representing some two clients per hour), the volume of sales for rentals per bath-year amounts to $114,062. Applying a 20% factor to account for other sales (refreshments, sadomasochist equipment,

pornographic materials, etc.), the total sales per bath-year can be estimated at $136,874. The total sales volume for the industry nationwide is
at least $27,374,800. For an industry that started in 1965 with a $15,000
investment, the homosexual baths are doing well indeed.

The third type of homosexual service to be analyzed is that of *homosexual prostitution*, which requires an estimate of the total number of
homosexual prostitutes. Although hard data in this regard are difficult to
obtain, a reasonable estimate is within the realm of possibility. It was
reported in 1977 that some 750 boys under 18 years of age were engaged
in prostitution in Denver, charging between $10 and $25 a "trick."[105] If
we assume half as many over-18 prostitutes, the total number in Denver
alone would be 1,125. *The Advocate* carries advertisements for "escort
services," sometimes 400 per issue. There are "model" or "escort" services
which cater to homosexuals in all major cities. One of the services in
Washington alone advertises a stable of twenty-five "male masseurs and
escorts" who provide "nude encounters and mutual massage" for the
appropriate fee. The Washington *Blade* regularly carries personal advertisements by some twenty of these individuals (at times two or three work
solo or in group sessions). Calls to several individuals and agencies revealed that the average price per encounter fluctuates between forty-five
and sixty-five dollars per hour, with several discounts offered for multiple-
hour deals and at "slow" hours (i.e., mornings). We found the average to
be fifty dollars per hour. An agency advertisement for the recruitment of
the "models" reads:

> No experience is necessary to work for [name of agency] and steadily make
> hundreds of dollars per week. We are the most professionally run agency in
> the city with the best dressed and most handsome male staff in this area. You
> can come by our offices in Georgetown for an interview any evening except
> Thursdays. Warning: No pot or drugs. We currently have openings for ages
> 18 to 34 who are clean, neat, friendly and good looking. Our models go out to
> male clients only—between 6 p.m. and 3 a.m. to their private homes. Appli-
> cants should call [telephone number] after 6:30 p.m. and ask for [name of
> person] which is busy only when another applicant is on the line. (Clients
> [telephone number] after 6.)[106]

This agency charges clients $50 per hour or $150 per evening. To make
three hundred dollars per week (a conservative figure), and assuming that
the agency retains 50% of the sales for administrative costs, overhead,
home-base personnel, and as profit, the "model" would have to engage
in twelve encounters per week or stay with clients for four complete
evenings (or any combination thereof). For the purpose of analysis, we
will utilize forty dollars as the average a homosexual prostitute realizes
per encounter for himself or his "agent," and twelve encounters per week
as an average per prostitute. Some perhaps can work harder, but it is

probable that certain forms of venereal disease, weather factors, and inherent biological limitations make twelve a reasonable figure.

The number of homosexual prostitutes in the Denver Standard Metropolitan Statistical Area (SMSA) per one million inhabitants in 1977 (population 1,464,000) can be estimated at 768.4. The total population residing in SMSAs and SCSAs (aggregates of contiguous SMSAs) of over one million inhabitants, according to the 1980 Statistical Abstract of the United States, was 91,867,000 (1978 population). In order to estimate the total number of homosexual prostitutes in the United States, we have assumed that the Denver SMSA proportion applies to SMSAs and SCSAs of over one million inhabitants and ignores the rest of the population. This assumption is extremely conservative for the following reasons.

First, Denver is not known to be an area of unusual homosexual activity. The same weight has been given to Denver as to New York, Boston, San Francisco or Los Angeles. Rural areas, where presumably there is a much smaller incidence of socially disruptive homosexual prostitution due to community pressures, other urban centers such as Rochester, Syracuse, Honolulu, Memphis, Hartford, Oklahoma City, Omaha, Sacramento, Reno, Las Vegas, and areas with fewer than one million inhabitants have not been counted. In fact, less than 50% of the population is included. Nor has the increase in population since 1978 has been taken into consideration. The numbers, moreover, are consistent with the high incidence of runaway youth, many of whom become prostitutes, and the information provided by homosexual publications.

Based on these assumptions, the total number of homosexual prostitutes in the United States can be estimated at no fewer than 70,591. (This is an extremely conservative figure; Robin Lloyd, author of *For Money or Love: Boy Prostitution in America*, estimated in 1976 that there were 300,000 boy prostitutes in the United States. Our figure of 70,591 *includes* adult homosexual prostitutes.) A more detailed study would probably yield a much higher figure. Still, the idea of over 70,000 persons—predominantly young people—making a living by the practice of homosexual prostitution would probably be quite disturbing to the majority of Americans. At twelve encounters per week, charging an average of $40 per encounter, the total dollar value of the business generated by 70,591 homosexual prostitutes is $1,762,000,000 per year. Table 15 shows the breakdown for each of the SMSAs and SCSAs considered. Due to the very conservative way in which the value was calculated, it can be safely asserted that the real figure is probably well over 3 billion dollars.

This does not take into consideration the cost of hotel rooms. Assuming that one-quarter of the encounters take place in hotel rooms rented at $20 per encounter for the specific purpose of having sex, homosexual prostitution generates no less than $220,244,000 per year in additional

THE HOMOSEXUAL NETWORK

TABLE 15

Economic Value of Homosexual Prostitution in SMSAs and SCSAs over 1,000,000 Inhabitants

SMSA/SCSA*	1978** Population (X 1,000)	Estimated Number of Homosexual Prostitutes	Estimated Value of Homosexual Prostitutes (X 1,000
Altanta (GA)	1,852	1,423	$ 35,518
Baltimore (MD)	2,145	1,648	41,134
Boston* (MA)	3,500	2,689	67,117
Buffalo (NY)	1,303	1,001	24,985
Chicago* (IL)	7,678	5,900	147,264
Cincinnati (OH)	1,646	1,265	31,574
Cleveland* (OH)	2,867	2,203	54,987
Columbus (OH)	1,089	837	20,892
Dallas (TX)	2,720	2,090	52,216
Denver (CO)	1,505	1,156	28,854
Detroit* (MI)	4,641	3,566	89,007
Houston* (TX)	2,793	2,146	53,564
Indianapolis (IN)	1,156	888	22,164
Kansas City (KS-MO)	1,325	1,018	25,409
Los Angeles* (CA)	10,784	8,286	206,819
Miami* (FL)	2,333	1,793	44,753
Milwaukee* (WI)	1,594	1,225	30,576
Minneapolis-St. Paul (MN)	2,063	1,585	39,562
New Orleans (LA)	1,141	877	21,890
New York* (NY-NJ-CT)	16,285	12,513	312,324
Philadelphia* (NJ-DE-PA-MD)	5,603	4,305	107,453
Riverside (CA)	1,385	1,064	26,557
St. Louis (MO)	2,386	1,833	45,752
San Antonio (TX)	1,038	798	19,918
San Francisco* (CA)	4,717	3,625	90,480
Seattle* (WA)	1,905	1,464	36,541
Tampa (FL)	1,396	1,073	26,782
Washington (DC-VA-MD)	3,017	2,318	57,857
Total	91,867	70,591	$1,761,951

*Standard Consolidated Statistical Areas
**Source: U.S. Bureau of the Census, 1980 Statistical Abstract of the United States.

revenues. Many of these funds (as well as those generated by the sexual encounters) are not taxed.

A fourth type of enterprise is the "service organization," involving a variety of nonprofit organizations that provide "educational" and "social" services to homosexuals. These service organizations have much more economic power than most people would suspect. According to the National Gay Task Force, there are some 3,000 homosexual organizations nationwide.[107] This figure was provided in connection with a Task Force project to prepare a computerized list of homosexual organizations. Naturally, the budgets of these organizations are not a matter of public record. However, the survey we undertook in preparation for this work provides some useful information. The average budget of a homosexual nonprofit organization was found to be $81,875. Thus the total economic power of homosexual organizations—exclusive of businesses—can be estimated at $245,625,000.

The various economic enterprises associated with homosexual pornography also provide considerable economic power. Unfortunately, it is nearly impossible to provide reliable figures. Large American cities have homosexual movie houses (in New York City alone there are no fewer than twelve). The movies shown are sold in film and videocasette forms for a price between $50 and $100 each. Porno shops also feature peep shows where customers watch short segments of films for a small price. There are hundreds of different books which sell at three to five dollars each. Glossy magazines featuring naked models, sometimes performing sexual acts, sell for up to ten dollars each. There are greeting cards, ornaments, chocolates shaped as fully stimulated genitals, equipment used in sadomasochistic practices, aphrodisiacs, and many other products which center in the practice of homosexuality. (Cf. chap. II.) The prices of these products far exceed their intrinsic value, the discrepancy probably being caused by market distortions based on societal disapproval. It is not difficult to appreciate, however, how the market in homosexual pornographic and sex-centered merchandise is worth millions of dollars.

It is clear from our discussion that from any point of view the homosexual movement represents an enormous economic force in America. It is reasonable to assume that the vast influence of homosexuality in our country—both social and political—relates directly to the economic power at the disposal of the movement. It must be acknowledged that there is no single source of coordination that can harness this economic power for the promotion of homosexuality. However, the homosexual ideology is sufficiently consistent and accepted widely enough that it is *as if* there were only a few decision-makers responsible for the movement as a whole.

Political Power

The homosexual movement does not consist of a ragged band of poor and oppressed individuals who are simply reacting with great rage and in anarchical fashion to unbearable injustice. Such a vision is designed to elicit the support of other Americans who have historically been part of groups that fit such a description. On the contrary, the homosexual movement represents large numbers of well-educated middle- and upper-class people. It has a coherent ideology and a vision of the future for America.

The movement has created a subculture which represents the seeds of future growth. This subculture encompasses some institutions which are solely designed to satisfy the needs of the homosexuals. Other homosexual organizations exist within other larger institutions. They are merely means by which the movement attempts to convert host institutions into tools for satisfying its sociopolitical needs, or perhaps to "homosexualize" such institutions completely, making them integral parts of the movement. The homosexual caucus within a church, for example, might work to make the homosexual ideology part of the tenets of the host church. This might be so repugnant to the traditional faith of the church that it is at best a long-range project. In the short run, it might suffice the goals of the movement to have the church implement elements of the prohomosexual program such as 1) affirmative action with regard to homosexuals in its employment practices, 2) incorporation of inclusive language in the services and/or sacred writings, 3) the ordination of females—especially female homosexuals—by those churches whose doctrines have traditionally prescribed male clergy only, 5) recognition of the church's homosexual groups as "legitimate" religious organizations, 6) support for prohomosexual legislation.

The homosexual ideology implies the intent to rearrange our perceptions, lifestyles, and legal system. As mentioned in chapter III, this change is revolutionary in the strict sense of the term. It requires, if it is to be effectively implemented, the careful and gradual application and transfer of power. The homosexual movement is thus not primarily a philanthropic or educational enterprise, but a hard-nosed political movement bent on changing our society. Most of this work portrays the various political ways in which the homosexual movement endeavors to impose its ideology. This section concludes with a short exposition on some of the manifestations of the political action of the movement, to complete an understanding of its nature.

The homosexual movement understands well that the key to its success lies in its ability to influence—and ultimately control—policymakers. In several cases, the movement has been extremely successful in its ability to influence political structures. Washington, D.C., is a prime example of a jurisdiction in which the homosexual movement has maximized its political clout. From an organizational viewpoint, the most important asset of the movement has been the Gertrude Stein Democratic Club. This is a well-organized and highly efficient political machine with roots in both the liberal establishment and the homosexual movement. (For example, Paul Kuntzler, a founder of the Club, is also a Director of the Gay Rights National Lobby and former president of the D.C. Chapter of Americans for Democratic Action.)[109] In 1978 Mayor Marion Barry was elected with the overwhelming support he received from the homosexual community. The 21 precincts where the homosexuals are concentrated—which represent 15 percent of the total electorate—gave 56 percent of their votes to Barry in the Democratic primary (the rest of the city voted only 30 percent for Barry). It is estimated that of 5,000 homosexual votes, Barry carried 4,000.[108] The movement contributed between $15,000 and $20,000 to Barry, distributed 35,000 leaflets and registered some 4,000 new voters. Homosexual bars staged pro-Barry fundraisers, joining the strictly political leadership in an all-homosexual effort to elect this liberal Democrat. Marion Barry has not forgotten that he is beholden to the homosexual leadership, and it is generally acknowledged that the homosexual movement has considerable input in major city-hall decisions, especially those affecting its interests.

Although not as important as in Washington, the homosexual vote in New York is not ignored by politicians. Although the minimal objective of the movement—the passage of prohomosexual legislation—has not been accomplished because of opposition by the Catholic Archdiocese, the homosexual vote has been actively sought. Prior to the 1977 mayoral election, candidate-to-be Herman Badillo indicated that "gays are a very important constituency; they vote passionately and are a key voter group."[110] Mayor Edward Koch—one of the main prohomosexual advocates in the U.S. Congress while he was a Representative—prepared to run for office under the assumption that there was a bloc of some 250,000 homosexual votes in New York City alone which he would actively seek.[111]

Influencing policymakers in America is accomplished primarily through the ballot box. On April 21, 1980, a Congressional briefing was held in support of prohomosexual legislation, at which the homosexual movement national leader Virginia Apuzzo pointed out the value of the homosexual vote:

> I am confident in telling you today that, despite your possible concern for your political future if you support civil rights for Gays, you have much more to gain by helping us than you have to lose. For every voter who may vote against you because of it, there will be many times more who vote for you because of it. We are 20 million strong and growing stronger. We have friends and family who love us and will stand with us. An attack on us will be seen as an attack on them, as well. We are good allies to have.[112]

The homosexual community's ability to deliver a significant number of votes has been skillfully exploited. For example, the Gay Rights National Lobby has published a monograph titled "Does Support for Gay Rights Spell Political Suicide?" It purports to demonstrate that support for prohomosexual legislation is at least not deleterious and at times even beneficial for politicians. A specific example is cited in an article friendly to the homosexual movement, which recounted the case of a Houston Councilman who referred to homosexuals as "oddwads" and lost his seat.[113] In response to a question from one of the champions of the homosexual movement in the U.S. Congress, Representative Ted Weiss, Art Agnos— California Assemblyman and secretary of the Democratic Caucus—has also acknowledged the value of the homosexual lobby.[114]

The political action of the homosexual movement also takes the form of pressure on existing parties to obtain their support for homosexual objectives. The movement achieved considerable success during the 1980 Democratic Convention by electing a significant number of homosexual delegates and having issues of importance to the movement made part of the party's platform.[115] Similar, although much less successful, efforts were undertaken within the Republican party. Steve Stahl, Christian Social Action Cochairman of the Metropolitan Community Church of Detroit, testified on homosexual affairs before the Republican National Platform Committee.[116] Being allowed to testify was in itself a form of recognition and acceptance of the homosexual movement as a legitimate political force. Stahl made the following report:

> I was well received by the committee and I feel that a strong blow was struck for Lesbian/Gay rights. After a brief oral statement recounting the Democrats' involvement in rights issues, I challenged the Republican Party to prove their interest in the rights of the nation's minorities.
>
> Undoubtably, [sic] they will be slow to action, but I feel that they are awakening to the realities of the '80s. We must continue to apply pressure on the Republican Party and be prepared to 'work' them against the Democrats. Both parties are keenly aware of the potential voting bloc our community represents.[117]

Another form this political pressure took was the passage of a resolution by all UFMCC Districts and Congregations recommending the incorporation of a prohomosexual plank in the Republican Platform.[118] Although the Republican Party never took a stand *against* homosexuality or homosexual behavior, the efforts of the homosexual movement were not successful.

The homosexual movement, as already demonstrated, is not representative of poor people. In point of fact, it represents a group whose income is clearly above the national average. Moreover, even in a purely organizational sense—rather than as individuals—the various components of the homosexual movement have large sums of money at their disposal. This is translated into both individual contributions by homosexual activists to candidates who favor (or are expected to favor) homosexual legislation, and contributions collected by homosexual organizations. On November 27, 1980, the National Convention Project sponsored a "Gay Vote USA Gala," a fundraising event in which the three leading Democratic candidates for the 1980 election, Jerry Brown, Ted Kennedy, and

The Homosexual Movement

Jimmy Carter were represented. The funds collected were used to further the political interests of the homosexual movement, while serving the candidates who were responsive to the call of the homosexuals with the opportunity to court their votes while expressing varying degrees of support for their ideology.[119] The decisive role played by the Gertrude Stein Democratic Club in the 1978 mayoral campaign in Washington, D.C., has already been noted.[120]

The homosexual-oriented Municipal Election Committee in Los Angeles had reportedly raised $200,000 for local candidates alone by 1980, while the National Convention Project had at its disposal some $100,000 to influence the major parties in the 1980 conventions.[121] The impact of homosexual dollars on the political process should not be surprising, since they have the money and, as a rule, political candidates are known to lend a friendly ear to their contributors.

The homosexual movement exerts its political clout in many ways. For example, it has been reported that the Harvard Law School has bowed to the pressure of the homosexual movement—exercised through the Harvard-Radcliffe Gay Students Association—so that only law firms which agree not to consider homosexuality as a factor in employment are allowed to use the university's placement service for employment interviews.[122] In this way, the movement accomplishes three objectives. First, an organizational component of the movement manifests its political clout. Feeding upon itself, this power gives its members and those affected by it the perception that the movement is not only real but productive. In other words, "nothing succeeds like success." Second, it makes a large and prestigious university a servant of the goals of the homosexual movement and an agent in the imposition of the homosexual ideology on the rest of society. Third, it transforms law firms into agents of the homosexual movement by making homosexuality acceptable as a lifestyle. This is a masterful use of the political power of what is probably a small group of students, and perhaps faculty members, in enrolling the support of powerful and respected institutions for their cause.

Part of the key to the political success of the homosexual movement is its organization. This organization and ability to work in close coordination is shown by some of the political accomplishments we have already seen. Apparently, homosexual organizations have little problem generating letters to Congress, educational institutions, the press, etc. *Gays on the Hill*, for example, provides instructions on the use and style of political correspondence. The results of a mail campaign against the Boston *Globe* illustrate the political power of the homosexual movement and its potentially chilling effects on a free press.[123] Apparently, the Boston *Globe* reported a figure for attendees at the March on Washington for Lesbian and Gay Rights that was considered unacceptably small by the leadership of the movement. The paper was inundated with protests which accused it of underplaying positive news of homosexuality and exercising censorship against the interests of the movement. The newspaper promptly capitulated, appointing a person to be "liaison" to the homosexual community. From another perspective, it appears that any news published by the Boston *Globe* bearing on homosexuality is now suspect, since there is a staff person whose apparent mandate is to promote the interests of the homosexual movement vis-à-vis the newspaper.

When all else fails, the homosexual movement has resorted to positive censorship in its attempts to keep views it considers obnoxious from the ears of the public. An example will suffice to show censorship as a political tool for enlisting the cooperation of hitherto unfriendly or neutral institutions in support of homosexuality. The following report appeared in *In Unity,* datelined Hartford. "The Gay Activist Alliance has convinced WOR-TV to edit and 'bleep' out anti-gay remarks made by Evangelist James Robinson [sic] on his weekly radio program. Robert Fennimore, general manager of WOR-TV, says 'If Robinson continues to attack homosexuals . . . he's going to be taken off the air.' "[124]

This success in having a radio station exercise positive censorship of the remarks of a minister whose opinions are deemed contradictory to the interests and/or ideology of the homosexual movement makes such a station, in fact, part and parcel of the political efforts to impose the homosexual ideology. Several passages from the Bible attack homosexuality quite harshly. While modern revisionists have attributed meanings compatible with the homosexual ideology to these passages, the plain meaning of the translations that have been in use for hundreds of years and their traditional interpretation must be acknowledged as the views handed down by many generations. The logic of the general manager of WOR-TV would demand that a minister should be expelled from the air simply for reading the Scriptures!

Various forms of pressure are used on institutions and individuals perceived as inimical to the homosexual movement, the degree of violence being a function of the movement's ability to utilize other more "efficient" and "peaceful" means. In the case of Pastor Fletcher Brothers (Rochester, New York) the clout of the movement at the state and local level motivated repeated "inspections," "threats to remove his church's tax-exemption," a sudden "$40,000 tax bill," etc.[125] Pastor Brothers had dared to object to the practice of homosexuality on biblical grounds and to the funding of homosexual organizations by tax dollars. The actions against Pastor Brothers are another form of political activity. While he worries about fighting the bureaucracy, the homosexual movement busily continues spreading its ideology.

In no way does this exposition exhaust the political activities of the homosexual movement. Demonstrations and marches are also political activities. The act of "coming out" by a single homosexual is regarded by

The Homosexual Movement

the movement as a political action. The homosexual movement is indeed political. Its aims are political, its methods are political, its success would bring a political change the dimensions of which one cannot even begin to imagine.

Notes

1. Bob McCubbin, *The Gay Question: A Marxist Appraisal* (New York, N.Y.: World View Publishers, 1979), p. 75.

2. Donald Webster Cory [pseud.], *The Homosexual in America: A Subjective Approach* (New York: Greenberg, 1951), quoted in Marotta, p. 7.

3. Ibid.

4. Marotta, p. 8.

5. *Workers World* (New York City), June 26, 1981.

6. *Gaynin'* 5 (Denver: Gay and Lesbian Community Center of Colorado, June 1981): 3.

7. *It's Time* 8 (New York: National Gay Task Force, January–February 1981): 2.

8. Ibid.

9. *Official Newsletter of the National Coalition of Gay STD Services* 2 (Arlington, VA: National Coalition of Gay STD Services, May 1981): 3.

10. *It's Time* 8 (March–April 1981): 1.

11. Ibid.

12. *Hearing*, p. 28.

13. Organizational brochure, International Gay Association, n.p.

14. *It's Time* 6 (June–July 1979): 2.

15. *New York Native*, April 6–19, 1981, p. 8.

16. Marotta, pp. 322–325.

17. Ibid., p. 325.

18. Ibid., p. 332.

19. Mrs. Valeska's appointment to the codirectorship of the NGTF and her previous accomplishments were reported in *It's Time* 6 (June–July 1979): 1.

20. Ibid.

21. Fundraising brochure (New York: National Gay Task Force), distributed in 1981.

22. *New York Native*, April 6–19, 1981, p. 9.

23. Ibid.

24. Ibid.

25. Ibid.

26. *Sentinel* (San Francisco) April 3, 1981, p. 1.

27. *Sentinel*, April 17, 1981, p. 1.

28. *Sentinel*, April 3, 1981, p. 1.

29. Ibid., p. 7.

30. *Sentinel*, June 12, 1981, p. 1.

31. Ibid.

32. Ibid., p. 7.

33. *New York Native*, April 6–19, 1981, p. 13.

34. *It's Time* 7 (February–March 1980): 1.

35. Ivan Illich, *Deschooling Society* (New York, N.Y.: Harper & Row, 1971).

36. News release, Gay Academic Union, April 10, 1981.

37. Gay Academic Union Interim Newsletter, Spring 1981, p. 3.

38. Ibid.
39. Ibid., p. 2.
40. *Interchange* 4 (Washington, D.C.: National Gay Student Center, Winter 1977).
41. Ibid.
42. Ibid.
43. Ibid.
44. Ibid.
45. Ibid.
46. Ibid.
47. Leaflet, Gay Teachers Association, New York City, November 25, 1980.
48. Promotional brochure, Gay Teachers Association of New York City, n.d.
49. Ibid.
50. Ibid.
51. Leaflet announcing the program of the Gay Task Force, American Library Association, for the 1980 Annual Conference of the ALA.
52. Ibid.
53. Ibid.
54. Ibid.
55. Letter to the author from Karen M. Keener, June 18, 1981.
56. Notes compiled by Karen Keener (Parkland College, Champaign, IL) entitled *Gay Events at NCTE,* the Palmer House, Chicago, November 25–27, 1976.
57. Ibid.
58. Personal communication.
59. James Abromaitis, "A Cult of Loving Brotherhood," *New Age,* November 1980. A reprint is furnished by the Loving Brotherhood (Sussex, N.J.) as part of its promotional package.
60. Letter from Ralph Walker to the author, June 4, 1981.
61. Promotional brochure, The Loving Brotherhood, Sussex, N.J., n.d.
62. *Sentinel* (San Francisco) April 3, 1981, p. 5.
63. Promotional brochure, National Association of Gay Alcoholism Professionals, Oakland, N.J., n.d.
64. *NAGAP Newsletter* 2 (Oakland, N.J.: National Association of Gay Alcoholism Professionals, Winter 1980–81): 1.
65. Ibid.
66. *NAGAP Newsletter* 2 (Oakland, N.J.: National Association of Gay Alcoholism Professionals, Spring 1981): 1.
67. Ibid., p. 4.
68. National Coalition of Gay STD Services Fact Sheet, Arlington, VA, n.d.
69. *Official Newsletter of the National Coalition of Gay STD Services* 2 (Arlington, VA: National Coalition of Gay STD Services, October 1980): 6.
70. Promotional brochure, Custody Action for Lesbian Mothers, Narberth, PA, n.d.
71. Ibid.
72. Ibid.
73. Letter to the author from Stephen Hunt, Codirector, Lambda Resource Center for the Blind (Chicago), July 29, 1981.
74. *Lambda Resource Center for the Blind Newsletter* (Chicago: Lambda Resource Center for the Blind), May 1, 1981.
75. Basic promotional leaflet and application for membership form, Parents of Lesbians and Gay Men, New York, N.Y., n.d.
76. Betty Fairchild, *Parents of Gays* (Washington, D.C.: Stone Age Trading Co., 1976), p. 12.
77. Basic promotional leaflet and application for membership form, Parents of Lesbians and Gay Men, New York, N.Y., n.d.

78. *In Unity*, November/December 1980, p. 11.

79. Parents and Friends of Gays, *About Our Children* (Los Angeles: Parents and Friends of Gays, 1978).

80. *New York Times*, August 8, 1977, p. 47.

81. Promotional brochure, Black and White Men Together, San Francisco, n.d.

82. *The Eulenspiegel Society's Newsletter* (New York, N.Y.: Eulenspiegel Society), Spring 1981, p. 6.

83. Ibid., p. 1.

84. Ibid.

85. "Introducing the North American Man/Boy Love Association," basic promotional brochure of the North American Man/Boy Love Association (New York), n.d. It is referred to hereinafter as NAMBLA promotional brochure.

86. *NAMBLA Bulletin* 2 (New York, N.Y.: North American Man/Boy Love Association, May 1981): 4.

87. NAMBLA promotional brochure.

88. *NAMBLA News* (Boston: North American Man/Boy Love Association), December 1980/January 1981, p. 24.

89. Promotional/information package, Rene Guyon Society, Beverly Hills: March 20, 1981.

90. *New York Times*, October 25, 1977.

91. Ibid.

92. "Gays: A Major Force in the Marketplace," *Business Week*, September 3, 1979, p. 118.

93. Audit Bureau of Circulation, *Advocate*, magazine publishers' statement for six months ended December 31, 1980.

94. Ibid.

95. Clarke Taylor, "Gay Power," *New York*, August 29, 1977, p. 46.

96. Ibid.

97. Ibid., p. 47.

98. Ibid., p. 45.

99. Ibid.

100. "In the Gay Camp," *Newsweek*, June 6, 1977, p. 19.

101. Ibid.

102. Donia Mills and Phil Gailey, "D.C. Homosexuals Increase Influence by 'Using System,' " *Washington Star*, April 9, 1981.

103. Joe Flower, "Gay in Business: The Prejudice and the Power," *San Francisco*, n.d. Reprinted in *Hearing*, p. 22.

104. U.S. Bureau of the Census, Retail Census Branch, 1977 Census of Retail Trade. Figures reported in the Geographic Area Series, October 1979.

105. *Denver Post*, June 12, 1977.

106. *Out Magazine* (Washington, D.C.), June 4, 1981, p. 26.

107. *It's Time* 8 (March–April 1981): 1.

108. Ralph H. Goff, "Gay Clout: Influence Felt in Local Elections," *Gays on the Hill* 3 (January 1979): 2.

109. Ibid.

110. Ken Lerer, "Gays—A New Key Voter Group," *New York*, May 30, 1977), p. 8.

111. Ibid.

112. Ken Spaatz, "Congressional Briefings Held for First Time Before Large Crowd in Washington," *A New Day* 4 (May and June, 1980): 4.

113. Flower, p. 20.

114. Statement of Art Agnos, *Hearing*, p. 15.

115. "Update: Detroit MCC and the Republican Convention," *CCSA: Meeting Human*

Needs 1 (Washington, D.C.: Commission on Christian Social Action, Universal Fellowship of Metropolitan Community Churches, April 1980): 4.

116. Ibid.

117. Ibid., p. 6.

118. Ibid., p. 4.

119. Congressional Research Service, "Presidential Candidates Speak to the Issue of Homosexual Rights," (Washington, D.C.: Library of Congress), April 18, 1980. Reprinted in *Hearing*, p. 117.

120. Goff, p. 2.

121. "A New Big Push for Homosexuals' Rights," *U.S. News and World Report*, April 14, 1980, p. 94.

122. "How Gay is Gay? Homosexual Men and Women Are Making Progress Toward Equality," *Time*, April 23, 1979. Reprinted in *Hearing*, p. 96.

123. *In Unity*, February/March 1980, p. 12.

124. *In Unity*, December 1979/January 1980, p. 11.

125. Connaught Coyne Marshner, "A Clash of Fundamental Forces in Rochester," *Family Protection Report* (Washington, D.C.: Free Congress Research and Education Foundation), August 1979, p. 8.

CHAPTER

V

The Goals of the
Homosexual Movement

The final cause of any social movement is a set of objectives, more or less specific in their expression, which constitutes the standard by which the movement's success is measured. Massive and diversified movements such as the one here considered do not have clearly articulated or universally accepted goals. This is especially true as the goals increase in specificity. After all, the goals of the homosexual movement are a synthesis of the goals of its individual members, who not only belong to other groups but who also have their own agendas. Homosexual organizations are created around specific concerns or geographical areas. These factors also influence the goals of these organizations and obviously have an effect on the goals of the movement as a whole, since each organization is the concrete expression of the movement within the various sociopolitical units and vis-à-vis other organizations or social structures which define its boundaries.

In addressing the goals of the homosexual movement, the most universal is discussed first, followed by specific examples of supportive goals in three specific areas. Inasmuch as there is no comprehensive expression of a program for the homosexual movement—its very nature precludes such a program—we may conclude that the boundaries between the various categories are not clearly defined, that specific examples may be fairly included in more than one category, and that the various subjects are not logically exhausted. This follows because the categories used here have been developed without reference to the subject at hand and have been adapted to suit the needs of the question under analysis. The objective of this chapter is not so much to present a comprehensive list of goals of the homosexual movement as to provide examples that will help the reader understand some of the deeply revolutionary changes advocated by this movement.

Three areas in which the homosexual movement is active are relevant in this section: ideological, political, and social. These three are naturally interrelated and difficult to distinguish when examining specific goals of the movement. The import of this classification is not to provide neat categories, for this would be a betrayal of reality, but to introduce a method for deepening understanding of the nature of the goals themselves. Thus categorization is a methodological tool rather than an ontological statement.

Ultimate Goal

The ultimate goal of the homosexual movement can be summarized in a very simple phrase:

ACCEPTANCE OF HOMOSEXUAL ACTS AS A NORMAL
VARIANT OF HUMAN BEHAVIOR AND OF HOMOSEXUALITY
AS AN ALTERNATIVE LIFESTYLE.

This goal obviously involves two distinct components. One refers to homosexual behavior and the other to the homosexual lifestyle. Although on the surface these are clear-cut notions, reality is not that simple. Homosexual behavior refers to the satisfaction of erotic desires by engaging in sexual activity with members of one's own sex (either factually or intentionally). The homosexual lifestyle refers to the active and open practice of homosexuality, as well as to the attendant cultural patterns "typical" of the homosexual community. "Normal" and "alternative" involve similar core concepts, that is, the notion that, although the homosexual behavior and lifestyle might statistically exist in a minority of cases—not a small minority according to the homosexual ideology—they are still within the order of nature. It is difficult to imagine a homosexual leader or movement that would disagree with this formulation. It is sufficiently vague to enable a multitude of individual cases and viewpoints to fall under its domain.

America, a Jesuit magazine which cannot be suspected of antipathy to the homosexual movement, has articulated this objective in no uncertain terms:

> But the ultimate objective of at least a significant segment of the movement for homosexual rights is not simply to establish legal protection for homosexuals against any discrimination based on their private lives, but also to win the

The Goals of the Homosexual Movement

eventual acceptance, on the part of both society and church, of homosexual behavior as a legitimate alternative that holds the full promise of human development and is in every way consistent with the Judeo-Christian ethical tradition.[1]

Nearly all the activities undertaken by the homosexual movement through its array of organizational components ultimately lead, directly or indirectly, to the accomplishment of this goal. In some cases, this relationship is rather obvious. Organized groups of homosexuals within various professional associations in the behavioral sciences lobby fiercely for "official declarations" by their parent organizations which resemble the dogmatic definitions of mainline churches. Organizations of homosexuals within churches seek justification in the Bible or the "evolving consensus of theologians" for the principle that homosexuality, if not individual homosexual acts, is perfectly within the order of nature. The concept of homosexual marriage (or "gay holy union"), widely accepted within various homosexual religious communities, has been developed as a means of assimilating homosexual relationships into the accepted range of sexual relations among human beings. Sex education centered on secular humanist principles rather than traditional morality has as one of its purposes to instill "toleration" and "understanding" in students for variant forms of "consensual" sexual behavior (i.e., homosexuality). Lack of an objective foundation for sexual behavior and insistence on the satisfaction of the self in sexual matters logically leads to the acceptance of homosexuality by naive students. The very blatant manifestations of its more extreme cultural expressions (camp, costumes, public expressions of physical affection, etc.) not only have a shock value, but are also geared to accustom the population at large to the open presence of homosexuals. Laws which imply the acceptance of homosexuals as a legitimate minority indirectly contribute to the acceptance of homosexuality. The imposition of "gay-speak" on the population frames the perception of the homosexual condition so as to make it impossible for the average user to conceive homosexuality as other than normal. Activities within homosexual organizations (open sex in bathhouses, homosexual prostitution, open search for sex partners in bars, "cultural" events, etc.) not only reinforce the homosexual condition in those affected by it, but accompany that reinforcement with principles and practices which, at least by implication, assert that homosexuality is normal. Finally, the ideology of the homosexual movement is nothing but a set of principles which logically imply the normality of the homosexual condition.

The ideological (i.e., nonobjective) and politically purposeful nature of the movement's primary goal becomes apparent when it is analyzed from two points of view. This goal is in reality an ethical statement, a command designed to alter both the behavior and the underlying perception of its recipients. The acceptance of homosexual behavior as normal implies not only the willingness to engage in social intercourse with individuals known or suspected to be homosexual, but the positive acknowledgement that when these individuals seek relief from their sexual urges, they do so without violating their own nature or the relationships demanded by the ontic structure of their sexuality. The acceptance of homosexuality as an alternative lifestyle implies the extension of American cultural pluralism to areas that have been considered manifestations of depravity, emotional disorders, and/or sociopathic personalities. The primary goal of the homosexual movement is thus a composite normative statement implying a judgment on present mores and a substantial attack on the traditional values of American society. On the surface it would appear merely to broaden the scope of existing values (e.g., compassion, acceptance, understanding, pluralism, etc.). In reality, it constitutes a radical challenge to established values and a demand that society redefine basic concepts which relate to sex as a core element in human personality.

Also noteworthy as revealing the primary ideological goal of the homosexual movement is the fact that it has become progressively more specific in its elements, to satisfy the needs of individual homosexuals or groups of homosexuals. Although the general concept of homosexual refers to the satisfaction of the sexual desires between persons of the same sex by certain erotic actions, how these relationships are established and what they entail are not clear. Within the framework of traditional morality, sex within marriage is eminently acceptable. Outside of the marriage contract, sexual relations may be normal in themselves but nonacceptable because they take place outside the context of the family. Homosexual relations are never acceptable. Once the principle of subjectivism is introduced, what is acceptable to one person (e.g., transgenerational sex) may be repugnant to another. Such elements in the homosexual lifestyle as causing physical harm to another *with his consent,* or a man to showing himself dressed as a woman, may be rejected by other homosexuals. When the homosexual movement works for the acceptance of homosexual behavior, does this include *all* forms of sadomasochism? Is the keeping of a fifteen-year-old boy by a wealthy "sugar-daddy" part of the "alternative lifestyle" to be accepted? From the viewpoint of the child and his keeper, certainly it is. There is little question that many homosexuals who are not inclined to transgenerational sex would reject such arrangements as illegitimate and recognize the inherent danger they pose to the homosexual movement at large. However, it is not possible to establish norms for answering these questions while maintaining logical consistency. At a meeting with the author, Adam DeBaugh of the UFMCC rejected adult-child relations as exploitative of the child. Still, they constitute the basis of the North American Man/Boy Love Association, an integral part of the homosexual movement.

The Goals of the Homosexual Movement

Theoretically, it is possible for all homosexual organizations to work for the transformation of society by the accomplishment of a broad goal to which all can subscribe. In practice, however, this goal must be divided into smaller and more manageable tasks or subordinate goals. In each organization and in each geographic area, homosexuals endeavor to come closer to their ideal by attempting to accomplish a variety of goals depending on their specific needs or interests. Thus the North American Man/Boy Love Association works for the acceptance of transgenerational sex in law and as a permanent feature of our culture, while Dignity tries to have one Catholic diocese after another drop its opposition to "gay rights" legislation, or establish an official church organization to relate to homosexuals according to the tenets of their ideology. In all cases, the final effect is the progressive transformation of society according to the homosexual conception, but each organization goes about this effort in its own peculiar way. From the point of view of tradition-minded organizations opposed to this process, this must be taken into consideration, since the challenge posed to society by the homosexual movement must be met according to the mode in which the challenge is posed, or efforts to meet such a challenge will be wasted. It is only by understanding what the specific homosexual organization *really* intends, and why it goes about its efforts in such a peculiar way, that the issues presented can be framed in an intelligible and winnable manner. For example, once the principles of secular humanism are accepted within the framework of psychology, it is nearly useless to respond to the challenge posed by the homosexual movement in asserting that homosexuality is not a mental disorder. Indeed, if man is the measure of all things, on what basis can it be decided that this man (i.e., this sadomasochistic boy-"loving" homosexual) is emotionally disordered, when he can "honestly" say that in killing a teenager he is only doing what to him comes "naturally"? The issue of whether or not homosexuality is a mental disorder must be framed in such a way as to reject the assumptions that allow homosexual organizations to assert that it is a normal variant of human sexuality.

The total transformation of society by the acceptance of homosexuality as an alternative lifestyle and of homosexual acts as normal is evident in the "1972 Gay Rights Platform." Adopted by a National Coalition of Gay Organizations in February of that year, it constitutes one of the most detailed outlines of the homosexualized society produced thus far by the movement. Although many of the elements of this list, considered in isolation, fall under specific categories within the various kinds of goals of the homosexual movement, taken as a whole these demands provide the reader with a vision of what the ideal society sought by the homosexual movement would be:

THE HOMOSEXUAL NETWORK

1972 GAY RIGHTS PLATFORM

DEMANDS:

Federal:

1. Amend all federal Civil Rights Acts, other legislation and government controls to prohibit discrimination in employment, housing, public accommodations and public services.
2. Issuance by the President of an executive order prohibiting the military from excluding for reasons of their sexual orientation, persons who of their own volition desire entrance into the Armed Services; and from issuing less-than-fully-honorable discharges for homosexuality; and the upgrading to fully honorable all such discharges previously issued, with retroactive benefits.
3. Issuance by the President of an executive order prohibiting discrimination in the federal civil service because of sexual orientation, in hiring and promoting; and prohibiting discriminations against homosexuals in security clearances.
4. Elimination of tax inequities victimizing single persons and same-sex couples.
5. Elimination of bars to the entry, immigration and naturalization of homosexual aliens.
6. Federal encouragement and support for sex education courses, prepared and taught by Gay women and men, presenting homosexuality as a valid, healthy preference and lifestyle as a viable alternative to heterosexuality.
7. Appropriate executive orders, regulations and legislation banning the compiling, maintenance and dissemination of information on an individual's sexual preferences, behavior, and social and political activities for dossiers and data banks.
8. Federal funding of aid programs of Gay men's and women's organizations designed to alleviate the problems encountered by Gay women and men which are engendered by an oppressive sexist society.
9. Immediate release of all Gay women and men now incarcerated in detention centers, prisons and mental institutions because of sexual offense charges relating to victimless crimes or sexual orientation; and that adequate compensation be made for the physical and mental duress encountered; and that all existing records relating to the incarceration be immediately expunged.

State:

1. All federal legislation and programs enumerated in Demands 1,6,7,8, and 9 above should be implemented at the State level where applicable.
2. Repeal of all state laws prohibiting private sexual acts involving consenting persons; equalization for homosexuals and heterosexuals for the enforcement of all laws.

The Goals of the Homosexual Movement

3. Repeal all state laws prohibiting solicitation for private voluntary sexual liaisons; and laws prohibiting prostitution, both male and female.
4. Enactment of legislation prohibiting insurance companies and any other state-regulated enterprises from discriminating because of sexual orientation, in insurance and in bonding or any other prerequisite to employment or control of one's personal demesne.
5. Enactment of legislation so that child custody, adoption, visitation rights, foster parenting, and the like shall not be denied because of sexual orientation or marital status.
6. Repeal of all laws prohibiting transvestism and cross dressing.
7. Repeal of all laws governing the age of sexual consent.
8. Repeal of all legislative provisions that restrict the sex or number of persons entering into a marriage unit; and the extension of legal benefits to all persons who cohabit regardless of sex or numbers.[2]

In a clear and explicit way, David Thorstad proclaims the ultimate aim of the homosexual movement:

1) The ultimate goal of the gay liberation movement is the achievement of sexual freedom for all—not just equal rights for "lesbians and gay men," but also freedom of sexual expression for young people and children. . . .

We should present ourselves not merely as defenders of our own personal rights to privacy and sexual expression, but as the champions of the right of *all* persons—regardless of age—to engage in the sexuality of their choice. We must recognize homosexual behavior for what it is—a natural potential of the human animal. The homoerotic capabilities of the human species, in all their wonderful variety, are not something to be justified, but to be explored and assimilated.[3]

While the ultimate stage of the homosexual society is not yet achieved, it must continue pressing for other "subordinate" goals that will hasten the accomplishment of the ultimate goal. It is in this spirit that the homosexual struggle continues. These individual subordinate goals of the homosexual movement can be included in three general areas: ideological, political, and social. As mentioned before, the various goals in these areas do not fit neatly into these categories. The following examples are offered to illustrate how the implementation of these goals contributes to the total breakdown of traditional mores rather than to provide an exhaustive list of subordinate goals.

THE HOMOSEXUAL NETWORK

Ideological Goals

The fundamental ideological goal of the homosexual movement can be summarized in a simple phrase:

PROGRESSIVE ACCEPTANCE OF THE VARIOUS
ELEMENTS OF THE HOMOSEXUAL IDEOLOGY.

The total acceptance of the homosexual ideology in terms of social behavior would signify the complete identification of our culture with the homosexual subculture. This is, of course, a utopian solution from both the theoretical and practical points of view. Heterosexual sex is based on the biological matrices of males and females, which are complementary and thus mutually interdependent. The homosexual ideology notwithstanding, homosexual sex is far closer to a psychocultural superstructure based on maladaptation than heterosexual sex could possibly be. In practice, even apologists for the homosexual movement realize that American society is not likely to become homosexualized. In fact, in no society is homosexuality the norm, since such a society would quickly disappear. From a practical standpoint, further attempts to impose the homosexual ideology are not likely to increase its acceptability. The essential contradiction between the homosexual ideology and traditional American values will probably result in an "antigay" reaction. William Bennett made this assertion in the Fall 1978 issue of *American Educator*:

> The gay rights movement will foster resentment; many citizens will not unfairly consider it to be a form of indecent exposure. More important, those who insist on making a deviant sexual preference a matter of public knowledge and discussion may get attention, but the public reaction will not be kind. By making overheated, active, public avowals, many leaders of the gay rights movement will bring about an equally public, equally active, and equally overheated condemnation. If pushed, most people will, not unreasonably, refuse to ratify and approve homosexuality.[4]

The intrinsic contradiction between the tenets of the homosexual movement and traditional American values is not hidden by homosexual leaders. The following exchange of views between Jeanne Cordova and Ivy Bottini is revealing. Both are recognized leaders of the homosexual movement in their own right:

> Cordova: We have to understand Bryant and her like in this political and economic context. A society propped up by a war-making economy (capitalism) turns inward upon itself during "peace" time.
> Bottini: I think they are testing the water with the gay issue. If the emotion can run high enough and they can get middle America hysterical enough

The Goals of the Homosexual Movement

over gays, they can get whoever they want next on the coattails of that
hysteria. Once the voters get out of control with fear, nobody's safe.

Cordova: It's also important to recognize that this wave of reaction is taking
the form of a *religious* war. Religion and patriotism are the hallmarks of the
right. They make the best banners precisely because they are so irrational.
You can't fight irrationality and hysteria with common sense or even guns.

Bottini: While we're sorting out the Constitution, there will be a lot of people
dying, or losing their jobs and careers.

Cordova: That's why I can't buy this, "the solution is to educate the silent
majority" line. Social change is a power struggle, not an educational program.
It's like Elaine Noble said in Denver, if the country was given the opportunity
to vote on the Bill of Rights, it would lose. Winning is not a matter of changing
people's consciousness.[5]

The question of "changing people's consciousness" (i.e., acceptance of
the homosexual ideology) remains an issue of vital concern for the movement. However, accepting traditional liberal dogma, social environmental
factors are deemed supreme and consciousness follows praxis. Nevertheless, the new consciousness must be present or the praxis will cease to
have a foundation. The reply to the above exchange by Judy Freespirit
makes this point abundantly clear. The homosexual movement must impose its program irrespective of the opinions of the majority: "There are
rights that we have to win and gains that we have to protect from erosion.
We need to take a good hard look at the Black Movement. They got
nowhere with 'good-image.' We need to get militant and start some fires.
First you get your rights and *then* you educate people."[6]

The transformation of the traditional consciousness into a "gay" consciousness cannot be expected to be a short-term phenomenon nor the
result of superficial measures. At any particular time, "liberated" homosexuals do perceive the need to institute whatever changes they can
accomplish in the order of society within the political limitations of the
moment. In the final analysis, what is sought is what they describe as a
"more just" society, in which antihomosexual prejudices are eradicated
by people with a new consciousness. Here is where the problem arises,
since from a traditional point of view discrimination against homosexuals
is not necessarily irrational. Thus the need to impose the homosexual
ideology is a precondition for the ultimate "liberation" not only of homosexuals but of heterosexuals as well.

There are various activities or factors which contribute to the acceptance
of the homosexual ideology. In some instances they act directly in making
this acceptance possible; more often than not the effect is indirect, at
times quite subtle. Included are:

- Continuing exposure to homosexual themes in the media, theater, and other
modes of communication.
- Reorganization of the legal system to suit the requirements of the homosexual
movement.

205

- Systematic affirmation of various propositions included in the homosexual ideology either directly or by implication.
- Use of inclusive language and/or practices which contribute to creating confusion in the roles of men and women within the family, church, economic units, governmental organizations, etc.
- Progressive weakening of family bonds by the institution of "open marriage," the increase and facilitation of divorce, the implementation of "children's rights," etc. The concept of alternative family (i.e., the redefinition of the family) appears to be vital to the homosexual movement.
- Continuing expansion of sexual subjectivism and moral relativism as acceptable tools for decision making, both within and without the sexual sphere.
- Acceptance and expansion of pornography as a "valid" expression of human feelings and/or a proper vehicle to satisfy a legitimate human need.
- Consistent utilization of expressions that imply the objectivity of the homosexual ideology (e.g., calling homosexuals "gay," homosexuals as a group a "minority," or homosexuality an "alternative lifestyle" rather than a disease or a perversion).

The means of communication (media, schools, churches, etc.) as well as the social organizations which formally validate behavior (churches, government, etc.) are quite important in the progressive acceptance of the homosexual ideology. One of the most important vehicles in this process is pornography, since it implies the principle that sex is acceptable so long as it suits the needs of each individual as defined by each individual, with no reference to an objective moral norm. Even the most casual observer of the homosexual subculture cannot fail to appreciate the pervasiveness of pornography in all its manifestations. "Gay movie houses" are in reality establishments where homosexual pornographic movies are exhibited. "Gay bookstores" as a rule sell hard-core pornography with other more "serious" materials. Conversely, "regular" porno shops as a rule have sections where materials specifically prepared for homosexuals are sold. Certain sections of the feminist movement have taken issue with the very existence of pornography,[7] although homosexual apologists have invariably rejected this position.[8] From the traditional point of view, this activity corrupts society by focusing human action on the unrestricted pursuit of pleasure while destroying the foundation of the family. Conventional individuals also see in pornography (as well as in all other aspects of the homosexual ideology) the destruction of society by the weakening of the moral fiber of individuals, a decrease in productivity, and the increasing inability of the people to defend themselves against aggression. (Thus the three classical areas of public policy—defense, economic, and social issues—are joined in the analysis of one primarily social issue.) The reader must take into consideration, however, that none of these issues appears to be relevant for the homosexual movement. The intensity with which it focuses its attention on the question

The Goals of the Homosexual Movement

of sexuality is so great that other areas of human interest seem to fade. Questions of ideology and the need to impose the ideological tenets of the homosexual movement color most of its activities. The homosexual leadership perceives as a great threat any and all attempts to question any of the basic tenets of the homosexual ideology.

Political Goals

Certain subordinate goals of the homosexual movement can be logically classified as political in nature. After all, the homosexual movement is fundamentally a political phenomenon. In general, the political goals of the homosexual movement pertain to the exercise of formal authority by the various jurisdictions of our political system.

PASSAGE OF PROHOMOSEXUAL LEGISLATION

Within the homosexual movement, no issue seems to have more importance than the passage of prohomosexual legislation. The universal denominators of these laws are: first, the acceptance of the principle that homosexuals constitute a legitimate minority; second, the concept that homosexuals have been unjustly discriminated against in the past and are thus entitled to special treatment under the law. In certain cases, this treatment extends to affirmative action programs in which homosexuals are actually preferred in the provision of services. This concept, however, is dangerous for the homosexuals themselves since, it forces them to disclose the nature of their sexual preferences.

The National Gay Task Force monitors the progress of the homosexual movement and has produced, partly with the help of CETA Title VI funds, a classification of the various areas typically covered by prohomosexual laws. The following listing will acquaint the reader with these areas as described by the NGTF:

> *Employment* means the provision or an offer to provide employment to an individual which includes opportunity for advancement based upon merit and/ or other established criteria and including all benefits of employment.

> *Public Employment* includes the above mentioned provisions for employment and in some specific cases requires that the City Manager (or other municipal official) include in all contracts, agreements and memoranda of understanding, the condition that contractors, in the performance of the contract, shall not discriminate on the basis of sexual orientation against any employee of, or applicant for employment with the contractor. Those contracts would extend and be applicable to all subcontracts.

> *Public Accommodations* includes all services or facilities which are generally

open to or offered to the public or which generally solicit public patronage or usage, whether operated for profit or not, e.g., theaters, hotels, retail stores, banks, hospitals, public conveyances, etc.

Housing describes any building or structure which is used or occupied or is intended, arranged, or designed to be used as a home, residence, or sleeping place of one or more individuals, groups or families, whether or not living independently of each other.

Education includes all public and private schools and training centers.

Real Estate Practices refers to exhibiting, listing, advertising, negotiating, agreeing to transfer, whether by sale, lease, sublease, rent assignment, or other agreement, any interest in real property or improvements upon that property.

Credit is defined as that credit which a person possesses as an individual and which is founded on the opinion held of their character or business standing. In many instances banking and insurance practices are also covered under the heading of "credit."

Union Practices refers to any person, employee representation committee or plan in which employees participate, or any agent or employee, which exists wholly or in part for the purpose of dealing with employers concerning grievances, labor disputes, wages, rates of pay, hours or other conditions of employment.

Affirmative Action Program describes a bona fide plan designed to overcome the effects of past discrimination and to take action not otherwise prohibited by any other ordinance or state or federal law to carry out such an affirmative action plan.[9]

Another area of legislative concern for the homosexual movement is the elimination of all legal restrictions on consensual sexual practices. Whether this elimination of legal restrictions is to apply to adults only or is also to be extended to minors depends on specific groups. Children's liberation organizations and "man/boy love" associations promote measures which eliminate transgenerational restrictions. In 1981 the Washington City Council was set to enact a measure which partially accomplished this goal (a committee of the council had approved such a bill) when public pressure forced a change, and a much "softer" bill was passed—only to be vetoed by the U.S. House of Representatives.[10] In New York a judge has legalized the use of children in pornographic films, opening the way for a great increase in "kiddie porn."[11] For proponents of transgenerational sex, this is undoubtedly only a step toward a more comprehensive change in legislation.

The extent to which the goal of prohomosexual legislation in the United States has been successfully accomplished is considerable. Table 16 displays the various jurisdictions in which a variety of prohomosexual measures have been enacted. It must be noted that many of these jurisdictions

The Goals of the Homosexual Movement

are "college towns" in which well-organized homosexual student organizations have managed to impose prohomosexual legislation on the permanent residents. In many of the larger jurisdictions, prohomosexual measures are the result of "executive orders" in which local legislative bodies have not had the opportunity of voting the measures up or down. In several cases, homosexual behavior has been legalized by liberal courts which have declared laws banning sex between persons of the same sex illegal for a variety of reasons.

It is a myth that the legislative power in America resides exclusively in the legislature. Many lawmaking activities in America reside in the courts, which have acquired increasing authority by judicial activism. Another source of legislative authority is regulatory and administrative agencies. Although in theory the lawmaking ability of these agencies is rooted in the legislative branches at the various levels of government, in practice the enabling legislation of these agencies is vague enough to make them legislators in their own right. The tendency of these agencies to respond to the pressure of constituent and single-interest groups predisposes them to enact measures in favor of the homosexual movement. This is caused by various factors, among which many years of liberal administration cannot be discounted. The tenor of federal regulation in America—especially the regulation of human behavior and social practices—is overwhelmingly liberal. Agencies as diverse as the Internal Revenue Service, the Legal Services Corporation, the Office of Personnel Management, the Federal Communications Commission, the Veterans Administration, the U.S. Bureau of Prisons, and a number of federal courts have been actively involved in prohomosexual "rule-making."

MULTIPLICITY OF POLITICAL GOALS
The political goals of the homosexual movement have been widely articulated in response to a variety of events and/or interests. At times, the specific nature of the group or leader articulating the goal makes it narrowly focused. In other cases, various goals or proposals are made covering broad areas of concern. James Tinney, a leader of Pentecostal homosexuals proposed the following list, presented to President Carter for consideration at an official meeting for homosexuals in the White House on April 28, 1980:[12]

- Appointment of homosexuals (both males and females) to all appointed governmental bodies;
- Amendment of the Civil Rights and Voting Rights Acts to cover homosexuals;
- Granting of equal time by the Federal Communications Commission to homosexuals when homosexual actions are criticized by preachers on radio and television;
- Recognition of homosexuals as a "class" in the challenge of licenses to radio and TV broadcasters by the Federal Communications Commission;

TABLE 16
Prohomosexual Legislation in the United States (June 1981)

Municipality	Year(s) Enacted	Public Employment	Public Accommodations	Employment	Housing	Education	Real Estate Practices	Credit	Union Practices	Affirmative Action Program	Homosexual Acts
Alfred, N.Y.	5/74	X	X	X	X	X	X	X	X		
Amherst, Mass.	5/76	X	X	X	X	X	X	X	X		
Ann Arbor, Mich.	7/72	X	X	X	X		X	X			
Aspen, Colo.	11/77	X		X	X		X	X	X		
Atlanta, Ga.	7/71	X									
Austin, Tex.	7/75	X									
Berkeley, Calif.	10/78	X									
Bloomington, Ind.	12/75	X	X	X		X	X				
Boston, Mass.	4/76	X								X	
Champaign, Ill.	7/77	X	X	X	X			X	X		
Chapel Hill, N.C.	9/75	X									
Columbus, Oh.	1/79		X		X			X			
Cupertino, Calif.	2/75	X								X	
Detroit, Mich.	1/79	X	X	X	X	X	X	X			
East Lansing, Mich.	5/73	X	X	X	X						
Evanston, Ill.	8/80	X			X						
Hartford, Conn.	4/79	X		X							
Honolulu, Hawaii	3/81	X									
Iowa City, Iowa	5/77	X	X	X				X			
Ithaca, N.Y.	9/74	X								X	
Los Angeles, Calif.	5/77	X	X	X	X	X	X				
Madison, Wisc.	3/75	X	X	X	X		X				
Marshall, Minn.	4/75	X	X	X	X			X			
Milwaukee, Wisc.	7/80	X									
Minneapolis, Minn.	4/74	X	X	X	X	X	X	X	X	X	
Mountainview, Calif.	3/75	X								X	
New York, N.Y.	1/78	X									
Palo Alto, Calif.	8/74	X				X					
Philadelphia, Pa.	10/80	X									
Portland, Oreg.	12/74	X									
Pullman, Wash.	4/76	X			X					X	
San Francisco, Calif.	7/78	X	X	X	X	X					
Santa Barbara, Calif.	8/75	X				X					

SOURCE: "Gay Rights Protections in the U.S. and Canada," June 1981.

The Goals of the Homosexual Movement

- Denial of federal funds to religious schools which discriminate against racial and sexual minorities [homosexuals]. This denial should include denial of all student loans and all other federal aid to students attending these institutions; [This goal implies forcing seminaries and other institutions that train church and synagogue personnel to accept practicing and avowed homosexuals as candidates for the ministry.]
- Elimination of homosexuality as a consideration in the admission of foreigners to the United States by the Immigration and Naturalization Service; and
- Issuance of a Presidential Executive Order abolishing discrimination against women and homosexuals in federal and public employment, education, housing and the armed forces.

In preparation for the March on Washington, held by homosexuals in 1979, a list of "demands" was issued by a National Conference celebrated prior to this event:

- Repeal of all anti-lesbian/anti-gay laws;
- Pass a comprehensive lesbian/gay rights bill in Congress;
- End discrimination in lesbian mother and gay father custody cases;
- Issue a presidential executive order banning discrimination based on sexual orientation in the Federal government, the military, and federally contracted private employment. [13]

U.S. News and World Report offered the following as the "top priorities" of the homosexual movement:

—A presidential order prohibiting discrimination on the basis of sexual preference in federal jobs and contracts. Current rules forbid such practices but exempt the Federal Bureau of Investigation, the Central Intelligence Agency and the State Department.
—Congressional passage of the lesbian-gay civil rights bill that would amend the 1964 Civil Rights Act to include homosexuals.
—Removal of the restriction that keeps declared homosexuals from entering the U.S. from foreign countries. [14]

In some instances, political goals are a matter of taking advantage of a particular circumstance. The inclusion of prohomosexual planks in the platforms of the Republican and Democratic parties in 1980 became an important goal prior to the conventions. The homosexual National Convention Project reportedly spent $100,000 to elect homosexual delegates to both conventions. [15] This was adopted as a major political goal for 1980 by the Gay Rights National Lobby. [16]

Very specific goals relate to the particular concerns of certain groups or localities.

- The North American Man/Boy Love Association has declared as its main goals the abolition of all age consent laws (allowing homosexuals to seek sexual relations with children of all ages) and the granting of freedom to male sex offenders who have not "resorted to violence."[17] (It is not clear what position NAMBLA would take in the case of consensual sex involving violence, especially if one of the partners suffers a serious injury or even death.)

- One Incorporated, a California-based group with Councils in New York, Michigan, Illinois, and Great Britain has adopted as a political goal the elimination of the "sex offender" register, a tool utilized by the police in tracking down sex criminals.[18]
- In New York City, the homosexual movement has made it a priority to place some of its members in key positions within the city government: "Gays must remain in city staffs, acting as liaisons in public offices and agencies."[19]

These examples provide the reader with a glimpse at the involvement of homosexual groups in the promotion of their political goals. However, their interest goes far beyond strictly "homosexual issues." Consistent with a general liberal orientation, homosexual organizations have adopted the goals of liberal America, including foreign policy issues which bear no apparent relationship with the traditional interests of homosexuals qua homosexuals.

BEYOND "HOMOSEXUAL" ISSUES

Although the homosexual movement directs most of its efforts toward the accomplishment of goals directly related to the sexual propensities of its members, there are other "nonhomosexual" issues which it commonly espouses. Specific policy items that yield corresponding political goals which the homosexual movement shares with the American left include: "women's rights, prison issues, rights of the handicapped, and immigration policy."[20]

The UFMCC Washington Office identified the following goals as part of the political agenda for the movement in 1979:

> Ratification of the Equal Rights Amendment
> Reform of the U.S. Criminal Code
> Continuation of "family planing funding" for materials designed to implement government-sponsored propaganda campaigns in the areas of abortion, homosexuality, and birth control
> Continuation of provision of free attorneys (via the Legal Services Corporation) to homosexuals for cases related to their condition.[21]

Many homosexual organizations have lobbied intensely in favor of the Equal Rights Amendment. This is an issue which on the surface appears unrelated to the interests of the homosexual community. Not only female homosexuals, but their male counterparts as well, support the passage of

The Goals of the Homosexual Movement

the ERA to such an extent that this has become not a feminist issue alone but one thoroughly identified with the homosexual movement. In addition to a virtual "payoff" to the feminist movement for the support homosexual organizations usually receive from their feminist counterpart, there are other factors which apparently have contributed to make the passage of the ERA a top homosexual priority, including the following.

- The confusion of sex roles and political authority's attempts to negate the effect of biological gender distinctions clearly benefits the homosexual movement and relates harmoniously to the homosexual ideology. (Heterosexual relations presuppose the basic sexual difference between the partners, their complementarity, and the biological openness towards new life implicit in each sexual act. These characteristics are clearly negated in homosexual relationships, autoeroticism, and abortion.)
- Female homosexuals (or at least their leaders) appear to be largely radical feminists.
- The ERA constitutes a frontal attack on the traditional family and its adoption would probably result in the forced legalization of homosexual marriages. According to a study published in the Yale Law Journal of January 1973:

> The Court's decision that the denial of marriage licenses to homosexuals does not abridge existing equal protection law would not save that practice from attack under the proposed Twenty-seventh Amendment. . . . The legislative history of the Amendment clearly supports the interpretation that sex is to be an impermissible legal classification, that rights are not to be abridged on the basis of sex. A statute or administrative policy which permits a man to marry a woman, subject to certain regulatory restrictions, but categorically denies him the right to marry another man clearly entails a classification along sexual lines. . . .
>
> The stringent requirements of the proposed Equal Rights Amendment argue strongly for . . . granting marriage licenses to homosexual couples who satisfy reasonable and non-discriminatory qualifications.[22]

It would be an oversimplification to assert that the great difficulties the feminist movement has encountered in the passage of the ERA have been the result of the association of this measure with homosexuality. However, this may have been a contributing factor. There can be little question, however, that the homosexual issue is just one of several radical issues which have resulted in the death of the ERA. Several years have now elapsed without one state having ratified the ERA; state ERAs have been defeated repeatedly in referenda; and a number of states have rescinded their previous ratification of the ERA. Liberals in Congress, pressured by the Carter White House, managed to extend the deadline for its ratification in a highly irregular and probably illegal maneuver which has proved unsuccessful.

Social Goals

There are a number of social goals espoused by the homosexual movement. Although they are closely connected with the political goals, the
specific characteristic of the social goals is that they are designed to directly
effect a transformation of social institutions and practices in harmony with
the tenets of the homosexual ideology and the needs of the homosexual
movement. As mentioned before, it is nearly impossible to delineate
precisely the boundaries between social and political goals, although it is
possible to perceive the difference in thrust between them. (E.g., while
the passage of the ERA was clearly a political goal and the acceptance of
same-sex "marriages" a social goal, there is little question that they were
related, in that passage of the ERA would almost certainly have legalized
homosexual "marriages".) The various social goals of the homosexual
movement presented here are offered by way of example and are limited
by reasons of space. Other social goals of the movement (e.g., homosexualization of the media, infiltration of cultural activities, etc.) which could
also have been included, have not been discussed.

STATEMENT OF HOMOSEXUAL SOCIAL GOALS
In November 1979, the National Gay Task Force conducted a survey
of its members, the results of which reveal the priorities of the very active
and socially conscious membership of the NGTF. They include consensus
on:

> The right of avowed homosexuals to be public school teachers
> Increase in the utilization of solar power
> Passage of the Equal Rights Amendment
> Adoption of children by homosexuals
> Passage of prohomosexual legislation
> Utilization of media to promote a positive image of homosexuals
> Elimination of "anti-gay" policies in federal agencies
> Utilization of the court system to advance the goals of the homosexual
> movement.[23]

Homosexual organizations with a narrower focus, such as the North
American Man/Boy Love Association, possess their own blueprints and
specific sets of activities for reshaping the United States to suit the sexual
needs of their members. The following outline was published by the
NAMBLA Journal as the social action agenda of the "Task Force on Child-
Adult Relations" (TFCAR). The general objectives of TFCAR are "to
improve the social status and public image of pedophiles, to eliminate
the legal sanctions against pedophile behavior, and to increase public

The Goals of the Homosexual Movement

awareness of children's emotional and sexual needs."[24] The activities proposed for the TFCAR are all designed to bring these goals to fruition.

1. Seeking to improve the public image of pedophiles through:
    A. Oversight of sex-education and psychology curricula in public schools, colleges and universities, seeking to eliminate old stereotypes and falsehoods regarding pedophilia and children's sexuality.
    B. Consultation with authorities on mental health and human sexual behavior to encourage a humane attitude toward pedophilia.
    C. Legislative lobbying to reduce legal sanctions against pedophile behavior in particular and all consensual sexual behavior in general, and to increase children's rights to self-determination.
    D. Liaison with feminist and other groups to establish the principle that the goals of all liberation groups are essentially the same: the elimination of sexist, authoritarian regimentation of human lives; and that the liberation of children is the *sine qua non* of all human liberation.
2. Publication and dissemination of literature supporting the goals of pedophile liberation.
3. Publication and dissemination of literature to increase public awareness of children's sexual and emotional needs, especially in the light of research on cognitive development.[25]

This outline was proposed by a man imprisoned for child-molestation, who apologizes in this way for his inability to implement these plans: "I regret that I cannot do so at the present time because I am in prison for 'crimes' of pedophilia."[26]

The ultimate social goal of the homosexual movement is the transformation of key social structures and our entire culture according to the pattern dictated by the homosexual ideology, to satisfy the individual needs of the homosexuals themselves—chiefly their sexual needs, but also the corporate needs of their organizations. Although not publicized widely, and normally unacknowledged, the foundation for a political and juridical system in which homosexuality is accepted as an alternative and legitimate lifestyle, and in which homosexual acts are not merely tolerated but positively accepted, requires the structural transformation of society and a profound alteration in the consciousness of its members. Jeff Greenfield published in the *Village Voice* an article which makes this point:

> What then is the nature of the oppression? Not that gays are excluded from the public life but that gays are forced to conceal their true nature. Why should gays have to hide their sexual preferences? Why should they have to be something in public that they are not in reality? . . .
>
> . . . But when a claim is made for government protection for the public assertion of private behavior, we are in a very different area—one in which the law has nothing to say.

To put the point as bluntly as possible: there is no civil right to feel comfortable about someone else's behavior: there is no constitutional right to be admired or respected when private preferences are made known to a public that doesn't approve of them.[27]

The implication is clear: unless society itself is transformed, the homosexual movement cannot hope to achieve lasting success. The National Gay Task Force has realized the nature of this challenge, targeting three key American institutions for "softening up" by a concentrated and aggressive campaign of systematic infiltration. According to the January-February 1981 issue of *It's Time* (newsletter of the NGTF): "work is progressing with NGTF's plans to target major American institutions for educational campaigns designed to make a positive impact on their perceptions of lesbians and gay men. Dr. Charles Hitchcock, the NGTF Public Education Consultant, reports that he has made religious, media, and educational institutions the foci of the program."[28]

The implementation of this program is designed to alter substantially the institutions themselves. It is a carefully designed plan, and these institutions can expect major pressure to "fall in line" in terms of the various homosexual issues. In a subsequent issue of *It's Time*, Hitchcock elaborated on the ways in which the NGTF expects to effect this social change.

> Individual programs are being designed for each specific institution. Components include a history of each institution's attitudes or policies on gay rights, identification of institutional decision-makers and decision-making processes, and a curriculum for an educational (training) program with appropriate materials and resource people identified," he added. "A prime example would be that of a national television network where, because of the lack of any stated policy or educational materials concerned with gay issues, individuals are left to their own personal whim or prejudice in dealing with gay stories and news items. In targeting such an institution for our program, we would, through staff meetings, educational seminars and the development of relevant educational materials, hope to have a major positive impact on how that institution deals with gay concerns—both internally and in it's [sic] entertainment programs and news coverage.[29]

These institutions have been well chosen in that they constitute the chief agents of socialization in America. Although the family is certainly a far more important socializing institution, families as such are not organized and thus not subject to this approach. As a matter of fact, the NGTF campaign can be easily conceived as directed not just to individuals but also to families, through which individuals are influenced and which are chiefly affected by church, school, and media. It is evident, however,

The Goals of the Homosexual Movement

that the homosexual movement does intend to alter radically the nature of American society.

THE SEARCH FOR ACCEPTANCE

In a sense, the homosexual movement and all of its activities may be interpreted as an effort to gain social acceptance for homosexuals. Traditional values in American society, held in great esteem by the vast majority of the population—although not necessarily by the elites—reject homosexual behavior as a perversion, an illness, and/or a form of criminally destructive activity. Since homosexual behavior (actual or intentional) is precisely the core concept which serves as a nucleus for the homosexual movement, it is only to be expected that tearing down the adverse value system is a goal of this movement. This is especially important in view of the fact that the rejection of homosexual behavior is not just an intellectual conclusion, although there are solid ethical, psychological, sociological, political, and theological grounds for such a rejection. The refusal to accept homosexual behavior is grounded in the need for sex definition and the threat to all psychosocial structures based on sexuality that same-sex practices imply. They involve not only the self, but the family and interpersonal relationships of many sorts. The rejection of homosexuality is as emotional as it is intellectual. For most Americans it is a "gut issue."

Against this overwhelming tendency born of the deep-seated need to protect oneself, one's children, and the very future of society, the homosexual movement labors to create the conditions that will enable its adherents to claim full equality, not just as human beings (no one has denied that homosexuals are persons) but as homosexuals. According to Barbara Gittings, a noted leader of the homosexual movement, "what the homosexual wants—and here he is neither willing to compromise nor morally required to compromise—is acceptance of homosexuality as a way of life fully on a par with heterosexuality, acceptance of the homosexual as a person on a par with the heterosexual."[30]

Most of this work is precisely about the efforts of many homosexual organizations to gain social acceptance. These efforts are exemplified by a suit on the part of a homosexual Eagle Scout to force his admission to the Boy Scouts organization.[31] Should he win the suit, other boys would be forced to associate with him (or leave the organization) and homosexuality would gain a measure of social acceptance. No different in kind is the goal of London's "Gay Sweatshop," a professional group of homosexual actors who use the theater to expose British children to "Feeling Different," a project in which children are made to explore the feelings homosexuals experience in social settings. Through discussions, role playing, and attendance at theater performances, the children are skillfully led to accept homosexuality.[32] Similarly, when Brother Joseph Izzo, CFX (a homosexual movement leader previously mentioned) asserts that many

Roman Catholic bishops are homosexuals,[33] it becomes difficult for followers of these bishops to reject homosexuality, since it affects people they have been trained to accept as models of holiness and as authority figures.

The acceptance of homosexuality would imply a revolutionary change in American social practices. This is, however, of vital importance to the homosexual movement. Its efforts in this regard are not only easily explainable, but also in a sense justifiable, if viewed as a necessary means for its survival.

EMPLOYMENT OF AVOWED HOMOSEXUALS

One of the social goals of the homosexual movement is to ensure the employment of avowed homosexuals throughout the private and public sectors alike. The question has never been whether homosexuals can be employed or not; it is obvious that they have always been able to find employment, as there is no evidence that among the unemployed there is a preponderance of homosexuals. Moreover, the affluence prevalent in the homosexual community, as seen in chapter IV, would seem incompatible with effective or extensive discrimination against homosexuals.

The question here is not simply one of securing employment for homosexuals, but of ensuring that avowed homosexuals remain in their jobs even after they have "come out." Additionally, positions from which the behavior of others can be shaped, or which have a special claim to respectability (law enforcement personnel, clergy, teachers, criminal justice system personnel, national security, etc.) are particularly important for the homosexual movement. There is little question that in the past homosexuals have occupied positions of responsibility at all levels of society. So long as a homosexual was discreet, he usually had few, if any, problems. If he was not sexually active, the problem simply could not arise. In especially sensitive cases, society frowned upon known homosexuals occupying specific positions, but unless a major scandal broke, there was little or no effort to uncover the sexual proclivities of individuals (and this happened only in certain kinds of jobs such as those mentioned immediately above).

The objective of having openly practicing homosexuals in positions where human behavior can be shaped, either directly or because the jobholder is a role model for others, can be easily understood once the need for acceptance on the part of homosexuals is acknowledged. The drive to accomplish this goal is relentless. New Ways Ministry, a Roman Catholic prohomosexual group, has sponsored a national symposium directed almost exclusively to the question of homosexual clergy.[34] A perusal of the documentation provided by most homosexual groups within the various denominations reveals an almost compulsory preoccupation with the question of ensuring the ordination of homosexual clerics. In a dif-

The Goals of the Homosexual Movement

ferent field, the efforts of homosexual radical activists to "open up" such agencies as the Federal Bureau of Investigation, the Central Intelligence Agency, the Defense Investigative Agency, the Armed Forces, and the Foreign Service have been notorious.[35] In California, the state, bowing to pressures from the homosexual movement, has a "gay protector" whose job is to ensure the permanence of open homosexuals in the civil service.[36] The importance of legitimizing homosexual teachers is underscored by the strenuous efforts of the movement's leadership in fighting instances of homosexual teacher dismissals. The importance of maintaining sodomy laws (which criminalize various homosexual acts) on the books if the homosexuals are to be kept out of the classroom is evidenced by the Minnesota case of *McConnell vs. Anderson*. In this decision, a man was deemed to be legally subject to dismissal from his teaching job after applying for a license to marry another man on the basis of his obvious intention to violate the state sodomy statute.[37] For many years, the New York City prohomosexual law has been defeated by community opposition—including Roman Catholics, Orthodox Jews, organized policemen and firemen—largely on the basis of the "employment clause" of the bill. "There is no doubt that the issue of jobs for homosexuals, especially jobs in the public sectors, such as teachers and firemen, is a political issue in New York State and has been since 1971."[38] Individuals and institutions interested in maintaining the traditional value structure of American society have much at stake in thwarting the homosexual movement's attempt to ensure the pervasive presence of avowed homosexuals in the working place. These efforts do not—and should not—include a systematic campaign to uncover "hidden homosexuals," as this would probably be counterproductive. In sensitive areas, such as law enforcement, education, religion, mental health, and national security, the presence of avowed homosexuals—especially individuals who insist on "converting" others to the homosexual ideology, who utilize their jobs for this purpose, or who try to approach coworkers sexually—is obviously contrary to the maintenance of a society based on traditional values. The best strategy to counteract the homosexual movement in this regard involves at least these three components:

- The creation of conditions that will make it impossible for homosexuals to "come out"
- The institution of measures that will reinforce heterosexual tendencies in individuals while discouraging overt or covert manifestations of homosexuality—even internal
- The implementation of an educational campaign designed to counteract the basic tenets of the homosexual ideology.

ACCEPTANCE OF "GAYSPEAK"

A clear goal of the homosexual movement is the incorporation of "gayspeak" into the speech patterns of the United States. This peculiar language of the homosexual subculture carries within itself—implicitly and explicitly—the various tenets of the homosexual ideology. Thus its use results in modifications in both the consciousness of the users and their behavior, to the benefit of the homosexual movement. (See chapter II.) It must be noted, however, that there are various elements of speech which must be adopted for a more efficient use of "gayspeak" in the social transformation of America according to the pattern of the homosexual movement:

Vocabulary. The use of certain words is important for the homosexual movement. Typical examples are "gay" to refer to a homosexual or as a qualifier of items associated with homosexuality; "holy union," "commitment" or "marriage" to refer to the pattern of consistent sexual intercourse between two persons of the same sex; "human rights" to refer to preferred legal status for homosexuals; "love" for the desire of a homosexual for sexual favors from or to a member of his own sex; "oppression" for the defensive reaction of individuals or groups to attempts by the homosexual movement to impose its ideology, and so on.

Inclusive Language. Although not directly related to homosexual issues, the use of inclusive language, as seen in chapter II, has a high priority for the homosexual movement. The sex role confusion which derives from, and is nearly the sole object of, the use of inclusive language is in harmony with the central feature of homosexuality, the disappearance of gender-specific roles in sexual relations (i.e., in homosexual relations there is neither "masculine" nor "feminine" as distinguished from the "opposite" sex, although the notions of "active" and "passive" are still valid). For a fuller understanding of this subject the reader is referred to Casey Miller and Kate Swift, *The Handbook of Nonsexist Language,* 1980. There are also a number of federal documents which instruct bureaucrats on how to write official documents designed to satisfy the language requirements of radical feminists and the homosexual movement.

Patterns of Expression. This refers not so much to the acceptance of individual words with a definite prohomosexual meaning as to the utilization of colloquial phrases, idiomatic expressions, modes of inflection, mannerisms, etc. which imply the tolerance of the homosexual lifestyle or its incorporation into our culture as a positive or at least neutral feature. The media are crucial in this regard, although other agents of socialization (e.g., schools) also make a significant contribution.

Homosexual movement efforts to impose "gayspeak" are difficult to counteract, although awareness of its nature and effects—especially on young persons—could dilute the impact of these efforts considerably. Should the use of "gayspeak" become prevalent, however, it is difficult to envision a practicable and effectual way for tradition-minded Americans to defeat the homosexual movement. For the present, the question of

The Goals of the Homosexual Movement

which has causal priority, the success of the homosexual movement, or the adoption of its language, must remain open.

EXTENDED CONCEPT OF "FAMILY"

There is no question that one of the top priorities of the homosexual movement is to force a "redefinition" of the American family away from the traditional husband-wife-children model to a more "functional" definition based on the notion of economic unit or any other basis that does not require heterosexuality as its foundation. The notion that a family must involve persons of both sexes is profoundly inimical to the homosexual movement. By their own definition, heterosexual relations are beyond their reach; thus the traditional family as a normative institution for human relations is unacceptable.

As early as 1970, elements within the homosexual movement had identified the family as inimical to its interests. At a convention in Philadelphia, the "Male Homosexual" workshop included the following as one of its demands: "The abolition of the nuclear family because it perpetuates the false categories of homosexuality and heterosexuality."[39]

The "Lesbian" workshop made a similar demand: "Destruction of the Nuclear Family: The nuclear family is a microcosm of the fascist state, where the women and children are owned by, and their fates determined by, the needs of men, in a man's world."[40] The "Women" workshop presented an equally radical plank which departed from the traditional model of the family in several respects and closed with a frankly prohomosexual statement:

> *Family:* Whereas in a capitalist culture the institution of the family has been used as an economic tool or instrument, not serving the human needs of the people, we declare that we will not relate to the private ownership of people. We encourage and support the continued growth of communal households and communal relationships and other alternative forms to the patriarchal family.
>
> We call for socialization of housework and child care with the sharing of all work by men and women.
>
> Women must have the right to decide if and when we want to have children. There is no such thing as an illegitimate child. There should be free and safe birth control, including abortion, available on demand. There should be no forced sterilization or mandatory birth control programs which are now used as genocide against third world sisters and against poor people.
>
> Every woman has the right to decide whether she will be homosexual, heterosexual, or bisexual.[41]

This philosophy, destructive of the traditional concept of the family and frankly subordinated to prohomosexual notions, made its way into official speech and thought. This has been discussed by Allan C. Carlson in *The*

Human Life Review, where he described the advent of "pluralism" in the concept of the family during the latter part of the 1960s:

> Semantic clarity progressively deteriorated over the next few years as the discipline embraced the heretofore unknown notion of "a pluralism of family forms." An important benchmark of such change was the Forum 14 Report of the 1970 White House Conference on Children, which celebrated a "pluralistic society of varying family forms and a multiplicity of cultures." Defining family as "a group of individuals in interaction," the Report described optional forms ranging from nuclear families to "single parent," "communal," "group marriage," and "homosexual" varieties.[42]

In 1972 the Chicago meeting of the National Coalition of Gay Organizations adopted the following demand: "Repeal of all legislative provisions that restrict the sex or number of persons entering into a marriage unit; and the extension of legal benefits to all persons who cohabit regardless of sex or numbers."[43] A 1976 article in the *Blade* pointed out various reasons for making same-sex "marriages" between homosexuals a social institution. Several are similar to those normally advanced to justify heterosexual marriages: love between those involved, the stability of the relationship, tax benefits, and others, one of which is particularly important in the context of this chapter. "The option of legal marriage for gays represents a social acceptance of a relationship which the individuals involved have taken seriously. Even for those gays who do not see legal marriage as necessary [it] is important on principle."[44] The change in social structures herein implied is undeniable.

At the 1980 White House Conference on Families, homosexual organizations and leaders labored with some success for the redefinition of the family in their own terms. Although homosexual relations are incompatible with the traditional families, the National Gay Task Force was reportedly one of forty-eight "diverse family-oriented" organizations that formed a coalition for the conference.[45] A group of forty-two national organizations (including the NGTF, Catholic Charities, the Synagogue Council, the Salvation Army, and the Future Homemakers of America) recommended that representatives of "same-sex couples" be part of the Advisory Council of the Conference.[46] At testimony offered during the preparatory hearings for the White House Conference on Families, homosexuals could testify confidently that "gay families share many of the attributes that characterize straight families, and that a broad definition of the family could easily include both homosexual and heterosexual relationships."[47] The NGTF could assert that it had "played a significant role in conference activities."[48] It is clear that redefining the family is by now a "traditional" issue of the homosexual movement.

From an ideological viewpoint, the homosexual attack on the family is

The Goals of the Homosexual Movement

rooted in the notion that if heterosexual relations were to be accepted as founded upon nature, and thus normative, homosexual practices would lose their legitimacy. Apologists for the homosexual movement—even those who otherwise profess allegiance to traditional beliefs—commonly join in the attack on the family. The contrast between those who continue to assert the validity of traditional morality and the defenders of the prohomosexual viewpoint (based on purely subjective criteria) is evident in the following *New York Times* story:

> The sanctity of family life, built on a model of heterosexuality, has come down through Christian history as an integral part of the faith that is deeply ingrained in most Christians.
>
> Under this view, a homosexual poses a threat to the accepted moral order and provides an illegitimate example for others to follow.
>
> The strongest attack on this view is mounted by those who proclaim, as their traditional coreligionists also do, that love is the guiding standard in all human relations but further believe that homosexual relationships can be loving and morally good.
>
> The Rev. John J. McNeill, a Jesuit, has become a leading exponent of the drive for reappraisal. In his recent book, "The Church and the Homosexual," Father McNeill, who admits to having homosexual preferences, contends that each relationship, homosexual or heterosexual, should be evaluated by its capacity to enhance human growth and that exploitation of one person by another is always destructive.[49]

Another reason why the family is attacked is the ideological need of the homosexual movement to obliterate sex distinctions. Such an organization as the Custody Action for Lesbian Mothers (CALM) (avowed purpose, to enable female homosexuals who have children to keep these children)[50] in practice foments sex role confusion, since in the American cultural matrix female homosexuals are considered incapable of inculcating in their children the traditional family values or of fostering a normal sexual identity. The open acceptance of female homosexuality which allows these homosexuals to keep their children implies that the sexual attraction of one woman to another, considered from a normative standpoint incompatible with the biological matrices of both women, is not, in fact, incompatible with these matrices. This is clearly self-contradictory.

Marotta's analysis of the "radical lesbian feminist" perspective points out the centrality of sex role rejection in the "homosexual liberation" process as early as 1970.

> The radical lesbian feminist perspective was powerful because it suggested that lesbians, heterosexual women, and male homosexuals were all kept from self-realization by the same phenomenon: conventional ideas about the nature of and the behavior appropriate for each sex. Some attempted to develop this

insight into the arguments, first, that women are oppressed because they are forced into limited and devalued roles, particularly those of sex object and child-rearer; second, that male homosexuals are denigrated and persecuted because they fail to conform to conventional male roles when expressing their sexual feelings and affections; and third, that lesbians suffer both because they are women and because as homosexuals they are denied even the meager rewards accorded females who succeed in roles deemed appropriate for women.[51]

This line of argumentation is common throughout the homosexual literature, although obviously not all authors are identified with the "radical lesbian feminist perspective." Ideologically, however, the notion of "conventional family" as normative is clearly inimical to the very existence of homosexuality as a condition and of homosexual behavior as its logical consequence. It is thus not surprising that the homosexual movement has established as one of its goals the demise of the family as the ideal American institution.

In order to define family with any degree of consistency in the context of the sexual needs of its members, the homosexual movement must promote the independence of the procreative and affective/supportive aspects of human sexuality in general and of family relationships in particular. Traditionally, both of these aspects have been considered essential according to the natural order. Inasmuch as homosexual relations are by nature nonprocreative, the concept of family must be radically altered to serve the needs of homosexuals. This was brought out in the testimony offered by the National Gay Task Force in connection with the White House Conference on Families:

> It seems to us that the notion of family involves two basic human needs: 1) The need of each individual to share love and caring with other human beings and to take responsibility in other people's lives; and 2) The need for children to depend on adults during their formative years, not only for their safety and survival but for the experience, love and caring that will enable them to make rewarding relationships with other human beings as independent adults. We believe that a working definition of "family" is any constellation of two or more individuals which meets one or both of these basic human needs.[52]

Within the homosexual subculture, the notion that homosexual liaisons can be given the rank of "family" is widely accepted. Homosexual religious institutions—autonomous or related to major denominations—provide the setting for rites of "union," the homosexual equivalent of marriage. Cases of "homosexual divorce" with suits for "palimony" or monetary compensation similar to alimony, have already taken place. One such case took place in the District of Columbia, where one homosexual sued another for $100,000 following the breakdown of their homosexual relationship.[53] This notion that homosexual couples do constitute a family has

The Goals of the Homosexual Movement

begun to make inroads outside the homosexual community. Diane Lebedeff, Housing Judge in Manhattan, has ruled that two homosexuals who "maintain a homosexual family unit" cannot be evicted from an apartment rented by one of them. This decision was greeted by Rosalyn Richter, executive director of the Lambda Legal Defense and Educational Fund—a homosexual organization—with words that clearly indicate its value in terms of the goals of the homosexual movement: "This is the first decision on this issue on the right of a homosexual family to remain as tenant. . . . This arises quite frequently."[54]

A variant of the "alternative family" proposed by the homosexual movement is the case of a female lesbian who has had children and begins to take on "lovers" while insisting on retaining the guardianship of her children. One such case is described in the *Boston Globe*, presenting the story of a divorced woman—Sarah—who had already told her ten-year-old son of her predilection for other women and the nature of her relationship with her "roommate," Lynn. This liberal publication portrays them as one happy family. "He not only accepts Sarah, but also accepts Lynn (not her real name), Sarah's lover and roommate for the past several months." Sarah is portrayed as a woman who feels "secure she is not only a fit but very loving parent."[55] Some of the family practices in Sarah's household would probably be considered improper by most Americans. About her son's relations with her and her homosexual mate, Sarah said that "he jumps into bed with us on weekends. . . . He feels so close to Lynn that he began calling her 'mother.' At first he corrected himself, but now he goes ahead. It seems natural to him."[56] In addition to such organizations as CALM, this concept is promoted by the practices of the Lesbian and Gay Parents Project, an offshoot of the Committee Against Sexism of the National Lawyers Guild.[57] Many feminist and homosexual groups have activities designed to promote this concept. For example, the Washington Area Women's Center sponsors a "Discussion/Support Group for Lesbian Mothers" which "will explore topics ranging from toys and games to relationships involving our children to parthenogenesis."[58] (This seems to refer to the artificial insemination of females as a way of eliminating completely the need for sexual intercourse in reproduction and family life. Although highly speculative, one can envision the day in which a female-controlled homosexual society would resort to amniocentesis to determine the sex of unborn children conceived in this fashion by female homosexuals. Most male children would be liquidated by abortion. Females would be reared as homosexuals and the few remaining males would be used as sources of spermatozoa for future implantations.)

Another important area in the redefinition of the family is the radical alternative to relations between children and their parents. Certain homosexuals have a vested interest in such a revolutionary change in the structure of the family. The North American Man/Boy Love Association, for example, has theorized on the nature of the family and the need to achieve "liberation" of children:

> With the decline of the extended family and traditional church influence, the state has increased its investment in maintaining a preferred family structure, i.e., male-dominated, heterosexual nuclear variety. The state continues to have a vested interest in regulating and channeling sexual activity into the type it can best control. The greatest threat to this hierarchical and repressive system is presented by sexual and affectionate personal relations outside the approved mode. Specifically, this means the freedom of those over whom the state still has greatest control (minors) and those with whom they would create their own lives.[59]

The "new" family is certainly not predicated on the traditional structure proposed by the Scriptures and enshrined by centuries of universal practice. In this progressive scheme, the natural foundation for family relations disappears, and in its place the autonomous self-defining will is enshrined as sole subjective master: "The child himself should have the right to decide whom to live with, whether a lesbian mother or a gay father, the 'natural' parents, a boy-lover, or someone else."[60]

It must be recognized that efforts to redefine the family are not the exclusive preserve of the homosexual movement. Feminists, the sex education establishment, and secular humanists also have much at stake in this process. From a traditional viewpoint, these forces can be fairly described as "antifamily," although many of them would protest this description. It is still too early to know whether the nature of the American family has been irretrievably modified, but they have had considerable success in their efforts at family "redefinition," if the rates of abortion, divorce, and use of artificial contraception are any indication. (If, in fact, the position that the traditional family is rooted in nature is true, the demise of the family would have disastrous—perhaps fatal—consequences to American society. At this point, however, from the point of view of empirical science, it is still too early to make definitive assertions.)

From an intellectual point of view, the acceptance of the concept of alternative families is not limited to such radical organizations as the National Organization for Women, which has indicated in its position paper on Lesbian Rights that "no single model or definition for family life can be justly applied to a diverse citizenry through legislation or the court system."[61] Martin Rock, coordinator of the Brethren/Mennonite Council for Gay Concerns, testified as follows at a public hearing held in Washington, D.C. by the White House Conference on Families: "We *are* families. We live as family units, sharing the same household and its expenses and duties, and sharing the responsibility for decisions; sharing

The Goals of the Homosexual Movement

resources, values, and goals; eating at the same table, enjoying the same friends, participating in church activities together, attending the same social functions, and taking vacations together."[62] These are indications that this mentality is starting to penetrate such "high" denominations as the Roman Catholic Church. For example, a 1981 set of guidelines on sex education published by the United States Catholic Conference was praised by New Ways Ministry's Father Robert Nugent, SDS, for its apparent acceptance of "alternate" lifestyles when speaking on the "centrality of family life." Nugent also points approvingly to a paragraph on the need to "understand and evaluate the . . . psychosexual processes of different sexual lifestyles."[63] New Ways Ministry has been able to cite two Catholic sources (one of them a bishop) which seemingly accept, at least in principle, the notion of alternative families, specifically in connection with homosexuality. According to Bishop Cletus O'Donnell of Madison, Wisconsin:

> . . . a family means more than a mother, father and two kids living happily in a single-family home. In our families we have to have room for widowed persons and divorced persons, for handicapped persons, and for persons with different sexual identities, for the gay people . . . In our programs we want married couples to minister to each other and single people to minister to each other and handicapped people and gays and all of the groups which make up the Christian community to minister to each other.[64]

An Archdiocesan Commission in Milwaukee presented similar ideas using the code word "sexual minorities" as a substitute for "homosexuals":

> While recognizing the value of the nuclear family, the reality of present society has necessitated the broadening of our concept and practice of family ministry to acknowledge other lifestyles, including, but not necessarily limited to, single parent families, childless couples, the widowed, the separated, sexual minorities, and single people. . . . [65]

Many other examples could be offered of the movement's success in advancing the principle of alternative families in the context of the homosexual condition. It is apparent from what has been presented, however, that this is a priority of the movement. Given the traditional concept that the family is the basic cell of society, it is most important for profamily advocates and intellectuals to understand the nature of the threat to the family that the homosexual movement represents.

IMPOSITION OF SEX EDUCATION: PANSEXUALISM

In chapter I of this work we had the opportunity to examine certain indicators in the American educational system that reveal an extraordinary acceptance for homosexuality in educational institutions. As schools are

227

a key component in the socialization of most Americans, it is not surprising that the homosexual movement has targeted them as potential vehicles for the spread of the homosexual ideology and of homosexuality itself. The former can be accomplished by the incorporation of prohomosexual ideas in the various curricula, the latter by creating an environment designed to strengthen any homosexual tendencies among students actually or even potentially affected by the homosexual condition, while sowing sexual confusion among other students. The transformation of the schools according to the needs of the homosexual movement is thus a major social goal of the homosexual leadership.

Schools are ideally suited to the purposes of the homosexual movement for various reasons and in several ways.

Curricula. The very purpose of the schools is the transmission of ideas, values, and attitudes. The homosexual ideology is precisely a composite of these items structured in a manner favorable to the homosexual movement. There is evidence that the schools have, in fact, been used to transmit the homosexual ideology, so much so that the Education Exploration Center (Minneapolis) has made one of its main projects the collection of articles which feature, among other subjects, "how to slip gay and lesbian issues into lesson plans."

> The Education Exploration Center is soliciting articles for a curriculum-anthology on teaching gay and lesbian issues in secondary and elementary schools. We want articles from teachers, students and parents—articles on experiences like being the only lesbian in the local PTA, how to slip gay and lesbian issues into lesson plans, student reactions to a gay speaker, coming out to other teachers or students, or how to organize a lesbian and gay teachers association. We're interested in your ideas for lesson plans on prejudice, stereotypes, civil rights, gays and lesbians in history, literature, science, etc., lesbian and gay culture, feminism, sex roles, the range of sexual behavior and how young people make decisions about their sexual values.[66]

Jean O'Leary and Bruce Voeller, then coexecutive directors of the National Gay Task Force, argued forcefully for the proposition that avowed homosexuals should be "entitled to use their own experience as an educational resource and/or advocate 'gay rights' in the classroom." They were responding to an article in the *American Educator* (official publication of the American Federation of Teachers) which pointed out various reasons why the use of the classroom for prohomosexual purposes was undesirable.[67] Even official agencies have advocated the use of schools for prohomosexual purposes. The Department of Human Resources of the State of Oregon advocated, in its "Final Report of the Task Force on Sexual Preference," the inclusion of homosexuality as a subject of study for children in the seventh grade and above who participate in sex education classes.[68]

The Goals of the Homosexual Movement

Personnel. Schools are compulsory institutions in which students are "forced" to stay for long periods of time under the supervision of adults not of their parents' choosing. These adults normally act as role models for the students and exercise considerable influence over them. The value of homosexuals in relationship with children was proposed eloquently by Andre Lorde, a female homosexual, speaking to the National Third World Lesbian and Gay Conference in Washington, D.C. in 1979:

> They [children] have a right to grow, free from the diseases of racism, sexism, classism, homophobia, and the terror of any difference. These children will take what we do and carry it on through their visions, and their visions will be different in turn from ours. But they need us as role-models, to know that they are not alone in daring to define themselves outside the approved structures. They need to know our triumphs, and our errors.[69]

The importance of the presence of homosexual teachers in the classroom is underscored by the strenuous campaign waged by the homosexual movement to defeat the Briggs Amendment in California.[70] In 1978 the name of California State Senator John Briggs became associated with Proposition 6 in a state-wide referendum. Proposition 6 would have excluded from employment by public schools individuals who "engaged in advocating, soliciting, imposing, encouraging or promoting private or public homosexual acts." The proposition was defeated by a joint effort of liberal and homosexual organizations. This case is only one of many in which homosexual organizations have endeavored to force schools to retain homosexuals as teachers.[71]

There are many examples illustrating the degree to which the concept that homosexual teachers belong in the classroom has infiltrated American institutions. For example, this practice has been defended in congressional hearings by the president of the American Psychiatric Association and the Stated Clerk of the General Assembly of the United Presbyterian Church in the U.S.A.[72] This prohomosexual viewpoint contrasts with the practices of societies which emphasize the need for strong and socially useful youth as a national policy. Socialist societies, for example, recognizing the potentially deleterious effects of homosexuals in the classroom, have a policy of "heterosexual teachers only." According to Fidel Castro, "we have considered it our duty to take at least minimum measures to the effect that those positions in which one might have a direct influence upon children and young people should not be in the hands of homosexuals, above all in educational centers."[73]

Although not as visible as teachers, counselors also play an important role in the formation of young people. It is to be expected, therefore, that the homosexual leadership will press for the employment of homosexual counselors. However, due to the "guidance" function of counselors, a stronger opposition still can be expected by tradition-minded parents and community leaders.

Literature. The homosexual ideology can be easily infiltrated, either subtly or openly, into texts and reference books alike. Until parents have the opportunity to play an effective role in selecting the kinds of books schools make available to—or even force on—their children, there is little likelihood that the use of prohomosexual books will cease in our schools. (Section 440B(4) of the Family Protection Act (S. 1378, 97th Congress) takes care of this problem by making it illegal "for any Federal, state or local educational agency or institution receiving any federal funds to . . . prohibit parental review of textbooks prior to their use in public school classrooms.")

Prohomosexual materials are already available in many American schools. For example, it has been reported that "San Francisco's schools are already adopting textbooks giving quasi-official sanction to homosexuality as an alternative lifestyle."[74] *Booklist,* the reviewing journal of the American Library Association recommended, in its June 1, 1979, issue, the use of *Sex, Telling It Straight* for children in grades 5 through 8. This work is openly prohomosexual and clearly teaches various tenets of the homosexual ideology.[75] Morton Hunt's *Gay: What You Should Know About Homosexuality,* intended for children as young as twelve years of age, is a frank exposition of how to engage in homosexual acts with exquisite detail.[76]

Libraries, both in and out of the schools, are not safe from the presence of prohomosexual materials. Homosexual organizations publish bibliographies for the use of sympathetic librarians and teachers willing to utilize their positions for the advancement of the homosexual cause. The Gay Task Force of the American Library Association has published a how-to manual on homosexualizing libraries. The following announcement describes this publication.

> A pamphlet of tips for the non-librarian on how to get gay materials into libraries is now available from the Gay Task Force of the American Library Association.
> Called *Censored, Ignored, Overlooked, Too Expensive? How to Get Gay Materials Into Libraries,* the pamphlet explains library selection policies in a general way and tells what an individual or a group can do to get a library to buy more gay books and periodicals. There are also sections on what to do if the library refuses your request, on why gay books are sometimes kept where you have to ask for them, and on donating materials to the library.[77]

Secular Humanism. The pervasiveness of secular humanism, which is taught in the schools as the unofficial religion of our society, makes educational institutions prone to accept substantial elements of the homosexual ideology with minimum difficulty. Rooted in a purely naturalistic

The Goals of the Homosexual Movement

conception of life and devoid of permanent ethical categories, secular humanism is ideally suited to incorporate the teachings of the homosexual movement. (Although not "officially" accepted as "state religion," secular humanism has acquired such a status for all practical purposes. Repeated court decisions—e.g., Arkansas Judge William Overton's decision against scientific creationism on January 5, 1982—have revealed this to be an incontestable fact.) While schools organized around religious principles (be they Muslim, Jewish, or Christian) would be virtually immune to the homosexual ideology, secular humanist ideas provide a fertile ground for it. This takes place in public and private schools alike. It is a well-known fact that there are many schools sponsored by churches in which some time is set aside for the "teaching of religious ideas," but which are otherwise not very different from publicly sponsored schools that teach secular humanism. The repeated attempts by secular humanists to thwart the popular movement to create Christian schools has as one of its causes the threat that the secular humanists perceive in these schools against their attempts to propagate their doctrine. Their repeated attempts to utilize the coercive power of the government for this purpose presents the greatest threat to freedom of thought in general and academic freedom in particular in the United States today.

Sex Education. The continuing spread of sex education offers the homosexual movement an ideal opportunity to establish its presence in the schools. Although a positive view of homosexuality and homosexual behavior can be presented in many subjects (e.g., literature, health, social sciences, etc.), sex education is perfectly suited to the purposes of the homosexual movement.

Although it is generally believed that sex education is promoted as an "option" for children whose parents believe this is a proper subject for the schools to address, optional sex education is, in fact, merely a temporary step in the long-term plans of the sex education establishment. Mary Calderone, speaking to the National Board and Staff of the YWCA at a 1975 briefing in New York City, openly advocated that children be forced to participate in sex education classes, as promoted by the Sex Information and Education Council of the United States, the oldest and most influential proponent of sex education in the country. "SIECUS presents impressive pleas for compulsory sex education in all public schools."[78] Calderone's idea of what sex education entails can be apprehended from her own statements:

- "Eroticism has been frowned upon, but there is nothing shameful about eroticism in young children."
- "Remember, you can't harm a child by telling it too much. You can overstimulate by ignorance, but not by information."
- "We find U.S. society still quite clearly divided into those who are pro-sex

and those who are anti-sex, and I am using the term 'sex' advisedly. It's the fear of eroticism that makes the anti-sexist, and I have a hunch that the people who feel this way probably have difficulties in their own sexual lives."[79]

Devoid of ethical connotations based on the natural law and/or accepted revelational morality, sex education becomes an appropriate tool for the spread not only of prohomosexual ideas, but of pansexuality, which can be defined as the notion that sex is not only pervasive but all-important, making the satisfaction of any and all sexual desires a sine qua non of human fulfillment.

The value of sex education has been noted by homosexual leaders everywhere. In an interview with the author, Adam DeBaugh indicated three school-related areas in which the Universal Fellowship of Metropolitan Community Churches has taken a position: "1) The church [i.e., the UFMCC] favors sex education in the schools; 2) the church disseminates materials prepared by population control groups, and 3) the church opposes prayer in the schools."[80] In a 1980 interview with *U.S. Catholic*, Catholic homosexual leader Brian McNaught was asked: "If the U.S. Catholic Conference called you in privately and asked you to draft a pastoral letter on homosexuality, what would be the ideal statement the bishops could make at this time, given the politics of it?" McNaught's response was unequivocal: "I would suggest initiating an immediate call for sex education in the homes and schools. Not just on homosexuality but on all aspects of human sexuality. The problem I'm seeing is that people just don't know what is going on sexually. It's not just a question of gay people; we Americans have one million cases of teenage pregnancy a year. One million."[81]

In 1981 the United States Catholic Conference did publish a document called *Education in Human Sexuality for Christians* which, while criticized by conservative Catholics,[82] has been praised by Father Robert Nugent, SDS, of New Ways Ministry as offering "new gay insights."[83]

Homosexual leaders are justified in their support of sex education, since empirical evidence indicates favorable outcomes for this movement when students are subjected to at least some forms of sex education. For example, a program developed by the University of Texas Medical Branch for eighth graders and scheduled for full integration in the curriculum by the fall 1979 semester was studied by Parcel and Luttman with the following results:

> However, in the experimental group [i.e. the students that went through the course] there was a fifty percent decrease in the feeling that masturbation in general is wrong, and an increase in the belief that masturbation was acceptable for oneself. This outcome was one of the goals of the course. The experimental group also developed a greater acceptance of homosexuality for others, while

The Goals of the Homosexual Movement

maintaining their previous feelings about homosexuality for themselves. Finally, the students in the experimental group became more comfortable with the idea of their future marriage partner having had sexual experience.[84]

The reader may have noticed not only that students developed in this-course definite ideas of what is right and wrong in sexual morality (i.e., the course is not value-free), but that the principle of subjective morality is introduced by the distinction of self and other when evaluating the homosexual condition.

Another study conducted by Hoch in 1971 on the results of a high school sex education class yielded comparable results: "Not only did the students' knowledge increase, but on questionnaire scales, the students demonstrated a significant increase 1) in their acceptance of family planning and contraception, 2) in their acceptance of others' homosexuality, and 3) in their confidence in making later sexual decisions."[85]

Even for college students, the effects of sex education consistently reveal similar results:[86]

Researcher(s)	Year	Results
Harold Bernard	1973	"During the course, students in the experimental group in comparison with students in the control group became more tolerant of homosexuality and masturbation."
Davidow	1976	"His findings indicate that the students in the course developed greater tolerance toward masturbation and premarital sex for others."
Rees and Zimmerman	1974	"At the end of the course, substantially greater percentages of the students felt that the following activities were normal: masturbation, oral sex, anal sex, sex during pregnancy and homosexuality."
Vennewitz	1975	"In general, the students became more liberal or tolerant of the sexual behavior of 'non-significant others,' and they also became more liberal toward their own nudity and mutual masturbation."

The following summary relates the educational areas described above to specific school-related objectives which favor the homosexual movement:

Areas	Objectives
Curricula	1. Incorporate elements of the homosexual ideology in the curricula.
	2. Foster acceptance of homosexuality by presenting it as "normal," "natural," or "very usual."
Personnel	1. Increase the number of openly homosexual teachers.
	2. Increase the number of openly homosexual counselors.
	3. Increase the number of prohomosexual school personnel.

Areas	Objectives
Literature	1. Develop textbooks and other reading matter which presents homosexuality in a positive light.
	2. Gain acceptance for these materials for classroom use.
	3. Infiltrate prohomosexual materials into libraries.
Secular Humanism	1. Continue pressing for an ever more open acceptance of the principles of secular humanism in American schools (e.g., by opposing prayer in the schools).
Sex Education	1. Promote sex education.
	2. Include a positive view of homosexuality and homosexual behavior in sex education curricula.

The homosexualization of schools can be best accomplished by homosexuals themselves, this process being not merely an "objective" or "dispassionate" exercise, but one which will necessarily involve the whole homosexual experience. The basic questions of homosexuality-centered education were formulated by the Gay Liberation Front in the first issue of *Come Out!*:

Because our oppression is based on sex and the sex roles which oppress us from infancy, we must explore these roles and their meanings. . . . Does society make a place for us . . . as a man? A woman? A homosexual or lesbian? How does the family structure affect us? What is sex, and what does it mean? What is love? As homosexuals, we are in a unique position to examine these questions from a fresh point of view. You'd better believe we are going to do so—that we are going to transform society at large through the open realization of our own consciousness. [87]

This fiery and bombastic oratory has yielded to more concrete and attainable objectives, although the ultimate purpose has undoubtedly not changed.

The 1979 promotional brochure of the New York City Gay Teachers Association proposes several goals and objectives, all designed to advance the homosexualization of our schools:

WHAT ARE THE GOALS OF THE G.T.A.?

The Gay Teachers Association has several primary objectives: to articulate the needs and problems of the city's 6,000 to 10,000 gay teachers; to insure the rights of both gay teachers and gay students within the school system; to work for positive changes in curriculum and materials; and to integrate gay teachers as a powerful voice within the gay rights struggle.

To these ends, the goal of the G.T.A. are as follows:

1. To provide a setting in which gay teachers can meet, share problems and ideas and give each other support.

The Goals of the Homosexual Movement

2. To conduct continuous negotiations with the New York City Board of Education and the United Federation of Teachers to obtain contractual guarantees of the right of gay teachers to teach in the city's public schools.
3. To work for the re-training of school administrators, teachers and guidance personnel to enable them to meet the needs of gay students for counseling and support.
4. To promote curriculum change in all subject areas to enable gay and non-gay students to gain a realistic and positive concept of current gay life styles and the historic contributions of gay people.
5. To lobby as a teacher organization for the gay rights bill.[88]

A complete program designed to enlist support for lesbianism has been conceptualized by Jean O'Leary and Ginny Vida, both of the National Gay Task Force. A leaflet describing this program was distributed at the June 25–26, 1979, Nebraska International Women's Year Conference at Lincoln. The following excerpt presents the basic components of this program:

Counseling: School counselors should be required to take courses in human sexuality in which a comprehensive and positive view of lesbianism is presented. (Colleges which do not offer such courses ought to design and provide them). Lesbians as well as heterosexual counselors should be represented on the guidance staff.

In addition, the names and phone numbers of gay counseling services should be made available to all students and school psychologists. Students should be given the opportunity, if they so desire, to contact these agencies.

No school counselor should ever refer a student to a psychotherapist for the purpose of changing her/his sexual preference from gay to straight. Such conditioning conveys to the student that her/his feelings of love are unworthy and unacceptable; it causes immeasurable conflict and ego damage, and can never be done in the name of mental health.

Sex Education: Courses in sex education should be taught by persons who have taken the human sexuality courses already mentioned. Students will thus be encouraged to explore alternate life styles, including lesbianism. Speakers from local lesbian organizations should be invited to these classes so that students can have their questions answered first hand.

Textbooks which do not mention lesbianism or which refer to it as a mental disorder should not be used in sex education courses. At the very least, teachers should expose the misinformation in these texts and provide additional reading material which includes a fair and positive view of lesbianism.

Lesbian Studies: Schools should set up lesbian studies programs in connection with women's studies programs to foster pride in the adolescent lesbian and to show heterosexual students that lesbians have made significant contributions to society. Learning about these contributions would foster positive feelings on the part of all students.

235

Libraries: School libraries should be supplied with bibliographies of lesbian literature and urged to purchase novels, stories, poetry, and nonfiction books that portray the joy of women loving women. The use of these books should be encouraged in literature and history classes.

Lesbian Clubs: Lesbian clubs should be established in the schools. These clubs would foster a community spirit among lesbians, who up until this time have been isolated due to the pressures of society. Such organizations would help lesbians to develop pride in their life styles, and to help overcome the prejudice of heterosexual students and faculty.[89]

There is no question that the homosexual movement fully intends to make the homosexualization of American schools a key component in its overall plan to mold our nation in its image and likeness. Whether it is successful depends not only on the skill and determination of the homosexual leaders and their allies, but on the resolve of parents to gain control over the educational system.

Notes

1. *America*, November 19, 1977.
2. Laud Humphreys, *Out of the Closets* (New York: Prentice Hall, 1972), pp. 165–167.
3. David Thorstad, "A Statement to the Gay Liberation Movement on the Issue of Man/Boy Love," *Gay Community News* (Boston), January 6, 1979, p. 5.
4. William Bennett, "The Homosexual Teacher," *American Educator* (Fall 1972), p. 24.
5. "Coalition Politics: A Necessary Alliance," *Lesbian Tide* 7 (Los Angeles: Tide Publications, September/October 1977): 5.
6. Ibid.
7. Michelle Turek, "SF Women Confer on Pornography," *Gay Community News* (Boston), December 23, 1978, p. 13.
8. Michael Bronski, "Notes and Thoughts by One Gay Man on Pornography and Censorship," *Gay Community News* (Boston), December 23, 1978, p. 11.
9. National Gay Task Force, "Gay Rights Protections" (New York, N.Y.: National Gay Task Force), June 1981.
10. "The Killing of D.C.'s Sex Law Reform," *Blade*, October 9, 1981.
11. "Court Strikes Down Law Preventing 'Kiddie Pornography,'" *Courier-Journal* (Rochester, N.Y.), May 20, 1981.
12. James S. Tinney, "A Pentecostal Statement on Gay Rights," *In Unity*, September/October 1980, p. 15.
13. "Dimensions of Future Political Battles," *Family Protection Report* (Washington, D.C.: Free Congress Research and Education Foundation), August 1979, p. 9.
14. "A New Big Push for Homosexual Rights," *U.S. News and World Report*, April 14, 1980, p. 94.
15. Ibid.
16. *Hearing*, p. 117.

The Goals of the Homosexual Movement

17. "Abolish All Age of Consent Laws and Free All Men Incarcerated for Non-Violent Sex Offenses," *NAMBLA News* (Boston), issue #4, December 1980/January 1981, p. 1.

18. "Five Ways You Can Help Remedy an Injustice in California," (Los Angeles: One Incorporated), n.d.

19. Matthew Daniels, "Gay Politics Goes Mainstream," *Advocate*, July 23, 1981.

20. R. Adam DeBaugh, "*Gays on the Hill* Proclaims *A New Day*," *A New Day* 3 (April 1979): 1.

21. R. Adam DeBaugh, "The 96th Congress: Prospects for Gay Rights Legislation," *Gays on the Hill* 3 (November-December 1978): 4.

22. Quoted in Phyllis Schlafly, *The Power of the Positive Woman* (New Rochelle, N.Y.: Arlington House, 1977), p. 91. This work should be consulted for a comprehensive analysis of the effects adopting the ERA would have on a variety of institutions and groups, including the homosexuals.

23. "Membership Survey Results," *It's Time* 7 (February-March 1980): 1.

24. Richard C. Bishop, "A Proposal for Pedophile Groups," *NAMBLA Journal* (New York, N.Y.), number 3, July 1, 1979, p. 5.

25. Ibid.

26. Ibid.

27. Jeff Greenfield, "Why is Gay Rights Different from All Other Rights?" *Village Voice*, February 23, 1978.

28. *It's Time* 8 (January-February 1981): 1.

29. Ibid. 8 (March-April 1981): 1.

30. Quoted in George A. Kelly, "The Political Struggle of Active Homosexuals to Gain Social Acceptance," *Homiletic and Pastoral Review*, February 1975, p. 9.

31. "Gay Eagle Scout Strikes Back," *Washington Post*, May 1, 1981.

32. "Homosexuals Charged with Exploitation of Children," *Catholic News*, February 3, 1977.

33. Letter of Brother Joseph Izzo, CFX, to *National Catholic Reporter*, November 13, 1981.

34. Steve Askin, "Gays in Religious Life Discussed at Meeting," *National Catholic Reporter*, December 3, 1981, p. 3.

35. *Washington Star*, April 10, 1981.

36. *Sacramento Union*, June 8, 1981.

37. David Stivison, "A Decade of Gay Teacher Cases," *Gay Community News* (Boston), March 3, 1979, p. 9.

38. Ken Lerer, "Gays—A New Key Voter Group," *New York*, May 30, 1977, p. 8.

39. *Quicksilver Times* (Washington, D.C.), November 24-December 4, 1970, p. 9.

40. Ibid.

41. Ibid.

42. Allan C. Carlson, "The Family: A Problem of Definition," *The Human Life Review*, Fall 1980.

43. "1972 Gay Rights Platform" reproduced in Laud Humphreys, *Out of the Closets* (New York, N.Y.: Prentice-Hall, 1972), p. 167.

44. Cheryl Kimmons, "The Case for Gay Marriage," *Blade*, June 1976, p. 6.

45. Report from a Texas delegate made available to the author.

46. News release, National Gay Task Force (New York City), July 10, 1978.

47. "Redefining the Family," *It's Time* 7 (February-March 1980): 1.

48. Ibid.

49. Kenneth A. Briggs, "Homosexuals Among the Clergy," *New York Times*, January 24, 1977, p. 12.

50. Promotional brochure, Custody Action for Lesbian Mothers, Narberth, PA.

51. Marotta.

52. National Gay Task Force, Testimony before the Senate Subcommittee on Human Development on the 1979 White House Conference on Families, January 1978.

53. LaBarbara Bowman, "From Altar to Palimony?" *Washington Post*, July 3, 1979.

54. Hal Davis, "Judge Bars Landlords from Evicting Gay Couples," *New York Post*, September 26, 1980, p. 9.

55. "A Devoted Mother Who's a Lesbian Is Honest with her Son," *Boston Globe*, February 8, 1979.

56. Ibid.

57. Ibid.

58. *In Our Own Write* (Washington, D.C.: Washington Area Women's Center), December 1981, p. 4.

59. "Abolish All Age of Consent Laws and Free All Men Incarcerated for Non-Violent Sex Offenses," *NAMBLA News* (Boston), issue #4, December 1980/January 1981, p. 1.

60. David Thorstad, "Man-Boy Love and Feminism," *NAMBLA News* (Boston), issue #4, December 1980/January 1981, p. 13.

61. National NOW Lesbian Rights Committee, "Position Paper on Lesbian Rights Issues" (Washington, D.C.: National NOW Action Center).

62. *Dialogue* 3 (Washington, D.C.: Brethren/Mennonite Council for Gay Concerns, March 1980): 2.

63. Rev. Robert Nugent, SDS, "Sex Education Guidelines: New Gay Insights," *National Catholic Reporter*, August 14, 1981.

64. Commentary on a statement by Bishop Cletus O'Donnell published in *Integrity/Dignity Newsletter* (Madison, WI), Winter 1980, reproduced in *A Time to Speak* (Addenda), p. 1.

65. Archdiocesan Commission for the Plan of Pastoral Action for Family Ministry, "Responding to the Call," *A Time to Speak* (Addenda), p. 4.

66. "Gay and Lesbian Curriculum Anthology," *Gay Insurgent* (Philadelphia), number 6, Summer 1980, p. 62.

67. Jean O'Leary and Bruce Voeller, Letter entitled "More on Homosexual Teachers" to *American Educator*, Winter 1978, p. 68.

68. Oregon, Department of Human Resources, "Final Report of the Task Force on Sexual Preference," December 1, 1978, pp. 11, 12, 19, cited in *Hearing*, pp. 131–132.

69. Andre Lorde, "When Will the Ignorance End?" *Gay Insurgent* (Philadelphia), number 6, Summer 1980, p. 13.

70. *Gays on the Hill* 3 (November-December 1978).

71. David Stivison, "A Decade of Gay Teacher Cases," *Gay Community News* (Boston), March 3, 1979, p. 9.

72. Prepared statement by William P. Thompson, Stated Clerk of the General Assembly, United Presbyterian Church in the U.S.A., *Hearing*, pp. 80–90.

73. Lee Lockwood, *Castro's Cuba, Cuba's Fidel*, quoted by Joe Nicholson, Jr., *Inside Cuba* (New York, N.Y.: Sheed and Ward, 1974), p. 118.

74. Joseph M. Sobran, "Capital M" (second in a two-part series entitled "Gay Rights and Conservative Politics"), *National Review*, March 17, 1978, reprinted in *Hearing*, p. 106.

75. "Telling It Straight," *Gay Teachers Association Newsletter* 4 (New York, N.Y.: Gay Teachers Association, June 1981): 2.

76. Morton Hunt, *Gay: What You Should Know About Homosexuality* (New York: Farrar, Straus & Giroux, 1977).

77. "How Gay is Your Library?" *Gay Insurgent* (Philadelphia), number 6, Summer 1980, p. 62.

78. Mary Calderone, excerpts from remarks reprinted by *YWCA Interchange* 3 (May/June 1976): 4.

79. Ibid.

80. Personal communication.

81. "Is Our Church Big Enough for Gay Catholics? Interview with Brian McNaught," *U.S. Catholic,* June 1980, p. 9.

82. Randy Engel, "A Critique of the USCC Sex Education Guidelines," *The Wanderer,* September 24, 1981, p. 9.

83. Rev. Robert Nugent, SDS, "Sex Education Guidelines: New Gay Insights," *National Catholic Reporter,* August 14, 1981.

84. U.S. Department of Health, Education, and Welfare, Public Health Service, *An Analysis of U.S. Sex Education Programs and Evaluation Methods,* by Douglas Kirby et. al., Contract No. 200-78-0804, Report No. CDC-2021-79-DK-FR (Atlanta), July 1979. See especially vol. I, chapter 2, Review of the Literature, p. 14.

85. Ibid.

86. Ibid., pp. 15–16.

87. Marotta, p. 101.

88. Promotional brochure, New York City Gay Teachers Association, November 1979.

89. Jean O'Leary and Ginny Vida, "Lesbians and the Schools," a leaflet distributed at the Nebraska International Women's Year Conference, Lincoln, Nebraska, June 25–26, 1979.

CHAPTER

VI

Homosexuality and Religion

The Importance of Religion for the Homosexual Movement

Organized religion is not only the social institution to which the greatest number of people belong voluntarily, it is probably the single most influential factor in the evaluation of behavior. In a collective sense, we find norms to validate our behavior in religious teachings. As individuals, even those who do not formally belong to a church or attend its services obtain much guidance from religious institutions in forming their consciences. Some try to escape the influence of religion and even pretend to renounce its sway; since individuality is only one facet of what it means to be human, this is patently impossible. One cannot escape history or one's cultural matrix.

As a manifestation of a deep-seated *Weltanschauung*, religion provides its adherents with precise rules which enable them to ascertain the ethical qualities of their behavior. Objectively, religion structures reality for the individual, categorizes the nature and value of his relationships, and provides the means by which he can transcend the limitations of his sense data. Subjectively, the individual surrenders his autonomy in the area of making judgments unfettered by intellectual faith, subjects himself to a code of behavior consistent with his newly found categories, and accepts his responsibility to seek self-actualization beyond ordinary experience. Religion does claim man's total adherence, while providing him with total liberation, both collective and individual.

However, man, being social and political by nature, cannot help but manifest his nature in a collective sense, especially when the dimension of human nature so manifested relates man to himself, his environment, and that which he posits as totally transcendent in the deepest and most universal sense. Thus religion must take the form of social organization of a kind which defines its nature and functions as extending beyond the state, family, purely voluntary associations, and units of production and service. Moreover, since religion is not based merely on the application of pure reason to empirical observations, but demands the involvement of feelings and the participation of the whole person in an all-encompassing experience, it can be neither discovered nor shared outside a community. This community must necessarily take the form of an organization, since the tenets of religion must be preserved and adapted to new circumstances in authoritative ways. For precisely this reason, religion, although founded on a rational basis, is nonrational in nature. There is no way of communicating religious beliefs, motivating the acceptance of ethical systems, or engaging in worship outside a historical and cultural stream in which the believer acquires religious meaning and finds it possible to adhere to a "truth" that is undiscoverable unless disclosed by others to the believer. (It should be noted here that for the purposes of this analysis, the objective validity of religion is not relevant. The dichotomy between objective and subjective, a fundamental distinction of the *philosophia perennis* which underlies Western religious thought, is fundamental in the analysis we are conducting. Since this work is addressed to people whose cultural matrix is Western, the dichotomy is taken for granted.)

The pervasive presence of religious organizations affects individuals not only as believers, but also as members of society. Even those societies which have formally abandoned the fundamental beliefs of Western religion, and even the individual leaders within those societies, retain the cultural matrix created by the very religious institutions and ideas they purport to reject. One has only to examine Marxist praxis to realize its close dependence on Judeo-Christian ideology: the need for justice, the preeminence of the poor, the role of the party as analog of the church, the eschatological nature of history, the ability of man to influence history, the linear nature of time, the objectivity of the real, and the acceptance of experience as valid are all examples. In a society such as the United States, where religion played a preeminent role in the foundation of the nation, and where there is a rather weak antireligious tradition, religious organizations have an even more fundamental role. It is true that forces representative of secular humanism (embodied by such institutions as Planned Parenthood Federation, the American Civil Liberties Union, Americans for Democratic Action, etc.) have tried to undermine the degree to which religion is an accepted factor in American life. In a formal sense they have succeeded to a great extent, inasmuch as there has been a rejection of customs and practices which, having their roots in religion, contributed to the intensification of the religious dimension in Americans, although they were in themselves secular and rational in nature. (It is ironic that secular humanist institutions are bent upon destroying the very foundations of Western civilization which have enabled them to exist. The values which these institutions purport to defend are founded—historically and rationally—upon the very notion of the supremacy of the transcendent which they abhor.) Their efforts have, in fact, been resented by a substantial proportion of the population, which has openly rejected the secularization of the churches and turned to traditional forms of religiosity. The secularization of churches cannot be quantified discretely, but is a more or less long-term process in which the secular humanist ideology and its representatives traditionally take the offensive role while certain elements within the churches try merely to defend whatever terrain has not been lost. Sometimes all the trappings of the traditional belief are kept while little or nothing remains of the formal doctrines. For the majority of the people, however, the religious institutions maintain at least some of their traditional roles as validators of behavior.

For society at large, religion remains *the* validator of behavior of choice. The social sciences, especially after the collapse of the "movement" which, during the 1960s and early '70s, failed to result in the "greening of America," are retreating in disarray. The term "social sciences" was always a misnomer for a peculiarly modern ideology, a form of speech without ontological content. Precisely because it is not an empirical science, religion has not only refused to disappear, but has managed to outlive the social sciences and retain its validity among the masses. We have already alluded to the discrepancy between the general public and the elites uncovered by the Connecticut Mutual Life Insurance Company report. The populist nature of American society will eventually force the elites to accept their irrelevance, however reluctantly. (The rage of Yale president A. Bartlett Giammetti against the mass-oriented Moral Majority in his message to the university's 1981–82 freshman class is only a sign of the uncontained anger caused by the realization of one's social irrelevance: cf. *National Review*, 9/18/81, p. 1059.) In the meantime, religious organizations provide the yardstick by which to measure behavior and are the basic agents in the construction of personal and social reality.

Religious organizations do not utilize purely spiritual means in the pursuit of their goals (although their ideology often sacralizes the secular means they employ). Thus these organizations have at their disposal substantial sums of money, means of communication, established procedures, bureaucracies, educational institutions, conference centers, and so on. Additionally, they enjoy the prestige and support won by many years of what is generally perceived as generous and unselfish service on behalf of the nation.

In relation to the homosexual movement, another factor must be con-

Homosexuality and Religion

sidered. Religion provides the strongest category by which human acts are evaluated—the virtuous/sinful continuum. Other categories such as healthy/diseased, decent/indecent, or legal/criminal have no immediate relevance in terms of conscience or a transcendent reality. Sinfulness is a particularly relevant concept, since it refers not only to the rationality of an act, but also to its effect on the universal order. There is no question that religious institutions have freely applied—according to the ancient traditions upon which they are based—the category of sinful when analyzing homosexual behavior. As a matter of fact, religious belief is probably the single most important factor in the near-universal rejection of homosexual behavior as acceptable. Even when the rejection is verbalized in psychological jargon or purely emotional expressions, one is likely to find at the roots the religious tradition that considers homosexual behavior as sinful.

While this religious rejection is usually presented as founded on written traditions accepted as completely authoritative, (and indeed the overwhelming preponderance of evidence indicates that these sacred writings do reject homosexuality unambiguously), still it is necessary to explore the rational foundations of this rejection, since religious literature cannot be produced without reference to an underlying rational ideology. It appears that, from an ideological viewpoint, the rejection of homosexuality by traditional religious organizations is based on several tenets, including:

The radical distinction between the objective and subjective orders, both ontologically and ethically;

The affirmation of a rational ordination in the objective order;

The dependence of ethically acceptable decisions on the objective order;

The ontological subordination of individual interests to the needs of the species in the rational design of human sexuality;

The subordination of personal satisfaction to human reproduction in matters of human sexuality, both ontologically and ethically.

While one can reasonably dispute any of these principles, it is clear that all of them have some rational basis; thus the religious rejection of homosexuality cannot be dismissed as arbitrary and irrational.

There is no question that the main stumbling block in the theoretical and practical acceptance of homosexuality by American society has been traditional religion. This has been perfectly understood by the leadership of the homosexual movement. For many years systematic efforts to utilize religion in support of homosexuality have been implemented not only by the founding of religious organizations which cater almost exclusively to homosexuals while purporting to justify their sexual propensities and activities, but also by the establishment of organizations within other religious institutions for the purpose of using them for the promotion of the homosexual ideology.

The importance of gaining the support of the churches, or at least neutralizing them, is widely acknowledged by homosexual leaders. At a Washington meeting of Friends for Lesbian and Gay Concerns (FLGC), a Quaker organization, concern was expressed for the apparent lack of support for homosexuality from the Friends Committee on National Legislation, an important body within the denomination.[1] The meeting was attended by Steve Endean, director of the Gay Rights National Lobby, who apparently prodded the attendees to enlist the collaboration of their church in the homosexual cause. Endean, according to the official newsletter of FLGC, "outlined for us the significance that such a position of support from FCNL would have on national legislators and other church lobby groups—some of which would be less timid about supporting gay rights if the Friends (FCNL) were doing so. The support of these church lobbies would be important in offsetting the negativism from the Christian right led by the Christian Voice, the new lobby set up to wage their war against us."[2] The clear implication is that homosexual Quakers should use their resources to set their religious organization against another—more traditional—Christian group and support the homosexual movement.

These efforts should not be surprising, since polls have indicated that people's views on the nature of homosexuality are affected by their religion. In a 1977 Minnesota Poll conducted by the *Minneapolis Tribune*, people were asked the following questions:

Do you think that the Bible says that homosexuality is a sin?

Do you yourself think that homosexuality is a sin?[3]

The following results were obtained:

	According to the Bible	Own Opinion
Yes, it is a sin	46%	47%
No	24%	42%
Don't Know	30%	11%
	100%	100%

Although it cannot be said that the same individuals who answered the first question affirmatively also answered the second affirmatively, the large and virtually identical proportion does suggest at least some overlap. It is also interesting to note that whereas many people did not know what the Bible teaches concerning homosexuality, many more people did have definite opinions on the morality of the condition.

Further indication of the influence of religion on people's attitudes toward homosexuality is seen in the fact that persons who consider homosexuality a sinful condition also tend to consider it abnormal. The relationship is clearly shown by the following results:

Homosexuality and Religion

| | Consider Homo-sexuality: | |
	A Sin	Not a Sin
Abnormal	81%	31%
Alternative Lifestyle	4%	43%
Neither	8%	23%
No Opinion	7%	3%
	100%	100%

While no causality is proven by these results, there is no question about the significant relationship between the two opinions.

We have already described the natural mechanisms by which religion exercises its influence on individuals and society. The supernatural element in man's transformation as the result of religious experience is discernible exclusively by faith and is beyond the scope of this work. The reader is cautioned that there is no implication in what we are discussing that denies or contradicts the existence of the supernatural. However, since it is by its very nature beyond the capability of empirical science to ascertain its nature or operations, it is not taken directly into consideration. From the standpoint of faith, the ultimate explanation for man's transformation is supernatural. However, there is no question that, according to most believers, the supernatural is made effective through quite natural means: "And how shall they believe in Him of whom they have not heard?" (Romans 10:14).

The homosexual ideology presents such a radical departure from traditional religious teaching—to the point of contradicting it—that it is necessary to introduce new principles that enable a total rejection of the traditional teachings while keeping all the appearances and control mechanisms of religion intact. Thus the new dogma of homosexuality can be enshrined. The principles in question are moral relativism and situation ethics, both of which fully satisfy the requirement that the practice of homosexuality be acceptable. A good example of the use of moral relativism is the testimony in favor of prohomosexual legislation offered by the Reverend Cecil Williams at a Congressional hearing where the following exchange took place:

Mr. Stephens: Let me ask questions of Reverend Williams. I think it unfortunate that you have experienced the prejudice and discrimination that you have and that people have been prejudicial to you in the name of the Scriptures. I, too, think it is abhorrent. But one thing which concerns me is the distinction between the behavior of people and what Scripture teaches. Are there certain moral absolutes which don't change from era to era?

Reverend Williams: There are no absolutes. All absolutes have to be looked at, criticized, reinterpreted, revised. That is why you have revised versions of the Bible. It is to reestablish, redirect, make relevant, the word in a different time and at a different condition and in different circumstances. That is merely one way of looking at it. There are no absolutes that should not and cannot be reinterpreted and redefined as well as to create different responses for the times during which people live.[4]

This is no less than a religious Copernican Revolution. Whereas traditional religion would use the Bible as a guide, we see here the Bible as the maidservant of the trends of the times. In other words, the Bible is placed at the service of the homosexual ideology. Any objective basis for religion disappears, sacrificed at the altar of the individual's sexual needs, however bizarre. The preoccupation of many in the homosexual movement with religion and Biblical teaching, the very need to reject traditional Biblical morality, bears witness to the importance attached to these teachings. In the final analysis, the minimal question is whether religious mechanisms can influence significantly the homosexual's need to seek actualization of his sexual desires either alone or with one or more partners. Maximally, the claim of religion to arrest or even to reverse homosexuality constitutes a challenge of incalculable magnitude to the homosexual movement. This question has already been examined in some detail. The reader is reminded of the virulent reaction to an article whose very title, "Homosexuals CAN Change," indicated the thesis that with God's help a person can cease to be homosexual.[5] Such a claim must be neutralized, for if it were to be accepted, there would be no reason for people to continue the practice of homosexuality and all claims of "goodness," "inevitability," etc., would have to be rejected. The homosexual movement would indeed come to a halt.

It might be argued that certain psychologists have asserted for many years not only that homosexuality is an illness, but that it can be cured, provided that the patient cooperates and submits himself to the appropriate treatment. Although the homosexual movement also rejects these claims vehemently, the reader is reminded that psychologists can claim only the use of purely human means (an explanation provided by a rational science) and that they posit the necessity of the patient's positive acts (often proceeding from a weakened will). Only religion can enlist the omnipotent power of the Divinity, provide its adherents with the sure explanation backed by infallible faith, and require no more than the passive opening of the spirit through prayer and the ardent desire to receive salvation and be delivered from sin. Religion is obviously a far greater threat to the homosexual ideology than is psychology.

The present state of flux in American society, and the progressive secularization of certain religious organizations, have made some of these

Homosexuality and Religion

institutions easy prey for the well-organized efforts of the homosexual movement. Its leaders have not only acknowledged the importance of this support, they use it prominently. The National Gay Task Force, for example, publishes a packet of documentation issued by representatives of groups as diverse as the Union of American Hebrew Congregations and the General Convention of the Episcopal Church, showing various degrees of support for the homosexual movement. This support is then used by the leadership of the movement in support of its goals. A letter from Steve Endean, Executive Director of the Gay Rights National Lobby, to the Washington *Star* in support of prohomosexual legislation is a good example of how this religious support is used.

> Many religious leaders, organizations and denominations, including the National Council of Churches, the National Federation of Priests' Councils and the Union of American Hebrew Congregations, have understood the distinction between support for civil rights legislation for gay people and any moral judgment about homosexuality. They do agree that discrimination is wrong and immoral.[6]

The support for the homosexual movement expressed by these religious leaders is thus not just an indication of their beliefs and perceptions, but first and foremost a political statement obtained for the purpose of furthering the cause of homosexuality. There is little question that in at least some instances the signers of these declarations are too naive to understand that they are being used to increase the acceptability of behavior they personally abhor. From a functional viewpoint this is basically irrelevant, since political analysis is not concerned with man's conscience except in terms of its effect on political behavior.

One result of the recognition of religion's importance in approving the homosexual ideology in America is the targeting of religious institutions for a prohomosexual "public education" campaign by the National Gay Task Force.[7] The campaign, directed by Dr. Charles Hitchcock, has as its goal "to make a positive impact on the perceptions of lesbians and gay men."[8] Its strategy indicates their perception of the nature and influence of churches and synagogues on American life and how they can be "turned around" to the point of view of the homosexual movement. In an interview which appeared in the National Gay Task Force's newsletter, Dr. Hitchcock was quite open about the project:

> "Identifying key institutions which are central to the general public's understanding of social issues, educating staff in those organizations, and soliciting positive policies and support for gay rights from these groups is the heart of our agenda," stated Dr. Hitchcock. "We know from our breakthroughs in changing policies with both the American Psychiatric Association and the Amer-

ican Psychological Association that such programs can have a major impact on public attitudes, government policies, and our ability to achieve gay rights."
"Individual programs are being designed for each specific institution. Components include a history of each institution's attitudes or policies on gay rights, identification of institutional decision-makers and decision-making processes, and a curriculum for an educational (training) program with appropriate materials and resource people identified," he added. "A prime example would be that of a national television network where, because of the lack of any stated policy or educational materials concerned with gay issues, individuals are left to their own personal whim or prejudice in dealing with gay stories and news items. In targeting such an institution for our program, we would, through staff meetings, educational seminars and the development of relevant educational materials, hope to have a major positive impact on how that institution deals with gay concerns—both internally and in it's entertainment programs and news coverage."[9]

It was also reported that the program had been prepared with the collaboration of "two former Presidential assistants, the Education Director of the Anti-Defamation League of B'nai B'rith and the National Urban League, officials of the Catholic Church, the United Methodist Church, and representatives of ABC, NBC, and Public Television."[10] Among the persons who participated in the interview process preparatory to the prohomosexual campaign were Rembert Weakland, Roman Catholic Archbishop of Milwaukee, Rabbi Barry Silbert of Moral Alternatives in Politics, and Dr. William Cate, the Director of the Council of Churches of Seattle.[11]

Churches, once they have been infiltrated by the homosexual movement, constitute one of its most important allies. Not only because of the ideological and human support they provide, but also on account of the availability of meeting rooms and other physical assets, the collaboration of churches can make the difference between the success and failure of a homosexual operation. A major demonstration against the Neighborhood Church, a Christian church in Greenwich Village that adheres to traditional teachings on human sexuality, was planned at a United Methodist Church facility, the Washington Square Church, also in New York City.[12] This was reported to a committee formed by groups as diverse as Dykes Against Racism Everywhere, Black and White Men Together, the Coalition of Lesbian and Gay Male Socialists, Radical Women, and the Workers World Party.[13] Tactically different, but still fully supportive of the homosexual ideology, was a church-sponsored ecumenical conference to "commemorate Gay Pride Month" which discussed ways to end "homophobia" in the churches.[14] In traditional language, this means making the churches subservient to the homosexual movement by accepting and promoting its ideology. The Strategy Conference on Homophobia in the Church was held May 4–6, 1979, in a retreat center in Potomac, Maryland.

Homosexuality and Religion

Its rationale: "Oppression of Gay people is on the rise in the churches and in response to this over 60 representatives of 16 Christian denominations met to begin developing strategies for combatting homophobia."[15]

The conference was not merely theoretical, but basically the task force of a small number of committed revolutionaries united by a total and ruthless determination to subvert the traditional ethical foundation of religion itself:

> For the first time, Gay and non-Gay people shared resources, experiences, tactics, ministry and support in a religious context that transcended denominational lines. About 25% of conference participants were not Gay. The conference was a celebration of the participants' ministries both to Lesbians and Gay men, non-Gay people, and the parent denominations themselves. The meetings included much music, prayer and sharing. Delegates affirmed that collectively they are the largest and potentially most influential force in the Gay movement and the Christian churches. Additionally, they have the potential to move the religious community into the full light of God's grace by achieving a full acceptance of God's love for all people.[16]

The code words utilized in describing the church's conversion to the homosexual ideology appear in the last sentence. This is a purely ideological expression designed, quite illogically, to create guilt among Christians who accept the teachings of the Bible at face value. As a matter of fact, people who reject homosexuality *and* who also have a Christian world view, *do not* deny that God loves homosexuals and heterosexuals alike. People who believe in traditional values necessarily accept that homosexuals are endowed with the same human dignity as heterosexuals. However, using human categories to describe what is transcendent, they would affirm that "God hates the sin while loving the sinner."

Adherents to religion, especially the religions of the Book (Christianity, Judaism, and Islam) believe not only that God is the ultimate cause of all reality—including history—but that He provides special guidance to the religious organization of each believer's choice. Religious ideologues of homosexuality extend this divine guidance to their own movement. Reverend William R. Johnson, the first homosexual minister ordained in the United Church of Christ and an activist in his own right, has indicated that he sees "women's liberation and gay liberation as movements of the Holy Spirit."[17]

In the same *New York Times* interview, Johnson indicates several factors which are important for the advancement of homosexuality in the church. They also constitute a model program for the conversion of a church into an agent of the movement.

1) On desensitization of the church to sexual ethics: "The church, and the heterosexual clergy, is still hung up on the Victorian ethic that sees

a conflict between being sexual and being Christian. I'm convinced that people are more upset about the fact that I am sexual and open about it than that I am homosexual."

2) Promotion of prohomosexual legislation by religious bodies as evidenced by the passage in 1975 of civil rights planks, including rights for homosexuals, by the National Council of Churches and by the Unitarian Church, the United Church of Christ and many local Quaker chapters even though the planks are secular and do not address the question of whether homosexuality is a sin.

3) Organization of official commissions or similar bodies within the church's ruling bodies, charged with studying the homosexual question. (Naturally, these groups should be dominated by persons sympathetic to the homosexual movement.) "Several church denominations have established committees to study homosexuality in the church."

4) Establishment of homosexual associations within the churches; Johnson notes approvingly "the creation for the first time of homosexual study groups or homosexual caucuses. Now numbering 13, these are secret associations of seminarians and clergy members where people may discuss confidentially their common fears of exposure, ostracism and oppression."

5) The ordination of homosexuals to the ministry, preferably "liberated" homosexuals who are identified with the movement's ideology: "At the time I was deciding to try to get ordained, everybody told me: 'Just pretend, hide the fact you're homosexual. That's what everybody else has done.' But I couldn't do it. I didn't see how I could be a person of God and not be honest about myself."

6) Willingness of homosexual clergymen to accept dual roles as leaders in the church and the movement, in fact, agents of the homosexual movement within their churches; as the interview concludes:

> After his ordination, Mr. Johnson said it became apparent that "the gay people were no longer willing to be shunted in the backrooms in the church today in an atmosphere of secrecy and guilt.
> "I got a tremendous amount of national publicity then, and that suddenly catapulted me into a position of leadership," he said. "I looked around and realized I was being considered a leader, and that I had to do something about it. I was getting hundreds of letters, and the question was, was I going to speak out about homosexuality and do what I had to do, or not?
> "I decided I had to do it."

Readers are reminded that if they belong to a religious body, whether parish, congregation, or temple, their organization is of great interest to, indeed is a target of, the homosexual movement, which works relentlessly to take over its structures for its own purposes. Johnson's priorities not only indicate how important the religious institutions are to homosexuality, but provide a checklist for ascertaining the degree to which a specific religious institution has been infiltrated by the homosexual movement.

Traditional Religious Positions Concerning Homosexuality

C. A. Tripp has correctly asserted, and the homosexual movement is quick to repeat, that many so-called primitive peoples have made homosexual practices, under certain controlled conditions, an accepted part of their culture.[18] However, from the point of view of either social evolution or revealed religion, the results of anthropological research on these peoples can hardly serve to provide guidance for contemporary society. From the standpoint of the Judeo-Christian or Islamic religions, the homosexual practices of these peoples would merely be a reflection of man's sinful nature in need of God's activity. From the point of view of social evolution, they represent the primitive stages of human society.

The bankruptcy of the behavioral "sciences" is due mainly to their radical inability to provide metaphysically certain solutions to transcendental problems confronting humanity. As is the case with other positive sciences, behavioral sciences can provide models of no permanent or absolute value. In fact, the word "science" is applied to behavioral sciences analogically. The models they offer have much less relationship to reality than those offered by the physical sciences. It would be far more appropriate to refer to the behavioral sciences as myths or poetry. This inherent deficiency is compounded by the fact that human nature seems to have some inherent self-contradictions which defy rational analysis (giving rise to the universal experience of alienation or angst) and by the unrealistic expectations of people who have accepted science as a source of "real" knowledge rather than "working" knowledge of no ontological value.

Advanced societies thus rely on religious tradition to provide the elements to make the necessary judgments. To the extent that the role of religion (and this word is used here in its widest sense, encompassing even the Marxist ideology) loses its hold on the mind of man, he is forced to seek other sources of total knowledge, since, even collectively, he cannot think through fundamental life problems. The final disintegration of thought and purpose occurs when man realizes that no empirical science, let alone the so-called behavioral sciences, can provide adequate guidance.

In America, however, although the forces of secular humanism have advanced considerably, religion remains the major factor determining thought and action for the majority of the people. In certain urban centers, this might not be apparent to "sophisticated" individuals, and some segments of the intellectual elites have altogether rejected religion as having any value beyond the power it exercises over the masses. However, this feeling is not shared by the majority of Americans, as demonstrated by the Connecticut Mutual Life Insurance Company Report. Thus it is necessary to examine the traditional Judeo-Christian position on homosexuality. This tradition originated some three thousand years ago and continues as a living stream of social consciousness. The history of Judeo-Christian thought itself is much too complex to be analyzed here, but it has considerable bearing on a current understanding, inasmuch as both Christians and Jews consider the Bible (or parts thereof) as normative. This tradition will be represented by excerpts from its most sacred texts, followed by two short sections presenting selected sacred writings of Islam, Hinduism, and Buddhism, which are relevant to our question.

THE JUDEO-CHRISTIAN TRADITION

Until very recently there was almost no question that the Bible condemned homosexual behavior and that, although its writers did not possess the contemporary sociopsychological frame of reference, homosexuality was a manifestation of man's sinful nature. Simultaneous with the appearance of the homosexual movement, and by a mysterious coincidence, certain biblical scholars who accept the critical approach to the Scriptures have concluded that all texts previously known to show homosexual behavior as wrong really referred to other matters. No one, apparently, has pointed out that these contemporary biblical scholars have reached conclusions that suit the needs of the homosexual movement. There is no indication that there is a "conspiracy" between the scholars and the homosexual movement; from the strictly religious point of view, however, this is an ominous phenomenon. According to the Judeo-Christian tradition, the Scriptures are the norm, and a function of religion is to interact with the world from the standpoint of faith. What seems to have happened is that biblical scholars have used the world as a guide and proceeded to reinterpret religion to suit the needs of the world. Otherwise, why only when the homosexual movement arose did scholars begin to interpret the Bible in harmony with the homosexual ideology? While not absolutely compelling, this observation makes all recent prohomosexual interpretations of the Bible highly suspicious.

Homosexual religious leaders (especially those who profess to be Christians) have publicized the prohomosexual interpretation of the Bible to such an extent that in certain circles it is fashionable to proclaim that homosexual behavior is perfectly acceptable from a biblical standpoint. A number of popular tracts (produced and distributed largely by homosexual organizations) presenting this viewpoint are available to the public, including:

Homosexuality and Religion

Reverend Dr. Norman Pittenger, *Homosexuals and the Bible*. The Universal Fellowship Press, Los Angeles, 1977.

Reverend L. Robert Arthur, *Homosexuality in the Light of Biblical Language and Culture*. The Universal Fellowship Press, Los Angeles, 1977.

Walter Barnett, *Homosexuality and the Bible: An Interpretation*. Pendle Hill Publications, Wallingford, Pa., 1979.

Ralph Blair, *An Evangelical Look at Homosexuality*. National Task Force on Student Personnel Services and Homosexuality, 1972.

These opinions have begun to filter down to authors whose main interest is not homosexuality. A typical example of an author who has accepted this revisionist position on homosexuality is Victor P. Furnish. The third chapter of his *The Moral Teaching of Paul* (Nashville, Tenn.: Abingdon, 1979) is an exposition of the typical prohomosexual interpretation of key Pauline texts.

In its most extreme forms, the prohomosexual position does not require the mental and linguistic gymnastics of critical biblical scholarship. The Reverend Cecil Williams, when challenged in his defense of prohomo-sexual legislation on biblical grounds, pointed out three basic principles by which a person can remain "committed" to biblical religion and still be prohomosexual:

1) "The Bible is not the word of God, but the word of men in which the contemporary word of God comes to men."
2) ". . . a Bible passage is to be interpreted in terms of experiences," and
3) ". . . we must see the Bible in light of our contemporary experience and knowledge."[19]

It is clearly beyond the scope of this work to exegete biblical passages or criticize the principles used by biblical scholars—prohomosexual or traditionalist—in their work. From a sociopolitical point of view, however, it is obvious that prohomosexual exegesis has meaning beyond the strictly religious. Inasmuch as religion is a major factor in creating man's aware-ness of the world and his evaluation of behavior, such exegesis has great significance. The following passages from the Bible have traditionally been offered as evidence that homosexual behavior is incompatible with the Scriptures. All of them have been reinterpreted, although in nearly all translations the homosexual meaning of the condemned behavior appears obvious. The King James version has been used for all texts, except for the passage from the Book of Wisdom, which is taken from the Confra-ternity version (Roman Catholic). Protestants do not accept this book as part of the Canon, while Roman Catholics do consider it inspired.

OLD TESTAMENT

Genesis 19: When Lot received angels disguised as men in his house at Sodom, the people of the town attempted to have homosexual sex with the angels. For this reason, God destroyed the town entirely. Sodom became the symbol of corruption and "sodomite" came to mean homosexual:

1 And there came two angels to Sodom at even; and Lot sat in the gate of Sodom: and Lot seeing them rose up to meet them; and he bowed himself with his face toward the ground;
2 And he said, Behold now, my lords, turn in, I pray you, into your servant's house, and tarry all night, and wash your feet, and ye shall rise up early, and go on your ways. And they said, Nay; but we will abide in the street all night.
3 And he pressed upon them greatly; and they turned in unto him, and entered into his house; and he made them a feast, and did bake unleavened bread, and they did eat.
4 But before they lay down, the men of the city, *even* the men of Sodom, compassed the house round, both old and young, all the people from every quarter:
5 And they called unto Lot, and said unto him, Where are the men which came in to thee this night? bring them out unto us, that we may know them.
6 And Lot went out at the door unto them, and shut the door after him.
7 And said, I pray you, brethren do not so wickedly.
8 Behold now, I have two daughters which have not known man; let me, I pray you, bring them out unto you, and do ye to them as *is* good in your eyes: only unto these men do nothing; for therefore came they under the shadow of my roof.
9 And they said, Stand back. And they said *again*, This one *fellow* came in to sojourn, and he will needs be a judge: now will we deal worse with thee, than with them. And they pressed sore upon the man, *even* Lot, and came near to break the door.
10 But the men put forth their hand, and pulled Lot into the house to them, and shut to the door.
11 And they smote the men that *were* at the door of the house with blindness, both small and great: so that they wearied themselves to find the door. . . .

24 Then the Lord rained upon Sodom and upon Gomorrah brimstone and fire from the Lord out of heaven;
25 And he overthrew those cities, and all the plain, and all the inhabitants of the cities, and that which grew upon the ground.

Genesis 19 : 1–11, 24–25

Leviticus 18, 20
Deuteronomy 23:   Legal prescriptions against the practice of homosexuality among the Hebrews:

22 Thou shalt not lie with mankind, as with womankind: it *is* abomination.
23 Neither shalt thou lie with any beast to defile thyself therewith: neither shall any woman stand before a beast to lie down thereto: it *is* confusion.

Homosexuality and Religion

24 Defile not ye yourselves in any of these things: for in all these the nations are defiled which I cast out before you:
25 And the land is defiled: therefore I do visit the iniquity thereof upon it, and the land itself vomiteth out her inhabitants.

Leviticus 18 : 22–25

13 If a man also lie with mankind, as he lieth with a woman, both of them have committed an abomination: they shall surely be put to death; their blood *shall be* upon them.

Leviticus 20 : 13

18 There shall be no whore of the daughters of Israel, nor a sodomite of the sons of Israel.

Deuteronomy 23 : 18

Judges 19: This story is similar to that of Sodom, in that the inhabitants of a town try to force a visitor to have homosexual sex. They are eventually punished by God after having raped and killed the visitor's concubine:

20 And the old man said, Peace *be* with thee; howsoever let all thy wants *lie* upon me; only lodge not in the street.
21 So he brought him into his house, and gave provender unto the asses: and they washed their feet, and did eat and drink.
22 *Now* as they were making their hearts merry, behold, the men of the city, certain sons of Belial, beset the house round about, *and* beat at the door, and spake to the master of the house, the old man, saying, Bring forth the man that came into thine house, that we may know him.
23 And the man, the master of the house, went out unto them, and said unto them, Nay, my brethren, *nay,* I pray you, do not *so* wickedly; seeing that this man is come into mine house, do not this folly.
24 Behold, *here is* my daughter a maiden, and his concubine; them I will bring out now, and humble ye them, and do with them what seemeth good unto you: but unto this man do not so vile a thing.
25 But the men would not hearken to him: so the man took his concubine, and brought her forth unto them; and they knew her, and abused her all the night until the morning: and when the day began to spring, they let her go.
26 Then came the woman in the dawning of the day, and fell down at the door of the man's house where her lord *was,* till it was light.

Judges 19 : 20–26

1 Kings 15, 22
2 Kings 23: Three kings are praised for having eliminated homosexuals who seemingly practiced homosexual sex in the very temple of God:

King Asa 12 And he took away the sodomites out of the land, and removed all the idols that his fathers had made.

1 Kings 15 : 22

King Jehoshapat 46 And the remnant of the sodomites, which remained in the days of his father Asa, he took out of the land.

1 Kings 22 : 46

King Josiah 7 And he brake down the houses of the sodomites, that *were* by the house of the Lord, where the women wove hangings for the grove.

2 Kings 23 : 7

Wisdom 14: In a passage similar to Romans 1, the author of Wisdom links idolatry with homosexuality:

26 Disturbance of good men, neglect of gratitude,
besmirching of souls, unnatural lust,
disorder in marriage, adultery and shamelessness.
27 For the worship of infamous idols is the reason and source and extremity of all evil.

Wisdom 14 : 26–27

NEW TESTAMENT

There is no record of Jesus having spoken directly about the morality of homosexuality. However, He did exalt the sex between man and woman within marriage. For centuries Christians have interpreted His teachings as meaning that any other form of sexual behavior is evil. St. Paul, however, is far more explicit.

Romans 1: In one of his most famous passages, St. Paul condemns both male and female homosexuality as contrary to the natural law. He teaches that idolatry results in the practice of homosexuality, as well as many other evil deeds:

21 Because that, when they knew God, they glorified *him* not as God, neither were thankful; but became vain in their imaginations, and their foolish heart was darkened.
22 Professing themselves to be wise, they became fools,
23 And changed the glory of the uncorruptible God into an image made like to corruptible man, and to birds, and four footed beasts, and creeping things.
24 Wherefore God also gave them up to uncleanness through the lusts of their own hearts, to dishonour their own bodies between themselves:
25 Who changed the truth of God into a lie, and worshipped and served the creature more than the Creator, who is blessed for ever. Amen.
26 For this cause God gave them up unto vile affections: for even their women did change the natural use into that which is against nature:
27 And likewise also the men, leaving the natural use of the woman, burned in their lust one toward another; men with men working that which is unseemly, and receiving in themselves that recompense of their error which was meet.

Homosexuality and Religion

28   And even as they did not like to retain God in *their* knowledge, God gave them over to a reprobate mind, to do those things which are not convenient;
29   Being filled with all unrighteousness, fornication, wickedness, covetousness, maliciousness; full of envy, murder, debate, deceit, malignity; whisperers,
30   Backbiters, haters of God, despiteful, proud, boasters, inventors of evil things, disobedient to parents,
31   Without understanding, covenantbreakers, without natural affection, implacable, unmerciful:
32   Who knowing the judgment of God, that they which commit such things are worthy of death, not only do the same, but have pleasure in them that do them.

Romans 1 : 21–32

Galatians 5:   A list of evil and godly behavior presents lustful actions as an example of sinfulness:

19   Now the works of the flesh are manifest, which are *these*; Adultery, fornication, uncleanness, lasciviousness,
20   Idolatry, witchcraft, hatred, variance, emulations, wrath, strife, seditions, heresies,
21   Envyings, murders, drunkenness, revellings, and such like: of the which I tell you before, as I have also told *you* in time past, that they which do such things shall not inherit the kingdom of God.
22   But the fruit of the Spirit is love, joy, peace, longsuffering, gentleness, goodness, faith,
23   Meekness, temperance: against such there is no law.
24   And they that are Christ's have crucified the flesh with the affections and lusts.

Galatians 5 : 19–24

1 Corinthians 6:   In another list of evildoers, both active and passive homosexuals are denied entrance to God's kingdom:

9   Know ye not that the unrighteous shall not inherit the kingdom of God? Be not deceived: neither fornicators, nor idolaters, nor adulterers, nor effeminate, nor abusers of themselves with mankind,
10   Nor thieves, nor covetous, nor drunkards, nor revilers, nor extortioners, shall inherit the kingdom of God.

1 Corinthians 6 : 9–10

1 Timothy 1:   In another "catalogue of sinners," St. Paul classifies homosexuals as "lawless," "disobedient," "ungodly," "sinners," "unholy," and "profane":

9   Knowing this, that the law is not made for a righteous man, but for the lawless and disobedient, for the ungodly and for sinners, for unholy and profane, for murderers of fathers and murderers of mothers, for manslayers,

10 For whoremongers, for them that defile themselves with mankind, for menstealers, for liars, for perjured persons, and if there be any other thing that is contrary to sound doctrine;

1 Timothy 1 : 9–10

2 Peter

Jude: At the time of Jesus, it was generally accepted that homosexuality was the crime for which the inhabitants of Sodom had been destroyed. Both Peter and Jude take for granted that homosexuality is contrary to God's law:

6 And turning the cities of Sodom and Gomorrah into ashes condemned *them* with an overthrow, making *them* an example unto those that after should live ungodly;
7 And delivered just Lot, vexed with the filthy conversation of the wicked:
8 For that righteous man dwelling among them, in seeing and hearing, vexed *his* righteous soul from day to day with *their* unlawful deeds:
9 The Lord knoweth how to deliver the godly out of temptations, and to reserve the unjust unto the day of judgment to be punished:
10 But chiefly them that walk after the flesh in the lust of uncleanness, and despise government. Presumptuous *are they*, self-willed, they are not afraid to speak evil of dignities.

2 Peter 2 : 6–10

7 Even as Sodom and Gomorrah, and the cities about them in like manner, giving themselves over to fornication, and going after strange flesh, are set forth for an example, suffering the vengeance of eternal fire.
8 Likewise also these *filthy* dreamers defile the flesh, despise dominion, and speak evil of dignities.

Jude 7–8

"Prohomosexual" Biblical Passages

In addition to stripping all the texts cited above of any antihomosexual interpretation by the skillful application of historical critical methods, the homosexual movement within the church has tried to use the Bible for its benefit. For example, prohomosexual exegetes point out that there might have been a homosexual affair between David and Jonathan.[20] Their contention is based on various texts, which are commonly used in religious services at which homosexuals "marry" each other:

1)   And it came to pass, when he had made an end of speaking unto Saul, that the soul of Jonathan was knit with the soul of David, and Jonathan loved him as his own soul.

258

2   And Saul took him that day, and would let him go no more home to his father's house.

3   Then Jonathan and David made a covenant, because he loved him as his own soul.

4   And Jonathan stripped himself of the robe that *was* upon him, and gave it to David, and his garments, even to his sword, and to his bow, and to his girdle.

1 Samuel 18 : 1–4

2)   16   So Jonathan made a *covenant* with the House of David, *saying*, Let the Lord even require it at the hand of David's enemies.

17   And Jonathan caused David to swear again, because he loved him: for he loved him as he loved his own soul.

18   Then Jonathan said to David, To morrow *is* the new moon: and thou shalt be missed, because thy seat will be empty.

1 Samuel 20 : 16–18

3)   25   How are the mighty fallen in the midst of the battle! O Jonathan, *thou wast* slain in thine high places.

26   I am distressed for thee, my brother Jonathan: very pleasant hast thou been unto me: thy love to me was wonderful, passing the love of women.

27   How are the mighty fallen, and the weapons of war perished!

2 Samuel 1 : 25–27

Obviously, none of these passages indicates anything but the existence of a strong affective relationship between these men. The reading of a sexual affair between them is absolutely gratuitous and unwarranted; it assumes that all strong personal relationships are sexual in nature.

Apologists of homosexuality have also alleged that St. Paul might have been homosexual. This is the contention of the anonymous author of *Prologue: An Examination of the Mormon Attitude Towards Homosexuality*. Based on St. Paul's recommendation of celibacy (1 Corinthians 8), the fact that he was not married, and his own statement that "Paul was very personally concerned about homosexuality,"[21] he concludes:

> In order to accurately account for his writings on homosexuality, one has to take into account Paul's problem. Whatever it was, he had a problem, and he comes within a hair's breadth of naming it, calling it his "thorn in the flesh." Many have tried to explain away this curious allusion to his problem by saying it was malaria or some other similar illness. Given Paul's explicitness, it is doubtful he would have alluded to something he could easily have stated outright and elaborated on. Malaria is not a satisfactory explanation to his euphemistic phrase. If Paul was struggling with homosexuality, his carefully disguised reference makes more sense. There are few Biblical authors whose personal lives come as close to approximating a struggle against homosexuality as does Paul's. No one in the Bible has as much to say on the subject as does Paul which only adds weight to the possibility. The knowledgeable homosexual

understands and appreciates what Paul says about homosexuality. (*Christianity Today*, Vol. 12:23, March 1, 1968) Many have gone through a similar effort. Paul evidently did not realize how transparent the doctrinal externalization of his personal battle was. The Brethren are alerted to this and are far more anxious to sweep it under the rug than Paul was.[22]

Likewise, the idea that Jesus and St. John the Apostle were homosexual lovers has been advanced in certain homosexual circles, based on the reference to the latter as the "Beloved Disciple." This idea was advanced in the following exchange during an interview with John McNeill, a "Pro-Gay Jesuit priest":

> *You are a practicing psychotherapist as well as a Jesuit scholar. Are you a Jungian?* My psychotherapeutic orientation, at least for now, is in the object relations school—more Sullivanian. But Jung had much to say. Each of the special qualities he attributes to the homosexual community is usually considered a striking characteristic of Christ himself, like the extraordinary ability to meet an individual's unique person free of stereotypes, or the refusal to accomplish goals by means of violence. The point I'm trying to make here is not, of course, that Christ was a homosexual any more than he was a heterosexual. His example clearly transcends our current homosexual-heterosexual dialectic. My point is that Christ was an extraordinarily free and fulfilled human being.

> *What about the many scholarly observations (including Boswell's) that Christ's most deeply intimate human relationship was with Saint John?* I think what we see in Jesus is the total freedom to love, to relate to *any* human being. Many priests have succeeded in incarnating these positive qualities of Christ. And, as we've said, many priests in many denominations are homosexually oriented. The gay community, if it were allowed to be itself, to develop its special qualities, has a major role to fulfill in helping to bring about the ideal that Christ represented.[23]

Most Christians would be shocked to see, and would probably consider it blasphemy, that a minister of the Gospel—prohomosexual or not— would not reject outright the intimation that Jesus was somehow affected by homosexuality, and that His relationship with His young disciple in any way resembled that of a pederast. In any case, just because two individuals of the same sex are personally close, it cannot be inferred that they are homosexuals. In the case of Jesus, the New Testament presents Him not only as God Himself, but as a model teacher and prophet. Even if no theological nuances are read into the Gospel of St. John, it can hardly be said that either Jesus or St. John are presented as homosexuals. McNeill's contention that Jesus transcends homosexuality and heterosexuality would seem to violate not only the ethical foundation of Christianity, but also the widely held Christian belief in the Incarnation.

Homosexuality and Religion

THE BIBLE AND HOMOSEXUALITY: CONCLUSIONS

In no instance does the Bible speak favorably of homosexuality. It does not remain neutral on the subject either, an indication that its authors certainly knew of the practice and addressed its ethical value. Although some homosexuals sought sex in pagan cultic settings and man/boy love was well known—and even accepted—in certain Greek circles, it is likely that the majority of homosexuals then, as now, simply looked for relief for their urges with other adult men and outside the temples. The Bible plainly condemns the practice. If the authors had accepted it, it is only reasonable that such acceptance would have been forthcoming. For the unbeliever, this argument will fail to be persuasive. The point is that the Bible does seem to teach that homosexual behavior is evil. Since the Bible has had such a tremendous impact in the ethical formation of America— and it can only be expected that this will continue—this conclusion is crucial in projecting future social behavior. The importance of the Bible is evidenced by the 1977 Minnesota poll mentioned earlier in this chapter. We have seen that the following table illustrates the responses given to the two questions:

Do you think that the Bible says that homosexuality is a sin?
Do you yourself think that homosexuality is a sin?

Response	According to the Bible	Own Opinion
Yes	46%	47%
No	24%	42%
Don't Know	30%	11%
	100%	100%

Statistical analysis of this table yielded the following results: $X^2 = 13.42$ with two degrees of freedom (df = 2). This is found to be significant at the .005 level for a coefficient of contingency, C = .2534. (A .005 level of significance far exceeds what is required in most social science studies.)

This indicates that the source of a person's opinion is statistically significant to the nature of these opinions when reason alone (i.e., own opinion) is compared with reason aided by revelation (i.e., according to the Bible). A detailed analysis of the calls indicates that ignorance of the biblical teachings significantly affects an individual's position concerning the issue of homosexuality. It also indicates that people who base their perception on their own opinion significantly tend to think that homosexuality is not a sin. From the point of view of traditional religion, it appears that the remedial action for ignorance about homosexuality is to study the Scriptures.

THE MOSLEM TRADITION

Islam categorizes itself as a religion of the Book. Muslims have great regard for Jesus, whom they consider a prophet together with Moses, Abraham, and other biblical figures. Although significantly different from Christianity and Judaism, historically and ideologically Muslims do have a legitimate claim to their contention that they have much to share with the other two religions. In America, Islam is particularly important because many Black people, in addition to immigrants and a few converts, also believe in Allah as preached by Mohammed.

Islam rejects homosexuality, and American Muslims have been in many instances at the forefront of the struggle against the homosexual movement. For example, it was partly as the result of the efforts of Abbas Shamsid-deen, a member of the American Muslim Mission in Baltimore, that local prohomosexual legislation was defeated in that city in 1980. He declared: "If this bill passes, how can we deny the civil rights of a child molester or a rapist?", adding that the law would "open the door for legal perversion."[24]

Such a strong position on the practice of homosexuality—which in Moslem countries involves severe penalties—is rooted in the clear teachings of the Koran. They are all based on Lot's story and will clarify the way in which this story was understood by Mohammed, very much in line with the traditional Christian interpretation of this passage. (Philo, many centuries later, also had the same interpretation in *On Abraham* (36:135).)[25] The following excerpts from the Koran have been taken from Mohammed Marmaduke Dickthall's interpretation.[26] They have been compared with Arberry's interpretation[27] and no significant differences have been found. There are eleven citations of Lot in the Koran. The following four explicitly reflect Allah's condemnation of the practice:

1) Sûrah VII: *The Heights*, Verses 80–84:
    80. And Lot! (Remember) when he said unto his folk: Will ye commit abomination such as no creature ever did before you?
    81. Lo! ye come with lust unto men instead of women. Nay, but ye are wanton folk.
    82. And the answer of his people was only that they said (one to another): Turn them out of your township. They are folk, forsooth, who keep pure.
    83. And We rescued him and his household, save his wife, who was of those who stayed behind.
    84. And We rained a rain upon them. See now the nature of the consequence for evil-doers!
2) Sûrah XI: *Hûd*, Verses 77–83:
    77. And when Our messengers came unto Lot, he was distressed and knew not how to protect them. He said: This is a distressful day.
    78. And his people came unto him, running towards him—and before then they used to commit abominations—He said: O my people! Here

are my daughters! They are purer for you. Beware of Allah, and degrade me not in (the person of) my guests. Is there not among you any upright man?

79. They said: Well thou knowest that we have no right to thy daughters, and well thou knowest what we want.

80. He said: Would that I had strength to resist you or had some strong support (among you)!

81. (The messengers) said: O Lot! Lo! we are messengers of thy Lord; they shall not reach thee. So travel with thy people in a part of the night, and let not one of you turn round—(all) save thy wife. Lo! that which smiteth them will smite her (also). Lo! their tryst is (for) the morning. Is not the morning nigh?

82. So when Our commandment came to pass We overthrew (that township) and rained upon it stones of clay, one after another,

83. Marked with fire in the providence of thy Lord (for the destruction of the wicked). And they are never far from the wrong-doers.

3) Sûrah XXVI: *The Poets*, Verses 160–175:

160. The folk of Lot denied the messengers (of Allah),

161. When their brother Lot said unto them: Will ye not ward off (evil)?

162. Lo! I am a faithful messenger unto you,

163. So keep your duty to Allah and obey me.

164. And I ask of you no wage therefor; my wage is the concern only of the Lord of the Worlds.

165. What! Of all creatures do ye come unto the males,

166. And leave the wives your Lord created for you? Nay, but ye are forward folk.

167. They said: If thou sees not, O Lot, thou wilt soon be of the outcasts.

168. He said: I am in truth of those who hate your conduct.

169. My Lord! Save me and my household from what they do.

170. So We saved him and his household, every one,

171. Save an old woman among those who stayed behind.

172. Then afterward We destroyed the others.

173. And We rained on them a rain. And dreadful is the rain of those who have been warned.

174. Lo! herein is indeed a portent, yet most of them are not believers.

175. And lo! thy Lord, He is indeed the Mighty, the Merciful.

4) Sûrah XXVII: *The Art*, Verses 54–58:

54. And Lot! when he said unto his folk: will ye commit abomination knowingly?

55. Must ye needs lust after men instead of women? Nay, but ye are folk who act senselessly.

56. But the answer of his folk was naught save that they said: Expel the household of Lot from your township, for they (forsooth) are folk who would keep clean!

57. Then We saved him and his household save his wife; We destined her to be of those who stayed behind.

58. And We rained a rain upon them. Dreadful is the rain of those who have been warned.

As with the Bible, there is not one passage that commends or promotes homosexual behavior or the affection between homosexual partners. This is most important, for, if American Christian churches were to cast their lots with the homosexual movement and if, in fact, homosexuality is contrary to the natural law, it is only to be expected that a fair number of individuals would seek refuge in other religious creeds that satisfy their need to raise children and develop strong family relations in agreement with the natural law. Islam might come to be perceived as such a creed.

Other Traditions

The overwhelming majority of Americans, whether or not they participate formally in a religious organization, belong to the Judeo-Christian tradition. Secular humanists, Marxists, and atheists of all sorts have in many instances consciously attempted to renounce this tradition. However, there is little doubt that they are still greatly affected by it. It will take many generations, if it is at all possible, before a significant number of Americans lose the ideological biases imposed by the Judeo-Christian tradition. Although not identical with this tradition, the Moslem tradition is organically connected with the dominant religious tradition, and it contributes to its understanding. For this reason, the sources of these two traditions have been cited whenever they have a direct bearing on the subject of homosexuality.

There are, however, many other civilized traditions which have also addressed this question. While it is not possible to cover them in any depth, a number of factors are starting to make them relevant in America's complex of religious thought. The "future shock" effect, as well as the increasing secularization of mainline denominations, have created a vacuum which is being filled by evangelicals—who can claim loyalty to the traditional principles—as well as by esoteric religions which increasingly claim the adherence of many Americans, especially young people.

There are two traditions which will be discussed briefly: the Hindu and the Buddhist. Although connected by common roots in the subcontinent, they are diametrically contradictory. If it is true that they possess a common mental structure, vocabulary, meditative practices, and, in many instances, share Sanskrit as a sacred language, they are as dissimilar to one another as orthodox Marxism is to Thomistic Scholasticism. In various forms, however, they have gained adherents in the United States.

Hinduism exists in many forms, from the Vedas and the Upanisads to

Homosexuality and Religion

Tantric Yoga, which emphasizes sexual mysticism and certain magical elements. The most popular form of Hinduism in America, however, is that preached by A. C. Bhaktivedanta Suami Prābhupādā, largely based on the Bhagavad-Gītā. As a form of yoga of renunciation (Gītā 6:3), the devotee is required to forgo sensual gratification. Self-actualization and identification with godhead require a godly life involving not only cultic practices and meditation, but also a high standard of ethical behavior. In his commentary on the Gītā, Śrīla Prābhupādā discusses the nature and uses of sex in three passages, in all of which Kṛṣṇa addresses Arjuna. This is particularly important since they believe that Kṛṣṇa is the supreme personality of godhead.

> Gītā, Chapter 4 (*Transcendental Knowledge*), Verse 26[28]
> Text: 26. Some of them sacrifice the hearing process and the senses in the fire of the controlled mind, and others sacrifice the objects of the senses, such as sound, in the fire of sacrifice.
> Purport (Excerpt): Sex life, intoxication and meat-eating are general tendencies of human society, but a regulated householder does not indulge in unrestricted sex life and other sense gratifications. Marriage on principles of religious life is therefore current in all civilized human society because that is the way for restricted sex life. This restricted, unattached sex life is also a kind of *yajña* because the restricted householder sacrifices his general tendency toward sense gratification for higher transcendental life.
> Gītā, Chapter 7 (*Knowledge of the Absolute*), Verse 11[29]
> Text: 11. I am the strength of the strong, devoid of passion and desire. I am sex life which is not contrary to religious principles, O lord of the Bhāratas [Arjuna].
> Purport (Complete): The strong man's strength should be applied to protect the weak, not for personal aggression. Similarly, sex life, according to religious principles (*dharma*), should be for the propagation of children, not otherwise. The responsibility of parents is then to make their offspring Kṛṣṇa conscious.
> Gītā, Chapter 10 (*The Opulence of the Absolute*), Verse 28[30]
> Text: 28. Of weapons I am the thunderbolt; among cows I am the Surabhi, givers of abundant milk. Of procreators I am Kandarpa, the god of love, and of serpents I am Vāsuki, the chief.
> Purport (Excerpt): Kandarpa is the god of love, the procreator. Of course, procreation is for begetting good children; otherwise it is considered sense gratification. When sex is not for sense gratification, it is a representation of Kṛṣṇa.

There are substantial differences, both conceptual and in terms of expression, between the traditional Western view of human sexuality and the viewpoint presented by Śrīla Prābhupādā; however, there are significant principles in which these traditions agree:

sexual acts are proper only within marriage;
unrestricted practice of sex is destructive and uncivilized;

separated from procreation, sexual acts are not proper;
the creative aspect of the sex act makes it a representation of the divinity.

While in traditional Western thought, de facto (as opposed to intended) nonprocreativeness in sexual intercourse is acceptable, this distinction is not apparent in the Hindu texts. This might be related to the acceptance of sense pleasure in the West and its rejection in the yoga of renunciation. The intrinsic and natural connection between sex and procreation is common to both, even if there are differences in emphasis.

As the reader can appreciate, the homosexual ideology fares no better with Hinduism than it does with traditional Judeo-Christian thought. Moreover, this is an indication that the rejection of homosexuality in the West is not a quirk of Western civilization, but part of the common heritage of mankind.

The *Buddhist* tradition, having a dominant existential dimension, is far less specific in terms of right and wrong, although the Second Holy Truth (suffering is rooted in desire) would indicate that homosexuality—at least as practiced in the West—is incompatible with the attainment of Nirvâna. However, the complexity and subtlety of Buddhist thought make it very difficult to make general or absolute assertions without misrepresenting its tenets. The concept of natural law in the sense of a blueprint for behavior based on the nature of things is nonexistent in Buddhism. Instead, the third of the "Five Precepts" mandated for all Buddhists, "not to indulge in illicit sexual relations,"[31] and the third of the "Ten Meritorious Actions," "to abstain from illicit sexual relations is good,"[32] are indicative not of the existence of absolute good and evil, but of the likely results of certain actions according to the principle of interdependent origins (pratîtya samûtpâda).

In general, Buddhism condemns debauchery and lust, although continence for its own sake is not exulted.[33] Marriage is the context in which sex is presented, and lust is generally rejected as a manifestation of suffering-related desire. In the words of the *Dhammapada*, a third-century B.C. collection of sayings attributed to the Buddha: (215) "From lust arises sorrow and from lust arises fear. If a man is free from lust, he is free from fear and sorrow,"[34] and (284) "As long as lustful desire, however small, of man for women is not controlled, so long the mind of man is not free, but is bound like a calf tied to a cow."[35] Attendees at homosexual baths would not fare well under this ethical system.

A very curious reference to homosexuality is found in the commentary to Lama Mipham's *The Wheel of Analytic Meditation* by Tarthang Tulku. The relevant passage is the second stanza, which starts the description of the method of meditation; this is followed by relevant excerpts from the commentary:

Imagining an image before one

Homosexuality and Religion

Of whatever is desired most
And distinguishing the five groupings of elements
Begin to analyse the imaginary body.[36]

The search for the nature of reality begins with the visualization of the most fascinating object of sexual desire. Men should take a woman as the object of meditation, women should take a man, and homosexuals one of their own sex. . . .

For a man, a woman is taken as the object of examination because she evokes the strongest emotional response in the mind. She is the giver of sexual satiety, she is the comforter, the mother, she is the origin of much energy. In youth particularly, the natural desire for a sexual partner, a mate with whom to procreate, is the dominant instinct. Woman is taken as the epitome of desirability, the strongest attachment of mind in the world of desire from which this meditation will lead.

Lust, which should not be confused with sexuality, is compared first to a honeyed razorblade which the foolish man, ignorant of the laws of karmic cause and effect, licks with his stupid tongue. Secondly, it is compared to the poison apple which looks so rosy and edible to the gullible but which is the cause of painful sickness. The man or woman that has his or her tongue lacerated is likely to refrain from a second attempt at savouring the honey, but the unfortunate who tastes the poisoned apple has no sure means of determining the source of the poison, and without a warning or an introduction to the honeyed razorblade, is likely to wallow in the juices of his own passion for many lifetimes.[37]

Although there is no expression of an ethical reflection on the homosexual condition in terms of the natural law—a concept alien to Buddhism— one can detect that sex between a man and a woman is in some sense normative. The purpose of concentrating on a same-sex partner as an object of meditation is not to elicit sexual desire, but to allow the meditator to realize the emptiness of his desire. The reader is cautioned that meditation, unlike Christian prayer, is in reality only an exercise in self-awareness, with no specific behavior to which it relates.

In none of the civilized religious or philosophical traditions we have examined is homosexuality accepted as a legitimate lifestyle. Although such an empirical examination cannot in itself produce the kind of certainty afforded by faith, it is safe to assert two things: the evidence indicates that the secular humanist affirmation that homosexuality is morally acceptable is a quirk in human thought, and religious and other institutions which have in some way compromised traditional thought with the homosexual ideology are bound to suffer as a consequence of their decision.

THE HOMOSEXUAL NETWORK

Notes

1. *Friends for Lesbian and Gay Concerns Newsletter*, 3 (Sumneytown, PA: Friends for Lesbian and Gay Concerns [Quaker], Autumn 1979): 2.
2. Ibid.
3. *Minneapolis Tribune*, August 28, 1977.
4. *Hearing*, p. 46.
5. Tom Minnery, "Homosexuals CAN Change," *Christianity Today*, February 6, 1981, pp. 36–41.
6. Letter of Stephen R. Endean, *Washington Star*, April 25, 1981.
7. *It's Time* 8 (January-February, 1981): 1.
8. Ibid.
9. *It's Time* 8 (March-April 1981): 1.
10. *It's Time* 8 (January-February 1981): 1.
11. *It's Time* 8 (March-April 1981): 1.
12. *Workers World* (New York, N.Y.), May 29, 1981, p. 2.
13. Ibid.
14. *A New Day* 3 (June 1979): 1.
15. Ibid.
16. Ibid.
17. Lacey Fosburgh, "From a Quiet Seminarian to Homosexual Spokesman," *New York Times*, January 25, 1977, p. 16.
18. Tripp, Chapter 5.
19. Statement of Rev. Cecil Williams, *Hearing*, p. 45.
20. Norman Pittenger, *Homosexuals and the Bible* (Los Angeles: Universal Fellowship Press, 1977), p. 10.
21. *Prologue: An Examination of the Mormon Attitude Towards Homosexuality* (Salt Lake City: Prometheus Enterprises, 1978), p. 26.
22. Ibid., p. 27.
23. "The Church Divided. A Jesuit Priest Who Begs to Differ: A Conversation with Father John McNeill and Dr. Lawrence Mass," *New York Native*, April 20–May 3, 1981.
24. *Baltimore Sun*, July 8, 1980.
25. The United Presbyterian Church in the United States, *The Church and Homosexuality* (New York, N.Y.: Office of the General Assembly, 1978), p. 18.
26. Mohammed Marmaduke Pickthall, *The Meaning of the Glorious Koran* (New York, N.Y.: New American Library, n.d.).
27. A. J. Arberry, *The Koran Interpreted* (New York, N.Y.: Macmillan, 1973).
28. A. C. Bhaktivedanta Suami Prābhupādā, translator and commentator, *Bhagavad-Gītā As It Is*, abr. ed. (New York, N.Y.: Bhaktivedanta Book Trust, 1968), pp. 80–81.
29. Ibid., p. 127.
30. Ibid., p. 172.
31. Alexandra David-Neel, *Buddhism: Its Doctrines and Its Methods* (New York, N.Y.: Avon Books, 1977), p. 150.
32. Ibid., p. 151.
33. Ibid., p. 167.
34. Juan Mascaro, trans., *The Dhammapada* (Harmondsworth, Middlesex, England: Penguin Books, 1973), p. 66.
35. Ibid., p. 76.
36. Lama Mipham, *The Wheel of Analytic Meditation*, trans. Tarthang Tulku in *Calm and Clear* (Emeryville, CA: Dharma Publishing Co., 1973), p. 43.
37. Ibid., pp. 58 and 59.

VII

Relationships Between Religious Organizations and the Homosexual Movement

The Homosexual Religious Network

INTRODUCTION

Churches are independent organizations, usually jealous of their identities and prerogatives. Nevertheless, they have sufficient communality of interests and a similar enough outlook on the human condition for the homosexual movement to approach each of them in pretty much the same way. Strategically, the approaches are almost identical; tactically, the movement is flexible enough to consider each church in terms of its individuality.

The point of contact between the homosexual movement and the religious establishment is a series of homosexual congregations or other religious units which cater fundamentally to the needs of homosexuals. Many such groups exist within other "normal" churches as foci for the spread of the homosexual ideology within the host churches. In other cases, they are independent congregations or they have federated. A prime example of the latter is the Universal Fellowship of Metropolitan

Community Churches. As Table 17 demonstrates, these groups may be found throughout the United States and involve most major denominations. On the surface, they are totally independent. In fact, they work pretty much in unison, if only because most of their members share the desire to seek sexual satisfaction with same-sex partners and accept the homosexual ideology. The key to their ability to act as a movement is *networking*, the existence of intimate working relationships among groups.

NETWORKING: THE UFMCC

At the center of the network of homosexual religious congregations is the Universal Fellowship of Metropolitan Community Churches (UFMCC), itself a network of autonomous religious congregations founded by a homosexual minister and providing a variety of services to homosexuals. A far-distant second to the UFMCC is New Ways Ministry (NWM), a Catholic homosexual center run by a priest and a nun, although it has no official or legal standing in the Church. These two institutions work in a close, harmonious relationship. Figures 3 and 4 are letters from UFMCC personnel to Father Robert Nugent, SDS, Codirector of NWM, which illustrate their close relationships. The April 22, 1980, letter from Kenneth Spaatz shows the role of NWM's codirector in preparing the "denominational statements" used in support of the prohomosexual federal legislation then pending in Congress. The common lobbying nature by these two "religious" organizations is obvious. The reader will note that in neither case is the priest addressed by his proper name or title, but as "Dear Bob."

The central role of the UFMCC in the assault on major denominations by the homosexual movement is shown by the following statement of Troy Perry, its founder. At the congressional briefing held on April 21, 1980, in support of federal prohomosexual legislation, Perry indicated that the homosexual organizations within several denominations are the result of UFMCC efforts and described how they have effectively worked to obtain the political support of these denominations:

> Our denomination has been instrumental in helping see that Gay caucuses in denominations such as the United Methodist Church, the United Presbyterian Church, the Presbyterian Church, USA, the Episcopal Church, and the Roman Catholic Church, have been formed to reach out to Gay men and Lesbians in those groups . . . . Many of these denominations have taken positions supporting Gay civil rights legislation . . . . I am here today to be their voice and to testify to you not only as a Christian, but also as a Gay male who is concerned with the rights of Gay men and Lesbians in this country—especially regarding the right to housing and jobs.[1]

The relationships between the UFMCC and other homosexual orga-

TABLE 17
Homosexual Congregations

State	Roman Catholic	Christian Science	Episcopalian	Lutheran	Presbyterian	Mormon	Seventh Day Adventist	Jewish	Metropolitan Community Churches	Other	TOTAL
Alabama	1		1						1		3
Alaska									1		1
Arizona	2		1		1	1			4	1	10
Arkansas									2		2
California	9	1	3	3	3	1	2	4	18	10	54
Colorado	2		1					1	3		7
Connecticut	3		2						2		7
Delaware											0
Washington, DC	1		1					2	1	1	6
Florida	3		2					1	10	1	17
Georgia	1		1	1					1		4
Hawaii	1		1						1		3
Idaho											0
Illinois	2		1	1	1				1	2	4	12
Indiana	3		2	1				1	2	1	10
Iowa	1								3		4
Kansas	1								1		2
Kentucky									1		1
Louisiana	1		1	1					1	1	5
Maine	1										1
Maryland	1		1					1	1	1	5
Massachusetts	3		1	1				1	2	2	10
Michigan	4		1	1				1	1	1	9
Minnesota	2		1	1					1	1	6
Mississippi											0
Missouri	3		1					1	5	1	11
Montana											0
Nebraska	1			1					1		3
Nevada	1										1
New Hampshire	1		1								2
New Jersey	4				1				1	1	7
New Mexico	1		1						1		3
New York	10	1	3	1	1			2	5	10	33
North Carolina	2		1						3	2	8
North Dakota				1							1
Ohio	5		2						6	3	16
Oregon	1								1		2
Pennsylvania	4		1					2	2		9
Rhode Island	1								1		2
Puerto Rico											0

TABLE 17 (*cont.*)

State	Roman Catholic	Christian Science	Episcopalian	Lutheran	Presbyterian	Mormon	Seventh Day Adventist	Jewish	Metropolitan Com. Churches	Other	TOTAL
South Carolina	1								1	1	3
South Dakota											0
Tennessee	1		1						3		5
Texas	9	1	1	1				1	5	6	24
Utah			1						1		2
Vermont			1								1
Virginia	2		1						3	1	7
Washington	1							2	1		4
West Virginia											0
Wisconsin	2		2	1					1	1	7
Wyoming	1										1
Totals	93	3	37	16	6	2	3	21	100	50	331

nizations within the various churches are intimate and far-reaching. They work together, support one another, and are the recipients of services in a variety of areas:

> In the area of cooperation with other gay religious organizations, Adam DeBaugh will be speaking at both the Integrity and Dignity national conferences this year and has addressed a number of local chapters of different religious gay organizations.
> All religious gay organizations received copies of the list of Members of Congress who are members of their respective religions. DeBaugh is assisting the Christian Church (Disciples of Christ) in the preparation of the report of their Human Sexuality Task Force, and he provided testimony for the consideration of the Executive Board of the Friends Committee on National Legislation (Quakers). We enjoy warm and close relations with many people in Dignity, both on the national and local levels. The Washington, D.C. chapter of Dignity contributed over $400 to the work of the Washington office as a result of DeBaugh's talk there last spring.
> Integrity has officially named Adam DeBaugh to be its spokesperson in Washington and is providing a very modest amount of money to help our work. While the amount of financial support is small ($100), it is an important contribution because of the significance of the continuing ecumenical ministry going forward in Washington.[2]

Perry can thus claim with some justification that he speaks not only for his "denomination," but for homosexuals in other denominations.

The building of such a network and the full participation of homosexual groups in general and the UFMCC in particular are high-priority items

Religious Organizations and the Movement

on the agenda of the movement. This is the specific responsibility of the UFMCC's Department of Ecumenical Relations:

Work With Other Denominations

The Department of Ecumenical Relations will coordinate many of the contacts between the Universal Fellowship of Metropolitan Community Churches and other denominational national staff, leadership, judicatories, boards and agencies. It will put our agencies and boards in touch with other denominational agencies doing similar work, for instance. It will help to explain the UFMCC to other religious bodies. It will work to educate the other religious bodies about areas of special concern and ministry to the UFMCC. It will formulate responses to be approved by the Board of Elders to actions by other denominations. It will "lobby the churches on Gay rights and other issues of concern to the UFMCC." In so doing, it will be undertaking part of the role of the Washington Field Office and thus save duplication of effort.

Religious Gay Organizations

The Department of Ecumenical Relations will work with the Gay caucuses of the other denominations (Dignity, Integrity, Affirmation, etc.), providing them with support, information, resources, and encouragement. This, also, is a task already assigned to the Washington Field Office and fits perfectly into the new joint role of this office.[3]

Adam DeBaugh pointed out in February, 1981, the following objective for the group: "For the immediate future, the UFMCC's Department of Ecumenical Relations plans to continue working with organizations with which we have been working in the past, and to pursue membership in the World Council of Churches, the National Council of the Churches of Christ in the U.S., and the National Council of Community Churches."[4]

In building its religious support network, the UFMCC has been a full participant in the Washington Interreligious Staff Council (WISC), a powerful but little-known group of church bureaucrats. It was also instrumental in the creation of the Interfaith Council on Human Rights, an organization founded to counteract the efforts of Christian Churches which organized the April, 1980, Washington For Jesus rallies.[5] There are many other religious groups with which the UFMCC maintains ties:

UFMCC people have represented the Fellowship at meetings of the Joint Strategy and Action Committee (a coalition of religious groups involved in a broad list of human concerns), the National Interfaith Coalition on Aging, the Commission on Women in Ministry (COWIM) of the National Council of Churches, the NCC's Commission on Family Ministries and Human Sexuality (where first the Rev. Ren Martin and now the Rev. Jim Glyer serve the Fellowship with distinction), the Criminal Justice Task Force (with the Rev. Bob Arthur ably witnessing the UFMCC's concern for prison ministry), and the National Council of Community Churches.[6]

Universal Fellowship of Metropolitan Community Church

110 MARYLAND AVE., N.E., WASHINGTON, D.C. 20002   (202) 543-2266

April 4, 1978

Reverend Robert Nugent, SDS
New Ways Ministry
3312 Buchanan Street, #302
Mount Rainier, Maryland 20822

Dear Bob:

      Thank you for your letter of March 30th. I was hoping
to see you at the Southeastern Conference of Lesbians and Gay Men
in Atlanta this past weekend, but I guess you were unable to make it
down there.

      Much is happening in the Washington office. Last September
Roy left to start a church in Norfolk, Virginia, and I am in the
process of searching for an administrative assistant.

      I will update your address on our mailing list. I am
sending you our latest issue of Gays On The Hill and our new
Writing To Congress pamphlet for you and Jeannine.

      We definitely have to get together soon to talk about
your new center and the continuing work here in the Washington
office. I will be out of town between April 6th and 17th, but
after that let's get together.

      Thank you for writing. God bless you in your ministry.

Shalom,

R. Adam DeBaugh
Social Action Director

encl:
RAD:rhg

Proclaim Liberation in the Land.

FIGURE 3
Letter from R. Adam DeBaugh to Father Robert Nugent, SDS.

(Letterhead)
Universal Fellowship of Metropolitan Community Cl. ·ches
Washington Field Office

22 April 1980

Fr. C. Robert Nugent, S.D.S.
New Ways Ministry
3312 Buchanan Street, #302
Mt. Ranier, Maryland 20882

Dear Bob:

　　　　Enclosed is as complete a packet on yesterdays Congressional Briefings on the National Gay Rights Bill as I can put together at this time.

　　　　Troy Perry's testimony enclosed is complete with addendums and includes the Denominational Statements on Gay Rights which you had specifically requested. The additional testimonies are extra copies which I was able to obtain yesterday and am forwarding them on to you for your own use and information.

　　　　I also want to take the opportunity to thank you for your valuable assistance in helping us put together the Denominational Statements.

　　　　If we can in some way for of further service to you, please don't hesitate to call.

　　　　　　　　　　　　　　　Sincerely,

　　　　　　　　　　　　　　　(No Signature)

　　　　　　　　　　　　　　　Kenneth G. Spaatz, Jr.

　　　　　　　　　　　　　　　Administrative Assistant

enclosures

FIGURE 4
Letter from Kenneth Spaatz, Jr. to Father Robert Nugent, SDS.

THE HOMOSEXUAL NETWORK

As the reader can appreciate, these groups are, although religious in appearance and perhaps inspiration, basically concerned with political and sex-related questions rather than with evangelism or spiritual growth, the traditional concerns of religion. Moreover, it can be anticipated that in supporting the political agendas of these groups or their participants, the UFMCC can later obtain reciprocal support for its own prohomosexual agenda. It is precisely in this give-and-take that networks are very productive for their members.

A similar list of organizations which, to one degree or another, are part of the UFMCC network of friendly religious supporters has been provided by DeBaugh:

> Such organizations include (but are not limited to) the National Council of Churches, the National Council of Community Churches, the World Council of Churches, the Ecumenism Research Agency, the NCC Commission on Women in Ministry, the NCC Joint Strategy and Action Coalition, the Washington Inter-religious Staff Council, and other national and international ecumenical and inter-religious organizations.[7]

The solidification of the homosexual movement's religious network has been shown by several events, all of which have been in some way related to the UFMCC. On April 28, 1980, a meeting of homosexual religious groups was held in the White House, part of the campaign of the UFMCC against the Washington For Jesus rally. Attendance at the meeting was varied, including representatives of twenty-one different homosexual religious organizations:

> The men and women attending the meeting were a varied group, not only being from many different religious backgrounds, but also being young and old, Gay and non-Gay, long-term activists and new faces. People attending the meeting included the Rev. Elder Nancy Wilson, clerk of the UFMCC Board of Elders, and R. Adam DeBaugh and Ken Spaatz, Director and administrative assistant of the UFMCC Washington Field Office; Dignity's president, Frank Scheuren, secretary, Elinor Crocker, and treasurer, Joseph Totten; Martin Rock, head of the Brethren/Mennonite Council on Gay Concerns; Raymond Spitale of Gay People in Christian Science; Dr. Ralph Blair and Dr. Wayne Swift of Evangelicals Concerned; Larry Neff and Barrett Brick of Bet Mishpocheh, the Gay synagogue in Washington; John Laurent of Affirmation: Gay and Lesbian Mormons; Bob Bouchard, of Kinship: Seventh Day Adventists; Bruce Grimes and Geoff Kaiser of the Friends Committee for Lesbian and Gay Concerns; Robert P. Wheatly of the Unitarian-Universalist Office of Gay Concerns; Gabriel Lanci, editor of Insight magazine, a Lesbian/Gay ecumenical quarterly; the Rev. William R. Johnson, of the Lesbian/Gay Ecumenical Center in formation in New York; Dr. James Tinney, a Black Pentecostal; the Rev. Robert Nugent, Sister Jeannine Gramick and Rick Garcia of the New Ways Ministry, a Roman Catholic peace and justice center with a special ministry to

Religious Organizations and the Movement

Lesbians and Gay men; Barbara MacNair, Rick Mixon and Sandra Rogers, of American Baptists Concerned; the Rev. Jan Griesinger and the Rev. Oliver Powell of the United Church of Christ Coalition for Gay Concerns; the Rev. Michael Collins, Peggy Harmon, Joan Clark and the Rev. Bill Matson of Affirmation: United Methodists for Lesbian and Gay Concerns; Howard Erickson and the Rev. John Backe, of Lutherans Concerned; Diane Stevenson and Dennis Buckland of the Unitarian-Universalist Gay Caucuses; William Silver and Sandy Brawders of Presbyterians for Gay Concerns; and Roger Conant, of Integrity.[8]

The meeting was intended not only to counteract a petition to President Carter signed by over 70,000 Christians in opposition to the granting of special legal privileges to homosexuals, but also as a vehicle for the strengthening of the homosexual religious network: "An additional reason for the meeting was that people from the major Gay religious organizations have never gotten together for a chance to get to know each other, to strategize for the future, and to plan for future ecumenical cooperation. The White House meeting afforded representatives from 21 Lesbian/Gay religious groups the opportunity to do so."[9]

Representing President Carter at the meeting were a Baptist minister, Reverend Robert L. Maddox Jr., Special Assistant to the President for Religious Affairs, and Allison Thomas on behalf of Assistant to the President Anne Wexler. Immediately after the White House meeting, the group retired to a local "leather bar" for a luncheon meeting ("leather" is homosexual argot for a variety of sadomasochism), described by *A New Day* as "the first time representatives of this many religious groups serving the Lesbian/Gay community had ever gathered for a meeting." Religious traditionalists would perhaps have found it significant that this crucial occasion for the establishment of the homosexual religious network took place in an establishment whose trademark is a young, musclebound, shirtless youth, wearing tight black pants and sporting a whip poised to strike, his genitals exposed and superimposed on an eagle, one of whose wings is about to enfold him.

The Strategy Conference on Homophobia in the Church (see chapter III) is another example of the homosexual religious network in action. The meeting was originally sponsored and funded by two traditional allies of the homosexual movement, the National Organization for Women and a fringe extreme leftist Roman Catholic group, the Quixote Center.[10] The UFMCC became a cosponsor of the meeting, contributing also to its funding. It is important to realize that this meeting was not an intellectual exercise, but that it had three clearly political and action-oriented objectives: 1) to raise the consciousness of the participants and those represented by the participants in various aspects of the homosexual ideology; 2) to form and cement the homosexual religious network; and 3) to develop and begin implementing an action plan to use the churches for the advancement of the movement's objectives. This is evident in the conclusions reached by the end of the meeting:

> With June being Gay Pride Month around the country the conference reached the following consensus:
>
> 1) that homophobia exists in the churches and promotes a state of sin and pain among Christians;
>
> 2) that we have a responsibility as Gay and non-Gay Christians to confront homophobia;
>
> 3) that we have the capability as Gay and non-Gay Christians to help the churches transcend the homophobic state of sin and pain;
>
> 4) that homophobia is part of the churches' politically expedient movement away from the whole Gospel along with racism, sexism, ageism, and classism, and is as contrary to the liberating Gospel of Jesus Christ as these other forms of oppression;
>
> 5) that as part of our strategy to combat homophobia we begin a process of interdenominational network building for purposes of mutual support, ministry and a sharing of resources and tactics;
>
> 6) and that we have developed a selection of strategies for exploration and implementation where applicable, by May 6, 1982.[11]

Attendees represented the following churches:

> The American Baptist Church
> The American Lutheran Church
> The Association of Evangelical Lutheran Churches
> The Church of the Brethren
> The Roman Catholic Church
> The Episcopal Church
> The Mennonite Church
> The Reformed Presbyterian Church
> The United Presbyterian Church in the U.S.A.
> The Presbyterian Church, U.S.
> The United Methodist Church
> The Seventh Day Adventists
> The Unitarian-Universalist Association
> The United Church of Christ
> The United Church of Canada.

Other homosexual-related groups represented included the UFMCC, Evangelicals Concerned, and New Ways Ministry. Although not connected with a church or religion, the National Gay Task Force was also represented, as were a number of other groups ostensibly without a direct interest in the homosexual ideology. They included the two original cosponsors (National Organization for Women and the Quixote Center) as

Religious Organizations and the Movement

well as "the Commission on Women in Ministry of the National Council of Churches, Men Allied Nationally for the ERA, Clergy and Laity Concerned [the remnant of a radical group of activist leftists opposed to the United States' efforts to defeat Communism in Viet Nam], the Center for Women Religious of Berkeley, and the Women's Ordination Conference."[12]

The third area which is crucial not only for the present vitality but also for the future growth and efficacy of the homosexual religious network is the UFMCC's recruitment and "activation" of homosexual seminarians. In a real way, it is in this hitherto little-known activity that the UFMCC is sowing the seeds of the future homosexual movement. This activity is also the duty of the UFMCC Department of Ecumenical Relations, whose responsibility is to:

> . . . assist and enable Gay women and men who are in seminaries, both UFMCC people and those from other denominations. We already have a network of UFMCC people who are studying at seminaries all across the U.S. and in other countries, in seminaries and schools of theology of many different denominations. The Department will try to identify our own people in seminaries, and help them educate other seminarians, faculty and staff. We can provide support for closeted seminary students and faculty. We can assist with providing materials, teaching classes and leading seminars. We can help, as many MCC students have done in the past, with the creation of Gay caucuses at seminaries. We can help build networks between Gay seminarians, not only in the UFMCC but in other denominations as well.[13]

The implication is that the churches cannot count on the unequivocal loyalty of the homosexual seminarians, here described as "our own people." The sexual propensities of these individuals are thus transformed, upon their "coming out," into political support for the homosexual movement.

The activities of the UFMCC among homosexual seminarians have begun to bear fruit in the form of periodic conferences. The following notice was published in an official publication of the UFMCC:

> The Third Lesbian and Gay Seminarians Conference has been scheduled for March 28 and 29, 1980, at Union Theological Seminary in New York City.
> The second gathering of Gay seminarians was held last fall in Cambridge, Massachusetts and was a significant success.
> Lesbians and Gay men who are in seminary are welcome to join the third conference at Union this spring. If you are interested, write . . .[14]

It is unlikely that individual donors or local congregations in denominations that support Union Theological Seminary are aware that the school has been used for the support of the homosexual movement . . . in the name of religion.

THE HOMOSEXUAL NETWORK

THE WASHINGTON INTERRELIGIOUS STAFF COUNCIL

In 1976, some two years after it was founded, the Washington office of the UFMCC joined the Washington Interreligious Staff Council (WISC). This event was noted by *Gays on the Hill*, which indicated that WISC had approved the UFMCC participation "unanimously."[15] To understand the significance of this occurrence, it is necessary to know what WISC is and how it works. Conversely, WISC can be used as an example of the homosexual movement's infiltration into and use of liberal coalitions in the pursuit of its goals.

The Washington Interreligious Staff Council is a coalition of national offices of mainline religious groups located in Washington. Although there are no ideological membership requirements in WISC, in fact it constitutes the vehicle by which the liberal bureaucrats of these offices share information and plan strategies to protect their interests and influence public policy according to the positions taken by the denominations. WISC was founded some twenty years ago and is composed of the national denominational offices represented by their staffs. Some of the member organizations are large and sophisticated; others are quite small and could not exercise appreciable influence unless such a vehicle as WISC were available: "WISC is unique in the breadth of its ecumenicity. It harbors bodies as disparate as the Union of American Hebrew Congregations, the Unitarian Universalist Association, the Roman Catholics, the National Association of Evangelicals, and a number of other ecclesiastical bodies. WISC, itself, does not appear in the Washington telephone directory."[16] WISC's basic organization is the plenary meeting attended by all members every other week to conduct routine business and receive reports of various task forces. While information exchange and decision-making take place at the plenary meeting, much of the detailed work is conducted by a number of task forces which concern themselves with such "basic priority areas" as:

U.S. food policy
U.S. foreign policy and military spending
health care
human services
employment and economic policy
criminal justice
civil rights and liberties
energy and ecology.[17]

It would be wrong, however, to assume that WISC is involved with issues only in a broad sense or in the abstract. In each of its basic priority areas, WISC's concerns are quite specific and partisan. Moreover, WISC does not have much involvement with administrative or regulatory activities,

Religious Organizations and the Movement

but concerns itself more with congressional action. From a strictly political viewpoint, WISC constitutes the focal point for a number of liberal coalitions, having close ties with other networks which includes both religious and secular groups. WISC maintains no relationship with conservative religious groups or with the Mormon Church. Apparently no attempts have been made to enlist the participation of these churches. One must conclude that WISC perceives its political agenda as incompatible with traditional Christian principles. After conducting an in-depth study of the political lobbying activities of the national staff of the United Methodist Church in Washington, Robert Wood reported:

> When I was there, the chairman of WISC was Rabbi David Saperstein. The address given to me by NCC was headquarters for the Union of American Hebrew Congregations. In its basement is housed the Leadership Conference on Civil Rights, which our Board of Church and Society helps support. (Here is another example of close alliances across religious lines characterizing social activists). However, a WISC staff member advised me that WISC headquarters are not actually located at the address furnished by NCC, but at 100 Maryland Ave., N.E.—the United Methodist Building, where I had been for two days! Finally I tracked down the "headquarters" of WISC—splattered among the groups assembled under our United Methodist roof.[18]

The modus operandi of WISC is also revealing:

> Corroborating what personnel at the UM [United Methodist] building had said, a WISC spokeswoman indicated that WISC personnel spend very much time meeting with each other under different committee, task force, or coalition labels. They rise to change hats, shuffle their papers, and trade places around the table. But when all are settled again, it is very nearly the same faces with only a new coalition name. For example, an April 1977 report listed Grover Bagby, Associate General Secretary for Church and Society's Division of General Welfare, as chairperson of WISC along with Saperstein. Bagby is also Issues Committee chairperson of WISC and on the Welfare Reform Committee. Luther Tyson serves on the Employment Programs Committee, and J. Elliott Corbett is on the WISC committee concerned with adequate housing. Barbara Weaver of the Board of Global Ministries Women's Division, whose law-of-the-sea "issues office" is provided by the Church and Society Division of World Peace, ties into WISC at the sea level.[19]

Good examples of church-sponsored coalitions are the Coalition for a New Foreign and Military Policy, Coalition to End Grand Jury Abuse, Religious Coalition for Abortion Rights, and Interreligious Task Force on U.S. Food Policy, all of them liberal in terms of goals and activities.

The political perception of these coalitions reveals the leanings of the coalitions themselves: "Down on the first floor, a spokeswoman for the Religious Coalition for Abortion Rights, a non-practicing Jew, indicated that abortion rightists, gays, and ERA proponents all face the same opposition from 'fundamentalist types.' "[20] Lack of knowledge of this modus operandi will lead a naive individual to conclude that there is considerable support for liberal causes on account of the large number of "coalitions," "committees," or "task forces" supporting the array of liberal goals, when in reality there is only a small number of paid employees of churches (and sometimes of federally funded programs) who "change hats" and constitute themselves in a myriad of seemingly independent groups. As a public relations gimmick, the system has some obvious merits. In the long run, however, it will result in a decrease in the real impact the denominations can have on the public arena. This, for two reasons. First, the old adage "You can fool all the people some of the time . . ." contains a kernel of truth. Inevitably, people will see through the hoax and come to realize that there is no real substance behind all the noise. Second, church bureaucracies are, like all bureaucracies, out of touch with the constituencies of their offices in terms of both feelings and perceptions. Eventually people realize that what the church bureaucracies advocate is not what the rank-and-file members are willing to support. This is rather dangerous for the leadership of the church (e.g., bishops, moderators, presidents, etc.). However, since they normally receive their information through the bureaucracies, which also prepare the agendas and reports, and manage the conferences, it is nearly impossible for the leadership of the churches to break this mold.

WISC is an organization that exerts incalculable influence, although it has a shadowy existence and almost negligible direct expenses. (It must be noted, however, that the various denominations in fact make considerable in-kind contributions in the form of staff time. In this way these religious institutions are de facto contributors to the typically liberal activities promoted by WISC.) Through WISC, the leftist church bureaucrats have managed to bypass the elected leadership of their denominations, not only in Washington-centered lobbying activities, but also in two other ways: First, by utilizing denominational social structures which these bureaucracies control by the use of mailings, newsletters, conferences, statements, briefings, news services, etc. Second, WISC has organized its own grassroots operation called IMPACT. This is an action network. Unlike WISC, IMPACT does have a budget (large amounts of money coming from the denominations and individual memberships) and a staff. IMPACT has its offices in the United Methodist Building in Washington, D.C., a center of much leftist political activity, both domestic and foreign, and which for many years housed the Washington offices of the UFMCC.

Wood has provided the following description of IMPACT's modus operandi:

Participants [members of IMPACT] are expected to communicate with their

Religious Organizations and the Movement

congressional representatives at least three times a year in response to the "Action Alerts" issued 8 to 12 times a year from the IMPACT office. A newly installed computer makes it possible for the seven WISC task forces to prod United Methodists in any congressional district to contact their elected representatives. Emphasis is especially upon "swing votes," and, as Hamlin [Joyce Hamlin, chairman of the Coalition for a New Foreign and Military Policy] expressed it to me, "More emphasis will help them [Congress] move in our direction."

Four times annually *Update* is published to report briefly on "a wide range of bills of concern." The May 1977 *Update* featured over three dozen issues grouped under the seven major headings.[21]

IMPACT is the route leftist church bureaucrats in Washington have chosen to avoid any interference by local pastors and the authorities within their denominations as they mobilize *individuals* in support of their attempts to influence the U.S. Congress. In theory, church bureaucracies exist to implement the policies of their denominations, since they are supposed to act under the supervision of church officials. In fact, the bureaucracies have frequently become policymakers. By their control over the flow of information, by the support they lend one another across denominational lines, and by their direct appeal to grassroots sympathizers, they constitute a clearly subversive segment within the array of religious institutions. The average member of a church is not aware that when he is making a contribution to his church, he might be supporting a leftist bureaucratic structure that not only does not respond to his interests or religious principles, but has its own agenda and the means by which to implement ideas he does not share.

A typical example is the case of the homosexual movement. There is every indication that the homosexual movement—through the UFMCC—has successfully infiltrated WISC and thus availed itself of the support of the church bureaucracies. The homosexuals' participation in WISC has been crucial in their ability to influence the national staffs of various denominations. According to R. Adam DeBaugh:

> Because of our location in the United Methodist Building and our membership and involvement in a number of ecumenical organizations and activities, the Washington Office is able to be very effective in working with other churches and denominations.
>
> Our activities in this regard are extensive. The Washington Office has for years been a member of the Washington Interreligious Staff Council (WISC), an organization of staff people from virtually all of the religious offices in Washington that work in public policy and advocacy areas. WISC meets on a regular basis and includes people from the Washington social action offices of all the mainline denominations, Jewish organizations, Quakers, Mennonites, Brethren, Unitarians, Evangelicals, and many other faith groups which are represented through their Washington offices.

UFMCC's Washington Office is very active in WISC's task force on civil liberties and civil rights, and through our efforts that task force has included Gay rights as a priority issue. We are also involved in the task force on public policy issues affecting women and the Director is a member of the IMPACT Publications Committee (IMPACT is an inter-religious constituency information and educational effort). Additionally, the Director attends meetings of the heads of WISC offices each month.

In addition to the meetings and organizational contacts, the Washington Office is involved on a virtually daily basis with staff people from other religious offices. Offices frequently consult our library and use our resources; we get frequent requests for information and counselling from other church offices. We have assisted in the preparation of national church studies on human sexuality for at least four denominations. Much of our work, however, is done by simple daily contact with us as a part of the community of faith. The educational value of this contact for national staff people from other denominations is tremendous.[22]

WISC is used by the homosexual movement not only to promote its ideology, but also to stimulate opposition to antagonistic forces. This is exactly what occurred when Christian Voice, a traditional morality-oriented organization, locked horns with the homosexual movement. WISC was duly mobilized to oppose the Christian group and support the homosexual movement:

DEBAUGH BRIEFS INTER-RELIGIOUS COMMUNITY ON CHRISTIAN VOICE THREAT: RESPONSE IS EXCELLENT

UFMCC Social Action Director R. Adam DeBaugh recently presented an in-depth report on the new Christian right to the Washington inter-religious community. . . .

DeBaugh's briefing on Christian Voice (see the last issue of A New Day) outlined the growth of the Christian Voice lobby. He showed WISC members that Christian Voice and its parent organization, the American Christian Cause, are opposed to virtually everything the WISC community supports and supports everything we oppose.

Members of the Washington inter-religious community packed the meeting for the initial briefing and many ordered the full packet of Christian Voice material DeBaugh made available (at $2.00 xeroxing costs). Interest was so high that WISC members requested a second meeting for the purposes of discussion about the newly active Christian Right, which was also held with DeBaugh leading the discussion.

The UFMCC Washington Office will continue to monitor the New Right and report to the moderate and progressive religious community in Washington about the threat of the right-wing Christians.[23]

The efforts of the UFMCC have paid off handsomely, not only in good

Religious Organizations and the Movement

will and sympathy, but in hard support for prohomosexual legislation. WISC's value for the homosexuals is evinced by the following report:

INTER-RELIGIOUS COMMUNITY GEARS UP TO SUPPORT SENATE GAY RIGHTS BILL

by R. Adam DeBaugh

The mainline denominations have begun to work for the up-coming Gay rights bill to be introduced in the U.S. Senate by Sen. Paul Tsongas.

Already a number of Washington offices of mainline, Protestant denominations have written all members of the Senate, urging them to co-sponsor the Tsongas bill when it is introduced.

The UFMCC Washington Field Office reported on the prospects for a Senate bill to the Washington Interreligious Staff Council (WISC), a coalition of Washington offices of religious denominations and organizations which work in public policy with the U.S. Congress. The UFMCC has been a member of WISC since 1975. A number of members of WISC have responded with information in their legislative newsletters to their constituencies about the upcoming Senate bill, advocating support for the legislation.

Other religious offices have sent letters to all 100 Senators, asking them to co-sponsor the Tsongas bill. The United Church of Christ Office for Church in Society sent letters to all Senators over the signature of the Rev. Barry W. Lynn, Legislative Counsel of the office. Rev. Lynn is also a very talented attorney who heads WISC's Civil Liberties/Civil Rights Task Force, of which the UFMCC Washington Office is a member.

Rev. Lynn wrote, "The United Church of Christ has in its heritage and in its theology a commitment to compassion for, and the liberation of, oppressed minorities. We believe that the continued legal discrimination against people solely on the basis of their sexual orientation is a great wrong that must be ended.[24]

The rest of this article indicates further support from the Unitarian Universalists, the Lutherans, the Presbyterians, and the National Council of Churches for Tsongas's prohomosexual legislation. By February 1980, the UFMCC had announced cosponsorship of the bill by Senators Patrick Moynihan (D-N.Y.) and Lowell Weicker (R-Conn.) and could produce quotes from strongly prohomosexual statements prepared by various denominations involved in WISC for an article headed "Religious Community for Senate Gay Rights Bill Continues."[25]

It is important to note that in obtaining this extraordinary support for homosexuality, the movement relies basically on daily contacts between UFMCC personnel and other church bureaucrats. A typical example of a person who has been deployed to influence religious and other organizations on behalf of the homosexual movement is Roy Birchard, Director of Church Relations of the UFMCC:

Working in the area of ecumenical cooperation, Church Relations Director Roy Birchard participated regularly as UFMCC representative to the Washington Interreligious Staff Council in its bimonthly meetings and in a weekly Tuesday morning Bible study organized among WISC members. In August, he met in Boston to plan cooperative endeavors with the officers of Dignity and the staff of Washington's Catholic Quixote Center working in the area of gay rights. Later in the year, he represented UFMCC at the East Coast Consultation on Sexuality of the United Church of Christ, the International Gay Jewish Convention, and an "alternate lifestyles" conference hosted by the American Baptist Churches. Throughout the year, he worked with officers of Integrity, Dignity, Evangelicals Concerned, the American Baptist Gay Caucus, Lutherans Concerned for Gay People, and the United Church of Christ Gay Caucus—assisting the latter two groups during their denominational conventions which were held in Washington.

With Elder Sandmire, he met in New York with staff of the National and World Councils of Churches, and the Joint Strategy and Action Committee about viable ways for UFMCC to continue developing relationships. In addition to attending ministers' and district conferences and two weekend programs at MCC New York, Birchard represented the Washington field office at a Tidewater Area Gay Conference in Norfolk, Va., and a benefit for MCC Philadelphia, Pa., worked with the Gay Activists Alliance of New York and New Jersey in planning a Supreme Court demonstration, and with the Rev. Michael Nordstrom who represented UFMCC at the President's Conference on Handicapped Individuals in Washington. Birchard also prepared a packet of statements by religious denominations on the gay question which was used by Rev. Perry in his White House meeting. (This packet is available for $2.00 and is periodically updated.)

During the first six months of 1977, Birchard also served as interim pastor of MCC Washington, D.C., and this task consumed the greater part of his energies. He was able, however, through this connection, to arrange a reception at the Hill office for Elder Freda Smith and the Rev. Ken Martin during MCC DC's Spiritual Renewal which was well attended by WISC staff persons and Congressional staff, and to arrange a memorable preaching engagement at MCC DC by Mrs. Cynthia Wedel, one of the six presidents of the World Council of Churches.[26]

The integration of the UFMCC and church bureaucrats appears to be total. The role of the UFMCC as spearhead of the homosexual movement within other religions is unquestionable. WISC provides the vehicle by which church bureaucrats have adopted homosexuality as yet another cause. This is extremely subversive from the point of view of traditional morality. The average member of a mainline church probably thinks that his representatives promote the morality his church has always preached. He certainly does not suspect that in reality his representatives have also become virtual agents of the homosexual movement.

Religious Organizations and the Movement

THE HOMOSEXUAL RELIGIOUS NETWORK IN ACTION

We have seen that at the national level the mainline churches have lent their support to the homosexual movement basically through WISC and IMPACT. The rejection of homosexuality is so pervasive in our society, however, that cooperation at such a "lofty" level would have few or perhaps even negative results unless the network were also operative at the grassroots level. In fact it seems clear that if the churches are to be totally incorporated into the struggle for the imposition of the homosexual ideology upon American society, support must be sought at all their organizational levels. In the first section of this chapter we provided evidence that some of the basic elements of a homosexual network exist within the churches. In describing the activities of homosexuality advocates within WISC and IMPACT, we encountered certain specific activities which illustrate the existence of considerable support for the homosexual movement at the highest level. The rest of this chapter will provide additional evidence of considerable support for, and indeed the existence of, a prohomosexual network within mainline churches. Documenting the existence of this network is vital for the efforts of profamily and other traditional morality-oriented religious activists, since only by uprooting this network and neutralizing the social structures in which it inheres (even to the point of disbanding them) will the traditional roles of the churches be restored. From the point of view of evangelism, this is a crucial outcome, since few Americans who accept traditional values—the majority of the people according to the Connecticut Mutual Life Insurance Company report—can be expected to convert to or remain in churches which disregard their feelings and sensitivities. Moreover, if homosexuality is contrary to the natural law, any support for the homosexual movement within the churches will weaken the allegiance of their adherents. No one can expect that believers will be willing to support churches that teach irrational doctrines. The alternative for churches is, of course, to accept the role of elitist institutions which involve only the cognoscenti, whose presumed deeper knowledge and lack of irrational prejudices allow them to accept homosexuality as an alternative lifestyle rather than the perversion, illness, or sin that the masses believe it to be.

One of the ways in which the homosexual movement becomes part of (sometimes even central to) religious networks is by working with other churches on "social action" projects. For example, the Metropolitan Community Church of Washington, D.C., is a member of the Downtown Cluster of Congregations.[27] From this position, the MCC of Washington began to provide staff and supplies for a charitable project of the Luther Place Memorial (Lutheran) Church, eventually joining the First Congregational United Church of Christ in a similar project. It is interesting to note that this last church is the host church for the MCC of Washington, and that it also worked with the Luther Place Memorial Church. The UFMCC set up a program for homosexual Cuban refugees with a federal grant of some $350,000. (Apparently Castro expelled from Cuba a large number of homosexuals during the spring of 1980 as part of a boatlift of refugees who arrived in Florida.) In conducting this program, the church announced that it had the cooperation of the Church World Service, the United States Catholic Conference, and the International Rescue Committee.[28] One way in which homosexual religious groups establish the network is by holding their meetings at churches, if possible of the same denominations to which the groups belong.

Homosexual religious organizations, needing recognition and support from as many sources as possible, often relate to or create other organizations to which individuals can belong without being threatened (i.e., being identified as homosexuals themselves). An example of the first is the National Ecumenical Coalition, Inc. (NEC). Figure 5 is a copy of a letter sent by this organization to New Ways Ministry, a Catholic pro-homosexual organization. Although the letter presents its support for the movement in terms of help to individuals in distress, the ultimate concern of its authors obviously is not to deal with the individual homosexual's hurt feelings, but to change public policy and cultural perception of the homosexual condition using religious concepts as the instrument to achieve this change. Another organization created to serve homosexual needs is the Inter-faith Council on Human Rights, founded by the UFMCC Washington office. This is a handy organization, without a homosexual "tag" in its name, to be used in activating the religious network in response to such events as the "Washington for Jesus" demonstration.[29] This council did plan a service for April 28, 1980. As reported by the UFMCC: "The service, planned as a response to the 'Washington for Jesus' activities, will present a different broad-based religious perspective on the issues to be attacked by the march."[30]

It is interesting to note that the issues addressed by the Christian rally, according to the same report, were: homosexuality, the Equal Rights Amendment, abortion, and pornography. Inasmuch as the "Washington for Jesus" activities opposed the "issues," it is reasonable to assume that the homosexual-sponsored coalition favored them.

It is impossible to cite all or even most of the instances in which homosexual religious organizations operate in network fashion, joining and being joined by other groups. However, the existence of a number of seemingly unrelated issues which homosexual organizations are ready to support provides the factor which makes networking much easier. Abortion, for example, is one of these issues. Homosexual actions do not result in pregnancy; thus it is difficult to understand why homosexuals would be so adamant in favoring "abortion rights." This becomes clearer upon examination of the WISC-originated Religious Coalition for Abortion

National Ecumenical Coalition, Inc.

GEORGETOWN STATION / POST OFFICE BOX 3554 / WASHINGTON, D.C. 20007

OFFICE OF THE EXECUTIVE DIRECTOR

June 27, 1978

The Reverend C. Robert Nugent, S.D.S.
The Reverend Sister Jeannine Gramick, S.S.N.D.
New Ways Ministry
3312 Buchanan Street #302
Mt. Rainier, Maryland 20822

Dear Father Nugent and Sister Gramick,

      We with the National Ecumenical Coalition, want to go on record as strongly advocating the elimination of ALL discrimination against homosexual men and women, that is based solely on the fact that they are homosexual. We are aware of the mockery, abuse, vindictiveness, and discrimination to which almost all homosexual persons have been subjected, especially when it is known that they are homosexual.

      We are profoundly sensible of the fact that church people throughout this nation have not found it easy to study and discuss the issue of homosexuality. However, we feel it is our duty to welcome them into Christian fellowship and love, to give them our understanding concern, compassion and love.

      We believe that any steps you can take toward achieving the objectives on the civil and constitutional rights of all gay men and women, will be most beneficial in achieving what we preceive to be a shared goal-dignity, love, and justice for all.

Yours in Christ,

The Reverend William E. Hibbs
Chairman-Co-Executive Director

Mrs. Nancy C. Ware
President-Co-Executive Director

WEH/hs

Let There Be Love. And Let It Begin With Me.

FIGURE 5
Letter from the National Ecumenical Coalition to New Ways Ministry.

Rights,[31] which includes such groups as the Union of American Hebrew Congregations, the United Methodist Church, and the United Church of Christ, which are also notorious for having favored prohomosexual legislation.

An even more interesting case is afforded by the issue of national defense. Presumably, nuclear attacks against American cities will not discriminate in favor of homosexuals. It is thus difficult to comprehend why the weakening of America can be in the interest of the homosexuals. Still, the staff of the Metropolitan Community Church of San Jose, California, has figured prominently in the Pacific Life Community Coalition, an organization formed by "concerned people who are developing non-violent methods of social change, and are working to dispel the myth that weapons provide security and jobs."[32]

In March 1979, the pastor of the prohomosexual church in San Jose led a march against Lockheed Corporation on account of Lockheed's participation in the construction of the Trident submarine. Having trespassed on Lockheed's property as an act of "civil disobedience," many of the participants were arrested, among them the pastor of the MCC of San Jose. The relationship with other leftist religious groups and individuals established by the homosexuals around this issue becomes clear in the report which appeared in the UFMCC publication:

> The evening prior to the march, the Rev. Anderson joined with people from the Catholic workers [this may be an allusion to the Catholic Worker, a well-known leftist group], Society of Friends, Baptist clergy, and others for worship and training sessions in non-violent action. After the arrests, approximately 125 people gathered across the street from the jail, keeping vigil, singing gospel music and liberation songs.[33]

The homosexual ideology is, of course, the top priority for homosexual religious organizations and the implementation of prohomosexual legislation one of the most important items in the movement's agenda. These concerns are brought to the fore by the activities of representatives of the homosexual movement who utilize a variety of settings to interact with other religious organizations and often turn them around to their peculiar viewpoint. A case in point is the Fellowship Commission of Philadelphia. The following report is reprinted in its entirety to exemplify the way in which these organizations are used by the homosexual movement for its own advantage:

PASTOR BORBE RAISING CITY'S CONSCIOUSNESS

MCC Philadelphia Pastor Don Borbe is one of three persons appointed to represent the gay community on the Fellowship Commission, an influential

Religious Organizations and the Movement

Philadelphia organization which monitors discrimination on a non-partisan basis among political parties and leaders.

The group, which represents all religious and ethnic groups of the city, had never before truly addressed itself to the inclusion of sexual minorities.

At a Commission meeting earlier this year, the Roman Catholic Archdiocese addressed the discrimination they were experiencing. The Rev. Borbe confronted the RCA with the fact that no organization has been more oppressive to gay people, and that he had been informed by a City Councilman's aide that the Archdiocese was the primary obstacle to the passage of a gay rights amendment in that city. Pastor Borbe further indicated that any group which so discriminated, especially those in positions of power, was hypocritical in any attempt to represent themselves as an oppressed minority.

The Rev. Borbe's challenge earned a great deal of support for gay concerns, even though there was little debate—the speaker from the RCA merely blushed and stated he was not qualified to speak on the RCA's position regarding sexual minorities.

At a more recent meeting, Pastor Borbe challenged the Board of Commissioners' presentation of the "priority of concerns for 1979," which failed to include sexual minorities. When a "Fair Election Campaign Practices Code for 1979" was presented, he again challenged them to include gay concerns. A debate ensued this time, with the Board defending its position, while three non-gay attorneys spoke in behalf of the gay community.

At the close of debate, a vote was taken, and the organization, founded in the early 1900's, officially went on record, for the first time, in support of prohibiting discrimination against sexual minorities. The additional significance of this step is that every politician will be made aware of gay concerns, and will be monitored by a very respected, powerful group.[34]

Colleges are important vehicles for the promotion of homosexuality, and the movement has used successfully the educational establishment's receptivity, not only to establish homosexual groups in college campuses, but to infiltrate significantly the campus ministry establishment. The UFMCC, for example, is a member of the National Institute for Campus Ministries: "For the second year in a row, NICM has had a Fellowship representative participating in its Summer Institute where one hundred college and university chaplains have gathered to develop and write specific plans for their ministry in the coming year, of course, reflecting the particular theologies, skills and settings of the writers."[35] In the pursuit of its goals, moreover, the homosexual movement counts on the collaboration of a number of significant institutions. "Project Identification" is a UFMCC sponsored operation aimed at reaching college students. The following description reveals the scope of this operation:

PROJECT IDENTIFICATION. Thanks to the cooperation received from the National Council on Higher Education, the National Student Association, the National Education Association, the National Gay Student Center, the College

Press Service, and the National Institute for Campus Ministries, the Fellowship has names of over 17,000 campus chaplains, educators, administrators, directors of student activities, counselors, campus newspaper editors, and leaders of gay-oriented groups who will receive one of four types of BCM letters during the first week of September (bulk rate mail) requesting their assistance with our program to reach the one million members of our community on the 4,500 campuses in North America.[36]

The reader has probably noticed how various organizations not usually identified with the homosexual movement have lent their expertise to a blatant attempt to influence American colleges in favor of the homosexual ideology. In fact, the movement has devised a set strategy for influencing college students in terms of its ideology, using religion as a convenient tool. The nature of this strategy is manifest in the following excerpt from the 1975–76 report of the Board of Campus Ministry of the UFMCC:

A major concern lies with the enlistment of leadership for campuses. The number of campuses on which UFMCC may build ministries is limited by the number of qualified persons who are available as campus representatives. Some of these will be laypersons and ministers in local churches. In other cases there is no local church near the campus and leadership will be developed from campus personnel or imported. Both of these models have been implemented in a few pilot ministries which are operating in the UFMCC program. As we have learned through experience in the Fellowship, it is best to wait to establish new ministries until stable and consistent leadership is available. Often such leadership becomes apparent, fortunately, as the new location and need for ministry is identified.[37]

Moreover, the concerns of the homosexual movement have become the concerns of the campus ministry establishment. The movement has made good use of this sympathy for its own purposes:

The Director recently attended a conference for one hundred selected Jewish and Christian campus ministers from the United States and Canada. It was held on the campus of Loyola University in Chicago. The conference lasted two and one-half weeks and was for the Director a time of extensive orientation and education in campus ministry. It was also an opportunity for establishing communication with many local ministers in other denominations and leaders in the field. The Director experienced enthusiastic acceptance of and response to the knowledge that UFMCC is active in campus ministry. There was remarkable openness and desire on the part of many conferees to learn about the special needs of gay people and about how they can minister to them or refer them to us for special needs. We expect that this cooperation and interaction will continue. The Director has been invited to write an article on ministry to gay people in a national campus ministry newsletter, as well.[38]

In many instances, the cooperation of nonhomosexual religious insti-

Religious Organizations and the Movement

tutions prepares the groundwork for the creation and progress of the homosexual religious network. In Seattle, for example, the Board of Directors of the Church Council of Greater Seattle created the Task Force on Lesbians and Gay Men. This is in reality a prohomosexual front, functionally an integral part of the movement. This is obvious from its activities, the "suggested readings" (all prohomosexual), its apparent inability to accept the traditional Christian position concerning the issue, and especially from its statement of principles:

WHERE WE STAND. . . .

As a task force, we share a commitment to address the needs and concerns of lesbians and gay men in the church and the community and to raise issues of injustice affecting the lives of lesbians and gay men. We support full civil and human rights for all persons, regardless of sexual preference. We encourage and support dialogue and study on the issues of homosexuality at denominational levels and within local congregations. We affirm and advance the full acceptance of lesbians and gay men within the life and work of the church.[39]

A crucial element in the building of the homosexual religious network is the seminary. After all, new generations of ministers are formed in these institutions, and their involvement with the movement is essential if it is going to be reasonably successful in churches. We already saw that the recruitment of homosexual seminarians is a priority of the movement. In other activities, many seminaries do not seem reluctant to cooperate with the homosexual movement, as outlined below.

Virtually every issue of *Bondings* (the publication of New Ways Ministry) reports the participation of its staff in seminary activities, especially Catholic seminaries in the Washington, D.C., area. (New Ways Ministry is strategically located near the Catholic University of America, in close proximity to numerous other universities and religious houses. In fact, this area probably has the largest proportion of seminaries in the country.)

The First National Symposium on "Homosexuality and the Catholic Church," sponsored by New Ways Ministry and featuring apparently all prohomosexual speakers, was originally scheduled to be held at the Holy Trinity Mission Seminary, a Roman Catholic institution located in Silver Spring, Maryland, on November 20–22, 1981.

Figure 6 illustrates an advertisement which appeared in *In Unity* inviting potential ministers in the Metropolitan Community Church to attend McCormick Theological Seminary, a Presbyterian institution. That would give them access to seminarians of many other denominations through the Chicago Cluster of Theological Schools, including the Bethany Theological Seminary (Church of the Brethren), the Catholic Theological Union (Roman Catholic), the Chicago Theological Seminary (United Church of Christ), the DeAndreis Institute of Theology (Roman Catholic), the Lutheran School of Theology at Chicago, the Melville Lombard Theological School (Unitarian Universalist), and the Northern Baptist Theological Seminary. There are many other examples of students openly preparing for the homosexual ministry in seminaries of major denominations. The following excerpt from the 1975–76 Report of the Director of Campus Ministry illustrates our point:

> A second pilot ministry has been established in cooperation with Good Shepherd Parish MCC in Chicago. It exists at the University of Illinois Chicago Circle Campus. Ms. Claudia Hendricks, a seminary student, is Campus Representative. Another example of campus ministry within the jurisdiction of a local church is that being founded at The American University here in Washington, D.C. by campus representative Louise Leopold, soon to graduate from Wesley Theological Seminary.[40]

An all-day conference on Gay Life Issues was held at the Episcopal Divinity School in Cambridge, Massachusetts, in November 1980. The use of the word "gay" to refer to the homosexual condition indicates the probable prohomosexual bias of the gathering.

Called:
Now it's time to begin preparing.
You don't want shortcuts.
Our ministry demands the fullest development of your potential for excellence . . . of God's gifts in you for others.

Good Shepherd Parish wants You to find Chicago.

A parish base for your education for ministry.

A working arrangement with McCormick Theological Seminary.

And cross-registration opportunities at:
Chicago Theological Seminary
University of Chicago Divinity School
Jesuit School of Theology
Lutheran School of Theology at Chicago
Bethany Theological Seminary
DeAndreis Institute of Theology
Meadville/Lombard Theological School
Northern Baptist Theological Seminary

For information write:
F. Jay Deacon
Good Shepherd Parish MCC
Box 2392   Chicago, Illinois 60690

FIGURE 6
Recruitment Advertisement for UFMCC Ministers.

Religious Organizations and the Movement

The degree of support which some of these activities enjoy is a measure of the homosexuals' skill in building up networks of supporters. New Ways Ministry's symposium, for example, was endorsed by a considerable number of organizations:

Association of Chicago Priests
Eighth Day Center for Justice
Glenmary Commission on Justice
Institute for Women Today
Milwaukee Justice and Peace Center
National Assembly of Religious Brothers
National Assembly of Women Religious
National Coalition of American Nuns
National Conference of Religious Vocation Directors of Men (NCRVDM)
National Federation of Priests' Councils
National Sisters Vocation Conference
P.A.D.R.E.S.
Parish Evaluation Project
Paulist Social Action Committee
Quixote Center
Religious Formation Conference
School Sisters of Notre Dame Provincial Team, Baltimore Province
School Sisters of Notre Dame, Chicago Provincial Council
Sisters of Mercy of the Union, General Administrative Team
Society of the Divine Savior Provincial Team, American Province
Washington Theological Union
Xaverian Brothers, American Central Province[41]

It is very unlikely that the members of these organizations know anything about the support they have offered to the homosexual movement. By skillfully working with the leadership or bureaucracy of the organizations, an impressive collection of endorsers has been put together. Naive readers, and perhaps even some segments of the official hierarchy of the Roman Catholic Church, are likely to be intimidated by this list. Seasoned political analysts would realize that in spite of its propaganda value, in reality it measures only the skill of the organizers in rounding up support for their project.

The support enjoyed by the homosexual movement in the official "religious" community is not limited to the more socially "acceptable" sex between "consenting" adults. The first conference of the North American Man/Boy Love Association (NAMBLA) took place at Boston's Community Church on December 2, 1978.[42] The idea of open sexual relations between adults and children is shocking enough to the sensitivities of most Americans. The thought that this is promoted on church grounds by an organization explicitly dedicated to this form of behavior would probably be considered beyond the realm of possibility by most people. Still, not only did the conference take place in a church, but church representatives also participated as speakers in the pederasts' affair where, according to *Gaysweek*, members "voiced their endorsement of love between man and boy." Among the speakers were Canon Clinton Jones, pastor of Christ Church Cathedral (Episcopal) in Hartford, Connecticut; Father Paul Shanley, representative of Boston's Cardinal Medeiros for sexual minorities (Roman Catholic); and Reverend Robert Whentley, from the national office of the Unitarian Universalist Church. The last speaker was reported to have made this comment on his having been propositioned by a 15-year-old boy: "If you don't think that was rather a shot in the arm for one who is fifty-eight, well, you're mistaken."[43]

The homosexual religious network is active and obviously very powerful. Its reach extends across denominational lines, and the loyalty of its members is probably directed toward the homosexual movement rather than toward the church or synagogue to which its members belong. This should not surprise anyone, since this loyalty is firmly rooted in sex drive, one of the strongest tendencies known to man.

Infiltration of Religious Bodies by the Homosexual Movement

The organizations by which religions express themselves socially can be most useful to the homosexual movement. Thus, as we have seen, strenuous efforts are made by "liberated" homosexuals within the various religious bodies (herein referred to collectively as churches, whether Christian or not) to alter the teachings and practices of these organizations for the benefit of the movement. There are two general ways in which the homosexual movement takes advantage of religious organizations: 1) by gaining recognition (positive acceptance) for the avowed and/or practicing homosexuals who are members of the churches, for homosexuals in general, for the practice of homosexuality, and for homosexual organizations; and 2) by utilizing the resources of the churches (physical, human, influence, connections, financial prestige, etc.) for the advancement of the homosexual ideology.

Each church or religious body in America of any significance has been the object of attention from the homosexual movement as a potential ally. Examples provided throughout this work clearly demonstrate that to one degree or another most churches have been infiltrated by the homosexual movement. The number and variety of religious bodies in America, however, preclude a comprehensive treatment of all of them in this work.

Religious Organizations and the Movement

Consequently, we have taken two religious bodies as case studies: the Roman Catholic Church and American Judaism. The former has been chosen as the largest American denomination (over 50,000,000 adherents) and one of the most influential churches in the nation. The latter has been selected because it is probably the only non-Christian religious group which is firmly established as part of the dominant culture in the United States.

The reader is cautioned, however, not to conclude that the Roman Catholic Church has been chosen as the most "homosexualized" church in the United States. Although within the Protestant tradition—using this word in its broadest sense—are found the clearest examples of rejection of homosexual behavior and even of the homosexual condition itself in fundamentalist preachers, mainline Protestant denominations are notorious for their willingness to compromise with the homosexual movement. For each example offered that shows elements within the Roman Catholic Church to be at the disposal of the homosexual cause, there are examples within Protestant denominations that show a far greater willingness to cooperate with the homosexual movement, even at the highest levels of authority. A short list of items will illustrate our point:

- Most denominations have "gay caucuses" or similar organizations which advocate the homosexual cause within the denomination. They tend to be much more accepted within the Protestant denominations than Dignity is by the Roman Catholic hierarchy.
- Although there is very little question that quasi-marriage rituals between homosexuals take place with Roman Catholic priests witnessing the union, there is no evidence of a Catholic priest performing such a service openly. Methodist minister Paul Abels has performed a number of "covenant services" for homosexual couples at the Washington Square United Methodist Church. The comment made by his bishop when he became aware of Abels's actions was reportedly: "We try to let Abels work things out in his own congregation."[44] In another instance, a homosexual "marriage" between the owner of a homosexual bookstore and his assistant manager was witnessed, at Washington's First Congregational Church, by the "pastor" of the local MCC on February 26, 1982.[45]
- No official body of the Roman Catholic Church has ever favored the ordination of homosexuals, although serious attempts are being made by agents of the homosexual movement to increase the acceptability of homosexual clergy in this denomination. Other churches have gone far beyond the record of the Roman Catholic Church. For example, the General Assembly Task Force on Homosexuality of the United Presbyterian Church voted in January 1978 to recommend the ordination of homosexuals.[46] In the Episcopal Church, Bishop Paul Moore ordained as a priest Ellen Barrett, reportedly a practicing homosexual,[47] and openly defended his action at a conference of bishops. In a sense, the Episcopal bishops condoned this, since they refused to take any action as a body against Bishop Moore.[48] William Reagan Johnson, an

avowed homosexual, was ordained a minister of the United Methodist Church in the early 1970s.[49] This ordination took place openly, after two years of strenuous efforts. Since that time, five female and one male homosexual have been ordained in the United Church of Christ. On Sunday, February 21, 1982, the governing body of the United Church of Christ in Maryland, the District of Columbia, and Northern Virginia decided to ordain to the ministry a woman known to be a homosexual, a member of the Emmaus United Church of Christ in Vienna, Virginia (a decision that motivated 20% of the members of the church to abandon it).[50]

- Protestant facilities are commonly used for homosexual events. The list of cases is much too long to be cited individually and includes not just small churches, but major facilities as well. Their use clearly exceeds the use of Roman Catholic facilities for the same purposes. The most glaring case of such use is the presence for many years of the UFMCC Washington Office at the United Methodist Building in Washington, D.C. Other examples abound. Whereas national Dignity conventions take place in hotels, Integrity—the Episcopalian counterpart of Dignity—held its 1980 convention at Emmanuel Episcopal Church in Boston.[51] The second national meeting of Lutherans Concerned—the homosexual group within Lutheranism—took place on June 19–22, 1980 at St. Mark's Lutheran Church in San Francisco.[52]

- In 1978, Boston's Committee for Gay Youth began to meet in the Arlington Street Church (Unitarian Universalist). After an organizational crisis, the group became the Boston Alliance of Gay and Lesbian Youth (BAGLY). Reportedly, BAGLY meetings are held at St. John The Evangelist Church (Episcopal) in the Beacon Hill section of Boston.[53]

- Whereas the Roman Catholic Church has been steadfast in its refusal to hire avowed homosexuals as teachers, the Stated Clerk of the General Assembly of the United Presbyterian Church in the U.S.A. offered testimony at a hearing in the U.S. Congress accepting the propriety of employing homosexual teachers.[54]

This is not to say that individual congregations or ministers favor homosexuality per se, or to make comparisons between one church and another. Should an exhaustive study of denominations be undertaken on an individual basis, adequate explanations would be found for both differences and similarities of approach to the homosexual movement. The import of our argument is that the homosexual movement does, in fact, exercise considerable influence over most churches, far beyond what their adherents suspect or are willing to tolerate. In the following case studies, therefore, it would be well to concentrate not so much on the specific ways in which Roman Catholic or Jewish institutions relate to the homosexual movement as on the manner in which similar or perhaps worse events occur within other denominations.

Religious Organizations and the Movement

Case Study: The Roman Catholic Church

INTRODUCTION

Among the various institutional expressions of the Christian faith, none is more influential, diffused, or visible than the Roman Catholic Church. Even in the United States, traditionally not a "Catholic" country, the Catholic Church constitutes a social force of vast proportions. It is by far the largest denomination, endowed with a multitude of institutions and a personnel which, thanks to the vow of celibacy, is theoretically committed to nothing but the work of the Church. The Catholic tradition, conscious of some two millenia of continuing historical experience, is rich in wisdom and understanding of the human condition.

The Catholic Church is well organized, although its legal system is sufficiently flexible to allow for many manifestations—ideological and organizational—within the bounds of orthodoxy. Roman Catholicism has a dual dimension. It represents a supranational body centered in Rome as the Mother Church, which claims universal and immediate jurisdiction over all its members. In this it is clearly different from the Episcopal communion or Eastern Orthodoxy, both of which represent coalitions or federations rather than institutions. At the same time, the Catholic Church is incarnated in each nation or culture according to the specific characteristics of this culture. Precisely because it is not tied to any particular country or culture, it takes on many of the characteristics of the countries in which it exists. Throughout its long existence, the Roman Catholic Church has learned that its survival is a function of its ability to respond to and identify with the specific needs of the countries in which it exists.

This vision of the Roman Catholic Church represents only the ideal the Church has set for itself. In reality, the Church is quite a human institution which, when analyzed in a purely secular framework, can appear indistinguishable from other human organizations. The Church exists as part of the historical process common to mankind and reacts to events in a human fashion even if, from the supernatural framework in which its members must view human events, the "signs of the times" acquire a completely different set of meanings. The Church thus constantly interacts with other institutions as a human agent in the historical process, even as she maintains a self-perception of eternal supernaturalism.

From a historical point of view, the Catholic Church is in the midst of a profound revolution measurable in decades rather than years, resulting from its attempt to react to three phenomena:

> *Secularization,* having its remote antecedents in William of Occam, which has become increasingly apparent since the Enlightenment, especially since Immanuel Kant.

Political Revolution, which can be traced to Marsilius of Padua, but which launched the contemporary era with the French Revolution.

Economic and Social Upheaval caused by technological and scientific innovations which, traceable to the advent of empiricism during the Renaissance, have been manifested in the Industrial Revolution of the nineteenth century and the Scientific Revolution of the twentieth century.

While the Catholic ideology precludes any fear on the part of the Church of anything that is "true" in human progress, in fact, Catholic thinkers have reacted in various ways to the challenges of history. Some have retreated in fear and become quite rigid, refusing to acknowledge even the existence of true historical development or its role in what their ideology would describe as "salvation history," let alone the potential benefits this development might represent. The underlying fear of some Catholic thinkers has been manifested in yet another way; they have decided that the solution is to embrace the world and reinterpret the traditional teachings of the Gospel according to the secular ideology of the new age. (This attitude exists also in many other denominations, but the traditional doctrinal discipline of the Roman Catholic Church makes it more noticeable in this church.) These individuals wish to be "modern," hence the name "Modernism" by which they became known some eight decades ago. In the intellectual life of the Church, this is not a long time; thus Modernism remained dormant after being thoroughly condemned by Pope Pius X in 1910. As the result of the upheaval caused by the Second Vatican Council, the Church is in considerable turmoil, caused— among other reasons—by the reappearance of Modernism.

In the United States, this turmoil is even more pronounced for a variety of reasons, some of which are common to all Western societies which have been waging an essentially defensive battle against Soviet imperialism. Lacking a consistent ideology, these nations have seen their former near-monopoly on leadership escape to an essentially multipolar world. In America the Roman Catholic Church is traditionally rooted in immigrant groups which brought the faith with them. Now the Church faces the prospect of many "ethnic Catholics" drifting away, as the cultural basis which reinforced their church affiliation disappears with the progressive "Americanization" of new generations. In addition, an institution as large as the Church reacts slowly to what is essentially a very fast sociopolitical process. While the mood of the country has moved decisively to the right, a growing number of bishops, the central bureaucracy of the American Church, and a number of Catholic leaders have moved increasingly to the left. This not only indicates that the Church is in a great deal of turmoil and unrest, but points to some of the root causes of that unrest.

The sheer size and importance of the Roman Catholic Church, and some of the characteristics of its present predicament, have singled it out

Religious Organizations and the Movement

for this study. At the present time, the Church's state of disarray makes Roman Catholicism an easy prey for the homosexual movement. As will become evident, the movement draws much support from the Catholic Church, although in several instances this Church has also been one of the main obstacles to the homosexual movement. From the point of view of traditional Christians, these instances have been precious few. However, they provide the necessary evidence that the homosexual movement is not invincible, and that religion is probably the key to its ultimate defeat. The fact that Catholicism possesses a powerful cultural structure presents the greatest challenge and opportunity for the homosexual movement. So long as the central Church authorities remain firm in the traditional teachings, rank-and-file Catholics *know* that their Church remains faithful. Thus dissent remains on the fringes and dissenters are generally seen as "oddballs." On the other hand, the generally authoritarian tradition of the Catholic Church in matters of faith and morals makes it theoretically easy for a movement like that of the homosexuals to change the direction of the whole Church by infiltrating—with personnel or ideology itself—its highest structures. For example, advocates of the "new sexual morality" came close to winning an impressive victory when the official commission they dominated recommended to Pope Paul VI the acceptance of their theories via the espousal of artificial contraception. The Pope rejected this recommendation and confirmed the traditional Christian teaching in his encyclical *Humanae Vitae*.

The homosexual movement has, in fact, been very successful in penetrating the Catholic Church and now derives considerable support from it. This does not imply that the Catholic Church has officially, or as a whole, supported the movement, but there is incontrovertible evidence that individuals—some of them highly placed within the Church—have served the movement. In many other cases, *institutions* within the Church have lent their support to homosexuality. Sometimes the homosexual ideology has infiltrated via the back door of feminism; at other times it has been embraced up front, on its own merits. Before discussing the nature and the results of this infiltration, however, it is important to present the teachings of the Catholic Church on the question of homosexuality, with a reminder of the turmoil in which Catholicism finds itself today. This might help explain why, in the face of clear and uncontroverted teachings, individual Catholics and Catholic institutions continue to support the teachings of the homosexual movement.

POSITION OF THE UNIVERSAL ROMAN CHURCH

For Roman Catholics, the Pope—Bishop of Rome—has universal and immediate jurisdiction over all the faithful and over local churches.[55] As the successor of Peter and visible head of the Church on earth, the Pope is considered to be supreme teacher of the Church, a primacy not only of honor but of jurisdiction. Although Catholics do not accept on faith all teachings from the Pope, he is considered to be the bearer of the teaching authority of the Church (technically called the ordinary magisterium) and is heard not merely with respect, but with some degree of internal assent as well, whenever he teaches the Church on matters of faith and morals.

The teachings of Rome are faithful to traditional biblical morality. In 1975 the Sacred Congregation for the Doctrine of the Faith—the teaching arm of the Pope—issued a declaration "On Certain Questions Concerning Sexual Ethics." This declaration was approved, confirmed, and ordered to be published by Paul VI on November 7, 1975.[56] The following excerpts of his declaration present explicitly the basic Catholic teachings on the morality of homosexuality:

HOMOSEXUALITY

8.   At the present time there are those who, basing themselves on observations in the psychological order, have begun to judge indulgently, and even to excuse completely, homosexual relations between certain people. This they do in opposition to the constant teaching of the magisterium and to the moral sense of the Christian people.

A distinction is drawn, and it seems with some reason, between homosexuals whose tendency comes from a false education, from a lack of normal sexual development, from habit, from bad example, or from other similar causes, and is transitory or at least not incurable; and homosexuals who are definitively such because of some kind of innate instinct or a pathological constitution judged to be incurable.

In regard to this second category of subjects, some people conclude that their tendency is so natural that it justifies in their case homosexual relations within a sincere communion of life and love analogous to marriage, insofar as such homosexuals feel incapable of enduring a solitary life.

In the pastoral field, these homosexuals must certainly be treated with understanding and sustained in the hope of overcoming their personal difficulties and their inability to fit into society. This culpability will be judged with prudence. But no pastoral method can be employed which would give moral justification to these acts on the grounds that they would be consonant with the condition of such people. For according to the objective moral order, homosexual relations are acts which lack an essential and indispensable finality. In Sacred Scripture they are condemned as a serious depravity and even presented as the sad consequence of rejecting God. This judgment of Scripture does not of course permit us to conclude that all those who suffer from this anomaly are personally responsible for it, but it does attest to the fact that homosexual acts are intrinsically disordered and can in no case be approved of.

MASTURBATION

9.   The traditional Catholic doctrine that masturbation constitutes a grave moral disorder is often called into doubt or expressly denied today. It is said that psychology and sociology show that it is a normal phenomenon of sexual development, especially among the young. It is stated that there is real and

serious fault only in the measure that the subject deliberately indulges in solitary pleasure closed in on self ("ipsation"), because in this case the act would indeed be radically opposed to the loving communion between persons of different sex which some hold is what is principally sought in the use of the sexual faculty.

This opinion is contradictory to the teaching and pastoral practice of the Catholic Church. Whatever the force of certain arguments of a biological and philosophical nature, which have sometimes been used by theologians, in fact both the magisterium of the Church—in the course of a constant tradition—and the moral sense of the faithful have declared without hesitation that masturbation is an intrinsically and seriously disordered act.

The main reason is that, whatever the motive for acting in this way, the deliberate use of the sexual faculty outside normal conjugal relations essentially contradicts the finality of the faculty. For it lacks the sexual relationship called for by the moral order, namely the relationship which realizes "the full sense of mutual self-giving and human procreation in the context of true love."

All deliberate exercise of sexuality must be reserved to this regular relationship. Even if it cannot be proved that Scripture condemns this sin by name, the tradition of the Church has rightly understood it to be condemned in the New Testament when the latter speaks of "impurity," "unchasteness" and other vices contrary to chastity and continence.

Sociological surveys are able to show the frequency of this disorder according to the places, population or circumstances studied. In this way facts are discovered, but facts do not constitute a criterion for judging the moral value of human acts. The frequency of the phenomenon in question is certainly to be linked with man's innate weakness following original sin; but it is also to be linked with the loss of a sense of God, with the corruption of morals engendered by the commercialization of vice, with the unrestrained licentiousness of so many public entertainments and publications, as well as with the neglect of modesty, which is the guardian of chastity.[57]

The teaching is very clear: sex is for marriage and homosexuality is evil. Part of this tradition, however, is that although any and all homosexual actions are of themselves evil, the tendency to engage in homosexual activities is evil in the sense that it leads people to engage in evil behavior, but no sin—in the sense of sinful action—is present so long as the homosexual does not yield to his sinful desires. Pope John Paul II confirmed this teaching in his 1979 visit to the United States:

Most recently the Pope himself spoke about homosexuality to the bishops of the United States in Chicago on October 4, 1979. He said, "As 'men with the message of truth and the power of God' (2 Cor 6:7), as authentic teachers of God's law and as compassionate pastors you also rightly stated 'Homosexual activity . . . as distinguished from homosexual orientation, is morally wrong.' In the clarity of this truth, you exemplified the real charity of Christ; you did not betray those people who, because of homosexuality, are confronted with difficult moral problems, as would have happened if, in the name of understanding and compassion, or for any other reason, you had held out false hope to any brother or sister. Rather by your witness to the truth of humanity in God's plan, you effectively manifested fraternal love, upholding the true dignity, the true human dignity, of those who look to Christ's Church for guidance which comes from the light of God's word."[58]

Commenting on the Pope's statement, Archbishop Quinn makes the appropriate distinction:

The recent teachings of the Church therefore re-echo the clear teaching of the Scriptures in declaring homosexual acts to be gravely evil and a disordered use of the sexual faculty. These same teachings, also, make clear the distinction between homosexual acts and homosexual orientation and counsel sensitive and positive pastoral care in helping individual homosexual persons in their journey of discipleship.[59]

Although John Paul II's statement is perfectly consonant with traditional Catholic teachings, religious elements within the homosexual movement referred to it as a "breakthrough" in their favor. *In Unity* quoted the Pope's statement and added the following commentary: "Leaders of Dignity have said this is the first time in history that a Pope has publicly stated, to the world, the distinction between the condition of homosexuality and acts of homosexuality."[60]

Although perhaps technically true, any person knowledgeable about traditional Catholic teachings knows that the distinction between vice and sin is standard in Catholic moral theology textbooks. Whereas ontologically the former fall into the category of "quality," the latter belong to the category of "action."

On occasion, the Vatican has taken action when Roman Catholics of some notoriety have expressed dissenting views, although the current turmoil has considerably diminished doctrinal discipline. A typical case is that of John McNeill, S.J., who is, according to a *New York Native* headline, a "pro-gay Jesuit priest."[61] A former seminary professor (Woodstock Seminary), Father McNeill has also taught in two other Jesuit institutions, LeMoyne College and Fordham University. He is also a founder of Dignity, the Catholic homosexual group. When Father McNeill published his masterpiece, the openly prohomosexual book "The Church and the Homosexual," the Vatican ordered him to refrain from speaking publicly on the subject of sexuality and ethics. Although this smells of censorship, it must be remembered that Father McNeill freely pledged— by his vows of obedience and special fealty to the Pope which Jesuits make—to obey such an order. The Vatican was acting fully within its rights to protect the faith and morals of Catholics, since Father McNeill's teachings not only differ from the moral doctrines of the Catholic Church,

Religious Organizations and the Movement

but would logically undermine the resolve of homosexual Catholics who, believing that they cannot change their sexual desires, try to live according to the dictates of the Bible as understood by the Church. The Vatican's order to McNeill was vehemently protested in prohomosexual circles and drew angry letters from a number of liberal religious personalities (e.g., William Sloane Coffin, Harvey Cox, John Bennett, and Robert McAfee Brown).[62] Dignity announced with obvious glee "we are not alone" when McNeill was characterized as a "qualified scholar and a prudent scholar," a person of "high integrity and a humble spirit" by the liberal theologians. By contrast, they describe the Vatican's action as placing a "most serious obstacle to the pursuit of truth" and exhibiting an "anti-intellectual spirit" that "embarrasses and damages the spirit and freedom of ecumenical conversation."[63]

A number of Roman Catholic "theologians" also protested, accusing the Roman Church of ignoring "scriptural and conciliar norms" and committing a serious injustice. Although no objective standard differentiates a theologian from the rest of the believers (only his recognition as such by others) this is a convenient label often utilized by liberals as a way of speaking authoritatively when they have no access to sources of ecclesiastical power. The protest statement in defense of McNeill was signed by:

> Elizabeth Carroll, R.S.M. Center of Concern;
> Margaret A. Farley, R.S.M., Yale Divinity School;
> Daniel C. Maguire, Marquette University;
> Marjorie R. Maguire, Ph.D.;
> Richard P. McBrien, Boston College;
> Richard A. McCormick, S.J., Georgetown University;
> Harry McSorley, S.T.D., St. Michael's College, Toronto;
> Christopher F. Mooney, S.J., University of Pennsylvania;
> Gabriel Moran, F.S.C., Boston College;
> Luke Salm, F.S.C., Manhattan College;
> Charles Curran, Catholic University of America;
> and Gregory Baum, McGill University.[64]

Father McNeill, the reader will notice, is the same person who indicated that Christ is exemplified by the homosexual movement. We encountered him in our discussion of alleged biblical sanctions for homosexual behavior (see chapter VI). By silencing McNeill, the Vatican has sent a signal to the Catholic Church and endeavored to teach actively, not just verbally, the traditional moral viewpoint on homosexuality. While the teaching is clear, the practical application has sometimes been confusing. As the rest of this chapter makes obvious, the record of the American Catholic Church is at best a mixed one.

POSITION OF THE ROMAN CATHOLIC CHURCH IN AMERICA

The American Catholic Church has set up a central office in Washington, D.C., which contains two distinct, though related, organizations: the National Conference of Catholic Bishops (NCCB), which comprises all the Catholic bishops in the United States, and the United States Catholic Conference (USCC), which comprises the central church bureaucracy and is the official arm of the NCCB. Speaking only descriptively, the NCCB represents the "board of directors" and the USCC the "staff" of one and the same corporation.

The Catholic Church in the United States, being in communion with and under the jurisdiction of the Vatican, adheres to the official teachings laid down by the Pope. However, the Catholic bishops have the responsibility of teaching in their own right, provided they exercise this office within the confines of orthodoxy. The bishops teach by applying Catholic teaching to the specific conditions of the people under their care, by amplifying the official teachings, and in some instances by breaking new ground.

As a group, the Catholic bishops have reaffirmed traditional morality: sex is for marriage and homosexual actions are sinful. The following excerpt from the pastoral letter "To Live in Christ Jesus" was approved by the bishops assembled in Washington on November 11, 1976, and sets forth the authentic teaching of the Catholic Church in the area of sexual morality:

> Our Christian tradition holds the sexual union between husband and wife in high honor, regarding it as a special expression of their covenanted love which mirrors God's love for His people and Christ's love for the Church. But like many things human, sex is ambivalent. It can be either creative or destructive. Sexual intercourse is a moral and human good only within marriage; outside marriage it is wrong.
>
> Our society gives considerable encouragement to premarital and extramarital sexual relations as long as, it is said, 'no one gets hurt.' Such relations are not worthy of beings created in God's image and made God's adopted children nor are they according to God's will. The unconditional love of Christian marriage is absent, for such relations are hedged around with many conditions. Though tenderness and concern may sometimes be present, there is an underlying tendency toward exploitation and self-deception. Such relations trivialize sexuality and can erode the possibility of making deep, lifelong commitments.
>
> Some persons find themselves through no fault of their own to have a homosexual orientation. Homosexuals, like everyone else, should not suffer from prejudice against their basic human rights. They have a right to respect, friendship and justice. They should have an active role in the Christian community. Homosexual activity, however, as distinguished from homosexual orientation, is morally wrong. Like heterosexual persons, homosexuals are called to give witness to chastity, avoiding, with God's grace, behavior which is wrong for

them, just as nonmarital sexual relations are wrong for heterosexuals. None-theless, because heterosexuals can usually look forward to marriage, and homo-sexuals, while their orientation continues, might not, the Christian community should provide them a special degree of pastoral understanding and care.[65]

The teachings are far clearer in a document addressed to priests who have to deal with homosexuals in counseling situations. This document reveals total and uncompromising adherence to the teachings of the Roman Church:

The *objective* morality of sexual acts is based upon the teaching of the Church concerning Christian marriage: Genital sexual expression between a man and a woman should take place only in marriage. Apart from the intentions of the man and of the woman, sexual intercourse has a twofold meaning. It is an act of union with the beloved, and it is procreative. Neither meaning may be excluded, although for a variety of reasons, the procreative meaning may not be attained. By their nature homosexual acts exclude all possibility of pro-creation of life. They are therefore inordinate uses of the sexual faculty. It is assumed, moreover, that the only ordinate use of the sexual faculty must be oriented toward a person of the opposite sex. Sexual acts between members of the same sex are contrary not only to one of the purposes of the sexual faculty, namely procreation, but also to the other principal purpose, which is to express mutual love between husband and wife. For these reasons homo-sexual acts are a grave transgression of the goals of human sexuality and of human personality, and are consequently contrary to the will of God.
The goals of human personality and sexuality demand that the exercise of the sexual faculty should take place within the family framework. The procreation and education of children is at least as important a goal in marriage as the expression of mutual love. But homosexual acts make the attainment of this goal impossible.
Homosexual acts are also a deviation from the normal attraction of man for woman, which leads to the foundation of the basic unit of society, the family. Two homosexuals cannot complement one another in the same way as male and female. Not surprisingly, lasting and fulfilling homosexual relationships are not found very often. . . .

That homosexual practices are a grave violation of the law of God is clear from the context in which St. Paul writes. Because the pagans had refused to worship the true God, God had given them up to the practice of vices, including unnatural forms. God had withdrawn his grace from them in punishment for their idolatry. (Romans 1:24–25)[66]

In view of this clear teaching, and mindful of the doctrinal discipline that is inherent in Roman Catholic teaching, dissent which would condone or even encourage the practice of homosexuality is clearly subversive. Some elements of this subversive component appear even in the USCC. The following set of recommendations, made by the leftist-controlled "A

Call for Action" Conference celebrated in Detroit on October 20–23, 1976 under the auspices of the USCC, reveals a profoundly prohomosexual mentality:

> . . . the Church actively seek to serve the pastoral needs of those persons with a homosexual orientation; to root out those structures and attitudes which discriminate against homosexuals as persons and to join the struggle by homosexual men and women for their basic constitutional rights to employment, housing and immigration.

> . . . that the Church encourage and affirm the pastoral efforts of Dignity, the organization of gay and concerned Catholics to reconcile the Church with its homosexual brothers and sisters.

> . . . that the Church provide pastoral care to all sexual minorities who are subjected to societal discrimination and alienation from the Church. Existing ministries of this type should receive recognition and support from Church members and leadership.

> . . . provide information, counseling and support for families who have members who are part of a 'sexual minority.'

> . . . eliminate every form of discrimination on the basis of . . . sexual orientation.[67]

There is evidence of other attempts by the homosexual movement (sometimes successful) to enlist the NCCB and USCC in support of its ideology. The instruments of this effort have been the organizations established by the homosexual movement within the Church: New Ways Ministry and Dignity. The following items will illustrate our point.

Father Robert Nugent, already identified as the Codirector of New Ways Ministry in Washington, D.C., and one of the leaders of the homosexual movement, serves as a consultant on sexual minorities for the USCC.[68] This relationship is good for leverage by the homosexual movement when Nugent makes presentations to Catholic audiences, since it provides him with a certain aura of authority on the subject. The Catholic rank and file would probably find it highly objectionable to have the priest-director of a prohomosexual center exert such influence on the official arm of the Catholic Church in the United States.

The Department of Education of the United States Catholic Conference has published a document on ministry to young adults under the title *Planning for Single Young Adult Ministry: Directives for Ministerial Outreach.* This work was partly produced by New Ways Ministry, which contributed to the section on "Single Young Adult Sexual Minorities."[69]

Dignity apparently maintains an ongoing relationship with both the NCCB and the USCC. During July 1981, Dignity's President, Frank Scheuren, met with then president of the NCCB, Archbishop John R.

Religious Organizations and the Movement

Quinn of San Francisco, and agreed to prepare a series of requests for the NCCB. Later, a meeting was held with Bishop Thomas Kelly, O.P., of the USCC and, as shown by a letter to Archbishop John R. Roach—the new presiding bishop of the NCCB—they intend to continue the relationship.[70]

The efforts of Dignity to influence NCCB and USCC date back as far as 1977. A key staffer at the Office of Public Affairs and Information of the USCC/NCCB turned out to be not only a leader of the Washington, D.C.,homosexual movement, but the president of Dignity. A memorandum prepared by this staffer in which he openly advocates the homosexual ideology is reproduced in Figure 7. This memorandum was sent to, among others, Bishop Kelly, Secretary General of the USCC. The individual in question was not only retained in the employ of the USCC, but transferred to a position where he apparently had access to sensitive information on Church finances.[71]

The challenge of the homosexual ideology to traditional religion in general and to the Catholic Church in particular goes to the very core of fundamental concepts, involving not only natural law principles, but biblical morality as well. Individual bishops or groups of bishops have responded to this challenge with varied forcefulness; while strictly speaking they have remained faithful to the teachings of the Church, in some instances elements of the homosexual ideology have been accepted, if not verbally, at least in terms of policies and practices. This is, of course, quite important, since proverbially actions send far stronger signals to friend and foe alike than words alone.

San Francisco's Archbishop John R. Quinn has enunciated the following teachings in a city that is acknowledged to be the homosexual capital of the United States:

The question then arises: What must be said to a subculture which advocates removing any distinction between homosexuality and heterosexuality? Given the fact that the authentic teaching of the Church clearly affirms the objective gravity of homosexual acts, what must be said in light of the growing acceptance of homosexuality as a legitimate and alternative lifestyle? . . .

At the same time, however, opposition to homosexuality as a form of conduct, opposition to homosexuality as an acceptable lifestyle, by the Church or by society cannot be regarded as a prejudice.
To agree that the persecution and harassment of homosexuals is incompatible with the Gospel is, therefore, not to say that the Church and society should be neutral about homosexual activity. The Church and society cannot and should not place the family, which is and always will be the basic unit of society, on a par with homosexual social units.
While we do not possess complete historical data on the subject, the fact is

that in no culture has homosexuality been the dominant form of sexual expression, and in Judaism and Christianity homosexual behavior has been clearly and consistently rejected as gravely contrary to the law of God. . . .

From the foregoing it is clear that the Scriptures, both the Old and the New Testament, reject and condemn homosexual acts. The Scriptures, it is true, do not explicitly deal with the question of homosexual attraction or with the issue of a homosexual lifestyle.

Nevertheless they do most clearly condemn an important element of that lifestyle, namely homosexual intercourse. Hence it is beyond dispute that there is a clear basis in Scripture for the consistent rejection of a homosexual lifestyle as it exists in the moral teachings of the Church, including the most recent Church teaching on the subject. . . .

The Church certainly does not condemn those who discover within themselves a homosexual attraction or inclination and it must work to foster better care and guidance for those men and women whom society has ostracized. The Church must continue to work toward better education about homosexuality. It must tirelessly try to help homosexual men and women accept and live up to the moral teaching which the Church has received from Christ.

But in no case can such acceptance or recognition of the homosexual person imply recognition of homosexual behavior as an acceptable lifestyle. The claim that homosexuality is simply a variant of normal sexual behavior and exists alongside heterosexuality as an equivalent expression of adult sexual maturation must be rejected. A normalization of homosexuality could only too early foster and make more public homosexual behavior with the result of eroding the meaning of the family.

Both from the religious point of view, as well as for the good of society itself, marriage and the family are realities that must be protected and strengthened. The family not only continues the human race but it also glues it together. The family is the basic and living example of social cohesion.

Thus the Second Vatican Council affirmed, "All . . . who exercise influence over communities and social groups should work efficiently for the welfare of marriage and the family. Public authority should regard it as a sacred duty to recognize, protect and promote their authentic nature, to defend public morality and to foster the progress of home life. . . .

Sexual intercourse cannot be legitimated merely by individual preference or on the basis of sociological surveys or because of mutual consent between two parties. Sexual intercourse is legitimate and morally good only between husband and wife. Thus while it is claimed that homosexuality in a few instances is more or less fulfilling for a limited number of individuals, the homosexual condition and homosexual behavior cannot be morally normative. . . .

On the other hand, when homosexual men and women claim that their way of life is a morally healthy one, insist on their intention to affirm and promote it publicly and ask that it be in some way approved by the Church, they are clearly in contempt of the Christian conscience and in conflict with the teaching of the Scriptures.[72]

UNITED STATES CATHOLIC CONFERENCE
OFFICE OF PUBLIC AFFAIRS
National Catholic Office for Information

INTEROFFICE MEMORANDUM

DATE: 770426

TO: Russ

FROM: John

SUBJECT: Dignity in Chicago

You will recall that before the bishops' meeting in November of '75, I memoed you on what I knew of Dignity's plans for a peaceful presence at the (then) Statler-Hilton during that week. My intention was to combat the rumors (which had by that time found their way into a couple national publications) claiming that Dignity was going to try to embarrass the bishops by picketting, name-calling and/or <u>every other tactic used by disgruntled folk during the turbulent sixties.</u>

This memo, likewise, is prompted by a desire to allay any possible fears and open an avenue for honest communication.

By way of background: The international office of Dignity is located in Boston (at least until our next convention this fall in Chicago). We have 60 chapters, with another nine in formation. The chapters are as autonomous in their relationship with Boston as are the dioceses in their relationship with Rome, if not more so, since chapter officers are elected locally (not appointed by Boston) and local organization varies from chapter to chapter. Some chapters have more of a relationship with their local chancery than with Dignity/ International. We have 5,500 dues-paying members including some 300 clergy/religious. It is estimated that approximately 12,000 people attend Dignity functions (it's rather common for a chapter to have almost as many "hangers-on" as dues-paying members).

Boston has asked the local chapter to handle Dignity's "presence" in Chicago next week.

Dignity/Chicago is a large, well-established chapter. I don't know off-hand how many members, but Chicago is a Catholic city. There was a Mass for the Gay Community in Chicago BEFORE there was a Dignity chapter organized in the city. (Chapter organization occurred in '72) The Mass is held at St. Sebastian's Church; the chapter has

/more

FIGURE 7
Internal USCC Memo Promoting Homosexual Organization.

purchased it's own vestments, sacred vessels, hymnals; it is, in reality, a floating parish within a geographical parish. (I plan to attend the Mass this coming Sunday evening--you are certainly welcome if you would like to attend.)

If the chapter is well organized, their "presence" at the bishops' meeting is not. Or perhaps it would be fairer to say that they are "late" organizers. Sunday the 17th (little more than a week ago) one of the Chicago members (not their president) called our chapter number, asking for information on Dignity's presence during the bishops' meeting in '75. One of our chaplains answered the phone but could not give information on the '75 meeting (it was before his time). He referred the caller to me.

As of the 17th, they had no reservation at the Palmer House (they plan to have a hospitality suite); they had not written to the General Secretary or anyone else here at the Conference to mention that they would be available to answer bishops' questions in Chicago; they had not contacted Father Myron Judy or anyone else who had really been involved in planning the November '75 presence. I, of course, suggested that they do all these things quam primum. I also let them know that they shouldn't expect miracles. There might not be any hotel rooms available at that late a date--and the hotel would undoubtedly check with the Conference before granting permission for a hospitality suite; they shouldn't feel "discriminated against" if the Palmer House says nothing's available or says the Conference will have to be consulted first.

I don't know if they have made any progress out there as yet--and I'm not likely to find out before the Sunday evening meeting and social after the Mass in Chicago.

The "coordinator" who called us on the 17th expressed the fear that a group other than Dignity might try to give the bishops some trouble. Seems a fellow named Joe Murray used to be a Dignity member but, because of his penchant for demonstrations, was always being voted down at Dignity meetings. (I remember that this gentleman tried to get the local chapter to picket last Spring's meeting in Chicago; he was overwhelmingly voted down at the Dignity meeting after the Mass for the Gay Community the Sunday before the bishops' meeting.) Dignity/Chicago is concerned because bishops and press may blame them if Joe Murray and his followers picket or otherwise try to cause a disturbance.

If you have any questions on any of the above, please ask.

Thanks.

cc: Bill, Bob, Fr. Kelly

bc: *NC News*

Religious Organizations and the Movement

Archbishop Borders of Baltimore was no less forceful in his struggle against the homosexual movement over a prohomosexual bill which was almost passed by the City Council:

> While gays and other supporters of the bill have stressed that it would merely safeguard their right to fair housing and job opportunities, the Archbishop declared that "to defend the fundamental rights of the human person is one thing. To approve or condone behavior that is socially destructive and directly opposed to the divine vocation upon which human dignity depends, under the guise of safeguarding fundamental human rights, is quite another."
> He pointed out that the Church has "constantly held that homosexual *orientation*, in and by itself and with no relation to homosexual *behavior*, is neither moral nor immoral. Just as constantly the Church teaches that homosexual behavior is immoral and socially destructive." . . .
>
> In civil law, he said, sexual orientation "necessarily indicates not only psychosexual attraction but also acts which flow from it. This is confirmed, for example, by one legal code that explicitly describes sexual orientation as 'the status of an individual as to homosexuality, heterosexuality or bisexuality by *preference or practice.*' "[73]

The bill was ultimately defeated, largely because of Archbishop Borders's efforts.

Boston's Cardinal Humberto Medeiros, in a document entitled "Pastoral Care for the Homosexual," has not only confirmed the traditional Catholic teaching, but has also outlined certain practical consequences he has drawn from this teaching. They have been summarized as follows:

> First, the Cardinal writes that there *is* no priest specifically assigned to ministry to homosexual people. If there has been any confusion about that in the past, it is now clear that the overall ministry of every priest extends to all people.
> Second, Cardinal Medeiros does not authorize any priest in his diocese to offer the Eucharist for any group who band together as homosexuals. Such groups tend to impede true human and spiritual development and he wants to integrate all into normal parish life.
> Third, the Cardinal instructs those who might recommend candidates for ordination that those who experience difficulty in handling sexual drives, or, are emotionally arrested, or, who have not moved beyond mere sexual preoccupation should not be recommended for a celibate life.[74]

The incompatibility between these conclusions and the homosexual ideology—let alone Dignity's demands—is obvious. The reader will recall that at the first conference of the North American Man/Boy Love Association, Father Paul Shanley of the Archdiocese of Boston was reported to have been the representative of Cardinal Medeiros for sexual minorities.

The opposition to the homosexual ideology by the Archdiocese of Philadelphia was highlighted in the appearance of an MCC minister at the Fellowship Commission.[75] This same staunch opposition was expressed by the late bishop James S. Rausch of Phoenix, who dismissed the local Dignity "chaplain" for asserting that 25 percent of all priests in the Phoenix area are "basically homosexual." According to *The Advocate*, "Bishop James S. Rausch of the Phoenix diocese and four other priests found Father [Andre] Boulanger guilty of heresy and dismissed him as pastor. Bishop Rausch said homosexual activity is 'objectively evil.' "[76]

In many other ways, Catholic bishops have upheld the traditional moral teaching of their church, as seen in the following examples.

A prohomosexual workshop was scheduled to take place on June 9, 1981, organized by Father Robert Nugent and Sister Jeannine Gramick of New Ways Ministry at St. Clement's Catholic Church in Chicago. The late Cardinal John Cody, Catholic Archbishop of Chicago, banned the program from any Catholic institution.[77] Rescheduled for Grace Episcopal Church, the program was cancelled again after its rector was discouraged from bringing in the Catholic program disapproved by the Archbishop. Eventually, an Episcopal church (Trinity Church) willing to sponsor the event was found. The array of individuals who protested Cardinal Cody's decision in a press conference is indicative of the networking groundwork done by the homosexuals.[78] The following persons appeared in the May 5 news conference:

Individual	Organizational Affiliation
John Malzone	Dignity Chicago
Daniel J. Daley	Chicago Call to Action (a network of ten leftist Catholic organizations)
Sheila Stoll Clark	National Organization for Women
Tracey Lee	Lesbian Community Center
Ann Greene	Parents and Friends of Gays
Rev. Grant Gallup	Integrity/Chicago

Connecticut's five Catholic bishops notified the state that they intended to disobey any law compelling them to employ or retain homosexual teachers in Catholic schools. They indicated that the Catholic moral position demands that children be kept from "persons or influences that might draw them toward the approval or practice of homosexuality."[79]

The Catholic bishop of Providence asked Catholic students to stay home and pray rather than attend a prom at which two homosexuals would appear as each other's "dates."[80]

The Minnesota Catholic Conference opposed actively the 1977 state prohomosexual bill that would have compelled Catholic schools to hire

Religious Organizations and the Movement

militant homosexuals as teachers. The argument offered was summarized thus:

> John Markert, MCC Executive Director, said in prepared testimony for the Senate Judiciary Committee that civil rights legislation for homosexuals cannot be compared with civil rights legislation for racial minorities.
> He said race is an "inseparable part" of personhood while homosexuality is a matter of conduct.
> "When civil rights legislation is extended to protect people on the basis of choice or conduct, several problems result.
> "This is true not only of homosexual conduct, but of many forms of heterosexual conduct as well, and indeed, of other forms of conduct which have nothing to do with sexual morality," he said.
> The spokesman for Minnesota's Catholic bishops said, "Generally speaking, a person chooses what kind of conduct he will engage in, and is therefore responsible for it, whereas he does not choose his race."
> Markert said civil rights legislation must protect the rights of persons on the basis of race and other human factors inseparable from personhood but it need not protect human persons on the basis of selective conduct.[81]

The Archdiocese of Miami suspended a priest who "came out of the closet" to indicate that he "felt like a hypocrite" when worshipping at a church which "persecutes gay men and women."[82]

The Catholic position on homosexuality has been summarized in a joint statement by the Archdiocese of New York and the Diocese of Brooklyn as part of their continuing campaign to resist the enactment of special legal rights for homosexuals:

> If the bill has an underlying purpose, to advocate and gain approval of homosexual behavior and lifestyle, then there is no way in which the Catholic Church in the City of New York may find it acceptable. And there is no way in which we can remain silent on the issue.
> The Catholic Church's moral teaching differentiates between "orientation" and "behavior" for both homosexuals and heterosexuals. While a person's orientation is not subject to moral evaluation, there is no doubt that a person's behavior is subject to evaluation. Homosexual behavior and an attendant homosexual life style is not in accord with Catholic moral teaching and is, in fact, harmful to all persons who become involved; heterosexuality is the norm for human behavior.[83]

Father Kenneth Jadoff, assistant director of the Office of Communications for the Archdiocese of New York, expressed the Catholic argument in the following way, while intending to speak for members of other faiths as well:

> Religious people maintain unequivocally that homosexual activity is gravely

immoral, violating the order of human sexuality ordained by the Creator. Without any unkindness toward homosexuals, the Jewish and Christian parents are conscience-bound to keep children in their formative years free from homosexual associations and influences. Parents' rights are unchallengeable in this regard.[84]

Canadian bishops have also supported the teachings of the Catholic Church in a clear and uncompromising way. Against attempts to include "gay rights" in the Ontario Human Rights Code, the Ontario Conference of Catholic Bishops declared that "a Catholic education system, Catholic organizations, and the official Church ministry must be free to exclude those who would publicly proclaim and indulge in homosexuality as a morally acceptable way of life."[85] They were opposed in this opinion by Father Tim Ryan, a Catholic priest representing Dignity, and by Ken Bhagan, a permanent deacon representative of an organization called Religious Leaders Concerned About Racism and Human Rights.

There are indications, however, that opposition to homosexuality by certain Catholic bishops is often soft at best. In many cases, elements of the homosexual ideology have been accepted, both by word and deed.

A *Time to Speak* is a booklet published by the Catholic prohomosexual center New Ways Ministry, with the subtitle "A Collection of Contemporary Statements from U.S. Catholic Sources on Homosexuality, Gay Ministry and Social Justice."[86] The biases of this booklet are obvious, since not one of the passages is in any way critical of homosexuality, although there are many authoritative quotes that could be used to illustrate the official position of the Catholic Church. The editors have been able to present statements by sixteen bishops which, in their obvious judgment, benefit the homosexual movement in some way. The following bishops have been cited:

Bishop	Diocese	Statement Date
Bernard J. Flanagan	Worcester	July 1, 1974
John Cardinal Krol	Philadelphia	August 13, 1974
John Cardinal Dearden	Detroit	August 20, 1974
Thomas J. Gumbleton	Detroit	October 2, 1974
Joseph L. Imesch	Detroit	October 2, 1974
Francis J. Mugavero	Brooklyn	February 11, 1976
Walter F. Sullivan	Richmond	August 26, 1977
Carroll T. Dozier	Memphis	January 22, 1978
John J. Roach	St. Paul/Minneapolis	January, 1978
Raymond G. Hunthausen	Seattle	August 25, 1978
John S. Cummins	Oakland	October 3, 1978
John Quinn	San Francisco	October 11, 1978
Juan Arzube	Los Angeles	October 20, 1978
Paul F. Anderson	Duluth	April 20, 1980
Rembert Weakland	Milwaukee	July 19, 1980
Cletus O'Donnell	Madison	Winter, 1980

Religious Organizations and the Movement

After Cardinal Medeiros removed Father Paul Shanley from his "job" as full-time minister to "sexual minorities," Sister Jeannine Gramick of New Ways Ministry produced a highly critical article against the Archbishop. In this article the nun listed a number of bishops who, in her perception, had in some way favored homosexuals. The following were included, although she contended there were "half a dozen more":[87]

Bishop	Diocese
George R. Evans	Denver
Joseph Gossman	Baltimore
Walter Sullivan	Richmond
Raymond G. Hunthausen	Seattle
John J. Roach	St. Paul/Minneapolis
Carroll T. Dozier	Memphis
John Quinn	San Francisco

Alleged support from any of the bishops in either list for the homosexual movement is questionable. It is apparent, however, that the movement has been able to utilize something they said or did for its own benefit. Some of these individuals may be surprised that they have been listed as supporters of the homosexual movement in some way. At the same time, a church can ill afford to have any of its hierarchs invoked as alleged proponents of the homosexual ideology or some of its components.

A typical example of a soft position on homosexuality is offered by Archbishop Rembert Weakland of Milwaukee. In an article published in his diocesan Catholic paper, Archbishop Weakland does not, in fact, openly dissent from the official teaching of his church. On the other hand, he uses all the arguments offered by the homosexual apologists.[88] The analysis on page 318 compares the arguments offered by the homosexual movement, the implications of these arguments, and the parallel passages in Archbishop Weakland's article.

It is not surprising that New Ways Ministry has reproduced and distributed this article as part of its prohomosexual campaign. Dignity also reproduced the article in its national newsletter.[96] The Archbishop's position may explain his apparent decision to permit a New Ways Ministry prohomosexual workshop scheduled at the Divine Savior Community House—a religious community—in Milwaukee. This workshop was identical to the one banned by Cardinal Cody in Chicago.[97] Weakland's position also explains his support for prohomoesxual legislation in the Wisconsin state legislature. According to the *Gay Community News*, he sided with mainline Protestant leaders against the fundamentalist Christian posi-

Homosexual Arguments	Implications	Archbishop Weakland's Language
1) In speaking of homosexuals, the word "gay" should be used, since it implies the joyful affirmation of one's sexual character.[89]	1) "Gay is good." Homosexuals are a legitimate minority.	1) Homosexuals consistently are called "gay people" throughout the article.
2) The Old Testament texts which seem to condemn homosexuality are not an expression of moral opposition to homosexuality but an expression of the needs of Israel to increase its population.[90]	2) Homosexuality per se is not condemned by the Old Testament.	2) "It is true that both in the Old and New Testament the condemnation of acts of homosexuality is strong. Current biblical scholarship has been of tremendous help in bringing these and similar texts into a total cultural context. Homosexuality in the Old Testament was also a 'national security problem' for a people constantly faced with a need for a male population sufficient to defend itself."
3) St. Paul does not condemn homosexuality as such, but only homosexual practices by heterosexuals. Since he knew no modern psychology, St. Paul did not have the concept of sexual orientation as opposed to sexual behavior.[91]	3) There is nothing wrong with homosexuality according to the New Testament. Religious people are thus free to affirm that homosexual behavior is acceptable and homosexuality implies a legitimate lifestyle.	3) "Jesus says nothing specific about homosexuality. But Saint Paul is quite explicit: he is indeed harsh with heterosexuals engaging in homosexual activity; he spoke out strongly against homosexual activity during his missionary journeys to those areas where such activity was associated with orgiastic pagan ritual sacrifices— as it had been, also, in Old Testament times. "All these texts do exist and cannot be taken lightly, even if our knowledge of psychology and the make-up of the human person is vastly different today from Saint Paul's."
4) The opinion that homosexual behavior is wrong, although currently the official position of the Catholic Church, is simply one of several positions. Responsible theologians disagree with this position which eventually will change.[92]	4) Homosexual behavior is morally acceptable.	4) "Current Church teaching which we Catholics must adhere to expects Gay people to remain celibate, a position which is difficult for them to accept, but, frankly, one which I cannot sidestep."

Religious Organizations and the Movement

Homosexual Arguments	Implications	Archbishop Weakland's Language
5) Homosexuality cannot be changed.[93]	5) People should accept their homosexuality. It is not an illness and God wants homosexuals to remain such.	5) "Theorists are divided as to the causes of a same-sex orientation. Whether it is biological or environmental, we must accept the fact that many have sincerely tried to be 'healed' of their 'sickness.' "Experience shows that very few, even with the best therapists, are capable of changing their sexual orientation. Many are coming to the realization that God loves them as they are and that He invites them to open out in concern for others. This movement of grace cannot be ignored or discounted. Many are seeking the opportunity to grow."
6) Homosexuals are not interested in having sex with children. They are not a threat to youth.[94]	6) Homosexuals should be hired as teachers, youth workers, etc.	6) "In justice, I would hope that we can grow beyond the myths surrounding the Gay person, myths, for example, that picture all Gays as perverters of children—a picture that simply is not true."
7) Homosexuals are responsible people who can do any job and occupy any social position.[95]	7) Homosexuals *as such* should be accepted without reservations at all levels of society.	7) "We must be concerned, also, about their rights. Consequently I cannot believe it is a Christian attitude that would block them from holding responsible positions in the community."

tion.[98] Figure 8 is a reproduction of Weakland's March 2, 1981, letter in support of this prohomosexual legislation.

Bishop Raymond G. Hunthausen of Seattle also wrote a letter of support for the movement's efforts to pass legislation in the State of Washington granting special privileges to homosexuals. This letter, dated July 1, 1977, seems to have been written to coincide with "Gay Pride Week." The introduction reads, "The Mayor of Seattle, along with many other mayors throughout the United States, has set aside a special week to call our attention to the injustices suffered by many homosexuals in our community."[99]

According to the *National Catholic Reporter*, Archbishop Hunthausen has become something of a cause célèbre for the New Left. He participated in a demonstration against the Trident submarine at a military installation which has been the object of leftist demonstrations since 1976.

(Letterhead)
Archdiocese of Milwaukee, 348 North Ninety Fifth Street,
P.O. Box 201R, Milwaukee, Wisconsin 53201, Phone 414/476
53201, Office of the Archbishop

March 2, 1981

The Reverend John Murtagh
Office of Human Concerns
731 West Washington Street
Milwaukee, Wisconsin 53204

Dear Jack,

It has recently been called to my attention that your
office has been seeking my opinion concerning Assembly Bill
#70 that is now being studied in the State Legislature.

I feel that your commission can in good conscience
support this legislation insofar as it bans discrimination
because of sexual orientation in the areas of employment,
housing, and public accommodations.

You will recall that the National Conference of Catholic
Bishops spoke to this issue in 1976. There has been no
change in the Catholic position concerning homosexual activity,
which has always been considered morally wrong; on the other
hand, it has also been consistent with Catholic teaching that
homosexuals should not be deprived of their basic human rights.
For this reason I feel that support of this Bill would be
indeed proper and consistent with previous positions that
the Church has taken.

Many thanks for your constant concern for so many
delicate issues.

Sincerely yours in the Lord,

(Signed: + Rembert G. Weakland)

Most Reverend Rembert G. Weakland, O.S.B.

Archbishop of Milwaukee

FIGURE 8
Letter from Archbishop Rembert G. Weakland Supporting Pro-Homosexual Legislation.

Religious Organizations and the Movement

On June 12, 1981, Archbishop Hunthausen, speaking to six hundred delegates at the Pacific Lutheran Convention of the Lutheran Church of America in Tacoma, called upon Christians to refuse to pay a substantial portion of their federal income taxes in protest against American defense efforts.[100]

There are other instances, as follows, which indicate a soft attitude toward homosexuality in a number of dioceses.

In several dioceses, the bishops have allowed churches to be used for homosexual masses and church property is regularly used to hold Dignity meetings, fundraisers, and other functions. According to Dignity, 75 percent of its meetings nationwide are held on Church property.[101]

For all its opposition to prohomosexual legislation, the performance of the Archdiocese of New York is not perfectly consistent. For example, St. Francis Xavier Church—a Jesuit parish—is regularly used for Dignity masses.[102] Other church facilities are also used for Dignity meetings. Father John McNeill, S.J., is allowed to preach homosexual-oriented retreats at the Manhattan House of Prayer,[103] while Fathers Robert Carter, S.J., and Bernard Lynch, SMA, function as clergy consultants to the Board of Dignity.[104] Father Carter is attached to the West Side Jesuit Community. Father Lynch, a Marist, was formerly part of the Mount St. Michael High School community. It has been reported that Father Lynch celebrates mass for vacationing homosexuals on Fire Island, a notorious homosexual hangout in the south shore of Long Island.[105] Both priests have faculties—i.e., authority to conduct religious services—within the archdiocese of New York.

These activities must be known and are presumably tolerated by the Archdiocese. Should there be any interest in suppressing them, the simple application of Canon Law would probably suffice without major difficulties beyond the need to cope with the pressure the homosexuals would exert.

A Dignity official asserted in a personal communication to the author that a Southwestern bishop ordained to the priesthood an avowedly homosexual man. Although no confirmation has been possible—thus the specifics of the case are not being divulged at this time—the seriousness of this item in terms of a breakdown in Catholic discipline demands that it be mentioned here.

On one occasion, a Catholic bishop has indicated that he supports the ordination of homosexuals. This happened when a committee of New England bishops rejected the ordination of homosexuals. Contacted by New Ways Ministry, Bishop Peter A. Rosazza, Auxiliary Bishop of Hartford, Connecticut, expressed support for the homosexuals' point of view in a letter which appears in Figure 9.

Dignity has reported that Bishop John Snyder of the Diocese of St. Augustine "is interested in formation of a [Dignity] chapter in the area,"

(Letterhead)

Most Rev. Peter A. Rosazza, D. D.

Auxillary Bishop of Hartford

Sacred Heart Rectory

49 Winthrop Street

Hartford, Connecticut 06103

January 30, 1980

Sister Jeannine Gramick, SSND

Rev. C. Robert Nugent

New Ways Ministry

3312 Buchanan St. #302

Mt. Ranier, Maryland 20822

Dear Sister and Father:

    Thank you for your well-prepared and thought out letter
reacting to the letter prepared by a committe of the Bishops
of the New England Region. Please note that the letter was
prepared by the committee appointed by the Bishops. This does
not mean that it was endorsed by every one of us. If so it would
read: ... a letter prepared by a committee and endorsed by the
Bishops of the New England Region.

    For my part I agree with your letter and am sympathetic
to your stance against the exclusion of homosexuals from Holy
Orders solely on the basis of sexual orientation. It is, I believe,
a case of being more Catholic than the Church.

    May the Lord continue to bless your work ... and let
us pray for each other and the people we try to serve in Jesus's
name.

                              Respectfully,

                              (Signature: + Peter A. Rosazza)

                              Most Rev. Peter A. Rosazza

FIGURE 9

Letter from Bishop Peter A. Rosazza to New Ways Ministry Defending Ordination of
Homosexuals as Catholic Priests. Source: Bondings.

Religious Organizations and the Movement

and that he had appointed "three religious, a nun and two priests," to help with the task of organizing the Catholic homosexuals in the diocese.[106]

Archbishop John L. May of St. Louis officiated at a vespers service for the St. Louis Chapter of Dignity where he preached a homily.[107] After the event was disclosed by the *St. Louis Globe-Democrat*, Father Richard Malone of the NCCB's committee on pastoral research and practices explained that the Archbishop was merely trying to " 'rescue' homosexuals from the clutches of some organizations that are ambiguous about the church's moral teaching."[108]

We have already seen that homosexual leaders have developed contacts with the Catholic hierarchy. By receiving these individuals in their capacity as leaders of the homosexual movement, bishops give the movement itself recognition and acceptability. Homosexual publications are quick to utilize these meetings for their own purposes. The following excerpt from Dignity's report of an Executive Board meeting which took place during Thanksgiving weekend, 1981, is quite revealing:

> WORK WITH THE HIERARCHY: Archbishop May will officiate at a vespers service with St. Louis Chapter sometime soon. This is only the latest in a continuing series of contacts between many chapters and their bishops. Frank Scheuren was scheduled to see Archbishop Kelly of the Washington office of the National Conference of Catholic Bishops the day after the Board meeting adjourned, and hopes to see the chairman, Archbishop Roach, sometime this winter. Dick Hitt, the Region IX director, reported that Archbishop Quinn has met repeatedly with Dick and San Francisco Chapter representatives, and has been positive and supportive, although not officially modifying his disturbing pastoral letter of 18 months ago.[109]

On July 28, 1980, a meeting took place in San Francisco between representatives of Dignity and two Catholic bishops. Archbishop Quinn of San Francisco and Bishop Roger Mahoney of Stockton, California, met with Frank Scheuren, national president of Dignity; Chris Patterson, regional director of Dignity's Region IX; and James Ehrhart and Kenneth Kamman, cochairmen of the San Francisco chapter of Dignity. The homosexual organization was quick to utilize the meeting for its own purposes. According to the Dignity newsletter: "The tone of the meeting was very pleasant. The representatives of Dignity, Inc. were able to give background information on their organization and provide an idea of where they feel there is a gap between the National Conference of Bishops and the workings of Dignity, Inc."[110] Moreover, it is apparent that the representatives of the Church were willing to accept input from the homosexual leaders on the direction the Church should take concerning the homosexuals: "The Archbishop has requested that Dignity, Inc. and Region IX of Dignity, Inc. and the local Chapters submit to him proposals as to how joint cooperation can be accomplished in the day-to-day pastoral ministry to our people. He expressed that this would be the beginning of an on-going dialogue between the parties concerned for the future concern of Gay Catholics and Gay Christians around the world."[111] The homosexual representatives, obviously, had good reasons to be satisfied with the meeting. They had not only been recognized by the leadership of the Roman Catholic Church, but they had been promised participation in episcopal decisions on the dealings of the Church with their own kind. From a political standpoint, this was bound to increase Dignity's power in homosexual and regular Catholic circles alike.

In certain cases, it is apparent that bishops have gone beyond having meetings or presiding over simple prayer services with the active participation of homosexual organizations. The center of Roman Catholic worship is the sacrifice of the Mass. Bishop Leroy Matthiesen (Amarillo, Texas) is reported to have celebrated a Mass for the homosexual community with several of his priests in August 1980.[112] The music for the service was provided by the choir of a homosexual organization. Matthiesen is the same bishop who has become one of the leaders of the Catholic antidefense movement by recommending that Catholics in his diocese working for a major defense contractor (Pantex Corporation) abandon their jobs.[113]

The official leadership structure of the Catholic Church seems to be waging a losing battle. Essentially reactive against a powerful and aggressive force, it is condemned to be defeated until it becomes both proactive and aggressive itself. Using another image, its behavior is reminiscent of that of the Kings of Israel and Judah who, while suppressing the idols of the Temple, still tolerated the high places.

INFILTRATION OF THE ROMAN CATHOLIC CHURCH BY THE HOMOSEXUAL MOVEMENT

From the perspective of the homosexual movement, the Catholic Church is an ideal institution from which to continue its seemingly inexorable advance. Once the principle "gay is good" is accepted, the rest is easy. Traditional Catholics recognize the truth of this premise; they understand that there is a struggle and that the Church is the immediate target. In this, both sides coincide. Naturally, the perceived desirability of the alternative outcome is diametrically opposed. Before proceeding to analyze the nature and characteristics of the infiltration of Roman Catholicism by the homosexual movement, the reader is referred to a reprint of an article wherein a homosexual parade is described by Dr. Timothy A. Mitchell, a traditional Catholic. The depth of feeling is obvious. This article has been reproduced in its entirety in the appendix and should serve as an introduction to the way in which militant homosexuals have

Religious Organizations and the Movement

managed to establish a pervasive presence in broad structures of the Roman Catholic Church.

Patterns of Collaboration. There are two major Catholic prohomosexual institutions, New Ways Ministry and Dignity, each of which will be discussed separately later. They are both very influential and exercise important leadership roles within both the Catholic Church and the homosexual movement.

The original tactic of the homosexual movement vis-à-vis all religions in general and Roman Catholicism in particular was one of confrontation. Radically antagonistic to homosexual practices, traditional religion constitutes the greatest single obstacle to the acceptance of the homosexual ideology. The homosexual movement was born of the turmoil of the sixties and was radically naive during its early stages. A confrontation that took place at Catholic University in 1970 exemplifies the attitude of the homosexual movement toward Roman Catholicism a decade ago. A conference on religion and homosexuality was being held under the leadership of Dr. John R. Cavanaugh, a noted Catholic psychologist who has written extensively on homosexuality. The meeting was interrupted by a violent demonstration organized by the D.C. Gay Liberation Front, who forced the audience to hear the following proclamation:

We are homosexuals!

As members of the Gay Liberation Front, we deny your right to conduct this seminar.

It is precisely such institutions as the Catholic Church and psychiatry which have created and perpetuated the immorality myths and stereotypes of homosexuality which we as homosexuals have internalized, and from which we now intend to liberate ourselves.

As homosexuals struggling to be free, we make the following statements:

1. We demand that you stop examining our homosexuality and become homosexual yourselves.
2. We do not seek acceptance, tolerance, equality or even entrance into your society with its emphasis on 'cock power' (read *male supremacy*). Liberation there would be impossible. For centuries, this system of power, dominance and possession has produced only genocidal wars, the profound oppression of women and racial minorities, and our own repression as homosexuals.
3. We hold the Catholic Church and the institution of psychiatry responsible for political crimes committed against homosexuals, such as imprisonment, blackmail, beatings, psychological rape, and loss of economic security. We also feel every gay suicide is a political murder.

As representatives of the sexist society that daily oppresses us, you are incapable of speaking for or defining the quality of our lives. ONLY WE AS HOMOSEXUALS CAN DETERMINE FROM OUR OWN EXPERIENCES WHAT

OUR IDENTITY WILL BE . . . AND THAT WILL HAPPEN IN THE NEW
SOCIETY WHICH WE WILL HELP TO BUILD.[114]

The first point of the proclamation was later "explained out" to mean that
listeners should examine their sexual feelings and accept any signs of
homosexuality they found. The original—and plain meaning—seems to
have been quite different.

Catholic leaders and organizations have shown such support for homosexuality—either directly or by implication—that New Ways Ministry
has been able to compile a source book of American Catholic prohomosexual sources, the already mentioned *A Time to Speak*. In addition to
the bishops named earlier in this chapter, the following sources of support
are also cited in chronological order:

Organization/Individual	Date
St. Vincent Hospital (New York City)	12/73
National Coalition of American Nuns	1974
National Federation of Priests' Councils	3/74, 7/77, 1978
The Advocate* (Newark, N.J.)	5/16/74, 12/13/78
Washington State Catholic Conference (Seattle)	3/76
USCC (Dept. of Education, Young Adult Ministry Board)	6/76, 5/30–6/3/79
Senate of Priests (Archdiocese of Baltimore)	7/9/76, 10/18/76
USCC (A Call to Action, Detroit)	10/76
Gabriel Moran, FSC	1977
Catholic Theological Society of America	1977
Office of the Vicar for Urban Ministry (Rochester)	3/1/77
Diocesan Social Ministry Commission (Richmond)	5/21/77
Phillip Keane, SS	6/77
National Assembly of Religious Brothers	6/77
Justice and Peace Center (Milwaukee)	7/77
Catholic Herald Citizen* (Madison, Wisc.)	7/2/77
Rev. Andrew Greeley	7/7/77
West Texas Catholic* (Amarillo)	7/17/77
Catholic Herald* (Sacramento)	9/1/77
Catholic Worker Community (Wichita)	10/4/77
Quixote Center (Mt. Rainier, Md.)	10/10/77
Commission on Social Justice (San Francisco)	10/12/77, 10/24/79
Diocesan Sisters' Council (Rochester)	11/12/77
Rev. Benno Salewski	1/22/78
Priests' Senate (Archdiocese of St. Paul and Minneapolis)	3/78, 6/21/79
National Assembly of Women Religious	3/78, 8/25/78
Sisters of St. Joseph of Carondelet	Summer, 1978
Office of Catholic Charities, Seattle	9/23/78
California Conference of Catholic Charities	10/3/78
America*	11/11/78
Priests' Senate (Diocese of Albany)	4/2/79
U.S. Catholic Mission Council	5/79
Archdiocesan Commission for the Plan of Pastoral Action for Family Ministry, Milwaukee	9/22/79

Religious Organizations and the Movement

The Criterion* (Indianapolis)	7/25/80
Theology of the Americas—Detroit II	8/5/80
Msgr. Harold Brienes	9/20/80
National Catholic Reporter*	11/20/80

*Denotes Catholic publication. All except *America* (a Jesuit publication) and the *National Catholic Reporter* are official church publications. Individuals have probably been included on account of their reputations as authors or because they represent official Catholic institutions.

This list is impressive not only for its length but on account of the geographical and institutional diversity it represents. Its obvious implication is that the homosexual movement is capable of influencing the Catholic Church.

There is a pattern of cooperative involvement, as seen below, between elements within the Roman Catholic Church and the homosexual movement.

- A number of priests act as "chaplains" or "consultants" for Dignity which, as we have seen, has access to Catholic churches in many dioceses where homosexual-oriented religious rituals are celebrated.
- Sky Anderson, pastor of the San Jose MCC, was reported to be working in collaboration with a priest and a nun in his campaign against Lockheed Corporation.[115]
- The Washington MCC works closely with the Carmelite Sisters of Charity in providing charitable services to poor residents of a shelter administered by these Catholic nuns.[116]
- A substantial number of licensed ministers of the UFMCC were originally Catholics, many of them apparently having had a seminary or convent background. In 1980, out of 173 licensed UFMCC ministers, 31 were former Roman Catholics.[117] In the current ecumenical climate, these individuals can be expected to maintain ties with their former church.
- New Ways Ministry has been allowed to offer its programs in a variety of Catholic institutions. The following list was provided to the author by the staff of New Ways Ministry and has been supplemented with information from *Bondings*, the group's official publication:

Diocese of Richmond, Virginia
Diocese of Harrisburg, Pennsylvania
Archdiocese of Los Angeles, California
Washington Theological Union, Washington, D.C.
Aquinas Institute, Dubuque, Iowa
Boston College
St. Mary's Seminary, Baltimore, Maryland
Dominican House of Studies, Washington, D.C.
Catholic University of America, Washington, D.C.
Theological College, Washington, D.C.
Conference of Major Superiors of Men, New York Region
Our Lady of the Holy Cross Abbey, Berryville, Virginia
United States Catholic Conference's Department of Education

Intercommunity Justice and Peace Center, New York, N.Y.
Parish educational programs in New Jersey, Maryland, Washington, D.C.,
  and Milwaukee
Marymount College, Tarrytown, New York
Mercy Center, Detroit
Glenmary Fathers and Brothers, Tupelo, Mississippi
East Coast Conference on Religious Education, Washington, D.C.
Holy Trinity Church, Georgetown, Washington, D.C.
Maryvale High School, Baltimore
Bishop McNamara High School, Forrestville, Maryland
Divine Savior Community House, Milwaukee
The Weber Center, Adrian, Michigan
Fifth Biennial International Convention, Philadelphia
Mt. Marie, Holyoke, Massachusetts
Notre Dame High School, Washington, D.C.
Conference of Women Religious, Philadelphia
Theological College, Washington, D.C.
Georgetown University, Washington, D.C.
St. Pius X Parish, Milwaukee
Sisters of Mercy of the Union, Silver Spring, Maryland
St. Mary's Academy, Leonardstown, Maryland
Martin Spalding High School, Glen Burnie, Maryland
Sisters of St. Joseph, Worcester, Massachusetts
Retreat for Gay Catholics, Indianapolis
Christ Church Parish, Washington, D.C.
Christian Brothers Retreat Center, Frederick, Maryland
National Organization for the Continuing Education of the Roman Catholic
  Clergy
Sisters of St. Joseph, Cleveland

- The list of "denominational gay caucuses and leadership" includes Brother
  Grant-Michael Fitzgerald, a member of the Roman Catholic "Society of the
  Divine Savior," to which New Ways Ministry Codirector Robert Nugent
  also belongs. The list was apparently part of the materials provided to the
  participants of a 1977 meeting of homosexuals in Denver.[118]
- The Washington Field Office Report (1976–77) of the UFMCC cited a Boston
  meeting between UFMCC Church Relations Director Roy Birchard, officers
  of Dignity, and the staff of Washington's Quixote Center to plan prohomosexual "cooperative endeavors."[119]
- Catholic clergy is sometimes present in a leadership capacity at homosexual
  meetings. For example, the Fifth Biennial Dignity International Convention
  (September 4–7, 1981) met in Philadelphia. Among the speakers at the
  convention were various Catholic clerics, including: the Reverend Declan
  Daly—himself a member of Dignity—leading a workshop on the liturgy;
  the Reverend Robert Hovda, a parish priest at St. Joseph's Church in New
  York's Greenwich Village, apparently charged with speaking on the nature
  of homosexual relationships between lay people and clerics ("Clerical/Lay
  Love Relationships"); and Brother William Roberts, a speaker on homosex-

uality and celibacy.[120] (A full agenda for this event appears near the end of this chapter.)

• Catholic parishes have participated in worship services of the UFMCC. For example, St. Peter Claver Parish in Baltimore merged its choir with that of the MCC Baltimore for a worship service which marked three days of "spiritual renewal" led by UFMCC founder Troy Perry on February 4–6, 1980. The combined choirs were directed by the Director of Music of the MCC Baltimore, Terry Snowden.[121]

• Catholic institutions have also been known to host homosexual social events, including dances where people presumably dance with members of their own sex. An example of such an event was the Inaugural Ball of Dignity/ Westchester Rockland, held in Rosary Academy in Sparkill, New York, on September 12, 1981. This affair was described in a homosexual publication as a "black and white dress" event where the music was provided by an "all-woman band."[122] Another example of a homosexual dance at a Catholic facility is the "Cabaret Night" sponsored by Dignity/New York at the St. Francis grammar school auditorium on 17th street between 6th and 7th avenues in New York City. According to a Dignity/New York invitation, this event would be "An evening of gutsy music and raucous music" and would take place on Wednesday, April 7, 1982.[123] An event of this nature on Wednesday in Holy Week would be extremely offensive to most Catholics. Holy Week is supposed to be a time of prayer and penance for Catholics. The holding of a homosexual musical affair in a Catholic grammar school would be considered by many Catholics as sacrilegious.

As a matter of fact, Roman Catholic facilities are regularly used for holding homosexual events—fundraisers, conferences, organizational meetings, workshops, and others. The number of instances is so large that it is impossible to cite them all. One example is the Massachusetts-based Center for Reflective Action, subsidized by the Sisters of St. Joseph of Springfield and the Sisters of Providence of Holyoke. The Center is a justice and peace organization that works through "schools, retreat centers, parish groups, religious communities and religious education programs."[124] In U.S. Roman Catholic jargon, "justice and peace" have become synonymous with radical left ideology and, in many instances, theology of liberation. "Justice and peace" centers have created an alternative structure within the Catholic Church which exists at all levels of Church organization and serves as a point of contact and network with the extreme political left. The Center for Reflective Action, for example, works with a number of leftist organizations:

American Friends Service Committee
Catholic Peace Fellowship
Interfaith Center for Corporate Responsibility
Bread for the World
United Farm Workers

Greater Springfield Council of Churches
Women's Ordination Conference
National Convergence of Justice and Peace Centers[125]

The Sisters of St. Joseph also staff the Genesis Spiritual Life Center in Westfield, Massachusetts, a multipurpose center originally established by this congregation.

Both the Center for Reflective Action and the Genesis Spiritual Life Center were made available for homosexual-oriented activities during the Columbus Day weekend, 1980. At the former, a one-day symposium was held. An examination of the materials provided to symposium participants reveals that it was really an exercise in the promotion of the homosexual ideology. The latter facility became the host of a "Dignity retreat" attended by more than fifty members of the organization's Region I (New England).[126]

Another indication of the pattern of collaboration between significant elements within the Catholic Church and the homosexual movement is the availability of prohomosexual materials at Catholic meetings. This is not a matter of individuals standing in doorways or on sidewalks handing out leaflets, but the fully accepted presence of representatives of the homosexual movement by Catholic agencies and national organizations. For example, during the March 1982 East Coast Conference on Religious Education in Washington, D.C., prohomosexual material was available at an official New Ways Ministry booth.[127] Homosexual booths were also installed at the National Catholic Charities 66th Annual Convention and at the 10th biennial meeting of the Association of Ladies of Charity of the United States. Dignity could boast that some "1600 Bishops, priests, nuns and laity from the U.S." had been reached at these events.[128] The value of being officially admitted to these functions comes not only from the resultant ability to influence the leadership of the Catholic Church, but from the fact that from a political point of view, this is equated with acceptance of the principle "gay is good," in practice if not in theory.

At times, even the bishops' conferences become the occasion for networking. As noted, the homosexual movement is closely related—ideologically and organizationally—with feminism. This relationship is then carried over to the Catholic Church. During the 1980 meeting of bishops in Washington, D.C., this relationship was cemented at a meeting which included Father Robert Nugent, SDS, and Sister Jeannine Gramick, SSND, for the homosexual movement and the leadership of the Women's Ordination Conference (WOC, a radical Catholic feminist organization). WOC was represented by, among others, Sister Joan Sobala, SSJ, a "chaplain" at the University of Rochester. The purpose of the meeting was "to explore ways of collaboration and to obtain support from WOC for the Catholic Coalition for Gay Civil Rights."[129] At this meeting, the homosexual movement was able to gain specific commitments from the WOC: "WOC will publish articles on homosexuality and will also offer New Ways printed resources to their readers."[130] There is evidence that WOC has indeed lived up to its commitment to the homosexuals: the January 1982 issue of *New Women New Church*, the publication of WOC, included an article by a female homosexual on the "Feminist Theological Perspectives of Lesbian and Gay Male Experience."[131] The same issue also published a very favorable report about the homosexual symposium sponsored by New Ways Ministry.[132] This should not be surprising, since the WOC sent a homosexual as a representative to the symposium who was also one of the speakers.

The evidence that there is a strong relationship between the movement to ordain women to the Catholic priesthood and the homosexual movement is obvious from the overlap between the Catholic homosexual network (the Catholic Coalition for Gay Civil Rights, of which more will be said later) and WOC. A comparison between the membership in WOC as of September 1977 and the current membership in the Catholic homosexual network reveals that fifteen percent of the members of WOC are also members of the homosexual organization. (Our analysis included a sample of members of WOC in eight States and the District of Columbia.)

Twenty-seven percent of the individuals whose names appeared in the Proceedings of the Second Conference on the Ordination of Roman Catholic Women which took place on November 1978 are also members of the Catholic homosexual network.

The leadership of the Women's ordination movement is closely connected with the homosexual movement. Thirty-three percent of the membership of the task force charged with organizing the 1978 conference of WOC are members of the Catholic homosexual network. The proportions for the WOC Advisory Board and the WOC Core Commission for 1979–1980 are even higher (fifty-seven and sixty-seven percent respectively.)[133] It is obvious that in terms of number of participants, increasing involvement in WOC correlates strongly with increasing involvement in the Catholic homosexual network.

It is difficult to imagine a logical relationship between the desire to engage in sexual intercourse with persons of one's own sex—for either males or females—and the question of the acceptance of females as part of the Roman Catholic clergy, unless all should be linked under the umbrella of "social justice." This could hardly be the case, however, since consistency would demand that practically every other issue be included as a suitable subject for adoption by both WOC *and* the Catholic homosexual movement acting in unison. Of course, as a matter of fact, this is not the case.

The relations between WOC and New Ways Ministry are obviously not a matter of a one-shot deal. This is clear from the following item, which appeared in a New Ways Ministry publication: "New Ways sent letters of congratulations to the new WOC Core Commission members and had a short visit at the New Ways house from Sr. Barbara Ferraro, a member of WOC Core Commission."[134]

What we have presented is merely a sampling of the many instances of cooperation between Roman Catholic institutions and leaders and the homosexual movement. Obviously, neither most Catholics nor most Catholic institutions would dream of becoming tools of the homosexual movement. However, the emergence of a pattern of collaboration between certain circles within the Church and the homosexual movement is unquestionable. The question, from the point of view of traditional Catholicism, is whether the Catholic Church will be strong enough to resist the attempts of a movement alien to its ideology and interests to utilize this ancient and venerable institution for its own political purposes.

Intellectual Infiltration. Ideologies are the foundation upon which human action rests. Institutions justify their actions by their ideologies, and so do individuals. The Roman Catholic Church is not immune to the need for an ideology that is not only faithful to her history and consistent with her interests, but also responsive to the needs of her social milieu. Ideology can be neither so fluid that it lacks consistency and continuity, nor so rigid that it becomes unresponsive. The inherent flexibility of the ideology of an institution committed to long-term survival like the Church, especially when doctrinal discipline is lacking, makes it vulnerable to attacks from such a quarter as that of the homosexual movement. In fact, this is what has taken place. The movement has much to gain from infiltrating the Church ideologically. At a minimum, many who would otherwise be unsympathetic to the practice of homosexuality can be confused and thus neutralized. Many others might perhaps be gained to the homosexual ideology, thereby establishing an intellectual foundation for across-the-board use of the Catholic Church. Above all, Catholic homosexuals will acquire justification for yielding to those tendencies which have historically been constrained. Several examples will show how the homosexual ideology has tried to extend its sway over Catholic thinking.

An editorial in *America*—a respected Jesuit publication—reveals how theological positions consonant with the homosexual movement have been accepted within the Catholic Church:

> The use of biblical injunctions against homosexuality by Anita Bryant and her followers was hopelessly fundamentalistic. Theological scholarship, whether scriptural or ethical, recognizes today that the application of Scripture texts that condemn homosexuality is dubious at best. The phenomenon of homosexuality, as it is understood today, covers too wide a range of inclinations and behavior patterns to be subject to sweeping condemnations. Furthermore, the overall tone and principal argument of the "Save Our Children" campaign not

only lacked Christian compassion toward homosexuals but also violated basic justice in perpetuating a lie. There is no scientific evidence to suggest that children are more likely to be molested by homosexuals than by heterosexuals.[135]

On a more practical level, Father Robert Nugent distinguishes three "current" theological positions concerning homosexuality: a) the "Magisterial" or official Catholic position that affirms that homosexual acts are intrinsically evil; b) the second or "mediating" position, which views homosexual acts not as objectively wrong but as a deviation from the norm (While not "ideal," in practice these acts might have to be tolerated for the overall good of the parties involved. . .); and c) the "relational" position which finds the value of sexual actions not in genital activity per se but in the quality of the relationships thereby established. Logically this position leads to the acceptance of homosexual relations as ethical so long as their quality is "good" or "acceptable."[136]

Presenting three alternative positions is a clever way of opening the door to acceptance of the morality of homosexual actions, since according to traditional Catholic moral teaching on probabilism, when there is disagreement among experts concerning the morality of a certain action, people are free to choose any "probable" opinion. The fact that the principle of probabilism does not apply in this case because the second and third opinions are not technically "probable" is never mentioned. In fact, *no* opinion contrary to what the Pope and bishops teach explicitly can be presented as "probable." The only Catholic opinions cited in a study commissioned by the Catholic Theological Society of America in support of the third opinion are Gregory Baum (a fallen-away priest) and a pro-homosexual "task force" of the Salvatorian Order, to which Nugent belongs.[137]

By attempting to use probabilism, Nugent nullifies the explicit teaching of the Catholic Church and gives license to homosexuals to seek relief from their sexual appetites so long as the relationship they establish satisfies the required criteria. In their critique of Archbishop Quinn's pastoral letter clearly condemning homosexuality, New Ways Ministry attempted to use the principle of probabilism (after accusing Quinn of being misleading, indicating that homosexuals would ignore the key direction of the document, and attacking his interpretation of the Bible):

New Ways also characterized as "disappointing" the response of Gay Catholics to the letter's recommendation that the only option for homosexuals is continence and celibacy. While clearly supporting such an option for some homosexuals, New Ways says that there are others who are aware of a solidly probable opinion among American Catholic moralists that "homosexual expression in the context of a faithful, stable relationship tending towards permanency is not beyond their moral reach," and that this option should have been noted in the Quinn letter.[138]

The key words here are "solidly probable opinion," with their implication of license. In any case, the attempt to justify not just homosexual practices but so-called homosexual marriages is undeniable.

One of the clearest examples of the acceptance of the homosexual ideology within the Catholic Church is *Human Sexuality: New Directions in American Catholic Thought*, the above mentioned study commissioned by the Catholic Theological Society of America.[139] The study was conducted by a five-member commission whose chairman was the Reverend Anthony Kosnik, a member of a national Catholic network of prohomosexuals (the Catholic Coalition for Gay Civil Rights). Another member of the commission is also part of this network. This is a rather confusing work that, under the guise of pastoral concern, eliminates every semblance of moral certainty. The Catholic Church as a whole rejected this study. The following excerpts from an official statement issued by the Archdiocese of New York reflect the manner in which it was received:

> The recently published *Human Sexuality: New Directions in American Catholic Thought* seeks to accommodate Church teaching in sexuality to modern sexual trends in America. In doing so, it has broken sharply with Catholic teaching and tradition. . . .
>
> The Committee of five authors of *Human Sexuality: New Directions in American Catholic Thought* tip the delicate and important balance between objective and subjective conscience, between action and intention, so much in favor of subjective conscience and intention, that the divine law and the human act are virtually emptied of significance. Their book's purely subjective definition of sexual love abolishes the objective criterion of openness to life which our tradition holds is a divinely ordained purpose of human sexual expression. The regrettable result is an all-inclusive list of sexual aberrations which the authors canonize in certain situations. . . .
>
> . . . does not represent the Catholic teaching in sexuality. If it is followed in practice it will seriously damage the lives of those who strive to put on the love of Christ which binds all the other virtues together and makes them perfect (Col. 3:14).[140]

An even more confusing work has been produced by Father Donald Goergen, O.P., also a member of the Catholic Coalition for Gay Civil Rights.[141] *The Sexual Celibate*, originally published in 1974, is well-known in clerical circles, having received favorable reviews from such Catholic periodicals as *Commonweal, America, The Long Island Catholic*, and others. It speaks, for example, of "healthy homosexuality in heterosexual persons" and "healthy homosexuality in homosexual persons."[142] The fol-

Religious Organizations and the Movement

lowing excerpt shows the tenor of this work, addressed primarily to priests and religious who intend to remain celibates all their lives:

> There are masculine homosexual men, as Robert Stoller points out: "One can have the rather comfortable identity of being a homosexual (even in the many cases where this is the end product of a stormy, neurotic personality development), just as one can have the rather comfortable identity of being a heterosexual." Homosexuality is not psychologically destructive if it does not destroy one's core gender identity—one's sense of maleness or sense of femaleness. A healthy homosexual person who has satisfactorily faced the task of sexual identity "considers himself to be a male and a man, though he clearly identifies himself as being a man of a particular class: homosexual." Even this particular classification is not the best way for a homosexual person to see himself. As pointed out above, homosexuality is not simply one classification. The task of sexual identity means being able to feel one's femaleness or one's maleness and at the same time accept one's degree of heterosexuality and one's degree of homosexuality, which degree cannot be best described simply as "I am heterosexual," or "I am homosexual." Here again maturity is bisexual.
>
> The supposed, stable, sexual (either heterosexual or homosexual) identity at which most people arrive can also be a defense due to enculturation and social expectations. Not that this is in itself destructive, but that conflicting tension can be as growth producing as stability. In our culture such a bisexual identity will contain a certain amount of instability. Sexual identity in its most mature phase means being able to *feel* that one belongs to and identifies with his or her own sex, male or female, which identity should not exclude feminine or masculine, heterosexual or homosexual, poles of personal life. Sexual identity which is achieved at the expense of, or to the exclusion of, one of these poles is as detrimental to human growth as is identity confusion.[143]

Father Charles Curran, a professor of Moral Theology at Catholic University of America, has taken a position which, in practice, coincides in several important points with the ideology of the homosexual movement. For example, during the homosexual symposium sponsored by New Ways Ministry in 1981, Father Curran offered the view that ". . . the normative ideal is heterosexuality but, because some people, through no fault of their own, are homosexual, homosexual actions in a committed relationship striving for permanency can be objectively good."[144]

The effects of the intellectual infiltration of the Catholic Church by the homosexual ideology are not merely theoretical, but strike at the very heart of Catholic life and tradition. An example of what the homosexual ideology can do to Catholic life is the case of the chaplain of Notre Dame University, one of the most prestigious Catholic institutions in the United States. In the February 1981 issue of *Notre Dame Magazine*, Father Robert Griffin, CSC, indicates that a young man came to confess to him that he was a homosexual and that he had been "unfaithful" to his regular sexual partner by having sex with another man. Father Griffin absolved him of his sin of "unfaithfulness." In Roman Catholic moral theology the sin of homosexual unfaithfulness does not exist; thus this absolution would not be recognized by Church authorities. The dialogue that followed, however, is even more surprising:

> My shriven penitent, having heartily resolved with the help of God's grace to do penance and to amend his life, said: "My roommate is thinking about becoming a Catholic, and he would like to talk to a priest. Could he come and talk to you?"
> "Actually," I said, "I'm not here regularly, but I'd be happy to give his name to one of the other priests. The pastor would be very happy to help him, I'm sure."[145]

It is significant that in the May 1981 issue of the magazine, two letters to the editor were reprinted in reply to Father Griffin's article. A letter from a priest was sympathetic to the prohomosexual position. Another letter, from a layman, correctly spelled out the traditional Catholic position:

A Confessor's Duty

I read with interest Father Griffin's article on the sacrament of reconciliation and a homosexual.
I believe Griffin's handling of that confession was misguided. The purpose of penance is to bring us closer to Jesus and to let us know that our sins are forgiven. However, a confessor is duty-bound to point out areas of sinfulness in our lives.
Certainly we must love the sinner but hate the sin. If a homosexual (or anyone) masks his sins and suppresses his conscience, a priest must point that out.
Rather than ignore the question, Father Griffin could have pointed out in a caring manner the wrongness of the homosexual's living arrangement. A new beginning might have been established—a beginning of inner healing under the guidance of the Holy Spirit.
If I were without sin, I could be both judge and stonethrower, but I am not. My sole purpose is to show how easy it is for us to hide our true beliefs, as I believe Father Griffin did. But we must live and love as Christians and help our brothers and sisters.[146]

Networking. In order to ensure effective action, the homosexual movement has made use of an endless number of networks and coalitions, some created solely around the issue of homosexuality while others include a multitude of other—usually leftist—issues. Throughout this work, but especially in this chapter, the existence of such networks within the Roman Catholic Church has been apparent. As is typical with the left, Catholic homosexuals have managed to create and participate in many networks

Religious Organizations and the Movement

and organizations. The movement has even created a special group for nuns who specialize in working with homosexuals: the Sisters in Gay Ministry Associated (SIGMA) has been established by New Ways Ministry.[147] When the time comes to sign petitions or send representatives to meetings, this multiplicity of names and organizational affiliation is very useful, since such names provide the impression of a widespread support that exists only on paper. Homosexual groups are very sensitive to this. For example, when Father Robert E. Burns, CSP, correctly related Dignity to the Catholic Coalition for Gay Civil Rights, Father Robert Nugent protested vehemently.[148] In fact, the relations—both ideological and organizational—are unmistakable; the Coalition is, in effect, a creature of New Ways Ministry.

The most important Catholic prohomosexual network is the Catholic Coalition for Gay Civil Rights, started in response to the "Call to Action Conference," a 1976 leftist meeting that took place in Detroit under official Church auspices. The Coalition's statement of principles constitutes a complete acceptance of basic principles of the homosexual ideology. By the end of 1981, 2,469 individuals and 150 organizations (including 36 Dignity chapters) had pledged to work for a special status for homosexuals under the law. The membership of the Coalition—a matter of public record—probably constitutes the backbone of the Catholic prohomosexual network. The fact that so many Catholic individuals and organizations have in some sense pledged support for the homosexual movement is a clear indication of the sanction it has within the Catholic Church. To provide an idea of the depth of support for homosexuality within the Catholic Church, the complete organizational list of endorsers is appended to the following list of Dignity chapters:

Dignity Chapters

Dignity/Albany	Dignity/Mission Valley
Dignity/Baltimore	Dignity/Orange County
Dignity/Bay Area	Dignity/Pittsburgh
Dignity/Boston	Dignity/Princeton
Dignity/Brooklyn	Dignity/Providence
Dignity/Buffalo	Dignity/Queens
Dignity/Canada/Dignite	Dignity/Region I
Dignity/Chicago	Dignity/Region V, Advisory Board
Dignity/Cleveland	Dignity/Region VI
Dignity/East Lansing	Dignity/Region IX, Advisory Board
Dignity/Fort Wayne	Dignity/Rochester
Dignity/Greensboro	Dignity/St. Louis
Dignity/Honolulu	Dignity/San Antonio
Dignity/Houston	Dignity/Toledo
Dignity Inc.	Dignity/Washington
Dignity–Integrity/Richmond	Dignity/Winnipeg

Dignity Chapters	
Dignity/Jersey City–Bayonne	Dignity/Wyoming
Dignity/Kansas City	Integrity–Dignity/Madison

Other Catholic Organizations

Alderson Hospitality House, Alderson, W. Va.
Appalachian Ministry, Griffithsville, W. Va.
APWC/Immaculate Heart of Mary Sisters
Archdiocese of New Orleans, Sisters' Council
Archdiocese of St. Louis, Council of Religious Women
Archdiocese of St. Paul and Minneapolis, Senate of Priests
ASC Pilgrim Ministries (Precious Blood Sisters)
Association of Chicago Priests
Boston Theological Institute, Women's Theological Coalition
Brothers for Christian Community, General Assembly, 1980
Brothers of the Sacred Heart, Pascoag, R.I.
Capuchin Gay Caucus
Cascade Community Church, Akron
Catholic Charities, Inc., New London (Conn.) District
Catholic Worker Farm, Sheep Ranch, Calif.
Catholic Worker House, St. Louis
Center for New Creation, Vienna, Va.
Center for Reflective Action, Holyoke, Mass.
Centre of Affirmation & Dialogue, Toronto, Ont.
Church of the Epiphany, Social Action Committee, Louisville
Community of the Holy Spirit, San Diego
Cornerstone Justice and Peace Center, Inc., Denver
Correctional Change Group, Worcester, Mass.
Des Moines Catholic Workers
Diocesan Criminal Justice Commission, Bridgeport, Conn.
Diocese of Brooklyn, Social Action Office
Diocese of Orlando, Ministry for Social Justice
Diocese of Pittsburgh, Sisters' Council, Peace and Justice Committee
Diocese of Richmond, Social Ministry Commission
Diocese of Rochester, Sisters' Council
Diocese of Syracuse, Justice and Peace Commission
Diocese of Trenton, Office of Diocesan Relations for Sexual Minorities
Dominican Students of the Province of St. Martin de Porres, Oakland, Calif.
East Lansing Peace Education Center
8th Day Center for Justice, Chicago
Emmaus Community of Christian Hope, Orange, N.J.
Emmaus House, Washington, D.C.
Futures Awareness Center, Mount St. Joseph, Ohio
Georgetown University, Office of Campus Ministry
Good Shepherd Catholics for Shared Responsibility, Alexandria, Va.

Religious Organizations and the Movement

Groundwork, Lansing
Handmaids of Mary, Sisters' Coalition for Justice
Las Hermanas, a national organization of Hispanic nuns
House of Community, Bemidji, Minn.
Institute for Peace and Justice, St. Louis
Jesuit Renewal Center, Milford, Ohio
Justice and Peace Center, Milwaukee
Manhattan College, Campus Ministry, Bronx, N.Y.
Martin Buber Institute, Columbia, Md.
Missionary Sisters of the Immaculate Conception, Provincial Council, W. Paterson, N.J.
Most Holy Sacrament Administrative Team
National Assembly of Religious Brothers
National Assembly of Women Religious, East Central Region
National Assembly of Women Religious, Executive Board
National Assembly of Women Religious, House of Delegates, 1979
National Assembly of Women Religious, Pittsburgh Chapter
National Center for Ministry, Milwaukee
National Coalition of American Nuns
Newman Center Staff, Columbia, Mo.
Newman Center Staff, Davis, Calif.
Newman Community, Chapel Hill, N.C.
New Ways Ministry, Mount Rainier, Md.
Orthodox Catholic Office for Peace and Justice, San Francisco
Passionist Social Concerns Center, Union City, N.J.
P.A.D.R.E.S.
Parents of Gays, Arlington, Va.
Paulist Social Action Committee, Storrs, Conn.
Parish Evaluation Project, Chicago
Pax Center, Erie, Pa.
Quixote Center, Mount Rainier, Md.
St. Francis Parish Team, Brant Beach, N.J.
St. Jerome Church, Pastoral Staff, Newport News, Va.
St. John's Student Parish, Campus Ministry Team, East Lansing
St. Joseph Parish, Pastoral Ministry Team, East Rutherford, N.J.
St. Joseph House, Minneapolis
St. Leander Parish, Social Concerns Committee, Pueblo, Colo.
St. Matthew Community, Brooklyn, N.Y.
School Sisters of Notre Dame, Baltimore Province in Bolivia
School Sisters of Notre Dame, Emmaus Community, Camden, N.J.
School of Applied Theology, Berkeley, Calif.
SIGMA (Sisters in Gay Ministry Associated)
Sisters of Charity of St. Elizabeth, Provincial Team, Northern Province, Paramus, N.J.
Sisters of Loretto, Cherry Street House, Kansas City, Mo.
Sisters of Loretto, Office of the Social Advocate, Denver
Sisters of Mercy, Social Concerns Committee, Burlington, Vt.
Sisters of Mercy of the Union, General Administrative Team

Sisters of Notre Dame de Namur, Province Team, Boston Province
Sisters of St. Dominic, Executive Committee, Racine, Wisc.
Sisters of St. Dominic of Marymount, Tacoma
Sisters of St. Francis, Alliance, Nebr.
Sisters of St. Francis, Tiffin, Ohio
Sisters of St. Joseph of Carondelet, Albany Province, Social Justice Secretariat
Sisters of St. Joseph of Carondelet, Social Justice Core Group
Sisters of St. Joseph of Carondelet, St. Louis Province, Social Justice Secretariat
Sisters of St. Joseph of Carondelet, St. Mary Star of the Sea Parish, Atlantic Mine, Mich.
Sisters of St. Joseph of Carondelet, Western Province, Social Justice Secretariat
Sisters of St. Joseph of LaGrange, Social Justice Committee
Sisters of St. Joseph of Orange, Social Concerns Committee, Orange, Calif.
Sisters of St. Joseph of Peace, Religious Development Team, Englewood Cliffs, N.J.
Sisters of St. Joseph, Third Order of St. Francis
Sisters of St. Joseph, Third Order of St. Francis, St. Francis Region
Sisters of the Presentation, Social Justice Committee
Sisters of Divine Providence, Provincial Administration, Melbourne, Ky.
Spokane Peace and Justice Center
St. Paul's University Catholic Center, Social Justice Committee, Madison, Wisc.
St. Paul's University Catholic Center, Staff, Madison, Wisc.
Third Life Center, Oakland, Calif.
Thomas Merton Center, Pittsburgh
University of Wisconsin, Campus Ministry, Whitewater
Villa Maria Retreat Center, Wernersville, Pa.
Women's Ordination Conference (WOC)
Whitehead Associates, South Bend, Ind.

The clergy and religious orders are widely represented in this coalition. The following table illustrates the minimum number of priests, brothers, and nuns among the coalition members. The figures are probably higher, since individuals might not have identified themselves as clerics or religious, and in many cases they have not clarified the order to which they belong.

A total of 1,353 priests, brothers, and nuns belong to this prohomosexual coalition. This represents 54.8 percent of the total membership of the organization, indicating the degree to which the homosexual ideology has penetrated the Catholic clergy. The names and numbers herein have been extracted from lists published in *Bondings*, the official publication of New Ways Ministry.[149]

The influence of the coalition as a nucleating factor in eliciting support for the homosexual movement is also undeniable. *A Time To Speak* contains two lists of prominent Catholics who have signed prohomosexual petitions. One is a "statement of concern" against the Vatican for ordering

Religious Organizations and the Movement

Clerics and Religious Members of the
Catholic Prohomosexual Coalition

Priests and Brothers*		Nuns	
Order	**Number**	**Order**	**Number**
Priests (no order indicated)	217	Not specified	106
Jesuits	64	School Sisters of Notre Dame	168
Franciscans	64	Sacred Heart	90
Dominicans	28	Dominicans	58
Holy Cross	21	Sisters of Mercy	42
Salvatorians	16	Franciscans	29
Oblates of St. Francis de Sales	15	Notre Dame	21
Oblates of Mary Immaculate	11	Immaculate Heart of Mary	18
Benedictines	11	Over sixty other orders	215
Augustinians	10		
Brothers (no order indicated)	19	Total	747
Christian Brothers	23		
Xaverian Brothers	9		
Over fifty other orders	98		
Total	606		

*Includes diocesan priests
NOTE: Four individuals who listed themselves under the acronym BFCC (Brothers for a Christian Community) have not been included inasmuch as this homosexual "order" is not recognized by the Church.

homosexual leader Father John McNeill, S.J., to stop speaking on sexual morality. The other is a declaration in support of the homosexual movement's failed effort to avoid the repeal of the Dade County prohomosexual ordinance in 1977. Six of the twelve signators of the former and five of the twelve signators of the latter are members of the coalition.[150]

Roman Catholic prohomosexual networking does not exist only at the national level, nor is it limited exclusively to Roman Catholics. At the local level, especially in areas where the homosexual movement is particularly strong, there are networks of priests, ministers, and religious who are active in support of the homosexual cause. An example is seen in Rochester, N.Y., where almost one hundred clergymen and nuns (including a large number of Catholic priests) signed a prohomosexual statement on March 1, 1977.[151]

Other examples of networking include the use of specific political issues to gain an entree with influential individuals and the participation in activities seemingly unrelated to the specific concerns of the movement. An example of the former is the Women's Committee Report submitted for the Executive Board Meeting of Dignity in Lubbock, Texas, in March 1981, requesting letters of support and thanks to Bishop Maurice J. Dingman on account of his activities in support of the Equal Rights Amendment.[152] The latter is exemplified by the sponsorship of Dignity/Chicago by the Chicago Call to Action, where it was seemingly accepted with other "grassroots" Catholic organizations gathered to implement the platform adopted by the 1976 Detroit Call to Action meeting. Hal Wand, Vice President of Dignity/Chicago and former editor of the national newsletter of Dignity, became a member of the organization's steering committee.[153]

Although national networks are bound to be more visible, it is the local groups and the painstaking work of establishing links with local organizations that can produce the "best" results for the homosexual cause.

It would be inappropriate to assume that specific members of the coalition, or of any other organization working with the homosexual movement, are actually homosexuals. In some other cases, however, it is clear that homosexuals have attempted to initiate Catholic social institutions—like Dignity—for the promotion of their ideology within the Church. Aside from Dignity, however, the homosexual movement expresses its presence within the Catholic Church in other ways, potentially more threatening to the life of the Church itself.

Homosexual Clergy. The attitude of certain elements within the homosexual movement seems to be that of the man who, having robbed a store, cried repeatedly, "Thief!" as he fled, in the expectation that somehow he could escape blame. By asserting that homosexuality is a pervasive phenomenon affecting many people or most people—perhaps, in some way, all people—they assume that somehow it will be made respectable. Moreover, by asserting the homosexuality of many people in certain positions (e.g., politics, education, religion, the judiciary), where they are expected to exercise authority, as well as serving as role models, two objectives are accomplished: first, whenever individuals within these groups act or speak against homosexuality or the movement, their authority is diminished, since their credibility has been diluted; second, their ability to serve as heterosexual models is also impaired, since people are led to believe that there is a substantial probability that they are homosexual.

In its attempt to infiltrate the Catholic Church, the homosexual movement has used this tactic by emphasizing the fact that there are homosexual priests, brothers, and nuns, by affirming the need to accept homosexuals for holy orders or religious profession, and by providing the existing homosexual clergy with structures in which to embrace—free of moral or social encumbrances—the homosexual ideology.

There can be no question that some members of the Roman Catholic clergy are homosexual. The process by which a person is prepared for vows or ordination cannot be perfect enough to weed out all homosexuals. In some instances, persons known to be homosexual by their superiors have been accepted, although this is not official Church policy. Two

Religious Organizations and the Movement

glaring examples of overemphasis on the subject of homosexuality and the clergy are Fathers Andre Boulanger and Richard Wagner. Boulanger is the former pastor of St. Edward's Church in Phoenix and a Dignity chaplain who, as we have already seen, reportedly asserted that "25 percent of all priests in the Phoenix area are basically homosexual."[154] Father Wagner is an avowed homosexual and a Missionary Oblate of Mary Immaculate who advertises as a "clinical sexologist" in *The Sentinel*, San Francisco's homosexual newspaper.[155] A doctoral candidate at the Institute for Advanced Study of Human Sexuality, Father Wagner not only appears to have close ties with the homosexual community in San Francisco, but has written an article in the *National Catholic Reporter* (a controversial radical leftist weekly) where he "suggested that sex should be available to ordained priests."[156] Father Wagner was scheduled to be a speaker at the September 1981 Dignity Convention in Philadelphia.[157] Shortly afterward, Wagner announced that, under the direction of Church authorities in Rome, he was being dismissed from his order.[158] In spite of this, Wagner was allowed into a Jesuit Church—Holy Trinity, Georgetown, Washington, D.C.—as main speaker after a mass and a "giant potluck" in celebration of the ninth anniversary of Dignity/Washington.[159]

One item on the homosexual movement's agenda for the Catholic Church is the ordination of homosexuals, connected, in a roundabout way, with the ordination of women. Although the policy of ordaining homosexuals has not been adopted by the Catholic Church, the movement has made great strides in this direction. It is now possible for New Ways Ministry codirector Sister Jeannine Gramick, SSND, to respond, apparently without fear of reprimand, to a public query by a Baltimore City Councilman as to whether female homosexuals should be allowed as nuns, that "such decisions were not based on considerations of sexual preference."[160] *America*, a Jesuit publication, has offered a qualified endorsement to the proposition that homosexuals should be ordained to the priesthood.[161]

It is apparent that in certain religious orders, homosexuals are already welcome as members. This was proposed in an open way by Gabriel Moran, FSC, a Christian Brother whose writings are widely read in religious communities. Speaking to the 1977 Conference of Christian Brothers, he intimated that religious communities were the ideal setting for homosexual relations.

It is not by accident that the word homosexual is generally used as a noun so that a person's being is totally classified by the category. I use homosexual here as an adjective to describe a sexual attitude which may apply to anyone but is a predominant attitude for millions of people in the U.S. This attitude is the basis of homophile relations, that is, sexual love between persons of the same sex. This love is especially threatening to the classification of people as married or single because the lovers are not isolated individuals nor are they getting together to have children . . . Responsible homophile relations are a dramatic example of mutual love. They show that patriarchal ownership is not necessary and that sex is not simply a contract for mutual exploitation . . . We are one of the few existing organizations that might provide a stable setting for the working out of homosexual love. . . . The existing organization of brothers has not been accepting of homosexual expression in the past. There is still a problem of structuring the organization to allow for this variation. Nonetheless it should not be necessary to exclude a person because he has developed a homosexual love for someone within or without the organization. For homosexual people who might wish to associate with us, we could provide aid, or at least protection from repression. There is no immediate solution for the person of homosexual orientation . . . An organization of religious brotherhood is a natural bridge for the meeting of straight and gay worlds.[162]

Parents of children attending a school staffed by Christian Brothers would probably object strenuously if the community should become a place that "provide[s] a stable setting for the working out of homosexual love. . . ."

Further, the author interviewed a young man who attended an orientation session for candidates of a major Roman Catholic religious order in Washington, D.C. The orientation team was described by the student as "basically sympathetic" toward the acceptance of confirmed homosexuals into the order. It included a theology graduate who was then waiting to be ordained and a priest who lectured on the subject of "celibacy and sexuality." This young man recalled the following statements made as part of the presentation:

Homosexuality or any other behavior against the vow of celibacy might have to be worked out. You could not be doing it all the time and stay.

Having homosexual sex might be necessary as part of a person's growth process. This is also true of heterosexuality. . . .

Homosexuality is something that should not be condemned. It might be necessary for the individual. . . .

The occasional practice of homosexuality should not be condemned. It is part of the growth pattern of the individual.

The young man stated that "homosexuality and heterosexuality were presented as two varieties of the same question."[163]

It is also apparent that in certain religious communities there is a short stated period during which a homosexual must be celibate if he is to be admitted.[164] However, there is no question of denying such a person admission on the basis of his sexual preferences. This policy is carefully kept under wraps. No indication is given as to the method used for

Religious Organizations and the Movement

ascertaining whether or not a homosexual has been sexually active. This question is highly important during the formation period, since religious congregations are unisexual. Whereas the problem does not arise for heterosexual persons, a religious house with several homosexuals obviously constitutes a veritable powderkeg, not only because of the danger of liaisons between the homosexuals, but also because of their potential for actually molesting heterosexual members of the community to whom they feel attracted. The fact that in some instances homosexuals *are* admitted to religious communities is consonant with available information. The following quote is taken from *Communication*, a newsletter for homosexual Catholic clergy: "I am finishing up my theological studies at the Jesuit School of Theology in Chicago. I was ordained last June. I work part time as assistant pastor of an inner-city parish in the Black community. I am gay. I have been out with my superiors since I was a novice, and, aware of my gayness, they have approved me for vows and now for ordination."[165]

Rumors of homosexuals—open and practicing—within the Jesuit order have transcended the sphere of ecclesiastical gossip. *Newsweek* reported that one of the reasons Pope John Paul II had to "take over" the Jesuit order by appointing a personal representative to manage its affairs was (quoting a Jesuit): "Even when Jesuits were denounced for having girlfriends—or boyfriends—Arrupe [the ailing superior general of the order] took no action."[166]

The attitude that made this possible cannot be called an isolated event. The following excerpt is from the discussion of a case involving the possibility of a Jesuit priest's homosexuality. The author is William A. Barry, S.J., Associate Professor of Pastoral Theology at Weston School of Theology and a staff member of the Center for Religious Development at Cambridge, Massachusetts. The case appeared in an internal publication for American Jesuits:

> A word about the acceptance of homosexuals into the novitiate. It should be clear that I do not favor the acceptance of those who have not yet come to grips with the issue of their sexual identity, or of those who are plagued by the destructive dynamics I have just mentioned. Neither of these restrictions is limited to the question of homosexuality. But there are young men who have come to terms with the fact that their sexual attractions are homosexual and who have arrived at a basic self-acceptance and who believe that they have a vocation to the Society of Jesus. I see no a priori reason to doubt the authenticity of the call. The all-male environment of a community may pose a difficulty, but fewer and fewer of our communities are like the cloistered hothouses of the past. These young men would, hopefully, not be afraid of developing close friendships with Jesuits for fear of homosexual implications. They may have to learn how to handle their feelings when offhand and cruel remarks about homosexuals are made. I would hope that their homosexual orientation is not

345

a dark secret they continually fear will be discovered, just as I hope that they need not feel it necessary to tell one and all. Whether a person is homosexual or heterosexual in orientation is not matter for public knowledge. For a Jesuit the main issue is that one can live with relative wholeheartedness a life of consecrated virginity in service of the Lord and his kingdom. Men with a homosexual orientation as well as men with a heterosexual orientation have been able to do so.[167]

The principle accepted here is the one espoused by Goergen. The "problem," in Barry's mind, is not homosexuality, but how "mature" the homosexual is. Whereas traditionally homosexuality has been considered a sign of immaturity, what we are now told is that there is another factor called "maturity" which determines the suitability of a man for the priesthood (or a woman for the sisterhood).

Addressing this question, a committee of New England bishops came to exactly the opposite conclusion. They asserted in a document entitled "Priestly Formation: Discerning Vocations":

A man who seems unable to come to heterosexual maturity should not be admitted. We recognize that there are various degrees of homosexuality and that generalizations cannot easily be made. We include in this statement anyone who while not engaging in homosexual activity is psychically homosexual and therefore unable to tolerate the demands of a celibate priestly ministry or of rectory living . . . Young men who are excessively effeminate should not be admitted. . . . because God calls real men and if there are not real men, there can be no call.[168]

The bishops have obviously rejected the notion of "homosexual maturity" which logically implies the fundamental principle of the homosexual ideology, "gay is good."

It was in connection with this document that Bishop Peter A. Rosazza dissented with the other bishops and accepted the principle that homosexuals are eligible for the priesthood.

Catholic priests are called to perform various functions which make it less than acceptable for most Catholics that avowed homosexuals be ordained to the ministerial priesthood, as distinguished from the "priesthood of the faithful" conferred by baptism. Catholic doctrine reserves the ministerial priesthood to men, and relatively few are ordained to holy orders. In addition to the general objection to homosexual practices on moral grounds, and the fact that priests are called to live as celibates in an all-male environment where other priests could become the objects of lust, priests act as counselors, confessors, teachers, and role models. In the exercise of all these functions, homosexuals are perceived as incapable—by their behavior or tendencies—to accurately portray the image of Jesus Christ. As the New England bishops said, ". . . because God calls real men and if there are not real men, there can be no call." This is essentially the reason why the Catholic Church teaches that women are not capable of being ordained to the priesthood validly.

Although not as strenuous as the efforts to achieve the ordination of women, there is a movement within the Catholic Church for avowed homosexuals to be accepted openly in all ranks of the clergy and religious orders. (We have established that this is already happening in secret.) On March 29, 1981, the New Ways Ministry codirectors piloted a workshop on "Homosexuality and Religious Life" for the Board of the Religious Formation Conference at the St. Thomas More House of Studies in Washington, D.C. The final version of the workshop is apparently aimed at vocation directors, formation personnel, etc. The target is obviously those who, in one way or another, can affect policy and make it possible for an ever-increasing number of homosexuals to join the ranks of Church personnel.[169] The subject was also scheduled as a major topic of discussion in the "First National Symposium on Homosexuality and the Catholic Church" to be held at Holy Trinity Mission Seminary in Silver Spring (November 1981), which will be described below.

Homosexual clergy and nuns within the Catholic Church do not stand in splendid isolation. Many are being helped in ways which are consonant with the Church's teaching. For example, the Reverend John Harvey, OSFS, has been extremely active in promoting programs to help homosexual clergy without condoning homosexual practices or in any way accepting the homosexual ideology. He has become "anathema" for the prohomosexual elements within the Roman Catholic Church. But at the same time, extensive and highly successful activities have been under way for several years to create a network of avowed homosexual clergy. In addition to what Dignity does by providing a church-related forum in which the homosexual ideology is refined and adapted to better relate to and influence the Catholic Church—and incidentally strengthen homosexual Church personnel in their condition—there are two other sources of organizational strength for the homosexual clergy and nuns: meetings and media. As usual, the bottom line of organization is communication (in Catholic modernist theological jargon the technical term is "sharing").

Apparently outside the supervision of Church authorities, it seems that a large number of meetings for homosexual clergy and nuns takes place on a regular basis. In some instances, they are advertised as "retreats," while in other cases they are called "gatherings." The naive reader might think that a retreat is exactly what a homosexual priest or nun needs to struggle with the seemingly overwhelming power of the compulsion to seek relief from sexual desires which are contrary to his commitment and to the natural law. However, it seems that this is *not* what takes place in these meetings. For example, an advertisement in *Communication* indicates that the "trialogue" method of the Marriage Encounter Movement

THE HOMOSEXUAL NETWORK

would be used. Those who have taken part in the Encounter know that trialogue means prayer by a couple (the word is derived from dialogue— a conversation between *two*—and means a conversation of three participants, i.e., a couple and God.) The implication is that the homosexual cleric and his "lover" pray together. . . . This is hardly what the average Catholic expects to happen in a retreat. Naturally, according to the homosexual ideology, this is not only natural but almost expected for "Christian couples."

Ascertaining when and where these meetings take place is not an easy matter, since efforts are made to keep them secret. The following 1979 meetings, however, have been documented:

Source	Available Data About the Meeting

Communication, 2/79 (Vol. 2, No. 5)	Midwest gathering, March 13–March 15; Bergamo Center, Dayton, Ohio
	Contact: Norb Brockman, S.M.
	    4435 E. Patterson Road
	    Dayton, Ohio 45430 (513) 426-2363

Communication, 2/79 (Vol. 2, No. 5)	Retreat for gay priests, brothers, and seminarians.
	May 29–June 1
	Beach Haven Terrace, NJ (1 block from beach)
	By: Revs. Robert Decker and Ed. Thompson
	Contact: Rev. Robert Decker
	    8 Ohio Avenue
	    Beach Haven Terrace, NJ 08008
	Style: Based on "Choice" Weekend and Marriage Encounter Trialogue

Communication, 4/79 (Vol. 2, No. 7)	Retreat for "gay" sisters directed by "Sr. Bernie," a "gay" sister. Weekend of May 4–6 in an undisclosed location in Maryland. Sponsored by New Ways Ministry.
Gayspring, 3/79 (Vol. 3, No. 1)	New Ways Ministry (Roman Catholic) has announced that they will be holding a conference/retreat for homosexual nuns this May.

The appendix includes a copy of *Communication* (Vol. 3, No. 5, February 1980) which includes a narrative of one of these secretive meetings. Page 8 of the same issue speaks about "a number of retreats in different parts of the country." Furthermore, in preparing this work, the author came across an announcement of a secret meeting of homosexual priests and nuns on the evening of December 10, 1978, in a Catholic high school in Washington, D.C. The announcement even mentioned which door to use, apparently in order to avoid detection, and gave the name and address of a "friar" in a religious house near Catholic University as the "contact" for the event. Whether the authorities of the religious order who staff the high school or of the Archdiocese of Washington knew about this event could not be ascertained.

348

Religious Organizations and the Movement

The homosexual clergy even has its own media. Published in the offices of Dignity Philadelphia, in the heart of the city's homosexual district, *Communication* is a monthly newsletter for homosexual clerics. The objectives of the publication are twofold. First, to foster the homosexual ideology among clerics and religious. This is very important since the teachings of the Catholic Church make no allowance for the practice of homosexuality among its personnel. Official church teachings must thus be counteracted. Second, the life of a homosexual priest or religious (of either sex) must be quite difficult. Life in community with members of the same sex who are forbidden objects of his sexual appetites, in addition to having to preach the doctrines of a Church which condemns what he seeks with the strongest passion, can become not only lonely but also tense. The "Catholic" solution for the problem would be to seek support from God in prayer, a spiritual counselor in the confessional, and sublimation of his desires in work for God and his fellow man. If he meets with other homosexuals, the clear objective should be, according to Church teaching, to offer and obtain support *away* from the practice of homosexuality. *Communication*, clearly an instrument of the homosexual movement, offers as an alternative the possibility of rationalizing homosexual behavior within the confines of Roman Catholicism.

Apparently local church authorities are not aware of the existence of *Communication*. Cardinal Kroll, the Archbishop of Philadelphia, is known as a man steeped in Catholic orthodoxy. He could hardly tolerate within his jurisdiction a publication by Church personnel which has affirmed: "Little does Cardinal Kroll know what great ministries bubble under his umbrella" in referring to the promotion of homosexuality by Catholic clergy. The removal of those responsible from the "service" of the Church would be a simple matter once the nature of their activities was ascertained.

The reader may find several issues of *Communication* reproduced in an appendix to this work. Sensitive individuals may wish to avoid reading this material.

There can be little doubt that there are homosexuals in Catholic rectories and convents. The situation has become so serious that even such a radical liberal publication as the *National Catholic Reporter* has expressed concern about this issue.[171] Although this publication has come out editorially in favor of prohomosexual legislation, it is obvious that a completely homosexualized clergy would make the Catholic Church totally ineffectual in promoting other liberal causes. Still, it is in the interest of the homosexual movement to "maximize" the proportion of homosexuals among priests and nuns. Therefore it is only prudent to look with suspicion at data which originate from spokesmen for homosexuality or homosexual organizations. The existence of homosexuals among Church personnel speaks of the human condition and the ability of man to rationalize. The practice of celibacy apparently creates a "convenient" cover for homosexuals. In the long run, however, it becomes a dangerous psychosocial trap. It is also obvious that the existing devices designed to screen out homosexuals unsuitable for the ministry are not perfect. Among other reasons, acceptance of the homosexual ideology by some of those specifically charged with the recruitment and formation of church personnel probably contributes to the problem.

Homosexual Orders. Even more secretive than the network of homosexual priests and nuns is the existence of religious communities organized exclusively for homosexuals. Patterned after legitimate orders, these organizations are not recognized by the Catholic Church. Although it is almost impossible to obtain any information on this matter, it is clear that these are not orders in the traditional sense of the term: the St. Matthew Community—located in Brooklyn and currently named Emmaus House—accepts men who have "chosen to live in permanent gay union," and in the Agape Community "lovers are of course welcome with or without their partners."

The available documentation on some of the organizations does not clearly reveal their homosexual nature. However, they have been included since they appear in the "Gay Religious Community File" of New Ways Ministry. The following are known to exist:

Agape Community, intended to be a spin-off of Dignity. The following excerpts have been taken from a description prepared by Robert Papi of Dignity Ottawa:

> Naturally, as we are primarily to be composed of homosexual men and lesbian women, members should have previously spent at least 1 year of regular attendance and participation in their local Dignity chapter. The same for our non-gay brothers and sisters who wish to join. This because part of our mandate is to fulfill the guidelines of the Dignity Statement of Position and Purpose. . . .
>
> Members will maintain as much as possible their present lifestyle, being of course, aware that they are witnessing to Christ hence they must give up those things in their lifestyle which would interfer [sic] with such a witness.
>
> While members may, if they choose, take personal promises of poverty, chastity and obedience, these are not required. While within the AGAPE COMMUNITY sex is to be kept in its proper perspective, members should seek to avoid the more destructive aspects of heavy cruising. Lovers, of course, are welcome, together or without their partners. However those not in a commitment relationship are not encouraged to undertake such a commitment simply to be part of the community. While ideally chastity or lover commitments are to be encouraged the community is open to all who seek to be witnesses to Christ. The AGAPE COMMUNITY, while closely associated with Dignity, and while members may remain part of Dignity and are encouraged to do so, does not come under the jurisdiction of Dignity. Rather the community is bound by its own infra-structure.[172]

Religious Organizations and the Movement

Members are urged to seek out a priest as their "spiritual director."

Augustinians of Charity, founded by two men who met while they were members of a "straight" religious community in California. Located in Charlestown, Massachusetts, this organization seems to have been directed by a priest from the Augustinians of the Assumption. Data on this order was obtained in a July 17, 1979, letter from one of its members to "Gerald," probably Gerald Moran, BFCC[173] (see below.)

The Order of Transformation, "composed of intelligent, energetic men who wish to devote two or more years of their life to the service of God and man in unique and creative ways."[174]

Emmaus House located in Brooklyn, New York, formerly called St. Matthew Community. This organization has extensive and well-drawn rules which are reproduced in their entirety in the appendix. The following excerpts from a promotional brochure designed to recruit "associate members" reveal some of the characteristics of the organization and its apparent acceptance by the local diocese. If the content of the brochure is accurate, it is inconceivable that Church officials would be unaware of a group engaged in the activities described below:

> The St. Matthew Community is made up primarily of gay Roman Catholics who serve the Church in a variety of ministries.
> We visit the sick, shut-ins, and those in need, both in hospitals and at home. We bring the Blessed Sacrament to them, and ensure that a priest is available if they need one. We share our time and prayers with them, giving of ourselves. . . .
>
> We work closely with our Roman Catholic parish, offering our various talents and abilities.
> We have public Mass celebrated weekly in our Community House, and more often as a priest is available. We have a lecture series conducted in conjunction with these Masses.[175]

According to the communication in which the change of name was announced, the organization "requested and received constructive criticism, advice, and workable guidelines to consider from diocesan officials, priests, religious, and friends."[176] It is also indicated that the community has been "given the opportunity to make our parish focus solid and meaningful by participating in worship at Sacred Heart Chapel." The establishment of a working relationship with Church officials is certainly beyond anything acceptable by the Catholic Church. The reference to "Sacred Heart Chapel" is obscure although it indicates that this homosexual order has established a relationship with a local church.

The Christian Community Association (CCA). Although centered in Calgary (Alberta, Canada), this organization has many members in the United States, counting as its "Chief Advisor" Brother William Roberts,

CSSR, of New York.[177] It was founded in May 1979 by "Brother" Gerald Moran, BFCC, a former member of a "straight" religious community. This organization promotes various levels of religious organization, the most advanced of which requires a fully monastic live-in lifestyle. The traditional vows (Poverty, Obedience, and Chastity) have been renamed "Sharing, Commitment, and Charity." The following quotes from the original document sent to inquirers interested in information about the Christian Community Association (November 1979) illustrate the character of the organization:

> Each religious house would be autonomous and set its own rules and regulations according to the wishes of the local members and the needs of the homosexual community being served. . . .
>
> It is my conviction that God is calling many gay Catholics to the religious life— again. I believe that homosexuality is a gift from God and that we have an obligation to use all our gifts in the service of humanity, and that this is one way in which we return our gift to God—through religious community. I believe that our unique situation (orientation) is a "call" in itself; a call to serve God and His people. . . .
>
> My concern is that religious houses be established as an alternative to present restrictive communities, so that the homosexual can fulfill (answer) God's call, serve humanity more completely and enjoy an environment in which we can communicate freely and openly with God and our neighbor through prayer, meditation, ministry.[178]

In the third issue of the CCA newsletter, Moran acknowledged that "I have long dreamed of forming a religious order for homosexuals, as some of you have also dreamed."

Membership in CCA has grown continuously since its foundation. A careful examination of several issues of its newsletter reveals considerable support from certain priests and religious. Gerald Moran belongs to the Brothers for a Christian Community, several members of which are also members of the Catholic Coalition for Gay Civil Rights. The nature of the relationship between CCA and BFCC, if any, is not clear. The Brothers for a Christian Community were sufficiently large and well organized to hold a "General Assembly" in 1980.

Morning Star Community. This final example of a homosexual religious community was founded in Kansas City some time during 1978. The very name of the organization is probably extremely offensive to Catholics, who use the title "Morning Star" to describe, as they believe, the ever-virgin Mother of Jesus. A letter by one of the members of the Morning Star Community to a Salvatorian Provincial is reprinted below (Figure 10). Written with frankness and candor, this letter sheds light on the degree to which homosexuality has infected the Catholic Church. It was

Religious Organizations and the Movement

made available to the author by Father Robert Nugent, SDS, a member of the Salvatorian Order and a founder of New Ways Ministry. The letter included the following handwritten note: "Dear Bob, I wrote and told him about you and that you would be interested. Take care! Myron." The provincial obviously knew where to refer the writer. It is instructive to note that the rule of the Morning Star Community is based on a document of the School Sisters of Notre Dame, the order of nuns which contributes the greatest number of members to the Catholic Coalition for Gay Civil Rights. Sister Jeannine Gramick, New Ways Ministry codirector, is a member of this order.

Unless the Catholic Church is to renounce some of its most strongly held beliefs, there is no possibility that homosexual religious orders will be approved. However, their existence illustrates the degree to which homosexuality has become acceptable in certain Church circles.

Within the homosexual movement, other efforts are underway to use religion and the idea of religious life to advance the movement in new and surprising ways. In an apparent attempt to mock the Catholic Church, certain homosexual males have organized themselves into such transvestite groups as the "Sisters of the Perpetual Indulgence," giving themselves such names as "Sister Hysterectoria," "Sister Sleeze," "Sister Missionary Position," "Sister Rosanna Hosanna Fellabella," "Sister Sit," "Mother Inferior," "Sister Atrociata," "Sister Appasionata," and others equally offensive. These individuals dress as nuns and are regular participants in homosexual events. Similar groups have sprung up in other parts of the country, as well as in Australia and Canada. In Virginia Beach, they have called themselves "Sisters of the Guiltless Procession" and in Atlanta, "Sisters of Perpetual Motion." It appears that Roman Catholic nuns have tried to establish a "dialogue" with the homosexual "sisters."[180] An indication of how well these "nuns" are accepted is the participation of "Sister Lovely Lashes" (of Washington's "Sisters of Constance Pleasure") at a public meeting attended by a high-ranking official of the Washington, D.C., city government. At a homosexual gathering held at the First Congregational Church in Washington on December 12, 1981, City Councilman John Ray was charged with drawing the winning ticket in a raffle from a bucket held by a bearded man dressed as a Roman Catholic nun.[181] These individuals are taken seriously within the homosexual movement. In Australia, two "sisters" provided the "blessing" for a National Campaign Against Police Harassment of Lesbians and Gay Men in a religious service featuring candles, incense, and the singing of the hymn "Thank You, Lord, for Gay Liberation."[182]

New Ways Ministry. In a sense, New Ways Ministry (NWM) is the dream of the homosexual movement come true. It embodies a nonprofit organization directed by a bona fide Catholic priest (Father Robert Nugent) and a real nun (Sister Jeannine Gramick), with a staff person who belongs to a non-canonical religious congregation (Brother Rick Garcia, BFCC), situated at the doors of the nation's capital (a block from the District line in Mount Rainier, Maryland) with easy access to the highest concentration of seminaries and religious houses in the United States. The group specializes in publishing prohomosexual literature with a Catholic flavor, lobbying for prohomosexual legislation, holding educational and religious meetings for homosexuals and their sympathizers, and generally promoting the movement's ideology. One of the group's most important activities is serving as a center for a very extensive network of homosexual and prohomosexual activists within the Church. In addition, the group provides the training ground for prohomosexual activists who spend time at its facilities as "interns."

NWM describes itself as "an organization founded in 1977 to serve as a bridge between gay and nongay groups . . . which has provided educational programs, resources, and consultation services for a wide variety of dioceses, seminaries, colleges, religious orders, universities, peace and justice groups, and has published documents from Holland and England."[183] The prohomosexual character of this organization is apparent to anyone reading its materials. An announcement for a June 1981 retreat to take place in an undisclosed "Catholic retreat facility in the Milwaukee area" indicated as topic "the meaning of gay spirituality for lesbians and gay Catholics," pointing out that there would be "presentations on the experience of being gay and Catholic, values in the gay world, how gay people relate to the Church, gay ministry and the coming out process."[184] Neither of the organization's founders, or for that matter its board members, staff, or interns, are on record so far as we could determine, as accepting the Catholic Church's official teaching that homosexual actions are intrinsically evil. We could not find any statements emanating from New Ways Ministry condemning or attacking *any* homosexual practices. Speakers at its functions and fundraisers include such people as Brian McNaught, an avowed active homosexual writer; Attorney Leonard Graff, who represented a homosexual student group against Georgetown University[185] and who has advertised in the *Washington Blade*;[186] Marry Puchall, a clinical psychologist who also advertises in the *Washington Blade*; Mary Mendola, a former nun, "one-time Catholic," and author of a major "study" of homosexual couples; and similar spokesmen for the homosexual ideology.

A typical expression of NWM's beliefs is its response to Baltimore Archbishop Borders when his opposition to prohomosexual legislation proved to be the key to its defeat. The reader will notice that, while NWM is quick to "acknowledge" the authentic teaching of the Church, there are no expressions of support for it. As a matter of fact, the excerpts which follow clearly show the prohomosexual bias of the group:

To claim that homosexual actions are immoral is certainly the perogative [*sic*]of

```
                                    Mr. Edward Freeman
                                    Morning Star Community
                                    4129 Harrison St.
                                    Kansas City, MO.64110


Very Rev. Myron Wagner, S.D.S.
1735 Hi Mount Blvd.
Milwaukee, WI.53208

29 January, 1979

Dear Fr. Wagner,
```

During 1978 I heard several references made of the
Salvatorians' work among homosexuals. Although none of us can
make any conclusive judgments regarding the theological and
pastoral labrynth of ministry to homosexuals, I feel great
solidarity with you and your congregation for your courage.
Just shy of wondering whether an irreparable wound had been
struck between the Church and the gay community when McNeill was
silenced, prejudice toward the ecclesiastical powers that be
led me to think that the Church was clearly charting a course
in unknown waters unknown even to God. So live and learn ...
I was wrong.

I'll get right down to my reason for writing. The diocese
of Kansas City, Mo. and the archdiocese of Kansas City, KS. are
seriously considering a joint venture in gay ministry. A priest
(Kansas City, KS.) has found a favorable response from both
bishops (John Sullivan, MO. and Joseph Strecker, KS.) after
approaching them with the prospect of such an outreach. In fact,
Bishop Sullivan has responded by including gay ministry as a
part of his recent administrative genius: the lay pastoral
ministry center. Many persons read the Kansas City area with
fundamentalist lenses, but because there is a marked confluence
of lifestyles in the metro area, tolerance seems to have the
upper hand. I think I say this primarily because Kansas City
Catholics have recently gone through the national ecumenical
charismatic conf. as well as the sticky mess between Sullivan
and Christ the King parish (NCR, Aug. and Sept. issues). This
leads me to think there is fertile ground here for making a
Catholic pastoral wedge in the gay community. Part of my reason
in writing is to pass along this info.

Specifically I want to draw your attention to a lifestyle
alternative for homosexuals in Kansas Ciy called Morning Star
Community. Morning Star is in its embryonic stage development,
not quite a year old. I consider it experimental, but it's not
likely to fold tomorrow due to financial commitments from
members and the prospect of new members month by month. The
community is residential (at the above address) and shares an
ecumenical Christian rule based on the S.S.N.S. document, You
Are Sent. Meals and prayers are in common on weekdays. Optional
meals and prayers are frequently attended on weekends, too. The
community numbers six members and one associate member presently
... a mixture of men and women. There is a lesbian couple in
the house, but the others are single. Not all the single persons
are celibate, but I can honestly say that I don't hear just talk
about chastity in this community. Thses people seem to think
deeply about their sexual activity in light of developing relationships which help them better understand God's grace.

FIGURE 10
Letter from Edward Freeman of Morning Star Community to
the Very Rev. Myron Wagner, SDS.

The gospel is active in this community. Some days I wake
up wondering whether the community is more a lost sheep or
prodigal or whether this small band of gay Christians is more
a herald for the Morning Star. But when I conjure up distinctions
like this I see that the only way to ministry in this generation
is to lose oneself in the labrynth ... we can't bind any wounds
from a distance: Emmanuel.

Is it possible that a Salvatorian who is currently involved
with ministry to gays might make a visit to the Morning Star
Community? I could arrange a visit to correspond with an overview
of gay ministry in both dioceses and/or a possible retreat for the
Kansas City Dignity chapter. If a visit is possible, we would want
to make the most of the exprience both for the Salvatorian and
all the gay Catholics in the area.

And consideration you can give my request is much appreciated.
You can see that I am rather proud of Morning Star Community.
Such a visit could bring meaningful learning between us and mean
the founding of similar communities wherever Salvatorians are
doing ministry among gays.

Keeping you in prayer and wishing you everything good.

Sincerely,

(Signature: Ed Freeman)

Edward Freeman

any particular religious group; but to claim that they are also "socially destructive" is a sociological, legal, psychological and anthropological judgment requiring concrete data from empirical sciences or human history. We believe there is no such proof at this time. All known societies and cultures have experienced the phenomenon of homosexual people and have responded to them with everything from punishment by death to toleration and control. Human societies have always been and will continue to be heterosexually oriented on the whole. In societies that have recognized the rights of the homosexual minority there is absolutely no proof whatsoever indicative of any socially destructive effects. . . .

Homosexual "practice" can also mean holding hands, embracing, same-sex dancing and other signs both moral and legal relating to the emotional-affective component of being homosexually oriented.

While we recognize and uphold the right of the Catholic Church to teach on the morality of homosexual acts and while we recognize this teaching, we believe it is a dangerous policy for a religious group to want to punish private behavior it judges "contrary to God's will," an attitude all too reminiscent of the Inquisition, the Reformation, witch burnings and Nazi Germany.[187]

In its response to the statement of New England bishops against the ordination of homosexuals, NWM openly advocated a policy of ordaining homosexuals, equating homosexuality with race: "We are disturbed when we hear you demanding 'heterosexual maturity' as a requirement . . . excluding a person solely on the basis of sexual orientation is as unjust and morally repugnant as excluding a person on the basis of skin color . . ."[188] Another argument to bolster its position used the assumption that homosexuality exists not only among priests, but among bishops as well: "Listen with trust and openness to the voices of your homosexually oriented brother priests and bishops who are free . . . to share with you their experiences of being chaste, happy and fulfilled ministers."[189]

The following statement of NWM, made in response to Archbishop Quinn's strongly antihomosexual letter, can be translated to common English as asserting the twin principles of the organization: 1) Homosexual actions are morally correct and to be approved according to "progressive" Catholic principles; and 2) The Catholic Church stands in need of and will continue to be educated concerning homosexuality.

The *Bay State Reporter* presented it in this way:

Gay Catholics, according to New Ways, will continue to strive "honestly, openly and concientiously [*sic*] to live morally healthy lives according to their own insights and within the limits of their sexuality" as well as "press the Catholic community for dialogue, reflection and understanding of sexual orientation and responsible moral behavior." It also expresses the hope that the letter and the responses it evokes will serve to help people reexamine positions and promote "open and trusting dialogue . . . which is so necessary for the whole Church as we move together in the fact of so many mysteries including homosexuality on our common journey to the Lord."[190]

Although NWM presents itself as a Catholic organization, the loyalties of the group are mixed at best. When the interests of the homosexual movement run contrary to the explicit teachings or the policy of the Church, one can almost predict where NWM will fall. In preparation for the fight against the Archdiocese of New York for its antihomosexual position, Brother Rick Garcia, BFCC, of NWM contacted the Archdiocese to request information on the Church's position on the City's proposed prohomosexual bill. This was part of a strategy devised by personnel of New York's National Gay Task Force. In a letter from the NGTF, Brother Garcia was instructed: "Of course, any and all expressions of support for the bill—especially to impediments such as the Archdiocese of New York— are extremely important. You might like to contact them and ask for their position on the issue; that will give you *exactly* what arguments they are using and make your rebuttal all the more pertinent."[191] Brother Garcia promptly followed the instructions in a letter to the Archdiocese and a "report" to the NGTF. These two letters, both dated January 9, 1981, are reprinted together so that the reader can contrast them in terms of style, intent, etc. (Figures 11-A and 11-B).

It is impossible to examine the homosexual movement within the Roman Catholic Church without taking NWM into consideration, but the status of the organization within the Church is far from clear. In June 1979, R. Adam DeBaugh reported that Father Nugent's faculties to exercise the ministry had been suspended and that he was under canonical discipline on account of his outspokenness within the homosexual movement.[192] Yet in his Baltimore testimony in favor of prohomosexual legislation, Father Nugent indicated that "I am officially assigned by my religious superiors to a ministry with homosexual people and I carry out this work as codirector of New Ways Ministry."[193] From the handwritten note added to the January 29, 1979, letter from Edward Freeman to the Very Reverend Myron Wagner, SDS, it is apparent that Father Nugent's superiors not only are aware of but also support this priest's activities (see Figure 8). As a matter of fact, Father Nugent seems to have left his original diocese (Philadelphia) to join the Salvatorian order in search of a freer environment which would enable him to work within the homosexual movement.[194] Father Nugent does not have faculties in the Archdiocese of Washington, where he resides and where New Ways Ministry is located.[195] Church authorities in Washington have circulated a letter clarifying that, in spite of its name and purported religious affiliation, New Ways Ministry has no official status as a Church organization.[196]

New Ways Ministry scheduled a "First National Symposium on Homosexuality and the Catholic Church" to coincide with the end of the official meeting of the Roman Catholic bishops in Washington on November 20, 1981.[197] The symposium was originally scheduled at a seminary, but apparently the response was so great that the facilities there were inadequate to the large number of registrants, mostly nuns and religious according to Sister Jeannine Gramick, SSND.[198] It is interesting to note that after the seminary proved too small, the group tried to move the event to the National 4-H Center. Upon examination of the subject to be discussed, the National 4-H Council decided not to accept the Symposium at the Center. After an unsuccessful attempt to force the National 4-H Center to accept the homosexual symposium via a court injunction, the event was moved to a commercial facility.[199] Meanwhile, Washington's Archbishop James Hickey wrote letters to all Catholic bishops in the U.S., as well as to religious personnel in the Washington area, indicating that New Ways Ministry's understanding of homosexuality was in clear conflict with Catholic teaching.[200] Two bishops had apparently accepted invitations to speak at the homosexual event, but were dissuaded from doing so when Hickey spoke with one of them and one of Washington's Auxiliary bishops spoke with the other.[201] Hickey's letter to the bishops clearly expressed his view that New Ways Ministry's position is unacceptable for Catholics:

> I must inform you that I found their (NWM's) position ambiguous and unclear with regard to the morality of homosexual activity. While presenting the teaching of the church as contained in the Declaration on Sexual Ethics of the Sacred Congregation for the Doctrine of Faith (1975), they present as viable other options which hold that it is morally permissible for homosexuals to live together in a sexually active, stable relationship.[202]

A measure of the support the homosexual movement can muster within the Catholic Church is provided by the attendance at the symposium. According to New Ways Ministry, 78 percent of the attendees were nuns, religious, or diocesan priests or brothers.[203] It was reported that ". . . the 150 participants were evenly divided between the sexes and that they included 18 major superiors of orders, 20 vocation or formation directors in religious orders, 13 representatives of diocesan organizations and 8 members of 'Dignity,' . . ."[204] Among others, the following religious orders were represented: Dominicans, Franciscans, Sisters of St. Joseph, Ursulines, Maryknolls, Paulists, Capuchins, Augustinians, Carmelites, and Christian Brothers.[205]

The importance of the event was noted by Dignity. In an article on one of the attendees, Andrew Humm of Dignity/New York commented approvingly: "She attended the recent New Ways Symposium on the Church and homosexuality in Washington. 'It was planned for 60 people and 180 showed up despite Archbishop Hickey's letter to all bishops

9 January, 1981

Fr. Damien
Archdiocese of New York (212) 371-1000
Office of Communications
1011 First Avenue,
New York, NY 10022

called Feb 27
will "resend" the
statement.

Dear Fr. Damien,

        Thank you for your phone call this afternoon. As per our conversation this afternoon, could you sent me a copy of the official position of the Archdiocese of New York on the anti-discrimination legislation relative to homosexually oriented women and men? I think the bill is Intro 384, but I'm not sure of the number this time around.

        We are a national Catholic center involved in education and ministry to sexual minorities, their families, friends and the larger Catholic community. We like to keep track of legislation relative to the human and civil rights of lesbians and gay men and the Church's response to it.

        I look forward to hearing from you soon regarding this matter. Thanking you in advance, I am,

Sincerely yours,

(Bro.) Rick Garcia, BFCC
New Ways Ministry Staff

FIGURE 11-A
Letter from New Ways Ministry Staff Regarding New York City's Gay Rights Bill
(Intro 384).

9 January, 1981

Jesse Lowen
National Gay Taskforce
80 Fifth Avenue
New York, NY 10011

Dear Jesse,

Many thanks for your prompt reply to my inquirey about the status of New York City's Gay rights bill and influence of the Archdiocese of New York City.

I have contact the Archdiocese Director of Communications and spoke with him about the Archdiocese official position. He will be sending me a copy of that position. With that in hand we will be better prepared to respond to its 'problem'.

I feel that New Ways Ministry can be of use in combatting the Archdiocese as we are a Roman Catholic organization involved full time in gay rights and gay ministry. We have prominent supporters within the Catholic Church all over the country and many in New York City.

If you hear of anything concerning this Intro or the Catholic Church's stand on it we would appreciate being made aware of it. If we can be of service to you in any way-please do not hesitate to contact us. I remain, fraternally yours,

In the struggle for justice,

(Bro.) Rick Garcia, BFCC
Staff, New Ways Ministry

FIGURE 11-B
Letter from New Ways Ministry Staff Regarding New York City's Gay Rights Bill
(Intro 384).

disavowing it and questioning New Ways' theology. And 75% of the participants were provincials, directors of formation, or major leaders in their communities. That's a sign of hope that Church leadership is responsive to the issue of homophobia.' "[206] Although it cannot be said that New Ways Ministry is a Catholic organization in any real sense of the term, its very existence is more than passively tolerated. Should Church authorities—especially the Archbishop of Washington, D.C.—desire to see the end of New Ways Ministry or the Catholic Coalition for Gay Civil Rights, the creative application of Canon Law would provide the required means. Such an application was utilized in the case of the Miami priest who, having made public confession of being a homosexual, was declared "pastorally unassignable" and relegated to "ecclesiastical limbo."[207] As religious, the codirectors of New Ways Ministry have vowed obedience to superiors who could be pressured effectively into recalling them and assigning them to legitimate ministries. After all, the Society of the Divine Savior and the Sisters of Notre Dame depend upon permission of the bishops to transact business as religious congregations. Should the hierarchy decide to "close down" New Ways Ministry, the Vatican would most likely strongly support such a move. In this regard, New Ways Ministry appears to be a case in which "lack of action" can be legitimately construed to be "passive encouragement."

Dignity. Dignity is by far the best known of all Catholic homosexual organizations and probably the largest homosexual religious group after the Universal Fellowship of Metropolitan Community Churches. Founded in 1969 by Father John McNeill, S.J., and others,[208] Dignity today has some 100 chapters in the U.S. and Canada,[209] organized into eleven regions run by "Region Directors," and an international President with an office in Washington D.C. (See appendix for Dignity addresses.) Dignity has some four thousand members and holds biennial conventions, the last of which met in Philadelphia in September 1981.[210] Purposes of Dignity are: "to unite all gay Catholics, to develop leadership, and to be an instrument through which the gay Catholic may be heard by the Church and society."[211] The organization has distinguished itself for its advocacy role in favor of homosexuals everywhere and for its boldness in opposing the Church when the interests or ideology of the homosexual movement have aroused the opposition of the Roman Catholic leadership.

The scope of this organization cannot be fully discussed in this section, which is meant to supplement what has been presented elsewhere in this work. It is necessary, however, to elucidate the position of Dignity in the area of sexual morality, inasmuch as the practice of homosexuality has been so explicitly and repeatedly condemned by the Church, part of which Dignity purports to be.

The Statement of Position and Purpose is as favorable to the practice of homosexuality as it could be without explicitly contradicting the teachings of the Church: "We believe that gays can express their sexuality in a manner that is consonant with Christ's teaching. We believe that all sexuality should be exercised in an ethically responsible and unselfish way."[212] While few people could disagree with the second sentence (unless prepared to advocate "irresponsibility" or "selfishness"), the first statement does seem to imply that Dignity accepts the practice of homosexuality as morally correct. The extensive research undertaken in the preparation of this work did not reveal any statement by Dignity or its officials that indicated acceptance of the Church's teachings in the area of sexual ethics.

The position of Dignity becomes clearer when various statements made by the organization or its leaders are examined. According to Dignity:

> As members of Dignity, we wish to promote the cause of the gay community. To do this we must accept our responsibility to the Church, to society, and to the individual gay Catholic to work for the acceptance of gays as full and equal members of the one Christ.
> We further believe that all sexuality should be exercised in an ethically responsible and unselfish way. The emphasis of Dignity is on the total human person, not just sexuality.
> We move towards a time when a gay Catholic life-style is accepted. Gays expressing their sexuality in a manner that is in harmony with Christ's teachings in an ethically responsible and unselfish way, can only bring that time closer to us.[213]
>
> For a gay Catholic who has come to an understanding of his-her sexual orientation and is attempting to integrate it into a full and active life within the Catholic community, the Sacrament of Penance becomes necessary—as in all cases—where there is some conscious awareness of having violated in a serious manner one's basic commitment to self-sacrificing love in the manner of Jesus Christ, either in the sexual realm or in any other aspect of the whole Christian life.
> As a result of a new consciousness on the part of some gay Catholics, sacramental confession can begin to take on a new dimension. The focal point would no longer be confessing one's homosexuality (or homosexual acts) but one's failure to live up to the demands of the Faith (including responsible sexual behavior) and on-going conversion as a homosexual. This new perspective can provide the religious situation in which a gay person can face and challenge his-her reactions to the pressures of living in an oppressive situation, such as loneliness, despair, sexual objectification, infidelity, animosity towards homosexuals, etc.[214]

Translated to "normal" English, this means that the only rule of morality is consensuality rather than the objective nature of the actions, and that homosexual behavior is to be accepted as a legitimate lifestyle.

The chairman of Dignity/Baltimore has emphasized in an interview the value of being homosexual from a Catholic viewpoint:

We are within the Roman Catholic Church, we participate at all levels. The only difference is that we are gay and lesbian, and we believe that is consonant with Christ's teachings.

Q. Why do you bother? Why don't you leave the church?
A. Because I feel that within my heart we are right, that a person can be gay and still be Christian, that there is not the hellfire and brimstone. I think the gay person has contributed a lot to society in the past and will continue to do so. God must have something in mind. Why is it in history that about 10 percent of the population is gay? In time there will be a vindication.[215]

The following is excerpted from a letter from Miller to the editor of a Baltimore publication: "As members of Dignity we are a gay presence in the Church and a Christian presence within the gay community. We are proud that we can bring Christian values and beliefs to the gay community and equally proud that we can bring our gayness before the Church."[216] The reader is reminded that "gayness" means that quality of a person which compels him to seek sexual intercourse with people of his own sex while accepting this condition as good in itself.

Although without great fanfare, Dignity seems to be actively involved in the "blessing of gay couples," or a commitment ritual identical to marriage between heterosexual couples in all but name. The appendix includes documents produced by Dignity/Los Angeles and Dignity/New York which describe the process by which two homosexuals can "marry" in Dignity-style (including "pre-matrimonial" instructions). The repeated protestations throughout the documents that a "gay union" is not a marriage the way the Church understands it are probably a way of avoiding conflicts with Church authorities. The ritual instructions include two options: the ceremony can take place during Mass and outside Mass. There is no indication that any Catholic bishop, even in such dioceses as Seattle, Milwaukee, Atlanta, Richmond, Jacksonville, or Miami where Dignity officials have pointed out some positive responses,[217] has ever authorized a priest to celebrate the rite of "gay union." On the other hand, Dignity Masses are often celebrated in private homes and in Catholic churches. Thus it is probable that homosexual "weddings" performed by Catholic priests do take place. In fact, the present state of disciplinary crisis affecting the Catholic Church makes it very likely that these rites are the rule rather than the exception. In any case, their very existence clearly indicates that Dignity's position calls for an unconditional acceptance of homosexual actions as normal and ethical.

A statement issued by Dignity/New York in the mid-1970s reveals the subversive nature of this organization:

The evidence seems to indicate that DIGNITY is the work of the Holy Spirit, the vehicle through which the Spirit is welding Gay Catholics into an identifiable community within the Church. More and more priests are being drawn into this work. More and more of them are coming to see the Gay Catholic in a fuller dimension, to show greater understanding and to offer far more realistic counseling in or out of the confessional. They are taking exception to the centuries-old stand of theologians. And they themselves, the theologians, are slowly re-thinking that position.[218]

The subversive character of Dignity is also seen in the testimony of one of its members, a New York nun apparently converted to the homosexual ideology in a course taught by Father John McNeill.[219] Sister Mary Lou Steele is a member of the Sisters of Charity in New York and former employee of the Archdiocese of New York. According to an article about her published by a Dignity newsletter:

> She thinks the best work Dignity can do is to liberate people from their hangups with the institutional Church. 'This community has the capacity for being an adult Christian community,' she maintains. 'If gay people would look at the way Latin-American Christians are living, they could learn a lot. Persecution can purify. I'm not saying that suffering is wonderful, but oppression can lead to a purity of faith you don't get any other way.'[220]

Sister Steele's career is dotted with instances of service to typically leftist organizations and prohomosexual groups. In addition to Dignity, she has been involved with the Catholic Peace Fellowship, the Catholic Worker, Clergy and Laity Concerned, Sisters in Gay Ministry Associated (SIGMA), and *Insight*, a Christian homosexual publication.[221] She is also the only nun who has been willing to testify in favor of prohomosexual legislation in the New York City Council.[222] Her reference to the "institutional" (as opposed to the "spiritual" Church), although typical of neo-Modernists, has no place in Catholic doctrine.

There is no question that Dignity's purpose is to make of the Catholic Church a tool of the homosexual movement. According to Dignity/Seattle, "DIGNITY's job is to point out the unmet needs of four to ten percent of the Church [the alleged homosexual Catholics], and that the current teaching must change."[223] This obviously implies that Dignity does not approach the Church to identify and accept Catholic teachings, but brings in its own ideas and agenda, working to bring the Church around to these new ideas. This attitude is so alien to traditional Catholic thinking that it places Dignity in a highly vulnerable position. This was demonstrated in a 1980 incident wherein Dignity and New Ways Ministry jointly published *Homosexual Catholics: A New Primer for Discussion*, a frankly prohomosexual booklet. At a meeting of Dignity's Executive Board in Vancouver B.C. on October 12, 1980, it was alleged that New Ways Ministry had failed to live up to their side of the agreement to be copublishers. Apparently, NWM was not supposed to fill any orders until Dignity had recovered its expenses. According to the minutes of the meeting, "Dignity Inc. has put up the front money, and the profits are to go to the authors."[224] However, "the problem began when New Ways sent out their own orders." Treasurer Joe Totten described the situation vividly: "It is more like the fall of Saigon . . . not a strain but a real demise."

The remaining minutes reveal that the financial problem was only part of the question; apparently, New Ways Ministry had also tried to exploit Dignity's weak ideological position for its own benefit. Errors in the original text have not been corrected:

> Frank Scheuren stated that the Primer came off the press, and before Dignity could do anything with it New Ways sent out a flyer to each Dignity Chapter. Jim Plack (R-6) "To claify this, is New Ways in your discussions, in part (feeling) that they don't want to co-ordinate with us, but they will use us as a catalist (for their sales), but that they want to control the situation? Is this an incorrect or correct evaluation?" Frank stated that "both cases are true."

> Joe Totten stated that he felt their first loyalty is to New Ways and that it was best to deal with them on a business level, with written contracts.

> Chris Patterson (R-9) stated that she felt that New Ways needed to be kept seperate from Dignity, and that they could be more effective that way.

> Jim Plack (R-6) asked Frank, "How do we direct chapters in this area, since we have a responsibility to Dignity Inc?"

> At this point, there was still a lot of people questioning what had happened to build up such a problem between the two organizations.

> Joe Totten stated that, "for example, The Conference of Evangelization, Bob Nugent gave the Director of that conference the opinion that Dignity Inc. was not a Catholic organization and was not in line with Catholic Teaching." It seems, Joe continued that Jeannine and Bob agree in concept on a face to face basis, but then . . . they go ahead with whatever will meet the needs of New Ways Ministry, not always considering the effects on Dignity.

> Frank, stated at this point that the officers simply wanted to make you (the board) aware of the problem. He recommended that any dealings with New Ways be done with a written contract. Dignity, had not done this, and now the officers were sorry. They had thought that they had had agreement, and find that each party is thinking something different.

Apparently, this was not the first time problems of this nature had arisen: "Frank stated that Dignity had gone to the Evangelization conference in previous years, and that if anyone should have been there (Dignity, New Ways, and Fr. Vince Inghiliterra were all trying to get in to set up booth) that Dignity should have been the one organization to get in. Frank felt that New Ways had closed the door on Dignity getting in, and as a result none of the groups got in."[225]

It is not surprising that political plays go on between organizations which have nearly identical goals and ideologies. Although the power for which they are competing is ecclesiastical, it is still power, and both Dignity and New Ways Ministry are essentially political organizations jockeying for positions within the Catholic Church. What the apparent rivalry between New Ways Ministry and Dignity reveals is not so much that they are rivals, or that Father Nugent and Sister Gramick might have behaved "dishonestly" in using Dignity's ideological weakness for their own purpose, but that Dignity's position is openly incompatible with that of the Catholic Church.

Still, Dignity is a highly successful organization. In a number of dioceses it seems to have the blessings of the bishop, and it is heard at the highest Church councils. One of its regional directors (the Reverend Pat Hoffman of Lamesa, Texas—Region VII) is a priest, and the organization counts on the support of chaplains and theological advisors. Churches are available for its uses. As Harry Dean, office manager of its international headquarters indicated to the author, "Dignity International has no official relations with the Catholic hierarchy, but in general the Church—unofficially—is encouraging of the movement."[226] In Seattle, for example, Father Ralph Carney is Vice-President of Dignity and Father Kirby Brown is its chaplain.[227] Father John Chancellor of Immaculate Conception Church celebrated Mass for Dignity on November 16, 1980. Apparently, Fr. Chancellor referred to his physical appearance during the Mass. *Dignity Seattle* commented in response that the priest "might be interested in knowing that he was the hands down winner of our best looking priest and most beautiful man contest."[228] At least five priests were scheduled to appear as speakers at Dignity's 1981 convention (John McNeill, S.J., Richard Wagner, OMI, Vincent Inghiliterra, Paul Shanley, and Robert Nugent, SDS), and the network of homosexual priests and religious was also to be a topic for discussion.[229] This indicates the great familiarity and a working relationship—on a personal level—between part of the clergy and Dignity.

One measure of Dignity's success is its ability to blend and work with other organizations which, although not in the mainstream of the Catholic Church, rally around issues that are more acceptable to the average Catholic than the defense of homosexual practices. An instance of such working relationships was a day of "study and prayer" concerning El Salvador which took place on March 27, 1982. This event was apparently part of a nationwide effort to elicit opposition to free elections in El Salvador, which eventually took place on March 28 and which resulted in a total defeat for the left. The "day" in question was held at St. Francis Xavier Church, a Jesuit parish in New York City which Dignity/New York uses for many of its functions. The program was staffed by a representative of the National Council of Churches, two sisters, one of them a member of Maryknoll, and a Jesuit priest. Among the guests announced in the program were Democratic representatives Gerry Studds of Massachusetts and Ted Weiss of New York, both cosponsors of prohomosexual legislation and known for their opposition to any aid to the people of El Salvador in their struggle against communist aggression. Although Dignity's name did not appear in the program, the invitation was mailed to members of Dignity/New York, a clear indication that Dignity shared its mailing list with organizers of the event. The invitation was made available to the author by a member of Dignity/New York, who received it in his capacity as a member of this homosexual organization.[230]

Dignity has close connections with other components of the homosexual movement. In April, 1982, the national Dignity organization mailed a subscription package for the *Advocate*, a large homosexual publication. The package included highly erotic illustrations, a letter from the publisher of the *Advocate*, a letter from the president of Dignity, and a coupon offer for a cut rate subscription.[231] The *Advocate* regularly publishes advertisements for homoerotic movies, homosexual prostitutes and men performing homosexual acts. In exchange for its favor to the *Advocate*, Dignity received credit to advertise freely in such a publication. Although Dignity does have the appearance of a Catholic organization—even as it maintains no formal relationships with the Church—it is obvious that it is a very peculiar form of Catholic organization.

In accomplishing its ultimate goal of making the Catholic Church useful to the homosexual movement, Dignity utilizes the standard practices of all pressure groups: organization, demonstrations, meetings, "retreats," person-to-person contacts, etc. Specifically, two strategies are used by Dignity:

On a *personal* basis, Dignity works to turn homosexuals into "gays" according to the tenets of the homosexual ideology, but using the Catholic Church as the sociocultural matrix: "The local effort is directed primarily to working with the individual, helping him/her to accept his/her homosexuality, helping each to be a better Christian."[232] As a priest preaching a Dignity Retreat indicated, "being gay is a blessing, not a curse."[233] In this view homosexuality not only satisfies the needs of the flesh (cf. Dignity's ritual of blessing gay couples in appendix), but also has the approval of God Himself.

Toward the rest of the Church, Dignity has applied great pressure (e.g., demonstrating, joining boycotts, writing letters, making public appearances) while simultaneously offering peace . . . if only the Church agrees to support, or at least not to oppose, the homosexual movement. This carrot-stick approach has been used unsuccessfully in New York, but apparently has been highly successful in Baltimore and other dioceses.[234]

368

Convention Workshop Status as of 2/15/81

Topic	Leader
Relationships: Establishing and Maintaining	Mary Mendola
Lifestyles: Alternatives to Monogamy	Eromin Center (T)
Coping with Stress: Breaking Up and Starting Over	Dr. Len Gershman
Gay/Lesbian Health Care	TBA
Women/Men Relationships: Male Perspective	TBA
Women/Men Relationships: Female Perspective	Barbara Gittings (T)
Spiritual Growth	(Rev.) John McNeill, S.J.
Married Gays	Pat Russoniello
Beatitudes: Magna Carta for Gay Rights and Morality	Dave Innocenti
Gay Morality/Ethics	TBA
Clerical/Lay Love Relationships	(Rev.) Declan Daly
The Tie That Binds: The Relationship Between Ex-Seminarians and Their Church	Brian McNaught, Tom Oddo (T)
Sexuality	(Rev.) Richard Wagner, OMI
Ageism/Aging	Mark Solomon
Celibacy	(Bro.) Bill Roberts
Ceremonies of Commitment	Dignity/Washington, DC
Prayerful Worship	(Rev.) Bob Hovda
Dignity: Permanent or Provisional?	Paul Diderich (T)
Repentance and Reconciliation: Sacramental Celebration	Jim Dallen
Ministry of/to the Chaplain	Mike McDonald
Chapters and Chanceries	(Rev.) Vince Inghiliterra
Gays and the New Politics	David Brudnoy, Ginny Apuzzo (T)
Ecumenism in the Gay Community	(Rev.) Paul Shanley, Louis Crew, Troy Perry, Frank Scheuren, Allen Bennett (T)
Chapter Public Relations	Hal Wand
Alcohol and Drug Abuse	Bill Lundgren
Coming Out (2 different workshops)	Gary McDonald
	(Sr.) Jeannine Gramick, SSND
Chapter Newsletters	Jim Highland
Lesbians and Organized Religion	Nancy Krody
Social Justice	Jim Wolfe (T)
Thomas Merton and Homosexuality	(Rev.) Bob Nugent SDS
Handicapped Gays and Lesbians	TBA
Leadership in Dignity	Deenie Dudley
Outreach: Designing and Implementing a Program for Chapters	Portland Chapter & Sue Woodruff
Assertion without Desertion	Sandra Boston (T)
Gay Clergy and Religious Network	*Communications**
The Development of Christian Morality, as Illustrated by Issues of Slavery, Democracy and Capitalism	Tim Ryan

*Probably a reference to the publishers of *Communication,* the newsletter for homosexual priests and nuns.

The list on page 369 of subjects and discussion leaders, proposed for Dignity's 1981 convention, illustrates the breadth of this organization's interests and its potential effect not only on the rest of the Church, but on society at large. Some of the names are already familiar to the reader, who is directed especially to the workshops on "Lifestyles: Alternatives to Monogamy," "Ceremonies of Commitment," "Clerical/Lay Love Relationships," and "Gay Clergy and Religious Network." In view of the official position of the Church on the morality of homosexual behavior, the very use of these subjects, with their obvious meaning for Dignity is nothing less than startling. [235]

Dignity is a large, powerful organization with its own dynamics, ideology, priests, ritual, and vested interests. Apparently, it encompasses all the peculiarities of the homosexual condition, as reportedly there is a club within Dignity for sadomasochists. [236] Should the bishops reassert their authority against its obviously subversive character, it is difficult to believe that Dignity will disband, or agree to become a Church instrument for inducing its members and other Catholic homosexuals to "fall in line." It is more likely that it would simply break away and become . . . a homosexual Catholic church. Naturally, Dignity would fight such a move, since its whole raison d'être is to make the Catholic Church useful to the homosexual movement. Once it was formally outside the Catholic Church, its usefulness to the movement would greatly decrease. If the Catholic bishops take a stand, however, the likelihood is that rank-and-file Catholics would support such a move.

Case Study: American Judaism

Although Jews play a very active role in American social and political life, their small number (less than 2.5 percent of the population) and traditionally nonproselitistic attitude has made most Americans unaware of religious developments within the Jewish traditions. Still less is known about the relationships between American Judaism and the homosexual movement.

THE TEACHINGS
The Old Testament, considered normative for Judaism, apparently condemns homosexuality without equivocation. Scholars who accept the critical method for understanding the Scriptures have managed to explain away the obvious meaning of the words, but in a question of this importance no passages can be cited which defend the practice of homosexuality,

while many passages indicate that it is incompatible with the law of God. These have been examined elsewhere.

It is important to note, moreover, that other ancient Jewish authorities are unanimous in their condemnation of homosexual practices. Philo, a Jewish philosopher, describes in this fashion the sexual excesses of the men of Sodom:

> They threw off from their necks the law of nature and applied themselves to deep drinking of strong liquor and dainty feeding and forbidden forms of intercourse. Not only in their mad lust for women did they violate the marriages of their neighbors, but also men mounted males without respect for the sex nature which the active partner shares with the passive. . . . Then, as little by little they accustomed those who were by nature men to submit to play the part of women, they saddled them with the formidable curse of a female disease.[237]

Another author, Josephus, is equally clear in his condemnation of homosexual practices. In *Jewish Antiquities* XV 28–29, he speaks approvingly of Herod's decision not to send young Aristobulus to Rome lest he be sodomized by Anthony. He also takes pride in the Jewish traditional abhorrence of homosexual acts and the death penalty attached to them according to the Code of Holiness (*Against Apion* II 199). Josephus's comment on the sin of the men of Sodom reveals how the traditional interpretation of the story in Genesis already existed at his time: "The Sodomites, on seeing these young men of remarkably fair appearance whom Lot had taken under his roof, were bent only on violence and outrage to their youthful beauty." (*Antiquities* I. 200–201).[238]

Even liberal Jewish authors concur that their tradition does not look favorably on homosexuality:

> References in Talmudic and post-Talmudic sources—likewise relatively few—remain consistent with the Biblical prohibition. Whatever the question at issue—whether two men may share the same blanket, or even be together in private; whether two women may sleep in the same room; whether climatic conditions stimulate homosexual temptation; whether Jews are likely to be influenced by the homosexual behavior of non-Jews; whether the age of the homosexual offender should be a factor in determining culpability; what the appropriate punishment is, in theory and in practice; whether the punishment should be the same for male and female offenders; whether rumors concerning a fellow Jew's homosexuality should be given credence; which privileges, communal and synagogal, should be denied to a homosexual—every single decision, pro or con, takes for granted that a homosexual act is a moral perversion, an outrageous and disgusting deed, a serious violation of the Torah's command and, therefore, a grave sin. It would, thus, appear absolutely clear that a Jewish

approach to homosexuality must end where and as it starts: with utter condemnation and categorical prohibition.[239]

Of the three branches of American Judaism, the Reformed is the most disposed to accept homosexuality, as will be seen later. At the other extreme, orthodox Jews have clearly indicated their decision to remain faithful to the Jewish tradition. Spokesmen for orthodox Judaism have been quick to speak their minds and act according to their convictions, as in the following cases.

Rabbi Manuel M. Poliakoff of Baltimore's Beth Isaac Adath Israel Congregation has indicated that for him homosexuality is a "mental disease" which must be opposed even by the coercive power of the state: "Don't say, 'Remove the hardship so you can continue with your disease' " was the language he used in opposition to Baltimore's prohomosexual legislation.[240]

Abraham Gross, spokesman for seven organizations representing a thousand rabbis and one-and-a-half-million orthodox Jews has indicated that "While we do not support the harassment of homosexuals, the Bible condemns the practice of homosexuality."[241]

One of the strongest Jewish spokesmen against homosexuality is Rabbi Abraham B. Hecht, president of the Rabbinical Alliance of America (500 rabbis) and spiritual leader of the congregation Shaare Zion in Brooklyn, New York. According to Rabbi Hecht, homosexuality must be stopped or "the institution of marriage will go out of style and children will become strange creatures—unwanted and unloved. Our country cannot afford the spread of this disease which is destroying the fabric of the traditional family unit."[242] Moreover, "We are not opposed to homosexuals. We are opposed to homosexuality as a way of life. We pity the poor who practice homosexuality and we are prepared to help them tear away from this sexual aberration. We are not discriminating against any minority. We are opposed to the philosophy of homosexuality."

The reason he disapproves of prohomosexual legislation is also clear:

> You are giving legal stature to an aberration. You don't give special rights to drunks or dope addicts and in this case you should not give special minority status to homosexuals.
> This would demolish family life, as children would see the homosexual lifestyle. We are also bringing the threat of child molesters into the backyard and hallways.
> Policemen and firemen are mature men and can physically reject any improper advances, but what about the poor innocent child? Who will protect them?

For this reason he assails religious leaders who do not oppose the rising tide of the homosexual movement. According to him, religious leaders

Religious Organizations and the Movement

"must come out forcefully with a very strong condemnation of homosexuality, so that there is no doubt in the minds of society as to the position of the spiritual and religious clergy leadership of this country." The basis of his argument is not only biblical; it is also centered in the natural law. Homosexuality, according to Rabbi Hecht, is a "deathstyle" and not a lifestyle, "for it stints everything the word life stands for—procreation, new life, vigor."

More liberal Jewish writers tend to be lenient on the question, although homosexuality is never elevated to the level of heterosexuality in terms of its normative nature. Matt's position, for example, would coincide with the traditional nonjudgmentality of Christian moralists: "God alone, therefore, has the ability and the right to judge a person's culpability; and that none of us humans, therefore, ought presume to judge a homosexual or automatically regard a homosexual as a sinner—since, as already implied, sin involves not only overt action but also intention, decision, and responsibility."[243] This might be an acceptable moral principle. In the public forum, however, it does not have much value, since the effects of behavior follow regardless of the intention of their author. Matt concludes, however, that all jobs (even those of teacher or rabbi) should be open to homosexuals,[244] and seems to accept the concepts of homosexual synagogues and marriages.[245] These ideas would be rejected by Jews of the orthodox tradition.

ORGANIZATIONS AND ACTIVITIES

Homosexual Jews have organized themselves in homosexual synagogues for the same reason that other homosexuals have founded organizations of all sorts. As part of the homosexual community, they believe that they are in need of expressing themselves in terms of their religion and also as homosexuals. This social expression is coextensive with acceptance of the homosexual ideology and the promotion of its tenets. As of September 1981 there were twenty-one homosexual synagogues in the United States and several others abroad. It appears that there is a rabbi in San Francisco who is openly homosexual. In Israel, the homosexual organization takes the name of "Society for the Protection of Personal Rights." (The reader may find in the appendix the names and addresses of homosexual synagogues.)

Homosexual synagogues sometimes meet in churches. Washington's Beth Mishpachah meets at Christ United Methodist Church and Chicago's Or Chadash meets at the Second Unitarian Church. If they belong to a wider body of religious organizations, it is usually the Union of American Hebrew Congregations, the "Reformed" branch of American Judaism. Jewish homosexual organizations have formed the World Congress of Gay and Lesbian Jewish Organizations, formed at a conference of homosexual

Jews held in response to the UN resolution declaring Zionism to be a racist ideology.[246]

The largest of the homosexual synagogues is New York City's Beth Simchat, which meets in Greenwich Village and has hundreds of worshipers at its Friday evening services. This organization is "involved in United Jewish Appeal fundraising efforts, tree plantings in Israel and offering classes in Hebrew."[247] The synagogue also has a side benefit probably not intended by its founders. As reported by the *New York Times*: "One trustee of the synagogue for homosexuals, for instance, mentioned off-handedly, 'My lover and I keep a kosher home now. We met at the synagogue. Everybody laughs because this is one of the traditional roles synagogues have always played.' "[248]

Homosexual synagogues engage in the same political activities as their counterparts in other religions. Providing "pride" and self-identity as homosexuals for their members is a crucial political function, since this is the movement's foundation. The Fourth International Conference of Gay and Lesbian Jews, for example, met at the Kibbutz Ma'aleh Ha Hamisha in the Judean Hills near Jerusalem on July 19–22, 1979. The discussion focused on three themes: Homosexuality in Israel, Law and Liberation, and Modern Perspectives in Judaism. According to published reports, the event received the full cooperation of the Israeli authorities.[249] The fifth international conference met in San Francisco during Labor Day Weekend in 1980. Scheduled to address the meeting was the first avowed homosexual to be appointed to the judiciary, California Superior Court Judge Stephen Lachs. It was expected that between three and four hundred persons would attend the event.[250]

Homosexual Jewish groups have, by definition, two allegiances. By the fact that they are Jewish, they belong to one of mankind's oldest and most respected traditions. On the other hand, their identification with the homosexual movement makes them part and parcel of a profoundly revolutionary phenomenon whose basis is a behavior form rejected by most people as individually and socially destructive. Still, the Jewish homosexual movement thrives. Bet Mishapachah (Washington's homosexual synagogue) is "a member of the Gay Community Center and maintains close contact with most of the gay groups in the Washington area." Additionally, it takes part in the annual "Gay Pride Day."[251] Numerous Jewish homosexual groups were reported to have taken part in the National March on Washington for Lesbian and Gay Rights in 1979.[252] The homosexual movement has also enjoyed the support of other Jewish organizations besides the synagogues specifically organized for homosexuals. The link between the homosexual movement and the Jewish community is the Union of American Hebrew Congregations (UAHC). Not only does this organization admit homosexual congregations to its membership, but in 1977 it took a clearly prohomosexual stand that, in the name of "civil

Religious Organizations and the Movement

rights" and "civil liberties," called for the recognition of homosexuals as a legitimate minority. Furthermore, UAHC has worked for the legalization of homosexual acts and called on its members to implement an educational campaign, aimed at both children and adults, to disseminate its stand.[253]

A few months prior to the UAHC resolution, the 88th Annual Convention of the Central Conference of American Rabbis (Grossinger, New York, June 1977) had called for similar measures, creating within itself a "Permanent Committee on Homosexuality" charged with the creation of homosexuality educational programs and the search for new avenues "whereby our Reform Jewish community can demonstrate by its own actions a greater degree of understanding of the problems of Jewish homosexuals."[254]

Antecedents to these resolutions had been the 1974 actions of the New York Chapter of the American Jewish Committee and the North American Jewish Students Network. The former limited itself to a very simple resolution calling for the passage of Intro 2, that year's version of a New York City prohomosexual law.[255] The latter sponsored a National Conference on Jewish Women and Men on the theme "Changing Sex Roles: Implications for the Future of Jewish Life." A resolution adopted unanimously by the conference accused unidentified Jews of persecuting homosexuals, calling for acknowledgement and acceptance of homosexual Jews as members of the Jewish community and for support of prohomosexual legislation.[256]

Since the Jewish community counts on its own internal resources to socialize its members, events in secular society do not seem to affect it as strongly as they do other ethnic or religious groups. On the other hand, should the homosexual ideology succeed in making inroads in traditional Jewish institutions, the effect could be geometrical, due to the proportionately high participation of Jews in the educational, social, and political life of the United States. Because of historical circumstances, Jews tend to be very sensitive to the need to assure civil/human rights for all people and to eliminate all forms of persecution. By framing the issue of homosexuality in terms of rights and persecution, the homosexual movement is likely to succeed in enlisting the help of significant elements within the Jewish community. On the other hand, the religious tradition from which Judaism has sprung strongly rejects homosexuality, and socially Jews tend to be family-oriented. If the issue is framed in terms of religion and the preservation of family values, the homosexual movement is likely to see itself soundly rejected by American Jews. This is certainly the case in Israel, where the homosexual movement does not even dare include the word "gay" in its name lest it be known for what it is.[257]

THE HOMOSEXUAL NETWORK

Notes

1. Testimony of the Reverend Elder Troy D. Perry, Founder and Moderator, Universal Fellowship of Metropolitan Community Churches, Congressional Briefings, April 21, 1981.

2. *Washington Field Office Report 1976–77*, (Washington, D.C.: Universal Fellowship of Metropolitan Community Churches), p. 95.

3. R. Adam DeBaugh, "Elders Form Department of Ecumenical Relations," *In Unity*, December 1979/January 1980, p. 16.

4. R. Adam DeBaugh, "The UFMCC to Apply for Membership in Major Ecumenical Organizations," *A New Day* 5 (February 1981): 2.

5. Ibid.

6. Ibid.

7. R. Adam DeBaugh, "Elders Form Department of Ecumenical Relations," *In Unity*, December 1979/January 1980, p. 16.

8. "Lesbian/Gay Religious Leaders Meet with White House Staff," *A New Day* 4 (May and June 1980): 2.

9. Ibid., p. 1.

10. R. Adam DeBaugh, "Representatives of 16 Denominations Gather to Discuss Homophobia in the Churches," *A New Day* 3 (June 1979): 1.

11. Ibid.

12. Ibid., p. 4.

13. "Rev. Elder Nancy Wilson and Adam DeBaugh Head New Ecumenical Relations Department," *A New Day* 3 (November 1979): 2.

14. *A New Day* 4 (January 1980): 1.

15. "Hill Office Begins Fourth Year!" *Gays on the Hill* 3 (October 1978): 1.

16. Robert D. Wood, "Our Washington Connection," *Good News* (Wilmore, KY: The Forum for Scriptural Christianity), July/August 1978, p. 46.

17. Ibid.

18. Ibid.

19. Ibid., p. 47.

20. Ibid., p. 44.

21. Ibid., p. 49.

22. R. Adam DeBaugh, "The Role of the Washington Field Office: Spreading God's Word, Proclaiming a New Day," *A New Day* (Special Issue, August 13–19, 1979), p. 1.

23. *A New Day* 3 (June 1979): 4.

24. *A New Day* 3 (November 1979): 4.

25. Michael K. Boockholdt, "Religious Community Backing for Senate Gay Rights Bill Continues," *A New Day* 4 (February 1980): 3.

26. *Washington Field Office Report 1976–77* (Washington, D.C.: Universal Fellowship of Metropolitan Community Churches, 1977), p. 95.

27. *CCSA: Meeting Human Needs* 1 (Washington, D.C.: Commission on Christian Social Action, Universal Fellowship of Metropolitan Community Churches, April 1980): 7.

28. *In Unity*, September/October 1980, p. 4.

29. Kenneth Spaatz, "Right-wing Christians Plan Washington March," *A New Day* 4 (February 1980): 4.

30. Ibid.

31. *Washington Star*, October 23, 1979.

32. *In Unity*, June/July 1979, p. 4.

33. Ibid.

34. Ibid., p. 5.

Religious Organizations and the Movement

35. Board of Campus Ministry, 1977 Report (Los Angeles, Universal Fellowship of Metropolitan Community Churches).

36. Ibid.

37. "Reports and Directives of the Seventh Annual General Conference" (Washington, D.C.: Universal Fellowship of Metropolitan Community Churches, 1976), p. 133.

38. Ibid., p. 134.

39. Promotional brochure, Task Force on Lesbians and Gay Men, Seattle, n.d.

40. "Reports and Directives of the Seventh Annual General Conference" (Washington, D.C.: Universal Fellowship of Metropolitan Community Churches, 1976), p. 135.

41. Promotional brochure, First National Symposium on Homosexuality and the Catholic Church (Mt. Rainier, MD: New Ways Ministry, 1981).

42. *Gaysweek*, February 12, 1979, p. 8.

43. Ibid., p. 9.

44. "Minister Sponsors Homosexual Rituals," *New York Times*, November 27, 1977.

45. Brad Green, "Gay 'Marriages': Delivering a Message," *Blade*, March 4, 1982, p. A-1.

46. *Good News* (Wilmore, KY: The Forum for Scriptural Christianity), July–August 1978, p. 57.

47. *Time*, January 24, 1977, p. 58.

48. "Episcopal Bishops are Divided on Ordination of Homosexuals," *New York Times*, October 4, 1977, p. 18.

49. Lacey Fosburgh, "From Quiet Seminarian to Homosexual Spokesman," *New York Times*, January 25, 1977, p. 16.

50. Mary Ann Mulligan, "Local Church Delegates Vote to Ordain Lesbian," *Fairfax (VA) Journal*, February 24, 1982.

51. *In Unity*, April/May 1980, p. 12.

52. Ibid., p. 13.

53. "BAGLY and the Gay Youth Movement in Boston Today," *Gay Community News* (Boston), March 20, 1982, pp. 8 and 9.

54. *Hearing*, p. 90.

55. *Codex Iuris Canonici* (Vatican City: *Typis Polyglottis Vaticanis*, 1974), p. 62, Canon 218.

56. *Vatican Declaration on Sexual Ethics* (Huntington, IN: Our Sunday Visitor, n.d.).

57. Ibid., pp. 11–13.

58. (Archbishop) John R. Quinn, "Pastoral Letter on Homosexuality" of May 5, 1980, *Monitor* (San Francisco), May 15, 1980.

59. Ibid.

60. *In Unity*, December 1979/January 1980, p. 10.

61. *New York Native*, April 20–May 3, 1981, p. 1.

62. *Dignity: Newsletter of the Gay Catholic Community* 9 (San Diego, March 1978): 4.

63. Ibid.

64. *A Time to Speak*, p. 4.

65. National Conference of Catholic Bishops, *To Live in Christ Jesus: A Pastoral Reflection on the Moral Life* (Washington, D.C.: United States Catholic Conference, 1976), pp. 18–19.

66. National Conference of Catholic Bishops, *Principles to Guide Confessors in Questions of Homosexuality* (Washington, D.C.: United States Catholic Conference, 1973), pp. 3–5.

67. *A Time to Speak*, p. 11.

68. Laurel Rowe, "Symposium Points to Need for Ministry to Gay Catholics," *Catholic Observer*, (Holyoke, MA), October 17, 1980.

69. "USCC Document on Young Adult Ministry," *Bondings*, Fall 1981.

70. Letter from Frank Scheuren to Archbishop John R. Roach, March 10, 1981.

71. "USCC/NCCB Staffer Lobbying for Homosexuality—to Retain Job Despite Activity," *CCPA News and Views* 2 (Washington, D.C.: Catholics for Christian Political Action, November 1978): 1.

72. (Archbishop) John R. Quinn, "Pastoral Letter on Homosexuality" of May 5, 1980, *Monitor* (San Francisco), May 15, 1980.

73. *Catholic Review* (Baltimore), July 25, 1980.

74. (Bishop) Austin Vaughan et al., "Qs and As," *Catholic News* (New York, N.Y.), October 18, 1979.

75. *In Unity*, (June/July 1979), p. 5.

76. *Advocate* (San Mateo, CA), September 6, 1978.

77. Lloyd Green, "Cardinal Cody Bars Workshop on Homosexuals," *Chicago Sun Times*, May 1, 1981.

78. *Bondings*, Spring-Summer 1981, p. 4.

79. NC News Service wire story, undated copy kept at New Ways Ministry's "Minneapolis File."

80. *Calendar* (New York City: Dignity/New York), July 1980, p. 9.

81. NC News Service wire story, May 10, 1977.

82. "Miami Archdiocese Boots Gay Priest," *Advocate*, January 7, 1982.

83. "Joint Statement on Intro 384 before the City Council by the Archdiocese of New York and Diocese of Brooklyn," April 17, 1978.

84. Kenneth Jadoff, "Catholics, Anita Bryant and the Gays," *Daily News* (New York, N.Y.), July 18, 1977.

85. John Bird, "Ontario Bishops Say Church Must Be Free to Exclude Homosexuals," NC News Service wire story, October 1, 1981.

86. *A Time to Speak.* There is an undated insert addendum to this document.

87. Jeannine Gramick, SSND, "Institutional Reprisal: The Fate of the Prophet," n.d.

88. (Archbishop) Rembert Weakland, "Herald of Hope. The Archbishop Shares: Who is Our Neighbor?" *Catholic Herald Citizen* (Milwaukee), July 19, 1980.

89. Interview with Adam DeBaugh by the author.

90. Ralph Blair, "An Evangelical Looks at Homosexuality," revised 1977, p. 3. Originally published as "The Gay Evangelical" in *Homosexuality and Religion*, Otherwise Monograph Series, no. 13, (New York, N.Y.: National Task Force on Student Personnel Services and Homosexuality, 1972).

91. Robert Nugent, SDS, Jeannine Gramick, SSND, and Thomas Oddo, CSC, *Homosexual Catholics: A New Primer for Discussion* (Washington, D.C.: Dignity, Inc., 1980), p. 12.

92. Ibid., pp. 4–8.

93. Tripp, chapter 11.

94. Rev. Andrew Greeley, article in the *Chicago Tribune*, July 7, 1977, reprinted in *A Time to Speak*, p. 6.

95. Statement of Judd Marmor, M.D., Past President, American Psychiatric Association, *Hearing*, pp. 65–66.

96. *Dignity* 11 (Washington, D.C.: Dignity, Inc.), September 1980.

97. *Bondings*, Spring/Summer 1981, p. 5.

98. "Wisconsin House Passes Gay Rights Legislation," *Gay Community News* (Boston), November 21, 1981.

99. Public letter from Archbishop Raymond G. Hunthausen, July 1, 1977.

100. *National Catholic Reporter*, July 3, 1981, p. 1.

101. *Dignity* 13 (Washington, D.C.: Dignity, Inc., January 1982): 1.

102. *Calendar* 6 (New York City: Dignity/New York), July 1980.

103. Ibid. 7 (August 1981): 4.

104. Ibid.

105. Ibid. 6 (July 1980): 2.

106. *Dignity* 12 (Washington, D.C.: Dignity, Inc., January 1981): 3.

107. Ibid. 13 (January 1982): 1.

108. Mark Neilsen, "Archbishop's Talk at Gay Service Eyed," *National Catholic Reporter*, February 19, 1982, p. 7.

109. *Dignity* 13 (Washington, D.C.: Dignity, Inc., January 1982): 1.

110. *Dignity* 11 (Washington, D.C.: Dignity, Inc., September 1980): 1.

111. Ibid.

112. Ibid.

113. Terri Goodman, "Target: Pantex, Oblates Grant Aid for Arms Workers," *National Catholic Reporter*, February 19, 1982, p. 2.

114. *Quicksilver Times* (Washington, D.C.), November 24–December 24, 1970, p. 5.

115. *In Unity*, August/September 1979, p. 8.

116. *In Unity*, January/February 1981, p. 27.

117. *In Unity*, February/March 1980, p. 19.

118. Convention materials made available to the author.

119. Washington Field Office Report 1976–77 (Washington, D.C.: Universal Fellowship of Metropolitan Community Churches, 1977), p. 95.

120. *Calendar* 7 (New York City: Dignity/New York, September 1981): 1.

121. *In Unity*, April/May 1980, p. 28.

122. *Calendar* 7 (New York City: Dignity, Inc., September 1981): 4.

123. "Welcome to Cabaret Night," *Calendar* 8 (New York City: Dignity/New York, April 1982): back of insert.

124. Promotional brochure, Center for Reflective Action, Holyoke, MA, 1980.

125. Ibid.

126. "New Ways Conducts Dignity Retreat Workshop in MA," a single sheet sent to the author by Margaret Johnson, Center for Reflective Action.

127. *Bondings*, Spring-Summer 1981, p. 1.

128. *Dignity* 12 (Washington, D.C.: Dignity, Inc., January 1981): 1.

129. *Bondings*, Winter 1980–81, p. 3.

130. Ibid.

131. Barbara Zanotti, "Feminist Theological Perspectives on Lesbian and Gay Male Experience," *New Women/New Church* 5 (Rochester: Women's Ordination Conference, January 1982): 6.

132. Barbara Zanotti, "Traversing New Ground," *New Women/New Church* 5 (Rochester N. Y.: Women's Ordination Conference, January 1982): 6.

133. Base data taken from Maureen Dwyer, *New Women/New Church/New Priestly Ministry*, Proceedings of the Second Conference on the Ordination of Roman Catholic Women, Rochester, especially pp. 173, 174, and 175.

134. *Bondings*, Winter 1980–81, p. 3.

135. *America*, June 25, 1977, p. 558.

136. *Bondings*, Winter 1980–81, p. 12.

137. Anthony Kosnik et al., *Human Sexuality: New Directions in American Catholic Thought* (Garden City, N.Y.: Doubleday, 1979), p. 229–231.

138. "Catholic Gay Group Calls Quinn Pastoral on Homosexuality 'Inadequate,' " *Bay Area Reporter* (San Francisco), June 19, 1980.

139. Anthony Kosnik et al., *Human Sexuality: New Directions in American Catholic Thought* (Garden City, N.Y.: Doubleday, 1979).

140. Untitled statement issued on July 1, 1977 by the Archdiocese of New York (Chancery Office).

141. *Bondings*, Winter 1980–81, p. 5.

142. Donald Goergen, *The Sexual Celibate* (Garden City, N.Y.: Doubleday, 1977), p. 99.

143. Ibid., pp. 106–107.

144. "Homosexuals and Religious Life," *The Tablet* (Brooklyn, N.Y.), December 26, 1981, p. 19.

145. Rev. Robert Griffin, CSC, "A True Confession," *Notre Dame Magazine* (Notre Dame, IN: Notre Dame University), February 1981.

146. "Letters," *Notre Dame Magazine* (Notre Dame, IN: Notre Dame University), May 1981.

147. *Bondings*, Spring/Summer 1980, p. 1.

148. "Letters to the Editor," *The Wanderer*, May 14, 1981.

149. Practically all issues of *Bondings* contain additional names of members of the network.

150. *A Time to Speak*, pp. 4 and 8.

151. "Statement of Support for Human and Civil Rights for Homosexual Persons by Clergy from Rochester and Monroe County," March 1, 1977.

152. Colette Satler (Pittsburgh) and D. Dudley (Atlanta), *Dignity Women's Committee Report*, submitted for Executive Board Meeting, Lubbock, TX, March 1981.

153. *Dignity* 12 (Washington, D.C.: Dignity, Inc., January 1981).

154. *Advocate* (San Mateo, CA), September 6, 1978.

155. *Sentinel* (San Francisco), June 12, 1981, p. 20.

156. Bill Kenkelen, "Priest Faces Ouster, Views on Gays Cited," *National Catholic Reporter*, July 31, 1981, p. 1.

157. *Bondings*, Spring/Summer 1981, p. 6.

158. Mark Brooks, "A Gay Priest Speaks Out: Censured and Censored," *Advocate*, December 10, 1981.

159. "Dignity Observes Ninth Anniversary," *Blade*, December 18, 1981.

160. Pamela Constable, "Hearing on City Gay Rights Measure is Sidetracked by Religious Disputes," *Sun* (Baltimore), July 3, 1980.

161. *America*, November 19, 1977, p. 346 (editorial).

162. Gabriel Moran, FSC, "Sexual Forms" (in *Sexuality*), Christian Brothers Conference, Lockport, IL, 1977, cited in *A Time to Speak*, pp. 10–11.

163. Personal communication.

164. Personal communication.

165. *Communication* 2 (Philadelphia: n.p., February 1979).

166. "Reining In The Jesuits," *Newsweek*, November 9, 1981, p. 81.

167. *Studies in the Spirituality of Jesuits* 10 (St. Louis: American Assistancy Seminar on Jesuit Spirituality, March/May 1978): pp. 127–128.

168. Origins (Washington, D.C.: United States Catholic Conference), January 3, 1980, p. 472.

169. *Bondings*, Spring-Summer, 1981, p. 3.

170. *Communication* 2 (Philadelphia: n.p., November, 1978).

171. " 'Play and Stay' Priests . . . ," *National Catholic Reporter*, October 16, 1981.

172. Typewritten document, original at the "Gay Religious Communities," file in New Ways Ministry, Mt. Rainier, MD.

173. Letter from Ray Tobin, AC, to "Gerald," dated July 27, 1979.

174. Letter written on the order's letterhead from Donald Lawrence, on file under "Gay Religious Communities" at New Ways Ministry, Mt. Rainier, MD.

175. Promotional brochure, "St. Matthew Community Associate Membership," Brooklyn, N.Y., 1978.

176. Official announcement, n.d.

177. *Community* (Calgary, Alberta, Canada: Christian Community Association), May 1980, p. 1.

178. Informational letter from Gerry Moran, BFCC, November 1979.

179. *Community* (Calgary, Alberta, Canada: Christian Community Association), Easter 1981 issue.

180. Bill Kenkelen, " 'Sisters of Perpetual Indulgence': Gays Poke Fun at 'Oppressive' Church," *National Catholic Reporter*, December 4, 1981, pp. 5 and 10. This leftist unofficial Catholic weekly devoted two full pages to these organizations.

181. "Lighting Candles: Celebrating Pride," *Blade*, December 18, 1981, p. A-21.

182. *Gay Community News* 9 (Boston), March 13, 1982.

183. Press release, "Catholic Gay Ministry Group Conducts Homosexuality Workshop," New Ways Ministry, April 9, 1981.

184. Press release, "Catholic Gay Ministry Group Sponsors Retreat," New Ways Ministry, April 10, 1981.

185. *Washington Post*, March 10, 1981.

186. *Blade*, June 26, 1981, p. A-7.

187. "Response to Archbishop Borders," New Ways Ministry, Mt. Rainier, MD, May 30, 1980.

188. *Bondings*, Winter 1979–80, p. 3.

189. Ibid.

190. *Bay Area Reporter* (San Francisco), June 19, 1980.

191. Letter from Jesse Lowen to Rick Garcia, December 12, 1980.

192. R. Adam DeBaugh, "Representatives of 16 Denominations Gather to Discuss Homophobia in the Churches," *A New Day* 3 (June 1979): 1.

193. Robert Nugent, SDS, untitled and undated testimony, (Mt. Rainier, MD: New Ways Ministry).

194. Personal communication.

195. Robert Nugent, SDS, Letter to the Editor, *National Catholic Register*, June 21, 1981.

196. Response of James Hitchcock to Robert Nugent, SDS, *National Catholic Register*, June 21, 1981.

197. Promotional brochure for the symposium.

198. Kim Shepherd, "Judge Delivers Setback to Catholic Group," *Blade*, November 20, 1981.

199. Ibid.

200. Letter from Archbishop James Hickey, "To the Priests, Deacons and to the Communities of Religious Women and Men in the Archdiocese of Washington," October 27, 1981.

201. Jim McManus, ". . . and gay symposium," *National Catholic Reporter*, November 13, 1981.

202. Ibid.

203. Catherine Barr, "Symposium Questions Traditional Ethics," *National Catholic Register*, December 6, 1981, p. 1.

204. Ibid.

205. Ibid.

206. Andrew Humm, "Mary Lou Steele, S.C. [*sic*]: Fighting Homophobia With Understanding," *Calendar* 8 (New York City: Dignity/New York, February 1982): 1.

207. "Catholic Priest Put in Limbo," *Blade*, December 18, 1981, p. A-9.

208. *New York Native* (April 20–May 3, 1981), p. 16.

209. *Blade*, September 11, 1981, p. A-13.

210. Ibid.

211. "Statement of Position and Purpose," (Washington, D.C.: Dignity, Inc., n.d.).

212. Ibid.

213. Quoted by Rev. Robert E. Burns, CSP, in "Concerning 'Gay' Rights," *Wanderer*, January 1, 1981.

214. Ibid.

215. Laura Scism, "A Gay Catholic Talks About the Church," *News American* (Baltimore), July 15, 1980.

216. Letters to the Editor, *The Review* (Baltimore), August 1, 1980.

217. *Blade*, September 11, 1981, p. A-13.

218. "What is Dignity?" (New York City: Dignity/New York). There is no date, but the text indicates that it was published ca. 1975.

219. Andrew Humm, "Mary Lou Steele, S.C. [sic]: Fighting Homophobia with Understanding," *Calendar* 8 (New York City: Dignity/New York, February 1982): 1.

220. Ibid.

221. Ibid.

222. Ibid.

223. "Church Authority . . . Helpful Guides or Big Daddy," *Dignity Seattle* November 1980, p. 3.

224. Minutes of the Meeting of Dignity's Executive Board, Vancouver, B.C., October 12, 1980.

225. Ibid.

226. Interview with Harry Dean, May 13, 1981.

227. *Dignity Seattle*, November 1980, p. 1.

228. Ibid., p. 5.

229. Dignity Workshop Status as of February 15, 1981.

230. "El Salvador: The Cry for Bread, the Cry for Justice, the Cry for Peace," promotional invitation for a day of study and prayer, March 27, 1982, at St. Francis Xavier Church, New York, N.Y., sponsored by Solidarity and New York Metropolitan Council of Bread for the World.

231. Undated cover letter to a marketing package distributed by the *Advocate*, signed by Frank Scheuren and sent to Dignity members in late April 1982: According to Scheuren's letter, "we assure you that this mailing was done by our staff . . ."

232. "What is Dignity?" (New York City: Dignity/New York). There is no date, but the text indicates that it was published ca. 1975.

233. *Dialogue* 4 (Washington, D.C.: Brethren/Mennonite Council for Gay Concerns, June 1981): 3.

234. "Baltimore Forms Catholic Gay Ministry," *Dignity* 13 (Washington, D.C.: Dignity, Inc., January 1982): 1.

235. List made available to the author by Dignity, Inc.

236. *Calendar* 8 (New York City: Dignity/New York, February 1982): insert.

237. Philo, *On Abraham* 135–136, cited by Victor Paul Furnish, *The Moral Teaching of Paul* (Nashville: Abingdon Press, 1979), p. 65.

238. Ibid., pp. 56, 57, 64, and 65.

239. Hershel J. Matt: "Sin, Crime, Sickness or Alternative Life Style?: A Jewish Approach to Homosexuality," *Judaism: A Quarterly Journal of Jewish Life and Thought* 27 (Winter issue, 1978): 14.

240. David Ahearn, "Gay Rights Bill Faces Broad Opposition," *News American* (Baltimore), July 8, 1980.

241. Vincent Cosgrove, " 'Harmful' Gay Rights Bill Ripped by Catholic Church," *Daily News* (New York, N.Y.), April 18, 1978.

242. "Orthodox Rabbis Fight Homosexual Battle," *Washington Star*, January 28, 1978.

243. Matt, p. 18.

244. Ibid., p. 21.

245. Ibid., p. 23.

246. Personal communication.

247. *New York Times*, October 25, 1977.

248. Ibid.

249. *Gaysweek*, April 16, 1979.

250. *In Unity*, September/October 1980, p. 13.

251. *Questions and Answers About Bet Mishpachah* (Washington, D.C.: Bet Mishpachah, n.d.).

252. *In Unity*, December 1979/January 1980, p. 18.

253. Complete text of official document contained in a package of materials distributed by the National Gay Task Force, New York, N.Y., 1979.

254. Ibid.

255. Ibid.

256. Ibid.

257. *Bet Mishpachah* (Washington, D.C.: Bet Mishpachah), July 1981, p. 6.

VIII

The Homosexual Movement and American Liberalism

There is little question that the homosexual movement is part and parcel of American liberalism. This does not mean that all liberals are homosexuals, that they necessarily accept the homosexual ideology, or that they actually sympathize with the movement. Nor does it mean that all liberal organizations do, in fact, support homosexuality. It does mean, however, that most homosexual organizations do support traditionally leftist positions, that they draw most of their support from liberal organizations, and that, in fact, they work together, forming a network in which homosexual organizations are an important component. In this chapter evidence will be offered to support these conclusions.

Survey Results

The survey of eighty randomly selected homosexual organizations undertaken as part of the research for this work shows these organizations to be biased in favor of liberalism. The survey included questions on social, economic, and foreign policy issues, selected according to the public issues that were being widely discussed when the survey was undertaken. Table 18 shows the distribution of responses for each of the

The Movement and American Liberalism

issues included in the survey. Respondents were given three choices: agreement or disagreement with the policies or no opinion on the subject at all. The only issue on which homosexual organizations did not favor the liberal line was that of "block grants." This is easily explained by the fact that homosexual organizations have much more influence on local governments than they have on the federal government. Since the effect of block grants is to shift the responsibility for allocating funds to the state and local bureaucracies, it is only natural that homosexual organizations would tend to support this policy. It is surprising, however, that in spite of the fact that block grants would mean such a budget increase, only 35% support them. On a related issue, 53% of the organizations indicated support for tax cuts. This reflects in part the class composition of the homosexual community (i.e., tax cuts would benefit homosexuals proportionately more than the rest of the population since they are wealthier). On the other hand, both liberals and conservatives in the U.S. Congress were proposing tax cuts while the survey was under way. What is significant is that 36% were opposed to *any* tax cuts at all (whether proposed by liberal Democrats or President Reagan). Another significant figure is the 14% no opinion response to the Family Protection Act issue. This

TABLE 18

Opinions of Homosexual Organizations Concerning Public Policy Issues

Area	Agree			Disagree			No Opinion	
Social Issues	N	%		N	%		N	%
Family Planning Services	73	91	*	2	2		5	6
Sex Education	78	98	*	0	0		2	2
Gun Control	66	82	*	12	15		2	2
ERA	76	95	*	2	2		2	2
Gay Rights	77	96	*	3	4		0	0
Family Protection Act	6	8		63	79	*	11	14
Abortion on Demand	76	95	*	1	1		3	4
Economic Issues								
Tax Cuts	42	53		30	36	*	8	10
Budget Cuts	6	8		65	81	*	9	11
Block Grants	28	35		24	30	*	28	35
Defense/Foreign Policy Issues								
Increased Military Spending	7	9		68	85	*	5	6
Dev. of Neutron Bomb	1	1		69	86	*	10	12
Military Aid to El Salvador	0	0		74	92	*	6	8

*Denotes liberal position on the issue.

probably reveals a lack of knowledge of the Act. The 15% response on the conservative side of the Gun Control issue probably reflects the fear of crime among homosexuals resulting from their vulnerability, caused in turn by social conditions.

The scores in the three areas were converted to a linear scale, as was the total score. The total range on each area and the total were divided into seven categories with adequate descriptors. Table 19 shows the scores assigned to each descriptor.

TABLE 19

Interpretation of Table 18

Descriptor	Range of Scores
Very Liberal	−7.16 to −10.00
Liberal	−4.29 to −7.15
Somewhat Liberal	−1.43 to −4.28
Neutral	+1.42 to −1.42
Somewhat Conservative	4.28 to 1.43
Conservative	7.15 to 4.29
Very Conservative	10.00 to 7.16

Tables 20 through 22 show the number of homosexual organizations, their percentages, and cumulative percentages that belong to each of the political categories.

TABLE 20

Ideological Distribution of Homosexual Organizations:
Overall Scores

Descriptor	Number of Organizations	%	Cumulative %
Very Liberal	40	50%	50%
Liberal	32	40%	90%
Somewhat Liberal	5	6%	96%
Neutral	1	1%	97%
Somewhat Conservative	1	1%	98%
Conservative	1	1%	99%
Very Conservative	0	0%	99%
Total	80	99%	—

* Categories do not add up to 100% due to rounding.

This table reveals that 90% of the homosexual organizations are liberal or very liberal and that only 4% are either conservative or neutral. Fully 50% of the homosexual organizations are very liberal.

The Movement and American Liberalism

TABLE 21

Ideological Distribution of Homosexual Organizations:
Social Policy Issues

Descriptor	Number of Organizations	%	Cumulative %
Very Liberal	73	91%	91%
Liberal	5	6%	97%
Somewhat Liberal	0	0%	97%
Neutral	0	0%	97%
Somewhat Conservative	1	1%	98%
Conservative	1	1%	99%
Very Conservative	0	0%	99%
Total	80	99%	—

* Categories do not add up to 100% due to rounding.

When social issues are considered by themselves, homosexual organizations are very liberal by an overwhelming majority. Moreover, they score consistently liberal on a variety of issues, indicating the pervasive acceptance of liberal positions within the homosexual movement. From a political point of view, the implication of this phenomenon is that elected officials or candidates whose point of view is to the center or right of the center can expect little support (if not outright opposition) from homosexual groups.

TABLE 22

Ideological Distribution of Homosexual Organizations:
Foreign Policy Issues

Descriptor	Number of Organizations	%	Cumulative %
Very Liberal	60	75%	75%
Liberal	10	12%	87%
Somewhat Liberal	5	6%	93%
Neutral	2	3%	96%
Somewhat Conservative	3	4%	100%
Conservative	0	0%	100%
Very Conservative	0	0%	100%
Total	80	100%	—

In terms of foreign policy, homosexual organizations are also overwhelmingly liberal; 93% of them identify with leftist positions, only 4% are somewhat conservative, and none scored conservative or very conservative. This does not mean that *all* homosexuals are liberal on foreign policy, but that homosexual organizations agree with leftist positions. This can only be expected to translate into political action in support of organizations which have a specific interest in promoting leftist causes. These homosexual organizations can also be expected to become part of left-leaning networks.

TABLE 23

Ideological Distribution of Homosexual Organizations:
Economic Policy Issues

Descriptor	Number of Organizations	%	Cumulative %
Very Liberal	11	14%	14%
Liberal	11	14%	28%
Somewhat Liberal	19	25%	53%
Neutral	15	18%	71%
Somewhat Conservative	16	20%	91%
Conservative	6	7%	98%
Very Conservative	2	2%	100%
Total	80	100%	—

The liberal complexion of the homosexual movement is obvious even in the area of economic policy. Although the survey was undertaken at a time when a wave of economic conservatism was sweeping America, over half the homosexual organizations proved to be liberal (average score - 1.48) and less than one-third were in any way conservative. It is significant that 28% were distributed at the liberal-very liberal end of the scale while less than 10% were either conservative or very conservative.

In order to examine the manner in which the various components of the political ideology affect one another, the X^2 test was applied and contingency coefficients were calculated whenever applicable. The following basic formulas were employed:

$$\chi^2 = \sum \frac{(0 - E)^2}{E}$$

$$C = \sqrt{\frac{\chi^2}{\chi^2 + N}}$$

Where 0 = Observed values
E = Expected values in a contingency table
χ^2 = Chi-square value
N = Total of all the values (80)
C = Contingency coefficient

Tables 24 through 26 and 27 through 29 show the pattern of interaction among the three components of political ideology in homosexual orga-

The Movement and American Liberalism

nizations. The first group of tables displays the number of organizations in each category, while the second group displays the proportions within each pair of categories. Analysis of these tables indicates that the social and economic policy views are related, but that social and foreign policy views are related with an even greater degree of significance. On the other hand, the foreign policy and economic policy components have no effect on each other. These findings are important in that they reveal that social policy issues are the center of the liberal character of the homosexual movement. Moreover, they also indicate that the strong liberalism of the homosexual movement in the social policy component apparently "spills over" into the other two components. It appears that the liberalism of the social issues component determines the liberalism of the economic and foreign policy components. Thus leftist opinions within the homosexual movement are not isolated views, but part of a frame of mind which is anchored in the social policy positions of the movement.

It is not surprising that the homosexual movement is liberal on social policy issues. After all, the movement is centered on a membership trait whose acceptance implies a veritable revolution in the nation's laws and customs in family relationships, sex-related questions, feminism, and many other elements of the social policy area. The relations between the social policy and the economic and foreign policy components, however, have serious implications for the practicioner of politics.

Traditionally, profamily, prolife, and other social conservatives have taken issue with the homosexual movement, while foreign and economic policy conservatives have tended to skirt it on the basis that homosexuality per se has no bearing on foreign policy or economics. Indeed, there is no logical reason why a homosexual cannot agree with supply-side economics or a strong defense policy against the aggressive advance of communism in Central America. However, homosexuality (the sexual attraction for people of one's sex) is not the same as the homosexual movement (a complex set of social institutions which accept and promote the homosexual ideology). The defeat of the homosexual movement—as opposed to the mere "conversion" of homosexuals to heterosexuality—is of great interest not only to the social conservatives, but to *all* political conservatives. Liberals have understood this well; thus the homosexual movement enjoys the support and reciprocates the help of liberals within the three components of political ideology. In fact, foreign and economic policy conservatives are indirectly benefitting by the anti–homosexual-movement activities of the social conservatives, since any weakening in the movement would result in an overall diminution of American liberalism's ability to impose its program. On the other hand, more forceful opposition to the homosexual movement by economic and foreign policy conservatives would be a logical line for them to follow.

TABLE 24

Interaction Between the Social Policy and Economic Policy Components (Number of Organizations)

Economic Policy	Social Policy: Very Liberal	Liberal	Somewhat Liberal	Neutral	Somewhat Conservative	Conservative	Very Conservative	Total
Very Liberal	11							11
Liberal	11							11
Somewhat Liberal	17	2						19
Neutral	14	1						15
Somewhat Conservative	15				1			16
Conservative	4	1				1		6
Very Conservative	1	1						2
Total	73	5			1	1		80

$\chi^2 = 26.29$
df = 18
Significant at the 90% level.
C = .497
Note: Columns that did not yield data were not considered in the analysis.

TABLE 25

Interaction Between the Social Policy and Foreign Policy Components (Number of Organizations)

	Social Policy							
Foreign Policy	Very Liberal	Liberal	Somewhat Liberal	Neutral	Somewhat Conservative	Conservative	Very Conservative	
Very Liberal	57	3						60
Liberal	10							10
Somewhat Liberal	4	1						5
Neutral	2							2
Somewhat Conservative		1			1	1		3
Conservative								
Very Conservative								
	73	5			1	1		80

$\chi^2 = 56.92$
df = 12
Significant at the 99.9% level.
C = .645
Note: Columns that did not yield data were not considered in the analysis.

TABLE 26

Interaction Between the Economic Policy and the Foreign Policy Components (Number of Organizations)

Foreign Policy	Economic Policy							
	Very Liberal	Liberal	Somewhat Liberal	Neutral	Somewhat Conservative	Conservative	Very Conservative	
Very Liberal	8	9	14	11	13	4	1	60
Liberal	3	1	2	2	1	1		10
Somewhat Liberal		1	3	1				5
Neutral				1	1			2
Somewhat Conservative					1	1	1	3
Conservative								
Very Conservative								
	11	11	19	15	16	6	2	80

$\chi^2 = 27.06$
df = 24
Not Significant

Note: Rows that did not yield data were not considered in this analysis.

TABLE 27

Interaction Between the Social Policy and Economic Policy Components (Proportions)

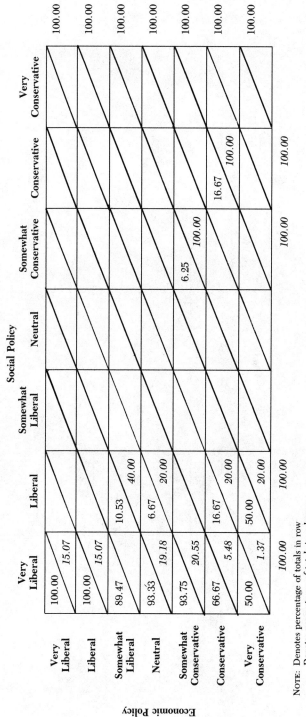

| | Social Policy | | | | | | | |
Economic Policy	Very Liberal	Liberal	Somewhat Liberal	Neutral	Somewhat Conservative	Conservative	Very Conservative	
Very Liberal	**100.00** / *15.07*							*100.00*
Liberal	**100.00** / *15.07*							*100.00*
Somewhat Liberal	**89.47**	**10.53** / *40.00*						*100.00*
Neutral	**93.33** / *19.18*	**6.67** / *20.00*						*100.00*
Somewhat Conservative	**93.75** / *20.55*				**6.25** / *100.00*			*100.00*
Conservative	**66.67** / *5.48*	**16.67** / *20.00*				**16.67** / *100.00*		*100.00*
Very Conservative	**50.00** / *1.37*	**50.00** / *20.00*						*100.00*
	100.00	*100.00*			*100.00*	*100.00*		

NOTE: **Denotes percentage of totals in row**
Denotes percentages of totals in columns

TABLE 28

Interaction Between the Social Policy and Foreign Policy Components (Proportions)

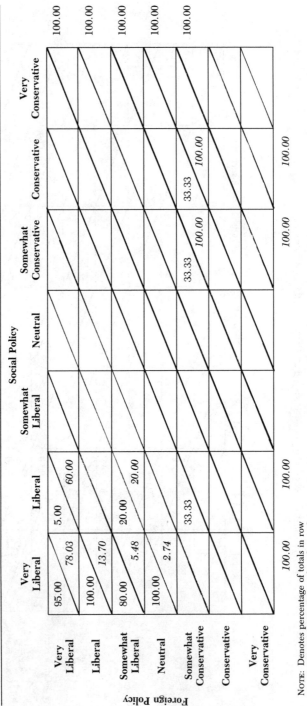

Foreign Policy	Social Policy							
	Very Liberal	Liberal	Somewhat Liberal	Neutral	Somewhat Conservative	Conservative	Very Conservative	
Very Liberal	95.00 / *78.03*	5.00 / *60.00*						100.00
Liberal	100.00 / *13.70*							100.00
Somewhat Liberal	80.00 / *5.48*	20.00 / *20.00*						100.00
Neutral	100.00 / *2.74*							100.00
Somewhat Conservative		33.33			33.33 / *100.00*	33.33 / *100.00*		100.00
Conservative								
Very Conservative								
	100.00	*100.00*			*100.00*	*100.00*		

NOTE: Denotes percentage of totals in row
Denotes percentages of totals in columns

TABLE 29

Interaction Between the Economic Policy and Foreign Policy Components (Proportions)

Foreign Policy	Economic Policy							
	Very Liberal	Liberal	Somewhat Liberal	Neutral	Somewhat Conservative	Conservative	Very Conservative	
Very Liberal	13.33 / 72.73	15.00 / 81.82	23.33 / 73.68	18.33 / 73.33	21.67 / 81.25	6.67 / 66.67	1.67 / 50.00	100.00
Liberal	30.00 / 27.27	10.00 / 9.09	20.00 / 10.53	20.00 / 15.33	10.00 / 6.25	10.00 / 16.67		100.00
Somewhat Liberal		20.00 / 9.09	60.00 / 15.79	20.00 / 6.67				100.00
Neutral				50.00 / 6.67	50.00 / 6.25			100.00
Somewhat Conservative					33.33 / 6.25	33.33 / 16.67	33.33 / 50.00	100.00
Conservative								
Very Conservative								
	100.00	100.00	100.00	100.00	100.00	100.00	100.00	

NOTE: Denotes percentage of totals in row
Denotes percentages of totals in columns

THE HOMOSEXUAL NETWORK

The Issues

Available evidence indicates that, on the basis of its issues, the homosexual movement is a well-integrated component of the American left. A casual examination of demonstrations against the Reagan conservative administration inevitably reveals the participation of homosexual organizations and the utilization of prohomosexual slogans. By way of contrast, the homosexual movement reached its maximum level of influence on the federal government during the liberal administration of Jimmy Carter. Moreover, the homosexual organizations have not limited themselves simply to promoting the homosexual ideology, but have adopted the agenda of American liberalism, including foreign and economic policy issues.

The 1981 Lesbian/Gay Pride Marches displayed liberal demands across the board. In Seattle, the demands were reportedly: "Stop the U.S. war drive," "Full reproductive rights for women," "Stop the cutbacks," and "Honor the Native treaties."[1] In San Francisco the themes included: "The unions are behind you" and "we gotta beat back the right's attack." One of the leaders of the march, Robin Tyler, spoke eloquently, "bringing the crowd to its feet with ovations, applause, cheers, and tears." She attacked the Family Protection Act, tying her opposition to traditional leftist slogans:

> Tyler scored the so-called Family Protection Act. "If the government is so concerned with the protection of the family, why do they continue to build nuclear power plants, why do they continue to poison our oceans, why do they continue to rape our land? If they are so concerned with children, why do they send baby formulas to Third World countries and murder hundreds of thousands of babies? Is that saving children?
>
> And why are they trying to make battering of children in schools legal once again? Why are they bent on starving our elderly to death, cutting back benefits to a disabled community that can barely survive on what they're getting now? Why, if children are so important to them, are they continuing to kill the children of El Salvador? Why on earth do they send our children to war, and then accost them when they come home so that Viet Nam veterans have to sit outside the White House and say, 'You've given us cancer—now pay for it!' "[2]

At the New York City parade, a female homosexual linked the homosexual struggle with world revolution as she called for support to "overturn the reactionary Reagan program":

> Our movement must never be pitted against other movements of oppressed peoples. While we are facing increasing attacks it's no accident that we're seeing attacks on women's rights, abortion rights, sterilization abuse, Reagan's cut-

backs. We're seeing the same type of repression all over the globe—in El Salvador, Africa, Latin America . . .

The struggles of all oppressed people wherever they are are the same struggles. . . . Sisters and brothers, in April there were rebellions in the Brixton section of London. What came out of those rebellions was a strong alliance between the lesbian and gay communities and Third World communities. We take responsibility for our own liberation. We have a responsibility to go out into our communities and say NO. Victory to all oppressed peoples![3]

It was no different in Phoenix where, according to reports, the rally which took place after the march was opened by Patricia Jackson, a representative of the Workers World Party: "Jackson, who opened the rally, got an enthusiastic response from the crowd when she showed how the budget cuts, racism, and the oppression of gay and lesbian people have common roots in the reactionary Reaganite program for dealing with the economic crisis."[4]

The ideological convergence between the homosexual movement and other leftist causes is seen in the list of thirteen topics which resulted from the second conference of the Mobilization for Survival, a group of 144 leftist organizations that met at the University of Chicago in December 1977. The topics were: "weapons facilities, the United Nations, the arms race, finances, religion, labor, feminism, the gay/lesbian issue, the Third World, South Africa, the right of service personnel to organize, a 'save our communities' project and militarism and the arms trade."[5] The agenda of the All Peoples Congress scheduled for October 16–18, 1981, in Detroit included the following items: "unemployment, racist violence, anti-Semitism, attacks on women's rights, lesbian and gay rights, and the military build-up."[6]

In preparation for the People's Anti-War Mobilization, a "city-wide conference" was held in Washington, D.C., on August 15, 1981. It took place at St. Stephen's Episcopal Church, often available for use by leftist groups. The structure of the conference called for a number of panels, formed by radical activists, union leaders, "gay and lesbian community spokespersons," and others. The following topics for discussion constitute a blueprint for an ideal leftist agenda:

CUTS IN SOCIAL SERVICES—food stamps, social security, programs for the disabled, healthcare and housing.

ATTACKS ON THE LABOR MOVEMENT—public employee unions, workers in social service programs, health & safety.

SEXUAL OPPRESSION—reproductive rights, equality in the workplace, the struggle of lesbians and gay men, and a report from the August 9 Women's Forum.

397

RACIST VIOLENCE—police brutality, government repression.

CULTURAL WORK IN OUR MOVEMENT—education, news & broadcast media, music and art.

U.S. BUILD-UP TOWARDS WAR—from the draft to Central America, South Africa, Palestine and Ireland.[7]

The overall goal for the program was "Fighting the Reagan Program." Unless the relationship among the social, economic, and foreign policy issues is understood, it is difficult to comprehend the structure of this agenda. The reader will notice the reference to "our movement" in the fifth point of the agenda. It is with this movement that the homosexual organizations have established a network.

Shelley Hamilton, a minister of the UFMCC, has articulated the following statement which links the goals of the homosexual movement with other issues: "People must deal with the chains that destroy us. Wrapped up in this sexist issue is the key to freedom. Contained within the bondage of sexism is racism and classism, homophobia, and the rape and plunder of our earth."[8]

Adam DeBaugh, in his interview with the author, admitted that the UFMCC in general takes positions on a variety of issues, invariably liberal. The church supports:

> Passage of the Equal Rights Amendment
> Gun Control
> End to the stockpile and use of nuclear weapons
> Constitutional amendment granting full voting rights to residents of the District of Columbia
> Opponents of prayer in the schools
> Sex education (The UFMCC distributes materials prepared by groups that favor population control.)

Additionally, the UFMCC strongly supports its pacifist members and is "concerned" about nuclear power and the whole nuclear energy issue. It also supports government regulation which has resulted in the opening of public buildings to handicapped persons.[9]

A telling example of the linkage of various leftist issues lumped together by the homosexual movement is seen in the publicity materials calling for a homosexual demonstration against the Neighborhood Church on Bleecker Street. Under the leadership of its pastor, the Reverend Roger Fulton, this Greenwich Village church has taken a position consistent with traditional Christian teachings. The response of the homosexual movement has been a series of demonstrations. The following issues were listed as those of the movement against the church, organized by a homo-

The Movement and American Liberalism

sexual organization: "affirmative action, busing, lesbians and gay males, abortion rights, and campaigns for capital punishment, increased militarism, etc."[10]

In their attack on the 1980 Washington for Jesus march organized by Christian churches to promote religious values in the nation's capital, the UFMCC Washington office indicated four areas on which the event would concentrate: homosexuality, the Equal Rights Amendment, abortion, and pornography. The linkage of these issues, counteracted by the homosexual-sponsored Interfaith Council on Human Rights, indicates that for the homosexual movement they are part of its own agenda.[11] Should the homosexual movement perceive that abortion is not one of its concerns—and logically there is no reason why the elimination of unborn infants should relate to the desire for same-sex intercourse—they would have clarified that they have no interest in promoting abortion.

The National Gay Health Coalition (NGHC), at a meeting in Newark, New Jersey, on April 5, 1981, established a Committee for Social Change and Political Action (CSCPA). This was the climax of increasing frustrations caused by the perception that Reagan Administration policies did not suit the interests of this homosexual organization. One might think that their complaint related to an antihomosexual position adopted by the Administration; no such events appeared in the announcement of the formation of the CSCPA. Instead, three items were mentioned: 1) The "inappropriateness" of the nomination of Dr. C. Everett Koop as Surgeon General; 2) Proposed federal budget cuts; and 3) The Administration's foreign policy, especially in El Salvador.

The statement of purpose of the CSCPA reads like a list of the concerns of any other leftist organization:

> The NGHC deplores and opposes the Reagan Administration's proposed diversion of federal funds for health and human needs to increased spending for nuclear weapons and other military purposes.
> The NGHC deplores and opposes the Reagan Administration's attack on human rights and erosion of personal choice in this country and abroad.
> The NGHC endorses the May 3rd March on Washington, DC for Peace, Human Needs, and Against War, and urge [sic] members and all gay health workers to march under the NGHC banner.
> The NGHC endorses the call for local demonstrations on May 9th issued by the Nationwide Action for a Fair Budget and urges all gay health workers to support such events in their own cities.
> The NGHC will be represented at the National Peoples Congress, and at the National Lesbian and Gay Rights Congress.[12]

The CSCPA was represented at the National Peoples Congress by a member of both Lesbian and Gay People in Medicine and the American

Medical Student Association. Its representative at the Lesbian and Gay Rights National Conference is involved with the Gay Public Health Workers, the American Public Health Association, the Lesbian and Gay Physician's Assistants, and the National Coalition of Gay Sexually Transmitted Disease Services.

In its assessment of the 96th Congress, the Washington Office of the UFMCC outlined its legislative agenda, a mixed bag of specifically homosexual and other matters, all of a liberal bent:

Approval of "gay rights" legislation
Ratification of the Equal Rights Amendment
Reform of the U.S. Criminal Code
Family Planning Services
Funding of educational materials on homosexuality
Federal funding of abortion and birth control services
Avoidance of "McDonald Amendment" kinds of surprises [sic].[13]

(The last item refers to an amendment introduced by Rep. Larry McDonald (D-Ga.) and approved by the Congress barring the Legal Services Corporation from promoting homosexuality.)

A review of homosexual literature and group activities reveals support for a variety of specific liberal issues across the board. The few examples offered below are provided just as a sampler.

The Loving Brotherhood, a New Jersey organization for homosexuals, published a list of leftist organizations out of concern for the war in El Salvador. The following groups were included: American Friends Service Committee, Fellowship of Reconciliation, Gandhi Peace Foundation, Institute for World Order, Mobilization for Survival, Pax Christi International, Planetary Citizens, Riverside Church's Disarmament Program, Stockholm International Peace Research Institute, and World Peace Makers.[14] These are all leftist groups.

The Gertrude Stein Democratic Club of Washington, D.C., opposed a populist move to increase parental control over children's education in Washington's "Tuition Tax Credit Referendum" in November 1981.[15] Homosexual opposition to parental control over education could only have been expected, since it is certain that no school in which parents have an effective voice would be able to impart prohomosexual education.

An antidefense demonstration of individuals and institutions has become a "Washington tradition." Protests before a prominent Washington hotel where an annual exhibit and professional meeting by defense contractors take place attract naive church groups, traditional liberals, and hardened leftists. Among the endorsers of the 1981 demonstrations were two officials of New Ways Ministry, Sister Jeannine Gramick, SSND, and Xaverian Brother Joe [sic] Izzo, as well as the Quixote Center.[16]

The Movement and American Liberalism

The UFMCC Washington Office has indicated that "women's groups, gay organizations and church groups" support the D.C. Representation proposed constitutional amendment.[17] The political consensus is that passage of such an amendment would merely increase the liberal representation in the U.S. Congress.

The Department of Christian Social Action of the UFMCC in its March 1981 mailing to its affiliates nationwide included pro gun-control material, including registration forms for the National Coalition to Ban Handguns.[18] It would be logical for this coalition to reciprocate the favor at a future date, supporting in some way the goals of the homosexual movement.

The "Board of Elders" of the UFMCC passed a resolution at its April 1980 meeting calling for an end to the hunting of harp seals in Canada. The Department of Christian Social Action of the UFMCC followed up by requesting that letters of support be sent to Canadian authorities.[19]

Throughout this work many other examples are offered that show the homosexual movement as liberal not only in terms of social policy issues, but in the economic and foreign policy areas as well. The liberalism of the homosexual movement, however, is not merely the result of philosophical conviction; it has been hammered out by years of working closely with leftist organizations.

Networking: The Organizations

The first printed issue of *Come Out!*, published on November 14, 1969, summarized the revolutionary aspirations of the homosexual movement:

> Because our oppression is based on sex and the sex roles which oppress us from infancy, we must explore these roles and their meanings . . . Does society make a place for us . . . as a man? A woman? A homosexual or lesbian? How does the family structure affect us? What is sex, and what does it mean?
> What is love? As homosexuals, we are in a unique position to examine these questions from a fresh point of view. You'd better believe we are going to do so—that we are going to transform society at large through the open realization of our own consciousness.[20]

Society, however, is too complex and vast to be radically transformed by one group or form of consciousness. Although social reformers start with the Utopian position that the key to revolution is in *their* hands and *only* in their hands, they quickly come to the realization that they must join forces with like-minded souls if their own agenda is to have chance of implementation at all. In this process, rationalization creates the perception that the agendas of other groups are also "logical." Formerly disparate groups begin to work together and coalitions are formed for the benefit of all concerned. It is no different with the homosexual movement, for homosexual organizations have allied themselves with groups concerned about issues that have no apparent relationship to the practice of having intercourse with a member of one's own sex.

Homosexual organizations actively seek the formation of such coalitions. In one issue of the newsletter of the National Gay Task Force (January-February 1981), the NGTF reported its participation in events of the National Association of Police Community Relations Officers, the Association of Women in Psychology, the National Women's Studies Conference, the Women in Law Conference, the Women's Leadership Network Conference, and the Interchange Resource Center. The newsletter also indicated that active support on specific issues was being sought from the National Education Association, the National Organization for Women, the National Association of Social Workers, and the American Federation of Teachers.[21] Homosexual groups are very conscious that they must seek the support of other liberal organizations. This was made clear at the 1982 biannual public meeting of New York City's Coalition for Lesbian and Gay Rights, an organization of several homosexual groups committed to the passage of prohomosexual legislation by the City Council. The main speaker at the February 20th meeting which took place at the "Gay Synagogue in the Westbeth Artists Housing Complex" on Bank Street (Greenwich Village) was David Rothenberg, a member of the City's Human Rights Commission. It was reported that at the meeting "Rothenberg emphasized that CLGR had to concentrate on 'building bridges of cooperation' to other minority groups in agitating for the passage of the city's proposed gay civil rights law."[22] In order to secure the cooperation of an efficient network of friendly organizations, moreover, it was pointed out that homosexual groups had to join forces with broad coalitions and be willing to support issues not "naturally" part and parcel of their own agendas:

> From the ideas expressed at the conference, it seems likely that a major item on the CLGR agenda will be reaching groups that have not been reached before, such as blacks, Hispanics and Asian-Americans, in an effort to create a stronger multi-issue coalition beyond the single issue of gay rights. "We have to be in touch with groups such as the Black and Puerto Rican Coalition of Legislators," said Rothenberg. "We have to be visible and audible. Gay activists have to become attuned to such issues."[23]

A prime example of a leftwing network in which homosexual organizations participate is the Interchange Resource Network, a coalition of liberal organizations founded in April 1978 "as a clearinghouse to disseminate information on the right-wing to moderate, progressive and liberal

The Movement and American Liberalism

groups."[24] In addition to the national organizations, there are state level organizations in Alaska, Arkansas, Illinois, Minnesota, Texas, Maryland, Washington, and Wisconsin. The national organization announced plans to add twelve more state affiliates in an August 1981 fund-raising letter.[25] Its bimonthly publication has been called by *Mother Jones* "outstanding" (May 1981). The membership of Interchange is representative of America's liberalism. On its board of directors sit representatives of leftist Catholic nuns (Network) with homosexual lobbyists (Gay Rights National Lobby), reformed rabbis (Union of American Hebrew Congregations) with radical feminists (National Organization for Women), trade unionists (United Auto Workers) with proabortionists. The following list of organizations provides an idea of the breadth of Interchange's membership, with its Board of Directors composed of individuals from such groups as:

The Kamber Group
Student National Education Association
National Education Association
National Women's Political Caucus*
NARAL (National Abortion Rights Action League)*
Network
United Presbyterian Church
AFSCME/PEOPLE
Union of American Hebrew Congregations
United Auto Workers
Committee on Students and Youth
National Association of Social Workers
Parents Without Partners
National Women's Conference Committee*
United States Student Association
Self Determination for D.C.
National Organization for Women*
National Consumers League
B'nai B'rith Women
Coalition of American Public Employees
Ms Magazine*
ACORN
Unitarian Universalist Association
Rural America
Lutheran Council, U.S.A.
Consumer Federation of America
National Council of Senior Citizens
National Council of Churches
Fellowship of Metropolitan Community Churches
Progressive Alliance
Gay Rights National Lobby

403

Americans Concerned About Corporate Power
Women's Division, United Methodist Church
Religious Coalition for Abortion Rights*
Americans for Democratic Action
Center for Third World Countries
Mormons for ERA
Columbia Associates
*Denotes proabortion group

The National Gay Task Force describes the Interchange Resource Center as "the group that we have been working with most closely."[26] The reader will notice that there are several homosexual groups represented on the Board of Directors. Most likely, there are other homosexual groups involved with Interchange. For example, the National Gay Task Force, which had a staff person as Interchange contact, is not represented on the Board. It is interesting to note that Interchange's headquarters are located at the National Education Association, a member of its board. The National Student Association (NSA) is also part of Interchange. The National Gay Student Center, a project of the NSA, publishes lists of homosexual student groups[27] and a newsletter called . . . Interchange. When the author called the NSA to request information on the National Gay Student Center he was referred to the "Interchange Resource Center at the NEA." The connections are obvious. On September 23, 1981, the Interchange Resource Center issued a statement against the Family Protection Act, accusing profamily advocates of causing problems for civil liberties advocates by "emotionalizing issues of Gay/Lesbian civil rights."[28] This was not a casual statement, but coincided with the date of a campaign against the Family Protection Act directed by the National Gay Task Force. Still, the leaders of Interchange seem to be fully aware that homosexual issues would not sit well with potential financial supporters. The August 1981 fundraising letter made no mention of homosexuality or the relationship between Interchange and homosexual organizations, although it mentioned prominently such issues as the ERA and abortion, which are also part of the homosexual movement's agenda.

Among the members of Interchange there are a number of leftist religious organizations and coalitions sponsored by these religious institutions. They provide the linkage between this secular network and the religious-oriented Washington Interreligious Staff Council (WISC), a parallel leftist coalition. The UFMCC participates in both networks. (See chapter VII for a full description of WISC and its relations with the homosexual movement.)

Liberal networking exists not only at the national level, but has its roots at the local level. The following excerpt from an article by Forrest J. Rode, President of the Sioux Empire Gay Coalition, reveals the inner workings of the network at the grassroots level:

The Movement and American Liberalism

I count among my friends the National Democratic Committeeman from South Dakota, the presidents of ACLU and NOW in Sioux Falls, and the coordinator of South Dakota Coalition for Freedom of Choice, a group advocating a pro-choice position on abortion. The members of Vermillion (S.D.) Gays and Friends also largely comprise the membership of their local chapters of ACLU and NOW. In 1976 I was the Sioux Falls coordinator for the Carter/Mondale campaign. The owner of our local gay bar, the Hitch'N Post, is a friend of our county sheriff. I have friends in Senator McGovern's office and worked with U.S. Rep. Tom Daschle when he was Sen. Abourezk's administrative aide.[29]

In Phoenix, several organizations (in addition to homosexual groups) were listed as "endorsers" of the first statewide "lesbian/gay pride" march in Arizona (1981). They included: American Civil Liberties Union, Arizona National Organization for Women, National Lawyers Guild, Movement for a New Society, Peoples Anti-War Mobilization, People Against Racism, and Workers World Party.[30] The Peoples Anti-War Mobilization in turn involves no less than two dozen organizations ranging from several locals of the American Federation of State, County, and Municipal Employees to the American Indian Movement and the homosexual "Dykes Against Racism Everywhere."[31]

The Mobilization for Survival has already been mentioned in connection with the Loving Brotherhood and the ideological convergence between the homosexual movement and the "New Left." The following leftist groups have provided the activists and ideologues for the Mobilization for Survival:[32]

War Resisters League
Chicago Peace Council
American Friends Service Committee
Fellowship of Reconciliation
Clergy and Laity Concerned
Women's International League for Peace and Freedom
Institute for Policy Studies
Movement for a New Society
New American Movement
Catholic Peace Fellowship
Gray Panthers
United Electrical Workers

An interesting case of network formation is Friends of Families, a leftist organization designed to be the counterpart of the conservative National Pro-Family Coalition. One of the most successful issues of the New Right is the defense of the family. The left has tried to seize this issue as an avenue through which it can press its own agenda. The leftist definition of family, however, is quite at variance with what most people would call family. By using the same word, however, "progressive" forces can obtain the support of individuals and organizations (e.g., churches) that normally would not work with them. Such an issue can become the core ideological concept which serves to nucleate a coalition in which diverse organizations participate and support each other. On January 12 and 13, 1982, a conference took place in Oakland, California, for the purpose of organizing the California branch of Friends of Families. According to a conference report, all the speakers at the event "were unanimous in their support of a progressive pro-families organization, an organization that attempted to understand what families needed and that was clearly on the side of all kinds of families, including single parent and gay families."[33]

Among the over eighty organizations represented at the conference were several homosexual groups. The membership of the conference included:[34]

> Planned Parenthood**
> Catholic Charities
> The Church and Society Network
> The San Francisco Council of Churches
> Equal Rights Advocates
> Reproductive Rights National Network**
> The Religious Coalition for Abortion Rights**
> The Salvation Army
> The Harvey Milk Democratic Club*
> Stonewall Democratic Club*
> Niagra Democratic Club
> The United Church Coalition
> United Methodist Women
> The Service Employees International Union
> American Federation of Teachers
> Graphic Arts International Union
> American Postal Workers' Union
> Amalgamated Transit Union
> Several Teamsters Union locals
> Contra Costa and Santa Clara Building Trades councils
> Hotel and Restaurant Employees locals
> United Auto Workers locals
> International Longshore and Warehousemen's Union local.
> *Denotes a homosexual group
> **Denotes a proabortion group

The conference report boasted that among the attendees one could find "several leadership people from the Union of American Hebrew Congregations, the United Church of Christ, the Lutherans, the Methodists, and the Catholic Church. A wide variety of social service organizations were also present."[35] One can safely assume that most Roman Catholics, as well as other Christians represented at the conference, would find it revolting to see the leadership of their churches (including Catholic Charities, an agency created to engage in charitable work) working with proabortion activists and various homosexual organizations in defense of the "gay family."

In response to the challenge presented by the Family Protection Act, the left has organized the Coalition to Stop the FPA. This effort is national in scope and also represents a good example of the participation of homosexual groups in the activities of the American liberal establishment. By November 1981, the coalition had fifty organizations in its membership and featured three main working groups in its structure: the Public Education Committee, the Legislative Lobbying Committee, and the Legal Research and Analysis Committee. Homosexual movement leaders figured prominently in the coalition: Lucia Valeska, director of the National Gay Task Force, as head of the Public Education Committee, and Mel Boozer, a Washington, D.C., leader, as a member of the Legislative Lobbying Committee. A partial list of coalition members exemplifies the involvement of homosexual organizations with other "more traditional" groups:[36]

> American Civil Liberties Union
> B'nai B'rith Women
> Lambda Legal Defense and Education Fund*
> Gay Rights National Lobby*
> National Organization of Lesbians and Gays*
> Ms Foundation**
> The National Association for the Advancement of Colored People (NAACP)
> National Gay Task Force*
> Fund For Human Dignity*
> National Education Association
> Women's Action Alliance**
> League of Women Voters**
> National Women's Law Center**
> Pennsylvania Coalition Against Domestic Violence
> Children's Defense Fund.
>   *Denotes a homosexual group
>   **Denotes a proabortion group

The political orientation of the National Gay Task Force is evident from its announcement that this coalition was part of its overall Campaign Against the Radical Right.[37]

Homosexual organizations have been active in numerous efforts to attack the Reagan Administration. The *Washington Post* reported their participation in a May 3, 1981 "March on the Pentagon" (rallying around causes ranging from gay rights to Palestinian autonomy) with other leftist organizations including: the New York chapter of the National Lawyers Guild, the Revolutionary Communist Party, the Black Veterans for Social Justice, and the American Federation of Government Employees.[38] In the fall of 1981, extensive anti-Reagan activities were scheduled nationwide. Among the groups reportedly involved in these efforts were: "trade unions and other organizations of the working class; women's groups; the gay and lesbian movement; the anti-draft movement; students; people on welfare; progressive religious forces; the anti-nuclear movement; the disabled; the elderly; and others."[39] This is probably a highly exaggerated statement designed to stimulate participation. However, within the veils of propaganda, the leftist complexion of the movement becomes readily apparent.

Networking has yielded the homosexual movement its intended political support. During the first part of 1980, the movement waged a fierce battle against religious forces in Baltimore (Christian, Moslem, and Jewish) for the passage of prohomosexual legislation. Many organizations went on the record in support of the homosexual movement. The following list was compiled from letters supplied to the author by New Ways Ministry. A single asterisk denotes letters addressed to Baltimore's Mayor, William D. Schaefer; a double asterisk denotes letters to the Coalition for Lesbian and Gay Rights.

These letters, most of them addressed to Mayor Schaefer, appear to have been the result of an orchestrated effort. This is just one example of the homosexual network in action.

There are a multitude of organizations at all levels which participate, in varying degrees, in this network. Some are offered here by way of example only. They are mentioned to acquaint the reader with the depth and breadth of support the homosexual movement has been able to muster in just a few short years.

One of the staunchest supporters of the homosexual movement is the American Civil Liberties Union, as seen in the article by Forrest Rode which indicated that in one South Dakota town a homosexual organization, NOW, and the ACLU are practically coextensive. The article gave the impression that the same individuals were at one moment the ACLU and at the next moment the homosexual organization. There are many ways in which the ACLU helps the homosexual movement. For example, *The Rights of Gay People: An American Civil Liberties Union Handbook* is a work highly valued in the homosexual community. Ira Glasser, as Executive Director of the ACLU, has lent his support to a fundraising letter of the Fund for Human Dignity, the "foundation of the National Gay Task Force."[41] This letter was reportedly mailed to some 600,000 individuals "including members of the American Civil Liberties Union."[42] The ACLU has obviously cooperated fully toward the financial survival of an important

408

Organization	Date, 1980	Support Language
Northeast Community Organization	March 10	"We urge your support and would like to know your current position on this bill."*
American Friends Service Committee	January 24	"The American Friends Service Committee urges your approval and backing of the ordinance."*
Baltimore Abortion Rights	March 24	". . . we support you 100%. You most definitely have permission to use our name."**
National Association of Social Workers (Maryland Chapter)	April 2	"In our view, this [discrimination against homosexuals] is an intolerable situation for a group of citizens who are productive, contributing members of society. We have a responsibility to affirm and openly protect the equal status of members of the gay and lesbian minority."
Young Women's Christian Association	April 3	"We urge you to consider supporting and signing the above legislation."*
Chesapeake Energy Alliance	March 16	". . . the Chesapeake Energy Alliance endorses the Coalition for Lesbian and Gay Civil Rights."
National Organization for Women (Baltimore Chapter)	March 25	"Baltimore NOW further unanimously endorsed the sending of a witness to the hearings before your Council, as well as a lobbying effort by its members in certain of the councilmatic [sic] districts."**
Presbytery of Baltimore (United Presbyterian Church, U.S.A.)	March 25	"It is my opinion that these positions of the highest Assembly of our church representing three million United Presbyterians throughout the country would indicate that the position of our church would be in support of the proposed ordinance and to prohibit discriminatory practices against homosexual persons."
Communities Organized to Improve Life, Inc.	February 19	"On March 18, 1980, [sic] the Board of Directors of COIL endorsed the Baltimore's Community Relations Commission's proposal to prohibit discriminatory practices against persons because of their sexual orientation."
Coalition of Peninsula Organizations	February 1	". . . we believe that Gay and Lesbian rights . . . should be protected by law."
Homewood Friends Meeting	January 25	". . . we ask for your endorsement of the measure to help insure its passage."*
Diocese of Maryland (Episcopal)	February 7	". . . the Episcopal Church is on record in support of civil rights for gay persons. . . . The passage of this ordinance would help to guarantee the civil rights of all our citizens."

homosexual organization. The ACLU also supports the movement in its willingness to provide legal counsel to homosexuals. In many cases the homosexual movement tries to have its ideology enshrined as law by judicial fiat. (One of the peculiarities of the American political system is the existence of judges as functionaries appointed for life who are not answerable to the people but who virtually have the power of legislating with little or no restriction.) In one case, the ACLU filed a $520,000 claim on behalf of Timothy Curran, reportedly an avowed homosexual, against Oakland's Mount Diablo Council of the Boy Scouts of America.[43] Curran had attracted attention when he insisted on attending his senior prom with another male as a "date." In another case, Arthur B. Spitzer, legal director of the ACLU, represented a homosexual mail clerk fired by the FBI.[44] The Agency paid over $20,000 to the homosexual, and the ACLU official praised the action as a "victory."

From an organizational point of view, the ACLU has also lent its support to the homosexual movement. In coordination with Amnesty International, the ACLU has set up a Gay Prisoner's Committee, under the aegis of the ACLU's National Gay Rights Project. Ostensibly, the purpose of the project is to "document incidents of selective abuse or discrimination suffered by lesbian and gay prisoners at the hand of police, the courts, jail or prison personnel, or other prisoners."[45] This project would by its nature be very useful in the subversion of legitimate authority by the homosexual movement, especially in light of the ACLU's avowed intention of using not only litigation, but also "lobbying and media techniques." The ACLU also announced that data it collected would be integrated with data available to Amnesty International.

The ACLU has issued statements in support of "gay rights" which are subsequently used in the promotion of prohomosexual legislation. For example, part of the support for New York State Assembly Bill No. 9996 was a statement by the ACLU.[46] The purpose of this bill was to facilitate the custody of children by a homosexual parent (male or female). The involvement of ACLU with the legislative process has proven very useful to the homosexual movement. The following report published by the National Gay Task Force's newsletters reveals the depth of involvement, not only of the ACLU, but of other left-wing organizations/politicians in efforts to promote the homosexual movement:

NGTF lobbyists had experience lobbying in New York City and State legislative bodies but recognized that that was limited background for tackling the United States Congress in a responsible and productive manner. Thus, the lobbyists initially spent a great deal of time conferring with several friendly members of Congress and their staffs. During earlier years, our lobbyists had been involved in candidate nights at the Gay Activists Alliance and some had been involved in one of New York's most powerful Democratic Party clubs, the Village Independent Democrats. Consequently, we had good ties to several members of New York's congressional delegations, particularly Edward Koch, Charles Rangel, Bella Abzug, and Herman Badillo. Additionally, our lobbying staff consulted at length, and continues to do so, with the very successful legislative experts at the National Organization for Women (N.O.W.) and the American Civil Liberties Union. Each of these organizations has full-time lobbying staffs in Washington, D.C. Karen de Crow, President of N.O.W., and Aryeh Neier, Executive Director of the National Headquarters of the ACLU, were wise and generous in their advice to us. Their staffs have been endlessly helpful.[47]

When the possibility introducing prohomosexual legislation in the Congress seemed poor, a successful technique was designed by the head of the ACLU. The NGTF came to refer to it as "Neier's technique": "Aryeh Neier of the ACLU argued that members of Congress should be approached with the Query, If five other members will join in cosponsoring, would you help introduce a gay civil rights bill? If several courageous members would act together, it would dilute the political toxicity of sponsorship."[48] Normally, the ACLU is associated with the defense of the Bill of Rights in court. Obviously, the extent of its interest and activities go far beyond such a narrow concern.

Another organization which has "distinguished" itself for its support of the homosexual movement is the Americans for Democratic Action (ADA), one of the most important and "prestigious" organizations of the American left. One of the items included in the ADA's 1980 voting record rating was the McDonald (D-Ga.) amendment to stop the Legal Services Corporation from using the courts for the promotion of the homosexual ideology. Homosexual issues are obviously important for the ADA. Like the ACLU, the ADA provides support that extends considerably beyond the "normal" political activities usually identified with this organization. On February 26, 1981, a meeting was held between representatives of the homosexual movement, certain New York City Councilmen, and representatives from selected organizations sympathetic to the homosexual movement. The purpose of the meeting was to map out a strategy for the promotion of prohomosexual legislation; the ADA was present.[49]

The ADA has also helped the homosexual movement in its antifamily efforts. As part of a continuing campaign to defeat the Family Protection Act, the National Gay Task Force held a press conference at the Capitol on September 23, 1981. Side by side with Lucia Valeska, Director of the NGTF, was a representative of the ADA. An ADA press release distributed at the gathering stated: "Americans for Democratic Action is glad to join the efforts of the National Gay Task Force. . . . The gay and liberal communities must strive together to inform concerned citizens everywhere."[50]

The Greater Washington Chapter of the ADA joined forces with the

Democratic Socialist Organizing Committee and the Gertrude Stein Democratic Club in opposing the 1981 Tuition Tax Credit initiative in Washington, D.C., and in proposing a united slate of candidates for the District of Columbia's Constitutional Convention.[51] This pattern of collaboration brings undeniable benefits to the homosexuals. Should the liberal-homosexual coalition be successful, the forthcoming constitution for the proposed State of the District of Columbia would logically enshrine in law not only the predictable liberal socioeconomic principles, but the basic tenets of the homosexual ideology as well.

It is interesting to note that Robert Drinan, a Jesuit priest and former Democratic representative from Massachusetts, was elected president of the ADA after he was barred by the Vatican from seeking reelection. Reports have circulated in leftist Catholic circles that Father Drinan was forbidden to run on account of his voting record in the area of abortion.[52]

There are many other liberal organizations which have close links with, or have supported, the homosexual movement. The reader may find in the appendix an alphabetical listing of organizations which have made representations *for the record* which, in the view of a homosexual source, tend to support the homosexual cause. There is no implication that any of these organizations or individuals intended to have their names associated with the homosexual movement, although in most cases statements have been offered by nonhomosexual organizations to be utilized by the homosexual movement for political purposes. The existence of such statements should surprise no one. The instances below show various ways in which nonhomosexual institutions relate, in a supportive way, to the homosexual movement. They are nonexhaustive and have been chosen to show the depth and breadth of support for the network. Many of these organizations and institutions are specifically leftist in political terms. Others are ostensibly nonpolitical, but have agendas and philosophies that help them identify with traditional leftist organizations. The former include such groups as the Center for Concern, Network, and Americans for Democratic Action. The latter include the social service establishment, the American Bar Association, the American Psychiatric Association, and others.

Organization/Individual	Date	Activity(ies)
National Council of Teachers of English	June 18, 1981	"In spite of the very narrow margin for approval of the Gay Rights resolution passed at the 1976 NCTE convention, the organization and particularly its executive personnel have cooperated very well with the Gay Caucus and the officially appointed Committee on the Concerns of Lesbians and Gay

Organization/Individual	Date	Activity(ies)
		Males in the English Teaching Profession."[53]
National Council of Teachers of English	November 7, 1979	NCTE funds survey on attitudes towards homosexuals among its members.[54]
Quixote Center (Mt. Rainier, Md.)	October 10, 1977	Letter to American Catholic bishops supporting the homosexual movement within the Catholic Church.[55]
	June 6, 1981	Sponsorship of Central American pro–Revolutionary Evening (a fundraiser) at Catholic University, Washington, D.C. (in the same hall used for a homosexual fundraiser described in chapter IX).[56]
	1979	Partial funding (with NOW), of a Strategy Conference on Homophobia in the Church.[57]
		Close ties with New Ways Ministry; Promotion of Catholic feminism; Statement in a personal interview with Quixote Center staff person: "Members of the Quixote Center see nothing wrong with the ordination of lesbians . . . Not to ordain lesbians (and women in general) is discriminatory."[58]
National Institute on Alcohol Abuse and Alcoholism	Spring, 1981	Liaison person with the National Association of Gay Alcoholism Professionals participates in NIAAA Advisory Council meetings.[59]
National Council on Alcoholism (various chapters)	May/June 1981	Representatives of homosexual organizations make presentations at NCA workshops.[60]
Pennsylvania Addiction Counselors Association	1981	Member of National Association of Gay Alcoholism Professionals elected President.[61]
Alcoholism Counselors Association, New York City Chapter	May 20, 1981	Homosexual organization's representative makes presentation.[62]
National Council on Alcoholism	December 1980	Statement praising homosexual organization effusively.[63]
New Democratic Coalition	May 1977	NDC lends itself to be the instrument of homosexual movement in pressuring New York's Governor Hugh Carey to pass pro-homosexual executive order.[64]

Organization/Individual	Date	Activity(ies)
American Bar Association	—	Establishment of ABA's Committee on Rights of Gay People. Committee chairman makes prohomosexual statements.[65]
American Social Health Association	—	ASHA works with various homosexual groups and refers clients to them.[66]
American Library Association	June 1, 1979	*Booklist*, the reviewing journal of the ALA, recommends prohomosexual text for grades 5 through 8.[67]
National Assocation for the Advancement of Colored People	August 1977	NAACP supports march of homosexuals at United Nations.[68]
Black Panther Party	1970	Close ideological and working ties between Black Panthers and the homosexual movement in the early '70s.[69]
National Association of Broadcast Employees and Technicians (a union)	August 1977	Local 16 of the NABET endorsed the Gay Activist Alliance's UN rally for its strike against ABC-TV.[70]
American Federation of Teachers	1977	The AFT hires a male teacher dismissed on grounds of "immorality." This was reported by the *New York Times* in an article on various instances in which homosexual teachers had been dismissed.[71]
National Education Association	—	NEA spends $50,000 defending the right of an avowed homosexual to teach and forcing a school district to rehire him.[72]
National Association of Social Workers	—	Statement: "NASW affirms the right of all persons to define and express their own sexuality. In choosing their own lifestyles, all persons are to be encouraged to develop their individual potential to the fullest extent possible as long as they do not infringe upon the rights of others."[73]
Madalyn O'Hair	—	Gay Atheists League of America granted the right to publish materials in the *American Atheist* and to use the motto "Freedom from Religion." Pledged to

The Movement and American Liberalism

Organization/Individual	Date	Activity(ies)
		cooperate with homosexual groups.[74]
Rev. Daniel Berrigan, S.J., Clergy and Laity Concerned Codirector; Rev. Paul Abels, Washington Square United Methodist Church	—	Endorsed declaration in support of Intro 384, a New York City prohomosexual bill.[75]
National Lawyers Guild	—	Promotion of female homosexual-led families by Lesbian and Gay Parents Project, an offshoot of the National Lawyers Guild's Committee Against Sexism.[76]
Dan Bradley, President, Legal Services Corporation	March 4, 1982	Joins Board of Directors of National Gay Rights Lobby.[77]
The *New York Times*	October 25, 1977	Publication of strongly prohomosexual article immediately prior to New York City's election. This article was seemingly designed to "get out" the homosexual vote as a bloc vote and thus influence the election in favor of the homosexual movement. No mention made of violence on the part of homosexual activists.[78]
	May 24 and October 24, 1977	Two editorials advocating a nondiscriminatory policy in the hiring of teachers. In both cases, the "opinion" of the American Psychiatric Association that homosexuality is not an illness is invoked.[79] One of the editorials ran just prior to the 1977 mayoral election.
National Catholic Reporter	November 21, 1980	Prohomosexual editorial in this radical leftist unofficial Roman Catholic publication.[80]

The information provided thus far reveals the existence of a complex network of left-leaning organizations which work in concert for the promotion of common issues and the development of mutual support. The homosexual movement is an integral part of this network. In this network, there is a division of labor based on interests, capabilities, and funding. Political in nature, the network exercises an influence far in excess of any grassroots basis. Much of its success is based on the fact that the American liberal network has managed to mix religion and politics to an unprecedented degree. Funds flow from religious institutions to centers of political action while a multitude of issues—elements of the homosexual ideology being just a few of them—are promoted across the board.

A typical example of the commingling of religion and politics is the Jesuit-sponsored "Center of Concern." Founded in the early seventies, it is largely funded by the Jesuits, the Maryknoll order, and the United Methodist Church.[81] The center is not presently involved in issues concerning homosexuality due only to the size of the staff, not as a matter of its acceptance of the traditional Christian position on this question. However, "since they are concerned with social justice and liberty for all, therefore they have strong feelings regarding the issue"[82] (of homosexuality). This does not mean, however, that the center is uninvolved with issues of interest to the homosexual movement. For example, on May 20 through 22, 1981, the center sponsored a "conference on women" with the participation of two female staffers from New Ways Ministry.[83] Its tenth anniversary was celebrated by a presentation from one of the world's foremost leaders of left-wing Catholicism, Cardinal Paulo Evaristo Arns of Sao Paulo, an influential exponent of the Theology of Liberation.[84] The Center of Concern was also involved with a number of other organizations and individuals whom the reader will recognize, in an October 20, 1981, seminar on a church document released shortly before that date.[85] This meeting reportedly included: The Institute for Policy Studies (organizer of the event), a left-wing think tank; the Reverend Robert Drinan, S.J., of the Americans for Democratic Action; The National Education Association; and Network, an organization of left-wing nuns.

A good example of a political coalition involving leftist, feminist, and homosexual groups at the local level is the list of those who endorsed Alexa Freeman, a Washington, D.C., Ward 2 candidate for the Constitutional Convention election which took place on November 3, 1981. According to a poster distributed throughout the ward and paid for by the Committee to Elect Alexa Freeman, the following groups endorsed her candidacy:

> DC Women's Political Caucus
> Ward 2 Neighborhood & Community Coalition
> DC Area Feminist Alliance
> Dupont Circle Political Action Committee
> Feminist Law Collective
> Gertrude Stein Democratic Club
> Americans for Democratic Action
> Democratic Socialist Organizing Committee
> Gay Activists Alliance
> National Lawyers Guild, DC Chapter[86]

Aside from two recognizably local groups, these organizations are clearly

The Movement and American Liberalism

linked with national groups or movements, among them the homosexual movement.

The reader will recognize many of the names among the following list of participants in the "Campaign to Stop the Arms Bazaar," the annual Washington, D.C., effort to interfere with a meeting of defense contractors:[87]

> Institute for Policy Studies*
> Coalition for a New Foreign and Military Policy*
> Robert Drinan, S.J.
> Walter Fauntroy
> New Ways Ministry*
> Brother Joseph Izzo, Xaverian Brother
> Committee Against Registration and the Draft*
> Maryknoll Fathers and Brothers*
> Holy Trinity Seminary*
> Capuchin College Justice and Peace Committee
> Carmelite Sisters of Charity
> Center for a New Creation
> Center of Concern
> Coalition Oscar Romero
> Committee in Solidarity with the People of El Salvador (CISPES)
> Fellowship of Reconciliation
> Mobilization for Survival
> National Organization for Women (DC Chapter)
> National Office of Jesuit Social Ministries
> Network
> Office of Social Development, Archdiocese of Washington
> People's Anti-War Mobilization
> Potomac Alliance
> Quixote Center
> SANE
> Sojourners Fellowship
> Washington Peace Center
> Washington Training Collective
> Women Strike for Peace
> Women's Pentagon Action
> World Peace Tax Fund
> World Peacemakers
> Organizations marked with an asterisk were listed with the names of one or more individuals; thus the organizational affiliation is unclear.

There was no indication that affiliations were listed "for identification purposes only," as is customary when no organizational affiliation should be inferred on a list of this nature. What is significant about this list is the pattern of networking that it reveals when examined in the light of groups involved in other leftist activities.

An example of a religious coalition involving homosexual groups and religious organizations that have indicated support for a purely political cause (the Equal Rights Amendment) is the list of Catholic supporters of the ERA circulated by the Women's Ordination Conference (WOC) during the latter part of 1981. In a package that not only requested support for the ERA, but also attacked the economic program of the Reagan Administration, Sister Maureen Fiedler, RSM, asked members of WOC to become active in a project of the National Organization for Women. The pro-ERA Catholic groups listed by WOC were:[88]

National Conference of Catholic Charities
Leadership Conference of Women Religious
National Assembly of Women Religious
National Coalition of American Nuns
National Federation of Priests' Councils
Conference of Major Superiors of Men
NETWORK
*Women's Ordination Conference
Priests for Equality
Padres
Las Hermanas
Women of the Church Coalition
St. Joan's Alliance
Religious Formation Conference
Center of Concern
Eighth Day Center for Justice (Chicago and New York City)
Intercommunity Center for Justice and Peace
Oregon Center for Peace and Justice
Institute for Education in Peace and Justice (St. Louis)
*Sisters of Loretto
Sisters of the Humility of Mary
Xaverian Brothers, American Central Province
Sisters of St. Joseph of Medaille (Cincinnati)
Paulist Social Action Committee
*Community of the Holy Spirit (San Diego)
*Sisters of Mercy of the Union (Generalate Team)
*New Ways Ministry
The Grail Movement
*Dignity, Inc.
Chicago Catholic Women
Association of Chicago Priests
Quixote Center
Justice and Peace Office (Winter Park, Fla.)
*Passionist Social Concerns Center
Medical Mission Sisters—Eastern District & Western District Assembly
*Sisters of St. Joseph of Peace—Center for Peace & Justice
Groups in italics endorsed the First National Symposium on Homosexuality and the Catholic Church

The Movement and American Liberalism

*Members of the Coalition for Gay Civil Rights (see chapter VII)

In addition to Dignity and New Ways Ministry (openly Catholic homosexual organizations) of a total of thirty-six pro-ERA groups, twelve are also members of the Catholic prohomosexual network Coalition for Gay Civil Rights. We have already encountered Network and Center of Concern; The National Conference of Catholic Charities represents the social service establishment within the Catholic Church. Brother Cornelius Hubbuch, Provincial of the American Central Province of the Xaverian Brothers, is also Secretary Treasurer of the Conference of Major Superiors of Men. These two organizations endorsed the First National Symposium on Homosexuality and the Catholic Church.[89] Sister Teresa Kane, president of the Sisters of Mercy of the Union, was a speaker at the same homosexual symposium. The "General Administrative Team" of her order endorsed the homosexual symposium and the "Generalate Team" of the order appears as a supporter of the ERA. Note the overlap between the organizations listed in italics and those indicated by an asterisk are also endorsers of the homosexual symposium. The overlap of these groups is obvious.

If the reader has reached the conclusion that America faces a broad composite of left-wing organizations, an interlocking complex of institutions bent on moving society toward the left—regardless of the ethos of most Americans—his conclusion is accurate. There is almost no evidence that this network has broad-based grassroots support. Essentially, it seems to be maintained by elites within the religious and social service establishments, funded by tax monies and church contributions under the approving gaze of the press. As a matter of fact, should the liberal press cease to report on the activities of this network it would, for all practical purposes, cease to exist.

The homosexual movement has benefited much from the support it enjoys from American liberalism. In turn, it has accepted in toto the liberal ideology. From a practical point of view this means that all conservatives—whether they focus on social, economic, or foreign policy issues—have much to gain by working together against what is really a united left-wing front that includes the homosexual movement.

Networking: The Individuals

Organizations are nothing but extensions of the relationships among individuals. The primacy of individuals in social and political activism is often lost because of our tendency to think of social structures as substantive. In reality, it is individuals who think, decide, and act when social or political action takes place. The problem with trying to describe activism in terms of individuals is that the number of actors and the detail of their actions is much too large to allow for an accurate and succinct presentation. In a movement as vast as the homosexual movement, this is even harder, inasmuch as there are a multitude of tendencies and interests within the general framework of the community. However, even a few examples of activists can show how the radical leftist origin of the movement, well documented by Marotta, has not been betrayed by the present leadership.[90] In the past affiliations and interests of its activists too, the homosexual movement shows itself still basically part of the American left. An interesting example of the convergence of leftist causes in a single individual is the case of "Brother" Rick Garcia, BFCC, a member of a Catholic religious order (not recognized by the Church) and a staffer at New Ways Ministry (NWM). According to *Bondings*, the publication of NWM, Garcia's experience included:

> Staff person and community organizer for the United Farm Workers
> Volunteer for the National Organization for Women
> Volunteer for the Gay Community Center (St. Louis)
> Organizer of Catholics who participated in the 1975 national ERA rally in Springfield, Ill.
> Charter Member and Treasurer of the St. Louis Task Force for the Ordination of Women
> Member of the Board of Directors of the Missouri Coalition for Human Rights
> Past President and Vice President of Dignity/St. Louis.[91]

Also associated with NWM is Brother Joseph Izzo, CFX, an avowed homosexual and counselor at Catholic University of America. Izzo is a member of the Board of Directors of NWM, Dignity/Washington, and the prohomosexual network Catholic Coalition for Gay Civil Rights. His other associations are revealing. He is a member of the Social Justice Committee of the Xaverian Brothers' American Central Province and of Pax Christi. "Social justice" committees have been set up throughout the Roman Catholic Church as a network from which to advocate leftist policies within and without the Church and as centers of liberal activism. Pax Christi is a left-wing Catholic organization that traditionally advocates positions inimical to national defense.[92]

Two examples of left-wing involvement within the United Fellowship of Metropolitan Community Churches are Frank K. Zerilli and R. Adam DeBaugh. The former is the executive secretary of the Fellowship office. According to *In Unity*, "besides being involved in gay rights, Zerilli is active in the anti-nuclear movement, minority rights and is pro-ERA."[93] DeBaugh directed the Washington Office of the UFMCC and is a major spokesman for the denomination. "A former administrative assistant to

The Movement and American Liberalism

Pennsylvania Rep. Robert Edgar, DeBaugh's background includes work in the civil rights, anti-war, farmworkers and women's movement."[94] Representative Edgar is a Democrat, known for his extreme liberal stands on most issues.

United Methodist Church's Joan Clark, who worked for six and a half years for the Women's Division of the Board of Global Ministries of the Church, has become something of a movement cause célèbre for being fired as a homosexual. According to an article in her defense written by the codirector of the Roman Catholic leftist Quixote Center, Clark "worked on such social justice issues as policy towards South Africa, hunger, the Equal Rights Amendment and reproductive choice"—i.e., abortion.[95] Fuller indicated that the Church's Women Division where Clark worked was "one of the most progressive and liberating areas of the Church." The reader can appreciate the repeated use of code words of the left in these descriptions.

In the purely secular arena illustrative examples also abound. (Note, however, that the left makes no distinction between religious and secular when describing left-wing activities, although this distinction is applied to conservative institutions. It is thus possible that in this case the distinction is meaningless from a liberal viewpoint.)

One of the founders of Washington's Gertrude Stein Democratic Club is Paul Kuntzler, who is also a former president of the DC chapter of Americans for Democratic Action and a member of the Board of Directors of the Gay Rights National Lobby.[96]

The organizers of the Harvey Milk Democratic Club of Los Angeles, Genevieve Vigil and Conrado Terrazas, formerly worked with the Campaign for Economic Democracy of radical activist Tom Hayden.[97] A leftist activist in his own right, Hayden is married to Jane Fonda of Viet Nam fame.

A special assistant to New York liberal Democratic Senator (and homosexual movement supporter) Daniel Moynihan was responsible for a "gay voter" drive that registered some 12,000 new voters in New York City in 1977.[98]

Lucia Valeska, the Executive Director of the National Gay Task Force has been described by the NGTF newsletter as having been "active in the 1960's in the civil rights and anti-war movements."[99]

The cases cited here do not "prove" that all individuals—or even all activists—within the homosexual movement are also active liberals. They are offered only as an indication that there is interpenetration between these movements and that in some of these individuals the aims of both movements support one another. It is evident that homosexual activists feel very comfortable with the American left, where they have their roots and from which they derive much of their support.

THE HOMOSEXUAL NETWORK

Congressional Support for the Homosexual Movement

Every two years, all members of the House of Representatives and one-third of the Senators must stand for reelection. In their desire to continue representing their constituents, they must act according to the needs/desires of significant forces within their districts or states, while keeping unpopular actions hidden from other constituents who might object to them. At the same time, they must act according to what is—in their judgments—in the best interest of the nation. Frequently this is not the case. In the political game, well-financed forces which have organized themselves and learned how to manipulate political resources can often exercise an influence well beyond their numbers or the rationality of their cause. In contemporary terms, where power seems to be the only goal of the politician, and logic or principle are at best convenient tools toward the conquest of power, this is not surprising.

The homosexual movement is no exception to this rule. The number of politically active avowed homosexuals is miniscule, and the tenets of the movement are contrary to what the majority of the population would accept. Nevertheless, its superb organization, the tenacity of its leaders and supporters, and the continuing drift toward the left that America has experienced during the past few decades—aptly exploited by homosexual leaders who have identified homosexuals as a "minority" deprived of "civil rights"—have elicited support for the movement in Congress.

For four "congresses" in a row (94th through 97th), prohomosexual legislation has been introduced in the House of Representatives. The main effect of these bills—always introduced as amendments to civil rights legislation—would be to enshrine homosexuals as a legitimate minority. Homosexuality would be considered by law on the same level as religion, sex, race, national origin, etc. Ideologically, the implication is national acceptance of the movement's belief, making "quasi-official" doctrine some of the most disputed conclusions of the behavioral sciences.

Although such legislation runs contrary to the beliefs of most Americans, it has obtained considerable support in the House. The efforts of the National Gay Task Force, the Washington Office of the United Fellowship of Metropolitan Community Churches, and the Gay Rights National Lobby have been crucial in this regard. However, without the continuing support of the liberal network that perceives in the homosexual movement a member and ally, it is not likely that these measures would have received any support.

The reader may find the names and other characteristics of the representatives who have sponsored prohomosexual legislation in Table 30. The Congress in which they sponsored the bills is indicated, as well as

TABLE 30

Supporters of Prohomosexual Legislation in the House of Representatives[100]

Representative	94th	95th	96th	97th	Party	State	Religion	ADA Rating
Bella Abzug	X	√	√	√	D	NY	Jewish	100
Les Aucoin		X	X		D	OR	Protestant	67
Herman Badillo	X	X	√	√	D	NY	None Recorded	95
Michael Barnes			X	X	D	MD	Protestant	92
Anthony Beilenson			X	X	D	CA	Jewish	91
Jonathan Bingham	X	X	X	X	D	NY	United Ch. of Christ	96
William Brodhead			X		D	MI	R. Cath.	91
George E. Brown	X	X			D	CA	Methodist	86
John Burton	X	X	X	X	D	CA	R. Cath.	91
Phillip Burton			X	X	D	CA	Unitarian	94
Shirley Chisholm	X	X	X	X	D	NY	Methodist	88
William Clay		X		X	D	MO	R. Cath.	85
Cardiss Collins		X			D	IL	Baptist	81
John Conyers		X	X	X	D	MI	Baptist	84
Ronald Dellums	X	X	X	X	D	CA	Protestant	96
Charles Diggs		X	X	√	D	MI	Baptist	58
Julian Dixon	√	√	X	X	D	CA	Episcopal	87
Robert Edgar			X		D	PA	Methodist	93
Don Edwards			X	X	D	CA	Unitarian	97
Walter Fauntroy	X	X		X	D	DC	Protestant	Not Rated
Victor Fazio	√	√		X	D	CA	Episcopal	87
Barney Frank	√	√	√	X	D	MA	None Recorded	None Available
Donald Fraser	X	X	√		D	MN	None Recorded	98
William Gray	√	√	X	X	D	PA	Baptist	86
S. William Green	√	√	X	X	R	NY	Jewish	73
Michael Harrington	X	X	√	√	D	MA	R. Cath.	100
Augustus Hawkins		X	X	X	D	CA	Methodist	85
Elizabeth Holtzman	X	X	X	√	D	NY	Jewish	100
Edward Koch	X	X	√	√	D	NY	Jewish	97
William Lehman		X			D	FL	Jewish	83
Mickey Leland	√	√	X	X	D	TX	R. Cath.	84
Michael Lowry	√	√	X	X	D	WA	Baptist	92
Edward Markey	√	X	X		D	MA	R. Cath.	90
Paul McCloskey	X	X	X	X	R	CA	Presbyterian	61
Stewart McKinney		X	X		R	CT	Episcopal	55
Abner Mikva		X	X	√	D	IL	Jewish	80
George Miller		X	X	X	D	CA	R. Cath.	91
Norman Mineta	X	X	X		D	CA	Methodist	87
Parren Mitchell	X	X	X	X	D	MD	Episcopal	83
Toby Moffett		X	X	X	D	CT	R. Cath.	97
Robert Nix	X	X			D	PA	Baptist	76
Richard Ottinger		X	X		D	NY	Jewish	91

TABLE 30 (*cont.*)

Representative	Congress				Party	State	Religion	ADA Rating
	94th	95th	96th	97th				
Charles Rangel	X	X	X	X	D	NY	R. Cath.	
Frederick Richmond	X	X	X	X	D	NY	Jewish	
Benjamin Rosenthal	X	X	X	X	D	NY	Jewish	
Martin Olav Sabo	√	√	X	X	D	MN	Lutheran	
James Scheuer		X	X	X	D	NY	Jewish	
Patricia Schroeder	X	X	X	X	D	CO	Congreg.	
James Shannon	√	√	X		D	MA	R. Cath.	
Stephen Solarz	X	X			D	NY	Jewish	
Fortney Stark	X	X	X	X	D	CA	Unitarian	
Louis Stokes		X	X		D	OH	Afr. Meth. Ep.	
Gerry Studds	X	X	X	X	D	MA	Episcopal	
Henry Waxman	X	X	X	X	D	CA	Jewish	
James Weaver			X		D	OR	None Recorded	
Theodore Weiss		X	X	X	D	NY	Jewish	1
Sidney Yates			X	X	D	IL	Jewish	
Totals	24	38	44	34*				

*Incomplete. More sponsors possible before the end of the Congress.
Note: √ indicates individual was not a member of that Congress.

their party, state, religious affiliation, and their average ADA rating. A total of fifty-seven individuals have allowed their names to be associated in this way with prohomosexual legislation.

Aggregate information on the same congressmen appears in Table 31. An analysis of this table reveals that the Democrats are overrepresented among the sponsors of prohomosexual legislation and that states where the homosexual movement is particularly well-organized (California and New York) are also overrepresented. When religion is taken into consideration, Representatives of the Jewish faith are in much larger proportion among supporters of the prohomosexual legislation than in the House at large.

The fact that proportions are higher in one group than in another does not mean that such a difference is statistically significant. A Z test is indicated to explore the significance of differences between proportions of logically dichotomous variables.[101] Table 32 shows the results of the Z test for each individual Congress according to political party.

Analysis of Table 32 indicates that support for the homosexual legislation has progressively increased, but that when measured by the absolute value of each proportion, the growth was much faster among Democrats than among Republicans. The very large value of Z indicates that political affiliation is a significant factor in this support, since the difference in proportions is statistically significant at practically any level.

TABLE 31

Aggregate Characteristics of Representatives Who Have Sponsored Prohomosexual Legislation

Party	N	% Of Supporters	% Of The Total House of Each Category*
Democrat	54	94.7	63.4
Republican	*3*	*5.3*	*36.6*
Religion			
Roman Catholics	*10*	*17.5*	*28.2*
Jewish	15	26.3	5.7
Other Christians	*28*	*49.1*	66.1
None Recorded	*4*	*7.0*	
State			
CA	14	24.6	10.0
NY	14	24.6	9.0
MA	5	8.8	2.8
IL	*3*	*5.3*	*5.5*
MI	3	5.3	4.4
PA	*3*	*5.3*	*5.8*
CT	*2*	*3.5*	*1.4*
MD	*2*	*3.5*	*1.8*
MN	*2*	*3.5*	*1.8*
OR	*2*	*3.5*	*0.9*
CO	1	1.8	1.2
DC	1	1.8	
FL	*1*	*1.8*	*3.5*
MO	*1*	*1.8*	*2.3*
OH	*1*	*1.8*	*5.3*
TX	*1*	*1.8*	*5.5*
WA	1	1.8	1.6

*Aggregate of 94th, 95th, 96th, and 97th Congresses.
Italics denote categories in which the proportion relative to the total number of sponsors of the homosexual act is smaller than the proportion of congressmen.

TABLE 32

Significance of Differences Between Proportions of Supporters of Prohomosexual Legislation in the House of Representatives by Political Affiliation

Congress	94th	95th	96th
% Democratic Supporters*	7.9	12.3	14.8
% Republican Supporters**	.7	1.4	1.9
Z	3.10	3.79	4.26
Level of Significance	.19%	.01%	`0

*Relative to all Democrats in the House
**Relative to all Republicans in the House.

Table 33 displays the results of analysis of difference in proportions based on the religious affiliation of congressmen who supported prohomosexual legislation. It reveals a steady increase in the support for prohomosexual legislation among all groups. Statistically, a level of significance below 5% is generally accepted as indicating that the difference in proportions is significant. Between 5% and 10%, the difference is questionable. Above 10%, differences are not considered significant. Analysis of significance indicates that the proportion of Catholic Representatives who have endorsed prohomosexual legislation is not significantly different from the overall proportion of Catholics in the Congress. Should the Catholic Church continue its present leftward move, it is conceivable that at some future date Catholic representatives would significantly favor homosexuality too. However, this is highly speculative, since the leftist course of the Catholic Church is a phenomenon affecting mainly clerics and religious—especially nuns. At the grassroots level, Catholics remain faithful to the traditional teaching. Legislators do not reflect the leadership of their churches but the characteristics of their culture. It is also possible that the continuing move to the left—in all areas of foreign policy—will result in an ever-diminishing respect for authority in the Church and even mass defections, probably toward evangelical Christianity. There is already evidence that large numbers of Roman Catholics relate better to evangelical preachers than to their own clergy.

In the case of non-Catholic Christians (to which the overwhelming majority of the "other" category belongs), the tests are inconsistent and no definite relationship can be said to exist between religious affiliation and prohomosexual legislation. In the case of Representatives of the Jewish faith, the situation is quite different. Not only has support increased in absolute numbers, but by the 96th Congress, over half the Jewish Representatives (52.2%) were sponsors of the prohomosexual bill. The level of significance for their Z was indistinguishable from 0.

There is nothing in the Jewish faith or culture that explains this support of homosexual legislation except for the way the homosexual movement has framed the issue in terms of discrimination and civil rights, about which Jews are—for very good reasons—quite sensitive. As a matter of fact, the Jewish religion and culture are essentially family-centered and responsive to a millenary tradition which consistently affirms that homosexual acts are wrong. It can only be expected that as the homosexual movement manifests the antifamily traits which are called for by its ideology and by the intrinsic fruitlessness of homosexual acts, Jewish legislators—insofar as they profess the values of the Jewish traditions—will become indistinguishable from other legislators.

This will require a rejection of the liberalism which is an intrinsic

The Movement and American Liberalism

TABLE 33

Significance of Differences Between Proportions of
Supporters of Prohomosexual Legislation in the House of
Representatives by Religious Affiliation

Congress	94th	95th	96th
Roman Catholics vs. All Others			
% of Catholic Endorsers*	4.0%	5.3%	6.9%
% of All Other Endorsers	6.1%	10.2%	11.2%
Z	− .86	− 1.64	− 1.34
Level of Significance	38.98%	10.10%	18.02%
Jews vs. All Others			
% of Jewish Endorsers	30.4%	37.0%	52.2%
% of All Other Endorsers	4.1%	6.9%	7.8%
Z	5.38	5.38	6.87
Level of Significance	`0	`0	`0
*Other** vs. Catholics/Jews*			
% of Other Endorsers	4.2%	7.6%	8.1%
% of Catholic/Jewish Endorsers	8.2%	10.8%	14.4%
Z	− 1.72	− 1.13	− 2.02
Level of Significance	8.54%	25.84%	4.34%

*Proportions in this table are relative to the total number Representatives in the category: e.g., 4% of Roman Catholics in the 94th Congress endorsed prohomosexual legislation.
**"Other" indicates neither Roman Catholic nor Jewish. The vast majority are Christians who are not Roman Catholics.

component of the homosexual movement. An analysis of the ADA scores reveals that co-sponsors of pro-homosexual legislation are significantly more liberal than the House as a whole. A t-test is normally conducted to analyze the differences between the mean values of a whole population and a sample of this population.[102] In the case at hand, it has been used to compare the mean ADA ratings for the 94th, 95th, and 96th congresses (1976, 1978, 1980) and the mean ADA ratings for Representatives who have sponsored prohomosexual legislation in the same congresses. The 97th Congress was not utilized, since no ratings have been issued as of this writing and the total roster of endorsers will not be known until the end of the Congress in 1982. Only 54 scores were utilized since there is no score for DC Delegate Walter Fauntroy.

The mean aggregate ADA score for the House was found to be 41.00. For the 54 endorsers of the pro-homosexual bill the mean was found to be 89.11, more than twice as large as the House score. The value of t was found to be 22.5061. For 53 degrees of freedom, the value of 22.5061 for t is so large that there is no question that the supporters of the

THE HOMOSEXUAL NETWORK

homosexual bill are liberal with a degree of certainty approaching and practically equal to 100%.

In the U.S. Senate, legislative support for the homosexual movement has been much less. It was not until the 96th Congress that prohomosexual legislation was introduced in the Senate, also under the guise of "civil rights" legislation. While prohomosexual efforts in the House have covered virtually all areas normally subject to civil rights legislation (public accommodation, education, employment, housing, etc.), the Senate bills have been much more moderate in scope, usually limiting themselves to the area of employment. Table 34 summarizes the support "gay rights" legislation has received in the Senate.

TABLE 34

Senatorial Support for Prohomosexual Legislation

Name	Congress 96th	Congress 97th	Party	State	Religion	Mean ADA Rating
Alan Cranston		X	D	CA	Protestant	84
Edward M. Kennedy		X	D	MA	R. Cath.	86
Daniel K. Inouye		X	D	HI	Methodist	67
Daniel P. Moynihan	X	X	D	NY	R. Cath.	62
Robert Packwood	X	X	R	OR	Unitarian	49
Paul Tsongas	X	X	D	MA	Greek Orthodox	83
Lowell P. Weicker	X	X	R	CT	Episcopal	59

SOURCES: *The Washington Blade* (Washington, D.C.) October 9, 1981, Alan Ehrenhalt, *Politics in America: Members of Congress in Washington and at Home* (Washington, D.C.: Congressional Quarterly Press, 1981)

Although not as pronounced as in the House, here also there is a marked tendency among homosexual bill sponsors to be liberal Democrats.

In addition to the "civil rights" legislation discussed thus far, prohomosexual legislation has also been introduced in both Houses to permit free entrance of homosexuals into the United States. In the House, such a measure was introduced in the 96th Congress by Rep. Anthony Beilenson (D-Calif.) and was basically sponsored by the same representatives who sponsored the "civil rights" legislation. Notable exceptions of representatives who *did not* cosponsor prohomosexual "civil rights" legislation, but who did cosponsor the bill to allow the entrance of homosexuals were: John Anderson (R-Ill.), Robert Matsui (D-Calif.), Barbara Mikulski (D-Md.) and Joel Pritchard (R-Wash.). These four Representatives can also be considered liberal (ADA ratings, 34, 92, 87, and 48 respectively). (John Anderson's ADA ratings are an extremely low 11 and 22 for 1979-80, when he announced no position in a large number of votes. In fact, Anderson ran for President as a liberal in the 1980 election.) In the Senate,

The Movement and American Liberalism

similar legislation was introduced by Alan Cranston (D-Calif.), also a liberal (ADA rating average, 84).

In addition to prohomosexual legislation, bills inimical to the interests of the homosexual movement have been introduced for consideration by conservative representatives and senators. In contrast to the prohomosexual legislation—which has never been reported to the floor—they have received much more favorable consideration. Legislation forbidding federal funds to be used for the promotion of homosexuality by the Legal Services Corporation—an amendment authored by Rep. Larry McDonald (D-Ga.)—eventually became law. It is interesting to note that while the McDonald Amendment was rejected by voice vote, it was adopted by recorded vote. This is a clear indication that certain members of the House personally favored a prohomosexual stand—i.e., the use of federal funds to promote homosexuality—but knew that their constituents would be seriously upset if they knew of their opinion. The 97th Congress vetoed a highly prohomosexual statute enacted by the District of Columbia by a large majority of the House of Representatives (the Senate, under the DC Home Rule Act, did not have to consider the measure). (According to the U.S. Constitution (ART. 1, SEC. 8), the U.S. Congress has jurisdiction over the District of Columbia. The D.C. City Council is thus a creature of the Congress and not of the people of the District.) The Family Protection Act, a measure which is concerned with issues far beyond the homosexual question, but which has been rightly diagnosed by the homosexual movement as the quintessential antihomosexual movement bill, was introduced in the 96th and 97th Congresses, in different versions, by a group of basically conservative legislators.

The following senators and representatives have been active in pressing Congress to enact measures antagonistic to the homosexual movement:

	Name	Party	State	ADA Rating Average
Senators:	Thad Cochran	R	MS	7.8
	Orrin Hatch	R	UT	8.2
	Jesse Helms	R	NC	2.6
	Roger Jepsen	R	IA	11.0
Representatives:	Edward Boland	D	MA	79.0
	Larry McDonald	D	GA	5.2
	Ronald Mottl	D	OH	47.3
	Steven Symms	R	ID	3.5

The activities of these legislators in opposing the homosexual movement naturally vary. Senator Jepsen, for example, is the author of the Family Protection Act, a measure of incalculable repercussions that would break the back of the homosexual movement by enacting traditional American family values as federal legislation. Representative Larry McDonald has

429

a long record as *the* principal opponent of the homosexual movement in the House of Representatives, being the author of more than half the congressional measures deemed inimical to the tenets of the movement. McDonald's actions in the Congress have won for him the appellation of "mouthpiece for the homophobic lobby Christian Voice" by *In Unity*, organ of the UFMCC.[103]

Table 35 is a summary of recent congressional measures which relate directly to the issue of homosexuality. The legislative numbers are only for the original bill. In some instances identical bills have been introduced by other members of Congress. These repetitions have not been included in the table.

The support the homosexual movement enjoys in the Congress is the result of hard work and organization on the part of its leaders. In some instances, homosexuals working for liberal congressmen have "come out" to begin lobbying openly on behalf of the movement; the importance of such an event cannot be overestimated and is appreciated by the movement. This happened in the cases of Craig Thigpen and Gary Aldridge, employed by two radical liberals, Senator Alan Cranston (D-Calif.) and Representative Bella Abzug (D-N.Y.). The importance of their presence in the Congress was duly noted by the UFMCC.[104] The value of homosexual lobbying activities has also been noted by liberal Democrat Art Agnos, California Assemblyman.[105]

The homosexual movement is well aware of the liberal nature of the support it enjoys in Congress. *Gays on the Hill* presented an analysis of the cosponsors of the 1974 House homosexual bill indicating that, of 21 cosponsors of the proposed legislation, 12 had received 100% ratings by the ADA and 14 had received 0% on the scale of Americans for Constitutional Action, a conservative group, in 1974.[106] Careful cultivation of this support and a consistent movement to the left by the homosexual movement has naturally resulted in ever-increasing support by liberal legislators. The problem of an increasingly conservative Congress is a difficult one for the homosexual movement to tackle. In the 1980 election, 18.2% of the sponsors of H.R. 2074—the "gay civil rights act"—were "retired." *Gays on the Hill* noted that eight prohomosexual Representatives did not return to the 97th Congress (Anderson, R-Ill.; Carr, D-Mich.; Corman, D-Calif.; Diggs, D-Mich.; Duncan, D-Ore.; Holtzman, D-N.Y.; Mikva, D-Ill.; and Nolan, D-Minn.) and asked for help by its supporters in obtaining additional sponsors.[107]

Although the homosexual movement has made considerable inroads in the U.S. Congress—after all, no one would have thought even ten years ago that U.S. congressmen and senators would use their positions to advocate homosexual "rights," or would seek the support of organized and open homosexuals—overall the movement has fared poorly. When-

TABLE 35

Summary of Congressional Measures Which Relate to the Homosexual Question

	Character*	Area of Interest	Summary	Disposition
94th Congress				
H.R. 166	+	Civil Rights	Extends civil rights to homosexuals making them a legitimate minority. Areas covered: public accommodations, public education, employment, housing, educational programs receiving federal assistance. Extended in H.R. 13019 to cover also public facilities and federally assisted opportunities.	Did not become law.
95th Congress				
H.R. 451	+	Civil Rights	Similar to H.R. 166 (94th Congress) above.	Did not become law.
H. Amendment 368	−	Housing	Forbids the use of federal money to make public housing available to homosexual couples. Presented in response to a HUD regulation that would have recognized certain homosexual couples as a "family."	Became section 408 of PL 95–119, 10/8/77.
H. Amendment 423	−	Legal Services	Forbids the Legal Services Corporation to promote homosexuality by entering into litigation concerning questions relating to the homosexual condition.	Approved by the House, eliminated from final approval in conference.
96th Congress				
H.R. 2074	+	Civil Rights	Similar to H.R. 166 (94th Congress) above.	Did not become law.
H. Congressional Resolution 166	+	Civil Rights	Establishes as the sense of the Congress that homosexual acts shall never receive special consideration under law.	No action taken.
H. Amendment 410	−		Similar to H. Amendment 423.	Approved by the House.

TABLE 35

Summary of Congressional Measures Which Relate to the Homosexual Question

	Character*	Area of Interest	Summary	Disposition
H.R. 6028	−	Family Protection Act	Seeks to strengthen family by various programs. Denies federal assistance to prohomosexual programs and declares the refusal to hire homosexuals to be legal.	Did not become law.
H.R. 6303	+	Immigration	Legalizes the entrance of homosexuals into the United States.	Did not become law.
S. 1808	−	Family Protection Act	Similar to H.R. 6028 (96th Congress) above.	Did not become law.
S. 2081	+	Civil Rights	Extends to homosexuals the right to be employed as a minority. Makes illegal the use of homosexuality as a criterion for deciding whether to employ a person.	Did not become law.
S. 2210	+	Immigration	Similar to H.R. 6303 (96th Congress).	Did not become law.
97th Congress				
H.R. 1454	+	Civil Rights	Similar to H.R. 166 (94th Congress)	No action at date of writing
H. Congressional Resolution 29	−	Civil Rights	Similar to H. Cong. Res. 166 (96th Congress)	No action at date of writing
H. Amendment 84	−	Legal Services	Similar to H. Amendment 423 (95th Congress).	Being considered by the Senate as of this writing.
H. Resolution 208	−	Criminal Law	Rejection of D.C. Sodomy Act which legalized a number of sexual acts including homosexual behavior, bestiality, etc.	Approved.
S. 1708	−	Civil Rights	Similar to S. 2081 (96th Congress,	No action at date of writing
S. 1378	−	Family Protection Act	Improved version of S. 1808 (96th Congress).	Hearing anticipated as of this writing.
H. R. 3955		Family Protection Act	Parallel measure to S. 1378 (97th Congress).	Hearing anticipated as of this writing.

*
  + Denotes a prohomosexual measure.
  − Denotes a measure inimical to the homosexual movement.

ever record votes have been taken, the overwhelming majority of the legislators has voted against the homosexual movement, an indication that senators and congressmen are well aware that Americans reject homosexuality. The conservative mood of the country, and the increasing organization of profamily forces and other conservative issues, with the emerging consensus that conservatism is a consistent philosophy (implying a close connection among social, economic, and foreign policy issues) does not augur well for the homosexual movement. It appears that in the Congress—a reflection of the nation as a whole—the pendulum has completed its swing to the left, and that a long-expected move to the right has begun. In a conservative environment, the homosexual movement is bound to lose ground and perhaps even disappear.

Support of the Homosexual Movement by Liberal Politicians

The homosexual movement has enjoyed the support of liberal politicians since its inception. This was the result of the consistent participation of politically active open homosexuals in leftist politics. During the 1940s, Henry Hay, an avowed homosexual, tried to found "Bachelors for Wallace," designed as a movement of homosexuals committed to support the leftist candidacy of Henry Wallace.[108] The climate of the United States in 1948 was inauspicious for homosexual political activism and the idea proved fruitless. By 1967 the situation had begun to change. New York City, under the leadership of liberal Republican Mayor John Lindsay, began implementing what appears to have been homosexual affirmative action. The Mattachine Society of New York was quick to claim credit for the success of its campaign geared to, among others, John Lindsay: "Mayor Lindsay has been on our mailing list for a very long time (at *least* since he voted, along with a very few others in Congress, against Dowdy, who was trying to illegalize the Washington Mattachine)."[109]

NATIONAL LEGISLATORS
Congressmen have supported the homosexual movement in ways far beyond the mere cosponsoring of bills. This support is not limited to members of the Democrat Party, but includes Republicans as well. Senator Edward Brooke (R-Mass.) is reported to have "blasted" the Defense Department for its policy of discharging homosexuals from the armed services. *Gays on the Hill* reported that Brooke had asserted: "Unless and until it can be determined that the personal and private lifestyle of such members of the Armed Services interferes with their ability to do

their job competently and loyally, the present policy is benighted, self-defeating, and not in the best interests of the United States of America."[110] The prime example of support for the homosexual movement is Senator Alan Cranston (D-Calif.), whose autographed portrait hangs behind the desk of the director of the Washington Office of the UFMCC. On July 11, 1977, Cranston's office was the setting for a conference sponsored by the National Gay Task Force having as its purpose "to draw upon the decades of experience of these leaders in developing the long-range and short-term goals of the gay-rights movement."[111] To a large extent, the leftist homosexual coalition seems to have formed right at the U.S. Congress. According to then Codirector of the NGTF Jean O'Leary, "they were seeking advice from the veterans of the black and women's rights campaigns on techniques for winning support and forming an alliance to help one another."[112] The majority of Cranston's constituents probably did not envision that their Senator in Washington would utilize his prestige and resources in helping forge a liberal homosexual coalition! The attendees and agenda of the conference provide further evidence of its nature. In addition to Cranston himself (who did not just lend his office, but who reportedly was present), the participants included the following:

Ruth Hinerfeld	First Vice President, League of Women Voters
Ruth Abrams	Executive Director, Women's Action Alliance
Eleanor (Ellie) Smeal	President, National Organization for Women
Aryeh Neier	Executive Director, American Civil Liberties Union
Jane Michaels	Executive Director, National Women's Political Caucus
Jean O'Leary	Co-Executive Director, National Gay Task Force
Bruce Voeller	Co-Executive Director, National Gay Task Force

The agenda of the meeting included the following items:

Dealing with coalitions of right-wing extremist groups opposing human and civil rights

Voter registration drives

Congressional and state legislation

Public education campaigns

Cooperation among and common goals of the various civil rights movement [sic]

Federal and State courts in relation to minority groups.[113]

A homosexual publication's report of this event ended on this note: "NGTF Co-Executive Directors Jean O'Leary and Bruce Voeller hailed the conference as a major step towards aligning and uniting civil-rights organizations in the United States, and applauded the other participants for their willingness to share ideas, resources and experience with a younger civil-rights organization, representing the gay-rights movement."[114]

An instance of what would normally pass as "constituent services" regularly performed by legislators, but with a twist that indicates Cranston's degree of support for the homosexual movement, occurred when Anthony Corbett Sullivan, an Australian national and allegedly a homosexual, tried to claim immigrant status on the basis that he was married to a U.S. citizen. The Internal Revenue Service refused to acknowledge Sullivan's right since his "spouse" whom he had "married" in Boulder, Colorado, was another man. Cranston was quick to pressure the INS to stop deportation procedures against the alleged homosexual. *Gays on the Hill* reported extensive pro-homosexual remarks by Cranston:

> Sen. Cranston's staff people met with Immigration authorities and he reports: "At my request, officials of the U.S. Immigration and Naturalization Service met with my staff in my Washington office to discuss the procedure of the Service in announcing its intended deportation of an Australian homosexual, Anthony Sullivan.
> "During the session my staff informed the Service of my strong feeling that the handling of this matter raises not only a question of taste, but of whether intolerant and bigoted persons made policy judgements that led to the deportation decision.
> "In response to my concerns, the Service has assured me that it will initiate a full and complete investigation of all actions that led to the deportation decision—and the manner of its announcement. Further, the Service has assured me that steps will be taken to determine the person or persons responsible for this ugly and insulting characterization of gay persons [as "faggots"], and that appropriate disciplinary action will be taken if warranted."[115]

The question here was not whether homosexuals should be admitted to the United States—seemingly Cranston's objective—but the nature of the family, and whether persons of the same sex can legally marry. This is of major concern to the homosexual movement. It would obviously be very advantageous for the movement if the INS were to recognize same-sex marriages as grounds for accepting immigrants.

There is some disparity between the "gay rights" bills in the House and the Senate. While the House bill covers several "civil rights" areas, the Senate version is restricted to employment. (Cf. Table 33 above.) *Gays on the Hill* reported how Alan Cranston had been instrumental in the strategy resulting in a more restricted Senate version as more likely to be eventually passed. Cranston apparently even went to the extent of assigning his staff—at government expense—to work with lobbyists of the homosexual movement in the actual drafting of the act:

> Alan Cranston of California has agreed to let his staff devote time to developing

a gay civil rights bill that will be able to receive broad bipartisan support. Sen. Cranston has agreed to explore with other Senators the possibility of their co-sponsoring such a bill. . . .

In order to create a bill that will garner broad support, Sen. Cranston's staff people, working with other Senate staff people and the National Gay Task Force, have decided that the first and most visible gay discrimination priority is in the area of employment. The staff had to build Federal legislative machinery that would best deal with this problem.

People working with the staff have come up with a formula and a bill is in the process of being drafted now. The legal complications, or [sic]course, are staggering. How do you deal with job discrimination in a way that doesn't force employers into an "Affirmative Action" program, in effect forcing people to come out in order to keep their jobs under a gay quota system? How do you protect people who want to come out from being fired, and people who are out from being denied jobs?

The formula that has been developed creates Federal machinery to allow gays to pursue complaints of discrimination with the Federal Government, but stops short of creating Affirmative Action programs. It involves both a reinterpretation of existing civil rights legislation in the past to include sexual and affectional orientation and preference, and a few new notions as well.[116]

Thus it is apparent that the reason why "gay rights" bills have specifically excluded affirmative action is not a desire to "soften" the bill, or make it more palatable to employers, but the need to protect homosexuals. Should affirmative action become the mechanism to guarantee the presumed right of homosexuals to be employed, individuals—homosexuals included—would be forced to reveal their sexual preferences. The accepted presumption that when applicants engage in sexual relations—if they so desire—they do so with members of the opposite sex would obviously have to be abandoned. In the meantime, *Gays on the Hill* reported, their cause had considerable support in the Senate:

Sen. Birch Bayh of Indiana and Sen. Mike Gravel of Alaska have said they would co-sponsor legislation in the Senate. Sen. John V. Tunney of California, Sen. Jacob K. Javits of New York, Sen. Hubert H. Humphrey of Minnesota, and Sen. Charles McC. Mathias of Maryland have all been supportive in the past. Sen. Lloyd Bentsen of Texas has been vaguely supportive of civil rights recently, possibly a function of his now defunct race for the Presidency.[117]

The Senator who first introduced prohomosexual legislation was Paul Tsongas (D-Mass.), one of the most liberal members of this body (ADA mean rating of 83). On September 19, 1979, Tsongas circulated a "Dear Colleague" letter in the Senate, announcing his intention to introduce the prohomosexual employment legislation. He used as an argument for recognizing homosexuals as a legitimate employment minority the favor-

The Movement and American Liberalism

able pronouncements issued by the American Psychiatric Association, the National Council of Churches, and the (Catholic) National Federation of Priests' Councils. (It is thus evident that such declarations have serious political implications.) Additionally, he invoked the alleged nondiscriminatory practices of certain corporations toward homosexuals:

> Non-discrimination in employment has also found wide acceptance within the business community. Among the many firms which have issued non-discrimination statements are AT&T, DuPont, Ford Motors, and IBM. This statement by Penn Mutual Life Insurance Company speaks to the sound reasons for business support for non-discrimination:
> "It is Penn Mutual's policy to provide equal employment and advancement opportunity for all employees, regardless of their race, color religion, sex, national origin, age, or sexual preference. Equality of opportunity is a sound business objective that, by allowing us to make effective use of our human resources, helps us secure profitable growth."[118]

Tsongas had defeated an openly female homosexual in a race for the Democratic nomination for the Senate in Massachusetts in 1978. Tsongas's homosexual bill was, according to the Washington office of UFMCC, the result of a campaign promise.[119] In a way, he was "atoning" for defeating Elaine Noble, the only avowed homosexual member of the State Legislature. Bill S. 2081 (December 5, 1979) was eventually introduced, cosponsored by fellow-liberal Senators Daniel Moynihan (D-N.Y.) and Lowell Weicker (R-Conn.). Following his remarks, Tsongas requested that a number of "letters of support" for the notions behind his bill be entered in the record. These letters included such bulwarks of American business as the Bank of America, American Telephone and Telegraph, Columbia Broadcasting System, Merck, DuPont, Levi Strauss, Weyerhaeuser, Western Electric, Warner Communications, General Foods, General Electric, and Mobil Oil.[120] Figure 12 is a reproduction of a letter from Paul Tsongas to Father Robert Nugent, S.D.S. The third paragraph of this letter does not indicate clearly whether Tsongas is speaking about the Salvatorians (Catholic order to which Nugent belongs), the homosexual community, the Catholic Church, or the people of Mount Rainier, Maryland. In any case, Tsongas is operating here as an advocate of the homosexual movement.

Although his record is not as prominent as that of Paul Tsongas, the senior Senator from Massachusetts, liberal Democrat Ted Kennedy, has also been a supporter of the homosexual movement. Figures 13 and 14 are letters from Ted Kennedy to Father Robert Nugent and Sister Jeannine Gramick. In these letters, Kennedy reveals himself as:

> A supporter of the homosexual movement
> Willing to support prohomosexual legislation

Accepting homosexuals as a legitimate minority comparable to racial or religious minorities
Favoring the admission of homosexuals to the United States
Opposed to efforts to ensure that schools are not open to avowedly homosexual teachers.

Senator Kennedy, with Governor Jerry Brown (D-Calif.) and President Jimmy Carter, were strong supporters of the National Convention Project, an effort to insert prohomosexual language in the platforms of the major political parties for the 1980 Presidential election. Supported by the Gay Rights National Lobby and the National Gay Task Force, the Project reportedly "was active with local gay groups in Iowa and has been successful in getting Democratic and Republican candidates to address Gay rights issues."[121] The kick-off event of the Project was a "celebration" at a Washington homosexual discoteque attended by Jerry Brown and representatives of President Carter and Senator Kennedy. The homosexual community hailed this event as a major achievement in its quest for recognition.[122]

Senator Kennedy, in his failed effort to obtain the Democratic nomination to the Presidency in 1980, revealed his depth of support for the homosexual movement as he courted it for votes and organizational support. Kennedy asserted that "I think . . . that there has to be elimination of all discrimination against gay rights in our society."[123] He also promised the National Gay Task Force to sign a prohomosexual Executive Order banning the homosexual condition as a factor when considering an individual for Federal employment and services.[124] Kennedy's position, similar to that of Brown, ensured that the 1980 Democratic Convention (unlike those of 1972 and 1976) would consider homosexual "rights" as an item in its platform. This was duly noted by the homosexual leadership, who saw the fruition of many years of hard work in the open support of their issues by two "serious" Presidential candidates.[125]

The subtitle of a lead article in It's Time, "[Kennedy] Promises Executive Order and Support for Platform Plank," became a reality in the Democratic Platform. The 1980 statement of beliefs and action program was openly prohomosexual. The issues which the homosexual movement traditionally considered its own became the credo of the then dominant party. All the traditionally liberal issues were presented to the American people by the Democrats: bigger government as *the* solution to social and economic problems, surrender to the demands of the environmentalists and antibusiness forces, and a no-win foreign policy. Of specific interest to the homosexual movement were:

Strong support for feminism scattered throughout the platform

(Letterhead)
United States Senate
Washington, D.C. 20510

January 15, 1980

Mr. C. Robert Nugent
New Ways Ministry
3312 Buchanan Street
Mount Ranier, Maryland 20822

Dear Mr. Nugent:

Thank you for your support of the gay rights legislation which I
recently introduced.

In my opinion, discrimination of any sort is a violation of an
individual's civil rights. In the past, I have taken a leadership
role in support of the rights of minorities, the elderly, women, and
the handicapped. Homosexuals are yet another group of Americans
whose civil rights are daily violated.

I encourage you to be active within your community on behalf of
gay rights.

Thank you again for contacting me. If I can be of further assistance,
do not hesitate to contact me.

                        Sincerely,

                        (Signature: Paul)

                        PAUL E. TSONGAS

                        United States Senator

FIGURE 12

Letter from Senator Paul Tsongas (D-Mass.) to New Ways Ministry. Source: Bondings.

(Letterhead)
United States Senate
Washington, D.C. 20510

December 26, 1979

The Rev. C. Robert Nugent
Sister Jeannine Gramick
New Ways Ministry
3312 Buchanan St., 302
Mt. Ranier, Maryland 20822

Dear Friends:

Thank you for giving me this opportunity to express my thoughts regarding discrimination against individuals based upon their sexual preference. I am well aware of the fact that members of the gay community are subject to discrimination in a number of areas, including employment, housing, and immigration, and am very concerned about the problems they face.

As one who has long been deeply committed to the civil rights of all persons, I have worked hard in the Senate to eliminate prejudice and discrimination against minority groups. Over the past two decades, this nation has made substantial progress in eradication discrimination against particular groups of Americans -- especially discrimination based on race, religion, and sex, and discrimination against the aged and the handicapped. We have also made great progress in protecting our citizens against unjustified inquiries into their personal lives. But it is clear that the battle against discrimination is far from won, not only in these areas, but in the area of sexual preference as well.

When a qualified individual is denied employment or a financially able person refused housing because of his or her race or sex or sexual preference, then we must all be concerned.

So, too, we must be concerned when an individual is denied permission to come into this country because of a statute based on outmoded medical and psychiatric views of homosexuality.

The Select Commission on Immigration and Refugee Policy, a commission which I fought hard to create and on which I am now currently serving, is involved in just such a review right now, of all the exclusion provisions contained in section 212 (a) of the immigration laws.

I believe that the Constitutional guarantees of equal protection and due process should protect individuals against such discrimination by the government. A person's ability and fitness -- not his or her race or sex or sexual preference -- are the only constitutional bases for government decisionmaking.

I have opposed efforts -- notably Proposition 6 in California -- which would have legitimized discrimination on the basis of sexual preference -- discrimination which deprives people of employment without regard to their individual fitness or ability. Measures such as these not only penalize the individual unfairly, but are a waste of talent and resources at a time when our country can ill-afford either. I am now, as I have been throughout my career in public service, firmly committed to the premise that ours must be a society in which the civil rights of all persons are respected.

Once again, I appreciate the opportunity to express these views. Best wishes for a successful meeting.

Sincerely,

(Signature: Edward Kennedy)

Edward M. Kennedy

FIGURE 13
Letter from Senator Edward Kennedy (D-Mass.) to New Ways Ministry
(December 26, 1979). Source: Bondings.

United States Senate

COMMITTEE ON THE JUDICIARY
WASHINGTON, D.C. 20510

June 11, 1980

C. Robert Nugent, S.D.S.
New Ways Ministry
3312 Buchanan Street, #302
Mount Rainier, Maryland 20822

Dear Father Nugent:

I would like to thank you, your co-director Jeannine Gramick, and Professor Charles Curran for sending me your insightful position paper, Human Dignity: Rights and Responsibilities, on the need to safeguard the civil liberties of homosexually oriented citizens.

I agree with your conclusion that our government has a serious responsibility to see to it that the "basic human equality of all its citizens before the law is never violated", and also that there is no discrimination permitted or sanctioned among citizens. Accordingly, I will support legislation based on these principles which will effectively eliminate discrimination against homosexually oriented individuals.

The New Ways Ministry should be commended for providing creative leadership in this sensitive area. I look forward to working with you on these serious and complex issues in the future.

With best regards,

Sincerely,

Edward M. Kennedy

FIGURE 14
Letter from Senator Edward Kennedy (D-Mass.) to New Ways Ministry (June 11, 1980).
Source: Bondings.

Support for the principle of abortion on demand with no recognized rights for unborn children

Total support for the Equal Rights Amendment, to the extent that Democrats opposed to the ERA were not to receive any financial or technical support from their party

Minimal support for the family, which went undefined (while family concerns were disposed of in twenty-two words, the ERA, abortion, and feminism were defended by the paragraph)

Specific support for recognition of homosexuals as a legitimate minority comparable to members of religious organizations, ethnic, or national groups

Acceptance of the principle that homosexuals should be allowed to enter the United States.

The Democrats indicated in reference to the last two points that "appropriate legislative and administrative actions to achieve these goals should be undertaken."[126] Approved by a convention dominated by leftist forces, and in which half the delegates *had* to be women (thus enshrining the principle of representation based on a quality other than ability to perform), this platform became a heavy burden for Jimmy Carter, set the tone of his campaign on principles rejected by most Americans, and was a factor in the President's ultimate rejection. The Democratic Platform represents a high point in the political achievement of the homosexual movement. It was so disastrous that it is unlikely the nation will ever be faced again with such a clear choice between the traditional ideas offered by the Republicans and the radical leftist principles of the Democrats. The existence of such ideas among Democrat leadership confirms what was revealed in the foregoing analysis of endorsers of homosexual legislation in the House of Representatives.

It is impossible to list the many ways in which liberal legislators support and have supported the homosexual movement or its agenda. A casual examination of homosexual publications, and even major newspapers, reveals the degree to which liberal congressmen and senators lend their names and prestige to the movement. Representatives Weiss (D-N.Y.) and Waxman (D-Calif.) helped organize a "Congressional Briefing" which took place on April 21, 1980.[127] This event served as an opportunity for leaders of the homosexual movement and supporters of their cause to propagandize their ideas in a "respectable" forum. Representative Augustus Hawkins (D-Calif.) held a hearing on H.R. 2074 (the prohomosexual rights bill) on October 10, 1980, and Theodore S. Weiss (D-N.Y.) on H.R. 1454 on January 27, 1982.

THE CARTER WHITE HOUSE

The Carter Presidency may be characterized by future historians of homosexuality in America as the "golden years" of the movement. The

The Movement and American Liberalism

relations between the Carter White House and the homosexual leadership bear witness to the incredible growth of the homosexual movement. From a group of "pariahs" and "perverts" (in the public's estimation) during the sixties, by the second half of the 1970s homosexual leaders saw the doors of the White House swing open. Their case was heard, their ideology accepted; the full weight of the federal government seemed to be poised to enact even the most controversial items of the homosexual agenda for America.

Jimmy Carter was elected as a "born again" Christian, on a campaign wherein he stressed morality and the need to purify the nation from the misdeeds of previous administrations. It is hard to imagine how he could combine his beliefs in Christian ethics with the homosexual ideology. (Even while President, Carter continued to teach Sunday School.) It is possible that he was defeated not only because of his obvious failures in both policy and administration, but also because of such glaring ethical inconsistencies as the profession of Christian ethics while cooperating fully with homosexuals and radical feminists.

The most obvious way in which Jimmy Carter helped the homosexual movement was by holding a number of formal meetings in the White House for movement leaders. On March 26, 1977, such a meeting was chaired by Midge Costanza, Assistant to the President for Public Liaison. In attendance were the codirectors of the National Gay Task Force—Jean O'Leary and Bruce Voeller—and eight other representatives of the homosexual movement. In an obvious attempt to increase O'Leary's and Voeller's power within the movement, Costanza gave them the right to select the eight additional representatives.[128] The March meeting followed a February 8, 1977, planning meeting between Costanza and the NGTF codirectors. Costanza assigned a person from her staff, Marilyn Haft, to work with O'Leary and Voeller and offered to engage in activities supporting the homosexuals: "I have been impressed with the presentation you have made and wish to explore more fully the role my office and I can play; specifically in facilitating meetings with those persons who will be most helpful to you in the areas we have reviewed."[129]

The "areas" mentioned referred to the agenda set for the March 26 meeting, which included:

1. Oppression, Discrimination and the Need for National Leadership and National Legislation.
2. Immigration and Naturalization.
3. Internal Revenue Service.
4. Defense Department.
5. The Federal Prisons.
6. U.S. Civil Rights Commission.[130]

It is interesting to note that the homosexual movement did, in fact, score significant victories in all these areas during the Carter years, undoubtedly with the help of the White House.[131] These meetings were not just exercises in public relations, but real working sessions in which much was planned and later implemented.

On December 19, 1980, there was another meeting in the White House. By then, Midge Costanza had "left" the Administration. Her successor, Anne Wexler, announced her intention to "continue our"—i.e., the White House's—"commitment" to the homosexual movement.[132] During the meeting, Margot Karle, representative of the Lambda Legal Defense and Education Fund (a homosexual organization), complained of the lack of cooperation of the Bureau of Prisons with a suit the NGTF and the UFMCC had instituted to force federal prisons to admit homosexual materials for the inmates: "Ms. Wexler and Malson both expressed surprise and dismay at the description of the suits and the policy of the Bureau to exclude all Gay publications and MCC ministers from Federal correctional institutions. They promised to look into the cases and asked for more information, which has been sent to them."[133] Eventually, the suit was settled out of court to the total satisfaction of the homosexuals. Attendees at the meeting are listed in the chart on the following page.

The turn of homosexual religious organizations came on April 28, 1980, when a group of homosexual religious leaders met at the White House with (Baptist) Rev. Dr. Robert L. Maddox, Jr., Special Assistant to the President for Religious Liaison, and Allison Thomas, an aide to Anne Wexler. (The reader may find a full description of this meeting in chapter VII.) Maddox addressed these guests, concluding with the cryptic remark: "I feel affirmed by you and I express my affirmation to you. This is a personal statement."[135] Maddox followed the meeting with a letter, no doubt encouraging to the homosexuals, which is reproduced in Figure 15. There is no question that many other informal meetings took place: "[Carter] has kept his first promise and the White House has never been so accessible or helpful to the Lesbian/Gay community as it has under the Carter Administration. . . . There have been numerous meetings with White House staff people."[136]

Several appointments made by Carter undoubtedly reflected the interests of the homosexuals and were probably designed to elicit their individual and organizational support during the 1980 reelection campaign:

The "Rev." Michael Nordstrom represented the UFMCC at the President's Conference on Handicapped Individuals.[137]

Jimmy Carter approved the appointment of Virginia Apuzzo, a homosexual political activist and former Catholic nun, to the 1980 Democratic Platform Committee.[138] The 1980 Democratic Platform had a marked pro-homosexual bias.

The Movement and American Liberalism

For the Government:	Anne Wexler	Assistant to the President
	Robert Malson	Assistant Director for Justice of the Domestic Policy Staff (Stu Eizenstat's office)
	Michael Chanin	Deputy Assistant to the President
	Allison Thomas	Special Assistant to Anne Wexler
	Scotty Campbell	Director of the U.S. Office of Personnel Management
For the Homosexuals:	Charles Brydon	National Gay Task Force
	Kay Whitlock	National Gay Task Force Board of Directors
	Steven Endean	Gay Rights National Lobby
	Billy Jones	National Coalition of Black Gays
	Joyce Hunter	National March on Washington
	Frank Scheuren	Dignity, Inc.
	Joseph Totten	Dignity, Inc.
	Mary Spottswood Pou	National Convention Project
	Terry DeCrescenzo	Gay Academic Union
	Margot Karle	Lambda Legal Defense and Education Fund
	H. Gerald Schiff	National Association of Business Councils
	Dr. Walter J. Lear	National Gay Health Coalition
	Carolyn Handy	National Convention Project, Gay Rights National Lobby, and avowedly homosexual Human Rights Commissioner, Washington, D.C.
	John Lawrence	Integrity, Inc.
	R. Adam DeBaugh	United Fellowship of Metropolitan Community Churches.[134]

Jean O'Leary, also an ex-nun and Co-Executive Director of the NGTF, was appointed by Carter to the National Commission for the Observance of the International Women's Year.[139]

When O'Leary resigned her position in protest against Bella Abzug's firing, Carter named in her stead a reportedly avowed female homosexual.[140]

Two female homosexuals were reportedly appointed by Carter to the President's Advisory Committee on Women.[141]

There are many other ways in which Carter helped the homosexuals. Anne Wexler indicated, in a letter to R. Adam DeBaugh, the President's support for Alan Cranston's bill to allow homosexuals to enter the United States. In her letter, Wexler invoked American obligations under the 1975 Helsinki Agreement.[142] (Since the Helsinki Agreement made no mention of homosexuals, it can only be inferred that the Carter White House had accepted the movement's premise that homosexuals constitute a legitimate minority and had extended this notion to international law!) Alan Parker, Assistant Attorney General under Carter, also sent a sup-

445

(Letterhead)
The White House
Washington

June 30, 1980

Dear Mr. Nugent:

Allison Thomas and I appreciated the
time with you and your colleagues at
our recent meeting. In an entirely
new way I felt your struggles and concerns. I look forward to continuing
this dialogue.

Please do not hesitate to call me if I
can be of assistance to you.

                    Sincerely,

                    (Signature)

                    Bob Maddox
                 Special Assistant
                  to Anne Wexler

The Reverend Robert Nugent, S.D.S.
New Ways Ministry
3312 Buchanan Street
Mt. Ranier, MD 20822

FIGURE 15
Letter from Rev. Bob Maddox to Father Robert Nugent.
Source: Bondings.

portive letter to Senator Cranston.[143] Even after Carter had been rejected overwhelmingly by the American people, reports of support for homosexual movement goals by his lame-duck Administration continued to circulate. The Department of Justice issued new guidelines to make it easier for homosexuals to enter the United States.[144] The new procedures made it virtually impossible for the Immigration and Naturalization Service to stop homosexuals at points of entry into the U.S. unless they repeatedly asserted the nature of their sexual propensities. Other federal departments which made prohomosexual decisions during the Carter Administration include the Internal Revenue Service, the Federal Communications Commission, the U.S. Navy, the Bureau of Prisons, the Job Corps, the Public Health Service, and the Agency for International Development.[145]

Jimmy Carter's position on homosexual issues as part of his 1980 reelection efforts was basically prohomosexual.[146] A campaign ad which appeared in a homosexual newspaper featured a picture of Rosalyn Carter with UFMCC founder Troy Perry and Dr. Newton Deiter.[147] Even the President's mother, "Miss Lillian" Carter, helped homosexual organizations in Los Angeles raise $120,000.[148]

Just before the Carters left the White House, the National Gay Task Force sent the President a well deserved letter of gratitude:

January 16, 1981

Dear President Carter:

On behalf of our members and staff, the National Gay Task Force would like to express its gratitude and heartfelt thanks for your successful commitment to open the government to all citizens, for your concern for human rights and justice and for the positive steps taken by your administration to advance the civil rights and human dignity of all gay people.

We particularly have appreciated your administration's openness in discussing gay issues, its opposition to employment discrimination in the federal government because of private non-job related behavior and the permission to enter the United States granted to gay Cuban refugees. Thank you for being a decent, caring and compassionate President, (sic) may the months and years ahead offer you personal fulfillment and satisfaction as you reflect on your achievements in the past four years, you may now look forward to the opportunity to enjoy life in ways that will be most meaningful to you and your family. Our hearts are with you.

Charles F. Brydon and Lucia Valeska
National Gay Task Force[149]

JERRY BROWN

On November 27, 1980, the National Convention Project sponsored a fundraising event at a homosexual discoteque. The only candidate to appear at the "Gay Vote USA Gala" was California's Governor Jerry Brown, who delivered a statement of commitment to some of the goals of the homosexual movement: "In his keynote address Brown said that he would fight for a gay rights plank in the Democratic Party and if elected would sign an executive order banning discrimination based on sexual preference in the federal government."[150] *In Unity* published a photograph of Jerry Brown with Larry Uhrig, "pastor" of the Metropolitan Community Church in Washington, D.C., where the event took place.

California is probably the state where homosexuals are best organized, especially in San Francisco and in Los Angeles. The leadership has access to the highest levels of the state government. Governor Brown has "distinguished" himself for the large number of avowed homosexuals he has appointed to state positions. They include:

- Mary Morgan, "a San Francisco attorney and prominent gay rights advocate." Her appointment as a San Francisco Municipal Court judge was recognized for its political importance for the movement by Morgan herself, who observed: "I think it's absolutely a step forward for the gay and lesbian community. I think it's important to have more lesbians and gays visible in our society so people can see there's not an enormous difference between us and we don't have anything to fear from each other."[151]
- Jerry Leaks, a Juvenile Court Commissioner and an activist in pro-homosexual organizations in California, was appointed to the Superior Court in Los Angeles.[152]
- Rand Schrader, president of the Board of Directors of Los Angeles Gay Community Services, was appointed judge of the Municipal Court of Los Angeles.[153]
- Ivy Bottini, reportedly also a homosexual, was named by Brown to the California Commission on Aging.[154]

On April 4, 1979, Brown issued an executive order (No. B–54–79) barring the consideration of homosexuality as a factor in the hiring of state employees. The implementation of Brown's order by the State's Personnel Board involved the creation of a *Sexual Orientation Project,* an office under the Public Employment and Affirmative Action Division of the Board. The first manager for the project was Leroy S. Walker, formerly a consultant with the State's Department of Fair Employment Practices.[155] According to Steve Phillips of the Board's Affirmative Action Division, Walker "was selected because of his action in the gay community . . . He was involved in gay rights issues."[156] The cost of the project is some $50,000 per year, of which nearly $30,000 is allocated to the manager's salary. Reportedly, one function of the manager is to sensitize employees and supervisors to the rights of homosexuals.[157] Translated into everyday English, this means propagandizing the ideology of the homosexual movement. An indication that this is, in reality, a major function of the project is the production at government expense of an official homosexual glossary, the first concrete achievement of the project. Compiled by Walker and others, "A Glossary of Terms Commonly Associated with Sexual Orientation" (California State Personnel Board, Sacramento, September, 1980) de facto, makes the homosexual ideology California's sexual orthodoxy.

WASHINGTON, D.C.

One of the jurisdictions in which the homosexual movement enjoys the strongest support is the nation's capital. Homosexual organizations are probably, after unions and certain churches, the most influential political force in city politics. The District of Columbia is also the most liberal jurisdiction of the union. It is not surprising that the homosexual movement has made congressional representation for D.C. an integral part of its agenda. Were the proposed constitutional amendment giving the District of Columbia two senators and a representative to be enacted, the homosexual movement would have "in its pocket" the D.C. congressional delegation. As a result of the great influence of the homosexual movement in Washington's political life, homosexuality flourishes in Washington and the city competes with New York and San Francisco for the title of "Gay Capital" of America.

The existence of such a politically powerful homosexual community in Washington is probably due to the transient nature of much of the city's population, the low quality of domestic political life, and the presence of numerous minority groups which are poor, unsophisticated, and largely inactive politically. The high cost of real estate has also resulted in the virtual inability of middle-class families (i.e., traditional families with children) to reside in the city. Groups of homosexuals, monied and without responsibilities beyond themselves, are able to share houses and apartments that normal American families cannot afford.

One of the main supporters of Washington's homosexual movement is Marion Barry, the city's mayor and former civil rights activist. In August 1980, a group of irate citizens—allegedly Marines—roughed up several homosexuals at one of their establishments, a bar strategically located near the Marine barracks. Marion Barry was one of the first "outsiders" to show up and express his "outrage" and support for the homosexuals.[158] Barry regularly issues proclamations commemorating "Gay Pride Weeks" to celebrate the Stonewall riot in New York commemorated annually in June.[159] He parades with the homosexuals and is often a speaker at homosexual rallies.[160] On the occasion of the first National Third World Lesbian/Gay Conference at the Harambee Hotel near Howard University in Washington, October 10–17, 1979, became "Gay Rights Awareness Week."[161] The UFMCC was honored by Barry on October 5, 1980, declared by the Mayor to be "Universal Fellowship Day."[162] The complete text of Barry's

THE HOMOSEXUAL NETWORK

resolution illustrates the depth of the Mayor's support for the movement and the nature of the UFMCC:

WASHINGTON, D.C.

UNIVERSAL FELLOWSHIP DAY
OCTOBER 5, 1980
BY THE MAYOR
OF THE DISTRICT OF COLUMBIA

A PROCLAMATION

WHEREAS, on Sunday, October 5, 1980, the members and friends of the Universal Fellowship of Metropolitan Community Churches will celebrate the 12th Anniversary of the founding of the church; and

WHEREAS, the Universal Fellowship of Metropolitan Community Churches is the largest international vehicle for public education about homosexuality; and

WHEREAS, the Universal Fellowship of Metropolitan Churches is a strong advocate for human rights and social justice at every level of existence; and

WHEREAS, the Universal Fellowship of Metropolitan Community Churches serves to inform and share with established church denominations in the process of breaking down the barriers which for centuries have excluded lesbian women and gay men and has brought human dignity and self respect to the gay and lesbian people of our city:

NOW, THEREFORE, I, THE MAYOR OF THE DISTRICT OF COLUMBIA, do hereby proclaim Sunday, October 5, 1980, as "UNIVERSAL FELLOWSHIP DAY" in Washington, D.C., and call upon all of our residents to join with me in honoring and commending Pastor Larry J. Uhrig and each member of the Universal Fellowship of Metropolitan Community Churches in recognition of the outstanding contributions which they make to their fellow citizens.

MARION BARRY, JR.
MAYOR
DISTRICT OF COLUMBIA

These "proclamations"—as well as others issued by politicians in other jurisdictions—are not to be taken lightly. They are read with pomp and glee at homosexual rallies. In the eyes of many, they represent the official recognition of the homosexual movement as a legitimate political force and, by implication, the practice of homosexuality as a normal variant of human sexual behavior.

Washington's City Hall is in constant communication with the homosexual community. Until she was fired (apparently for showing interest in running against D.C. Delegate Walter Fauntroy) Marie Dias, a highly paid city official, was Marion Barry's staff liaison with the homosexual movement, the elderly, Hispanics, and the "women's community" (i.e.,

450

radical feminist organizations).[163] Her termination on May 27, 1981, was seized by leaders of the homosexual community as the opportunity to request that a homosexual be appointed in her place. The letter was signed by Melvin Boozer, President of the Gay Activists Alliance; Tom Chorlton, President of the Gertrude Stein Democratic Club; Don Bruce, President of the Gay Restaurant Owners of Washington; Larry Uhrig, pastor of the Washington Metropolitan Community Church; Clint Hockenberry, President of the Gay and Lesbian Pride Week; Irving Embrey, President of the DC Sports Association; J. Carlson, proprietor of a bar, and the editor of *Out*, a prominent local homosexual publication. By June 8, a list of prospective candidates for the job had been drawn for presentation to the mayor. The arguments used for the homosexuals' request were direct and unambiguous: 1) A homosexual could best represent the interests of the homosexual movement, certainly better than a heterosexual ever could; 2) "Lesbians and Gay men make up one of the Mayor's key constituencies in this city. . . . There is no reason why we should not be in a high position on the Mayor's staff."

This second argument was offered by a representative of the Washington Chapter of the National Organization of Lesbians and Gays,[164] setting the framework for Barry's response which—not unexpectedly—was positive. By September 11, the *Washington Blade* was announcing to Washington's homosexuals that Barry had committed himself to appoint a "gay liaison."[165] As an added incentive to his homosexual constituency, Barry also announced that he had assigned a District government official to look for a public building to be given to the homosexuals for a "community center" of their own.

The Mayor has "stacked" municipal commissions with representatives of the homosexual movement to such an extent that a system of movement nominees seems to have been worked out. Don Michaels, editor of the *Washington Blade*, is a member of the Committee on the Issuance and Use of Police Passes.[166] Homosexuals also sit on the Board of Library Trustees and the Juvenile Justice Advisory Committee. Frank Kameny is a member of the D.C. Human Rights Commission to which he was originally appointed by Mayor Walter Washington.[167] The Gay Activists Alliance is responsible for most of the appointments through its Mayoral Appointments Project: "So far, the GAA project has secured the appointment of over two dozen Gays to positions with the city. Roehr has as his goal placement of Gays on other Boards and Commissions with direct impact on the economic and professional life of the city."[168]

In addition to boards already mentioned, the GAA claimed credit for positioning homosexuals in the following organizations:

Mayor's Committee on Child Abuse and Neglect,
Board of Appeals and Review,

Citizen's Traffic Board,
Mayor's Mini Art Gallery Committee.

The GAA has also nominated homosexuals for the Mayor's Committee on Downtown Redevelopment, the Board of Psychologist Examiners, the D.C. Human Rights Commission, the Arts and Humanities Commission, and the Mayor's Committee on the Handicapped. (The D.C. Human Rights Commission nominee was described by the *Washington Blade* as "active with WPFW," which is the local affiliate of Pacifica, a radical leftist radio network which broadcasts a weekly a homosexual program.) At one time the GAA was actively recruiting homosexuals otherwise qualified and willing to serve on the Registered Nurses Board, the Physical Therapists Board, and the Rentals Accommodation Commission. [169]

There are many indications of Barry's support for the homosexual movement. Under Marion Barry, for example, the D.C. Corporation Counsel supported two homosexual groups—the Gay People of Georgetown and the Gay Rights Coalition of Georgetown University Law Center—in their struggle against Georgetown University. [170] The university refused to recognize the homosexual groups as legitimate student organizations, since this would have forced this Catholic school to provide the homosexuals with a portion of student activity funds, which conflicted with the Catholic philosophy of the school. With the help of the official D.C. attorney, the university lost the suit in the D.C. Superior Court. Another example of official support for the homosexuals is the full cooperation the city provides to homosexual rallies and parades, well beyond what the strict interpretation of the law would require. The homosexual festival which ended the 1981 Gay and Lesbian Pride Day took place at a public school: Francis Junior High. [171] At the festival, Barry voiced his gratitude to the homosexuals: "You should let people know you will support your friends and punish your enemies. That's how it works." [172]

Support for the homosexual movement is widespread throughout the city's highly liberal political establishment. On April 9, 1981, the Gertrude Stein Democratic Club held a well-attended black tie banquet "to pay homage to a decade of Gay political achievement." [173] The *Washington Blade* made clear the liberal nature of the event as well as the ample support the movement has among Washington liberals:

> Stein Club members also intended the banquet to be a visible sign of Gay political clout in an era of conservative politics, a meaning expressed in the banquet slogan, "We've Just Begun."
> Many mainstream Democrats apparently agreed with that slogan. In attendance were Congressmen Walter Fauntroy (D.C.), Barney Frank (MA), Ted Weiss (NY), and Mickey Leland (TX). Ann Lewis, Political Director of the Democratic National Committee, attended as representative for Chairman Charles Manatt.

The Movement and American Liberalism

Representatives from the Americans for Democratic Action, the American Civil Liberties Union, and other progressive groups were present.
Washington politicians were well represented with Mayor Marion Barry, seven city council members, and a host of other local Democrats in attendance.
Councilmembers present were Dave Clark (D-Ward 1), John Wilson (D-Ward 2), Charlene Drew Jarvis (D-Ward 4), Nadine Winter (D-Ward 6), Betty Ann Kane (D-At Large), Hilda Mason (Statehood Party-At Large) and Council Chairman Arrington Dixon. In addition, Sterling Tucker, former Council Chairman and asst. secretary of HUD under President Carter, put in an appearance. . . . Representatives of Councilmen Jerry A. Moore (R-At Large) and H. R. Crawford (D-Ward 7) attended as well.[174]

The support for homosexuality in Washington is not merely symbolic, although the homosexual leadership appreciates any signs of recognition, waiting until later to reap the benefits of favorable policies or legislation. In addition to appointing numerous homosexuals to city offices, the liberal politicians who run Washington tried to deliver for the movement D.C. Act 4–69, signed into law by Marion Barry, which contained specific provisions of great importance to the homosexual movement. As it was originally proposed by Councilman David Clarke (D-Ward 1), who represents one of the most heavily homosexual areas of Washington, the bill would have legalized "kiddie sex" and incest (both heterosexual and homosexual). Reportedly, Clarke argued that "teen-aged sexual activity that is consensual is not an area for criminal law."[175] The City Council was ready to approve the measure as proposed when a news story alerted the community.[176] Community pressure (spearheaded by churches) forced the liberals to pass, instead of the original bill, their "fall back" position, which, although not as radical as the original bill, still suited well the goals of the homosexual movement in the following particulars:

By removing all sanctions against homosexual conduct in the District of Columbia;

By legalizing adultery, fornication, and bestiality;

By legalizing sexual advancement of a teacher against a teenager over seventeen, so long as no "force" was used (The difference in age and social standing between the individuals involved make the absence of some element of force highly questionable here.);

By reducing drastically the penalties for forcible rape; and

By allowing wives to bring charges against their husbands under a multitude of circumstances (even if the husband had allegedly intoxicated his wife for the purpose of having sexual intercourse). (Although not of direct interest to the homosexual movement, the deleterious effect such a provision would have on family life makes it very attractive for the movement.)

By the time D.C. Act 4–69 reached the Congress, profamily forces nationwide had mobilized considerable opposition to the bill. These efforts were spearheaded by the Moral Majority. In accordance with the D.C. Home Rule Act, the House of Representatives had the opportunity to review the D.C. Act 4–69. It was soundly defeated. The homosexuals well understood the nature of their defeat. Although they had tried to frame the issue in terms of home rule or self-determination, the true nature of the question was clear in the first issue of the *Washington Blade* immediately after the repeal of the prohomosexual statute. Under the headline "A contest between two rival lobbies," the first two paragraphs of the story read: "The issues in the House of Representatives floor debate of the D.C. Sexual Reform Act were clear cut: traditional morality vs. the District's right to self-government. But behind the scenes the contest was between the relative strength of two lobbies: The Moral Majority and the Gay Rights National Lobby."[177] Although the participation of the homosexuals was kept in the background during the debate, after the veto all veils were lifted: "The vote was also a setback for Washington's politically influential Gay community. Gay leaders had played a significant role in drafting the legislation and, with the cooperation of city officials, had quietly orchestrated the lobbying effort to save the legislation after it came under attack from Jerry Falwell's Moral Majority."[178]

The nation's capital probably represents the extreme case of a local government under the spell of the homosexual movement. In this sense, Washington is unique. In another sense, the District of Columbia reflects what is happening, on a lesser scale, in many other communities throughout the United States. It is too early to say whether the influence of the homosexual movement has reached its apex in Washington, or whether other communities will follow its lead and enshrine homosexuality de facto as an acceptable lifestyle and homosexuals as a legitimate minority.

NEW YORK, N.Y.

New York City is not Washington, D.C. With a population thirteen times as large, and seemingly insurmountable difficulties, the city remains—in spite of major shifts in population—a mosaic of well-established and old neighborhoods. Solid political traditions, ethnic political involvement, and stable family-centered religious groups (both Roman Catholic and Jewish) have provided a solid barrier against which the homosexual movement, largely centered in fashionable Greenwich Village, has made few inroads. The homosexuals are well organized and count on the support of their traditional allies: the ACLU and other liberal elements of the political spectrum.

This picture contrasts with the paradox of a city with a well-recognized liberal tradition which is virtually run by liberals. Inasmuch as city politicians are liberal, they do support the homosexual movement. This support has been thwarted year after year by opposition from the police-

The Movement and American Liberalism

men, firemen, Catholics, and Orthodox Jews. Liberal politicians, however, have continued to "pay their dues" to the homosexual movement.

In New York, as in Washington and elsewhere, the Mayor proclaims homosexual "holidays" as city celebrations. Mayor Edward Koch proclaimed June 1981 "Gay Arts Festival Month." He also gave his blessing to the June 29 "Gay Pride March" and proclaimed November 22 and 23, 1980, "Gay Market Weekend," a celebration which featured a "gay business exposition" at a public grade school (Public School No. 3) in Greenwich Village. [179] Edward Koch is a supporter of the homosexual movement from his days in the House of Representatives. Not only was his name then associated with prohomosexual legislation, but he devised the strategy that called for explicit exclusion of affirmative action provisions in homosexual "rights" legislation as a way of making it more palatable to his fellow Representatives. [180] One of his first acts as Mayor was to issue a "gay rights ordinance" pertaining to municipal hiring practices, although homosexual leaders complained openly about his "lukewarm" support even after he appeared before the Greater Gotham Business Council to call for the passage of prohomosexual legislation by the City Council "as a matter of conscience."[181]

The participation of avowed homosexuals in city government is important for the movement. In making room for them, liberal politicians render a much-needed service to the homosexual cause:

Manhattan Borough President Andrew Stein has been one of the most supportive. His office is a key to city government for gays, especially since Manhattan has more visible gays than the other boroughs. Stein has worked with gays since his election four years ago, and continues to support the emergence of a stronger gay constituency. "The New York City gay population is only starting to realize its political potency," says Stein. "You have to get involved in the whole system. The idea is to register more gays and get more active in voting—and let the body politic know that this is happening. The gay community still has a long way to go in terms of organization."

In New York, this political muscle is being developed by a growing network of gays working in city government. Gay politics is replacing the smoke-filled room with the steam-filled room, and gay social encounters can produce miracles. "We are in all the agencies," notes Bob Mehl, until recently Andrew Stein's liaison to the gay community. "A well-placed phone call, a talk over a beer at Ty's, a chance meeting in the steamroom at Man's Country can work wonders." ["Ty's" is a homosexual bar; "Man's Country" is a homosexual bathhouse. Both are listed in the *Gayellow Pages* as "Gay or lesbian-owned business . . . serving all people."]

With Mehl in Stein's office and Herb Rickman as special assistant to the mayor, the gay community made some gains. Open gays now serve on the community boards; police are trained about gays and gay lifestyles; city officials have been made more aware about violence against gays. [182]

Stein is a liberal Democrat and President of the Borough of Manhattan. When Thomas Burrows resigned as special assistant to the codirector of the National Gay Task Force, Charles Brydon (in protest against Brydon's letter discouraging the introduction of prohomosexual legislation in the 97th Congress as a tactical maneuver), Stein promptly hired him as liaison to the homosexual movement. According to Stein, "Mr. Burrows will be available to assist me in making this office more responsive to Manhattan's lesbian and gay community."[183]

In New York City, homosexuals are welcome as teachers in the public schools. Apparently, the policy of the City's School Board was called into question in 1979, motivating a request for a clarification by Mayor Koch. The public school system's Chancellor Frank J. Macchiarola responded in a way that won the approval of Meryl Friedman of the Gay Teachers Association of New York City. According to Macchiarola:

> In no instance has sexual orientation been raised as a bar to entrance into our service. In no cases are employees subject to disciplinary action of any kind on account of sexual orientation.
> The New York City Public Schools judge each and every one of our students and teachers on an individual basis. We do not discriminate because of belief or because of the attitudes of our employees in matters that are personal and private.[184]

Perhaps the most interesting case of support for the homosexual movement by a New York City liberal politician is the statement mentioned earlier made by Harrison Goldin, City Comptroller, at a meeting of the Greater Gotham Business Council. According to Goldin, "It would make good sense financially to include the gay community in the national promotion of New York City as a tourist attraction."[185] It is hard to imagine that many Americans would be interested in visiting New York City on the basis of its homosexual bars or bathhouses. The fact that such a statement could be made by a New York City liberal politician is an indication, however, of the degree of support they are willing to offer the homosexual movement.

SUMMARY

The support of liberal politicians for the homosexual movement has been shown with some detail in certain cases. It would be a mistake, however, to conclude, that this close connection exists only in New York, California, and Washington. In any jurisdiction where homosexuals are organized and liberals control the government, it is safe to assume that there is a connection. Reasons of space preclude a wider treatment of the subject, although the patterns of support uncovered immediately above exist throughout the country. A few examples show the pervasive nature of this phenomenon:

- In Sacramento, Mayor Isenberg (a liberal Democrat) declared a "Gay Pride Week" during June 1981 to commemorate the Stonewall riot.[186]
- Mayor Dianne Feinstein (San Francisco) not only indicated her support for national prohomosexual legislation,[187] but actually led a homosexual march.[188]
- Under the leadership of Mayor Feinstein, sixteen homosexuals (nine males and seven females) were inducted into the San Francisco Police Department.[189]
- In Los Angeles a testimonial dinner was held in January 1981 in honor of Ivy Bottini, previously mentioned, as a "long-time lesbian activist." A booklet was printed to honor Bottini, filed with advertisements paid by Los Angeles's liberal establishment, including U.S. Representative Henry Waxman, the city comptroller, five councilmen, six state assemblymen, and the local state senator (Alan Sieroty), also a Democrat.[190]
- Los Angeles County Supervisor Ed Edelman participated in the Gay Pride and Festival Parade in West Hollywood in June 1980.[191]
- Mayor W. H. McNichols, Jr. of Denver wrote an official letter welcoming the 8th Annual General Conference of the UFMCC, which met in Denver on August 1 through 7, 1977. (See Figure 16). The letter offered attendees Denver's "numerous cultural and recreational facilities." The delegates' interests may be ascertained from the map of Denver distributed to them. The facilities pointed out by the map (see Figures 17-A and -B) are mainly homosexual bars and bathhouses. These are probably not the facilities Mayor McNichols had in mind when he wrote his letter.
- Colorado's Governor Richard D. Lamm extended a similar welcome also offering delegates "the many recreational opportunities Colorado has to offer." (See Figure 18)
- March 25, 1979, marked the anniversary of Stan Harris's arrival in Baltimore from Adelaide, South Australia. He is an MCC "minister". Mayor William Schaeffer (a liberal Democrat) declared that date the "Reverend Stan Harris and Metropolitan Community Church Day" in Baltimore. Representing the Mayor at the celebration, Edwin Dean thanked the MCC for its work in the area of "juvenile services."[192] (In reporting this story, *In Unity* did not specify the "services" to juveniles which elicited this expression of gratitude.)
- In April 1979 the UFMCC opened a local church in Ann Arbor, Michigan. The Michigan State House passed Resolution No. 39 to commemorate this event; the resolution was formally presented by liberal state representative Perry Bullard.[193]
- On February 15, 1978, George McGovern (then Democratic Senator from South Dakota), acknowledged leader of the liberal faction of the Democratic Party, was the star speaker at a rally held by the Los Angeles New Alliance for Gay Equality. He spoke against a referendum question designed to eliminate homosexual teachers from public schools. Also in attendance were:

MAYOR

City and County of Denver

CITY AND COUNTY BUILDING · DENVER, COLORADO · 80202

AREA CODE 303 297-2721

August, 1977

Greetings!

It is a pleasure and a privilege for me to extend a warm
welcome to all in attendance at the 8th Annual General
Conference of the Universal Fellowship of Metropolitan
Community Churches which is meeting in Denver August 1-7.

I hope that all delegates to this Conference, family
members and guests, will have the time to take advantage of
the numerous cultural and recreational facilities which our
beautiful city and State have to offer our guests.

All citizens of our city welcome you and hope that this
international Conference will be fruitful and pleasant
for everyone.

Sincerely yours,

W. H. McNichols, Jr.
M A Y O R

FIGURE 16

Letter of Denver's Mayor W. H. McNichols welcoming the attendees at the 8th Annual
General Conference of the UFMCC.

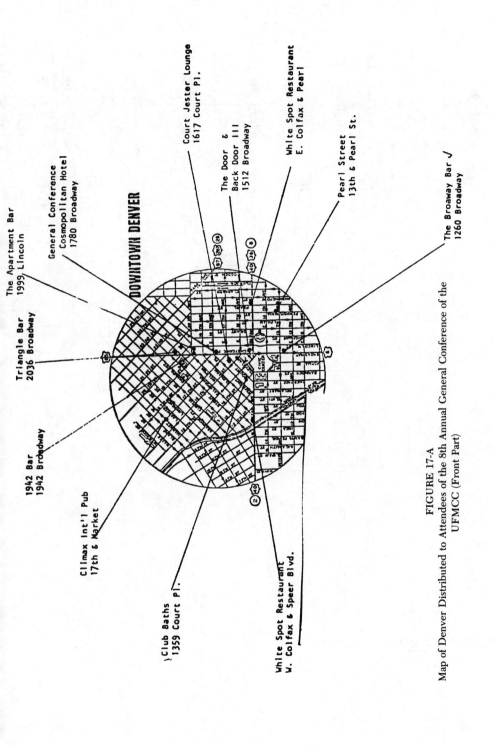

DOWNTOWN DENVER

Court Jester Lounge
1617 Court Pl.

General Conference
Cosmopolitan Hotel
1780 Broadway

The Door &
Back Door III
1512 Broadway

White Spot Restaurant
E. Colfax & Pearl

The Apartment Bar
1999 Lincoln

Pearl Street
13th & Pearl St.

Triangle Bar
2036 Broadway

The Broaway Bar
1260 Broadway

1942 Bar
1942 Broadway

Climax Int'l Pub
17th & Market

Club Baths
1359 Court Pl.

White Spot Restaurant
W. Colfax & Speer Blvd.

FIGURE 17-A
Map of Denver Distributed to Attendees of the 8th Annual General Conference of the
UFMCC (Front Part)

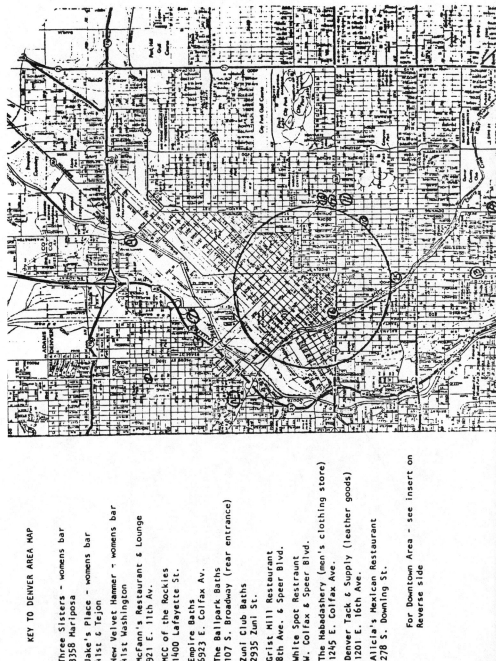

KEY TO DENVER AREA MAP

7. Three Sisters - womens bar
    3358 Mariposa

8. Jake's Place - womens bar
    41st & Tejon

9. New Velvet Hammer - womens bar
    41st Washington

10. McFann's Restaurant & Lounge
    921 E. 11th Av.

11. MCC of the Rockies
    1400 Lafayette St.

12. Empire Baths
    6923 E. Colfax Av.

13. The Ballpark Baths
    107 S. Broadway (rear entrance)

14. Zuni Club Baths
    2935 Zuni St.

15. Grist Mill Restaurant
    8th Ave. & Speer Blvd.

16. White Spot Restraunt
    W. Colfax & Speer Blvd.

17. The Habadashery (men's clothing store)
    1245 E. Colfax Ave.

18. Denver Tack & Supply (leather goods)
    1201 E. 16th Ave.

19. Alicia's Mexican Restaurant
    278 S. Downing St.

    For Downtown Area - see insert on
    Reverse side

State of Colorado

EXECUTIVE CHAMBERS

DENVER

RICHARD D. LAMM
Governor

August 1, 1977

GREETINGS:

As Governor of the State of Colorado, I am pleased to welcome all of you who have come to Denver to attend the 8th Annual General Conference of the Universal Fellowship of Metropolitan Community Churches.

The religious community plays an important and integral role in today's complex urban society--a role that we recognize and appreciate. Through your church, you are able to provide guidance and counseling to many people who might otherwise be neglected. Through your leadership, you have the opportunity to teach and reinforce the moral and ethical guidelines for living set down in the Ten Commandments, the simplest and best set of laws known to man.

I hope you will have time during your busy schedule to enjoy some of the many recreational opportunities Colorado has to offer--from the Denver Museum of Natural History to the scenic splendor of the Rocky Mountains.

My best wishes for a successful, educational, and enjoyable Conference.

Sincerely,

Richard D. Lamm
Governor

FIGURE 18

Letter of the Governor of Colorado, Richard D. Lamm, welcoming delegates to the 8th General Convention of the UFMCC.

Troy Perry, founder of the UFMCC
Zev Yaroslavsky, Los Angeles City Councilman
Joel Wachs, Los Angeles City Councilman
Peggy Stevenson, Los Angeles City Councilwoman
Ed Edelman, Los Angeles County Supervisor
Mel Levine, California Assemblyman
Willie Brown, California Assemblyman
Michael Roos, California Assemblyman
Art Agnos, California Assemblyman
Burt Pines, California State Democratic Chairman
Alice Travers, State Democratic Caucus Chairman
Mervyn Dymally, California Lieutenant Governor
Anthony Beilenson, U. S. Representative
Paul McCloskey, U. S. Representative[194]

Among the sponsors of the event were well-known entertainers including Warren Beatty, Shirley MacLaine, Barbra Streisand, and Marlo Thomas.[195]

- Against solid Republican opposition, liberal Democrat Hugh Carey, Governor of New York, nominated Richard Hongisto as the State Corrections Commissioner.[196] Hongisto is a former sheriff of San Francisco known for his "vocal, public support" for "gay rights."
- The introduction of pro-homosexual legislation in Illinois has been the result of the efforts of two liberal Republicans, State Representatives Elroy C. Sandquist Jr. (13th District) and Susan Catania (22nd District). Mrs. Catania endorsed five separate bills in the 82nd Illinois Legislature (HB-0357 through HB-0361) in which homosexuality was recognized as a reason for providing persons affected by this condition special protection under the law. She is apparently also an ERA and gun control advocate.[197] On November 11, 1981, a cocktail party was held at BJ'S, a homosexual bar in downtown Chicago. The party was held as a fund-raiser for OPEN (the Organization to Promote Equality Now), a homosexual Political Action Committee formed a few days before the event. The featured guest—and sharer in half the proceeds from the party—was Susan Catania.[198] Her allotment was to be utilized in her eventually unsuccessful campaign for lieutenant governor.

There are many ways in which liberal politicians contribute to the ultimate goal of the homosexual movement: the acceptance of the "gay lifestyle" as part of American society and of homosexual acts as normal variants of human behavior. The following list summarizes these ways. Naturally, some liberal politicians have contributed more to the homosexual movement than others. Many have avoided the issue altogether. However, there is myriad evidence that the several ways by which the liberal political establishment contributes to the homosexual movement include:

Promoting prohomosexual legislation
Attacking profamily legislation
Issuing orders or regulations which favor the homosexual movement
Providing public funding for homosexual organizations
Nominating avowed homosexuals for public positions
Issuing declarations on the occasion of homosexual celebrations

The Movement and American Liberalism

Participating in homosexual events: rallies, marches, "religious" services, etc.
Meeting in their official capacities with leaders of the homosexual movement
Hiring avowed homosexuals for their staffs
Creating offices and positions to deal with the homosexual question in a way favorable to the homosexual movement.

The homosexual movement is aware that its future is with American liberalism. The fact that Political Action Committees (PACs) are the contemporary way to influence legislators has not escaped the leaders of the homosexual movement, which has organized PACs of its own. An indication of this awareness is a rating chart on liberal PACs published in *The Advocate*.[199] The ratings given to the various PACs are additional indicators of the support enjoyed by the homosexual movement vis-à-vis American liberalism:

Organization	Politician/Personality Identified with Organization	Rates for	
		"Gay Issues"	Effectiveness
Americans for Democratic Action PAC	Rev. Robert Drinan, S.J., ADA President	A	A −
Americans for Common Sense	George McGovern	B −	B
Committee for American Principles	Birch Bayh	C +	C +
Committee for Future America	Walter Mondale	D −	C
Democratic Study Group	—	C	B
Democrats for the '80s	Pamela Harris	C +	B
Democratic National Committee	Jim Foster	B +	B −
Fund for a Democratic Majority	Sen. Edward Kennedy	B −	B
Human Rights Campaign Fund	—	A +	B
Independent Action	Morris Udall	B +	B +
National Abortion Rights League PAC	—	B +	B +
National Committee for an Effective Congress	Russell Hemenway	C	A
National Organization for Women PAC	Eleanor (Ellie) Smeal	B	B −
National Women's Political Caucus PAC	—	B +/A −	B
Parker-Coltrane PAC	Rep. John Conyer (D-MI)	Too new to rate	
People for the American Way	Norman Lear	A	A
Progressives-PAC	Vic Kamber	B	B

Note: Pamela Harris is the wife of Averell Harriman. Jim Foster is reportedly a homosexual activist. Russell Hemenway was campaign manager for Adlai Stevenson in the 1950s. Vic Kamber reportedly has close connections to organized labor political committees.

Notes

1. *Workers World* (New York, N.Y.), July 3, 1981, p. 4.

2. Ibid.

3. Ibid.

4. Ibid.

5. *Persuasion At Work* 4 (Rockford, IL: Rockford Institute, April, 1981): 2.

6. *Workers World* (New York, N.Y.), July 3, 1981, p. 7.

7. Handbill announcing the city-wide conference, St. Stephen's Church, Washington D.C., August 15, 1981, circulated in Washington, D.C. during the summer of 1981.

8. *In Unity*, August/September 1979, p. 20.

9. Personal interview with Adam DeBaugh, May 14, 1981.

10. Handbill circulated in Greenwich Village during the early part of June 1981.

11. *A New Day* 4 (February 1980): 4.

12. *Official Newsletter of the National Coalition of Gay STD Services* 2 (Arlington, VA: National Coalition of Gay STD Services, May 1981): 6.

13. R. Adam DeBaugh, "The 96th Congress: Prospects for Gay Rights Legislation," *Gays on the Hill* 3 (November-December 1978): 4.

14. *The Loving Brotherhood Newsletter* 5 (Sussex, N.J.: The Loving Brotherhood, June 1981): 3.

15. Leaflets handed out by representatives of the Gertrude Stein Democratic Club in front of voting centers throughout the city showed the homosexuals' position.

16. Promotional brochure distributed during the demonstration in front of the Sheraton-Washington Hotel.

17. *Gays on the Hill* 2 (August-September 1978): 1.

18. *CCSA: Meeting Human Needs* 2 (Washington, D.C.: Commission on Christian Social Action, Universal Fellowship of Metropolitan Community Churches, March 1981): 3.

19. Ibid. 1 (May and June 1980): 4.

20. Quoted in Marotta, p. 101.

21. *It's Time* 8 (January-February 1981): 3, 4.

22. Bob Nelson, "CLGR Charts Course for '82," *Gay Community News* (Boston), March 6, 1982.

23. Ibid.

24. *It's Time* 8 (January-February 1981): 4.

25. Fundraising letter from Interchange dated August 1981. Interchange is located at 1201 16th Street, N.W., Washington, D.C.

26. *It's Time* 8 (January-February 1981): 4.

27. "Gay Student Groups," (Washington, D.C.: National Gay Student Center, January 1977), 5th ed.

28. Statement by the Interchange Resource Network, Washington, D.C., September 23, 1981.

29. Forrest J. Rode, "Gay in Rural America," *It's Time* 6 (June-July 1979): 4.

30. *Workers World* (New York, N.Y.), July 3, 1981, p. 4.

31. Ibid., p. 7.

32. *Persuasion At Work* 4 (Rockford, IL: Rockford Institute, April 1981): 1, 2.

33. "A Report on the Outcome of Friends of Families Conference, January 12–13, 1982" (Oakland, CA: Friends of Families, n.d.).

34. Ibid.

35. Ibid.

36. *Task Force Report* 8 (New York, N.Y.: National Gay Task Force, November/December 1981).

37. Ibid.

38. Mike Sager, "25,000 Demonstrators March on the Pentagon," *Washington Post*, May 4, 1981.

39. A handbill entitled "People's Anti-War Mobilizer," distributed by the People's Anti-War Mobilization, New York, N.Y., June 1981.

40. New Ways Ministry, "Baltimore" file.

41. Fundraising letter, Fund for Human Dignity, New York, N.Y., n.d., p. 2 at margin.

42. *It's Time* 8 (March-April 1981): 1.

43. *Washington Star*, May 1, 1981.

44. *Washington Star*, April 10, 1981.

45. News release, American Civil Liberties Union, reproduced by *In Unity*, September/October 1980, p. 9.

46. New York State Assembly, "Memorandum in Support of Legislation," Assembly No. 9996, Albany, N.Y., February 8, 1978.

47. *It's Time*, Special Bonus Issue, 1976, p. 1.

48. Ibid., p. 2.

49. Andy Humm, "Gay Rights Bill," *New York City News*, March 10, 1981.

50. News release, Americans for Democratic Action, Washington, D.C., September 23, 1981.

51. Handbill distributed throughout Washington, D.C. on election day.

52. *National Catholic Reporter*, October 9, 1981, p. 8.

53. Letter of Karen M. Keener to the author, June 18, 1981.

54. Memorandum to members of the National Council of Teachers of English, Lesbian/Gay Caucus, from Karen M. Keener, Cochairman, November 7, 1979, p. 2.

55. Letter from the Quixote Center to American Catholic Bishops, excerpt reprinted in *A Time to Speak*, p. 5.

56. Handbill advertising the event.

57. R. Adam DeBaugh, "Representatives of 16 Denominations Gather to Discuss Homophobia in the Churches," *A New Day* 3 (June 1979): 1.

58. Personal interview conducted with staff person of the Quixote Center in preparation for this work on June 25, 1981.

59. *NAGAP Newsletter* 2 (Oakland, N.J.: National Association of Gay Alcoholism Professionals, Spring 1981): 2.

60. Ibid., p. 7.

61. Ibid.

62. Ibid.

63. Ibid., Winter 1980–81, p. 2.

64. Ken Lerer, "Gays—A New Key Voter Group," *New York*, May 30, 1977, p. 9.

65. "A New Big Push for Homosexuals' Rights," *U.S. News and World Report*, April 14, 1980, p. 94.

66. Letter to the author from the Director of the VD National Hotline, June 15, 1981.

67. *Gay Teachers Association Newsletter* 4 (New York, N.Y.: Gay Teachers Association, June 1981): 2.

68. *New York Times*, August 21, 1977, p. 37.

69. *Quicksilver Times* (Washington, D.C.), November 24-December 4, 1970, p. 9.

70. Clarke Taylor, "Gay Clout," *New York*, August 29, 1977, p. 47.

71. *New York Times*, October 4, 1977, p. 24.

72. "Homosexuality Goes to School," transcript of program #26 in the series "Options in Education" (Washington, D.C.: National Public Radio), April 19, 1976, p. 6.

73. Univ. of Connecticut, Graduate School of Social Work (West Hartford), Summary, Title XX Training Grant "New Perspectives on Lesbians and Gay Men," n.d.

74. Thom Willenbecher, "A G.A.L.A. Goodbye to God . . . Gay Atheists Come out," *Advocate*, January 10, 1980.

75. Handbill containing declaration and endorsers, distributed by the Religious Coalition for Gay Concerns, New York, N.Y.

76. *Boston Globe*, February 8, 1979.

77. "Legal Services Head Joins GRNL Board," *Advocate*, March 4, 1982.

78. Grace Lichtenstein, "Homosexuals In New York Find New Pride," *New York Times*, October 25, 1977.

79. *New York Times*, May 24, 1977 and October 24, 1977.

80. *National Catholic Reporter*, November 21, 1980.

81. Personal interview with Peter Henriot, S.J., Director of the Center of Concern, June 29, 1981.

82. Ibid.

83. *Bondings*, Spring-Summer 1981, p. 3.

84. *The Catholic Standard*, May 7, 1981.

85. *Washington Post*, October 24, 1981.

86. Campaign poster advocating the election of Alexa Freeman, November 1981, Washington, D.C.

87. The list of endorsers appears in a leaflet distributed at the demonstration in front of the Sheraton-Washington Hotel.

88. Undated package of information soliciting support for the Equal Rights Amendment mailed by the Women's Ordination Conference, Rochester, N.Y., in late 1981.

89. First National Symposium on Homosexuality and the Catholic Church (November 20–22, 1981), held in the Washington, D.C. metropolitan area. Promotional brochure and program distributed by New Ways Ministry, Mt. Rainier, MD.

90. Marotta.

91. *Bondings*, Winter 1979–80, p. 2.

92. *Bondings*, Winter 1980–81, p. 9.

93. *In Unity*, April-May 1980, p. 10.

94. "Our Man on Capitol Hill," *Christopher Street*, October 1978.

95. *A New Day* 3 (June 1979): 2.

96. *Gays on the Hill* 3 (January 1979): 2.

97. Austin Scott, "L.A. Homosexuals Create Own Brand of Political Activism," *Los Angeles Times*, March 15, 1981.

98. Clarke Taylor, "Gay Power," *New York*, August 29, 1977, p. 45.

99. *It's Time* 6 (June-July 1979): p. 1.

100. Americans for Democratic Action, Washington, D.C. congressional ratings for the various congresses.

101. James L. Bruning and B. L. Kintz, *Computational Handbook of Statistics* (Glenview, IL: Scott, Foresman & Co., 1977), p. 222.

102. Ibid., p. 8.

103. *In Unity*, December 1979/January 1980, p. 10.

104. *Gays on the Hill*, vol. 1, number 1 (n.d.), p. 1.

105. *Hearing*, p. 15.

106. *Gays on the Hill*, vol. 1, number 4 (n.d.), p. 4.

107. *A New Day* 5 (February 1981): 6.

108. Bob McCubbin, *The Gay Question: A Marxist Appraisal* (New York, N.Y.: World View Publishers, 1979), p. 75.

109. "New York City Hiring Policy," *Mattachine Society of New York Newsletter* 12 (January-February 1967): 1, quoted in Marotta, p. 43.

110. *Gays on the Hill*, vol. 1, number 2 (n.d.), p. 2.

111. *The Scene #69* (Denver: Gay Community Center of Colorado, July 15-August 4, 1977.

112. *Rocky Mountain News* (Denver), July 12, 1977.

113. *The Scene #69* (Denver: Gay Community Center of Colorado, July 15-August 4, 1977).

114. Ibid.

115. *Gays on the Hill*, vol. 1, number 2 (n.d.), p. 2.

116. *Gays on the Hill* 1 (March 1976): 3.

117. Ibid., p. 4.

118. Letter of U.S. Sen. Paul Tsongas (D-MA) to all other members of the U.S. Senate, September 19, 1979.

119. "Sen. Paul Tsongas to Introduce Gay Rights Bill in the Senate," *A New Day* 3 (November 1979): 1.

120. *Congressional Record*, December 5, 1979, pp. S17870–S17871.

121. *A New Day* 4 (February 1980): 2.

122. Ibid.

123. Don Michaels, "Sign of Kennedy Support Surfaces in Post," *Blade*, June 24, 1980, p. 3.

124. *In Unity*, April/May 1980, p. 12.

125. "Kennedy Pledges Support," *It's Time* 7 (February-March 1980): 1.

126. 1980 Democratic Platform text, p. 15. The complete text appears in the *36th Annual Almanac, 96th Congress, 2nd session—1980* (Washington, D.C.: Congressional Quarterly, 1981), pp. 91-B to 121-B.

127. "Dear Colleague" letter of April 15, 1980 from U.S. Rep. Theodore Weiss (D-NY) and Henry Waxman (D-CA) to the members of the U.S. House of Representatives.

128. Letter of Midge Costanza to Jean O'Leary and Bruce Voeller, Washington, D.C., February 8, 1977.

129. Ibid.

130. Ibid.

131. Some of these victories, closely paralleling the meeting agenda, were utilized by the NGTF in its fundraising efforts. Cf. National Gay Task Force's 1981 fundraising brochure.

132. *A New Day* 4 (January 1980), p. 2.

133. Ibid.

134. Ibid.

135. *Bondings*, Spring-Summer 1980, p. 6.

136. *A New Day* 4 (September 1980): 1.

137. Universal Fellowship of Metropolitan Community Churches, "Washington Field Office Report 1976–77," Washington, D.C., p. 95.

138. Andrew Humm and Betty Santoro, "If We Gay Men and Lesbians Stand Up," *New York Times*, November 1, 1980. Humm and Santoro wrote this article as representatives of the Coalition for Lesbian and Gay Rights, which comprises 47 groups. Humm is also a noted leader in Dignity/New York.

139. Handout distributed at the Nebraska International Women's Year Conference which took place in Lincoln, June 25–26, 1977.

140. "Homosexuals!! An Official American Family Unit??," Texas, 1977. Position paper prepared by a Texas delegate who has requested anonymity to the White House Conference on Families.

141. *A New Day* 4 (September 1980): 2.

142. Letter from Anne Wexler to Adam DeBaugh, quoted in *A New Day* 4 (August 1980): 5.

143. Letter from Alan A. Parker to U.S. Senator Alan Cranston (D-CA), reproduced in *A New Day* 4 (August 1980): 5.

144. *A New Day* 4 (December 1980): 3.

145. Fundraising brochure, National Gay Task Force, also cf. *A New Day* 4 (September 1980).

146. Congressional Research Service, "Presidential Candidates Speak to the Issue of Homosexual Rights" (Washington, D.C.: Library of Congress, April 18, 1981).

147. *In Unity*, February-March 1980, p. 12.

148. Ibid.

149. *It's Time* 8 (January-February 1981): 1.

150. *In Unity*, February/March 1980, p. 14.

151. "Brown Appoints Lesbian to Court in San Francisco," *Washington Post*, August 28, 1981.

152. *In Unity*, December 1979/January 1980, p. 11.

153. *In Unity*, September/October 1980, p. 12.

154. Ibid.

155. Memorandum of Ronald M. Kurz (Executive Officer, California State Personnel Board) to all state agencies and employee organizations of April 30, 1980.

156. "Gay Protector," *Sacramento Union*, June 8, 1981.

157. "Protecting Gay State Workers," *San Francisco Bee*, March 24, 1981.

158. *Washington Star*, April 9, 1981.

159. *Washington Post*, June 22, 1981.

160. Ibid.

161. *In Unity*, December 1979/January 1980, p. 4.

162. *In Unity*, November/December 1980, p. 22.

163. "Mayor Urged to Name Openly Gay Liaison," *Blade*, June 12, 1981, p. A-3.

164. Ibid.

165. "Barry Promises Gay Liaison," *Blade*, September 11, 1981, p. A-5.

166. "D.C. Homosexuals Increase Influence by 'Using System,' " *Washington Star*, April 9, 1981.

167. *Washington Star*, April 10, 1981.

168. "New Slate of City Appointments Set," *Blade*, May 1, 1981.

169. Ibid.

170. "Homosexuals Win Bias Suit Against GU," *Washington Post*, March 10, 1981.

171. "Parade and Festival Highlight Gay and Lesbian Pride Events," *Washington Post*, June 22, 1981.

172. Ibid.

173. "A Sign of Clout in a Conservative Era," *Blade*, April 17, 1981, p. 1.

174. Ibid.

175. "D.C. Panel Backs Bill to Legalize Sex Between Consenting Children," *Washington Post*, June 25, 1981.

176. Ibid.

177. "The Killing of D.C.'s Sex Law Reform," *Blade*, October 9, 1981.

178. Ibid.

179. *Newsletter of the Council for Community Consciousness, Inc.* (New York, N.Y.: Council for Community Consciousness, June 8, 1981), p. 2. The Council's address is P.O. Box 150, Gracie Station, New York, N.Y., 10028.

180. *Gays on the Hill*, volume 3, number 1 (n.d.), p. 2.

181. Matthew Daniels, "Gay Politics Goes Mainstream," *Advocate*, July 23, 1981.

182. Ibid.

183. *Gay Community News* (Boston), July 18, 1981.

184. *Gay Community News* (Boston), February 17, 1979.

185. *In Unity*, December 1979/January 1980, p. 11.

186. Peter Anderson, "Wrath Toward the Gays," *Sacramento Union*, June 17, 1981.

187. *Hearing*, p. 49.

188. *In Unity*, February/March 1980, p. 12.

189. Ibid.

190. Austin Scott, "L.A. Homosexuals Create Own Brand of Political Activism," *Los Angeles Times*, March 15, 1981.

191. Ibid.

192. *In Unity*, June/July 1979, p. 4.

193. *In Unity*, August/September 1979, p. 6.

194. *Gay Community News* (Boston), March 1978; *Los Angeles Herald Examiner*, February 16, 1978.

195. Official invitation for the event.

196. *Gaysweek* 3 (April 16, 1979).

197. "Some Questions About GOP Lt.-Gov. Candidate Susan Cantania," an unsigned, undated leaflet circulated during the 1982 Illinois campaign for Lieutenant Governor.

198. Stephen Kulieke, "State's First Gay Political Action Committee Formed," *Chicago Gaylife* 7 (November 6, 1981).

199. Larry Bush, "Making the Grade: Liberal Political Action Committees and Gay Rights," *Advocate*, March 4, 1982, pp. 15 ff.

CHAPTER

I X

The Funding of the Homosexual Movement

There is no question that the homosexual movement has relatively large sums of money at its disposal. Homosexuals tend to be wealthier than the rest of the population, and vast sums are generated by homosexuality-related businesses, in both the "taxed" and the "underground" economies (cf. chapter IV). Moreover, the homosexual movement is an integral part of the American left. This relationship, plus the "big government" principle that is the cornerstone of liberal philosophy, has resulted in the availability of substantial funds for homosexual organizations. In the case of student organizations, funding is the result of the common practice of distributing student activity fees receipts to the various campus organizations. As the result of court actions based on the movement's influence on university administrators, monies paid by students or their parents for "student activities" may end up promoting the homosexual ideology. Due to successful efforts undertaken during the Carter Administration, the IRS recognizes homosexual organizations as "charitable" for tax purposes (501(c)(3) status), which constitutes an incentive for wealthy homosexuals to contribute to them.

The gross annual income of the homosexual movement—exclusive of profit-making organizations (businesses)—was estimated in chapter IV to be $245,625,000. This figure is an approximation at best, since it is based on the assumption that the gross income of the 3,000 homosexual organizations listed by the National Gay Task Force is equal to the gross income of organizations surveyed for the preparation of this work. Considering that $81,875 is a rather small budget for an organization, this assumption is reasonable. However, without a careful examination of the NGTF list, it cannot be posited with certainty. Statistically, only if the survey sample had been taken from the NGTF list would the figure of $245,625,000 be acceptable without further questions. In the absence of other information, it is reasonable to state that a quarter of a billion dollars is spent annually by homosexual nonprofit organizations in the pursuit of their goals.

Survey Results

TAX STATUS

The tax-deductible status of contributions made to certain homosexual organizations places certain restrictions on their activities. In many cases however, these restrictions are ignored. Nonprofit organizations are those which do not declare a "profit" to be shared by their owners. By their charter, any funds left after expenses are paid belong to the organization rather than to anyone else and must be used in the pursuit of its goals. There is no universal legal prohibition against nonprofit organizations engaging in lobbying activities (i.e., trying to influence legislation). Certain nonprofit organizations have been classified by the Internal Revenue Service as "501(c)(3)." As mentioned above, contributions made to these organizations are deductible from the income of the donors for tax purposes. The practice of homosexuality is also promoted in profit-making establishments, many of which are merely centers for the procurement of sexual partners or facilities for sexual acts of various kinds.

Most people would agree that the Internal Revenue Service stretched the meaning of "public interest" when it decided to accept homosexual organizations as 501(c)(3). Organizations typical of the category include hospitals, churches, and schools. The freedom of action of 501(c)(3) organizations is restricted in terms of lobbying activities: substantial allocation of their resources in this area should result in the loss of such privileged status. The rationale behind this limitation is that it is unfair for taxpayers to support interest groups involved in lobbying.

The survey preliminary to this work included questions pertaining to the legal status and related activities of the homosexual organizations queried. All the organizations questioned indicated that they were nonprofit. This provided a measure of reassurance to the designers since the universe had been chosen from organizations believed to be non-profit. Other questions asked whether the organizations were 501(c)(3) and whether they invested a substantial amount of resources in lobbying. Tables 36

and 37 display the raw data and the percentages corresponding to responses to the above questions. The results indicate three significant
findings:

Seventy-eight percent of the organizations are 501(c)(3). This is a very
high percentage, corresponding to 305 organizations of the original universe of 394. It indicates a high degree of awareness of the value of this
status by the leadership of the homosexual movement.

TABLE 36

Tax Status vs. Lobbying Activities (Raw Data)

Is the organization 501(c)(3)?		YES	NO	
Does the Organization Invest Substantial Resources in Lobbying?	YES	30	8	38
	NO	32	10	42
		62	18	80

TABLE 37

Tax Status vs. Lobbying Activities (Percentages)

Is the organization 501(c)(3)?		YES	NO	
Does the Organization Invest Substantial Resources in Lobbying?	YES	79% / 48%	21% / 44%	100%
	NO	76% / 52%	24% / 56%	100%
		100%	100%	

Forty-eight percent of the homosexual organizations that have the 501(c)(3)
status also invest a substantial proportion of their resources in lobbying.
This corresponds to almost 191 organizations in the original universe.

More than one-third of *all* the homosexual nonprofit organizations are
both classified as 501(c)(3) and engaged in lobbying activities.

Questions concerning tax status were asked very early in the interview,
while those relating to potentially illegal activities were left for the end
of the interview, to minimize the probability that the responses would
affect each other.

OVERALL LEVELS OF FUNDING

Six different sources of funding for homosexual organizations were identified during the interview process. In order of decreasing importance
relative to the total funding, these sources are: individual donations, state
and local governments, the federal government, client fees, foundations,

TABLE 38

Funding of Homosexual Organizations by Source of Funding

(1) Source	(2) N	(3) %N	(4) N % of Sample	(5) Total Funding of the Sample (80 Organizations)	(6) % of Funding From Source	(7) Mean Level of Funding From Source	(8) Estimated Total Funding of The Universe (394 Organizations)
Federal Government	24	14.20%	30.00%	$1,207,375	18.43%	$50,307	$ 5,946,322
State/Local Governments	37	21.89%	46.25%	$1,781,375	27.20%	$48,145	$ 8,773,272
Foundations	12	7.10%	15.00%	$ 132,300	2.02%	$11,025	$ 651,578
Churches	7	4.14%	8.75%	$ 80,375	1.23%	$11,482	$ 395,847
Client Fees	27	15.98%	33.75%	$1,043,000	15.92%	—	$ 5,136,775
Individual Donation	62	36.69%	77.50%	$2,305,575	35.20%	—	$11,354,956
TOTALS	169	100.00	—	$6,550,000	100.00	—	$32,258,750

All figures expressed are per annum, covering the June 1980–81 period.

NOTES: (1) Sources of Funding: It is possible for an organization to have various sources of funds or receive multiple contributions from the same type of source.

(2) Number of organizations receiving funds from each source: The total exceeds 80 due to multiple funding in most organizations

(3) Percentage of grants per source assuming that each source provides one grant per organization: (e.g., the federal government provides 14.04% of all grants made to homosexual organizations).

(4) Percentage of organizations receiving funds from each source: (e.g., 30.00% of the homosexual organizations receive federal monies).

(5) Total funds received by all the organizations in the sample from each source: (e.g., the 24 organizations in the sample received a total of $1,207,375 from the federal government).

(6) Percentage of the total funding of homosexual organizations from each source of funds: (e.g., 18.43% of all funds received by homosexual nonprofit organizations proceeds from the federal government).

(7) Funding provided to each organization by each source of funding: Assuming one grant per organization per source of funding, this represents the average value of each grant. Only the first four rows of this column are significant, since there are many "clients" and "individual donors" per organization.

(8) Total funding received by all 394 organizations in the original universe: This column is obtained by multiplying column (5) by 4.9925 (= 394/80).

and churches. Table 38 presents the funding of the homosexual movement by sources of funding.

The main source of funding of the homosexual movement is the American taxpayer. The federal government provides 18.43% of the funding and the state and local governments 27.20%. The latter sum indicates the high degree of influence of homosexual organizations at the state and local levels through their grassroots network. The total funding directly from tax sources—probably in the form of grants and contracts—amounts to 45.63% of the total income of homosexual nonprofit organizations. It is probable that a large portion of the funds labeled "state and local" are ultimately federal in origin, the state and local jurisdictions being merely conduits for federal monies.

Almost half the homosexual organizations (46.25%) receive state/local funding and nearly one-third (30%) receive federal funds. A total of 44 organizations was found to receive both federal *and* state/local funds. This means that over half the homosexual nonprofit organizations in the original universe (55%) receive tax dollars. Although churches provide a small proportion of the funds (1.23%), they contribute to a larger proportion of organizations (8.75%). The same is true of foundations, which contribute 2.02% of the funds, but to 15.00% of the organizations. This suggests that both foundations and churches provide "seed money" in the form of small grants of approximately $11,000 each (see column 7), and that this money is then "leveraged" to obtain much larger grants from the government. There is evidence of this in the case of New Ways Ministry, normally supported by small contributions from church sources and individual donations.[1] These contributions enabled the organization to seek and obtain a much larger ($38,000) federal grant.[2] The $50,000 level in government grants (Table 38, column 7, rows 1 and 2) are merely average values. Much larger grants have undoubtedly been made to homosexual organizations as shown below.

It is interesting to note that if funds are divided into public and individual, the homosexual organizations receive approximately half from each group. "Public" funds in this context refer not just to "tax" dollars, but also to church or foundation funds. In the final analysis, these two sources partake of the tax system, since donations to them are always tax-deductible. In another sense, they are "respectable" institutions which are expected—no less than the government—to fund only activities which are in the public interest. These "public" funds amount to 48.88% of the total funding of homosexual organizations. Private funds (client fees and individual donations) amount to 51.12% of the total funding. Some of these funds are also tax-deductible—especially in the case of 501(c)(3) organizations—and probably in most cases they come from homosexuals, although this cannot be known with certainty.

Over one-third of the funds (35.20%) are provided by "individual do-

The Funding of the Movement

nations," either from members of the organizations, procured through fundraisers, or simply solicited among friends and sympathizers of the homosexual cause. Over three-quarters of the homosexual organizations (77.5%) receive funds from individual donors. Many of these funds may come from owners of homosexual businesses (bars, bookstores, porno shops, bath houses, "escort" services, etc.). This would represent a link between homosexual businesses and nonprofit organizations. The high proportion and absolute level (over $11 million) of individual contributions reflects the high level of commitment to the movement of many homosexuals, the high organizational level of the groups involved, and the affluence of many homosexuals. The client fees in many cases reflect payment for VD-related services.

The figures which appear in Table 38, column 8, represent the floor (or minimum) of contributions in each category; i.e., the federal government contributes no less than $5.9 million to homosexual organizations, the churches no less than $400 thousand, etc. Inasmuch as some organizations might not have been included in the original universe of 394 organizations, actual figures are probably much higher. It is most likely that if the National Gay Task Force's list of 3,000 organizations had been utilized, the figure would have been higher, perhaps as high as one-quarter-billion dollars. (Statistically, if the NGTF listing contains *all* the organizations of our universe of 394, the grand total would certainly exceed $32.2 million.)

BUDGET SIZES

The sizes of homosexual organizations vary widely. Their budgets also vary radically, from small operations with no paid staff offering services during early evening hours, and perhaps not on a daily basis, to large and well-run organizations with highly diversified staffs, office procedures, etc. Table 39 presents the frequency distribution of organizations by budget size. This data is also presented in graphic form in Figure 19. The obvious characteristic is that funds are controlled by a small number of organizations. In effect, 11.25% of the organizations receive less than one-third of one percent of the funds, and 70% of the organizations receive approximately one-quarter of the funds. On the other hand, less than one-third of the organizations controls approximately three-quarters of the funds. In total dollars, 44 small organizations receive approximately $111,000 of $32 million of total funding for all organizations, while the 120 largest organizations control nearly $24 million dollars.

This disparity in the distribution of funds suggests that successful organizations within the homosexual movement have access to large sums of money, while others remain quite small. The proliferation of small organizations—i.e., those with budgets under $20,000 a year, which constitute 40% of the total number—reflects great organizational dynamism

TABLE 39

Number and Funding of Homosexual Organizations by Budget Size

Budget Range × $1,000	Number of Organizations in the Sample	% N	Cum. %N	Funding of Organ. In Sample of 80 × $1,000	Estimated Number of Organizations in the Universe	Estimated Funding of Organ. in the Universe 394 × $1,000	% of Funding	Cum. % of Funding
<5	9	11.25	11.25	$ 22.5	45	$ 110.8125	.3%	.3%
5 – 20	23	28.75	40.00	$ 287.5	113	$ 1,415.9375	4.4%	4.7%
21 – 100	24	30.00	70.00	$1,440.0	118	$ 7,092.0000	22.0%	26.7%
>100	24	30.00	100.00	$4,800.0	118	$23,640.0000	73.3%	100.0%

Mean: $81,875/program
Median: $60,000

The Funding of the Movement

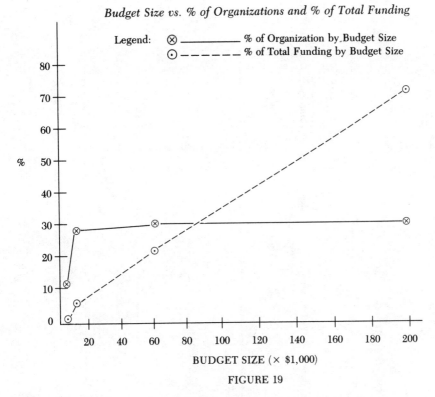

Budget Size vs. % of Organizations and % of Total Funding

FIGURE 19

in the field of homosexuality. Many new organizations are, perhaps, continually in formation. While some disappear, others undoubtedly remain and grow to become veritable community multiservice centers. This pattern of funding strengthens the notion that "seed money" is provided for homosexual organizations—by churches, foundations or wealthy homosexuals—which develop the skills and organizational structure necessary to procure larger funding.

The fact that a few large organizations control most of the budget makes the homosexual movement vulnerable to "defunding," since it is possible to make large cuts in the total budget of all homosexual organizations by cutting off a relatively small number of groups. From a political standpoint, it is easier to cut the budgets of fewer organizations—even if the total amount is larger—than to attack a large number of small organizations. This strategy for defunding the homosexual movement would be useful for those interested in both cutting budgets and curtailing as much as possible the acceptance of the homosexual ideology.

Tables 40 and 41 present the relationship between the sources of funds and the size of the budgets of the various organizations. It is apparent

TABLE 40
Sources of Funds vs. Total Annual Budget (Totals)

Sources of Funds

Total Annual Budget (× $1,000)	Federal	State/Local	Foundations	Churches	Client Fees	Individual Donations	TOTAL
<5	—	2	—	—	2	8	12
5–20	3	6	4	4	3	21	41
21–100	5	11	3	1	7	17	44
>100	16	18	5	2	15	16	72
	24	37	12	7	27	62	169

TABLE 41

Sources of Funds vs. Total Annual Budget (Percentage)

Sources of Funds

Total Annual Budget (× $1,000)	Federal	State/Local	Foundations	Churches	Client Fees	Individual Donations	TOTAL
<5	— / —	16.67% / 5.41%	— / —	— / —	16.67% / 7.41%	66.67% / 12.90%	100.01
5–20	7.32% / 12.50%	14.63% / 16.22%	9.76% / 33.33%	9.76% / 57.14%	7.32% / 11.11%	51.22% / 33.87%	100.01
21–100	11.36% / 20.83%	25.00% / 29.73%	6.82% / 25.00%	2.27% / 14.29%	15.91% / 25.93%	38.64% / 27.42%	100.00
>100	22.22% / 66.67%	25.00% / 48.65%	6.94% / 41.67%	2.78% / 28.57%	20.83% / 55.55%	22.22% / 25.81%	99.99
	100.00	100.01	100.00	100.00	100.00	100.00	

Note: Difference from 100.00 due to rounding.

TABLE 42

Number of Funding Sources by Budget Size

Sources of Funds

Total Annual Budget (× $1,000)	1	2	3	4	5	6	
<5	6	2	1				9
5–20	11	7	4	1			23
21–100	14	3	4	3			24
>100	1	6	9	5	3		24
	32	18	18	9	3		80

TABLE 43

Percentage of Funds From the Federal Government vs. Total Annual Budget

Total Annual Budget (× $1,000)	% of Funds Contributed by Federal Government						
	0	1–20%	21–40%	41–60%	61–80%	81–100%	
<5	9						9
5–20	20	3					23
21–100	19	4	1				24
>100	8	7	4	2	2	1	24
	56	14	5	2	2	1	80

$\chi^2 = 28.74$
df = 15
Significant at the 2.5% level.

TABLE 44

Percentage of Funds From State and Local Government vs. Total Annual Budget

Total Annual Budget (× $1,000)	% of Funds Contributed by State/Local Government						
	0	1–20%	21–40%	41–60%	61–80%	81–100%	
<5	7	1				1	9
5–20	17	1	2		1	2	23
21–100	13	2	4		2	3	24
>100	6	5	7	4	2	2	24
	43	9	13	4	5	6	80

$\chi^2 = 27.40$
df = 15
Significant at the 5% level.

TABLE 45

Percentage of Funds From Tax Revenues vs. Total Annual Budget

	% of Funds Contributed by Tax Revenues (Federal Plus State/Local)						
Total Annual Budget (× $1,000)	0	1–20%	21–40%	41–60%	61–80%	81–100%	
<5	7	1				1	9
5–20	15	3	1	1	1	2	23
21–100	12	2	4	1	2	3	24
>100	2	3	4	7	4	4	24
	36	9	9	9	7	10	80

$\chi^2 = 28.60$
df = 15
Significant at the 2.5% level.

TABLE 46
Percentage of Funds From Client Fees vs. Total Annual Budget

	% of Funds Contributed by Client Fees						
Total Annual Budget (× $1,000)	0	1–20%	21–40%	41–60%	61–80%	81–100%	
<5	7				1	1	9
5–20	20	2			1		23
21–100	17	4				3	24
>100	9	8	3	3	1		24
	53	14	3	3	3	4	80

$\chi^2 = 32.73$
df = 15
Significant at the .5% level.

TABLE 47

Percentage of Funds From Foundations vs. Total Annual Budget

	% of Funds Contributed by Foundations						
Total Annual Budget (× $1,000)	**0**	**1–20%**	**21–40%**	**41–60%**	**61–80%**	**81–100%**	
<5	9						9
5–20	19	1	2	1			23
21–100	21	3					24
>100	19	4	1				24
	68	8	3	1			80

$\chi^2 = 8.43$
df = 9
Not significant
Note: Columns that did not yield data were not considered in this analysis.

TABLE 48

Percentage of Funds From Churches vs. Total Annual Budget

	% of Funds Contributed by Churches						
Total Annual Budget (× $1,000)	0	1–20%	21–40%	41–60%	61–80%	81–100%	
<5	9						9
5–20	19	4					23
21–100	23					1	24
>100	22	2					24
	73	6				1	80

$\chi^2 = 8.13$
df = 6
Not significant.
Note: Columns that did not yield data were not considered in this analysis.

TABLE 49

Percentage of Funds From Individual Donations vs. Total Annual Budget

Total Annual Budget (× $1,000)	% of Funds Contributed by Individual Donations						
	0	1–20%	21–40%	41–60%	61–80%	81–100%	
<5	1	2			1	5	9
5–20	2	2	1	3	1	14	23
21–100	7	2	2	2	1	10	24
>100	8	7	2	4	1	2	24
	18	13	5	9	4	31	80

$\chi^2 = 21.61$
df = 15
Not significant.

that, from the point of view of the number of contributors, tax dollars are more important for large homosexual organizations than for the smaller ones. Whereas two-thirds of the federal grants and half the state/local grants are made to the largest organizations—which comprise less than one-third of all the organizations—two-thirds of all the smallest organizations and half the next-sized ones are funded by individual donations. Moreover, the relative importance of federal and state/local contributions to the homosexual movement increases with the total budget of the organizations (from 12.50% to 66.67% and from 5.41% to 48.65% respectively). In the case of individual contributions, their relative importance diminishes with the size of the organization's annual budget (from 66.67% to 22.22%).

Multiple funding sources are common among homosexual organizations (Table 42). Forty percent of the organizations (32 out of 80) rely on three or more sources. Large organizations tend to rely on multiple sources of funding more than small ones. Whereas 53.13% of the organizations which have annual budgets under $20,000 per year rely on one source of funds, 68.75% of organizations with budgets over $20,000 per year rely on two or more sources of funds. In the case of organizations with budgets over $100,000 per year, the percentage of multifunded organizations rises to 95.83% (70.83% receive funds from three or more sources). Multiple funding sources normally correlates positively with financial security, since it makes the defunding of organizations much more difficult.

Tables 43 through 49 present cross tabulations which relate the size of the organization with the relative importance of the funds received from particular sources. The X^2 values and significance of the relationships are included at the bottom of each table. It is apparent that in the case of government funding of homosexual organizations, at any level of government, the relative importance of the funding relates significantly to the size of the organization. This means not only that the bureaucracies tend to fund homosexual organizations, but that they do take the importance of their contributions into consideration when making these decisions. In the case of client fees, the significance found may be attributed to the fact that only large organizations tend to provide the services (e.g., VD diagnosis and treatment) for which homosexuals are willing to pay, and that these organizations need other resources to continue in existence. In the case of churches, foundations, and individual donations, no significance means that the funding sources provide monies to the organization independent of the values of their contributions. This militates against the idea of churches and foundations providing "seed money" for homosexual organizations. Although there is some indication that they do so, it cannot be asserted conclusively.

An important question to be explored is the possible relationship between the organization's political stand and the sources of funding. Table

The Funding of the Movement

51 presents the results of the survey. An χ^2 analysis of this table reveals that there is no apparent relationship between these two variables. This is probably because support for homosexuality, rather than political ideology, is the distinguishing feature of these organizations and that homosexuality is overwhelmingly significant as a descriptor. This conclusion is confirmed by a comparison between the proportions of organizations at the various levels of political opinion and the proportions of the numbers of funding sources relative to the total number of funding sources. As is evident from Table 50, these proportions are very similar:

TABLE 50

Numbers of Organizations and Funding Sources for the Various Levels of Political Opinion

	Organizations		Funding Sources	
	N	%	N	%
Very Liberal	40	50.00	87	51.48
Liberal	32	40.00	68	40.24
Somewhat Liberal	5	6.25	10	5.92
Neutral	1	1.25	2	1.18
Somewhat Conservative	1	1.25	1	.59
Conservative	1	1.25	1	.59
Very Conservative	—	—	—	—
Total	80	100.00	169	100.00

Federal Funding of the Homosexual Movement

There is no question that the federal government has been, for the past few years, in the business of funding the homosexual movement. Whether this pattern will continue during and after the Reagan Administration, and whether any changes are due to a newly found recognition by the federal government that homosexuality is not in the public interest, remain to be seen.

During the Carter Administration the number of homosexual organizations applying for federal grants was so large that the UFMCC Washington office counted among its "constituent services" "tracking the progress of grant applications to Federal agencies."[3] The Center for Disease Control scheduled a meeting for providers of VD services to homosexuals to help the agency in its funding activities.[4] In such meetings, bureaucrats come to know potential applicants for funds, and informal arrangements for

TABLE 51

Political Stand of Homosexual Organizations vs. Funding Sources

Political Stand	Sources of Funding						TOTAL
	Federal	State/Local	Foundations	Churches	Client Fees	Individual Donations	
Very Liberal	14	21	6	3	16	27	87
Liberal	8	11	6	3	8	32	68
Somewhat Liberal	1	2		1	3	3	10
Neutral	1	1					2
Somewhat Conservative		1					1
Conservative		1					1
Very Conservative							
Total	24	37	12	7	27	62	169

$\chi^2 = 14.45$
df = 25
Not significant.
Note: The row that did not yield data was not considered in this analysis.

The Funding of the Movement

future funding are made, for obviously funds must be available before these meetings are held. The availability of such funds motivated a homosexual group to publish the official guidelines for proposal preparations in order to stimulate other homosexual organizations to apply for federal funding.[5]

Another indication of the use of federal funds by the homosexual movement is the reaction of the homosexuals not just to the "conservatism" of the Reagan Administration, but to the budget cuts proposed by the President. The homosexual movement has been a leading participant in practically every demonstration against the Reagan budget cuts. This concern was voiced by the liaison of the homosexual movement with the National Institute of Alcohol Abuse and Alcoholism—a federal agency—at a May 27, 1981, meeting of the NIAAA Advisory Council.[6] In a related development, and fearing the effect of the budget cuts on organizations advocating homosexuality, Steve Endean of the Gay Rights National Lobby launched a project designed to build a data base of homosexual programs funded by the federal government.[7] The implication is clear that there are many such programs. It is true that the 1981 budget cuts have been received within the homosexual organizations as a major threat to their existence. For example, the May 1981 issue of a homosexual organization newsletter requested its readers to submit ideas—for publication—of alternative ways to fund the homosexual movement during the years of Reagan austerity.[8] It must be recalled, however, that it was under the Reagan Administration that the UFMCC received a $370,500 grant.

Although no conclusive proof can be offered to explain why the federal government has provided extensive funds to homosexual organizations, it is reasonable to attribute it to four general causes.

Increased acceptability of homosexuality in general and of the homosexual ideology in particular. As homosexual practices come to be viewed as a "normal variant" of human behavior, federal bureaucrats lose their reluctance to fund organizations based on this practice.

The liberal ideology that has pervaded the federal government for decades. As soon as homosexual organizations began to approach the federal government for funds in a manner not obviously designed to threaten its stability, it became advantageous for bureaucrats to make the funds flow. After all, it is the business of the liberal bureaucracy to hand out funds. Without this practice, it would lose its very raison d'être.

The support of the homosexuals by liberal politicians, who expect in turn to be supported by the homosexuals. Chapter VIII offered examples of liberal politicians helping the homosexuals raise funds. The case of homosexual fundraisers sponsored by New York City liberal Democrats (Brooklyn Democrat boss Meade Esposito, his Bronx counterpart, Pat Cunningham, Manhattan's Frank Rosetti, and New York City Council President Paul O'Dwyer) provides another example.[9] It is reasonable to assume that liberal politicians supportive of the homosexual movement, when in power, will help homosexual organizations receive federal funds.

The existence of an increasing number of avowed homosexuals within the bureaucracy. This is due to increasingly liberal hiring policies promoted successfully during the Carter Administration.[10] It can only be expected that these homosexuals will help their organizations during the funding process. Their openness about their sexual condition probably serves to neutralize the natural inhibitions people would normally have about championing the homosexual cause.

A factor that has increased greatly the availability of funds for the homosexual movement, as noted early in this chapter, is the recognition of homosexual organizations by the Internal Revenue Service as eligible for 501(c)(3) status. The position of the IRS on homosexual organizations was made in Ruling 78–305, applying the 501(c)(3) classification to organizations that "foster an understanding and tolerance of homosexuals."[11]

As we have seen, in many cases the obligations incurred by this status have not have followed by homosexual organizations. Although no definite determination can be made without an exhaustive examination of the office's records—and such a determination would not be final without the decision of the courts—it appears that one organization claiming special tax status while lobbying extensively is the Washington Office of the UFMCC. On many occasions the office has solicited funds claiming the special status: "Tax deductible contributions are welcome and will help us to continue our work,"[12] and "Contributions to this office can be large or small, and donations in any amount are tax deductible."[13]

Yet this same office makes no secret of its lobbying activities. Among these activities it lists: "Lobbying Congress for gay civil rights, women's issues and other issues of concern for the UFMCC. The gay rights work is done following the leadership of the Gay Rights National Lobby and in cooperation with them."[14] On a specific legislative item, the following was published in the office's newsletter: "Though the McDonald amendment passed the House in 1977, it was not introduced in the Senate after heavy lobbying by the UFMCC Washington Field Office and other groups."[15] Moreover, the lobbying is done in the traditional way: "In the next Congress, we will begin to target some specific Congress people for special attention in the hopes that they will support the gay rights bill."[16]

These quotes have been taken from publications of the office involved, and are thus a matter of public record. It is suspicious that the IRS apparently did not investigate the case, although the support the homosexual movement had during the Carter Administration provides at least a partial explanation for this ostensible lack of official concern.

The Funding of the Movement

THE CASE OF THE CUBAN REFUGEES

In the spring of 1980, some 125,000 refugees came to the United States from the Communist island of Cuba. Political oppression, cultural backwardness, the complete lack of freedom, and a chaotic economic situation served as catalysts for the "Mariel exodus," named for the fishing village in northwestern Cuba from which the refugees left in a makeshift flotilla. Castro utilized this exodus to expel thousands of homosexuals from the island. The total number cannot be determined with any accuracy, but Dale Leeche has indicated that between 10,000 and 12,000 homosexuals were among the refugees.[17] According to Bob Scott, director of the UFMCC Cuban Relief Fund, the number of refugees needing help as of the late summer of 1980 was between 3,000 and 5,000.[18] The ideologies of the left promote homosexuality, and other forms of behavior traditionally considered aberrant in Western societies. In Communist countries, however, homosexuality is considered a social disease. At one point, for example, known homosexuals were interned in concentration camps in Cuba for "rehabilitation."

As soon as it became evident that there were homosexuals among the newly arrived Cuban refugees, various homosexual organizations became actively involved. Since the majority of the refugees came to South Florida, the Dade County Coalition for Human Rights was one of these. Eventually, it was to be rewarded with a contract by the U.S. State Department.[19] The National Gay Task Force became involved on the legal status of the homosexuals, as did Dignity.[20] The Universal Fellowship of Metropolitan Community Churches, however, sought out homosexuals as its "natural constituents," finally receiving a sizable grant for the resettlement of Cuban homosexuals. The State and Immigration Departments apparently were only too glad to accept the "help" offered by American homosexuals. According to *In Unity*, they earned the title of "Saviors of the Gay situation" from these federal agencies.[21]

The UFMCC presented a proposal for the placement of fifty Cuban homosexuals at a total cost of $123,500 to the federal government. A grant award for three times this amount was made to the "UFMCC Cuban Relief Fund" of Santa Monica on March 31, 1981, to be spent over the following twelve months. According to the notice of grant award: "The purpose of this grant award is to resettle *150 Gay Cubans* from Fort Chaffee to the following locations: Chicago, Ill., Baltimore, Md. and San Francisco, California."[22] According to the approved budget, the cost per homosexual was to be $2,470 for a total of 150 individuals. The services to be provided included: staff services, transportation, temporary accommodations, food, clothing, counseling and referral, coordination with local agencies and "other" services.[23]

The original notice of grant programs contained very precise information on the nature of the proposals required by the government.[24]

Government Requirement	UFMCC Proposal
(1) Description of grantee organization, background, affiliations, and experience	Not included
(2) Project plan and description including:	
(a) Resettlement plan	Very sketchy, vaguely including what is to be done but no methodology or principles of operation. E.g. no methodology of counseling, interviewing, etc.
(b) Follow-up plan	None indicated
(c) Sponsorship breakdown plan	None indicated
(3) Listing of proposed subgrantees or subcontractors	None indicated. There is no indication that subcontractors or subgrantees will not be used. Although there are allusions that the homosexuals will be referred to other services, these are not identified nor are the customary letters of agreement or support from other community agencies included.
(4) Time Schedules	No clear timelines or schedule of performance
(5) Estimated number of individuals to be resettled in each planned resettlement location	No indication of how many homosexuals will be resettled in Baltimore or Chicago.
(6) Detailed budget with justifications	No detailed explanation provided for many items, e.g., Basis for the sort of individual items provided. Level of effort of staff persons not provided No justification for "Administrative costs."
(7) Description of financial resources available to the applicant to assure the sound establishment and maintenance of the proposed effort, including a description of the extent to which funds have either been sought by or have been made available to the applicant from other federal programs.	None indicated
(8) Estimate of voluntary services and donated resources to be made available for this effort.	None indicated
(9) Plans for continuing the effort beyond the end of grant support under the program.	None indicated

The Funding of the Movement

According to the notice "an application for a grant should contain a detailed description of the proposed project or effort which meets the applicable requirements described in this notice."[25] In fact, the proposal presented by the UFMCC was not only written in very poor English, but did not correspond to the outline prescribed by the Cuban/Haitian Task Force (the federal agency administering the program). An analysis of this proposal as compared to the government requirements reveals its fundamental flaws[26] (see page 494).

The proposal of the UFMCC is seriously deficient in other respects. In addition to a description of duties, job descriptions in federal proposals normally include the required qualifications for the various positions or résumés of the persons to be hired. By the use of these procedures, federal agencies can be assured that competent individuals will occupy the various positions, avoiding the misuse of funds. The UFMCC proposal included neither of those items, and the grant award documents did not require the grant administrator to approve or examine proposed staff. This means that the UFMCC could have employed totally unqualified persons working minimally for the project, or actually engaged in a full-time job on other UFMCC tasks, without the government having the control necessary to correct any abuses. Measurable objectives were neither offered by the UFMCC nor required by the government. Reporting requirements within the program period were limited to quarterly financial line item reports and final reports, programmatic and financial, to be submitted within 90 days *after* the completion of the program. With no specific provision for what was to be included in the program, it is conceivable that all the funds could have been spent by the UFMCC after providing almost no services to the refugees.

The UFMCC proposal was a mere nine-page document—budget included—totally inadequate by any professional standard. It basically proposed to house large groups of homosexuals in centers in three cities (in one case, a former convent). The prospect of centers full of homosexuals would probably be unacceptable to most neighborhoods. (Popular conception of homosexuals as promiscuous would lead some to think of these centers as orgy facilities.) When such centers are paid for by tax dollars, the idea would certainly be rejected by the majority of Americans. In any case, the award of this grant—both in terms of the project itself and the manner in which the grant was made—reveals the preferential treatment the homosexual movement enjoys within the federal bureaucracy.

In addition to the large sums involved, other benefits were received by the UFMCC as the result of this grant:

First, it gave the leadership of the UFMCC the possibility of providing its "constituents" with a number of jobs. Persons hired by the UFMCC as staff for its projects develop or strengthen a relationship with the sponsoring organization. Federal grants have been a traditional way of funding the left in the United States. This grant to the UFMCC (and other grants to be examined later) is in the line of a well-established tradition.

This grant also provided a measure of much-needed recognition for the UFMCC. Homosexual organizations in America are acutely aware that for the majority of the population they exist beyond the pale of acceptability. It is true that many organizations and their leadership recognize homosexual organizations as legitimate, but this is largely an elitist position, as seen in the Connecticut Mutual Life Report. For most people, neither the homosexual lifestyle nor homosexual organizations are accepted or legitimate. Two *In Unity* articles emphasized the aspect of implied respectability: "The UFMCC Refugee program will be working in conjunction with the Carter Administration's Interagency Task Force, with the International Rescue Commission [*sic*] and with the U.S. Catholic Conference . . .,"[27] and "The UFMCC is working with nine agencies. 'We have gotten the most cooperation from Church World Services.' "[28]

With the grant, the UFMCC probably cleared $30,000 for its services. In the original budget, one-third the size of the final grant, the final line item on the budget was $10,000 for "Administrative Costs." These costs are not justified in the budget and presumably represent monies retained by the UFMCC for its use.

The final outcome of this analysis is that the UFMCC was given $370,500 by the federal government under very loose conditions and in response to a very deficient proposal. For the homosexuals this grant has been a major victory and possibly the foundation for future and even larger grants. It is possible that austerity programs will deny the UFMCC this opportunity; this depends to a large measure on political conditions. Should the homosexual movement prevail in its goal of making homosexual sex acceptable, further funding is in store. Should profamily forces succeed, or should economic and foreign policy conservatives come to realize the homosexual movement is inimical to their interests, the movement will find it more difficult to obtain federal funds in the future. A swing of the political pendulum back to the left will undoubtedly increase the chances of future federal funding.

CETA

By far the most important source of federal funds for the homosexual movement to date has been CETA, an acronym for "Comprehensive Employment and Training Act." Under this act, over $50 billion were spent between 1973 and 1981 by the federal government on "creating jobs" for unemployed individuals. The theory behind CETA is that if unemployed persons are provided with work experiences, the probability of their finding unsubsidized employment increases. This program was created in response to the chronic unemployment affecting certain pop-

The Funding of the Movement

ulations and geographic areas within the United States (without reference to the fact that unemployment originates in the persistent interference with the market by the federal government). CETA not only did not diminish the unemployment problem, but by helping to create an ever-larger federal deficit, it aggravated the economic conditions that had created unemployment in the first place. CETA did not become the cradle of trained "employable" persons, but the source of a larger group of people dependent on the federal government for their livelihood. CETA jobs became the epitome of nonproductive activities, and the program was quickly converted to a massive transfer-of-wealth scheme. For liberal politicians, CETA became a form of patronage and a vehicle for satisfying political debts.

Structurally, CETA funds are disbursed through "prime sponsors" to organizations which are then alloted "CETA slots" or individual jobs. The prime sponsors vary from one area of the country to another. A prime sponsor may be a county, township, city, or similar entity. Organizations can be private nonprofit organizations, community groups, churches, etc. CETA workers are supposed to be "chronically unemployed," although conditions for eligibility have changed as abuses have surfaced. Traditionally, CETA has been plagued with scandals, emerging as the "ultimate pork barrel" and the vehicle of choice for funding the left. In all steps in the CETA ladder, prime sponsors and funded organizations are entitled to a "cut" of the total budget for "administrative purposes." In practice, this has been a way of funding the organizations themselves—over and above the obvious benefits that accrue to any prime sponsor as a result of controlling a large number of jobs. This structure makes it extremely difficult to document which organizations have received CETA grants since the Department of Labor—which administers CETA—is often unable to identify the ultimate grantees. For the local politicians, CETA provides patronage without the responsibility of taxing the population directly. The federal government can thus claim to be solving the unemployment problem while politicians can help their favorite groups without any obvious connection to the damage being done to the national economy through excessive taxation and large budget deficits. Politicians who favor the homosexual movement—or even those who simply do not have the will to resist its pressure—are thus able to provide funds for homosexual organizations with minimum flack from their constituents, since these funds are not raised locally. Meanwhile, the federal bureaucrats can claim innocence, since they did not approve the funding. They can always allege that it was a "local matter."

This lack of accountability is probably the best explanation for the many grants—some of them sizable—that have been provided to homosexual organizations under CETA. These are difficult to document, since no center of responsibility exists for CETA. The following list illustrates the variety of homosexual projects which have received CETA funds. The common thread through these projects is the promotion of homosexuality as an acceptable lifestyle which these projects make possible. Theater groups carry the homosexual ideology to their audiences. Counselors employed by homosexual organizations cannot be expected to apply the principles of traditional psychology. In all cases, CETA workers employed by homosexual organizations contribute to the ultimate goal of these organizations.

Perhaps the largest homosexual recipient of CETA's largesse has been the Los Angeles Gay and Lesbian Community Services Center housed in a two-story building in Hollywood, California. The organization is large enough to require not just an executive director, but also directors of finance and development.[29] In a letter of June 15, 1981, a staff person in the Employment and Social Services Department Center indicated that "the LAGLCSC is a nonprofit community service organization presided over by a dedicated group of volunteers representing much of the Gay leadership in various professions in Los Angeles. Founded approximately ten years ago, it now receives public funding from various governmental agencies as well as direct contributions from members of the public."[30]

The Center is well known throughout the homosexual community, even outside the Los Angeles area and California. It is supported not only by homosexuals, but by many other prominent individuals. The Center is the organization for which Lillian Carter helped raise $120,000 at a Beverly Wilshire gala in October 1979. Other known liberal politicians joined the President's mother in this event, including Governor Jerry Brown, City Attorney Burt Pines, District Attorney John Van de Kamp, and California State Assembly Speaker Leo McCarthy.[31]

According to *In Unity*, much of this funding was obtained with the help of Morris Kight, one of its founders, an activist in the Democratic party who was eventually made a member of the Los Angeles County Commission on Human Relations by Supervisor Ed Edelman.[32] The reader may recal Edelman as a supporter of a homosexual fundraiser described in chapter VIII.

Forty of the eighty-four employees of the center were paid by CETA prior to the Reagan budget cuts. The total amount of the CETA grant for the homosexual center has been reported at various levels. According to the Los Angeles *Times*, at one point the amount was $50,000.[33] James Bovard, writing for *Inquiry* magazine, reported it to be $640,000.[34] According to CETA rules, the "cut" for the grantee in these cases, taken "off the top," is 15%. In the former case, this "cut" for the center would have been $7,500, in the latter case, $96,000.

There are many other examples of CETA funding of homosexual enterprises, several of them listed below. In some cases, the "projects" would probably be considered extraordinary by any measure. In other cases, the CETA employees performed routine tasks. It was always important for the movement to have a veritable army of federally paid agents working on behalf of the "gay lifestyle":

CETA is reported to have provided $41,000 to a feminist collective performing naked for female-only audiences in the "Leaping Lesbian Follies."[35] Funding was provided to "Virago"—a 15-member theatre group—through the City of Denver.[36]

The Staff Artist for the UFMCC Publications Department, Dan Sims, was reportedly paid by CETA funds. *In Unity* specifically reported that Sims was not on the Fellowship payroll.[37]

The Project Open Employment of the National Gay Task Force was funded for some sixteen months by a CETA Title VI grant.[38] Reportedly, five individuals were hired.[39] The purpose of the project was to obtain data favorable to the concept that homosexuals are a legitimate minority, one of the core ideas of the ideology of the homosexual movement.

The City of Seattle provided CETA funding, through its City's Summer Youth Employment Program, for a project of the Seattle Gay Community Center. The project consisted of a program for fourteen homosexual youth (males and females alike) who developed a play—appropriately called "Lavender Horizons"—featured at the city's Cornish Auditorium on August 21, 1980.[40]

Four "counselors" at a Dade County (Florida) homosexual center were reportedly paid with CETA funds.[41]

The CETA grants provided to the Gay Alliance of Genesee Valley (Rochester, N.Y.) in 1978 more than trebled the organization's budget. The Alliance's copresident, Sue Cowell, could boast: "We were the first New York State gay organization to get CETA money, maybe one of the first in the country."[42]

The many scandals and abuses in the use of CETA funds, as much as the evident failure of this program to achieve its stated goals, made it a prime target for "radical surgery" under the Reagan budget cuts. To the extent that CETA is in place, however, homosexual organizations have benefited largely from this program.

OTHER FEDERAL FUNDING

There are many other ways in which the federal government funds the homosexual movement *directly*. Although action-oriented projects like those funded by CETA and the homosexual refugees program are important, another need of the homosexual movement is to provide its ideology with a "factual" or "scientific" basis. The federal government has also been involved in funding projects designed to provide an intellectual foundation for the homosexual ideology. The normal practice with federal grants and contracts is to use part of the budget to support the sponsoring organizations. By providing these grants, the federal government guarantees the continuance of certain organizations. Moreover, the principal investigators are frequently the officers of the organizations involved. Thus the federal government also directly provides the salaries of the leadership of these organizations. Examples abound:

- The National Institute of Mental Health funded a project "to study and document cases of discrimination based on sexual orientation and/or social sex-role stereotypes, in public and private institutions that render services to the public."[43] Such a study would appear to provide the basis for accepting homosexuals as a legitimate minority whose rights have been violated. The recipient of the grant was the Center for Homosexual Education, Evaluation, and Research (CHEER) at San Francisco State University of California. The principal investigator was John P. DeCecco and the co–principal investigator Michael G. Shively, Director and Associate Director of CHEER. It has been reported that the size of this grant was $50,000.[44] Since then, CHEER has reportedly changed its name to the less conspicuous CERES (Center for Research and Education and [sic] Sexuality), in which the word homosexual does not appear. According to Louie Crew of the National Council of Teachers of English (Committee on the Concerns of Lesbians and Gay Males) CHEER is centered in the Psychology Department of the university and is "run by gay males." (Letter of Louie Crew to the author of April 10, 1978.)
- CHEER was the recipient of another grant award of the National Institute of Mental Health. The purpose of the grant was "to study the life-span experiences and current adaptations of men and women sixty and older and to determine the effects of different sexual orientations."[45] The problem of aging homosexuals who find themselves deprived of the family they never formed is very crucial for the homosexual movement. This problem, as much as the almost exclusive emphasis on sensual gratification, might explain the virtual worship of youth by homosexuals.
- In 1978 Sister Jeannine Gramick, SSND, and Father Robert Nugent, SDS, became project director and research assistant of a two-year, $38,000 study funded by the National Institutes of Health of the then Department of Health, Education and Welfare.[46] The grant was funneled through the Dignity Chapter in San Diego, California, although Gramick and Nugent are codirectors of New Ways Ministry, the Catholic homosexual center located in Mount Rainier, Maryland. The obvious prohomosexual bias of the study on the "coming out process and coping strategies of homosexual women" is obvious in the announcement made by Nugent on the basic presupposition of the study. According to Nugent, this study would "proceed from an assumption that being homosexual is a valid expression of a person's lifestyle involving more than the simple notion of sexual preference rather than from the illness approach."[47] From such an assumption, only conclusions consonant with the homosexual ideology could emerge, since the basic principles of the ideology are already implicit in the study.
- Title XX funds provided to the University of Connecticut School of Social Work for the purpose of developing a course entitled "New Perspectives on Lesbians and Gay Men."[48] This Title XX Training Grant is intended to

The Funding of the Movement

create a regular course to be offered regularly in the curriculum of the School of Social Work.[49] A description of the course as it appears in the summary furnished by the school and the recommended readings for the students reveal that the course assumes, or actually teaches, substantial elements of the homosexual ideology.[50] By participating in this course—originally developed with federal funds—homosexual students will naturally find their propensities strengthened and justified while heterosexuals will come to accept the homosexual ideology as the "scientific" and "modern" outlook.

On June 30, 1981, the Alcohol, Drug Abuse and Mental Health Administration (U.S. Department of Health and Human Services) made a one-year grant of $41,365 to the Gay Community Services of Minneapolis for a "study on aging and the affectional preferences of minorities" (Grant No. 5 T 15 MH 15711-03).[51]

State and Local Funding

The main fundor of leftist social programs in America has historically been the federal government, though state and local governments have always provided some funding for these programs as well. With the advent of "new federalism" during the Nixon Administration, the states have become an integral part of the federal government's funding activities. Unless very specific details of the grant action are known, it is often nearly impossible to ascertain whether the funds are federal, state, or local in origin. From the political point of view, this is often irrelevant, since government grants are not necessarily related to the needs of the target population. As a rule, grants measure the degree of influence grantees have on the bureaucracy or the politicians. At the state or local level, a grant to a homosexual group measures any of three factors:

1. The degree to which the homosexual ideology has found acceptability in the funding agency;
2. The influence (political or otherwise) the homosexual organization has on the local bureaucracy and/or politicians; and/or
3. The degree of penetration of the agency by homosexuals committed to the movement's ideology.

These are not isolated factors; they influence one another, resulting in the astonishing phenomenon of millions of dollars (no less than $8.7 million according to our survey) of state or local funds being funneled annually into the promotion of the homosexual ideology.

Homosexual projects funded at the state and local levels are as varied as those funded by the federal government. For example:

The District of Columbia funded a food project for needy women to be operated jointly by the Metropolitan Community Church and the First Congregational Church. Although only $2,000 was involved, it enabled the MCC to establish a "track record" working with a church generally accepted by the community.[52]

The D.C. Community Humanities Council—a program sponsored by the federal National Endowment for the Humanities—granted $6,000 to the Stonewall Nation Media Collective to produce four prohomosexual radio programs focusing on such issues as adoption of homosexual youth by other homosexuals and female homosexuals becoming mothers via artificial insemination with the issue of male homosexuals (thus avoiding the need for heterosexual intercourse).[53]

The Title XX grant to the University of Connecticut School of Social Work was actually made by the Connecticut Department of Human Resources.[54]

In San Francisco, the coroner's office is reported to have organized a workshop for sadomasochists on how to have their preferred variety of sex without injuring one another. The reason apparently offered was that 10 percent of the homicides in San Francisco are the result of sadomasochistic homosexual practices. The costs for the course, however, were paid by the San Francisco taxpayers.[55] From the point of view of the homosexual movement, this course was important in that it provided the seal of "official respectability" to a homosexual practice particularly frowned upon by the population at large.

One of the first assignments of the first manager of the Sexual Orientation Project, a California state office, was the production of "A Glossary of Terms Commonly Associated With Sexual Orientation," which virtually enshrined the homosexual "lingo" as California's newspeak. This document was financed with state funds. The Sexual Orientation Project is financed by state revenues.[56]

The Lesbian-Feminist Study Clearinghouse, located at the University of Pittsburgh, indicated in a communication to the author that it is "not supported, in name, or financially, by the University," a state institution.[57] However, although funds are perhaps not directly transferred from the University to the Clearinghouse, financial support is certainly provided. For example, the Clearinghouse's address reads "University of Pittsburgh." The envelope used was franked by a meter rented by the University (PB Meter 677127, Pittsburgh, PA) and the staff member who wrote indicated that the University provides academic credit for work undertaken at this homosexual clearinghouse. Additionally, a part-time student is provided as part of the work-study program. This type of arrangement, in the context of the homosexual ideology, is "beneficial" to all parties involved, allowing the Clearinghouse to remain "a covert, file cabinet operation" as described to the author.[58]

The San Francisco State University sponsors the Center for Research and [sic] Education and Sexuality (CERES), mentioned above, formerly called the Center for Homosexual Education, Evaluation and Research.[59] The center conducts studies and publishes scholarly material of interest to the homosexual movement. Among the publications are the *Journal of Homosexuality* and a series of monographs including such titles as "Homosexuality and the Philosophy of Science," "Homosexuality and History" and "Homosexuality and Psychotherapy." Its proposed projects include the "Archives of Homosexuality" and a study of sadomasochism. A completed study of female homosexuals has been described thus by the center: "Purposes: to determine what physical sexual activities a sample of lesbians engage in and the attitudes of these women toward various aspects of lesbian sexuality."[60] The center does not appear to be a "neutral" or purely "scientific" institution. The prohomosexual ideological bias of the institution is evident from a project funded but not completed as of this writing, described as *Civil Liberties and Sexual Orientation Handbook:* "Purpose: To provide guidance to those men and women who believe their rights have been abridged because of their biological sex, social sex role, or sexual orientation and information on how to identify and document discriminatory acts and take the appropriate action for protection of their rights."[61]

The Gay and Lesbian Community Services Center of Los Angeles—already mentioned as one of the largest recipients of CETA funds—received in 1980 a $50,000 grant from California's Office of Statewide Health Planning and Development.[62]

The Boston Homophile Alcoholism Treatment Center has received state funds in the past,[63] but apparently its place has been taken by the Homophile Community Health Service, a federally funded agency.[64]

Also located in Massachusetts, the Minority Council on Alcoholism-Community Training and Resource Center has, according to a homosexual publication, a special homosexual program.[65]

Pride Foundation, Inc., a San Francisco homosexual organization, was reported as requesting $27,750 "to develop a 'social environment' services program" at its outpatient services for alcoholic homosexuals, which would include a "disco."[66] It was subsequently reported that the organization had acquired a "huge convent" where it intended to house male and female homosexuals in two separate sets of quarters starting in the fall of 1981. (It is difficult to see the reasoning behind this separation. Ordinarily, male and female populations are separated to avoid promiscuous situations. In the case of homosexuals, this problem could only be expected to arise with same-sex individuals and hardly at all between male and female homosexuals who would normally feel no physical attraction to one another.) The Pride Foundation was also reported to be seeking city and county funds to expand its services.[67]

Church Funding of Homosexuality

Most churchgoers would probably be very surprised—if not upset—if they knew that monies they contribute during Sunday services are diverted to homosexual organizations, or that facilities built and supported with church funds are used by homosexual organizations to procure funds with which to carry out their activities. After all, the nearly universal belief of people who attend church services—other than those in churches organized by homosexuals—is that homosexual practices are an abomination, that homosexuality is a perversion of human nature, and that the Scriptures of all religions reject homosexuality. Yet our survey revealed that a number of homosexual organizations (8.75%) are partially funded by churches. Although the percentage of church funds (no less than $395,847) flowing yearly to homosexual organizations is small compared to their gross income (a mere 1.23%), the symbolic value of this funding is extraordinary for the homosexual movement. If the validators of behavior from an ethical standpoint (i.e., religious institutions) are willing to provide financial support for homosexual organizations, the most elementary logic dictates that homosexual practices themselves must be acceptable. Documenting such support, however, is not easy. Church leaders, even those who are inclined to accept active homosexuality as a valid "alternative" lifestyle, *know* that the faithful will object to the diversion of church funds toward homosexual organizations. However, enough has been published to make it incontestable that church funds are indeed being used for the promotion of the homosexual ideology.

The simplest and "cleanest" way for a church to provide financial support for homosexual organizations is to allow its facilities to be used for homosexual fundraisers (cf. chapter VII). For example, on Wednesday, May 7, 1980, the Parish Hall of Christ Episcopal Church in Georgetown (Washington, D.C.) was used to stage a musical comedy "cabaret style" to raise funds for New Ways Ministry.[68] The work was presented by the Georgetown Workshop Theatre. As noted above, Catholic University of America (also in Washington) lent the Caldwell Auditorium—located in the building where church law and theology are normally taught—also for the same purpose.[69] The evening was also used to propagandize in favor of the homosexual ideology. Three frankly prohomosexual "experts on the subject" discussed the topic "Lesbian/Gay Coupling: Can It Work?" Catholic University has become a center of prohomosexual and other feminist activities, and has lent its facilities for other political leftist events.

504

The Funding of the Movement

The school has also been utilized to raise funds for "Catholics for ERA," a Catholic radical feminist organization, in an event that featured Theresa Kane, the nun who acquired national notoriety for "standing up to Pope John Paul II" on national television.[70] (Theresa Kane was also scheduled to be a panelist on a prohomosexual symposium sponsored by New Ways Ministry in November 1981.)

There are instances, however, in which church funds actually flow for homosexual organizations, usually for specific projects. For example, the Washington office of the UFMCC, as reported in *Gays on the Hill*, received a contribution from a "straight church" in Milwaukee. The name of the church was intentionally not revealed, probably because the donation was made without the knowledge of the majority of church members. The editor of the prohomosexual newsletter was quick to draw the logical consequence in support of the homosexual ideology: "There is support for our work in other churches."[71]

Wesley Theological Seminary, a United Methodist institution in Washington, D.C., gave Jeannie Boyd Bull—a theology student for the UFMCC—an "Urban Ministries Grant" to direct an MCC Washington project.[72]

The Provincial Council of the Eastern Province of the Claretians (a Roman Catholic order) donated $3,000 to the national network of prohomosexual Catholics' "Catholic Coalition of Gay Civil Rights." The chairman of the province's "Justice and Peace Committee" wrote to the network leaders: "The Provincial appreciates your efforts to minister to gays, to create a relationship of concern between the Church and gays, and to afford basic human rights to gays. We hope our help will make a contribution to that end."[73] There is little doubt that the function of the prohomosexual Catholic network was not solely to express the opinions of its members but also to seek funds for the movement. *Bondings*, the publication of New Ways Ministry, expressed this function clearly: "We are also contacting other religious communities who have already endorsed the Coalition for financial support."[74]

The Church World Service, an arm of the National Council of Churches, donated $30,000 to the UFMCC for its program with Cuban homosexuals.[75]

A similar grant of $8,000 was provided by the American Baptist Churches of the U.S.A.[76] The two grants were apparently linked and required the establishment of a close relationship between the UFMCC and the American Baptist Churches. According to John Chasteen, an MCC layman: "To qualify as a resettlement unit under Church World Service, the American Baptist Churches in effect 'adopted' the MCC as one of its own."[77]

An article in the *National Catholic Reporter*, a radical leftist publication, indicated that New Ways Ministry was funded by the School Sisters of

Notre Dame and the Salvatorian order.[78] This has been vehemently denied by Sister Jeannine Gramick, SSND: "Although both codirectors have received encouragement and support from their religious superiors for their assigned ministry, New Ways is not supported financially by their religious congregations. We here at New Ways depend primarily on donations and stipends from retreats and workshops to fund our works. . . ."[79] This cannot be independently verified, since financial data of the three organizations involved are not a matter of public record. The author was personally informed by Father Nugent, codirector of New Ways Ministry with Sister Gramick, that the organization obtains substantial donations from religious orders. It would be surprising if the orders which have provided the personnel and many individual supporters for New Ways Ministry did not contribute financially to this organization.

There are instances of cross-funding. A typical example is the grants which Dignity (Catholic homosexuals) and Integrity (homosexual Episcopalians) have made to the Washington office of the UFMCC.[80]

An interesting approach to church funding of homosexuals is provided by George W. Casper, treasurer of Integrity. In this instance, strictly speaking, no church money is given to a homosexual organization, but the church is used as a cover for individuals interested in taking advantage of the tax status of churches and/or making their money available to a homosexual organization without fear of discovery. Casper is very explicit in his advice:

> For potential donors of large sums, or for the very careful, I recommend that you channel your contribution to the discretionary fund of a priest whom you trust to a high degree, or I can recommend several such priests to you if you desire. Your check should be payable to "St. W——'s Discretionary Fund, Rev. J——, trustee" and designate your contribution to be given to Integrity, Inc. The trustworthy priest will then transmit a different check to Integrity, drawn on his discretionary fund in the same amount.
> This procedure is perfectly acceptable and is also a useful technique for persons who need to maintain a degree of "closetedness" in their financial matters.[81]

A similar system was suggested by *Gays on the Hill.* Apparently, the Washington Square United Methodist Church in New York City has offered itself as a conduit for funds to "Affirmation," a homosexual organization for Methodists. The instructions offered were also quite explicit: "Checks can be made out to the Washington Square United Methodist Church so that they can be tax-deductible, and the checks should indicate on the bottom left memo section that they are for Affirmation."[82]

From a financial point of view, church funds are not critical for the survival of the homosexual movement. Nevertheless, the fact that churches are willing to finance the homosexual movement is of the utmost impor-

The Funding of the Movement

tance for its social and political survival. In the eyes of a substantial number of Americans, many politicians are greatly discredited; it is expected that they will do virtually anything for the sake of votes. However, church leaders are not generally expected to behave in a manner contrary to the principles of religion. Yet in the perception of vast numbers of Americans, funding homosexual organizations probably qualifies as antireligious behavior.

Other Forms of Direct Funding

In addition to government and church funds, the homosexual movement also derives considerable funds from other private sources. A great part of these funds come from individuals and cannot be traced. The decision of the IRS to grant homosexual organizations 501(c)(3) status has accelerated the size and number of these donations. Funds are also provided by organizations, including a number of foundations. For example, the Mildred Andrews Fund, a Cleveland Foundation, awarded a grant to the Mariposa Foundation (a homosexual group) for the production of a statue glorifying homosexuality.[83] The sculpture is intended for Christopher Street Park in Sheridan Square, New York City, across from the Stonewall Inn where the Stonewall riot took place. Copies of the sculpture are intended for public display in Washington, D.C., and California.[84] In another case, the Playboy Foundation has repeatedly funded the UFMCC to produce the *Prisoner's Yellow Pages* for distribution in the nation's jails.[85]

Organizations for homosexual college students are funded by the colleges themselves. The official publication of the National Gay Student Center has indicated that "most homosexual groups have no problems with either recognition or funding."[86] Special events, on the other hand, are likely to be funded on a one-at-a-time basis by groups having a special interest in the events themselves. For example, the Strategy Conference on Homophobia in the Church (May 4–6, 1979) was initially funded by the National Organization for Women and the Quixote Center.[87] The National Organization for Women would logically have an interest in promoting this conference, as the ideological and organizational relationships between feminism and homosexual activism are readily apparent. Moreover, traditional religion is the clearest ideological opponent of both. Therefore, it is in the interest of feminist organizations to "soften up" the churches by infiltrating their theology and social structures with forms of thought and behavior which, while logically dependent on feminism, are intrinsically incompatible with the very roots of religion. The Quixote Center is also a logical candidate for funding the conference. A Catholic organization interested in the promotion of "social justice," the Quixote Center is the parent group of New Ways Ministry,[88] having distinguished itself for its promotion of the ultimate form of feminism in the Roman Catholic Church—the ordination of women to the priesthood—and strident religiopolitical activism against any support for the people of El Salvador in their struggle for national survival against Communist aggression. The initial cosponsors of the event were later joined by New Ways Ministry and two Episcopalian "advocates" of the homosexual movement, the Church and Society Network and the magazine *Witness*.[89]

Organizations without a direct interest in the issues typically identified with homosexuality, and which normally would not be expected to do so, support homosexual causes. For example, the National Council of Teachers of English (NCTE) funded a questionnaire on attitudes toward homosexuals for its members. This was disclosed in a memorandum for Karen Keener, cochairwoman of the homosexual organizations with the NCTE, to its membership. Keener indicated that she had worked directly on this project.[90] Funding for the "Gay Task Force" of the American Library Association is provided directly by the ALA through its Social Responsibility Roundtable Division.[91] This degree of commitment of the ALA toward the homosexual interest group within its ranks has serious implications of interest to the American people, since the members of the ALA—the nation's librarians—manage the vital resources, public and private libraries, through which reading materials become available to millions. The influence of librarians on the intellectual climate of the country is probably as pervasive as it is unappreciated. A substantial penetration of the ALA by the homosexual movement would probably signal a substantial increase in books favorable to homosexuality in the library shelves. Another organization, the National Association of Gay Alcoholism Professionals, has reported that the New Jersey Alcoholism Association provides funds for contracts to several local National Council on Alcoholism affiliates which require the provision of specialized services to homosexuals.[92]

Any funds provided to homosexual organizations are used in some way for the promotion of the homosexual ideology. At a minimum, they serve to provide the movement with an aura of legitimacy and homosexual behavior with the seal of social approval. When the funds come from governmental agencies, society at large and each taxpayer become, in effect, fundors of the homosexual movement. If the social consensus approved active homosexuality and its attendant lifestyle, this would be a legitimate—thought not necessarily ethical—political process. Inasmuch as most Americans reject the practice of homosexuality, this is a clear violation of the rights of the majority and a continuing source of social disruption.

The Funding of the Movement

Indirect Funding of Homosexuality

In order to support the homosexual movement, it is not necessary to provide monies directly to homosexual organizations. As a matter of fact, it is probable that the monetary value of in-kind or indirect contributions to the homosexual movement far exceeds the funds received directly. When a church lends space or rents it below cost to a homosexual organization, this church is clearly subsidizing the organization in question. When a government agency provides staff support to advance the homosexual ideology through the courts or the regulatory process, the taxpayers are subsidizing the homosexual movement. Similarly, when a governmental agency publishes a book or pamphlet supportive of the homosexual ideology, the taxpayers are in reality subsidizing the homosexual movement, albeit in an indirect way. Indirect funding is not limited to instances in which a specific homosexual organization benefits as the result of the activities of other organizations or individuals. It also includes instances in which prohomosexual actions of nonhomosexual organizations create conditions favorable to or supportive of the homosexual movement.

THE CASE OF THE LEGAL SERVICES CORPORATION

A typical case of governmental support for the homosexual movement is provided by the Legal Services Corporation (LSC). An independent corporation funded by the federal government for the purpose of providing legal services to poor people, the LSC has in fact become a fundor of groups of leftist activist lawyers throughout the United States. The modus operandi of the LSC is to fund grantees, organizations who are supposed to deliver the direct services to the poor. Inasmuch as the homosexual ideology is an integral part of the liberal agenda for America, the LSC lawyers have tried to promote significant elements of this ideology through the courts and the regulatory process alike. These activities have provoked a strong adverse reaction from grassroots organizations and political leaders, including the Conservative Caucus. However, although the Reagan Administration was officially committed to defunding the LSC, as of this writing this objective had not been accomplished, and the activities of the LSC continue. As mentioned earlier, Dan Bradley, former president of the Legal Services Corporation, is a member of the Board of Directors of the Gay Rights National Lobby (see chapter VIII). Bradley has admitted to being a homosexual.[93]

There are two ways in which the LSC has supported the goals of the homosexual movement without having to transfer any of its funds to homosexual organizations. LSC attorneys have litigated in favor of homosexuals qua homosexuals. It has been reported that LSC lawyers have argued in favor of individuals receiving disability payments because they are homosexuals.[94] A case in point is that of a Helena (Montana) male homosexual who attempted to "become a woman" by undergoing castration and receiving massive doses of drugs. A Social Security Administrative law judge eventually granted disability benefits to this individual.[95] The place and cost of the operation were recorded in an article reproduced in the *Congressional Record*: "In Hartford, Connecticut, a legal services lawyer has demanded that the taxpayers foot the $10,000 bill for a sex-change operation for some 35-year-old guy who likes to prance around in women's clothes."[96] The LSC action not only cost the taxpayers, but was aimed at forcing the public to recognize the desire to "change one's sex" as a legitimate choice by paying for "medical procedures" to satisfy that desire. In another case, LSC lawyers reportedly used federal funds to argue in court for the "upgrading of Armed Forces discharges for persons thrown out of the service because of homosexuality."[97]

Another way in which the LSC has promoted the homosexual ideology is by attempting to issue regulations which presuppose the acceptance of basic principles of the homosexual movement. This is done by adding homosexuals to the list of "legitimate" minorities. The proposed civil rights regulations of the LSC, published for comment in March 1981, include the following statement of purpose: "The purpose of this part is to prevent discrimination by legal services programs supported in whole or in part by Legal Services Corporation funds in the delivery of services or in employment on the basis of race, religion, color, age, sex, marital status, national origin, handicap, political affiliation or sexual orientation. . . ."[98] Should the LSC be allowed to adopt this rule, the federal government would thereby be accepting the principle that homosexuals are a legitimate minority for civil rights purposes. This principle of the homosexual ideology is accepted in an even clearer form in the definitions section of the proposed rule: "(a) 'Protected Groups' means those groups which have been historically subjected to discrimination on the basis of race, color, national origin, sex, religion, or sexual orientation."[99] The concept that homosexuals have been discriminated against arbitrarily throughout history is admitted as a fact. The proposed regulations, moreover, not only prescribe that homosexuals shall be accepted as a legitimate minority in the provision of legal services [Secs. 1624.1, and 1624.5(a)] but they are recognized as a minority potentially capable of receiving, as a class, the benefits of the services provided by LSC grantees:

> (b)(1) A recipient, in determining the type of services, aid or benefits which will be provided, or the manner in which such services, aid or benefits shall be offered, may not directly or through contractual or other arrangements, utilize criteria or methods of administration with the purpose of subjecting individuals to discrimination on the basis of race, religion, color, sex, age, marital status, national origin, handicap, political affiliation or sexual orientation or which have the effect of substantially impairing accomplishment of the ob-

jectives of the program with respect to individuals on one of the bases outlined above.[100]

LSC aims to extend its prohomosexual policies to organizations with which its recipients, also called grantees, have contracts, or with which they have any other relationship:

> (c) A recipient may not participate in any contractual or other relationship with persons, agencies, organizations or other entities, such as, but not limited to, employment and referral agencies, labor unions, organizations providing or administering fringe benefits to employee of the recipient, and organizations providing training and apprenticeship programs, if the practices of such person, agency, organization or other entity have the effect of subjecting qualified applicants or employees to discrimination on any of the bases enumerated in this subpart.[101]

The power of these regulations, backed by the $300 million which LSC has been distributing annually (likely to be much reduced in fiscal 1982) has not been unnoticed by political commentators. The LSC proposed these regulations in the face of considerable opposition within and without the Reagan Administration. Such an action was called "waving the red flag at Reagan" by a Washington political columnist.[102]

The value of the LSC is appreciated by the homosexual movement and its opponents as well. Rep. Larry McDonald (D-Ga.) has tried repeatedly to stop the use of LSC funds for the promotion of homosexual causes.[103] Opposition by prohomosexual legislators has made McDonald's work tedious, if not difficult. (Although his proposals to bar the use of federal LSC funds for prohomosexual purposes have been rejected by voice vote, record votes have invariably resulted in their approval. This is indicative that legislators realize the real wishes of their constituents.) In 1980 Senator Lowell Weicker (R-Conn.) managed to amend McDonald's proposal, making it virtually ineffective, which was applauded by the homosexual press.[104] *Workers World* and the *Village Voice*, well-known for their prohomosexual sentiments and editorial policies, have made clear that one of the reasons why LSC is valuable is precisely in its ability to serve the homosexual cause.[105]

PUBLIC FUNDS
Tax dollars are not only utilized in the promotion of the homosexual ideology by direct contributions to homosexual organizations, although such contributions constitute a major portion of the total funding of the movement. Since they are less obvious, indirect contributions are not as taxing to the various jurisdictions from a public relations point of view. Still, they benefit the homosexual ideology not only for their intrinsic

value, but for the recognition and acceptance which are normally craved by homosexual organizations.

It is relatively easy for various units of government to contribute to the intellectual foundations of the homosexual ideology by funding "unbiased" research and sources of information. For example, Governor Milton J. Shapp established, on February 11, 1976, the Pennsylvania Council for Sexual Minorities, which explicitly included a number of homosexuals. The very existence of this state organization, with the clearly prohomosexual mandate given it by the Governor, implies acceptance of key points of the movement's ideology by the state. This is confirmed in the publication of a frankly prohomosexual booklet by Pennsylvania's Department of Education. *What is a Sexual Minority, Anyway?*[106] constitutes a virtual endorsement of significant elements of the homosexual ideology. It provides a bibliography and list of resources which are clearly one-sided (all sources cited being sympathetic to the homosexual movement).

In preparation to hearings for Intro 1017 (New York City's 1981 prohomosexual legislation), the city's Commission on Human Rights joined forces with the homosexual Coalition for Lesbian and Gay Rights in administering and evaluating a survey. This was done, at least partly, at the public's expense. Normally, surveys involve the administration of objective instruments in order to ascertain the nature of a social phenomenon. In this case, the questionnaire assumed the existence of such discrimination and was intended to "prove" it. Even where subjects might not be troubled by the assumed "discrimination," the idea is planted in their minds in an open way. The instruction to the subjects is explicit: "As you read the questionnaire, try to recognize the ways in which anti-gay discrimination may have shaped your life. We often avoid situations in which we expect to experience discrimination. We also tend to ignore the real basis for other people's failures to give us equal treatment."[107] The following questions reveal one of the purposes of the survey as the recruitment of homosexuals willing to testify at hearings in favor of Intro 1017:

Would you be willing to discuss the case of discrimination in further detail with a representative of the Coalition or the Commission on Human Rights? Yes _____ No _____

Would you be willing to submit written signed testimony to the City Council on your case? Yes _____ No _____

If not, would you be willing to submit written unsigned testimony? Yes _____ No _____

Would you be willing to testify openly at City Council hearings about your experiences? Yes _____ No _____

The Funding of the Movement

If not, would you be willing to testify if you could remain anonymous?
Yes _____ No _____

If you are willing to testify in some way or provide other information, please give us the following information:

Name_____ Telephone # _____
Address_____
_____

The cover letter was signed by Larry Katzenstein, Director of Research of the Commission of Human Rights. This provided the survey with an aura of scientific objectivity. In reality, however, the public was paying for a prohomosexual public relations effort and a gimmick to recruit witnesses for a public hearing. Such a survey lends itself to providing impressive statistics, duly relayed by the sympathetic press, which contribute to creating the impression that homosexuals are a legitimate minority subject to unreasonable discrimination.

Funding for sex education, especially when dealing with homosexuality itself or with gender identity, constitutes an indirect way by which public funds are utilized in the promotion of the homosexual ideology. The Women's Equity Act is a typical case of educational efforts which contribute to the homosexual ideology. It seems clear that gender identity confusion correlates positively with homosexuality.[109] Thus the Women's Educational Equity Act Publishing Center (Newton, Mass.) distributes a large array of materials designed to "combat sexism" and promote "sex equity." In addition to promoting sex role confusion, these materials tend to enshrine feminism and establish the foundation for the acceptance of principles of the homosexual ideology through the schools.[110]

Titles sold by the Women's Educational Act Publishing Center include: "New Pioneers: A Program to Expand Sex-Role Expectation in Elementary and Secondary Education," "Sexism in the Classroom," "Thinking and Doing: Overcoming Sex-Role Stereotyping in Education," and "Teacher Skill Guide for Combatting Sexism." As the last title indicates, the purpose of these programs is not just to impart knowledge, but to alter the values of teachers and students as well. Additionally, the Department of Education publicizes "model programs" developed in various school districts which also contribute to sex role confusion.[111]

Government-owned facilities can also be used in a manner that glorifies the homosexual subculture. Mention has been made of the National Park Service exhibit at the Colonial National Historical Park in York, Virginia, which stressed the presumed participation of homosexuals in colonizing the state. Apparently there was no historical foundation for the exhibit, which was closed because of public protest.[112] Public facilities are also

513

available to the "Gay Men's Choir," which has performed in both Lincoln Center (New York City) and the Kennedy Center (Washington, D.C.). The implications of this use of public facilities by avowed homosexuals has not escaped the attention of concerned citizens.[113]

There are many other instances in which public funds are used to support the homosexual ideology throughout this work. They include such items as the use of state college facilities to conduct homosexual courses or hold meetings of homosexual organizations; the airing of programs which promote or accept implicitly the homosexual ideology by public radio; the open or covert practice of hiring homosexuals qua homosexuals for public service jobs; the use of space on Capitol Hill to hold "hearings" or "congressional briefings" which are really platforms from which the leadership of the homosexual movement can propagandize its principles; the use of public schools for homosexual rallies and/or exhibits; the use of homosexuals qua homosexuals in speaking engagements in school assemblies or classrooms, and others.

It is evident that public authorities have supported the homosexual movement in a variety of ways. This support is largely responsible for the degree of acceptance of homosexuality as an "alternative lifestyle" in modern America. The use of schools is particularly important in this regard, since education is crucial in the formation of new generations.

CHURCH FUNDS

The help of churches, though, is the most important and sought-out support by the homosexual movement. Churches find it most difficult to provide direct funds for homosexual organizations. On the other hand, it appears that considerable nonfinancial support is offered by otherwise conventional religious organizations. Favorable articles in the religious press, the use of church facilities, and the willingness of church personnel to lend their personal and organizational prestige to homosexual causes benefits movement in no small measure. It is impossible to be exhaustive about indirect church funding for the homosexual movement. The following examples are meant to be illustrative of specific instances and in no way portray a complete picture.

A typical example of a church subsidizing the homosexual movement is the case of the United Methodist Church's building on 110 Maryland Avenue, N.E. in Washington, D.C. (see chapter VII). Located in an enviable position a short distance from the Capitol, the building served for several years as headquarters of the Universal Fellowship of Metropolitan Community Churches Washington Field Office. A center of homosexual advocacy and lobbying, this office served as a facility from which considerable influence could be exercised on the Congress, the White House, national offices for various religious bodies, and the community at large.[114] In a sense, it was the center of the Washington homosexual

The Funding of the Movement

Although in 1976 the United Methodist Church had passed a resolution forbidding church monies to be used for "gay causes,"[115] on February 1, 1980, the United Methodist Board of Church and Society started charging the UFMCC $6.50 per square foot for prime Capitol Hill office space. Prior to this date, the rent had been only $5.00 per square foot.[116] Without the "subsidy" of the church, the UFMCC would have been forced to pay as much as $20 to $25 per square foot for the same space.[117]

New Ways Ministry has used religious facilities for some of its pro-homosexual activities. The Sisters of St. Joseph of Springfield (Massachusetts), as indicated earlier, fund the Center for Reflective Action used for a homosexual symposium.[118] In some instances, local church authorities are willing to lend their facilities, but public pressure or direct orders from higher church authorities make such a use impossible. This was the case of the pastors of St. Clement's Church (Roman Catholic) and Grace Episcopal Church, who agreed to allow a New Ways Ministry workshop to take place on church property but cancelled the offers under pressure from their respective bishops.[119] The authorities of the Holy Trinity Seminary (Roman Catholic) in Silver Spring (Maryland) were willing to allow a prohomosexual symposium to take place on its premises, but later denied their permission for the event, in this case because of excessive registrations.[120]

Church support does not have to be related to religious activities of homosexual groups. While religious homosexual groups are normally instruments of the movement for the infiltration and utilization of churches, these groups, in fact, usually engage in a variety of prohomosexual political activities. In this case, they can also at times receive the support of their "host" churches. (As a matter of fact, this use of churches for prohomosexual political activities is a primary reason for the existence of homosexual groups in the churches.) Typical cases occurred at the Florida Avenue Friends Meeting in Washington and the Homewood Friends in Baltimore. These two churches reportedly provided the space necessary for the training of marshals for the 1979 March on Washington, one of the largest events ever sponsored by the homosexual movement.[121]

There are instances in which church facilities are used by homosexual groups which are not church related and for purely secular or political activities. This use can only be justified on the basis of the acceptance by these churches of some elements of the homosexual ideology. Warren Methodist Church in Denver is advertised by the Gay and Lesbian Community Center of Colorado as the setting for weekly meetings of the "Men's Coming Out Group."[122] "Parents of Gays" (POG) meetings are held in various churches throughout the New York City metropolitan area: the Community Unitarian Church in White Plains, (New York), the First Methodist Church in Westport, (Connecticut), the Unitarian Universalist Fellowship in Huntington, (New York), and the Metropolitan-

Duane Methodist Church in New York City.[123] The support sometimes goes beyond simply lending the organization space for meetings:

> Starting out on what we hope will be another successful year, we recall that for POG's entire 8-year history our meetings have been made possible by the hospitality of Metropolitan-Duane United Methodist Church. We are not sponsored by, and indeed have no connection with, the Church, which makes even more extraordinary its generosity and support in making our meeting room available every month and (until we established our post office box two years ago) letting us use its office as our mailing address. Our heartfelt thanks to the pastor, Rev. David Vernooy, to the Trustees and Lay Leaders, and to the congregation for their vital contribution toward making NYCPOL&GM, Inc. possible.[124]

The reader is reminded that POG is not a self-help group where parents with the "problem" of having a homosexual child meet—like alcoholics who attend AA meetings—in order to seek solutions. POG is a full-fledged prohomosexual group, an integral part of the movement.

An extreme case of use of church facilities by a prohomosexual group is the case of the Washington Square Church, a New York City United Methodist facility, used for the planning of a demonstration against the Neighborhood Church.[125] The protest was scheduled because of the Neighborhood Church's traditionalist stand on homosexuality.

There are instances in which the support of churches for the homosexual movement takes the form of advocacy with funding sources. We already indicated the importance of federal funding, especially from CETA, for the homosexual movement. The case of Sister Mary Claude Loeb, a Roman Catholic nun who appeared at a hearing of the City Council in Rochester on January 23, 1979, to promote continuing CETA funding for the Gay Alliance of Rochester, represents a glaring example of a church professional using her prestige and influence (the Catholic Church is very influential in this city) to serve the homosexual movement.[126]

These examples are only single instances of what seems to be a widespread phenomenon: the willingness of pastors to let church facilities be used to advance the homosexual ideology by homosexual organizations. From the point of view of the churches themselves, this is a dangerous phenomenon. The great majority of religious persons perceive homosexual activity as sinful and destructive and understand homosexuality to be a perversion, an illness, or perhaps a combination of both. It appears that they may not be inclined to support churches which positively contribute to organizations having a diametrically opposite point of view to their own in such sensitive matters. At the same time, religious people who are convinced that homosexual behavior is evil have an ideal way of making their views known in an effective manner by withdrawing their support

The Funding of the Movement

from churches, and religious organizations which maintain a pattern of relationships collaborative with the homosexual movement.

PRIVATE FUNDS

The homosexual movement has always been able to count on the material resources of many organizations, usually without the knowledge of their memberships. The very complexity of modern society has made it possible for the bureaucracies which administer them to engage in practices that, if known, would in all likelihood be thoroughly rejected.

An example of such an organization is the YWCA of Austin, Texas. A Texas profamily activist has informed the author that the Gay Community Services of that city is supported to a great extent by the local YWCA.[127] The *Gayellow Pages* lists the Austin Gay Community Services at 2330 Guadalupe Street, which is also the address of the University YWCA.[128]

Support can be offered under many guises. National Public Radio (NPR) and the Institute for Educational Leadership of George Washington University coproduced the openly prohomosexual radio program for the series "Options in Education" already discussed. NPR is funded by the Corporation for Public Broadcasting (itself funded by the federal government) and by private contributions. George Washington University is a private institution which, like all institutions of higher education, benefits from a preferential tax status. According to the program's transcript, "Options in Education" is funded mainly by the National Institute of Education (a federal agency) with additional monies provided by Carnegie Corporation of New York and the Corporation for Public Broadcasting.

Space has been made available by various organizations for the benefit of the homosexual movement almost since its inception. One of the first meetings of homosexuals after the Stonewall riot took place at Freedom House in New York City, the usual place for the monthly public lectures of the Mattachine Society of New York.[129] The Law School of New York University provided the setting for a national conference entitled: "Law and the Fight for Gay Rights" on March 10–11, 1979. The sponsors of the event were the Lesbian and Gay Law Student Association of New York University, the Rutgers Gay Caucus, and the Lambda Legal Defense and Education Fund.[130]

Just as federal agencies commission "studies" designed to justify their own existence by "proving" the need for services, private organizations utilize the same technique to satisfy special groups. An interesting case in which such a study was used for the benefit of the homosexual movement is offered by a project completed by professors of social welfare at the University of California in Berkeley and the University of Illinois at Chicago Circle for the San Francisco United Way.[131] The results of the survey are typical of similar efforts traditionally undertaken by the social services establishment: the researchers concluded that there is a need for expanding existing services, creating specialized services for homosexuals, and training existing service providers in the need of homosexuals. The benefits of such recommendations for the homosexual movement were they to be enacted, are obvious:

Further identification of homosexuals as a minority;

Dissemination of the homosexual ideology through the training programs; and,

Additional jobs and funding at the disposal of homosexual organizations.

A different, though quite effective way, of promoting the homosexual ideology is exemplified by the National Education Association. This organization has already been presented as a supporter of the movement. In a further effort on its behalf, the NEA is reported to have spent over $50,000 trying to force a school district to rehire a homosexual.[132] Had the NEA been successful, its efforts would have also greatly benefited the homosexual movement. A decision favorable to the NEA would have meant the recognition of "gay rights" by the courts, an outcome greatly desired by homosexual leaders.

Notes

1. Personal communication to the author by Father Robert Nugent, codirector of New Ways Ministry.

2. Wire story carried by *NC News*, November 8, 1978.

3. *A New Day* 3 (April 1979): 2.

4. *Official Newsletter of the National Coalition of Gay STD Services* (Arlington, VA: National Coalition of Gay STD Services), vol. 2, January 1981, p. 12 and May 1981, p. 9.

5. Ibid., vol. 2, September 1980.

6. *NAGAP Newsletter* 2 (Oakland, N.J.: National Association of Gay Alcoholism Professionals): 2.

7. Ibid. 2 (Winter 1980–81): 3.

8. *Official Newsletter of the National Coalition of Gay STD Services* 2 (Arlington, VA: National Coalition of Gay STD Services, May 1981): 2.

9. Ken Lerer, "Gays—A New Key Voter Group," *New York*, May 30, 1977, p. 9.

10. *Hearing*, pp. 108–110.

11. Internal Revenue Service, Ruling 78–305, 1978–2, Cumulative Bulletin 172 (Washington, D.C., 1978).

12. *Gays on the Hill* 1:4.

13. Ibid. 3 (November-December 1978): 5. The identical language is used in *A New Day* 3 (April 1979): 5.

14. *A New Day* 3 (April 1979): 2.

15. Ibid. 4 (August 1980): 1.

16. *Gays on the Hill* 1:4.

17. Dale Leeche, "Presence of Jesus Seen at Cuban Refugee Camp," *In Unity*, September/October 1980, p. 4.

18. T. Earlye Scott, "Gay Cuban Refugees," *In Unity*, September/October 1980, p. 5.

19. *It's Time* 8 (January-February 1981): 3.

The Funding of the Movement

20. R. Adam DeBaugh, "Lesbian and Gay Cuban Relief," *CCSA: Meeting Human Needs* 1 (Washington, D.C.: Commission on Christian Social Action, Universal Fellowship of Metropolitan Community Churches, July 1980): 1.

21. Scott, p. 5.

22. U.S. Department of Health and Human Services, Cuban/Haitian Task Force, Notice of Financial Assistance Awarded, Award No. CHTF-81-G023, March 31, 1981.

23. Ibid.

24. *Federal Register,* vol. 46, no. 45, March 9, 1981, pp. 15685–15854.

25. Ibid.

26. For the complete text of the UFMCC document, see the final grant proposal submitted by the Metropolitan Community Church and funded by the Cuban/Haitian Task Force (later named the Office of Refugee Resettlement), Department of Health and Human Services.

27. Leeche, p. 4.

28. Scott, p. 5.

29. Letter from Robert J. Goldenflame to the author, June 15, 1981.

30. Ibid.

31. Austin Scott, "LA Homosexuals Create Own Brand of Political Activism," *Los Angeles Times,* March 15, 1981.

32. *In Unity,* September/October 1980, p. 13.

33. Ibid.

34. James Bovard, "Tales from the CETA Crypt," *Inquiry,* August 3 and 24, 1981.

35. Ibid.

36. Reported by a Texas delegate to the International Women's Year meeting in Houston.

37. *In Unity,* June/July 1978, p. 14.

38. *It's Time* 8 (January-February 1981): 1.

39. Reported by a Texas delegate to the International Women's Year meeting in Houston.

40. *In Unity,* November/December 1980, p. 19.

41. *Family Protection Report* (Washington, D.C.: Free Congress Research and Education Foundation), August 1979, p. 6.

42. Ibid.

43. Center for Homosexual Education, Evaluation and Research (San Francisco), Summary of Projects, sent to the author in June 1981.

44. *Family Protection Report* (Washington, D.C.: Free Congress Research and Education Foundation), August 1979, p. 6.

45. Center for Homosexual Education, Evaluation and Research (San Francisco), Summary of Projects, sent to the author in June 1981.

46. Wire story carried by NC News Service, November 8, 1978.

47. Ibid.

48. *NAGAP Newsletter* 2 (Oakland, N.J.: National Association of Gay Alcoholism Professionals, Spring 1981): 6.

49. Personal communication from Carolyn Gable of the School of Social Work, University of Connecticut.

50. University of Connecticut, Graduate School of Social Work (West Hartford), *Summary,* Title XX Training Grant "New Perspectives on Lesbians and Gay Men"; see also the course outline, syllabus, required and suggested readings furnished by the school. Documents undated, but supplied to the author by the school in July 1981.

51. "ADAMHA Awards In FY 81–82, As Of May 19, 1982 By FY, Inst., State, City, Institution," p. 557. A computer printout provided by the U.S. Department of Health and Human Services, Washington, D.C.

THE HOMOSEXUAL NETWORK

52. *Washington Post*, August 7, 1981.

53. *Advocate*, September 18, 1980.

54. Personal communication from Carolyn Gable, School of Social Work, University of Connecticut.

55. *Journal* (Manitou Springs, CO), June 1, 1981, p. 5. See also the *Sacramento Bee*, March 13, 1981.

56. *Sacramento Bee*, March 19 and 24, 1981.

57. Letter to the author from Jannie Giacrusso, staff, Lesbian-Feminist Study Clearinghouse, University of Pittsburgh, PA, July 24, 1981.

58. Ibid.

59. Letter to the author from Michael Shively, Associate Director, Center for Research and Education and Sexuality (San Francisco), June 3, 1981.

60. Center for Homosexual Education, Evaluation and Research (San Francisco), Summary of Projects, sent to the author in June 1981.

61. Ibid.

62. *Official Newsletter of the National Coalition of Gay STD Services* 2 (Arlington, VA: National Coalition of Gay STD Services, January 1981): 2.

63. *Gay Community News* (Boston), February 17, 1979.

64. As reported to the interviewer for our survey.

65. *NAGAP Newsletter* 2 (Oakland, N.J.: National Association of Gay Alcoholism Professionals, Spring 1981): 2.

66. Ibid. 2 (Winter 1980–81): 3.

67. Ibid. 2 (Spring 1981): 5.

68. *Bondings*, Winter 1979–80, p. 3.

69. *Bondings*, Spring-Summer 1981, p. 3.

70. Ibid.

71. *Gays on the Hill* 1:4.

72. *In Unity*, January/February 1981, p. 18.

73. *Bondings*, Winter 1979–80, p. 5.

74. Ibid.

75. *A New Day* 5 (February 1981): 1.

76. *Los Angeles Times*, April 10, 1981, p. 16.

77. Ibid.

78. Joan Turner Beifuss, "Gays 1980: 'Out of Both Closet and Confessional,' " *National Catholic Reporter*, November 21, 1980.

79. Sister Jeannine Gramick, SSND, Letter to the editor, *National Catholic Reporter*, January 9, 1981.

80. *Washington Field Office Report 1976–77* (Washington, D.C.: Universal Fellowship of Metropolitan Community Churches, 1977), p. 95.

81. *Integrity Forum: For Gay Episcopalians and their Friends* 7 (Oak Park, IL: Integrity, Epiphany, 1981): 5. (Epiphany corresponds to the calendar month of January.)

82. *A New Day* 3 (June 1979): 3.

83. "Sculpture Honoring Gays Soon to be Unveiled," *Advocate*, September 18, 1980.

84. Ibid.

85. *In Unity*, December 1979-January 1980, p. 11.

86. *Interchange*, vol. 4, issue 1 (Washington, D.C.: National Gay Student Center, a project of the United States National Student Association, Winter 1977).

87. *A New Day* 3 (June 1979): 1.

88. Beifuss.

89. *In Unity*, April/May 1979, p. 5.

90. Memorandum from Karen Keener (Communications Division, Parkland College, Champaign, IL), Cochairman, Lesbian/Gay Caucus, National Council of Teachers of Eng-

lish, to members of the caucus, November 7, 1979, p. 2. (Committee on the Concerns of Lesbians and Gay Males Report).

91. National Gay Task Force (New York, N.Y.), "About our Group," a section printed in the back of the leaflet distributed by the Gay Task Force during the 1980 Annual Conference of the American Library Association.

92. *NAGAP Newsletter* 2 (Oakland, N.J.: National Association of Gay Alcoholism Professionals, Winter 1980–81): 4.

93. Phil Gailey, "Homosexual Takes Leave of a Job and of an Agency," *New York Times*, March 31, 1982.

94. Michael E. Hammond, *Missionaries for Liberalism: Uncle Sam's Established Church* (Vienna, VA: Conservative Caucus Research, Analysis and Education Foundation, n.d.), p. 2.

95. *Clearinghouse Review*, January 1980, p. 715. Cited in "Legal Services Corporation Reauthorization (H.R. 2506)," Republican Study Committee, Washington, D.C. 1981), p. I-34.

96. Patrick Buchanan, "A Brief Look at Legal Aid Horror," *Congressional Record*, March 26, 1981, p. E 1387.

97. Hammond.

98. Legal Services Corporation 45CFR Part 1624, "Comprehensive Civil Rights Regulations," *Federal Register*, vol. 46, no. 55, March 23, 1981, Washington, D.C., p. 18056.

99. Ibid.

100. Ibid., p. 18057.

101. Ibid.

102. Walter Pincus, "Legal Services Corp. Suits Itself, Waves Red Flag at Reagan," *Washington Post*, March 30, 1981, p. A3.

103. *In Unity*, November/December 1980, p. 18.

104. *A New Day* 4 (December 1980): 3.

105. "The Emasculation of Legal Services," *Village Voice*, July 28, 1981. Kathy Durkin, "Reagan Targets Legal Services," *Workers World*, June 26, 1981, p. 3.

106. Pennsylvania, Department of Education (Executive Office), "What is a Sexual Minority Anyway?"(1980).

107. Isaiah E. Robinson, Jr. et al., Cover Letter to the 1981 *Anti-Lesbian and Anti-Gay Discrimination Survey*. Robinson signed the letter in his capacity as Chairman of the New York City Commission on Human Rights.

108. New York City Commission on Human Rights, *Anti-Lesbian and Anti-Gay Discrimination Survey*, questionnaire (New York: New York City Commission on Human Rights, 1981).

109. Brad Prunty, "Gender Role/Identity Discord," *Gay Community News* (Boston), February 17, 1979.

110. U.S. Department of Education, Women's Educational Equity Act Program, *Resources for Sex Equity: 1980–81 Catalog* (Newton, MA: Women's Educational Equity Act Publishing Center, n.d.).

111. Laurie R. Harrison et al., *Programs to Combat Stereotyping in Career Choice* (Palo Alto), American Institutes for Research, 1980). Performed under U.S. Office of Education Contract No. 300–78–0471.

112. "Gays' Colonial Role Questioned; Park Service Closes Va. Exhibit," *Washington Star*, June 24, 1981.

113. Newsletter, Council for Community Consciousness (New York), July 13, 1981.

114. For a full description of the UFMCC Washington Field Office see "Hill Office Begins Fourth Year!" *Gays on the Hill* 3 (October 1978).

115. *A New Day* 3 (June 1976): 2.

116. *A New Day* 4 (January 1980): 1.

117. Based on figures published for real estate rental costs in the same area by local newspapers.

118. Registration form of the symposium, *Ministering to Gay Catholics*, Borgia Conference Center, Mont Marie, Holyoke, MA, 1980. Cosponsors were Dignity and the Center for Reflective Action (Sisters of St. Joseph).

119. *Gaylife*, May 8, 1981.

120. "Center Bars Symposium on Gays," *Washington Post*, November 21, 1981.

121. *Friends for Lesbian and Gay Concerns Newsletter* 3 (Symneytown, PA: Friends of Lesbians and Gays Concerned [Quakers], Autumn 1979): 1.

122. Promotional brochure (Denver), Gay and Lesbian Community Center of Colorado, n.d.).

123. Newsletter (New York: New York City Parents of Lesbians and Gay Men), no. 47, April 1981, p. 1.

124. Ibid., no. 44, January 1981, p. 1.

125. "Protest Violence against Lesbians, Gays in New York," *Workers World*, May 29, 1981, p. 2.

126. Area Statements of Support for Gay and Lesbian Persons: Speaker at City Council Hearings on CETA Funding for the Gay Alliance of Rochester, NY. (A Xeroxed collection of prohomosexual statements issued by religious persons/institutions of the Rochester area, n.d.).

127. Personal communication.

128. *Gayellow Pages: The National Edition* (New York: Renaissance House, 1980), p. 268.

129. Marotta, p. 78.

130. *Gay Community News* (Boston, MA), February 17, 1979.

131. "Bay Area Blacks Special Social Services for High Gay Population," *Behavior Today* 12 (New York, N.Y.: ADCOM, March 23, 1981): 7, 9.

132. "Homosexuality Goes to School," transcript of program #26 in the series "Options in Education" (Washington, D.C.: National Public Radio), April 19, 1976, p. 6.

I

Alleged Supporters of the Homosexual Movement/Ideology

American society has traditionally rejected homosexuality as a lifestyle and judged homosexual acts to be destructive and antisocial by nature. The increasing complexity of this society has established barriers between "the grassroots" and "social leaders." This breakdown of the social fabric, and the pervasive influence of an ideologically biased media, have enabled social and political leaders to be responsive to pressure groups rather than to the perceived interests of their natural constituents.

This phenomenon is compounded in the case of the homosexual movement by the almost compulsive need of its leaders to obtain and publicize the support of influential individuals and organizations. The following list presents a number of individuals and organizations not self-identified as homosexual, which, according to homosexual sources, have made statements favorable to one or more aspects of the homosexual ideology or the interests of the movement. In some cases the individuals or organizations listed below may not have intended that their names be used in support of the homosexual ideology or movement; they may not even be aware of this use. Nevertheless, they have been included by elements within the homosexual movement on behalf of the movement. The number next to each name corresponds to the source from which the name was taken according to the following code:

CODE	SOURCE
1	National Gay Task Force, Gay Civil Rights Support Statements and Resolution Packet, Volume 1
2	National Gay Task Force, Corporate Business Support Statements Packet
3	*A Time to Speak*, New Ways Ministry, Mt. Rainier, MD
3A	*A Time to Speak*, Addenda, New Ways Ministry, Mt. Rainier, MD
4	*Bondings*, Winter 1980–81
5	National Gay Task Force Supplement
6	*Bondings*, Spring-Summer 1981
7	*Bondings*, Fall 1981
8	*Bondings*, Winter 1981–82
9	*Bondings*, Spring-Summer 1980
10	*Bondings*, Winter 1979–80

Name	Location	Date	Source
The Advocate	Archdiocese of Newark, NJ	May 16, 1974 December 13, 1978	3, 5 3A
Albany, Diocese of (RC)* Priests' Senate	Albany, NY	April 2, 1979	3A
Alderson Hospitality House	Alderson, WV		4
America (Editorial)		November 11, 1978	3A
American Airlines Neil W. Byl	New York, NY	February 27, 1975	2
American Anthropological Assn. 1970 Annual Meeting	Washington, D.C.	1970	1
American Association for the Advancement of Science	Washington, D.C.	January 31, 1975	1
American Association of University Professors			1
American Bar Association Alicia V. Pond	Chicago, IL	August 8, 1973	1

*Roman Catholic

Homosexual Movement/Ideology

Name	Location	Date	Source
American Broadcasting Companies, Inc. Peter Cusack	New York, NY	April 10, 1975	2
American Civil Liberties Union	New York, NY	April 13, 1975	1
American Federation of Teachers David Selden	Washington, D.C.	1970	1
American Jewish Committee Daniel S. Shapiro	New York, NY	May 20, 1974	1, 5
American Library Association	Chicago, IL	June 1971	1
American Medical Association E. M. Steindler	Chicago, IL	June 19, 1975	1
American Personnel and Guidance Assn.	Washington, D.C.	April 7, 1971	1
American Psychiatric Association John P. Spiegel	Washington, D.C.	June 30, 1975 December 15, 1974 March 25, 1975	1
American Psychological Association	Washington, D.C.	January 24, 1975	1
American Public Health Association	Washington, D.C.	November 19, 1975	1
American Telephone and Telegraph Co. John D. deButts	New York, NY	March 4, 1975	2
Anderson, Bishop Paul F. (RC)	Duluth, MN	April 28, 1980	3A
Appalachian Ministry	Griffithsville, WV		4
Arzube, Bishop Juan (RC) Auxiliary Bishop of Los Angeles	Los Angeles, CA	October 20, 1978	3A
Association of Chicago Priests	Chicago, IL		4
Avon Products, Inc. Paul A. Abodeely	New York, NY	February 27, 1975	2
Baltimore, Archdiocese of (RC) Senate of Priests, Clergy Education Committee	Baltimore, MD	July 9, 1976 October 18, 1976	3 3A
Bank of America William J. A. Weir	San Francisco, CA	March 6, 1975	2

Name	Location	Date	Source
Baum, Gregory McGill University		October 31, 1977	3
Boston Theological Institute, Women's Theological Coalition	Boston, MA		4
Boyle, Rev. Eugene		June 3, 1977	3
Bridgeport Diocesan Criminal Justice Commission (RC)	Bridgeport, CT		4, 9
Brooklyn, Diocese of (RC) Social Action Office	Brooklyn, NY		4
Brothers for Christian Community 1980 General Assembly		1980	4, 9
Brothers of the Sacred Heart	Pascoag, RI		4
Cafferty, Margaret		June 3, 1977	3
California Conference of Catholic Charities		October 3, 1978	3A
Callahan, Rev. William, SJ		June 3, 1977	3
Capuchin Gay Caucus			8
Carroll, Elizabeth, RSM Center of Concern		October 31, 1977	3
Cascade Community Church	Akron, OH		4
Catholic Charities, Inc. New London District	New London, CT		4
Catholic Herald (Editorial)	Sacramento, CA	September 1, 1977	3
Catholic Herald Citizen -Editorial -Msgr. Andrew Brienes (article)	Madison, WI	July 2, 1977 September 20, 1980	3 3A
Catholic Theological Society of America *Human Sexuality: New Directions in American Catholic Thought*		1977, Paulist Press	3
Catholic Worker Community	Wichita, KS	October 4, 1977	3
Catholic Worker Farm	Sheep Ranch, CA		4, 9
Catholic Worker House	St. Louis, MO		4
CBS Drew Q. Brinckerhoff	New York, NY	June 24, 1975	2

Homosexual Movement/Ideology

Name	Location	Date	Source
Center for New Creation	Vienna, VA		4
Center for Reflective Action	Holyoke, MA		4, 10
Central Conference of American Rabbis Rabbi Elliot L. Stevens	New York, NY	June 28, 1977	5
Centre of Affirmation and Dialogue	Toronto, Ontario		4, 9
Christian Century, The Elliott Wright		March 3, 1971	5
Church of the Epiphany Social Action Committee	Louisville, KY		4
CitiCorp. Lawrence Small	New York, NY	March 11, 1975	2
Commonweal -Editorial		May 24, 1974	5
-Fr. Gregory Baum (article)		February 15, 1974	5
Community of the Holy Spirit	San Diego, CA		4, 9
Cornerstone Justice and Peace Center, Inc.	Denver, CO		4
Correctional Change Group	Worcester, MA		4
Coston, Carol, OP		June 3, 1977	3
Criterion, The (Editorial)	Indianapolis, IN	July 25, 1980	3A
Cummins, Bishop John S. (RC) Bishop of Oakland, CA	Oakland, CA	October 3, 1978	3A
Curran, Fr. Charles Catholic University of America		October 31, 1977	1
Davis, Rev. William, SJ		June 3, 1977	3
Dearden, John Cardinal Archbishop of Detroit Letter to Detroit Priests	Detroit, MI	August 20, 1974	3
Des Moines Catholic Worker	Des Moines, IA		4, 9
District of Columbia, Board of Education Marion Barry, Jr., Pres. D.C. Board	Washington, D.C.	May 23, 1972	1
Dominican Students of the Province of St. Martin de Porres	Oakland, CA		4

Name	Location	Date	Source
Dozier, Bishop Carroll T. (RC)	Memphis, TN	January 22, 1978	3
Eastern Airlines William R. Howard	Miami, FL	February 26, 1975	2
East Lansing Peace Education Center	East Lansing, MI		4, 9
Eighth Day Center for Justice	Chicago, IL		4
Emmaus Community of Christian Hope	Orange, NJ		4
Emmaus House	Washington, D.C.		4
Episcopal Church, The 65th General Convention	Minneapolis, MN	September 1976	1, 5
Flanagan, Bishop Bernard J. (RC) Diocese of Worcester, MA Letter to Dignity President	Worcester, MA	July 1, 1974	3
Futures Awareness Center	Mt. St. Joseph, OH		4
Georgetown University Office of Campus Ministry	Washington, D.C.		4
Glenmary's Commission on Justice	Neon, KY		4, 9
Good Shepherd Catholics for Shared Responsibility	Alexandria, VA		4
Greeley, Fr. Andrew *Chicago Tribune*		July 7, 1977	3
Groundwork	Lansing, MI		4
Gumbleton, Bishop Thomas J. (RC) Archdiocese of Detroit	Detroit, MI	October 2, 1974	3
Handmaids of Mary (RC) Sisters' Coalition for Justice			8
Las Hermanas			8
Honeywell C.E. Brown	Minneapolis, MN	February 28, 1975	2
House of Community	Bemidji, MN		4
Hovda, Rev. Robert		June 3, 1977	3
Hunthausen, Archbishop Raymond G. (RC) Archbishop of Seattle	Seattle, WA	August 25, 1978 July 1, 1977	3A 5
IBM Jerry G. Anderson	Armonk, NY	March 5, 1975	2

Homosexual Movement/Ideology

Name	Location	Date	Source
Imesch, Bishop Joseph L. (RC) Archdiocese of Detroit	Detroit, MI	October 2, 1974	3
Immaculate Heart of Mary Sisters/APWC (RC)			7
Jesuit Renewal Center	Milford, OH		4, 9
Keane, Philip, SS *Human Sexuality*		June 1977, Paulist Press	3
Kelleher, Maureen, RHSN		June 3, 1977	3
Krol, John Cardinal (RC) Archdiocese of Philadelphia	Philadelphia, PA	August 13, 1974	3
Lutheran Church in America, The	New York, NY	July 2, 1970	5
McBrien, Richard P. Notre Dame University, Notre Dame, IN		October 31, 1977	3
McCormick, Richard A., SJ Georgetown University		October 31, 1977 June 3, 1977	3 3
McDonald's Linda B. Gelbard	Oak Brook, IL	March 9, 1975	2
McSorley, Harry, STD St. Michael's College, Toronto		October 31, 1977	3
Maguire, Daniel C. Marquette University		October 31, 1977	3
Manhattan College Campus Ministry	Bronx, NY		4
Martin Buber Institute	Columbia, MD		4
Medeiros, Humberto Cardinal (RC) Archdiocese of Boston	Boston, MA	March 11, 1974	1
Medinger, Daniel *The Times Review*	LaCrosse, WI	June 1, 1978	3A
Michigan, Diocese of (Episcopal) Executive Council	Detroit, MI	May 1974	1, 5
Milwaukee Archdiocesan Commission for the Plan of Pastoral Action for Family Ministry (RC)	Milwaukee, WI	September 22, 1979	3A
Milwaukee Justice and Peace Center Newsletter	Milwaukee, WI	July 1977	3

APPENDIX I

Name	Location	Date	Source
Minnesota Catholic Conference Rev. Benno Salewski		January 22, 1978	3
Missionary Sisters of the Immaculate Conception (RC) Provincial Council	West Paterson, NJ		4
Mooney, Christopher F., SJ Univ. of Pennsylvania		October 31, 1977	3
Moore, Bishop Paul (Episcopal) Bishop of New York		May 11, 1974	5
Moran, Gabriel, FSC -Statement on Fr. John McNeill		October 31, 1977	3
-"Sexual Forms," Christian Brothers Conference	Lockport, IL	1977	3
Most Holy Sacrament Administrative Team			7
Mugavero, Bishop Francis J. (RC) Pastoral letter	Brooklyn, NY	February 11, 1976	3, 5
Myers, Bishop C. Kilmer (Episcopal) Diocese of California		October 1, 1977	5
National Assembly of Religious Brothers (RC) -Bro. Robert McCann, FSC	Buffalo, NY	March 4, 1978	5
-Resolution	Providence, RI	June 1977	4
National Assembly of Women Religious (RC) -East Central Region			4
-Executive Board			4
-House of Delegates		1979	4
-Pittsburgh Chapter			4
-S. Kathleen Keating, National Chairperson			3
-Resolution	Pittsburgh, PA	August 10–13, 1978	3A
National Catholic Reporter	Kansas City, KS	May 17, 1974 November 21, 1980	5 3A
National Center for Ministry	Milwaukee, WI		4
National Coalition of American Nuns (RC) Resolution		1974	4
National Conference of Catholic Bishops	Washington, D.C.		

Homosexual Movement/Ideology

Name	Location	Date	Source
-U.S. Catechetical Directory		November 17, 1977	3
-"To Live in Christ Jesus" A Pastoral Letter on Moral Values		November 11, 1976	3
National Council of the Churches of Christ	New York, NY		1
National Education Association Martha L. Ware	Washington, D.C.	September 9, 1974	1
National Federation of Priests' Councils (RC)	San Francisco	March 21, 1974	1, 3
Priest: USA (Editorial)		July 1977	3
National Organization for Women	Washington, D.C.	November 3, 1975	1
Newman Center Staff	Columbia, MO		4
	Davis, CA		4
Newman Community	Chapel Hill, NC		4
New Orleans, Archdiocese of Sisters' Council (RC)	New Orleans, LA		4
North American Jewish Students' Network	New York, NY	April 1974	1, 5
O'Brien, David J.		June 3, 1977	3
O'Donnell, Bishop Cletus (RC)	Madison, WI	Winter 1980	3A
Orlando, Diocese of (RC) Ministry for Social Justice	Orlando, FL		4, 10
Orthodox Catholic Office for Peace and Justice	San Francisco, CA		6
P.A.D.R.E.S.			4
Parish Evaluation Project	Chicago, IL		4
Passionist Social Concerns Center	Union City, NJ		4
Paulist Social Action Committee	Storrs, CT		4
Pax Center	Erie, PA		4
Pittsburgh, Diocese of (RC) Sisters' Council, Peace and Justice Committee	Pittsburgh, PA		4
Precious Blood Sisters (RC) ASC Pilgrim Ministries			4
Procter & Gamble Co. J. H. Percival	Cincinnati, OH		2

Name	Location	Date	Source
Quinn, Bishop John R. (RC)	San Francisco, CA	May 15, 1980 October 11, 1978	3A 3A
Quixote Center	Mt. Rainier, MD	October 10, 1977	3, 4
Richmond, Diocese of (RC) Diocesan Social Ministry Commission	Richmond, VA	May 21, 1977	3, 6

Roach, Archbishop John J.
  (RC)
Archbishop of St. Paul
  and Minneapolis
		January 1978	3

Rochester, Diocese of (RC)
-Diocesan Sisters' Council
-Office of Vicar for
  Urban Ministry, Ecumenical
  Clergy Statement
	Rochester, NY
	Rochester, NY
		November 12, 1977
		March 1, 1977
			3, 6
			3

St. Francis Parish Team	Brant Beach, NJ		6
St. Jerome Church Pastoral Staff	Newport News, VA		4
St. John's Student Parish Campus Ministry Team	East Lansing, MI		4
St. Joseph House	Minneapolis, MN		4
St. Joseph Parish Pastoral Ministry Team	East Rutherford, NJ		4
St. Leander Parish Social Concerns Committee	Pueblo, CO		4, 10

St. Louis, Archdiocese of
  (RC)
Council of Religious
  Women
	St. Louis, MO		4

St. Louis Institute for Peace and Justice	St. Louis, MO		9
St. Matthew Community	Brooklyn, NY		4
St. Paul and Minneapolis, Archdiocese of (RC) Senate of Priests		March 1978 June 21, 1979	3 3A
St. Paul Citizens for Human Rights Sr. Janet Mathison Msgr. Jerome Boxleitner	St. Paul, MN	January 24, 1978	3
St. Paul's University Catholic Center -Social Justice Committee -Staff	Madison, WI		4, 9

Homosexual Movement/Ideology

Name	Location	Date	Source
St. Vincent's Hospital	New York, NY	December 1973	3
Salm, Luke, FSC Manhattan College		October 31, 1977	3
San Francisco, Archdiocese of (RC) Commission of Social Justice	San Francisco, CA	October 12, 1977 October 24, 1979	3 3A
School of Applied Theology	Berkeley, CA		4
School Sisters of Notre Dame (RC) -Baltimore Province in Bolivia	Baltimore, MD		4, 9
-Emmaus Community	Camden, NJ		4
Seattle, Archdiocese of (RC) Office of Catholic Charities	Seattle, WA	September 23, 1978	3A
Sisters in Gay Ministry Associated (SIGMA)			4
Sisters of Charity of St. Elizabeth (RC) Provincial Team, Northern Province	Paramus, NJ		4
Sisters of Divine Providence (RC) Provincial Administration	Melbourne, KY		4, 9
Sisters of Loretto (RC) -Cherry Street House -Office of the Social Advocate	Kansas City, MO Denver, CO		4 4
Sisters of Mercy (RC) Social Concerns Committee	Burlington, VT		6
Sisters of Mercy of the Union (RC) General Administrative Team			4
Sisters of Notre Dame de Namur (RC) Province Team, Boston Province	Boston, MA		4, 10
Sisters of St. Dominic (RC) Executive Committee	Racine, WI		4
Sisters of St. Dominic of Marymount (RC)	Tacoma, WA		4

Name	Location	Date	Source
Sisters of St. Francis (RC)			
-Alliance, NE			4
-Tiffin, OH			4, 9
Sisters of St. Joseph (RC)			4
-Third Order of St. Francis, St. Francis Region			
Sisters of St. Joseph of Carondelet (RC)			
-Albany Province, Social Justice Secretariat	Albany, NY		4, 10
-General Chapter in Los Angeles	Los Angeles, CA	Summer 1978	3A
-St. Louis Province, Social Justice Secretariat	St. Louis, MO		4
-St. Mary Star of the Sea Parish	Atlantic Mine, MI		4
-Social Justice Core Group			8
-Western Province, Social Justice Secretariat			4
Sisters of St. Joseph of LaGrange (RC) Social Justice Committee			8
Sisters of St. Joseph of Orange (RC) Social Concerns Committee	Orange, CA		4
Sisters of St. Joseph of Peace (RC) Religious Development Team	Englewood Cliffs, NJ		4, 10
Sisters of the Presentation (RC) Social Justice Committee			4
Society of Friends	Various cities	1972, 1973, 1974	1, 5
Spokane Peace and Justice Center	Spokane, WA		3
Sullivan, Bishop Walter F. (RC)	Richmond, VA	August 26, 1977 March 7, 1976	3 3A
Syracuse, Diocese of (RC) Justice and Peace Commission			7
Third Life Center	Oakland, CA		4, 9
Thomas Merton Center	Pittsburgh, PA		4
Times Review, The Daniel Medinger	LaCrosse, WI	June 1, 1978	3A
Trenton, Diocese of (RC) Office of Diocesan Relations for Sexual Minorities	Trenton, NJ		4

Homosexual Movement/Ideology

Name	Location	Date	Source
Turner, Mary Daniel, SND		June 3, 1977	3
Union of American Hebrew Congregations	New York, NY	November 1977	5
Unitarian Universalist Association Raymond C. Hopkins	Boston, MA	June 3, 1973	1, 5
United Church of Christ	New York, NY	July 1, 1975	5
		July 5, 1977	5
United States Catholic Conference	Washington, D.C.		
-"A Call to Action"	Detroit, MI	October 20–23, 1976	3
-Dept. of Education,		June 1976 and	3, 5
Young Adult Ministry Board		May 30–June 3, 1979	3A
United States Catholic Mission Council		May 1979	3A
United States Civil Service Commission News Release	Washington, D.C.	July 3, 1975	1
University of Wisconsin	Whitewater, WI		
-Campus Ministry			4
-Shalom Ecumenical Campus Ministry			9
Villa Maria Retreat Center	Wernersville, PA		4, 10
Washington State Catholic Conference	Seattle, WA	March 1976	3
Weakland, Archbishop Rembert (RC) Archdiocese of Milwaukee	Milwaukee, WI	July 19, 1980	3A
West Texas Catholic	Amarillo, TX	July 17, 1977	3
Whitehead Associates	South Bend, IN		4
Women's Ordination Conference (WOC)			7
Young Women's Christian Association 26th National Convention	New York, NY	March 1973	1

APPENDIX

11

Homosexual Rights and the Foundations of Human Rights

Robert Reilly

Reprinted from *Family Policy Insights,* a publication of the Free Congress Research and Education Foundation, Washington, D.C., volume 1, number 3, December 10, 1981.

Writing about homosexuality has become a growth industry, one writer has quipped. Indeed, there has never been a time in our nation when we have been so publicly preoccupied with this subject. All of a sudden, the love whose name dare not be spoken is being shouted, if not from the rooftops, at least from the streets in demonstrations, from the platforms in political rallies, and from the pages of various popular and intellectual journals. One wonders why.

One reason is that the subject of homosexuality, much like that of abortion, has become inextricably enmeshed in the political rhetoric of rights. Rights, as the Declaration of Independence tells us, are founded firmly in and are fully dependent on the "Laws of Nature and of Nature's God." Anyone whose claim can be asserted on the level of a right, therefore, gathers a tremendous moral and political impetus for his cause. For this reason, activist homosexuals are attempting to identify themselves as the new civil rights movement.

Homosexual Rights

This attempt demands especially close scrutiny, because it questions the meaning of concepts critical to our moral and political understanding of ourselves, including the very understanding of that "Nature" upon which our founders thought our existence as a free people depends.

The case for homosexuality begins with seeming modesty. Its proponents contend that sexual choices are private, and that therefore homosexuals should be left to their own sexual predilections. Live and let live. At the same time, they insist they are the objects of discrimination and wish to enact remedial legislation. This very complaint, however, reveals that there is a public aspect to their private choice. First of all, they must be identifiable to others as homosexuals; otherwise it would be impossible to discriminate against them. In many cases this public aspect takes the form of the homosexual telling others that he is a homosexual: "coming out of the closet" as it is called. Why should a homosexual feel impelled to do this, especially if he expects discrimination as a result? After all, the hidden homosexual who has not "come out of the closet" enjoys the privacy of concealment. One reason homosexuals take this risk has been made fairly clear by militant homosexual organizations: by so doing homosexuals wish not only to be tolerated in terms of their private sexual behavior, they wish to have that behavior publicly vindicated and recognized as normal.

This is hardly a strange desire. Man is a social being. Though parts of his life take place in private, in the normal course of things even those private aspects have public manifestations. Indeed, public, social life is organized in such a way to ensure privacy for certain things. We learn what should be private from the public way in which certain privacies are protected. So by private we do not mean things which are nobody else's business. The private, in this sense, is everybody's business.

For example, certainly the sexual intimacy between a husband and wife is held to be private and inviolate. But what are the public manifestations of this privacy? Obviously, wedding rings, children, private property, homes, schools, communities—the whole structure of society, in fact, is built to protect and maintain the conditions for that intimacy and its results. The whole social and political order is supportive of this privacy. It is encouraged and protected by law because it is held to be of benefit to all.

This is the kind of support and acceptance which homosexuals are seeking. This is seen in their desire to have their relationships legally recognized as marriages, or to have the ability to adopt children, etc. This makes somewhat specious the claim that all that is at stake in the homosexual controversy is the right to privacy. The clandestine homosexual does not claim a "right" to do the things he wishes to conceal and so claims no public protection for his privacy. As a result, he implicitly acquiesces in society's implied judgment of his actions as wrong. Many homosexuals no longer find this concession tolerable. And by advancing their cause on the level of moral principle ("gay rights") they insist on not only a repeal, but a complete reversal of that public judgment. In the same way we once learned of the inherent goodness of married life, we must now be taught the "new morality" of homosexuality. Ironically, the logic behind this process of the legitimization of homosexuality undercuts any objective standards by which we could judge the legitimacy of anything.

THE MORAL VIEW IMPLIED BY LEGAL NEUTRALITY

Why this should be so requires some understanding of the moral foundations of law and its prescriptive nature. The legal protection of heterosexual relations between a husband and wife involves a public judgment on the nature and purpose of sex. That judgment teaches that the proper exercise of sex is within the marital bond, because both the procreative and unitive purposes of sex are best fulfilled within it. The family alone is capable of providing the necessary stability for the profound relationship which sexual union both symbolizes and cements, and for the welfare of the children which issue from it.

The legitimization of homosexual relations changes that judgment and the teaching which emanates from it. What is disguised under the rubric of legal "neutrality" toward an individual's choice of sexual behavior is in fact a demotion of marriage from something seen as good in itself and for society, to just one of the available sexual alternatives.[1] In other words, this "neutrality" is not at all neutral; it teaches and promotes an indifference, where once there was an endorsement. Since that endorsement purported to be based upon knowledge of the objective good of marriage, it taught not only that marriage is good, but that we can know what is good. The latter is, in a way, a far more critical lesson.

The implied indifference in a law which is "neutral" to one's choice of sexual alternatives teaches that we are incapable of knowing in an objective way the goodness or evil of these sexual alternatives, and that therefore their worth can only be determined subjectively by the private individual. An example of a similar teaching is provided by the legalization of pornography, which preceded and prepared the ground for the homosexual cause. Go into almost any grocery store or newsstand and you will see side by side on the shelf *Playboy* and *Good Housekeeping*. What does any sensible person learn from seeing this odd juxtaposition? Certainly the way of life espoused by *Playboy* is inimical to good housekeeping. Yet there they are together, take your pick.

In other words, the person learns, if only by osmosis, that it is a matter of public indifference as to whether one properly uses or abuses sex. More accurately, legal commerce in pornography teaches that no such distinction exists. Once this teaching has been learned, where does one draw

538

the line? If heterosexual sex is only a form of play or recreation, what could be wrong with a little sodomy? Or even incest?

So, far from not embodying any moral view, legal "neutrality" gives public status to and fosters a highly subjective view of life, which, of course, extends to things other than sexual behavior. As Germain Grisez writes, "One cannot long adopt certain specific moral precepts without adopting the entire view from which such precepts rise."[2] Evelyn Waugh said much the same thing in his satiric way when asked why there were no good professional proofreaders left in England. "Because," he responded, "clergymen are no longer unfrocked for sodomy." One cannot abandon one standard without affecting all others.

NATURE AND THE NATURAL LAW

In order to understand what is at stake, it might be well to review briefly what the natural law understanding of "Nature" is and the kinds of distinctions an objective view of reality enables us to make in regard to our existence in general and to sexuality in particular. At the same time, we shall see how, once the objective status of Nature is lost or denied, one is incapacitated from making such distinctions and, in fact, from possessing any true knowledge about ourselves or the world.

Man first deduced the existence of Nature by observing order in the universe. The regularity with which things happen could not be explained by random repetition. All activity seems governed by a purpose, by ends to which things are designed to move. In nonhuman creation this design is manifested through either instinct or physical law. Man, however, possesses free will. He alone can choose the means to his end or choose to frustrate his end altogether. This, of course, is why "moral" laws are applicable only to man. That man can defy the moral law in no way lessens the certainty of its operation. In fact, man not so much breaks the moral law as the moral law breaks man, if he transgresses it. In short, when we speak of man's nature, we mean the ordering of man's being toward certain ends. It is the fulfillment of those ends which makes man fully human.

Since Socrates, we have called man's end "the good." The good for man, Aristotle tells us, is happiness. However, happiness is not whatever we say it is, but only that thing which will by our nature truly make us happy. (That good, the theologians tell us, is God.) Aristotle explains that happiness is achieved only through virtuous actions—the repetition of good deeds. Deeds are considered good and bad, natural and unnatural, in relation to the effect they have on man's progress toward his end. So, it is through Nature that we come to understand the proper use of things.

The case for homosexuality is a vulgarization of a philosophical anarchism which denies the existence of Nature and therefore the ability to discriminate between the use and abuse of things. This is popularly manifested in the most frequent defense of homosexuality, which takes the form of an anthropological survey of societies which invariably produces a tribe or two in which homosexual behavior is accepted as normal. This is offered as proof that either homosexuality is an expression of natural law, or that such a variety of human behavior proves there is no such thing as natural law. The first conclusion is simply a way of robbing the word Nature of its meaning, by including within its definition anything man is capable of doing. But this approach becomes less attractive when we recall that, besides sodomy, it includes incest, human sacrifice, and mass suicide, for all of which there are numerous historical—and some recent—examples. The second conclusion errs by supposing that there can be a natural law only if it is universally acknowledged and adhered to. This overlooks the fact that man is unique in that he can affirm or deny his Nature. However, his denial of his Nature in no way refutes its existence, any more than the denial of the law of gravity will keep one from falling.

It is ironic that the proponents of homosexuality so often point to ancient Greece as their paradigm because of its high state of culture and its acceptance of homosexuality. Ancient Greece's greatest contribution to western civilization was philosophy, which discovered that the mind can know things, as distinct from just having opinions about them, that objective reality exists, and that there is some purpose implied in its construction. The very idea of Nature and natural law arose as a product of this philosophy, whose first and perhaps greatest exponents, Socrates and Plato, were unambiguous in their condemnation of homosexuality as unnatural: "The intercourse of men with men, or of women with women, is contrary to Nature, and . . . the bold attempt was originally due to unbridled lust" (*Laws* 636C; see also *Symposium of Xenophon,* 8:34, Plato's *Symposium,* 219B-D).

THE NATURE OF SEXUAL ACTS
Perhaps it would be appropriate here to sketch very briefly and only partly (space does not allow for more) what the nature of sexual acts is. We can begin with the overwhelmingly obvious fact that human bodies are better designed for heterosexual intercourse than for homosexual. As George Gilder puts it: "Procreative genital intercourse stands at the crux of sexual differentiation, and is the normative pinnacle of sexual relationships to which all other sexual energies aspire, and from which they flow."[3] And William May expresses the combined unitive and reproductive nature of the sexual act: "There is something of paramount human significance in the fact that one special kind of touch, the touch of coital sex, not only requires for its exercise a difference between male and female, but also is an act that of its own inherent dynamism is capable of expressing an intimate, exclusive sharing of life and love between a man and a woman

and at the same time is capable of communicating that life and that love to a new human being."[4]

As procreative, this pinnacle of sexual relationships is naturally ordered to the family, the structure of which places a couple in a context larger than themselves. Compared with the act of marital union, homosexual acts are, as Michael Novak has pointed out, "self-centered in a way that is structural, independent of the goodwill of the individual."[5] They have in them an inescapable element of solipsism. "The other side of the bed is occupied, as it were, by more of the same—the same half of humanity, instead of the other half for whom each person is constitutionally seeking."[6] The renunciation of the other half leaves homosexuals bereft not only of a role in continuing the human race, but of the personal growth entailed in adjusting oneself, as Samuel McCracken expresses it, "to someone so different from oneself as to be in a different sex entirely."[7]

REJECTION OF THE NATURAL LAW

To see more specifically the way in which nature is removed as an objective standard, we may turn to an example provided by Professor Berton Leiser, who offers a fairly typical argument against natural law in his chapter on homosexuality in *Liberty, Justice, and Morals*, a college textbook. He quotes Pope Pius XI as a representative of the natural law position: "Private individuals have no other power over the members of their bodies than that which pertains to their natural ends."[8] Leiser goes on to question: "Is it true that every organ has one and only one proper function?"[9] He gives the example of a woman's eyes as well adapted to seeing, but also well adapted to flirting. He then asks, "Is a woman's use of her eyes for the latter purpose sinful merely because she is not using them, at the moment, for their primary purpose?"[10] Similarly, he questions whether any use of sex can be condemned because it is not being used for its principal procreative purpose: "Why should any other use of these organs, including their use to bring pleasure to their owner, or to someone else, or to manifest love to another person, or even, perhaps, to earn money, be regarded as perverse, sinful, or unnatural?"[11]

The natural law theory which Leiser here pretends to debunk is a straw man. The natural law argument has never been (nor is it in any way suggested by Pius XI's statement) that there is one and only one purpose or function of an organ, but that within the other ends an organ may be intended to serve by Nature, there is a hierarchy which subordinates some ends to others. (While flirting with one's eyes is not unnatural, it is certainly subordinate to seeing. In fact, one can hardly flirt with one's eyes while at the same time not seeing. Strange, indeed, would be the person who flirted with her eyes so as to impair her sight.) Moreover, this hierarchy is arranged according to the one final end which is expressive of the whole nature of man: the good of which Socrates spoke or the God of revealed religion.

But the real crux of the natural law position is that, however many purposes an organ (or any other natural object) has, those purposes originate in Nature and not in man's desires. Leiser, on the other hand, contends that "the purpose or function of a given organ may vary according to the needs or desires of its owners."[12] With this argument he justifies the use of sex not only "for pleasure, or for the expression of love" but "for some other purpose"[13]—whatever that may be. Homosexuality, under this dispensation is not wrong, because there is no "objectively identifiable quality in such behavior that is unnatural."[14] This removal of the objective quality of human acts leaves the true reality of things residing in man's desires. This results in the reduction of morality to human intentions. In other words, an act such as sodomy has no meaning in and of itself, apart from the meaning it happens to be given by the person acting, i.e., what he intends or desires the act to be. As a consequence of this, we are unable to say that the act of sodomy is inherently wrong (or right), but are required to look to the person performing the act. It is according to his interior disposition or desires that the act becomes evil or good. (It should be carefully noted here that while the natural law position emphasizes the moral nature of an act, it does not disregard the intent of the actor. Indeed, the very idea of a moral act presupposes that the necessary conditions for a moral act are present, i.e., a thorough understanding by the actor of what it is he is doing, full and free consent in the performance of the act, etc. But at the same time, when we say that an act is objectively good or evil in itself, we mean that intention cannot change the goodness or evil of the act. A good intention (love) cannot change an evil act (sodomy) into a good act. It will harm the nature of the person acting and the person acted upon, regardless of intent. However, intention may affect the guilt or innocence of the actor, e.g., if the person is not fully aware of the evil of the act or does not perform it with full consent.) But by what standard are these desires to be judged? If human acts are not objectively good or evil and only individual desires are real, how can distinctions between desires be made? This is the existential dilemma created by the abandonment of the objectivity of Nature. Since the moral quality of an act cannot be discerned, one is left with a quantitative standard of intensity. How intensely (genuinely) is the desire felt? Adultery, incest, pederasty, masturbation—according to the school of desire, no moral distinction can be made between any of these acts and, say, the act of marital union. This is sexual equality with a vengeance.

The wider social and political implications of this moral egalitarianism are not hard to deduce. If there are no preexisting, intelligible ends toward which man is ordered by nature, every individual must invent, in an

Homosexual Rights

arbitrary and subjective manner, some ends by which to guide his actions and order his life. The way one lives then becomes a matter of "life-style." The elevation of the words "life-style" to their present prominence is an indication of total loss of any serious meaning in one's choice of how to live. What used to be man's most profound ethical concern has been reduced to an element of fashion. The choice of homosexuality or family life becomes equally "valid" in this denatured context. If the concept of an intelligilble common good is denied, so are the moral grounds for social approval or disapproval of personal behavior. With each person a law unto himself, political community becomes impossible. (In another, very literal way, political community is impossible for homosexuals. Aristotle begins his *Politics* with the first condition for the existence of a polis—a man and a woman in the family. As to what sort of citizen a homosexual would make, try to imagine a polis composed only of homosexuals. Like the Shakers, such a community would have to rely for its continued existence on recruitment alone.)

And here we finally arrive upon the supreme irony which makes the homosexual's appeal to gay "rights" so grotesque. Our rights reside in and derive from the "Laws of Nature and of Nature's God," to which the Declaration of Independence refers for our justification as a new nation. Yet the proponents of homosexuality are supporting a cause which can succeed only by obliterating that very understanding of "Nature" upon which our existence as a free people depends. The moral view from which their vindication of homosexuality emanates is one which ultimately makes impossible the very conception of rights. Their appeal to rights subverts the rights to which they appeal. Yet it would be wrong to assign the major share of blame for this to the homosexual apologists. Homosexuality is simply the latest in a series of causes célèbres which are the logical consequences of the loss of objective reality, a loss that is transforming the right to life into death (abortion), liberty into license, and the pursuit of happiness into hedonism.

It should be emphasized that this critique of homosexuality is not an attack on homosexuals. This would, of course, be hard to believe for anyone who has collapsed the distinction between the nature of an act and the person performing the act. It is this vital distinction which allows one to judge the act, not the person. (It is also this distinction which removes any moral onus from a person whose homosexuality or, say, alcoholism, is no fault of his own. But a genetic condition of homosexuality or alcoholism does not deprive a person of his free will, so the person is still morally responsible for homosexual acts or drunkenness. Of course, if one has no free will (which is suggested by those who declare sexual restraint or abstinence to be impossible), then any notion of morality becomes absurd.) Who but an omniscient God could finally judge the adulterer, or murderer, or sodomist as to the true condition of his soul?

But this in no way means that man cannot come to an understanding of the moral nature of an act, that he cannot know that adultery, murder, and sodomy are great evils.

Nor is this argument against homosexuality meant to suggest that homosexuals should have anything but the full exercise of their civil rights, as should any other citizen. Rights, since their source is Nature, are, after all, universal by definition. It is the espousal of fictitious and self-contradictory "gay rights" that must be opposed because it elevates homosexuality to, and advances it on, the level of moral principle. This claim threatens the health of the whole community, not because it would mean a wholesale defection to the ranks of the homosexuals, but because the teaching itself is pernicious and will affect and form the attitudes of the body politic in other matters as well.

Each distinction we erase makes it harder for us to see or make other distinctions. The ability to discriminate is, of course, essential to the ability to choose. If we lose it, the change in our own character cannot help but profoundly change the character of our government. And what sort of government do you suppose it would be?

Notes

1. Francis Canavan, "The Dilemma of Liberal Pluralism," *The Human Life Review*, vol. V, no. 3, summer, 1979.

2. Germain Grisez, "Moral Systems: The New and the Old," *Faith and Reason*, vol. III, no. 4, winter, 1977. p. 65.

3. As quoted by John F. Harvey, "Human Sexuality and the Homosexual: A Critique," *Faith and Reason*, vol. IV, no. 3, fall, 1978, p. 28.

4. William May,"Male and Female: The Sexual Significance," *Proceedings*, First Convention of the Fellowship of Catholic Scholars, April 1978, p. 64.

5. Michael Novak, "Men Without Women," *The American Spectator*, vol. XI, no. 10, October 1978, p. 16.

6. Andre Guindon, *The Sexual Language* (University of Ottawa Press, 1976), p. 339.

7. Samuel McCracken, "Are Homosexuals Gay?" *Commentary*, vol. LXVII, no. 1, January 1979, p. 27.

8. Burton M. Leiser, Liberty, Justice, and Morals (Macmillan, 197?), p. 51.

9. Ibid.

10. Ibid.

11. Ibid., p. 52.

12. Ibid.

13. Ibid.

14. Ibid., p. 53.

544

The "Gay Pride" March: Not Just Another Parade

Dr. Timothy A. Mitchell

The homosexual movement is multifacetic. This article presents a classic confrontation between the forces of traditional faith and "liberated" homosexuals. It has been reproduced with the permission of the *Wanderer*, a Catholic publication in St. Paul, Minnesota, where it appeared originally on August 6, 1981.

NEW YORK—Commemorating the anniversary of the resistance to a police raid at the Stonewall Inn in 1969 and proclaiming a liberated "gay" lifestyle, an estimated 50,000 homosexuals marched up Fifth Avenue in New York City on June 28th. It was, in the view of Judy Pomerantz, writing in a Greenwich Village weekly, the *Villager,* a "glorious celebration, reflecting the struggle to understand ourselves, to be understood and respected, and to formulate a society of people-loving-people."

There were different emphases afoot, according to Miss Pomerantz. For behind "the broad lavender banner, lesbians and feminists chanted for power and . . . were trying to communicate issues of broader concern" while the men, "some felt, were here to parade their liberated sexuality only." But as a number of reports and eyewitness accounts indicate, both a "liberated sexuality" and some "issues of broader concern" (though not the ones Miss Pomerantz had in mind) were in grand abundance.

A liberated sexuality was in evidence for all to see. The advance guard of the parade was a thin man with a powdered face, wearing a full ankle-length dress and bonnet, who came skating up the street and proceeded to perform a series of vulgar gyrations while facing St. Patrick's Cathedral.

In front of the cathedral, several persons handed out leaflets extolling pedophilia while a group called NAMBLA (the North American Man-Boy Love Association) marched in back of a sign reading "Man-Boy Love is Beautiful." Many of the men walked arm in arm with boys, and one spectator spotted a couple of young lads dressed only in bathing suits.

But the men were not alone. Marching along with them was a contingent of homosexual women, carrying a cloth banner nearly the width of the street which read: "Lesbian Chicken Lovers." Behind the banner was a tot about five or six holding a sign with this message: "Chicken-Dyke."

On the other end of the spectrum were representatives from SAGE, a senior citizens group, who passed St. Patrick's chanting, "Two, four, six, eight—how do you know your grandma's straight?" And Judy Pomerantz informs us that on one "corner stood an elderly woman carrying a placard 'Grandmas for Gays.'"

Most bystanders, however, as Dudley Clendinen of the *New York Times* reported, "watched in silence and reserved judgment." But, he added, the "sight of some of the signs and some of the groups—some, for instance, with leather and chains—stopped East Side joggers in their tracks and drew one woman in a pink bonnet and mesh pink gloves to wag a finger: 'It's in the Army, for you guys. They'll knock the devil out of you!'"

And as "some elderly women in the park watched a stream of shirtless young men in shorts pass," one of them, Clendinen noted, said: "I just can't believe it. So many naked people. I'm surprised that they allow it." Another bystander, meanwhile, claimed that when the "parade ended in Central Park . . . many of the participants engaged in public sex acts."

THE GRAND MARSHAL
So much for the "liberated sexuality" and "the pride and happiness of being gay—and being Out," about which Miss Pomerantz wrote. There were, as she noted (although in a different context and not among women alone), "issues of broader concern."

These issues have again taken on the ugly overtones of being antireligion, anti-Catholic, and anti-God. Their focal point once more was St. Patrick's Cathedral, as a number of participants, perhaps encouraged by the skating gyrator and the "gay grand marshal," had their day as they marched by the most prominent Catholic church in New York City.

After the gyrating skater made his mocking gestures, the grand marshal appeared in a huge black limousine and sought to place a bouquet of

The "Gay Pride" March

flowers at the main door of the cathedral which, if successful, would have made St. Patrick's a part of the proceedings. He did not succeed because Andy McCauley, an attorney who has run for the State Assembly, several judgeships, and district attorney for Manhattan, stepped in and took the flowers from him. A melee followed and the police had to lead McCauley away.

Later, members of a "Catholic" homosexual group identified as Dignity approached the entrance of the cathedral to light a candle, again implicating the Church in the proceedings and again McCauley intervened and was led away. According to the *New York Times*, a "chorus of cheers went up from the cluster of homosexual Catholic groups massed in front of St. Patrick's as the New York City Gay Men's Choir passed . . . 150 voices strong, singing, 'I'll make a brand new start of it in old New York. If I can make it there, I'll make it anywhere.' "

Afterward, some of the marchers moved the police barricades from the sidewalk up to the steps leading to the cathedral. Herb McKay, a captain in the fire department and the father of seven children, said, "they have no right to do that." The marchers then began to drape a long black banner over the barricades. At that point, McKay, a member of the Knights of Columbus, removed it so as not to allow St. Patrick's Cathedral to be made into a reviewing stand. A part of the crowd around the cathedral, apparently forgetting about formulating "a society of people-loving-people," reacted feverishly—grabbing McKay and tearing the jacket from his back. The police had to escort him to the relative safety of the paddy wagon.

DESECRATION
The parade went on, the scene of a series of deeply offensive incidents. For example, the Gay Socialists came by carrying red banners and shouting what one bystander described as "their hatred of the Church and religion." The Gay Militant Atheists stopped while passing the cathedral and frantically chanted: "Smash the state, smash the Church, death to the Church." One person carried a picture of Adolph Hitler with the caption: "Adolph Hitler a Catholic leader," while a man dressed as a nun holding a cross upside down danced as he passed St. Patrick's, and another sarcastically asked "Pope John Paul, are you gay?" as his fellow paraders sang: "Two, four, six, eight, how do you know the Pope is straight?" One newspaper woman, hearing the latter sentiment, shook her head and recalled this taunting ditty leveled at the Cardinal of New York two years ago: "Cardinal Cooke, Cardinal Cooke, where are you, where are you? Hiding in your closet, hiding in your closet. Shame on you, shame on you."

Nor was that all. One collection of marchers, nearing the cathedral, was clearly heard by several witnesses to yell, "burn it down, burn it down," while others held a sign which succinctly spelled out what one viewer told this reporter he thought was the purpose of the parade: "Put the Holy Ghost in the closet." Still others, standing on the steps of the cathedral, hoisted placards that read: "Ignorance and Immorality Taught Here"; "Cardinal Cooke, Take a Look"; "Tax Churches"; and "No Subsidies for Oppressors."

When it was all over, St. Patrick's Cathedral, as the nondenominational Council for Community Consciousness, Inc., pointed out, was "desecrated—literally ablaze with signs and banners; including 'God is Gay.'" The "gay flag," replete with lavender stripes and fifty sex symbols, had hung from its portals, and leaflets proclaiming that the love about which Christ preached includes homosexual love were strewn on its steps.

Thus ended what one observer termed "Gay Desecration Day." That night the television coverage, which as a policy presents both sides of such events, virtually ignored these insults and blasphemies even though they were dramatic and newsworthy. As a result, viewers of the nightly news saw mostly pictures of ordinary marching bands similar to a memorial parade, with but a glimpse, on one channel, of two men hugging affectionately.

Yet the brazenness of those who congregated about St. Patrick's made the Gay Pride Parade neither "gay" nor something to be proud of. Just two-and-a-half weeks after flyers advocating man-boy love had been distributed around the cathedral, four men were arrested in what the *New York Post* referred to as the cracking of a "nationwide ring which promotes sex between men and boys," which involved a "score of eight-to-15-year-old boys, mostly from New Jersey."

The cathedral, thus, was not only desecrated but had become, as it were, a drop-off point for literature promoting acts that are unlawful. And this, as one press assistant who is Jewish noted, is both appalling and an attack upon biblical values. And here is a thought worth pondering.

St. Patrick's, like every such edifice in Christendom, is a monumental biblical message carved in stone; and it is a message that is diametrically opposed to the "gay" lifestyle that was being celebrated. The "celebrators" know this. And for this reason, their blasphemies should be seen for what they are and not minimized as the silly antics of some frustrated "alternative lifestylers" suffering from an edifice complex.

APPENDIX

IV

Communication

Communication is an underground publication that circulates among certain homosexual priests and nuns of the Roman Catholic Church. It is *not* a publication approved by the Church. As it is secretive by its very nature, it is impossible to know whether Church authorities are aware of its existence.

Vol 4
Number 6

252 S. 12th St.
Phila. Pa. 19107

MMUNICATION

A dialog on the relationship between personal sexuality and ministry
for the purpose of building community among gay clergy and religious.

Hello,

    Here we are again. In a few short weeks the drama and passion
of Good Friday, and the splendor and the hope of Easter will reveal
again the cost and rewards of discipleship. We find parallels in
our own life th the pain, the loneliness, the powerlessness of Jesus.
Good Friday is a terrible, intense day; but not one without hope.
Just around the corner is a day of liberation and freedom. Good
Friday takes a lot out of you; but the promise of Easter is to restore
what you have lost, a hundredfold. But what happens in the meantime.
What happens on Holy Saturday? "What happens when the last vestige of
energy is spent in facing one's own particular passion? Is there
nothing left but a peculiar silence of spirit; we are entombed like
Jesus, feeling no pain, hunger, passion or joy. Perhaps those of us
who are more "activist" can end up feeling this way for a time. (althoug
the feeling of "burn-out certainly can happen in any aspect of our
particular ministry.)

    I don't know of any answers to these questions, but thinking about
them made me wonder about what must have happened to the community of
believers that had gathered around Jesus on the first " oly Saturday".
What were their thoughts and feelings about the day before? About the
future? If the leadership of their charismatic rabbi had been abruptly
removed, how would they function. Maybe Easter really began on Saturday
for thᵃt community as they began to resurrect themselves as leaders and
teachers. We don't really know. History and the Gospels are silent
on this point. Sometimes it seems that the most interesting and importa
things aren't mentioned. Maybe they are too mundane or insignificant.
But human lives are filled with seemingly insignificant things and
events that shape and influence the "big events".

    We as gay persons have also been entombed in silence. Until
recently our stories could not be told , sometimes not even to ourselves. Our own unique meaning, our own unique Passion and Resurrection
could not be shared. This silence did not mean that we were dead or
not present; only that there weren't words enough to speak our experience
or if there were, there was no one there to record them.

    One priest from the East Coast speaks of his experience, and we
record it here for you.

550

Communication

I've just returned from the woods where I've been reading
Teresa of Avila's life. It makes me long for closer union
with God, realizing how much a beginner I am in prayer. But
questions arise. Teresa is a contemplative nun; I am not
She lived in the 16th century. I am a man of the 20th
century, with all its global awareness and responsibility.
I feel called to help develop a spirituality which is able
to be embraced by laity as well as religious; one which will
see the holiness of the earth, marriage and history. Teresa's
way. attractive and challenging as it is (along with Augustine
and Ignatius) seems to see married life as second best, a
distraction from God.

But where did I learn to pray or thirst for God (or Justice
for that matter)? I did not pop out of a rock, or parachute
to earth from on high. My parents taught me my faith.
Their example made me look to Christ as a Leader. Two of
the clearest examples of prayer I have are from them--one
from my mother, the other from my dad. I remember sitting
next to my mother at daily Mass as a schoolboy. She was
usually pregnant. I vividly recall one morning looking
at the priest with her, him elevating the host for adoration.
Just as the bells were about to ring to signify God's presence
among us, I heard a sound come from within my mother--a baby's
cry To this day I cannot forget that, nor what it tells
me about God and holiness.

> As I began to work in my father's restaurant, I would
> get up early with him--5 am some mornings--though I
> usually tried to sleep in until the last minute. When
> I came down into the darkened living room, my father
> was always sitting in a chair in the corner. "Daddy
> why don't you sleep a little longer?" I'd ask. I don't
> remember what he said, but I thought even then that
> it was probably the one time during the day he got to
> be alone. Was he praying? I don't know. But some
> times when I just sit now, I think of him. Maybe
> that is especially when God can speak to us.

These moment, this life, I learned from my parents. They
certainly had their faults, as I have mine. But can their
holiness, their way of marriage and family be any less pleasing
to God than mine? I can't believe that.

> And what of gay people of whom I am one. Must we
> all be religious in order to really please God. What way
> of holiness can there be for us as well as celibate
> religious life? I do not know. There are so few
> examples because so many prayerful gay people are
> hidden, closeted in a society and church that would
> have us not exist. Can we ask God for guidance on this.
> Can we ask God to show us a way to express our sexuality

in a way that is holy, a way that calls us to sacrifice as our parents had to for us? Only in some self-
transcending way, it seems, will gay people's sexual
expression be a way to union with God. Children almost
force parents to a self-transcending relationship. What
will force ours?

All of this I ask as a person who has experienced same-sex sexual
expression and found it to be beautiful--even holy--in some of
my relationships. But now the Lord calls me to celibacy, to
make myself like Him, a eunuch. I only beg Him--If this life
of mine is holy and prayerful now--to make the sexual expression
of my gay brothers and sisters equally holy, to show us the
way it can be so--if it be His Will.

Coming as this letter does in the Springtime, it does bring
to mind all sorts of thoughts about young things. This priest's
question about transcendence and children is a challenging one to us.
But at least one answer is close at hand for us. Just because
we have not brought children into the world physically, does that
mean that we have none. We think of parenting too often as the
exclusive perogative of biological parents. Although many of us
work with children as teachers or counselors, its sometimes difficult
to speak the words gay and children in the same breath. The straight
world has too many sick and perverted images of us in regard to
children. But many of us can remember our own youth, the feeling that
we were different, not like the others. I can remember the hidden
playtime explorations with my girlfriends. I knew even then that
this was something to confess. I knew I never would. Even before
I had a name for "it". We do have children. They are gay or are
at least dealing with gay feelings. They do not for the most part
have role models to show them how to grow up to be ethically responsible, "self-transcending" gay persons. Their heterosexual peers
need those role models too, so that they can grow up as free and
loving human beings too.

I don't pretend to know a lot about Youth Ministry, but
certainly a lot of you out there do. If you have had any sucess
in developing programs or approaches to young gay people please
feel free to share. There is one social service program here in
Philadelphia which is starting to respond to the need of gay, lesbian
and sexual minority adolescents. Anyone interested in this pilot
program should contact The Eromin Center, 1735 Naudain St. Phila. Pa.
19146. Also, Bro. Bill Roberts has a couple articles on gay youth
and counseling, which can be obtained by writing him at 323 E. 61st
Street, NY. NY. 10021.

Before we close out this issue we have a few reminders of
upcoming events, as well as some requests from some of our readers.

Communication

4

**Remember the New Ways Ministry retreat for lesbian religious May 29-31, in the Baltimore-Washington area. The cost is $50. By the way, if you are wondering what to do with all that money you saved during Lent (cf. our last issue) by giving up chocolate bars, New Ways is in need of financial assistance to continue their work. Contact New Ways Ministry 4012 29th St Mt. Ranier Md.

** Speaking of Financial support, thank you again for the support you've given us. I will have a financial report in the next issue.

** We got a great letter from someone in Houston with a whole long list of names. Welcome Houston. Keep it up. You've got your own local network going there.

** Don't forget the Dignity Covention. Details are in the back of this issue. We will be there. We hope you will be too.

**Anyone who wishes to communicate with a priest from South Dakota, (preferably someone in South Dakota) send a letter in care of Communication. Mark the outside of the envelope <u>Attention: South Dakota</u>. and we will forward.

We have a couple of short letters to share with you before we close out this issue. The first is from Rev. Richard Wagner, who as we mentioned in the last issue has come under fire for his dissertation on gay priests.

> I guess that I have known all along that something like this would happen. I must say however, I was a little unprepared for the ugliness. Churchmen, not the laity have been the most abusive. Dishonesty and fear rule.
>
> The reason I write to you is to let you know that my dissertation has been published as a monograph and is available in a limited edition, to those interested. This was the easiest and quickest way to have it disseminated in light of the fact that the Church has made a number of attempts to suppress it. If you think your readership would be interested, they can receive a copy by sending $10.95 to
> Specific Press
> 1523 Franklin St.
> San Francisco CA 94109 (make checks payable to Specific Press)

5

We also rec ived a letter from a priest in Ireland who has had some severe health problems followed by some difficulties with depression. He describes his session with a psychiatrist.

In the session with the psychiatrist I was attending, the question of celibacy came up. I said that I was celibate anu gay. I never thought I would hear the proposal that was put to me, "Would you ever consider aversion therapy?" No way would I consider such treatment. I am happy being gay but feel so isolated and alone here in a religious community in Ireland.

Tonight I thought I would write to you and ask your prayers. I feel I have brothers and sisters who understand, and this thought gives me strength and courage.

With that thought we take our leave of you. We hope that this season of renewal and liberation gives you strength and courage. We leave you with a gift of poetry for Easter. (Please don't forget to check out the convention details on the back of this issue)

What are you calling forth from within me
My clowning around hero?
The Messianic secret, the scholars call it
Might be more properly called
"God in the closet?"

Like some uptight but none-the-less loveable
Religious men I've known,
You found it necessary to hide
Who you were,
You ran
From those who wanted to crown you king
(or Queen)
Because the timing would have been all wrong.
What would your mother say?
Not that you were ashamed of being God;
Its just that you weren't sure she could handle it
It was love that kept you closeted.
I bet you were also scared like me.
So you stuck to the message.
Excited words about a kindgom
You figured that would be safe.
After all who could be against love
and peace and healing
And chasing daemons out of nice people?
You could always talk about those things
And nobody would see through your mask.
How could they see
The heart of God
In a simple message
Like that?

But,
It was when the message challenged folks
That your cover was blown,
That you got dragged out of the closet
That they saw you for who you were:
A changer of hearts,
A lover of the oppressed,
A breaker of bread,
A rriddle maker:
What dies and then rises?
What size must your faith be to move a mountain?
What makes the first last and the last first?
Give up?
The answers are in me,
And to get them,
You've got to get me first.

And so they did.
And your hang-ups were hung up
For all of Jerusalem (city of Peace) to see.

And even your mother found out.
And she was able to handle it.

Hookers and thieves and
Those who sold out to the oppressors--
Your friends--
Beheld your secret.
And began to shed <u>their</u> masks.

VOL. 3, NO. 5
FEBRUARY
1980

252 S. 12 ST.
PHILA., PA.
19107

MMUNICATION

A dialog on the relationship between personal sexuality and ministry for the purpose of building community among gay clergy and religious.

Hello Everybody,

Happy February! Please skip the next few pages until you have an hour or two of solitude. When Brother Paul asked me to edit the article on masturbation the first thing that ran through my head was the comment one Sister made-- "Masturbation?...Why it's part of the bath!" Sooo...empty your head of all concerns, worries, struggles and goals. Pour yourself a glass of wine, put on some soft music. Now step into a warm bath filled with bubbles or baby oil. Ahhh! Now read on with a Brother from the East Coast:

In the years before I came out, masturbation was my only sexual outlet. After reading Don Goergen's book (Sexual Celibate) and examining my own masturbatory behaviour, I came to see it as a substitute for my need to be touched affectionately. Being Italian I tend to be a very tactile person and really thrive on touching and being touched. Since I was very much deprived of physical affection--particularly from men, masturbation became the way in which I stayed in touch with my body, my fantasies and my sexuality. When I finally accepted my gayness and began to be sexually involved with others, I have noticed a sharp decrease in masturbatory behaviour. I much more prefer making love to another man than doing a "solo flight". I have noticed too, that during the times in my life when I was involved in a secure friendship which provided me with my recommended minimum daily requirement of hugging, carressing, massage, etc., that my genital needs tended to decrease. So I would have to vote for the side of the argument which would say that masturbation can be a positive contribution to one's psycho-sexual health providing it is a way of remaining sensual/ sensuous, and of keeping in touch with the beauty of the human body. It is also a much better tranquilizer or sleeping pill than any of the chemical substitutes. Well brothers and sisters in the very Incarnate Christ, thanks for giving me another opportunity to share my story.

ed. note: Those tactile non-Italians who feel compelled to respond to this letter please note that we will not feel obliged to print any defense of Irish, Welsh, Chinese, Black, German et al. sensuality!

This man raises several good points for discussion. One of these points relates to masturbation as a substitute. Some of my own ethical questions around masturbation concerns this issue. Is it a practice which allows me to maintain my singleness or is it a substitute for relationships with other people (whether sexual or otherwise)?

Communication

A Brother from New York relates the following story:

> I had an astonishing conversation with another Brother today
> which says something about celibacy and our lifestyle. We
> were talking about religious and clerics who got involved
> with other people. He said that he would much rather that
> they drank, gambled or did a solitary vice rather than get
> involved with another person because it is wrong to involve
> another person in sin. I asked him: "Isn't there some
> chance that involving yourself with another person may
> assist you to grow as a human being?" He did not think this
> was any excuse. He would rather see non-human involvement.
> He made these solitary options for pleasure look like mastur-
> bation although this would be anathema to him since it is
> sexual.

Here we seem to have a preference for solitary pleasure (and vice!)
in every other situation than the sexual. I wonder what makes solitary
sexual pleasure so awful when solitary gambling or drinking is not? And does
this force us into the r diculous position of looking upon the seduction of
a friend into a hot fudge sundae 'trick' in the same moralizing ways we do
about sexual pleasure? The concern for the other person's holiness here seems
to be a deceptive mask for the Thomas a Kempis fear thet we--holy as we are by
ourselves!--will be debauched every time we go out among men! God save us!

A priest from Virginia shares his thoughts:

> One thing about masturbation--you don't have to look your best!
> The quote is from Boys In The Band. Perhaps it is a fitting
> start. Masturbation is something one does by himself (or herself).
> At least that's how I view it. Mutual masturbation, I feel,
> is or can be the act of making love to or with someone else.
> Can masturbation be making love to yourself?

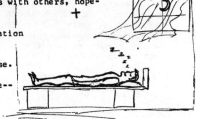

> I generally tend to shy away from doing things by myself.
> Life and its many beautiful activities are so much more
> interesting and better when shared with someone else. This
> includes sex. So in general I do things with others, hope-
> fully others I really love.

> All this comes from a stance of masturbation
> as a non-sinful act. I don't have tons
> of guilt when I engage in masturbation.
> Many times I feel great peace and release.
> But I don't fantasize on myself. When
> I'm masturbating I'm always with someone--
> at least in my mind. It sometimes is a
> sign that I miss someone very much and
> yearn to have sex with him.

> I also feel it can be a sign of frustration. Things are not
> going well in one's life. I know when I'm frustrated I tend
> to masturbate. When I'm joy-filled I never do. Often when
> I masturbate I ask myself, "Hey, what's eating you?" "What
> is wrong in my life? Who am I missing? Why am I doing this?"
> In this regard masturbation is a good and healthy sign to get
> your act together. Life can and should be more than what you
> are going through experiencing.

-3-

A Brother from New England joins the conversation:

Why is it that whenever I do masturbate I have guilty
feelings, at my age of thirty? Also, to have wet dreams
at a certain age...I find that when I have wet dreams
it is because I haven't masturbated in awhile. The reason
why I masturbate are times when I am lonely for companionship,
for someone my age or a gay religious, or that I'm down in
the dumps, discouraged from a failure. I do fantasize a lot
about other peoples' penises and bodies of friends and looking
at gay porno magazines. But I find myself in this rut
because I'm lacking in my spiritual life as a religious.
How does one overcome this masturbation problem or is it a
natural thing for gay religious? Please help.

At an institute for American Catholic Church leaders sponsored by the
House of Affirmation in New England this past month, the following ideas
were offered on the subject of masturbation: Infants masturbate to get their
genitals to work; it is necessary, same as oral stimulation. A non-masturbation
may be more pathological than masturbation. The disturbed adolescent does not
masturbate. Fantasy is the key which directs libido outward from oneself.
Normally then, this fantasy is replayed in relations with others beyond masturbation.
Thus masturbation is a normal activity. The question we rather need to ask is:
Is it compulsive? Masturbation puts a pattern, an 'engram' on the brain. This
pattern/engram develops a habit which has to be searched into its meaning.
What motivates it? What alternative engrams can we place on the brain if in
fact it is compulsive for us? Genital expression of any sort is a vehicle for
expressing many emotions; it is not just for reproduction. It may signify a
receiving and giving of affection/intimacy, though not necessarily achieving it.
It may be our way of demonstrating our adequacy as a male or female. It can be
an expression of aggressive emotions too. At the root of most sexual problematics
is that often it is an expression of aggression rather than affection...
FUCK YOU, as they say!

Is masturbation a problem then, a sign of frustration, or an indication of
psycho-sexual health? It can be all of these things of course, sometimes all of
these simultaneously. It may be important for us to know and discern that there
are many levels of motivation that can be influencing the same action. We have
one last comment on this from a reader in the Midwest. (Thank God the East isn't
alone in its horniness!)

The topic of masturbation...oh dear!
I haven't done much reading on the "theory",
but my "clinical" experience is widespread
(so to speak) and varied!! I don't see it as
the ideal but I see no reason for guilt.
Maybe if you say "I enjoy it and the fantasies
associated with it" you are healthy. You
certainly are open to your sexual feelings and needs.

This past Summer a PH. D. candidate in Sociology visited us as
a vocational prospect. His dissertation topic was on an area of
gay sexuality. His remark to me was that he felt that gay
celibates are especially to be open to the "richness" of fantasy
life that can accompany masturbation. He felt it to be developed

Communication

as your own personal technique. Well, I wouldn't want to push
that to egotism or eccentric limits so much that a person becomes
isolated from others. No one can live in just a fantasy island,
despite what T.V. says! But fantasy is a very real and a rich
part of human life.

I would invite someone much more educated in Theology and
Psychology to speak to this topic from what, for instance,
Thomas Aquinas said about 'phantoms' or fantasies of the
imaginative faculty of the mind. In other words, I remember
being raised in the Catholic system that prepared one for
Penance by calling to mind any enjoyment in "illicit sexual
thoughts/desires" as part of the Laundry List of sins! What
are we saying about this today? My guess is that psychologists
insist how "natural" a part of life fantasies, and sexual ones
at that, really are! What is sin? What is O.K.?

Enough! I think I've brought home my main point. Masturbation
as a human reality has to be considered a normal and natural
activity not to be done in a void of love of God and neighbor.
If it keeps one self-centered, not loving, then it is not O.K.
But if one loves God, loves self and others and appreciates his
"naturalness" (and always puts his envelopes in the collection
each and every Sunday..."a good Catholic!"), then keep it up.
This side of heaven, and especially for us celibates, masturbation
is about the only (imperfect) form of sexual outlet.

Is this true? Is masturbation normal for others but still somehow
imperfect for celibates in the most traditional sense of the word? We'll
close with a small anecdote by way of one of our priests in the Southwest.
One day upon arising, his local pastor was stricken with severe pains in the
groin area, causing him to double up in the foetal position on the floor.
His curate managed to get him into a car and take him to the emergency ward of
the local hospital, pajamas and all. Somehow after examining him, the doctor
screwed up his face and asked him: "Father, do you ever masturbate?" "No",
said the embarrassed pastor, gritting his teeth. The reply: "You are suffering
from semen back-up! My God, Father, you have to exercise that thing once in
awhile!" We have no idea if this is apocryphal, but it sure lightens the topic!

---------- ----------- ------------

That's enough of masturbation for now. Time to move onto another topic.
We would like to share with you a synopsis of our winter gathering in New Jersey.
Twelve of us gathered for three days after Christmas at a private secluded house
by the shore. All of us were men--a few brothers, a few priests, both diocesan
and religious, and a deacon. All of the cooking was done by the retreatants.
The total cost was $35.00 due to the availability of the house for a very low fee,
the fact that two of us did the facilitation and a third person planned the menus,
bought the food and coordinated the food preparation. We preceded this gathering
with mail-outs of three short articles on aspects of celibacy, morality and politics
in the gay movement.

I will try to be brief in sharing an overview of what we did but feel this
will be helpful to any of you wishing to have a gathering of your own. The "three
days" were divided into an evening arrival where we simply had a meal and provided
some "icebreaker" introduction exercises followed by some prayer around a fire
where we mentioned some of our hopes for our time together.

The next two full days were divided more or less along the following lines:
<u>First Day</u>--a look at the 'public' struggles of gay priests and religious, especially
focusing on those of seminarians coming up through the gauntlet. A set of sociodramas
that illustrated some of the problem situations we may find ourselves in (cf. below).
Later that day we envisioned alternatives, how we might form some kind of 'gay
religious space', i.e. a gay religious household?, a gay religious and priests
organization?, a guideline for vocation directors in regard to gay candidates?
Liturgy was held before dinner with a predetermined theme. We finished the
evening with refreshments and games.

    <u>Second Day</u>--we took a look at the personal relationship struggles of gay
religious and priests. An exercise was done whereby we looked at how we approach
risk and its two possible outcomes, relationship or rejection. Then we divided
into three groups to discuss this--those among us who are in a lover relationship
or looking for one, those among us who are trying to live a traditional celibate
life, and those among us who are not looking for a lover but who are open to genital
relationships on a more casual basis. Later on in the day we dramatized the
advantages and problems of each approach, talked about how each of these three
approaches to being a gay priest or religious got reinforced, and what was needed
beyond that. We also discussed what problems might exist <u>between</u> these different
approaches to the celibacy expectation. This day was finished with a liturgy of
healing where we anointed each other with oil on the forehead or hands and
proceeded into a Eucharist set in the midst of our evening meal (cf. last month).

    The morning before we departed we discussed where we would go from here--
what next? Also, an evaluation and sharing of the highs and lows of our time
together, and a closing liturgy. There was not much time for privacy as you can
see. Nor even for a special emphasis on prayer. That was not the style of this
particular gathering. However, it was surely prayerful both in formal prayer
times and even woven through our whole encounter with one another as you will
sense from the following letters from a few of the participants:

    Dear Paul, I can hardly believe that it has been
a week since the gathering of the brothers in Ocean City.
There was so much that I wanted to say that Saturday
morning when you asked did everyone have anything to say.
But being an emotional (very) person, I just felt that
the mental exhaustion was too much and I would start crying again. But I did
feel that something should have been said about Friday morning. I suppose that
being with the brothers was the best thing that could have happened to me at
that time. This situation (his recent break-up with a lover) had been ignored
since September in a large effort to forget so much. But the realization came
the morning we were speaking about relationships and risks. Sure there was
support from friends, but the hope that maybe it was not so, or just a bad
dream and I would wake up soon, was always present. Being alone and having to
face it, and yet knowing there was strong support downstairs, just took me one
step further. The realization that this relationship was over and I did not hate
anyone, I was not angry with anyone, especially myself...knowing that God had
brought me to a place where help and support was so available, that this was not
the end of the world...that it was a risk I took, that even He took a risk and
it turned out to be a crucifixion...But the greater risk was the Resurrection...

    Maybe I am getting older and a little wiser. That morning I tried to look
at the positive side of this relationship. Would I ever have known tenderness,
compassion, the warmth of arms around me on a cold night, the voice that said:
"Don't be afraid, I'm here.", or "You have to get up, you have your obligations

Communication

-6-

and duties at the church"...or even words that said I love you? How many gay
religious and clergy go all their lives not even hearing them, not knowing how
to seek them? How many had friends come to their room and comfort them and hold
them as you, Bob and Bill held me?

So we have come away with the realization that
Our Father does love us and is good to us, his
special sons and daughters. I wanted to say so
many things...Bob said, "You know you had us all
for support." The patience, the understanding
are an important part of our group. I knew that
this was the time and the place to look at the end of a relationship, my first
relationship and a very important one to me. The charismatics have a saying--
"Lord, make him whole!" I want you to know that is how I felt when I left
Saturday morning. I felt whole and good about all that happened to me in the
past four months. Each of you has become an important part of my life, I
remember you in my daily prayers...With the deepest affection and regards...

Another participant writes:

> I'm sure somewhere there were more dramatic comferences given.
> On retreats of yore there were more bodies, more food, more
> drinking...But I've never felt the closeness, the drawing
> together, the real listening, the real love that quietly
> flooded in, unnoticed at first but felt with such power that
> I treasure the feeling, the reality still. Yes I was loved,
> forgiven, listened to, affirmed. And I experienced the totally
> human feeling of doing the same to others. We received and
> we gave. Yes, there were twelve of us who came in from the
> cold, and together we became thirteen. We had Christ there
> with us. So to all who came, worked, laughed, cried and prayed...
> all I can say is thanks. And God, let's not let this die...
> let's do it again and again!

The last bit of information I wish to give you on our Winter gathering is
the following more detailed description of the sociodramas we staged on the first
morning. You will surely get a kick out of imagining how we threw ourselves into
these with gusto. This brief sketch may also provide an example for you to try
out with a group of yourselves (House Chapter?, Day of Recollection?, etc.!!!)

Sociodramas are short roleplays where we act out a situation we may encounter
in our real lives. The purpose of doing this, other than to get us interacting
in a playful way, is 1) to get us to reflect as a group on the problem that is
portrayed so that we may be better prepared for alternate solutions if and when
the problem actually comes upon us, and 2) to get us to share our feelings in
regard to the problem rather than to simply share ideas. Each of these take
approximately 30 minutes to do after you explain the basic concept of sociodrama--
5 min. to define the roles for a given exercise, 5 min. for the volunteers to get
set into their roles, 10 min (approx.) for the actual roleplay, 10 min. to debrief
the feelings and insights afterwards (participants first, spectators second). N.B.,
You "cut" the roleplay in midstream rather than playing it out to its last word.

Setting # 1--The scene is a religious order's annual screening meeting for
candidates to their novitiate. Three members of the screening board sit in chairs
behind a table as each candidate comes before them (individually, each as a separate sociodrama). The board members are the following: JACK, the Director of
Novices. He is gay himself, very closeted, and a subscriber to Communication.

561

BILL, the local house superior. He is heterosexual, involved in peace and justice work, open to trends, even verbally supportive of homosexual people, but expects traditional celibacy. BRUCE, the Vocation Director. He too is heterosexual, and frankly down on gays. He thinks they cause problems in seminaries and his policy to this date has been to screen them out.

The candidates that come before this board have all had psychological tests beforehand and have spoken to a psychiatrist employed by the order. No major problems appeared on these tests and they have been passed on by the psychiatrist to this second stage of the order's screening process. All of the candidates have some homosexual dimension to their lives, but only the first, Dennis, has anything explicit about this showing up on the papers before the screening board. The candidates are: 1) DENNIS--He is gay and proud of it. Has lots of gay experience in his 27 years, is butch-looking but not especially attractive. Dennis wants to be ordained so he can further the cause of gay rights in the Church. He intends to be celibate. 2) DAVID--Thinks he may be gay but has very little overt experience. David is a 22 year old college graduate who is somewhat effeminate, naive and innocent. He never mentions the gay side of himself to anyone. 3) JAY-- A very good looking 18 year old boy. He has had a lover for the past two years, a priest who lives nearby and taught him in high school. Enjoys this relationship tremendously but feels guilty about it and somewhat unsure of how this fits in with his goal of being a priest.

Setting # 2--The scene is a Midwestern chancery office. Three diocesan priests sit behind a table waiting to receive another priest, Tim, who is a member of their diocese and has been summoned by the chancellor. The three board members are the following: MONSIGNOR GEORGE--He is the chancellor, a 50 year old distinguished looking gay man. He is very closeted and deeply ashamed of his occasional encounters in book stores in nearby states. LARRY--A 65 year old heterosexual pastor who has had Tim as a curate for the last four years. Larry is an overweight, compassionate and instinctively pastoral man, but traditional in his values. PETER--A 37 year old pious, earnest, heterosexual classmate of Tim's who teaches Theology at the local seminary.

1) The priest who comes before them is TIM, a 36 year old self-confident and amiable priest of average looks. He is an excellent curate in the parish and has great rapport with the teen-agers there. His pastor, Larry, knows he is gay since Tim confided in him, and though they are good friends Larry never asks Tim any questions about his gay life. Tim is in a lover relationship with a parishioner for three years now and has never felt happier in his life. His lover has an excellent job and they spend two days a week off together in the privacy of his lover's fine home. They are very discreet. Tim comes before the board and is confronted for the first time with the challenge of his being homosexual and involved in a relationship. His accuser is his classmate who contacted the chancellor who in turn called in his pastor over this. No evidence is mentioned, though the classmate claims it is common knowledge among the seminarians and even a number of the parishioners and is beginning to cause a scandal. (Run through the ten minute roleplay on this and debrief it).

2) As a second step if you have time after the first, the group is told that after Tim is dismissed with an assurance that a judgment will be made on his situation by the three man board, he receives a call later that afternoon from the chancellor. He is informed kindly but firmly that he is being transferred to a parish 150 miles away starting next week..."for your own good!" Tim is so stunned that he cannot even reply properly, gets off the phone and calls a few of his priest friends who know the score about him. The participants are told that they are among this group of friends (do this in groups of three), and are meeting without him to discuss how they might support him given their real situation right now. How will your group respond to Tim's call for help? Share in these small groups for 20-30 min., then in larger group for a half hour.

Communication

Enclosed in this month's mailing is a press release from New Ways Ministry
in response to the New England bishops' recent letter on the discernment of vocations
to the ministerial priesthood. One section of this long letter from the bishops
which appears in full in the January 3, 1980 issue of <u>Origins</u> is quoted below:

> A man who seems unable to come to heterosexual maturity should
> not be admitted. Young men who are truly homosexuals should
> not be admitted. We recognize that there are various degrees
> of homosexuality and that generalizations cannot easily be made.
> We include in this statement anyone who, while not engaging in
> homosexual activity, is psychically homosexual and thereby
> unable to tolerate the demands of a celibate ministry or of
> rectory living.

Obviously we strongly disagree and are quite worried about the ramifications
of such a publicly stated policy of discrimination by some of the highest authorities in our Church. It betrays a faulty psychological basis as well as a
refusal to acknowledge the experience of many priests and religious to the contrary.
For the moment we feel that the New Ways Ministry response is the best synthesis
of our feelings on the matter and we gladly pass them on to you. (feel free to
use their single sheet in any way you wish) More on this in the next issue.

Exciting things are in the making for a number of retreats in different parts
of the country coordinated by some of you. Hopefully these will take place
sometime this May. We will pass the details on to you as soon as they become firm,
by next issue if all goes well.

Lastly (Dear Lord, will we ever have a six page issue again?), as an entree
to our next few themes, here is an excerpt from a recent letter:

> As I have been unconsciously (certainly not consciously!)
> open a bit more, fellow-brothers are coming to me more,
> and sharing parts of their lives. My personal disappointment
> in the dialogue in Communication is the failure to speak to
> this. There are two unspoken issues--community and support
> on the one hand, and the real values of celibacy on the other.
> Both, I feel, are left out of what has been talked of in the
> newsletter. That bothers me because I feel the importance
> of both. Of course, I didn't write in anything either, so I
> shouldn't complain! I am encountering, at least in (my religious
> community), a number of faithful, integrated, celibate gay men.
> Why don't more of our correspondents meet them also? I
> suspect that there are many kinds of gay space, and the "actives"
> don't dialogue with those who are continent. My community is
> very good space for being gay and a religious.

With this priest's questions in mind, we propose the following themes for
our next few issues:

COMMUNITY AND SUPPORT AMONG GAY CLERGY AND RELIGIOUS

POSITIVE REASONS FOR (AND EXPERIENCE OF) CELIBACY

n.b. We will continue the masturbation dialogue as well...

Until March then dear brother and sister in the gay side of Christ, remember.
"You are from the earth and you shall return to the earth." So this Lent, why
not get back in touch with the earth?--grow a plant, start a compost heap, take
a walk in the woods...stand tall in Our Lord who is always with us. Love in Him,

Volume 4
Number 1

October, 1980

252 S. 12ᵗʰ St.
Phila. Pa
19107

MMUNICATION

*A dialog on the relationship between personal sexuality and ministry
for the purpose of building community among gay clergy and religious.*

Hello, my brothers and sisters,

My name is Joe, your editor for October. I've been a bene-
ficiary of this newsletter from the beginning; it's about time
I did something in return. I get a big lift every time the
newsletter comes. I hope this issue will do the same for you.

The theme I would like to run through is the variety of ways
in which we clerical and religious gay people cope with the crazy
world we live in. We can't live on hope alone. There has to be
enough of love, satisfaction and fulfillment in our actual life
<u>now</u> to keep us sane and reasonably happy. Pie in the sky is not
enough. How else can we thank the Lord daily, sing and dance
in His presence, and help our Christian people to do the same?

The obvious fact is that we gay people live in a fairly
hostile world, in a fairly hostile country and in a fairly hostile
Church. Secrecy and masking is second nature to us.
We feel we have enemies all around us. (and we do)
Our neighbors, many of them, still believe all sorts
of bizarre things about us. And a good number are
ready to persecute us (in Bible-supported ways, of course) if they
find out about us.

So in the midst of this scorpion-infested gloomy desert, how
actually are we to manage? How do you squeeze enough out of the
present situation to keep yourself alive? Let's look at some ways
we have of coping and (even)keeping ourselves joyful with the life
God gives us.

COMING OUT PART-WAY

There is no doubt that a measure of "coming-out" does a
lot to relate us to the real world and make up happy. A fellow
religious once told me bluntly, "Your going to have to get out of
your box." It was the best advice he could have given me. Thank
God, for the last seven or eight years, I've ventured out of"my
box" in more and more ways. Such venturing out has chased away
most of my old fears and done me a world of good.

The thing to remember is that there are a hundred degrees of
"coming out" and that you should venture to do only that degree
that you're capable of. For some, that degree may be to march
down the street with a placard saying, GAY IS GOOD. For another

2

the degree of coming out may be to confide in a trusted friend.
For still another person, the step to take may be as simple and
decisive as admitting to yourself, in the quiet of your own heart,
"I am gay, and God made me so for His own good purposes. I thank
Him and I love myself, and my sexual leanings are OK. I'm going
to find God's grace in them.

MINISTRY TO OUR GAY BROTHERS AND SISTERS

One way of partially coming out to our families and religious
communities is to express an interest in gay civil rights and gay
ministry. This does not mean you have to say you're gay--in fact,
in most cases you won't want to make public statements about
your orientation. Just state your convictions about justice for
gay people,(and if you're up to it) let
your friends draw their own conclusions.
Of course this goes only for those of us
who are hardshelled, independent, and bold. Let him/her who can
do it, do it.

The umbrella of gay ministry works very well and you don't
have to feel guilty about using it. If you were or are, black.
wouldn't it be natural for you to minister to blacks? So why
shouldn't you minister to the huge TEN PERCENT or more out there
who need comfort, who are waiting for you to dry the tears from
their eyes as soon as you dry your own? As for criticism from
those around you, "Blessed are you when they shall revile you and
persecute you and speak all that is evil against you, untruly,
for my sake. Be glad and rejoice, for your reward is very great
in heaven." (Matt 5:11-12). At the same time you have no obliga
tion to go public about your private life and you will get a lot of
strength   out of ministering to gays and being with them.

A SUFFICIENT NUMBER OF STRAIGHT AND GAY FRIENDS

I am blessed with the friendship of two straight priests who
are like brothers to me. They also help me in my ministry to
gays. These two priests are my vital connection to the (majority)
straight world.   And you, are you, too, graced with a friend?--
a sister, a brother, a priest you can confide in?
                        Also crucial to survival, coping, and being happy
                        is a sufficient number of friends who are gay.
                        They are our brothers and sisters in a special way.
                        They are--(Are you willing to admit it?) mirrors
                        of ourselves. Their ways--cute, macho, androgynous
                        timid, colorful, gentle, stylish, physically
proud, artistic, paranoid, activist, or whatever--are what we are
when we are fully ourselves. Being with gay friends, holding their
hands, kissing them, embracing them,--above all, rapping with them
about our feelings--is a sharing of authentic life.

But now I'm thinking also of those of you who are hemmed in
by your convent, monastery, or rectory--those of you who can't

make any of the above moves. Can I sincerely recommend a severe
abnegation of your gay life? (I'm not speaking necessarily of an
active sexual life.) Yes, I think I can, as long as you accept
yourself completely, are happy in the celibate state, and have
some connection with the gay world, be it by correspondence,
magazines, visits to another area, or friends in your own locality--
in short, an understanding of yourself that will not thwart your
nature. If you have none of the above, I advise you to make a
change in your life--you have to survive, and you don't have to
apologize for trying to.

 I know a religious community of twenty men in which
half at least are gay. Unfortunately, most of these
men wouldn't admit their orientation to themselves.
They are psychologically stunted human beings, eccentric
alcoholic, strangers to themselves.   They are fossilized
in their present condition. If any of you out there are
living in a circumstance like this, MOVE OUT! Find an
excuse to get out and save yourself. I you have an
enlightened superior, tell him/her the actual reason.
You, like any of God's plants and animals need a certain
amount of space, air, nourishment and freedom. These
you have a right to. You're not asking a special favor.

GOD AND YOUR GAYNESS IN THE SAME BREATH

        Highest notch in this survival-happiness effort is the
opportunity of integrating faith in God with your sexual identity.
Sad to say, neither the Church nor the straight world will help
you here. Putting yourself together has to be done by yourself,
and yet not without the help of other believing people. Organizations like Dignity, Integrity, MCC are very important to us.
Most of us were taught that God is up and sex is ↑
way, way down Then we grow up with our heads in   ↓
the upper regions of faith and our bodies in the
sexual underground, with fantasies that would fill a porno book,
and a body pulsating with secret insistent desires. God is
good and sex is bad, and they're both inside of me--Lord, what a
mess!

        The only way we're going to survive and be happy is to put
these two big pieces of our lives together. That beautiful
face we love should speak to us of God's goodness and compassion.
That body we long to embrace should be praying to God beside us.
Sex and God have to come, somehow, in the same package.

DONT ACCEPT A NEGATIVE JUDGMENT ABOUT YOURSELF FROM ANYBODY

        You can help this survival-happiness process very much
by refusing to have or accept negative judgments about yourself.
To hell with them! They are the demons that throw you into the
water or fire, and that Jesus comes to cast out. Sex is good not
bad. My body's real neat not dirty. My desires are natural, not

4

perverted. Gay people are great--all of them--as long as they
hunger for true love and justice. God's grace is as much in them as
in flowers, gamboling sheep and children.
Glory be to God for dappled various, gay
folks!. Negative spirit of false guilt
and body hate, I rebuke you! (Are you
still with me gang? Almost got carried away by the exorcism.)

And do my spiritual and sexual sisters and brothers, this is
the way I'm trying to put myself together. It's working. It will
work for you too. Speak to the Lord about yourself; cast your
burden on Him. Tell Him He put you into this untidy world and He's
got to help you manage not only survival, but also a good measure of
happiness. Complain to the Lord like the Hebrew psalmists, then
turn to the pursuit of goodness and the joy it brings.

My close embrace and love to you all.

Joe

Joe's article speaks a great deal about coming out and about
coping and surviving. Now, sometimes it feels like coming out is
just about the least likely way to survive. (In fact, I've heard
someone in that situation being described as a "herring among the
barracuda"--Gulp) But as Joe pointed out there are many degrees and
ways of coming out and of surviving. All of them
require some risk and some disclosure.(even if
it is only self-disclosure) Not all of these ways
require a full page ad in the NCR! It really
depends upon you and your situation. But perhaps it helps to have
concrete examples to bounce around.

I think that a few of my own experiences were similar to
some of the suggestions that Joe made. So, at the risk of this
sounding like an essay on "What I did over my summer vacation", I'll
try to share a few of the things I did over my summer vacation.

When I started my studies in pastoral ministry this summer,
I made a commitment to be as honest as I could about what I felt
was a call to a ministry of "sexual justice", especially for women
and for gay persons. Sometimes that decision involved some uncomfortable situations. I don't mean to imply that it was a totally
excruciating experience. I was graced with some support and
encouragement from sometimes unexpected sources. However, there
were enough rough spots to make me feel very alone and isolated at
times.

For some people the connection of "gay ministry" with
social justice was a new idea. Other people shifted the subject (if
not their seats)when the word gay was mentioned. Once I came
to the startling conclusion that a classmate thought I was another

5

Anita Bryant type, out to "cure" people. (That was the unkindest
cut of all, and unleashed a torrent of words on just who needed to
be "cured" in a homophobic society.)

But there was a peculiar kind of grace at work in all this.
The person that I had lost patience with became one of the most supportive people to me during the summer. A woman I barely knew told
me that her consciousness had been raised about gay people, simply
by hearing a prayer for the gay community during a liturgy. Another
asked me about some concerns she had about negative aspects of gay
life. I think she left knowing that there was another side. I
was able to share with another person the role that Dignity played
in my life in being a joyful, prayerful, faith community.

I'm not suggesting that everyone go this route. Often it is not
possible or wise. I'm certainly not as open in my work situation
as I was at school. (although this is changing too.) I think that
the trick is to really listen to where people are at, and push them
one step further. Many of my classmates were concerned about social
justice and were open to hearing my story. Not everyone, of course,
was in that space, but maybe next year. . . I do have to disagree
with one point that Joe made. You don't have to be "hard-shelled"
"independent" or "bold". All you have to be is willing to become
"a herring among the barracuda". (It helps if you can swim fast.)

I feel funny rattling on about myself, but one other thing
happened this summer that I would like to share with you as well.
While I was going through a sort of "public disclosure" I was also
having private struggles about my own sexuality. Fortunately, I
had friends who listened and help me sort through all the confusing
and contradictory feelinga about my own bisexuality. No one
had any "answers"--least of all me--but I at least feel more comfortable with my lesbian side now. I somehow feel the two "comings
out" were somehow connected. Maybe getting in touch with my feelings
made speaking out a more natural thing. Perhaps, discovering that
the world wasn't going to end if I publicly supported gay rights,
made me more willing to deal with myself. Perhaps both were operating. I know that both struggles are a process which is only just
beginning.

Finally, even those times when I was alone, pacing back
and forth in my room at night, trying to put it all together, I
came to the realization that I was really
loved by God. Not in spite of all my troubles
and worries, and not in spite of who I was,
but because of the struggles and because of
who I was. I ended the summer feeling like
a tigress. Well so much for my vacation stories. I do want to
express my appreciation to Joe for his excellent article. I hope
it sparks as much in you as it did for me.

✳ ✳ ✳   Clare

Communication

6

We received a couple of special requests that we wanted to pass on to you. The first comes from Arizona.

 I have a special request that I would like to make to your readership. I am an Episcopal priest and active in the local Dignity chapter. Recently the priest who has been saying Mass for us for some time was transferred from Phoenix, and we are looking for someone to fill his place. There is very limited support for Dignity in this diocese and we recognize that someone volunteering to minister to our Chapter would be doing so out of the mainstream of the Church here, but we are hoping that maybe there is someone here who reads this Newsletter who may be able to make contact with us.

If any of you know anyone who might be interested, or if you yourself can help please contact:

> Roy Wood
> 3421 N. Hayden Rd.
> Scottsdale AZ 85251

The second request comes from a dear friend, Bill Roberts. He is interested in hearing from anyone willing to discuss a support network for traditional celibates. He writes.

> The gay celibate is still needful of more support and peer communication. Perhaps this can be accomplished through COMMUNICATION. However, as I attend COMMUNICATION events, I find myself severely outnumbered by those religious who have chosen a different path in regards to celibacy. In other words the support and interaction I need is lacking.

Bill's address is

> Brother William Roberts
> 321 East 61st St.
> New York, New York 10021

New Ways Ministry is repeating their ad for the Catholic Coalition For Gay Civil Rights in the National Catholic Reporter next month. Donations are needed to help underwrite the cost. If you are one of those "hardshelled" "independent" or "bold" types, and haven't yet endorsed the statement, contact New Ways Ministry
> 4012 - 29th St.
> Mt. Ranier, Md. 20822

Well thats about all for this month folks. Next month's issue will not have a theme. Just a juicy selection of your letters. J.E. and I hope the year' s starting out well for you and that you keep us in your prayers as we do in ours

Clare + J.E.

APPENDIX IV

252 S. 12th St.
Phila., Pa. 19107

Dear friend,

Thank you for your inquiry about COMMUNICATION. As you can see from the sub-heading of the enclosed issue(s), we hope to further a dialogue on the relation-ship between personal sexuality and ministry. At this time in history we see a cultural awakening to new and good meanings of homosexual behaviour, and also celibacy being questioned as a necessary prerequisite for the ministry. Without wanting to judge alternative paths individuals may take, we hope the sharing of our experiences with one another will build a sense of community among gay religious and priests, and assist us in discerning our own personal choices on this journey. Our dialogue may serve as a catalyst for heterosexual religious and priests to do likewise, thus fostering a greater sexual integrity among the leadership of our church.

Very often, because of our public role, gay **religious and priests** are unable to find safe forums for testing experiences, even with people like ourselves. We want COMMUNICATION to be part of that confidential space, both for those of our readers who are able to be more public about their homosexuality, as well as for those who for one reason or other presently do not choose to be so.

COMMUNICATION is not officially connected with the national gay Catholic organization known as Dignity, though many of our readers are members or chaplains. Some of our readers pointedly choose not to be so connected. However, the dialogue this newsletter generates began at some of the National Dignity conventions and will probably find special elaboration at such conventions in the future. We hope to be a means of continuing the dialogue in between.

Our method of disseminating this newsletter is important for you to know since it tells you as much about us as the contents do. We have grown to over two hundred readers --almost exclusively gay Brothers, Sisters, seminarians and priests--since our beginning in October of 1977. Other than names gathered at Dignity Conventions, our mailing list has grown primarily from your showing your copy to an interested brother or sister. They would subsequently write to us asking to be included. On a few occasions our existence and our address was announced at a gathering of sympathetic listeners such as a Regional Dignity meeting or the Catholic Campus Ministers Association Meeting. This personal involvement of yours in our growth and the confidentiality and responsibility it suggests has always seemed to us to be the best and most organic way to grow.

There is of course a chance even in such a process for one or other of us to pass the newsletter or the delicate ideas presented in it to someone indis-creetly. By this I mean that the person who receives it may be an inappropriate participant in our dialogue because they are rigid and homophobic, or simply because they misconstrue our personal sharing as theological doctrine.

We cannot completely prevent this possibility of course, nor even the risk that such a person might bring our monthly nosegay to the attention of someone in the hierarchy or public media who would make trouble for us. Neither do we want to constantly run screening processes on everyone who writes: "I've heard of your newsletter and would like..." We simply have to trust that you and even a potential antagonist would recognize what we are primarily about and respect our confidentiality without which we would be quite different.

Nobody's **name is printed under** their letter. Names aren't printed for any reason unless that is agreed upon, even then with great caution for your sake and ours. We expect and presume that nothing is reprinted from our newsletter without permission, especially any personal letters. We send it out in a first class mailing so it is returned to us if unable to find you, and we stamp it "Personal" on the front.

Our policy then, until you hear otherwise, is to assume that anyone who knows of our existence and writes us to receive the newsletter is sympatico unless we know otherwise. We take this risk because of our conviction that God is behind all true dialogue, especially one as vulnerable as this.

If you are interested in receiving this each month (ten issues per year); please send in the tear-off at the top of this page with $5-$10.00 for mailing and printing costs (all labor is volunteer). Make checks payable to COMMUNICATION. We look forward to some of your ideas and experience enlightening others on this adventurous road we travel together in Christ.

Love and joy to you,

"Brother Paul & Clare

(if not already sent)　　　　　PLEASE PRINT

NAME:＿＿＿＿＿＿＿＿＿＿＿＿＿＿＿＿　　Amount: $＿＿＿＿

ADDRESS:＿＿＿＿＿＿＿＿＿＿＿＿＿＿＿＿＿＿＿＿＿＿
(include zip)

V

Homosexual Marriage Rituals

In many homosexual circles religious ceremonies where two homosexuals express and make a commitment to each other on a more or less permanent and exclusive basis are purposely called by names other than "marriage." However, the parallel between these ceremonies and normal weddings between men and women is undeniable. The following rituals and rules for the preparation of homosexual couples prior to these ceremonies illustrate the extent to which the practice of homosexuality is becoming institutionalized in America.

Committee Statement

In light of the Dignity, Inc. Statement of Position and Purpose, we believe that God, through the action of the Christian community, sustains the free and deliberate choice of two people to live together in love. The couple's commitment to each other expresses and calls the couple to reflect Christ's love to one another and to the greater community, thus expressing the ongoing covenant between God and God's people. We believe the Christian community has the pastoral responsibility to affirm and support lesbian and gay couples who have undertaken to live the Christian life together in love, truth, and fidelity. Therefore we believe *Dignity/New York*, as a community, has the pastoral responsibility to publicly witness and support the commitment of lesbian and gay couples.

PROCEDURES AND OPTIONS

Members of Dignity/New York who wish to celebrate their commitment publicly within our community should have known each other for at least one year and/or lived together for six months. The couple shall select a sponsor(s) who is a member of Dignity/New York. This sponsor shall know the couple, know the resources available to the couple, and will act as a liaison between the couple and the Liturgy committee regarding the ceremony.

While it is the couple who makes the commitment to each other, and it is God who actually blesses the commitment of the two people, it is the Dignity/New York community who calls the blessing of God on the couple and their commitment and witnesses that commitment. The ceremony will take place where the community usually meets for its religious celebrations.

For practical purposes, the couple shall take from the community witnesses who will act on behalf of the community as a whole. One of these witnesses will be a member of Dignity/New York and the couple may choose other witnesses.

The material which follows suggests the likely elements in a service of commitment with choices within each:

Introduction: A witness should introduce the couple to the community, calling
   to mind the significance of the commitment to be made.
Questions of Intent: To be asked by the sponsor.
Readings: At least two from the Bible.
Forms of Exchange of Promises: To be made by the couple.
Prayers of Offering: To be made by the couple.
Prayers of Blessing: To be made by the witness(es).
Thanksgiving.

One of the clergy consultants will be present when the couple, with the representative of the Liturgy Committee, coordinate the planning of the ceremony.

Dignity's Participation in Blessing Gay Couples

Dignity's Position: The Roman Catholic Church's Canon Law states that: "Marriage is a contract by which two competent persons of *opposite sex* give to each other the exclusive and irrevocable right over their bodies for the procreation and education of children (Canon 1012 and following)." Preserving this Church definition of marriage, Dignity will only partici-

Homosexual Marriage Rituals

pate in blessing gay "unions" and will strive to maintain a clear distinction between the two, especially avoiding any simulation of the Rite and ceremonies associated with heterosexual marriage. Nevertheless, Dignity recognizes many social and psychological similarities and parallels between heterosexual marriage and gay "unions" and that, above all, they both need the blessing of God and the celebration and support of a Christian community, family, and friends.

While gay "unions" are free of the terms dictated by the Church and State for marriages, they are contracts and/or covenants and, thus, each couple must determine, beforehand, the mutual terms of their commitment.

Dignity will follow these guidelines in blessing gay couples:

1. Both of those making the commitment must be over 18 years of age.
2. One member of the couple must be a member of Dignity or a Catholic.
3. The couple must have the intention of making a serious commitment to join their lives together for a long period of time.
4. They should be invited to attend some Dignity functions (Mass, raps, meetings, etc.), so that they can witness the Christian community in action, and understand the need of support from the community.
5. They must meet with a priest and two members of the Dignity community three times in at least two-week intervals to discuss the following topics:

First Meeting: To determine the contract or covenant by which they wish to live. Such subjects as: work, money, property, living together, obligations (parents, children, etc.), debts, wills (lawyers), a physical exam (doctors), fidelity, and any special problems they may have (drugs, alcoholism), etc. This counseling session with a priest and the two members of Dignity is offered with the hope that the couple entering this relationship will realize the deep obligations and problems they will be assuming. Many questions will be raised in their minds. It is up to the couple to go home from these sessions and decide on their contract or covenant, their life style, and how they will meet their problems and obligations.

Second Meeting: The priest, the two Dignity members, and the couple will discuss religion and their Faith. It should be stressed that this ceremony is a religious one, and has no civil ramifications. The couple will have the opportunity to revitalize their Faith, and see the part their Faith could play in their daily lives. Any questions or doubts they have about their Faith will be discussed. If the couple to be blessed wish to meet privately with the priest, this will be arranged.

Third Meeting: Plan the ceremony [*sic*] with the priest and the Dignity members. It is absolutely necessary for the couples being blessed, and the community of Dignity, to realize the difference between contracts of heterosexual marriage and that of a gay "union." The customs and/or elaborate ceremony that have grown up surrounding marriage must not be imitated. The spirituality of the Blessing, the sharing of their love with their friends and the community, should be stressed. It would be more Christian and more meaningful if simple declarations of love, the blessing of God and the community of their friends, with some social reception, take place celebrating the occasion.

A Ceremony of Blessing Couples

This ceremony is only a suggestion, a guideline. The ceremony and all of its details should be worked out by the couple, the priest, and the Dignity couple. Locations: a) Before the General Meeting, b) at Home, or c) at some other appropriate place.

1. During Mass after the Gospel: Sermon
                                    Announcement or Greeting
                                    The Blessing
                                    Congratulations or Kiss of Peace
2. Outside Mass: Greeting or Announcement
                   Scripture or other Readings
                   Sermon
                   The Blessing
                   Congratulations or Kiss of Peace

AN ANNOUNCEMENT: In the Spirit of Christian love, N. & N. wish to announce their intention to join their lives together, and ask the Christian community of Dignity and their friends for their prayers and support.

A GREETING: We are gathered here to bless the love between N. & N. They have chosen to share their lives and have asked you their friends to bless and support them in their love for each other. They realize how difficult it is for a couple to truly love, care, and be faithful to each other. They call upon this Christian community, you, to give them the prayers, love, support, and friendship they need, to continue growing in their love. N. & N. have joined their lives hoping that through their love and mutual support they can achieve salvation of body and soul and lead happier, fuller lives. Let us give them our prayers, and good wishes, and the encouragement they need to grow, strengthen, and be happy in their love for each other.

SERMON: On love and the necessity of Love in our lives, Etc.

PRIEST AND COMMUNITY BLESSES THE COUPLE: May take the form

574

of the Prayer of Faithful, [*sic*] or any form the Couple and Priest agrees on.

    KISS OF PEACE: An opportunity for the Priest and guests to congratulate the Couple.

A Sample Exchange of Commitment for Celebrations of Commitment

Father Paul, Father Mel, Jim, Neal, and friends, we thank you for joining us today to witness our expressing the love we have for each other. We are sure you realize this is not the first time we have expressed our love for each other, nor is it the first time we have prayed for God's blessings. What makes this day different is that this time we are doing it in the presence of our friends. It is not by chance that we discovered our love for each other. We believe it is the fulfillment of God's plan for the two of us.

    It is our prayer that as we grow and change, our love may continue to flourish. Together with God's love we will take care of each other, support and help each other in times of stress and pain, rejoice during periods of peace and thanksgiving. It is our intention to continue our obligations to our families, friends, the gay community, and to those in need.

    Sid, the degree of love I give is determined by my own capability. My capability is determined by the envirement [*sic*] of my past existence and my undersranding [*sic*] of love, truth, and God. I will give you as much love as I can. If you show me how to give more, then I will give more. I can only give as much as you need to receive or allow me to give. If you receive all I can give then my love is endless and fulfilled.

    Marty, I love you from the depths of my being. I promise to do my best and to strive continually for your happiness and physical and spiritual well being. For me to love, is to commit myself freely and without reservation. Whatever your needs are, I will try to fulfill them and will bend in my values depending on the importance of your need. If you are lonely and need me, I will be there. If in that loneliness you need to talk, I will listen. If you need to listen, I will talk. If you need the strenght [*sic*] of human touch, I will touch you. If you need to be held, I will hold you. I will lie naked in body with you if that be your need. If you need fulfillment of the flesh, I will give you that also, but only through my love.

An Exchange of Vows

At the entry of the priest all STAND and he will welcome the couple and the congregation. A hymn may be sung.

The priest then says:

In the presence of God we have come together to witness the celebration
and blessing of the union which exists between N & M, which they now wish
to offer to God for blessing and renewal.

In this service we remind ourselves of our human vocation which is to love
God and to love our neighbour. God has created us to love. We are to respond
in many ways, always remembering that in our relationships with others the
marks of true love should be self-sacrifice, committment [*sic*], respect, mu-
tuality in giving and receiving, and the avoidance of all coercion, exploitation,
and superficiality.

From the earliest times people have made solemn vows in the sight of God
and before witnesses. The story of David and Jonathan reminds us of one such
vow, solemnly made before God, calling on him to bless the love they swore
to each other for ever.

We have come here in order that N & M can bear witness to their love,
and so we share in their happiness and witness their exchange of vows because
we believe that God who is love and truth sees into our hearts, recognises [*sic*]
our humanity, and accepts the offering they are making.

The priest then says to the couple:
You are about to make a solemn vow. Do you believe God has called
you to live together in love?

Couple: WE DO.
Priest: Do you ask for his blessing?
Couple: WE DO.
Priest: Will you swear to remain faithful to each other, never allowing any
other relationship to come before the one you are now to affirm?
Couple: WE WILL.
Priest: Will you give yourselves to each other wholeheartedly and without
restraint?
Couple: WE WILL.
Priest: Will you do all in your power to make your life together a witness
to the love of God in the world?
Couple: WE WILL.
The priest then asks each partner seperately: [*sic*]
Will you N, give yourself wholly to M, sharing your love and your life, your
wholeness and your broken-ness, your success and your failure?
Answer: I WILL.
All SIT for the Lesson(s).
The priest (or some other) will give the Address.
*Each partner then makes her/his vow to the other taking her/his right hand
and saying:*

I, N vow to you, M, in the sight of God and before these our chosen witnesses,

Homosexual Marriage Rituals

that I shall love, honour and cherish you all the days of my life until death divides us.

The priest blesses the rings:

Bless, O Lord, these rings, that those who give and receive them may live in your peace and continue in your love all the days of their life, through Jesus Christ our Lord.

All say: AMEN.
The giver places the ring on the other's finger, saying:

This ring is a sign of all that I am and all that I have; receive and treasure it as a sign and a pledge of the love I have for you.

The couple alone KNEEL, and the priest says:

Will you now offer your life together to God?

Couple: God our Father,
            we offer to you our lives and our love for each other.
            Forgive what we have been,
            consecrate what we are,
            order what we shall be.   Amen.
The priest then blesses them, saying:

Almighty God who has given you the will to do all these things, grant you strength to perform them, perseverance to keep them, patience and courage to complete them; and the blessing of God Almighty, Father, Son and Holy Spirit be upon you to guide and protect you both, today and always.

All say: AMEN.
ALL STAND. The couple join hands and the priest says to the congregation:

Will you who are witnesses to this exhange [sic] of vows do all in your power to support and strengthen N & M in the days ahead?

All say: WE WILL.
Priest: God has called us to live in peace, joy, love, and holiness. The peace of the Lord be always with you.
People: AND ALSO WITH YOU.
The people greet the couple and each other. They then sign a commemorative card which is given to the couple. A hymn may be sung.

All KNEEL or SIT and the priest leads the people in prayers for the couple.*
There is then a period of silence, after which all say:

>Our Father in heaven,
>hallowed be you [*sic*] Name,
>your kingdom come,
>your will be done
>on earth as in heaven.
>Give us today our daily bread.
>Forgive us our sins
>as we forgive those who sin against us.
>Do not bring us to the time of trial
>but deliver us from evil.
>
>For the kingdom, the power and the glory
>are yours
>now and forever.   Amen.

The priest then gives the blessing.

*If there is to be a Communion Service it follows here, beginning at the Offertory. The Lord's Prayer is then said in its usual place in the service.

This is just one of a number of services currently in use. It is included to give members some basis for discussion at the September gathering and is not intended to be definitive.

APPENDIX
VI

Homosexual Religious Orders: Sample Rule and By-Laws

According to traditional Catholic doctrine, the concept of a religious order *for* homosexuals is profoundly self-contradictory. Such institutions do exist, although not recognized by the Church. The reader is asked to give particular attention to Article X of the Rule.

The Rule and By-Laws of the St. Matthew Community

THE RULE OF THE ST. MATTHEW COMMUNITY

Preamble: The Rule and life of the professed members of this Roman Catholic Community is to live the Holy Gospel of Jesus Christ, as witnesses of God's presence in the world, as instruments of God's love and peace, and in the service to all people.

Professed members of this Community are to be a sign of joy and peace and love among people. Let them open themselves to all that is human: let them not seek to abandon the world but to transform it. They are to be present to the time in which they live, adapting themselves to the conditions of the moment.

Grateful to God for what God has given them, let each professed member of the Community share their abundance, faith, and joy in liberation through Christ where the greater need exists.

Chapter One: WAY OF LIFE

ARTICLE I. *Undiscriminating love of neighbor.*

All members of the Community shall strive to be the first among Christians to discover Christ in their neighbors and in strangers. For each person is an image of God, their difference in color or race, or sex or age; their difference in speech or dress or custom: is but a reflection of the richness of God, in whom there is neither Greek nor Hebrew, male nor female, old nor young, freeperson nor slave, gay nor non-gay. Let no professed member of the Community harbor prejudice, openly or inwardly, in their heart but rather let them strive, by words and actions, to heal the wounds of prejudice and discrimination.

ARTICLE II. *Love for each other.*

Wherever members of this Community are located or meet one another, let them act toward one another like members of a family. Each should with assurance make their needs known to the other, and if anyone of them falls into illness or any other misfortune, the rest should wait on this one as they themselves would want to be helped.

ARTICLE III. *Personal prayer life.*

A personal prayer life and a program of Scriptural study is required of each member of the Community, and will be developed with the aid of a qualified spiritual counselor of the Roman Catholic Faith. A qualified spiritual counselor of the Roman Catholic Faith is required for each member of the Community.

ARTICLE IV. *Sacrament of Reconciliation.*

Each member of the Community shall receive the Sacrament of Reconciliation at least during the Major seasons of the Church Year. (Advent and Lent.)

ARTICLE V. *Attendance at Mass*

All members of the Community recognize that daily attendance at Mass is an ideal to be encouraged, but due to our secular working conditions this may not be possible. The possibility is to be determined by each individual member of the Community.

All Masses sponsored by the Community, however, shall be attended by each member of the Community.

ARTICLE VI. *Devotions toward the Blessed Virgin and to St. Francis of Assisi*

Homosexual Religious Orders

Private devotions of some type is expected of each member of the Community toward the Blessed Virgin and St. Francis of Assisi, who are patrons of the Community.

ARTICLE VII. *Love for the Church*

Each member of the Community shall pray daily for those in authority in the Church (that is the Pope, and the Bishop of the Diocese, all Clergy and Religious of the Church), e.g. one Our Father.

Respect for those in authority in the Church will be shown by all members of the Community.

ARTICLE VIII. *Humility*

Each member of the Community agrees to work continually toward achieving an attitude of humility in their lives and actions.

ARTICLE IX. *Christian Apostolate*

Individual Ministries

Each individual in the Community shall develop over a period of time their individual apostolic ministries with the co-operation of their spiritual director and the co-ordinator of the Community.

Community Ministries

The general ministry of the Community is:

1) to bring Christ's presence to the gay community and the non-gay community wherever it feels Spirit is guiding.
2) to make the official Roman Catholic Church more aware of and responsive to the needs of the gay community as the Spirit directs.
3) to foster a personal growth and to support each member spiritually.

ARTICLE X. *Traditional Vows and Commitments*

Some of us have accepted celibacy, without denying that sexual feelings exist within each of us. Celibacy has been a charism of the Church since its beginning for the purpose of serving both God and the Christian Community with total commitment. However, some of us have not accepted a commitment of celibacy. Some members of the Community have chosen to live in a permanent gay union. They hope to be a sign of total, permanent, and faithful union to others. All of us are striving to live out the Gospel in our lives as we feel Spirit is directing us.

Any member of the Community may appeal to the Bishop of the Diocese to take private vows of celibacy, obedience, or poverty after they have received the approval of their confessor and spiritual director, and have informed the Community of their intentions. The Community shall provide every effort at its means to encourage and spiritually support any member who takes these vows with the approval of the Bishop of the Diocese.

Chapter Two: ADMISSION TO THE COMMUNITY

ARTICLE XI. *Basic Requirements*

1) A person must be a practicing Roman Catholic.
2) A person must be at least 21 years of age, and show ability to make mature decisions.
3) A person must be willing to participate in a period of training and instruction and service as outlined in the By-Laws of the Community.

Chapter Three: COMMUNITY STRUCTURE

ARTICLE XII. *Officers*

1) The Community shall have a Co-ordinator, whose responsibilities shall be as follows:

Official spokesperson for the Community. In this role the Co-ordinator is to reflect the mind of the Community.

The Co-ordinator is the Chairperson for all Community Meetings.

The Co-ordinator has the responsibility to take a personal interest in each individual member of the Community to be sure they are living the Rule.

The Co-ordinator shall have the responsibilities and duties as outlined in the By-Laws of the Community.

2) The Community shall have a Secretary and a Treasurer, whose responsibilities shall be clearly outlined in the By-Laws.

ARTICLE XIII. *Spiritual Director of the Community*

The Spiritual Director of the Community should be a priest of the Diocese, and should provide a channel of communications between the Community and the Bishop of the Diocese in which the Community resides.

ARTICLE XIV. *Organization*

The By-Laws of the Community shall govern the organizational structure of the Community.

ARTICLE XV. *Amendment of the Rule*

The Rule as adopted on June 11, 1978 shall not be changed except by unanimous consent. Additional Articles may be enacted by a two-thirds vote of the full membership of the Community as outlined in the By-Laws.

(Signed)

Donald M. Thienpont   *Daniel J. Ventrelli*
Kevin Clifford Burke   *James Jarman*

THE BYLAWS OF THE ST. MATTHEW COMMUNITY
Section I. *ARTICLES OF ORGANIZATION*
A. The name of the organization shall be St. Matthew Community.
B. The principal office of the St. Matthew Community shall be located in Brooklyn, New York, in Kings County.
C. The St. Matthew Community is organized exclusively for charitable

and religious purposes, in accordance with section 501 (c) (3) of the Internal Revenue Code of 1954.

D.   The names and addresses of the persons who are the initial trustees of the St. Matthew Community are:

James Jarman
Daniel Ventrelli
Kevin Burke
Donald Thienpont

All residing at 146 Bond Street, Brooklyn, New York 11217.

E.   No part of the surplus of the St. Matthew Community shall inure to the benefit of, or be distributable to its members, trustees, officers or other individuals, except that the St. Matthew Community shall be authorized and empowered to pay necessary expenses for the welfare of its members, such as rent, food, etc.

No substantial part of the activities of the St. Matthew Community shall be the carrying on of propaganda or otherwise attempting to influence legislation, and the Community shall not participate in or intervene in (including the publishing or distribution of statements) any political campaign on behalf of any candidate for public office.

The St. Matthew Community shall not carry on any activity not permitted of organizations under sections 501 (c) (3) or 170 (c) (2) of the Internal Revenue Code of 1954.

F.   Upon the dissolution of the St. Matthew Community, the trustees shall, after paying or making provisions for the payment of all liabilities of the Community, dispose of all assets exclusively for the purposes of the Community in such a manner or to such organizations organized and operated exclusively for charitable or religious purposes as shall at the time qualify as an exempt organization under section 501 (c) (3) of the Internal Revenue Code of 1954. Any assets not so disposed shall be disposed by the Court of Common Pleas of the County in which the Community is then located, in accordance with this article.

G.   IN WITNESS WHEREOF WE HAVE HEREUNTO SUB-SCRIBED OUR NAMES ON THIS 20TH DAY OF FEBRUARY 1978.
(Signed)

Donald M. Thienpont   *Daniel J. Ventrelli*
Kevin Clifford Burke   *James Jarman*

Section II. *MEMBERSHIP*

A.   Application for membership in the St. Matthew Community is open to practicing Roman Catholics who shall desire, and can demonstrate an aptitude for life in a Religious Community, and who shall have attained an age of mature decision (at least 21 years of age) and who shall be willing and able to abide by the Rule and By-Laws of the Community.

B.   The Community shall establish requirements for receiving new members. Applications for membership in the St. Matthew Community will be received by the Co-ordinator, and the Co-ordinator, together with the Spiritual Director of the Community will review the applicant's Spiritual, Educational, Personal and Financial background and stability, and will present the applications and the applicant to the members of the Community at a Community meeting. A vote will be taken at a Community meeting, and if the applicant is found to be acceptable, the Applicant shall begin a period of training and testing under the guidance of the Co-ordinator, of not less than six months. (After which) the Community shall request the applicant to begin a period of conditional membership, living in the Community, for a period of not less than one year. (After which) if the applicant and the Community are in agreement, the Applicant shall be installed at the Annual Anniversary Celebration of the Community. During the period of conditional membership the Applicant may be granted permission to vote, but not to hold office in the Community.

C.   Full members of the Community, as well as conditional members, shall financially contribute to the Community. The contribution shall help cover the cost of the Community facilities and the current ministries of the Community. Each person is expected to strive toward a commitment to poverty, however, the financial contribution offered to the Community is determined solely by the individual member.

D.   The St. Matthew Community shall have a class of membership called: ASSOCIATE MEMBERSHIP. Associate Membership is open to all who desire to support the programs and ministries of the Community. Associate Membership minimal dues shall be $10.00 per annum. Associate Members receive our newsletter and all important mailings of the Community. All Associate Members are personally remembered in the prayers and masses of the Community during the year. No voting privileges are reserved to this class of membership.

Section III. *OFFICERS*

A.   The election of officers shall take place at the Quarterly Meeting in October. Officers shall serve for a period of one year, beginning on the first Sunday in Advent.

B.   A Co-ordinator shall be elected. The Co-ordinator shall preside at all Community meetings, and shall be the official spokesperson for the Community. The Co-ordinator shall administer the Rule of the Community, encouraging each member to obtain their greatest benefit from the Rule. The Co-ordinator shall meet for at least one half hour weekly with each member of the Community, privately for discussions about the member and their relationship to the Community. The Co-ordinator shall be responsible for the training of new members.

C.   The Secretary shall receive all motions, and officer's reports, and place them on the agenda for Community meetings. The Secretary shall make note of all reports and resolutions of the Community meetings, and provide the minutes thereof, before the next meeting, to each member of the Community.

The Secretary shall be the official custodian of the Articles of Organization, the By-Laws, and the Rule. Additionally, the Secretary shall keep the minutes of all meetings as a part of these permanent records.

The Secretary shall keep a file of all news clippings related to the Community, a photograph file, and a file of all commercial transactions including the lease, loan obligations, product instructions, guarantees, and all other documents as may be entrusted to the Secretary for safe keeping.

D.   The Treasurer shall keep all of the financial books of the Community, and will make a weekly financial report at the Community meetings. The Treasurer shall receive all monies, keeping a record of donations, and issuing receipts for the same.

The Treasurer shall establish and present to the membership at a Community meeting, a budget for the calendar year, and that upon Community approval of the budget, shall make appropriations as it shall prescribe.

At least two signatures must appear on all checks issued.

Section IV. *SPIRITUAL DIRECTOR OF THE COMMUNITY*

A.   The Community shall choose a Spiritual Director, who shall serve the Community for as long a period as the Community desires, and the Spiritual Director is willing to serve.

B.   The Spiritual Director of the Community should be a priest of the Diocese, and should provide a channel of communication between the Community and the Bishop of the Diocese in which the Community resides.

C.   The Spiritual Director shall oversee the religious life of the Community and of its individual members, in accordance with the Rule of the Community.

He will encourage each member to counsel with him privately, and/or to have a priest as a confessor and a spiritual director.

D.   The Spiritual Director will ensure that the Eucharist is celebrated within the Community.

E.   The Spiritual Director shall receive monthly reports of the state of the Community from the Co-ordinator, and he shall be welcome at all meetings and activities of the Community.

Section V. *QUARTERLY MEETING*

A.   A Quarterly (organizational) Meeting shall be conducted four times each year, on the last Sunday in October, January, April, and July, unless otherwise specified by the Co-ordinator, or by request from a majority of the members of the Community, given to the Co-ordinator to call a special Quarterly Meeting.

B.   The business of the October Quarterly Meeting shall be devoted primarily to the election of officers, presentation of new members, and establishment of new chapters of the Community.

C.   The Quarterly Meeting is the only forum at which the By-Laws or the Rule may be amended. By-Law amendments must be moved and seconded, and must be approved by a two thirds vote of the full membership. It requires two Quarterly Meetings and a two thirds vote of the full membership at each of those Quarterly Meetings to add Articles to the Rule. However to change the Rule as adopted on June 11, 1978, requires a unanimous consent.

D.   The election of officers, the repeal of a motion already passed, a recall action, or any other official action, with the exception of actions on the Rule and By-Laws, shall require a majority vote of the full membership.

E.   The order of business at the Quarterly Meeting shall be: 1) The Co-ordinator's Report, 2) The Minutes, and the Secretary's Report, 3) The Financial and Treasurer's Report, 4) All old Business, and 5) New Business.

Section VI. *COMMUNITY MEETINGS*

A.   The full members of the Community shall meet weekly at the call of the Co-ordinator to hear the regular business of the Community.

B.   The Community Meeting is empowered to make all decisions regarding the operation of the Community, and of the Household, its ministries, both Community and Individual, and its business and financial affairs, and to develop all public activities.

C.   Each item placed before the Community Meeting shall be in the form of a motion, either with a second, or as a part of an officer's report, and shall require a majority vote from the members present for passage.

E.   The order of business at the Community Meeting shall be as follows: 1) The Co-ordinator's Report, 2) The Minutes and Secretary's Report, 3) The Financial and Treasurer's Report, 4) Old Business, and 5) New Business.

Section VII. *DISCIPLINE*

A.   The Co-ordinator may convene a Special Meeting, upon due notice to all full members, for the purpose of disciplining a member or officer of the Community, or for settling any dispute that may arise between members.

A petition from a majority of the full members may request the Co-ordinator to call such a meeting.

B.   Only the action of the entire Community, meeting in a special session may discipline or remove an individual's membership. The individual will be given every opportunity to present their case.

Section VIII. *COMMUNITY RESPONSIBILITY*

A.   As a sign of love for each other, and as a sign of the love that God has granted to us, each member and conditional member of the Community agrees to regularly complete their duties in the House. Failure to do so will be a matter of disciplinary action.

Section IX. *CHAPTERS*

A. The Community will be open to the establishment of other Chapters within the Community.

Section X. *RATIFICATION.*

A. Section I of these By-Laws, entitled "Articles of Organization" was ratified on the 20th day of February, 1978, by the undersigned.

B. Sections II thru X of these By-Laws, entitled "The By-Laws of the St. Matthew Community" were ratified on the 18th day of June, 1978, by the undersigned.

C. The Rule of the St. Matthew Community was ratified on the 11th day of June, 1978, by the undersigned.

(Signed)

Donald M. Thienpont *Daniel J. Ventrelli*
Kevin Clifford Burke *James Jarman*

APPENDIX
VII

Dignity Chapters, U.S. and Canada

ALABAMA IV

DIGNITY/Birmingham
5005 2nd Ave. N
Birmingham, AL 35212

ARIZONA VIII

DIGNITY/Phoenix
P.O. Box 21091
Phoenix, AZ 85036
602/967-3557

DIGNITY/Tucson
P.O. Box 27929
Tucson, AZ 85726
602/745-1812

CALIFORNIA IX

DIGNITY/Bay Area
P.O. Box 5127
San Francisco, CA 94101

DIGNITY/Central Valley
P.O. Box 9192
Fresno, CA 93791

DIGNITY/Inland Empire
P.O. Box 1001
Riverside, CA 92502

DIGNITY/Los Angeles
P.O. Box 27516
Los Angeles, CA 90027
213/467-8911

DIGNITY/Mission Valley
P.O. Box 902
Campbell, CA 95009
408/374-6111

DIGNITY/Orange County
P.O. Box 1818
Santa Ana, CA 92701
714/972-1509

DIGNITY/Sacramento
P.O. Box 161765
Sacramento, CA 95816
916/448-3777

DIGNITY/San Diego
P.O. Box 33367
San Diego, CA 92103
714-231-6609

Dignity Chapters

DIGNITY/San Fernando Vly.
Box 2871
Van Nuys, CA 91401
213/781-1370

COLORADO VIII

DIGNITY/Denver
P.O. Box 2943
Denver, CO 80201
303/377-2733

CONNECTICUT I

DIGNITY/Fairfield City
Box 348
Belden Station
Norwalk, CT 06852

DIGNITY/Hartford
P.O. Box 72
Hartford, CT 06141
203/233-8325

DIGNITY/New Haven
P.O. Box 285
West Haven, CT 06516

DISTRICT OF COLUMBIA III

DIGNITY/Washington
4550 MacArthur Blvd.
No. 206
Washington, D.C. 20007
202/332-2424

FLORIDA IV

DIGNITY/Miami
P.O. Box 370397
Miami, Fl 33137
305/674-8339

DIGNITY/Jacksonville
Box 225
Jacksonville, FL 32202

DIGNITY/Suncoast
P.O. Box 3306
Tampa, FL 33601
813/238-2112

KANSAS VI

DIGNITY/Wichita
P.O. Box 995
Wichita, KS 67201
316/265-4778

GEORGIA IV

DIGNITY/Atlanta
P.O. Box 14342
Atlanta, GA 30324
404/874-1694

ILLINOIS VI

DIGNITY/Chicago
P.O. Box 11261
Chicago, IL 60611
312/549-2633

DIGNITY/E. Central IL
Gay II Office #270, U of I
Urbana, IL 61801

INDIANA V

DIGNITY/Ft. Wayne
P.O. Box 11676
Ft. Wayne, IN 46859
219/484-5634

DIGNITY/Indianapolis
P.O. Box 831
Indianapolis, IN 46206

DIGNITY/Muncie
P.O. Box 2111
Muncie, IN 47302

IOWA VI

DIGNITY/Siouxland
P.O. Box 1711
Sioux City, IA 51102

LOUISIANA   VII

DIGNITY/New Orleans
P.O. Box 50723
New Orleans, LA 70150
504/522-9823

MAINE   I

DIGNITY/Central Maine
P.O. Box 7021
Lewiston, ME 04240

MASSACHUSETTS   I

DIGNITY/Boston
355 Boylston
Boston, MA 02116
617/536-6518

DIGNITY/Merrimack Val.
P.O. Box 321
Methuen, MA 01844

DIGNITY/Springfield
P.O. Box 1604
Springfield, MA 01101

MARYLAND   III

DIGNITY/Baltimore
P.O. Box 1243
Baltimore, MD 21203

MICHIGAN   V

DIGNITY/Detroit
P.O. Box 32874
Detroit, MI 48232
313/567-4210

DIGNITY/E. Lansing
P.O. Box 1431
East Lansing, MI 48823

DIGNITY/Flint
G-2474 S. Ballenger
Flint, MI 48507

DIGNITY/Grand Rapids
P.O. Box 1373
Grand Rapids, MI 49501

MINNESOTA   VI

DIGNITY/Fargo
Box 83
Morehead, MN 56560

DIGNITY/Twin Cities
P.O. Box 3565
Minneapolis, MN 55403
612/825-3110

MISSOURI   VI

DIGNITY/Kansas City
P.O. Box 10075
Kansas City, MO 64111
816/756-2363

DIGNITY/Mid Missouri
P.O. Box 991
Columbia, MO 65205

DIGNITY/St. Louis
P.O. Box 23093
St. Louis, MO 63156

NEVADA   IX

DIGNITY/Las Vegas
1605 E. Charleston Blvd.
Las Vegas, NV 98104

NEW JERSEY   II

DIGNITY/J.C. - Bayonne
Box 301 Pt. Station
Bayonne, NJ 07002
201/436-6259

DIGNITY/Jersey Shore
P.O. Box 824
Asbury Park, NJ 07712
201/988-9510

Dignity Chapters

DIGNITY/Metro N.J.
261 Central Ave. Box 35
Jersey City, NJ 07307
305/674-8339

DIGNITY/Princeton
P.O. Box 665
Princeton Junctn., NJ 08550
609/921-2565

DIGNITY/So. Jersey
8 East Ohio Ave.
Beach Haven Terrace, NJ 08008

NEW MEXICO   VIII

DIGNITY/N. Mexico
P.O. Box 1703
Albuquerque, NM 87103
505/831-3513

NEW YORK   II

DIGNITY/Albany
Box 6166
Albany, NY 12206
518/482-7820

DIGNITY/Brooklyn
c/o Sr. Moira 107 St. Felix
Brooklyn, NY 11217

DIGNITY/Buffalo
P.O. Box 75 Ellicott Sta.
Buffalo, NY 14205
716/884-5631

DIGNITY/Mid Hudson
P.O. Box 1344
Kingston, NY 12401

DIGNITY/Nassau
P.O. Box 48
East Meadow, NY 11554

DIGNITY/New York
P.O. Box 1554 FDR Sta.
New York, NY 10150

DIGNITY/Queens
P.O. Box 1060
Woodside, NY 11377

DIGNITY/Rochester
17 S. Fitzhugh St.
42 Tyler House
Rochester, NY 14614
716/232-2521

DIGNITY/Suffolk
P.O. Box 621P
Bayshore, NY 11706
516/666-6098

DIGNITY/Westchester-Rockland
P.O. Box 576
Bronxville, NY 10708
914/623-5824

NEBRASKA   VI

DIGNITY/Omaha
P.O. Box 31201
Omaha, NE 68131
402/345-7169

NORTH CAROLINA   IV

DIGNITY/Greensboro
P.O. Box 13014
Greensboro, NC 27405
919/275-2061

DIGNITY/Raleigh
P.O. Box 10613
Raleigh, NC 27605
919/834-8942

OHIO   V

DIGNITY/Central Ohio
P.O. Box 2591
Columbus, OH 43216
614/276-7615

DIGNITY/Cincinnati
P.O. Box 983
Cincinnati, OH 45201
513/621-4026

DIGNITY/Cleveland
P.O. Box 18479
Cleveland, OH 44118
216/791-0942

DIGNITY/Dayton
P.O. Box 55
Dayton, OH 45401
513/293-4186

DIGNITY/Toledo
P.O. Box 1388
Toledo, OH 43603
419/960-3997

OREGON X

DIGNITY/Portland
P.O. Box 5427
Portland, OR 97228
503/636-0356

PENNSYLVANIA III

DIGNITY/North E. PA
P.O. Box 1651
Wilkes-Barre, PA 18703
717/822-7269

DIGNITY/Central PA
P.O. Box 297 Fed. Sq. Sta.
Harrisburg, PA 17108
717/232-2027

DIGNITY/Philadelphia
252 So. 12th St.
Philadelphia, PA 19107
215/546-2093

DIGNITY/Pittsburgh
P.O. Box 991
Pittsburgh, PA 15230
412/682-0165

RHODE ISLAND I

DIGNITY/Providence
P.O. Box 2231
Pawtucket, RI 02861
401/724-0132

SOUTH CAROLINA IV

DIGNITY/Piedmont
P.O. Box 5572
Greenville, SC 29606

TEXAS VII

DIGNITY/Austin
P.O. Box 4357
Austin, TX 78765

DIGNITY/Dallas
P.O. Box 19703
Dallas, TX 75219
214/526-3231

DIGNITY/El Paso
P.O. Box 26523
El Paso, TX 79926

DIGNITY/Ft. Worth
P.O. Box 296
Bedford, TX 76021

DIGNITY/Houston
P.O. Box 66821
Houston, TX 77006
713/528-7644

DIGNITY/Lubbock
P.O. Box 5460
Lubbock, TX 79417
806/763-6111

DIGNITY/Outreach
12222 Goit Road
Dallas, TX 75251
214/233-3100

DIGNITY/Palo Duro
P.O. Box 1035
Canyon, TX 79015

Dignity Chapters

DIGNITY/San Antonio
c/o Valdez 310 Gardina
San Antonio, TX 78201
512/735-7191

TENNESSEE   IV

DIGNITY/Memphis
P.O. Box 3733
Memphis, TN 38103
901/274-4528

VIRGINIA   IV

DIGNITY/Richmond
P.O. Box 5351
Richmond, VA 23220

DIGNITY/Tidewater
P.O. Box 434
Norfolk, VA 23501
804/623-4075

WISCONSIN   VI

DIGNITY/Milwaukee
P.O. Box 597
Milwaukee, WI 53201
414/845-1490

DIGNITY/Madison
723 State St.
Madison, WI 53703

WASHINGTON   X

DIGNITY/Seattle
P.O. Box 1171
Seattle, WA 98111

WYOMING   VIII

DIGNITY/Wyoming
P.O. Box 2415
Cheyenne, WY 82001
307/632-6007

CANADIAN CHAPTERS   XI

DIGNITY/Calgary
Box 1492 Station T
Calgary, AB T2H 2H7
403/269-7542

DIGNITY/Edmonton
P.O. Box 53
Edmonton, AL T5J 2G9
403/433-3559

DIGNITY/Montreal/DIGNITE
3484 Peet St.
Montreal, PQ H3A 1W8
514/481-2397

DIGNITY/St. John's
Box 1475 Sta. C
St. John's, NF A1C 5N8

DIGNITY/Toronto
P.O. Box 249 Station E
Toronto, ON M6H 4E2
416/960-3997

DIGNITY/Vancouver
P.O. Box 3016
Vancouver, BC V6B 3X5
604/684-7810

DIGNITY/Winnipeg
P.O. Box 1912
Winnipeg, Man R3C 3R2
204/452-3782

DIGNITY EXECUTIVE BOARD   *Current on 10 February, 1981*

Region	Director	Region	Director
I	Ed Dempsey 75 Bushnell Road Hartford, CT 06114 203/247-3378	XI	Ken Delisle 3-197 Furby Street Winnipeg, Man R3C 2A6 204/772-4322
II	Bob Hunter 42 Shore Lane Bayshore, NY 11706 516-666-6091		

III — Kevin McAnnally
1833 S. St., N.W. #1
Washington, DC 20009
202/265-1942

IV — Jack Jacknik
330 W. Brambleton Ave.
Norfolk, VA 23510
804/627-9182

V — Ron Schulte
2112 St. James Ave. #4
Cincinnati, OH 45206
513/221-2349

VI — Jim Plack
1020 Jones #3
Sioux City, IA 511505
712/252-1088

VII — Fr. Pat Hoffman
Box 599
Lamesa, TX 79331
806/872-7100

VIII — Bob Edgerly
Box 410
Boulder, CO 80306
303/440-4425 (h)
303/492-6501 (o)

IX — Chris Patterson
Box 33721
San Diego, CA 92103
714/692-9912

X — Ernest Neumann
6181–175 A Street
Surrey, BC V3S 4S3
604/574-5174

DIGNITY OFFICERS

President — Frank P. Scheuren
PO Box 53156
Atlanta, GA 30355
404/252-5210

Secretary — Elinor M. Crocker
Apt.319
1500 Mass. Ave., NW
Washington, DC 20009
202/223-2575

Treasurer — Marvin P. Marks
17344 W. Twelve Mile
Road, Suite 200
Southfield, MI 48034
313/559-5720

Past President — Paul C. Weidig
7770 Sierra Drive
Roseville, CA 95678
916/791-4984

DIGNITY, INC. OFFICE

DIGNITY/Inc.
Suite Eleven
1500 Massachusetts Ave., NW
Washington, D.C. 20005
202/861/0017

APPENDIX

VIII

Integrity
Chapters, U.S.

NORTHEASTERN REGION

Integrity/Albany
23 Knights Bridge
Guilderland, NY 12084
Bill Reedy, Jr.
518-456-3843

Integrity/Boston
P.O. Box 2582
Boston, MA 02208
Lee Ridgeway

Integrity/Burlington
P.O. Box 11
Winooski, VT 05404
Bruce M. Howden
802-864-7198

Integrity/Central New Jersey
P.O. Box 1432
New Brunswick, NJ 08903
Ronald W. Miller
609-683-0305
W. Keith McCoy
201-249-9782

Integrity-Dignity/Concord
P.O. Box 521
Concord, NJ 03301
Skip Ordway
603-485-3144

Integrity/Hartford
P.O. Box 3681
Central Station
Hartford, CT 06103

Integrity/Long Island
P.O. Box 192
Roslyn, NY 11576
Leslie Hopkins
516-621-7427

Integrity/New Haven
P.O. Box 1417
New Haven, CT 06506

Integrity/New York City
G.P.O. 1549
New York, NY 10001
Sister Brooke Bushong, C.A.
212-522-7097
Mason Martens, Program
   Coordinator
212-873-7443

Integrity/Philadelphia
3601 Locust Walk
Philadelphia, PA 19104
David Lauer
Richard Keiser
215-386-5180

Integrity-Dignity/Rochester
42 Tyler House
17 S. Fitshugh St.
Rochester, NY 14614
Jack Lowe
716-232-6521

SOUTHEASTERN REGION

Integrity/Atlanta
P.O. Box 13603
Atlanta, GA 30324
Michael Phillips
404-352-2649

Integrity/Baltimore
1319 N. Calvert St.
Baltimore, MD 21202
Tom Frasier

Integrity/Dallas-Ft. Worth
(no address given)

Episcopal Integrity/Houston
P.O. Box 66008
Houston, TX 77006
Jason Cabot
713-960-0733

Integrity/Knoxville
1624 Coher Ave.
Knoxville, TN 37917
Jim Fleenor

Integrity/Miami-South Florida
123 N.E. 36th St.
Miami, FL 33137
Allen Timberlake
305-757-0690
Bob St. Aubin
305-576-4216

Integrity/Montgomery
3653 Woodley Rd. #9
Montgomery, AL 36116
Dr. Lloyd C. Williams

Integrity/New Orleans
4611 Baronne St.
New Orleans, LA 70115
Rev. Bill Richardson, Jr.
504-899-2549

Integrity-Dignity/Richmond
P.O. Box 5351
Richmond, VA 23220
William A. Harrison, Jr.

Integrity-Dignity/Tampa Bay
209 Columbia Dr.
Tampa, FL 33606
Joe Ball
813-251-0150

Integrity/Unifour
P.O. Box 853
Hickory, NC 28601
Gary Mann

Integrity/Washington, D.C.
2112 32nd St., S.E.
Washington, D.C. 20020
Wayne Schwandt
202-583-2158

CENTRAL REGION

Integrity/Bloomington
701 Hawthorne Lane
Bloomington, IN 47401
Rev. James K. Taylor
812-334-2921

Integrity Chapters

Integrity/Central Indiana
c/o All Saints Episcopal Church
1537 Central
Indianapolis, IN 46202

Integrity/Central Wisconsin
Rt. 3, Box 31
Stevens Point, WI 54481
Kathryn Jeffers
715-344-5950

Integrity/Chicago
P.O. Box 2518
Chicago, IL 60690
James Edminster
312-477-4196

Integrity/Cleveland
c/o Trinity Cathedral
2021 E. 22nd St.
Cleveland, OH 44105
Donald Comes
216-249-3539

Integrity-Dignity/Madison
723 State St.
Madison, WI 53703
Steven Webster

Integrity/Milwaukee
Write to Rev. Russell Allen
Episcopal Milwaukee Area University Chaplaincy
804 E. Juneau Ave.
Milwaukee, WI 53202
414-272-8028

Integrity/St. Louis
1049 S. Taylor
St. Louis, MO 63110
Chris Butler
314-533-4439

Integrity/Southern Ohio
2351 Beechmont Ave. Apt. 15
Cincinnati, OH 45230
Robert F. Diehm

Integrity/Twin Cities
P.O. Box 882
Minneapolis, MN 55440
Collin Neal
612-545-4806
Rev. John Rettger, Chaplain
612-784-3330, 9AM-Noon M-F

WESTERN REGION

Integrity/Albuquerque
4328 Pan American N.E. #315
Albuquerque, NM 87107
Dan Swearingen
505-881-4129

Integrity/Denver
815 E. 18th Ave., Apt. 3
Denver, CO 80218
William Whitlock
303-831-4604

Integrity/Honolulu
St. Andrew's Cathedral
Queen Emma Square
Honolulu, HI 96813
Bill Potter
808-537-9478

Integrity/Los Angeles
3000 Griffith Park Blvd. #3
Los Angeles, CA 90027
Tom Johnson
213-662-5979

Integrity/San Diego
c/o Episcopal Community Services
601 Market St.
San Diego, CA 92101
David Todd

Integrity/San Francisco
P.O. Box 3339
San Francisco, CA 94119
Rev. Susan Bergmans
415-525-2459 or 415-776-5120

IX

Homosexual Synagogues, International

AM TIKVA
P.O. Box 11
Cambridge, MA 02138

BEIT HAVERIM
B.P. 397
75013 Paris Cedex 13
FRANCE

CONG. BETH AHAVA
P.O. Box 7566
Philadelphia, PA 19101

BETH CHAIM
P.O. Box 66734
Houston, TX 77006

BETH CHAVERIM
P.O. Box 90
Balwyn, Vic 3103
AUSTRALIA

CONG. BETH CHAYIM CHAD.
6000 W. Pico Blvd.
Los Angeles, CA 90035

CONG. BETH SIMCHA
11/75 O'Brien St.
Bondi Beach NSW 2026
AUSTRALIA

CONG. BETH SIMCHAT TORAH
P.O. Box 1270, G.P.O.
New York, NY 10001

BET MISHPACHAH
P.O. Box 1410
Washington, D.C. 20013

CHUTZPAH
c/o Gottlieb
Unit 5, 19 Glen Ave.
Randwick, NSW 2031
AUSTRALIA

Homosexual Synagogues

CONG. ETZ CHAIM
19094 W. Dixie Hwy.
N. Miami Beach, FL 33180

ETZ HAYYIM FELLOWSHIP
P.O. Box 14258
Dinkytown Station
Minneapolis, MN 55414

TIMOTHY GOLDARD
BM JGG
London, England
WC1V 6XX

HA-CHUG
P.O. Box 69406
Vancouver, BC
CANADA V5K 4W6

HAVURAH OR B'EMEK
P.O. Box 11041
Ft. Wayne, IN 46855

HATIKVAH HASHALOM
c/o Gerald Gerash
1360 Corona
Denver, CO 80218

JEW GAYS OF CENTRAL MD.
c/o Gay Community Ctr.
P.O. Box 74
Baltimore, MD 21230

JEWISH LES-FEMINISTS
c/o Ocean Park Comm. Ctr.
245 Hill St.
Santa Monica, CA 90405

LAMBDA CHAI
P.O. Box 351
Farmington, MI 48024

THE LOST TRIBE
c/o Naphtali Offen
863 Waller St. #1
San Francisco, CA 94117

NACHES - GJDG
P.O. Box 298, Station H
Montreal, Quebec H3G 2K8
CANADA

CONG. OR CHADASH
c/o 2nd Unitarian Church
656 W. Barry
Chicago, IL 60657

ST. LOUIS GAY HAVURAH
P.O. Box 9235
St. Louis, MO 63117

SEATTLE JEWISH LESBIAN
  GROUP
c/o Judith Klein
1516 18th Ave.
Seattle, WA 98122

CONG. SHA'AR ZAHAV
P.O. Box 5640
San Francisco, CA 94101

SJALHOMO
Postbus 2536
1000 CM Amsterdam
NETHERLANDS

SOC. PROTECTION PERSONAL
  RIGHTS
P.O. Box 16151
61161 Tel Aviv, ISRAEL

CONG. TIKVAH CHADASHAH
P.O. Box 2731
Seattle, WA 98111

ZIONIST UNION OF GAYS
c/o Roz Regelson
245 E. 21st St.
New York, NY 10010

APPENDIX

X

Homosexual Student Groups, U.S. and Canada

CALIFORNIA

Gay Students Union
Student Union No. 301
Univ. of Southern California
Univ. Park
Los Angeles, CA 90007

Gay Liberation Front
East Los Angeles College
5357 E. Brooklyn
Los Angeles, CA 90022

Gay Students Union
UCLA
308 Westwood Plaza
Los Angeles, CA 90024

Gay Sisterhood - UCLA
Women's Resources Ctr.
90 Powell Library
405 Hilgard Ave.
Los Angeles, CA 90024

Gay Students Union
Box 499
Occidental College
Los Angeles, CA 90041

Gay Caucus
The People's College of L.A.
2228 W. 7th St.
Los Angeles, CA 90057

Gay Awareness Program - USC
c/o Sal Licata
2257 Gower St.
Hollywood, CA 90868

Gay Discussion Group
Winnett Center 218-51
California Technical Inst.
Pasadena, CA 91109

Gay Law Students Assoc.
618½ E. Lomita Ave.
Glendale, CA 91205

Gay St. Union-Claremont College
McAllister Center
Columbia Avenue
Claremont, CA 91711

Gay Students Union
Univ. of California
c/o Associated Students
Riverside, CA 92507

Homosexual Student Groups

Gay St. Union - Fullerton College
c/o Gordon Magnusson
610 Magnolia
Brea, CA 92621

Gay Students Union
Student Activities Office
California State Univ.
Fullerton, CA 92634

Gay Students Union
Student Activities
University of California
Irvine, CA 92664

Gay People's Union
Box 15048
University of California
Santa Barbara, CA 93107

Gay Students at Hastings College
 of Law
198 McAllister St.
San Francisco, CA 94102

Gay Students Coalition
c/o Student Activities
City College of San Fran.
50 Phelan Avenue
San Francisco, CA 94112

Gay Liberation Front
c/o Student Activities Bldg.
San Francisco State College
San Francisco, CA 94132

Gay People's Union
Stanford Univ.
P.O. Box 8265
Stanford, CA 94305

Gay Seminarians
Graduate Theological Union
2441 LeConta
Berkeley, CA 94709

Gay Students Union
Eshelman Hall - 3rd Floor
University of California
Berkeley, CA 94720

Gay Student Union
Sonoma State College
c/o Student Activities
Rohnert Park, CA 94923

Lesbian & Gay Men's Union
Student Affairs Office
Cabrillo College
6500 Sogurd Dr.
Aptos, CA 95003

Gay Students Union
Sonoma State College
Sonoma, CA 95476

Gay Students Union
c/o Student Activities
10 Lower Freeborn Hall
University of California
Davis, CA 95616

Gay Liberation Front
Sacramento State College
Sacramento, CA 95816

Gay Students Union
Sacramento City College
Student Activities
1835 Freeport Blvd.
Sacramento, CA 95822

COLORADO

Boulder Gay Liberation
P.O. Box 1402
University of Colorado
Boulder, CO 80302

Gay Students Association
Metropolitan State College
Student Activities Ctr. Rm. 140
710 W. Colfax
Denver, CO 80214

Gay Alliance
Box 210 Activity Ctr.
Colorado State Univ.
Fort Collins, CO 80523

CONNECTICUT

Gay Liberation
Trinity College
c/o Kalos Society
Hartford, CT 06101

Univ. of Conn. Gay Alliance
c/o Women's Ctr.
Storrs, CT 06263

Gay Liberation Front
Inner College
Univ. of Connecticut
Storrs, CT 06268

Wesleyan Gay Alliance
Women's Ctr.
Wesleyan Station
Middletown, CT 06457

Gay Women's Group
3438 Yale Station
New Haven, CT 06520

Gay Alliance at Yale
Yale Station
P.O. Box 2031
New Haven, CT 06520

Gay Alliance
Univ. of Bridgeport
Student Center
Bridgeport, CT 06602

DELAWARE

Gay Community at Newark
Univ. of Del.
P.O. Box 4533
Newark, DE 15213

FLORIDA

Gay Academic Union
Student Activities Office
Florida Atlantic University
Boca Raton, FL 33432

Gay Coalition
CTR 2466
University of South Florida
Tampa, FL 33620

GEORGIA

Committee on Gay Education
P.O. Box 2467
Georgia Univ. Station
Athens, GA 30601

Gay Liberation
Box 1203
Fort Valley State College
Fort Valley, GA 31030

ILLINOIS

NIU Gay Liberation Front
c/o Bruce Wade
318 S. 1st St., No. 7
DeKalb, IL 60115

Northwestern Gay Liberation
Norris Center
Northwestern Univ.
Evanston, IL 60201

Circle Campus Gay Liberation
Room 518
750 S. Halsted St.
Chicago, IL 60607

Loyola Univ. Gay Students
5866 N. Broadway
Chicago, IL

Univ. of Chicago Gay Liberation
1212 E. 59th St.
Chicago, IL 60637

Homosexual Student Groups

Giovanni's Room
7109 N. Glenwood
Chicago, IL

Univ. of Chicago Gay Liberation
Room 301
1212 E. 59th St.
Chicago, IL 60690

G.A.C. of Loop College
c/o U.F.G.O.
P.O. Box 872
Chicago, IL 60690

Gay Law Students Assoc.
c/o U.F.G.O.
P.O. Box 872
Chicago, IL 60690

Friends
c/o Jim Nixon, V.P.
P.O. Box 296
Macomb, IL 61455

Gay Peoples Alliance
University Union
Illinois State Univ.
Normal, IL 61761

Gay People's Alliance
284 Illini Union
University of Illinois
Urbana, IL 61801

Students for Gay Liberation
Student Activities Office
Box 67.124
Southern Illinois Univ.
Edwardsville, IL 62025

S.I.U. Gay Liberation Org.
3rd Floor, Student Center
Southern Illinois University
Carbondale, IL 62901

INDIANA

Gay Activists Union
Ball State Univ.
Muncie, IN 47306

Gay People's Union
Earlham College
Richmond, IN 47374

IOWA

Gay Community
Grinnel College
P.O. Box 1285
Grinnel, IA 50112

Gay Liberation Front
University of Iowa
Student Activities
Iowa Memorial Union
Iowa City, IA 52240

KANSAS

Lawrence Gay Liberation Front
Room B-112, Kansas Union
University of Kansas
Lawrence, KS 66044

Children of Sappho
Kansas State Univ.
Manhattan, KS 66502

Gay People of Emporia
Student Organizations Office
Kansas State College
Emporia, KS

KENTUCKY

Gay Liberation Front
Univ. of Kentucky
Box 1615
Lexington, KY 40501

Gay Students Coalition
University of Kentucky
120 Student Center
Lexington, KY 40506

LOUISIANA

Tulane Univ. Gay Students Union
c/o Associated Student Body
University Center
New Orleans, LA 70118

MAINE

Gay People's Alliance
Student Union
Univ. of Maine
Portland, ME 04101

Wilde-Stein Club
c/o Memorial Union
Univ. of Maine at Orono
Orono, ME 04473

MARYLAND

Gay Student Alliance
Student Union Bldg.
Univ. of Md.
College Park, MD 20742

Gay Student Alliance
Box 2244
Towson State College
York Road
Towson, MD 21204

Gay People's Group
Student Activities Office
Prince George College
301 Largo Rd.
Largo, MD

MASSACHUSETTS

People's Gay Alliance
RSO 368 Student Union
Univ. of Massachusetts
Amherst, MA 01002

Gay Women's Caucus
RSO 367, Lincoln Ctr.
University of Mass.
Amherst, MA 01002

Student Homophile League
University of Mass.
RSO 368, Lincoln Ctr.
Amherst, MA 01002

Hampshire Gay Friends
P.O. Box 607
Hampshire College
Amherst, MA 01002

Holyoke Homophile League
c/o Bruce McKeon
15 Berkeley St.
Easthampton, MA 01027

Student Homophile Arts
Emerson Union
96 Beacon St.
Boston, MA 02116

Gay People's Group
Univ. of Massachusetts
Ctr. for Alternatives
100 Arlington St.
Boston, MA 02116

Harvard-Radcliffe Gay Student
  Assoc.
Phillip Brooks House
Harvard Univ.
Cambridge, MA 02138

MIT-Student Homophile League
142 Memorial Drive Rm. 50–306
Cambridge, MA 02139

Tufts Gay Community
Student Activities Office
Tufts Univ.
Medford, MA 02155

Gay Liberation - Williams Col.
c/o Rick Schneider
Spencer House
Williamston, MA 02167

Homosexual Student Groups

Homophile Union
Box B28 Chesnut Hall
Boston College
Boston, MA 02167

Northeastern Gay Students Org.
c/o Student Federation
Rm. 152 Ell. Center-N.E. Univ.
Boston, MA

Mytilene Society
Women's Ctr.
Wellesley College
Wellesley, MA 02181

SMU Gay Alliance
SMU Campus Center
North Dartmouth, MA 02747

MICHIGAN

Gay Liberation Front
325 Michigan Union
Univ. of Michigan
Ann Arbor, MI 48103

Gay Liberation Front
Box 23, S.C.B.
Wayne State Univ.
Detroit, MI 48202

Gay Liberation Movement
309 Student Services Bldg.
Michigan State Univ.
E. Lansing, MI 48824

Central Mich. Gay Liberation, Inc.
Box 34 - Warriner Hall
Central Michigan University
Mt. Pleasant, MI 48859

Mountain Women's Collective of
  Central Michigan Univ.
c/o P. Shepard
204 G Parkplace
Mt. Pleasant, MI 48858

MINNESOTA

Gay Liberation
B-67, Coffman Union
University of Minnesota
Minneapolis, MN 55455

Metro Gay Students Union
Metropolitan St. Junior College
50 Willow St.
Minneapolis, MN 55403

Gay Consciousness Group
Student Union Activities Office
Box 58
Mankato State Univ.
Mankato, MN 56001

MISSISSIPPI

Mississippi Gay Alliance
c/o Liz Landrum
P.O. Box 4470
Miss. State Univ.
State College, MS 39762

MS State Gay Counseling & Proj-
  ects
P.O. Box 4470
Mississippi State University
Jackson, MS 39762

MISSOURI

Gay Peoples Alliance
Box 1068
Washington Univ.
St. Louis, MO 63130

Gay People's Union - UMKC
c/o Gay People's Union
3825 Virginia
Kansas City, MO 64109

NEW HAMPSHIRE

Gay Student Organization
c/o Memorial Union
Univ. of New Hampshire
Durham, NH 03824

NEW MEXICO

Gay Liberation
Univ. of New Mexico
New Mexico Union
Albuquerque, NM 87106

NEW JERSEY

Rutgers Activists for Gay Educ.
Box 6 Student Center
350 High St.
Newark, NJ 07102

Alternate Sexual Life Styles Assoc.
Ramapo College
505 Ramapo Valley Rd.
Mahwah, NJ 07430

Gay Activists Alliance
William Paterson College
Student Center
Pompton Rd.
Wayne, NJ 07470

Student Homophile League
Fairleigh Dickenson Univ.
Teaneck Campus
Teaneck, NJ 07666

Gay Alliance of Princeton
306 Green Hall Annex
Princeton Univ.
Princeton, NJ 08540

Rutgers Univ. Homophile League
RPO 2901
Rutgers University
New Brunswick, NJ 08903

Rutgers Univ. Coalition of Lesbians
c/o Women's Center
Livingston College
New Brunswick, NJ 08903

NEW YORK

Gay Medical Students
c/o Gay Men's Health Project
247 W. 11th St. (basement)
New York, NY

606

Gay People's Union of NYU
Box 13, Room 810
566 LaGuardia Place
New York, NY 10003

Gay Student Liberation
New York University
Loeb Student Center, Box 13
566 LaGuardia Pl.
New York, NY 10017

Gay Men's Alliance
Hunter College
695 Park Ave. Rm. 124
New York, NY 10017

Lesbian Rising Collective
Hunter College
Women's Ctr.
New York, NY

Lesbian Activists at Barnard College
Room 106, McIntosh Center
New York, NY 10027

Gay People at Columbia—Barnard
103 East Hall
Columbia University
New York, NY 10027

Gay People at City College
Findlay Student Center
CCNY
Convent Ave. & W. 135th St.
New York, NY 10031

Gay Liberation
Staten Is. Comm. College
Student Activities
715 Ocean Terrace
Staten Island, NY 10301

Gay Men's Collective
Richmond College
Student Govt., Rm. 542
130 Stuyvesant Place
Staten Island, NY 10301

Homosexual Student Groups

Lesbians United
Student Govt. Rm. 542
Richmond College
130 Stuyvesant Pl.
Staten I., NY 10301

Gay People at Lehman Col.
Bedford Pk., Blvd. W.
Bronx, NY 10468

Gay Liberation Front
Long Island Univ.
Student Activities
385 Flatbush Ext.—Zeckendorf
  Campus
Brooklyn, NY 11201

Pratt Gay Union
Student Affairs
Pratt Institute
Brooklyn, NY 11205

Gay People at Brooklyn Col.
Student Activities
La Guardia Hall
Brooklyn College
Brooklyn, NY 11210

Queens Lesbian Feminists
Box 117 Student Union Bldg.
Queens College
Flushing, NY 11367

Gay Community at Queens Col.
Student Activities
Queens College
Flushing, NY 11367

Hofstra United Gays
Box 67, Center Bldg.
Hofstra Univ.
Hempstead, NY 11550

Gay Liberation Front
SUNY Stony Brook
Stony Brook Union
Stony Brook, NY 11790

Gay Liberation Front
Bard College
Box 87
Annandale-on-Hudson, NY 12504

New Paltz Gay Liberation
CPO 1022
State Univ. College
New Paltz, NY 12561

Vassar Gay Liberation
Box 907
Vassar College
Poughkeepsie, NY 12601

Individual Sexual Freedom Coalition
Nassau Community College
Stewart Avenue
Garden City, NY 13045

Gays for Human Liberation
Hewitt Union Bldg.
Oswego State University
Oswego, NY 13126

Gay Freedom League
Tilden Cottage
109 College Place
Syracuse, NY 13210

Gay Liberation
c/o Mike Reckewes
Herkimer College
Herkimer, NY 13350

Potsdam-Canton Gay Comm.
c/o College Union
State University College
Potsdam, NY 13676

Harpur Gay Liberation
Campus P.O. Box GLF
SUNY Binghamton
Binghamton, NY 13902

607

Gay Law Students
Box 10, Norton Union
SUNY Buffalo
Buffalo, NY 14213

Student Alliance for Gay Equality
c/o USG
State Univ. College
1300 Elmwood Ave.
Buffalo, NY 14222

Gay Liberation Front
SUNY Buffalo
Box 10, Morton Union
Buffalo, NY 14260

Gay Freedom League
SUNY Brockport
Brockport, NY 14420

Gay Freedom Coalition
Box 38, College Union
SUC Geneseo
Geneseo, NY 14454

Geneva Gay Liberation
Box 359
Hobart College
Geneva, NY 14456

Fredonia Homophiles
Student Activities
SUNY Fredonia
Fredonia, NY 14603

Gay Liberation Front
Univ. of Rochester
201 Podd Union, Box 6913
River Campus
Rochester, NY 14627

Alfred Gay Liberation
Box 472
Alfred, NY 14802

Cornell Gay Liberation
Sheldon Court 221
410 College Avenue
Ithaca, NY 14850

Radicalesbians
24 Willard Straight Hall
Cornell University
Ithaca, NY 14850

NORTH CAROLINA

Guilford Gay Alliance
P.O. Box 17724
Guilford College
Greensboro, NC 27410

Carolina Gay Association
Student Union, Box 39
Univ. of North Carolina
Chapel Hill, NC 27514

Duke Gay Alliance
7686 College Station
Durham, NC 27708

OHIO

Gay Activists Alliance
Ohio State University
1739 N. High St., Box 3
Columbus, OH 43210

Gay Union
Box 9 Univ. Hall
Bowling Green State Univ.
Bowling Green, OH 43402

Gay Liberation
Oberlin College
Box 30, Wilder Hall
Oberlin, OH 44074

Gay Liberation Front
Kent State University
Room 8, Student Activities Center
Kent, OH 44242

Gay Rights Organization
Kilcawley Center
Youngstown State Univ.
Youngstown, OH 44503

Homosexual Student Groups

Gay People of Oxford
c/o Together
12 S. Campus
Oxford, OH 45056

Univ. of Cincinnati Gay Society
Student Affairs
Tangeman Univ. Ctr.
Cincinnati, OH 45221

Antioch Radicalesbians
Women's Ctr.
Antioch College Union
Yellow Springs, OH 45387

Gay Liberation Front
Antioch College
Antioch Union
Yellow Springs, OH 45387

Lutherans Concerned for Gay People
Box 22, Hamma School of Theology
Springfield, OH 45504

Lesbian Collective
Women's Ctr.
Baker Tr.
Ohio Univ.
Athens, OH 45701

Gay Activists Alliance
c/o United Campus Ministry
18 N. College St.
Athens, OH 45701

OKLAHOMA

Gay Comm. All. for Sexual Freedom
c/o Women's Studies Center
Ellison Hall
Univ. of Oklahoma
Norman, OK 73069

OREGON

Gay People's Alliance
Portland State Univ.
Room 422, Smith Center
Portland, OR 97207

Gay Students Union
c/o Student Activities
Southern Oregon College
Ashland, OR 97820

PENNSYLVANIA

Gay Students at Pitt
Box 819 Student Union
University of Pittsburgh
Pittsburgh, PA 15234

Homophiles of Indiana Univ.
Box 1588
Indiana Univ.
Indiana, PA 15701

Homophiles of Penn State
P.O. Box 218
State College, PA 16801

Shippensburg Students for Gay Rights
c/o CUB
Shippensburg State College
Shippensburg, PA 17257

Student Homophile League
c/o Le-HI-HO
P.O. Box 1003
Moravian Station
Bethlehem, PA 18015

Bryn Mawr-Haverford Gay Peoples Union
Haverford College
Haverford, PA 19041

Swarthmore Gay Liberation
Swarthmore College
Swarthmore, PA 19081

Gays at Drexel
Creese Student Center
Drexel University
3210 Chestnut Street
Philadelphia, PA 19104

Gay Students at Temple Univ.
Room 205, Student Activities
13th & Montgomery
Philadelphia, PA 19122

Gays at Penn
University of Pennsylvania
3601 Locust Walk, Room 4
Philadelphia, PA 19174

PUERTO RICO

Frente de Liberacion Homosexual
Universidad de Puerto Rico
c/o Junion Sanchez
Calle Tetuan 313
San Juan, PR 00901

RHODE ISLAND

Kingston Gay Liberation
University of Rhode Island
Memorial Union
Kingston, RI 02881

Brown Univ. Gay Liberation
Student Activities Office
Providence, RI 02912

SOUTH CAROLINA

Gay Liberation Front
c/o Scottie Harrison
Box U-1869
Univ. of South Carolina
Columbia, SC 29408

TENNESSEE

Gay People's Alliance
c/o Knoxville Lesbian Collective
1210 Forest Avenue
Knoxville, TN 37916

TEXAS

Gay Activists Alliance
Box 441 Univ. Ctr.
Univ. of Houston
Houston, TX 77004

Gay/Texas
Office of Student Activities
Univ. of Texas
Austin, TX 78712

VERMONT

Gay Student Union
Billings Ctr.
Univ. of Vermont
Burlington, VT 05401

VIRGINIA

Gays Against Discrimination
c/o The Parthian Shot
N. Virginia Community Coll.
8333 Little River Turnpike
Annandale, VA 22003

Students for Gay Awareness
Box 176
Shenandoah College & Conservatory of Music
Winchester, VA 22601

Gay Student Union
P.O. Box 3610
Univ. Station
Charlottesville, VA 22903

Gay Liberation Group
College of William & Mary
Campus Center
Williamsburg, VA 23185

Homosexual Student Groups

Gay Alliance of Students
Virginia Commonwealth Univ.
c/o Sam Gage
1214 W. Franklin St., Apt 7
Richmond, VA 23220

Gay Alliance at Virginia Tech
210 Squires Student Center
Virginia Polytechnic Inst.
Blacksburg, VA 24061

WASHINGTON

Gay Students Association
SB 29 HUB
University of Washington
Seattle, WA 98195

Gay People's Alliance
Viking Union, Room 233
Western Wash. State College
Bellingham, WA 98225

Gay Resource Center
CAB 305
Evergreen State College
Olympia, WA 98501

Gay People's Alliance
3rd Floor-Compton Union
Washington State University
Pullman, WA 99163

WASHINGTON, D.C.

Gay People's Alliance
Room 435, Marvin Center
George Washington Univ.
800 21st St., NW
Washington, D.C. 20006

WEST VIRGINIA

Homophile Awareness League
c/o Bruce Severino
10 Glenn Street
Morgantown, WV 26505

WISCONSIN

Gay Students Association
Box 10 Student Union
Univ. of Wisc.
Milwaukee, WI 53211

CANADA

Gay People
University of British Columbia
Vancouver 8, BC

Gay People of Simon Fraser
c/o Student Society
Simon Fraser University
Burnaby, BC

Campus Gay Club
Student Union
University of Manitoba
Winnipeg, Manitoba

Gay Alliance at York
CYSF, CS105
York University
4700 Keele Street
Downsview, Ontario
M3J 1P3

Homophile Association
"The Ontarian" Office
University of Guelph
Guelph, Ontario

Queens Univ. Homophile Assoc.
Student Affairs Centre
Queens University
Kingston, Ontario

Homophile Association
c/o University Comm. Center
University of W. Ontario
London, Ontario

Gays of Ottawa
Carleton University
c/o Student Activities
Ottawa, Ontario

Gay People of Carlton
c/o CUSA
Carleton Univ.
Colonel By Drive
Ottawa, ONT K1S SB6

Homophile Association
12 Hart House Circle—SAC Office
University of Toronto
Toronto, Ontario

Lakehead Gay Liberation
Student Union
Lakehead Univ.
Thunder Bay, ONT

Gay Liberation Movement
c/o Federation of Students
Campus Center
University of Waterloo
Waterloo, Ontario

Gay McGill
Univ. Ctre. Rm. B-41
3480 McTarish
Montreal, QUE H3A 1X9

Gay Students Alliance
Box 3043
Saskatoon, Saskatchewan

Homosexual Political Organizations, U.S.

DEMOCRATIC

Alice B. Toklas Memorial Democratic Club
Box 11316
San Francisco, CA 94101
415/836-0704

Barbary Coast Democratic Club
c/o 990 Geary St., Suite 403
San Francisco, CA 94109
415/885-1001

Harvey Milk Gay Democratic Club
330 Grove St.
San Francisco, CA 94102
415/863-6831, 621-5722

Minutemen Democratic Club
277-B Shipley St.
San Francisco, CA 94107
415/495-7182

Susan B. Anthony Democratic Club
Box 2066
San Jose, CA 95109
408/289-1088

Gertrude Stein Democratic Club
No Address
Washington, D.C.

The Gay Democrats of Greater Seattle
Emery Bushong (206) 623-1239
Tim Mayhew (206) 323-4453

Lesbian and Gay Democrats of Texas
c/o Allan G. Calkin
4423 Cole, #111
Dallas, TX 75205
214/526-8345

L.I.F.E. Democratic Club
P.O. Box 27071
Kansas City, MO 64110
Gerry Young
816/753-8762

Long Beach Lambda Democratic Club
Box 14454
Long Beach, CA 90803

California Democratic Party Gay Caucus
3165 Larga Ave.
Los Angeles, CA 90039
213/661-3339

Stonewall Democratic Club
Box 39495
Los Angeles, CA 90039
or
1428 N. McCadden Place
Los Angeles, CA 90028
213/660-2987

Fruitridge Democratic Club
Box 2103
Sacramento, CA 95810

First Tuesday Democratic Association
Box 7032
Atlanta, GA 30357
404/885-1382, 876-5372

Gay Independent Democrats
Box 91
Rutgers Student Center
New Brunswick, NJ 08903
201/249-2627

Lambda Independent Democrats
22 Tompkins Pl.
Brooklyn, NY 11231
Peter Vogel, Pres.

Gay and Lesbian Independent Democrats
c/o 59 W. 82nd St. #1
New York, NY 10024
Jim Levin, Pres., 212/799-4558

Walt Whitman Democratic Club
1719 Rodman St.
Philadelphia, PA 19146
Jeff Britton, Pres., 215/735-0904

REPUBLICAN

New Era Young Republican Club
c/o Box 251 Cooper Station
New York, NY 10003
212/475-5137

Concerned Republicans for Individual Rights
P.O. Box 14174
San Francisco, CA 94114
415/626-1443

Teddy Roosevelt Republican Club
c/o Rev. Ray Broshears
990 Geary St., Suite 403
San Francisco, CA 94109
415/673-8184

Republican Alternative Committee
Box 91
Austin, TX 78767
512/472-2020

Lincoln Republican Club of Southern California
Box 3719
Los Angeles, CA 90028
213/275-2357
Bob Appel, Pres.

Walt Whitman Republican Club
P.O. Box 50295
Washington, D.C.
703/528-2168
202/966-8873

NON-PARTISAN

Cambridge Gay Political Caucus
Box 218
Cambridge, MA 02141
617/491-0968

Capital District Gay Political Caucus
Box 131
Albany, NY 12201
or
332 Hudson Ave.
Albany, NY
518/462-6138

Colorado Citizen's Caucus
Box 18701
Denver, CO 80218

Political Organizations

Portland Town Council Political
Action Committee
320 SW Stark St., #506
Portland, OR 97204
503/223-8299

Cleveland Gay Political Union
c/o GEAR
P.O. Box 6177
Cleveland, OH 44101

Dallas Gay Political Caucus
Box 35011
Dallas, TX 75235
214/528-4233
Don Baker or Bill Nelson

Gay Political Caucus
Box 3887
Houston, TX 77001
Lee Harrington, Pres.
713/658-4224 (work)
      523-4400 (home)

SEAMEC
(Seattle Municipal Elections Committee for Gays)
526 Smith Tower
Seattle, WA 98104
206/682-6044

Mass. Gay Political Caucus
Box 179
118 Mass Ave.
Boston, MA 02115
671/242-3544

N.Y. Political Action Council
1841 Broadway, #808
New York, NY 10023
Sandy Gold,
212/222-4076

Gay Political Union
c/o Jim Owles
61 Jane St.
New York, NY 10014
212/741-3677, 212/675-9228

Gay Political Caucus, Albany
Gary Pavlic 518/434-4062 (h)
518/370-7680 (w)

Gay Political Caucus, Rochester
Rochester NY
Patty Evans 716/436-2524

Municipal Elections Commission of
Los Angeles
c/o Gay Community Services Cen-
ter
Box 36777
Los Angeles, CA 90038

Lesbian and Gay Political Caucus
Box 822
Austin, TX 78767
512/478-8653

Gay Voter's League of California
c/o 2778 Shipley St.
San Francisco, CA 94107
415/637-8184

Gay Voter's League of San Francisco
c/o Box 1428
San Francisco, CA 94101
415/885-1001

APPENDIX
XII

Homosexual Interest Groups, U.S. and Canada

ACADEMICS

(See also: Scientists, Seminarians, Teachers and Social Workers)

Caucus of Gay Men's and Lesbian's Concerns of the Speech Communications Association
Randall Majors
Northeastern Illinois University
5500 N. St. Louis Ave.
Chicago, IL 60625
312/583-4050 - Ext. 536

Committee on (Concerns of) Lesbians and Gay Males in the English Profession
c/o Dr. Richard J. Follett, Co-Chair
7501 E. Treasure Dr., PH "E"
North Bay Village, FL 33141
305/864-7625

Gay Academic Union
National Headquarters
Box 927
Los Angeles, CA 90028
(Contact national headquarters for local chapters)

Gay & Lesbian Task Force of American Library Association
c/o Barbara Gittings
Box 2383
Philadelphia, PA 19103
215/471-3322

Sociologist's Gay Caucus
440 East 87th Street
New York, NY 10028

Sociologists' Gay Caucus
University of Windsor
Windsor, Ontario N9B 3P4
510/253-4232 - Ext. 109

James Zais
1545 18th St., NW
Washington, D.C. 20036
202/462-5879 or 233-1950
(Historians & Political Scientists)

Homoseuxal Interest Groups

ARTISTS

Alliance of Gay Artists (AGA)
c/o J. Smith
7959 Woodrow Wilson Fr.
Los Angeles, CA 90046
213/851-7722

BOOKSELLERS

American Booksellers Association
Gay Caucus
P.O. Box 248
Belvedere, NJ 07823
201/475-5718

BUSINESS

Golden Gate Business Assoc.
South Bay 1288 Isengard St.
San Jose, CA 95121
408-629-1606

Greater Gotham Business Council
Box 751 - Chelsea Station
New York, NY 10011

Hudson-Mohawk Business & Prof.
  Assoc.
P.O. Box 1816
Albany, NY 12201

Key West Business Guild
Box 1208
Key West, FL 33040

Metropolitan Business Assoc.
24 North Wabash - Rm. 823
Chicago, IL 60602
312/878-3020

Provincetown Business Guild
Box 421
Provincetown, MA 02657
617/478-2313

Greater San Diego Business Assoc.
2440 Chatsworth Blvd.
San Diego, CA 92106

Stanford University Gay Business
  Students Association
Stanford University Graduate School
  of Business
Box 9606
Stanford, CA 94305

Realty Referrals
P.O. Box 14221
Portland, OR 97214
503/239-5051

COUNSELORS

American Association of Sex Edu-
  cators, Counselors & Therapists
AASECT-GLB Caucus
Gay, Lesbian & Bisexual Caucus
P.O. Box 834
Linden Hill, NY 11354

Gay Caucus of the National Association of Alcoholism Counselors
c/o Rooney
4201 So. 36th Street
Arlington, VA 22206

National Association of Gay Alcoholism Professionals
Box 376
Oakland, NJ
201/337-1087

National Coalition of Gay and Les-
  bian Counselors
P.O. Box 14662
San Francisco, CA 94114

GOVERNMENT

Advocates for Gay and Lesbian State
  Employees (ALSE)
c/o Boyce Hinman
Sacramento, CA
916/965-6851

HEALTH WORKERS

Bay Area Physicians for Human Rights
P.O. Box 14546
San Francisco, CA 94114

Capitol Area Physicians Association
P.O. Box 32068
Calvert Station
Washington, D.C. 20007

Caucus of Gay Public Health Workers
206 North 35th St.
Philadelphia, PA 19104

Gay Health Professionals Group
Stan Whittemore, M.D.
563 Clayton Street
Denver, CO 80206
303/399-4520

Gay People In Health Care
74 Grove St., Rm 2RW
New York, NY 10014
212/499-1453

Gay Task Force of the National Drug Congress c/o Beatty
3621 Brookridge Terrace - Apt. 103
Harrisburg, PA 17109

Lesbian and Gay People in Medicine/NY
(No address)
212/789-1927

National Gay Health Coalition
55 West 26th Street #402
New York, NY 10010
212/725-0114

Northern California Dentists for Human Rights
P.O. Box 14575
San Francisco, CA 94114
415/673-3189

Southern California Dental Society for Human Rights
256 South Robertson Blvd.
Beverly Hills, CA 90211
213/652-6459

LAW

American Civil Liberties Union/Gay Rights Chapter
633 South Shatto Pl. Suite 207
Los Angeles, CA 90005
213/466-6739

Gay Caucus of American Bar Assoc.
c/o E. Carrington Boggan
5 East 57th St.
New York, NY 10022
212/935-9380

Gay Law Students Association
Box 872
Chicago, IL 60690
312/327-9896

Gay Law Students Association
Hastings College of Law
198 McAllister
San Francisco, CA 94102
415/557-1950

Gay & Lesbian Legal Association
Boston University
c/o Stewart Mittler
14 Grove St.
Boston, MA 02114

Gay Rights Caucus San Diego
1456 5th Ave.
San Diego, CA 92101
415/621-3900 9 a.m.–5 p.m.

Lawyers for Human Rights
Box 480318
Los Angeles, CA 90048

Lesbian & Gay Caucus
Northeastern University School of Law
400 Huntington Ave.
Boston, MA 02115

Homoseuxal Interest Groups

Lesbian & Gay Law Students of New York University
33 Washington Sq. West, #1C
New York, NY 10011
212/598-7542

Lesbian & Gay Legal Worker's Group
c/o Gerald Gerash
1535 Grant St., Suite 180
Denver, CO 80203

Minnesota Gay Bar Association
3244 1st Avenue
Minneapolis, MN 55408

National Lawyers Guild Gay Caucus
c/o Paul Alberts
236 Day Street
San Francisco, CA 94131
or
558 Capp Street
San Francisco, CA 94110
415/285-5066

National Police-Gay-Lesbian Orientation Program
P.O. Box 42010
San Francisco, CA 94101

New York Law Group
Box 1899
New York, NY 10017
(Lawyers & Students)

The Lesbian & Gay Rights Caucus
Antioch School of Law
Box 207
1624 Crescent Place, NW
Washington, D.C. 20009

MEDICAL STUDENTS
Gay People in Medicine Task Force
American Medical Student Assoc.
P.O. Box 131
Chantilly, VA 22021
703/968-7920

NURSING
Gay Nurse's Alliance
P.O. Box 8166
UT Station
Knoxville, TN 37916
615/637-8845
(Note: Regional offices can be contacted through this address)

Lesbian & Gay Caucus of the American Academy of Physician Assistants
c/o Ron Vachon
Fenway Community Health Center
16 Haviland St.
Boston, MA 02115
617/267-7573

PSYCHIATRISTS
Gay Caucus of the American Psychiatric Assoc.
c/o Emory Hettrich
144 East 36th St.
New York, NY 10016

Gay, Lesbian & Bisexual Caucus of the American Psychiatric Association
c/o Dr. Richard Pillard
6 Bond St.
Boston, MA 02118

PSYCHOLOGISTS
Association of Gay Psychologists
Alan Malyon, Ph.D, President
8430 Santa Monica Blvd., #200
Los Angeles, CA 90069
213/657-4275 (h)
    657-1670 (w)

Association of Gay Psychologists
463 West Street, #A627
New York, NY 10014
ATTN: Jack Doren

New York Association of Gay Psychologists & Gay Psychotherapists
,c/o Georgia Simari
255 Avenue of the Americas, #13
New York, NY 10014
212/255-6647

SCIENTISTS

Lesbian & Gay Associated Engineers and Scientists
P.O. Box 70133
Sunnyvale, CA 94086

National Organization of Lesbian and Gay Scientists
P.O. Box 39528
Los Angeles, CA 90039

Triangle Gay Scientists
Box 1137
Chapel Hill, NC 27514
(Physical, Biological, Mathematics and Engineering fields)

Washington Area Gay Scientists (WAGS)
P.O. Box 4614
Arlington, VA 22204

SEMINARIANS

Gay Seminarians
c/o Chicago Theological Seminary
P.O. Box 2073
Chicago, IL 60690
312/477-3177
528-3064

SOCIAL WORK

Association of Gay Social Workers
c/o Mike Weltmann
315 South 15th St.
Philadelphia, PA 19102

Association of Lesbian & Gay Social Workers
110 East 23rd St., #502
New York, NY 10010

The Association of Social Work Educators Concerned with Gay Issues
c/o Dr. Ray Berger
Social Work Program
Florida International University
North Campus
North Miami, FL 33181

Council on Social Work Education Task Force on Lesbian/Gay Issues
c/o I.H.I.
490 West End Avenue
New York, NY 10024

Lesbian Committee of National Assoc. of Social Workers
c/o Susan Frankel
79 Madison Avenue
New York, NY 10016

National Association of Lesbian and Gay Gerontologists
3312 Descano Drive
Los Angeles, CA 90026

TEACHERS & SCHOOL WORKERS

Boston Area Gay & Lesbian Schoolworkers (BAGL)
P.O. Box 178
Astor Station
Boston, MA 02123

Homoseuxal Interest Groups

Gay Caucus
National Council of Teachers of
English c/o Dr. Louis Crew
P.O. Box 754
Stevens Pt., WI 54481
or
Dr. Julia Stanley
Department of English
University of Nebraska
Lincoln, NE 68508

Gay Teachers Association
c/o Marc Rubin
204 Lincoln Place
Brooklyn, NY 11217
or
Meryl Friedman
282 Garfield Place
Brooklyn, NY 11215
212/499-1060

Gay Teachers Association
c/o UFGO - Box 872
Chicago, IL 60690

Gay Teachers Caucus of the National Education Association
32 Bridge Street
Hackensack, NJ 07601
201/489-2458

Gay Teachers of Maryland
P.O. Box 12
Randallstown, MD 21133
301/889-6872
   521-2590

Gay Teachers & School Workers
Coalition
c/o Gay Switchboard Message Center
Box 365
625 Post Street
San Francisco, CA 94109
415/771-9700 - Ext. 60

Gay Teachers & Schoolworkers
625 Post
Box 365
San Francisco, CA 94109
415/626-3131

John Gish
32 Bridge St.
Hackensack, NJ
201/489-2458

GTLA (Gay Teachers of Los Angeles)
Box 10024
Glendale, CA 91209

Lesbian School Workers
Box 23984
Oakland, CA 94623

VETERANS

Gay Veterans Action
c/o David Krause
25 Parade Place
Brooklyn, NY 11226
212/284-0812

ONOMASTIC INDEX

Onomastic Index

Onomastic Index

Kosnik, Rev. Anthony, 334.
Krause, David, 621.
Kretz, Selma, 54.
Krody, Nancy, 369.
Krol, John Cardinal, 316, 348, 529.
Kuntzler, Paul, 188, 421.

Lachs, Stephen M., 23.
Laing, R.D., 106.
Lamm, Richard D., 457.
Lanci, Gabriel, 276.
Landrum, Elizabeth, 605.
Lasswell, Harold D., 77.
Lauer, David, 596.
Laurent, John, 276.
Lawrence, John, 445.
Leaks, Jerry, 448.
Lear, Norman, 463.
Lear, Walter J., 445.
Lebedeff, Diane, 225.
Lee, Tracey, 314.
Leeche, Dale, 493.
Lehman, William, 423.
Leiser, Berton, 541.
Leitsch, Richard, 87, 95, 101.
Leland, Mickey, 423, 452.
Leopold, Louise, 294.
Levin, James, 614.
Levine, Melvin, 462.
Lewis, Ann, 452.
Licata, Sal, 600.
Lindsay, John, 111, 433.
Lloyd, Robin, 185.
Loeb, Sister Mary Claude, 516.
Lorde, Andre, 229.
Lowe, Jack, 596.
Lowry, Michael, 159, 423.
Lundgren, William, 369.
Luttman, David, 232.
Lynn, Barry W., 285.
Lynch, Rev. Bernard, SMA, 321.

Macchiarola, Frank J., 456.
MacNair, Barbara, 277.
Maddox, Robert L., 277, 444.
Magnusson, Gordon, 601.
Maguire, Daniel C., 305, 529.
Maguire, Marjorie R., 305.
Mahoney, Bishop Roger, 323.
Majors, Randall, 616.
Malone, Rev. Richard, 323.
Malson, Robert, 444, 445.
Malyon, Alan, 619.
Malzone, John, 314.
Manatt, Charles, 452.

Mann, Gary, 596.
Marsilius of Padua, 300.
Markey, Edward, 423.
Markert, John, 315.
Marks, Marvin, 594.
Marmor, Judd, 106, 107, 113, 128.
Marotta, Toby, 63, 85, 128, 130, 137, 147, 223, 420.
Martello, Leo, 78–79.
Martens, Mason, 595.
Martin, Kenneth, 286.
Martin, Rev. Ren, 273.
Mason, Hilda, 453.
Masters, William H., 101.
Mathias, Charles, 436.
Mathison, Sister Janet, 532.
Matson, William, 277.
Matsui, Robert, 428.
Matt, Herschel J., 91, 373.
Matthiesen, Bishop Leroy, 324.
May, Archbishop John L., 323.
May, William, 540.
Mayhew, Tim, 613.
McAnnally, Kevin, 594.
McBrien, Richard P., 305, 529.
McCann, Brother Robert, FSC, 530.
McCarthy, Leo, 498.
McCauley, Andrew, 547.
McCloskey, Paul, 423, 463.
McCloskey, Peter, 158.
McCormick, Rev. Richard A., SJ, 305, 529.
McCoy, W. Keith, 595.
McCracken, Samuel, 541.
McDevitt, Kathy, 98.
McDonald, Gary, 369.
McDonald, Lawrence, 400, 411, 429, 511.
McDonald, Michael, 369.
McGovern, George, 405, 457, 463.
McKay, Herbert, 547.
McKeon, Bruce, 604.
McKinney, Stewart, 423.
McNaught, Brian, 111, 114–115, 124, 232, 354, 369.
McNeill, Rev. John, SJ, 88–89, 223, 260, 304, 305, 321, 341, 362, 365, 367, 369, 530.
McNichols, W.H., Jr., 457.
McSorley, Rev. Harry, STD, 305, 529.
Medeiros, Humberto Cardinal, 296, 313, 317, 529.
Medinger, Daniel, 529.
Mehl, Robert, 455.
Mendola, Mary, 354, 369.

Onomastic Index

Reedy, William, Jr., 595.
Rees, Bill, 233.
Reeves, Tom, 97
Regelson, Roz, 599.
Reid, John, 86.
Reilly, Robert, 536–544.
Rettger, Rev. John, 597.
Rice, Charles, 91.
Richardson, Rev. William, Jr., 596.
Richmond, Frederick, 424.
Richter, Rosalyn, 225.
Rickman, Herbert, 455.
Ridgeway, Lee, 595.
Roach, Archbishop John R., 309, 316, 317, 323, 532.
Roberts, Bro. William, 328, 352, 369, 552, 569.
Robertson, Marc (pseudonym), 102.
Robinson, James, 192.
Rock, Martin, 226, 276.
Rode, Forrest J., 404, 408.
Rogers, Sandra, 277.
Rohl, Randy, 16.
Roiphe, Anne, 97.
Rooney, 617.
Roos, Michael, 462.
Rosazza, Bishop Peter A., 321, 322, 346.
Rosetti, Frank, 492.
Rothenberg, David, 41, 157, 402.
Rubin, Marc, 112, 129, 621.
Russoniello, Pat, 369.
Ryan, Father Tim, 316, 369.

Sabo, Martin Olav, 424.
St. Aubin, Bob, 596.
Salewski, Rev. Benno, 326–530.
Salm, Rev. Luke, FSC, 305.
Sandmire, Rev., 286.
Sandquist, Elroy, C., Jr., 462.
Saperstein, David, 281.
Schaefer, William, D., 408, 457.
Scheuren, Frank, 276, 308, 323, 366, 369, 424, 445, 594.
Schiff, H. Gerald, 445.
Schneider, Rick, 604.
Schrader, Rand, 448.
Schroeder, Patricia, 424.
Schulte, Ron, 594.
Schwandt, Wayne, 596.
Scott, Bob, 493.
Segal, George, 41.
Seift, Katherine, 220.
Selden, David, 525.

Severino, Bruce, 61.
Shamsid-deen, Abbas, 262.
Shanley, Father Paul, 296, 313, 317, 367, 369.
Shannon, James, 424.
Shapiro, Daniel S., 525.
Shapp, Milton J., 512.
Shepard, P., 605.
Shively, Michael G., 500.
Siegel, Paul, 4, 117.
Sieroty, Allan, 457.
Silbert, Barry, 248.
Silver, William, 277.
Silverman, Merv, 53.
Silverstein, Charles, 18.
Simari, Georgia, 620.
Small, Lawrence, 527.
Smeal, Eleanor, 434, 463.
Smith, Freda, 286.
Smith, J., 617.
Snowden, Terry, 329.
Snyder, Bishop John, 321.
Sobala, Sister Joan, SSJ, 330.
Sobran, Joseph, M., 69.
Socarides, Charles, 95, 104–105.
Solarz, Stephen, 424.
Soloman, Marc, 369.
Spaatz, Kenneth, 270, 276.
Spiegel, John, P., 525.
Spitale, Raymond, 276.
Spitzer, Arthur B., 410.
Springman, William, 90, 98–99.
Stahl, Steve, 190.
Stanley, Julia, 621.
Stark, Fortney, 424.
Starr, Adele, 173.
Steele, Sister Mary Lou, 365.
Stein, Andrew, 455.
Steindler, E.M., 525.
Stevens, Rabbi Elliot L., 527.
Stevenson, Diane, 277.
Stevenson, Peggy, 462.
Stokes, Louis, 424.
Stoller, Robert, 335.
Stone, Irving, 136.
Stone, Judy, 32.
Studds, Gerry, 368, 424.
Sullivan, Bishop Walter, F., 316, 317, 534.
Sullivan, Anthony Corbett, 435.
Swearingen, Daniel, 597.
Swift, Wayne, 276.
Symms, Steven, 429.
Szasz, Thomas, 106.

ORGANIZATIONAL INDEX

Organizational Index

Association of Ladies of Charity of the United States, 330.
Association of Lesbian & Gay Social Workers, 620.
Association of Social Work Educators Concerned with Gay Issues, 620.
Association of Women in Psychology, 402.
AT & T (see American Telephone & Telegraph), 437.
Atlas, 182.
Augustinian Order, 359.
Augustinians of Charity, 351.
Augustinians of the Assumption, 351.
Austin Gay Community Services, 517.
Avon Products, Inc., 525.

Bachelors for Wallace, 433.
Ball State University, 603.
Baltimore Abortion Rights, 409.
Baltimore City Council, 313.
Baltimore Province in Bolivia: School Sisters of Notre Dame, 533.
Bank of America, 437, 525.
Barbary Coast Democratic Club, 613.
Barnard College, 606.
Bay Area Physicians for Human Rights, 618.
Beacon Theatre: NYC, 39.
Beit Haverim (France), 598.
Bet Mishposheh, 276, 373–374, 598.
Beth Chaverim (Australia), 598.
Beth Chiam (Texas), 598.
Beth Isaac Adath Israel Cong., Baltimore, 372.
Beth Simchat, NYC, 374.
Bethany Theological Seminary, 293.
Bishop McNamara High School, Forrestville, Md., 328.
Black and Puerto Rican Coalition of Legislators, 402.
Black and White Men Together (BWMT), 173–174, 248.
Black and White Men Together International Convention, 148.
Black Movement, 205.
Black Veterans for Social Justice, 408.
B'nai B'rith Anti-Defamation League, 128, 248.
B'nai B'rith Hillel Foundation (Princeton University), 91.
B'nai B'rith Women, 403, 407.
Board of Appeals and Review (Washington D.C.), 451.

Board of Campus Ministries of the Universal Fellowship of Metropolitan Community Churches, 292.
Board of Church and Society: United Methodist Church, 281, 515.
Board of Commissioners: City of Philadelphia, 291.
Board of Education: NYC, 162–163, 235.
Board of Elders: Universal Fellowship of Metropolitan Community Churches, 276.
Board of Global Ministries: United Methodist Church, 118.
Board of Global Ministries Women's Division: Washington Interreligious Staff Council, 281.
Board of Library Trustees: City of Washington, D.C., 451.
Board of Psychiatric Advisors: Mattachine Society, 92.
Board of Religious Formation Conference: St. Thomas More House of Studies, Washington, D.C., 347.
Bob Jones University, 123.
Boston Alliance of Gay and Lesbian Youth, 298.
Boston Area Gay and Lesbian Social Workers, 162, 620.
Boston City Hospital: ICU, 18.
Boston College, 305, 326, 605.
Boston Gay and Lesbian Advocates and Defenders, 152.
Boston Homophile Alcoholism Treatment Center, 503.
Boston Opera House, 39.
Boston Theological Coalition, 526.
Boston Theological Institute: Women's Theological Coalition, 337.
Boston University, 618.
Boston's Committee for Gay Youth, 298.
Boston's Community Church, 295.
Boulder Gay Liberation: University of Colorado, 601.
Bowling Green State University, 608.
Boy Scouts of America, 217, 410.
Bread for the World, 329.
Brethren/Mennonite Council for Gay Concerns, 226, 227.
Brigham Young University, 135–136.
Brooklyn College, 607.

633

Organizational Index

635

Organizational Index

Continental Life Insurance Company, 182.

Continuing Education Committee of the APA, 120.

Contra Costa Building Trades Council, 406.

CORE, 128.

Core Commission: Women's Ordination Conference, 332.

Cornell Gay Liberation, 608.

Cornell University, 608.

Cornerstone Justice and Peace Center, 338, 527.

Correctional Change Group, 338, 527.

Council for Community Consciousness, Inc., 548.

Council of Churches, 330. (see also: National Council of Churches, World Council of Churches)

Council of Churches (Seattle), 248.

Council of Europe, 156.

Council of Religious Women, 532.

Council on Social Work Education Task Force on Lesbian/Gay Issues, 620.

Country Experience for Young Womyn, 97.

Criminal Justice Commission: Diocese of Bridgeport, 526.

Criminal Justice Task Force, 273.

Cuban/Haitian Task Force, 495.

Cuban Relief Fund: Universal Fellowship of Metropolitan Community Churches, 493.

Cumberland High School, R.I., 15–16.

Custody Action for Lesbian Mothers (CALM), 223.

Custody Action for Lesbian Mothers (CALM) Philadelphia, Pa., 169.

Dade County Coalition for Human Rights, 493.

Dallas Convention Center, 39.

Dallas Gay Political Caucus, 615.

Daughters of Bilitis, 147.

David the Matchmaker, 166.

Davis City Council (Calif.), 98.

DeAndreis Institute of Theology, 293.

Defense Investigative Agency, 219.

Democratic Caucus, 190.

Democratic Convention (1980), 157, 158, 438.

Democratic National Committee, 452, 463.

Democratic Party, 211, 433, 448, 498.

Democratic Platform Committee (1980), 444.

Democratic Socialist Organizing Committee, 412, 416.

Democratic Study Group, 463.

Democrats for the '80s, 463.

Department of Christian Social Action of the Universal Fellowship of Metropolitan Community Churches, 401.

Department of Ecumenical Relations: Universal Fellowship of Metropolitan Community Churches, 272, 279.

Department of Education: United States Catholic Conference, 308, 326.

Department of Fair Employment Practices: State of California, 448.

Department of Health, Education and Welfare, U.S., 19, 500. (see also U.S. Dept. of Health and Human Services)

Department of Health's Venereal Disease Control Unit: State of California, 53.

Department of Human Resources: Oregon State, 228.

Department of Human Services: State of New Jersey, 15.

Des Moines Catholic Workers, 338, 527.

Det Norske Forbundet av '48 (Norway), 155.

Dignity, 15, 44, 124, 129, 201, 272, 273, 276, 286, 297, 298, 304, 305, 308, 309, 313, 314, 316, 317, 321, 324, 325, 326, 328, 329, 330, 337, 341, 342, 343, 347, 350, 359, 362–363, 364, 365, 366, 367, 368, 369, 370, 419, 493, 502, 566, 569, 570.

Dignity (Albany), 338, 591.

Dignity/Atlanta, 589.

Dignity/Austin (Tex.), 592.

Dignity (Baltimore), 338, 363, 590.

Dignity (Bay Area), 338, 588.

Dignity/Birmingham, 588.

Dignity/Boston, 338, 590.

Dignity (Brooklyn), 338, 591.

Dignity (Buffalo), 338, 591.

Dignity/Calgary (Canada), 593.

Dignity (Canada) Dignite, 338.

Organizational Index

Organizational Index

Gay Democrats of Greater Seattle, 613.
Gay Discussion Group: California Technological Institute, 600.
Gay Educators Association, 162.
Gay Fathers Coalition: Washington, D.C., 169.
Gay Freedom Coalition SUC Genesco, 608.
Gay Freedom League, 607.
Gay Freedom League: SUNY Brockport, 608.
Gay Health Professionals Group, 618.
Gay Horizons, Inc., 170.
Gay Independent Democrats, 614.
Gay Law Students Association, 618.
Gay Law Students Association (Calif.), 600.
Gay Law Students Association: UFGO, 603.
Gay Law Students: SUNY Buffalo, 608.
Gay, Lesbian & Bisexual Caucus of the American Psychiatric Association, 619.
Gay Liberation: Ft. Valley State College, 602.
Gay Liberation: Herkimer College, 607.
Gay Liberation: Oberlin College, 608.
Gay Liberation: Staten Island Community College, 606.
Gay Liberation: Trinity College, 602.
Gay Liberation: University of Minnesota, 605.
Gay Liberation: University of New Mexico, 606.
Gay Liberation: Williams College, 604.
Gay Liberation Front: Antioch College, 609.
Gay Liberation Front: Bard College, 607.
Gay Liberation Front: East Los Angeles College, 600.
Gay Liberation Front: Inner College University of Connecticut, 602.
Gay Liberation Front: Kent State University, 608.
Gay Liberation Front: Long Island University, 607.
Gay Liberation Front: N.Y., 63, 78, 109, 137–138, 234.

Gay Liberation Front: Sacramento State College, 601.
Gay Liberation Front: San Francisco State College, 601.
Gay Liberation Front: SUNY Buffalo, 608.
Gay Liberation Front: SUNY Stony Brook, 607.
Gay Liberation Front: University of Iowa, 603.
Gay Liberation Front: University of Kentucky, 603.
Gay Liberation Front: University of Michigan, 605.
Gay Liberation Front: University of Rochester, 608.
Gay Liberation Front: University of South Carolina, 610.
Gay Liberation Front: Wayne State University, 605.
Gay Liberation Group: College of William and Mary, 610.
Gay Liberation Movement, 85.
Gay Liberation Movement: Michigan State University, 605.
Gay Liberation Movement: University of Waterloo (Canada), 612.
Gay McGill: McGill University (Canada), 612.
Gay Medical Students: Gay Men's Health Project, New York, 606.
Gay Men's Alliance: Hunter College, 606.
Gay Men's Choir, 514.
Gay Men's Chorus, 41.
Gay Men's Collective: Richmond College New York, 606.
Gay Men's Health Project: New York, 606
Gay Militant Atheists, 547.
Gay Nurses Alliance, 619.
Gay Nurses Alliance East, 166.
Gay Nurses Alliance of Brownsville (Texas), 148.
Gay Nurses Alliance West, 166.
Gay Outreach Program: San Francisco Police Department, 22.
Gay Parent Custody Fund (Denver, Colorado), 169.
Gay Parent Legal and Research Group (Lynnwood, Washington), 169.
Gay People at Brooklyn College, 607.

Organizational Index

Organizational Index

Graduate School of Social Work: University of Connecticut, 119.
Graduate Theological Union, 601.
Grail Foundation, The, 418.
Graphic Arts International Union, 406.
Gray Panthers, 405.
Great American Lesbian Art Show (GALAS), 41.
Greater Gotham Business Council, 154, 455–456, 617.
Greater San Diego Business Association, 617.
Greater Springfield Council of Churches, 330. (see also: Council of Churches, National Council of Churches, World Council of Churches)
Groundwork, 528.
Groundwork: Lansing, 339.
Guilford Gay Alliance: Guilford College, 608.

HA-CHUG (Canada), 599.
Hamma School of Theology, 609.
Hampshire College, 604.
Hampshire Gay Friends: Hampshire College, 604.
Handmaids of Mary: Sisters Coalition for Justice, 339, 528.
Harpur Gay Liberation: SUNY Binghamton, 607.
Harvard Divinity School, 88.
Harvard Law School, 191.
Harvard-Radcliffe Gay Students Association, 191, 604.
Harvard University, 604.
Harvey Milk Gay Democratic Club, 159, 406, 421, 613.
Hastings Center: Institute of Society, Ethics and the Life Sciences, 105.
Hastings College of Law, 601, 618.
Hatikvah Hashalom (Colorado), 599.
Haverford College, 609.
Havurah Or B'Emek (Indiana), 599.
Health Services Administration: NYC, 111.
Herkimer College, 607.
High Sea Islanders, 181.
Hitch'n Post Bar, 405.
Hobart College, 608.
Hofstra United Gays, 607.
Hofstra University, 607.
Holiday Inn, 182.

Hollywood Police Department, 57.
Holy Cross, Society of the, 341.
Holy Trinity Church, Georgetown, Washington, D.C., 328, 343.
Holy Trinity Mission Seminary, 293, 347.
Holy Trinity Seminary, 417, 515.
Holyoke Homophile League, 604.
Homewood Friends (Baltimore), 515.
Homewood Friends Meeting, 409.
Homophile Association: University of Guelph (Canada), 611.
Homophile Association: University of Toronto (Canada), 612.
Homophile Association: University of Western Ontario, 611.
Homophile Awareness League: West Virginia State University, 611.
Homophile Community Health Service, 503.
Homophile Union: Boston College, 605.
Homophiles of Indiana University, 609.
Homophiles of Penn State, 609.
Homosexual Community Counseling Center, 117.
Hope College, 22.
Hotel and Restaurant Employees Union, 406.
House of Affirmation, 558.
House of Community, 339, 528.
Housing and Urban Development, 431.
Houston Gay Political Caucus, 152.
Howard University, 449.
Hudson-Mohawk Business & Professional Association, 617.
Human Rights Agency of San Francisco, 131.
Human Rights Campaign Fund, 463.
Human Rights Commission: Washington, D.C., 445.
Human Sexuality Task Force: Christian Church/Disciples of Christ, 272.
Humbolt State University, 90.
Hunter, College, 606.

IBM, 437, 528
Illinois State University, 603.
Immaculate Conception Church, Seattle, 367.

Organizational Index

Jesuit Renewal Center, Milford, Ohio, 339, 529.
Jesuit School of Theology: Chicago, 345.
Jew Gays of Central Maryland, 599.
Jewish Congregations, 271–272.
Jewish Les-Feminists (Calif.), 599.
Job Corps, 447.
Joint Strategy and Action Coalition: National Council of Churches, 276.
Joint Strategy and Action Committee: Universal Fellowship of Metropolitan Community Churches, 273, 286.
Justice and Peace Center, 125, 326, 339.
Justice and Peace Commission: Diocese of Syracuse, 338, 534.
Justice and Peace Committee (Claretians), 505. (see also: Claretian Order)
Justice and Peace Office, 418.
Juvenile Court, San Francisco, 448.
Juvenile Justice Advisory Committee, Washington, D.C., 451.

Kamber Group, the, 403.
Kansas State College, 603.
Kansas State University, 603.
Kennedy Center: Washington, D.C., 39, 40, 514.
Kent State University, 166, 608.
Key West Business Guild, 617.
Kingston Gay Liberation: University of Rhode Island, 610.
Kinsey Institute, 132.
Kinship: Seventh Day Adventists, 276.
Knights of Columbus, 183.
Knoxville Lesbian Collective, 610.

Lakehead Gay Liberation: Lakehead University, 612.
LAMBDA CHAI (Mich.), 599.
Lambda Independent Democrats, 614.
Lambda Legal Defense and Education Fund, 407, 445, 517.
Lambda Resource Center for the Blind, 168, 170.
Las Hermanas, 339, 418, 528.
Lavender University of the Rockies, 116.
Lawrence Gay Liberation Front: University of Kansas, 603.

Law School of New York University, 517.
Lawyers for Human Rights, 618.
Leadership Conference of Women Religious, 418.
Leadership Conference on Civil Rights, 281.
League of Women Voters, 86, 407, 434.
Leaping Lesbian Follies, 499.
Legal Research and Analysis Committee, 407.
Legal Services Corporation, 209, 212, 400, 411, 415, 429, 431, 509, 510, 511.
Legislative Lobbying Committee, 407.
Lehman College, 607.
Le Moyne College, 304.
Lesbian Activists at Barnard College, 606.
Lesbian Alliance (Iowa), 167.
Lesbian and Gay Associated Engineers and Scientists, 620.
Lesbian and Gay Caucus, 618.
Lesbian & Gay Caucus of the American Academy of Physician Assistants, 619.
Lesbian & Gay Democrats of Texas, 613.
Lesbian and Gay Law Students Association of New York University, 517, 619.
Lesbian and Gay Legal Workers' Group, 619.
Lesbian and Gay Men's Union: Cabrillo College, 601.
Lesbian and Gay Parents Project: National Lawyers Guild, 225, 415.
Lesbian and Gay People in Medicine, 399.
Lesbian and Gay People in Medicine/New York, 618.
Lesbian and Gay Physician's Assistants, 400.
Lesbian and Gay Political Caucus, 615.
Lesbian and Gay Rights Caucus, 619.
Lesbian and Gay Rights Conference, 400.
Lesbian Collective: Ohio University, 609.
Lesbian Committee of the National Association of Social Workers, 620.
Lesbian Community Center, 314.

Organizational Index

McCormick Theological Seminary, 22, 293.
McDonald's, 529.
McGill University, 305, 526, 612.
Medical College of Georgia, 102.
Medical Mission Sisters-Eastern District & Western District Assembly, 418.
Men Allied Nationally for the ERA, 279.
Mennonite Church, 278.
Men's Coming Out Group, 515.
Merck, 437.
Mercy Center, Detroit, 328.
Methodist Church, 406.
Metro Gay Students Union: Metropolitan Street Junior College, 605.
Metropolitan Business Association, 617.
Metropolitan Community Church (MCC), 22, 79, 138, 271, 272, 293, 294, 314, 315, 329, 556. (See also: Universal Fellowship of Metropolitan Community Churches)
Metropolitan Community Church: District of Columbia, 125.
Metropolitan Community Church: New Orleans, 20.
Metropolitan Community Church: NYC, 286.
Metropolitan Community Church: Philadelphia, Pa., 286, 290.
Metropolitan Community Church: Raleigh, North Carolina, 46.
Metropolitan Community Church: San Jose, California, 290, 326.
Metropolitan Community Church: Toronto, Ontario, Canada, 65.
Metropolitan Community Church: Washington, D.C., 286, 287, 326, 448, 451, 502.
Metropolitan-Duane Methodist Church, 515–516.
Metropolitan State College, 601.
Michigan State Legislature, 457.
Michigan State University, 605.
Michigan Women's Music Festival, 148.
Midwest Lesbian-Feminist Conference, 148.
Mildred Andrews Fund, 507.

Milwaukee Archdiocesan Commission for the Plan of Pastoral Action for Family Ministry (Roman Catholic), 529.
Milwaukee Justice and Peace Center, 295, 529.
Minnesota Catholic Conference, 314, 530.
Minnesota Gay Bar Association, 619.
Minneapolis Police Department, 22–23.
Ministry for Social Justice: Diocese of Orlando, 338, 531.
Minority Council on Alcoholism-Community Training and Resource Center, 503.
Minutemen Democratic Club, 613.
Missionary Oblates of Mary Immaculate, 343.
Missionary Sisters of the Immaculate Conception, 339.
Mississippi Gay Alliance: Mississippi State University, 605.
Mississippi State Gay Counseling & Projects: Mississippi State University, 605.
Mississippi State University, 605.
Missouri Coalition for Human Rights, 420.
Mobil Oil, 437.
Mobilization for Survival, 397, 400, 405, 417.
Modern Language Association, 42.
Moral Majority, 7, 40, 242, 454.
Mormon Church (Church of Latter Day Saints), 103, 271–272, 281.
Mormons for ERA, 404.
Morning Star Community, 352, 353.
Most Holy Sacrament Administrative Team, 339, 530.
Mount Diablo Council of the Boy Scouts of America, 410.
Mt. Marie, Holyoke, Mass., 328.
Mount St. Michael High School, 321.
Mountain Women's Collective of Central Michigan University, 605.
Movement for a New Society, 405.
Ms Foundation, 407.
Municipal Court of Los Angeles, 448.
Municipal Election Committee (Los Angeles, Calif.), 191.
Municipal Elections Committee of Los Angeles, 615.
Mytilene Society: Wellesley College, 605.

Organizational Index

National Urban League, 248.
National Women's Conference Committee, 403.
National Women's Conference (1977) International Women's Year, 158.
National Women's Law Center, 407.
National Women's Political Caucus, 158, 403, 434, 463.
National Women's Studies Conference, 402.
Navy, U.S., 14. (see also: Armed Forces, U.S.)
Neighborhood Church, the, 102, 248, 398, 516.
Network, 403, 416, 417, 418, 419.
New American Movement, 405.
New Democratic Coalition, 413.
New England Lesbian and Gay Conference, 126, 147.
New Era Young Republican Club, 614.
New Jersey Alcoholism Association, 508.
New Left, 130.
New Mexico Coalition of Lesbian and Gay Rights, 158.
New Paltz Gay Liberation, 607.
New Ways Ministry, 80, 122, 125, 218, 227, 232, 270, 276, 278, 288, 293, 295, 308, 314, 316, 317, 321, 325–326, 328, 330, 331, 332, 333, 337, 339, 340, 343, 347, 350, 353, 354–357, 358, 359, 362, 365, 366, 367, 400, 408, 413, 416, 417, 418, 419, 420, 500, 504, 505, 506, 508, 515, 524, 553, 569.
New Ways Symposium on the Church and Homosexuality, 359.
New York Association of Gay Psychotherapists and Psychologists, 620.
New York Law Group, 619.
New York Political Action Council, 615.
New York University, 606, 619.
New York City Board of Education, 162, 163, 235.
New York City Commission on Human Rights, 512, 513.
New York City Council, 365, 402, 455.
New York City Gay Men's Choir, 547.
New York City Gay Teachers Association, 152, 234.

New York City Health Services Association, 111, 134.
New York City Health Systems Agency, 158.
New York City Human Rights Commission, 402.
New York City School Board, 456. (see also NYC Board of Education)
New York Gay Men's Health Project, 52.
New York State Court of Appeals, 89.
New York State United Teachers, 163.
New York Times, 25.
New York University, 517.
Newman Center Staff, 531.
Newman Center Staff: Columbia, Md., 339.
Newman Center Staff: Davis, Calif., 339.
Newman Community, 531.
Newman Community: Chapel Hill, 339.
News Release, 535.
Niagara Democratic Club, 406.
Nineteen-seventy-two Gay Rights Platform: National Coalition of Gay Organizations, 201–202.
NIU Gay Liberation Front, 602.
Nixon Administration, 501. (see also: White House)
Non-Sexist Child Development Project: Women's Action Alliance, NYC, 20.
North American Conference of Homophile Organizations (NACHO), 87–88.
North American Jewish Students Network, 375, 531.
North American Man/Boy Love Association (NAMBLA), 80–82, 96–97, 107, 173, 176–177, 179–180, 200, 201, 211–212, 214–215, 226, 295, 313, 546.
North Carolina State University, 46.
Northeast Community Organization, 409.
Northeastern Gay Students Organization, 605.
Northeastern Illinois University, 616.
Northeastern University, 605.
Northeastern University School of Law, 618.

Organizational Index

Organizational Index

Religious Coalition for Abortion Rights, 281, 288–290, 404, 406.

Religious Formation Conference, 295, 418.

Religious Leaders Concerned About Racism and Human Rights, 316.

Renaissance House, 149.

Rene Guyon Society, 173, 177–180.

Reproductive Rights National Network, 406.

Republican Alternative Committee, 614.

Republican National Platform Committee, 190.

Republican Party, 190, 211.

Research and Education SIG: San Diego Gay Academic Union, 161.

Research and Forecasts, Inc., 7.

Retreat for Gay Catholics, 328.

Revolutionary Communist Party, 408.

Richmond College, Staten Island, NYC, 606–607.

Riksforbundet for Sexuellt Likaberattigande (Sweden), 155.

Riverside Church, NYC, 400.

Riverside Church's Disarmament Program, 400.

Rochester City Council, 516.

Roman Catholic Church, xv, xviii, 80, 227, 270, 271, 272, 278, 280, 295, 297, 298, 299, 324–325, 326, 332, 342, 347, 357, 358, 370, 406, 413, 419, 420, 426, 437, 508, 549, 572, 581. (see also: Catholic Church, American Catholic Church, Archdiocese and Diocese listings, Pope, Vatican, Religious Orders under their respective titles)

Rural America, 403.

Rutgers Activists for Gay Education, 606.

Rutgers Gay Caucus, 517.

Rutgers Summer School of Alcohol Studies, 167.

Rutgers University, 606.

Rutgers University Coalition of Lesbians: Livingston College, 606.

Rutgers University Homophile League, 606.

Sacramento City College, 601.

Sacramento State College, 601.

Sacred Congregation for the Doctrine of the Faith, 302.

Sacred Heart Chapel, 351.

Sacred Heart Sisters, 341.

St. Clement's R.C. Church, 515.

St. Edward's Church, Phoenix, 343.

St. Francis Grammar School, NYC, 329.

St. Francis Parish Team: Brant Beach, New Jersey, 339, 532.

St. Francis Xavier Church, NYC, 321, 367.

St. Jerome Church, Newport News, Va., 532.

St. Jerome Church Pastoral Staff, Newport News, Va., 339.

St. John's Alliance, 418.

St. John's Student Parish; Campus Ministry Team, East Lansing, 339, 532.

St. John the Evangelist Episcopal Church, 298.

St. Joseph House, Minneapolis, 339, 532.

St. Joseph Church, NYC, 328.

St. Joseph Parish, East Rutherford, N.J., 532.

St. Joseph Parish, Pastoral Ministry Team, East Rutherford, N.J., 339.

St. Leander Parish, Pueblo, Colorado, 532.

St. Leander Parish Social Concerns Committee, Pueblo, Colorado, 339.

St. Louis Gay Huvurah, 599.

St. Louis Institute for Peace and Justice, 532.

St. Louis Provence Social Justice Secretariat, Sisters of St. Joseph of Cardondelet, 534.

St. Louis Task Force for the Ordination of Women, 420.

St. Mark's Lutheran Church, San Francisco, 298.

St. Mary Star of the Sea Parish, Atlantic Mine, Michigan, 340.

St. Mary Star of the Sea Parish, Sisters of St. Joseph of Carondelet, 534.

St. Mary's Academy, Leonardstown, Md., 328.

St. Mary's Seminary, Baltimore, 326.

St. Matthew Community, Brooklyn, 339, 350, 351, 532, 579–587.

St. Michael's College, 305, 529.

St. Paul's Citizens for Human Rights, 532.

Organizational Index

Sisters of Divine Providence, 340, 533.

Sisters of the Guiltless Procession, 353. (organization of male homosexuals; not a Roman Catholic order)

Sisters of the Humility of Mary, 418.

Sisters of the Immaculate Heart of Mary, 341.

Sisters of Loretto, 339, 418, 533.

Sisters of Loretto; Cherry Street House, 533.

Sisters of Loretto; Office of the Social Advocate, 533.

Sisters of Mercy, 339, 341, 533.

Sisters of Mercy of the Union, 295, 339, 418, 419, 533.

Sisters of Mercy of the Union: Silver Spring, Md., 328.

Sisters of Notre Dame, 341, 362.

Sisters of Notre Dame de Nahur, 340, 533.

Sisters of Perpetual Motion, 353. (organization of male homosexuals; not a Roman Catholic order)

Sisters of Providence, 329.

Sisters of the Perpetual Indulgence, 353. (organization of male homosexuals; not a Roman Catholic order)

Sisters of the Presentation, 340, 534.

Sisters of St. Dominic (Dominicans), 533.

Sisters of St. Dominic (Dominicans) of Marymount, 340, 534.

Sisters of St. Joseph, 328, 329, 330, 359.

Sisters of St. Joseph; Third Order of St. Francis, 340, 534.

Sisters of St. Joseph of Carondelet, 326, 534.

Sisters of St. Joseph of Carondelet, Albany Province; Social Justice Secretariat, 534.

Sisters of St. Joseph of Carondelet; General Chapter, Los Angeles, 534.

Sisters of St. Joseph of Carondelet; Social Justice Core Group, 340.

Sisters of St. Joseph of Carondelet; Western Province Social Justice Secretariat, 340, 534.

Sisters of St. Joseph of La Grange, 534.

Sisters of St. Joseph of La Grange; Social Justice Committee, 340.

Sisters of St. Joseph of Medaille, 418.

Sisters of St. Joseph of Orange, 534.

Sisters of St. Joseph of Orange: Social Concern Committee, 340.

Sisters of St. Joseph of Peace, 340, 534.

Sisters of St. Joseph of Peace: Center for Peace and Justice, 417.

Sisters of St. Joseph of Springfield, (Mabs.), 515.

Sisters in Gay Ministry Associated, (SIGMA), 337, 365, 533.

Sixth International Conference of Gay and Lesbian Jews, 148.

Sjalhomo (the Netherlands), 599.

Skyline High School, Los Angeles, California, 16.

Social Action Committee: Church of the Epiphany, Louisville, 338.

Social Action Office: Diocese of Brooklyn, 338, 526.

Social Concern Committee; Sisters of Mercy, 533.

Social Justice Committee, 532.

Social Justice Committee: Xaverian Brothers, 420.

Social Justice Core Group: Sisters of St. Joseph of Carondelet, 534.

Social Justice Field Office: Universal Fellowship of Metropolitan Community Churches, 85.

Social Ministry Commission: Diocese of Richmond, 338.

Soc. Protection Personal Rights, (Israel), 599.

Social Responsibilities Roundtable Division; American Library Association, 163, 508.

Social Security Administration, 510.

Social Work Program; Florida International University, 620.

Society for the Protection of Personal Rights (Israel), 373.

Society of Friends, 290, 534.

Society of Jesus (Jesuits), 341, 345, 416.

Society of the Divine Savior, 295, 328, 341, 362.

Sociologist's Gay Caucus, 616.

S.O.H. (Switzerland), 155.

Sojourners Fellowship, 417.

Sonoma State College, 601.

South Dakota Coalition for Freedom of Choice, 405.

Organizational Index

Organizational Index

Washington Area Women's Center, 225.

Washington City Council, 208.

Washington for Jesus, 273, 276, 288, 399.

Washington Interreligious Staff Council (WISC), 273, 276, 280–282, 282–283, 284, 285, 286, 287, 404.

Washington Peace Center, 417.

Washington Square Church, 248, 516.

Washington Square United Methodist Church, 297, 415, 506.

Washington State Catholic Conference, 326, 535.

Washington State University, 611.

Washington Supreme Court, 101.

Washington Theological Union, 295, 326.

Washington Training Collective, 417..

Washington University; 606.

We Are Everywhere,' 155.

Weber Center, Adrian, Michigan, 328.

Wellesley College, 605.

Wesley Theological Seminary, 294.

Wesleyan College, 602.

Wesleyan Gay Alliance Women's Center, 602.

Westbeth Artist Housing Complex, 402.

Western Electric, 437.

Western Washington State College, 611.

West Side (NYC) Jesuit Community, 321.

West Virginia State University, 611.

Weston School of Theology, 345.

Weyerhaeuser, 437.

White House, 3, 22, 77, 157, 209, 213, 276, 277, 286, 396, 442–444, 447, 514.

White House Conference on Families, 17, 124, 157, 173, 222, 224, 226.

Whitehead Associates, 340, 535.

Whitman-Walker Gay Men's Venereal Disease Clinic; Washington, D.C., 168.

Wichita Gay Community Association, 148.

Wilde-Stein Club, Orono, Maine, 148, 604.

William Patterson College, 166, 606.

Williams College, 604.

Winnett Center California Tech, 600.

Wisconsin State Legislature, 317.

Woman's Division; Board of Global Ministries of the United Methodist Church, 118.

Women in Law Conference, 402.

Women of the Church Coalition, 418.

Women Strike for Peace, 417.

Women's Action Alliance: NYC, 20, 407, 434.

Women's Division of the Board of Globan Ministries: United Methodist Church, 404, 421.

Women's Educational Equality Act Publishing Center, Newton, Mass., 513.

Women's International League for Peace and Freedom, 405.

Women's Leadership Network Conference, 402.

Women's Ordination Conference, 125, 279, 330–331, 332, 340, 418, 535.

Women's Pentagon Action, 417.

Women's Resources Center UCLA, 600.

Women's Studies Program, 158.

Woodstock Seminary, 304.

WOR-TV, 192.

Workers World Party, 248, 397, 405.

World Congress of Gay and Lesbian Jewish Organizations, 373.

World Council of Churches, 155, 156, 273, 276, 286.

World Health Organization, 156.

World Peace Makers, 400, 417.

World Peace Tax Fund, 417.

WPFW, 452.

Xaverian Brothers, 39, 295, 341, 418, 419, 420.

Yale Divinity School, 305.

Yale University, 602.

York University, 611.

Youngstown State University, 608.

Young Adult Ministry Board: USCC, 326, 535.

Young Women's Christian Association, 157, 231, 409, 517, 535.

Zionist Union of Gays, NYC, 599.

GEOGRAPHICAL INDEX

Geographical Index

Buffalo, N.Y., 186, 338, 530, 591, 608.
Burlington, Vt., 339, 533, 610.
Burnaby, B.C., Canada, 611.

Calgary, Alta., Canada, 351, 593.
California, 23, 71, 148, 154, 159, 160, 161, 162, 166, 167, 173, 174, 176, 178, 181, 182, 185, 186, 210, 212, 219, 229, 230, 253, 271, 290, 298, 309, 316, 317, 323, 326, 327, 338, 339, 340, 343, 364, 374, 396, 406, 410, 418, 424, 447, 448, 449, 456, 457, 493, 498, 500, 502, 503, 507, 517, 526, 527, 531, 532, 533, 534, 553, 588–589, 594, 597, 598, 599, 600–601, 613–614, 615, 617, 619–620.
Cambridge, Mass., 279, 294, 345, 598, 604, 614.
Camden, N.J., 339, 533.
Campbell, Calif., 588.
Canada, 155, 173, 176, 177, 292, 305, 316, 338, 350, 351, 362, 401, 593, 599, 611–612, 616.
Canyon, Tex., 592.
Carbondale, Ill., 603.
Central America, 389, 413.
Champaign, Ill., 210.
Chantilly, Va., 619.
Chapel Hill, N.C., 210, 339, 531, 608, 620.
Charlestown, Mass., 351.
Charlottesville, Va., 610.
Cheyenne, Wy., 593.
Chicago, Ill., 51, 161, 168, 170, 186, 292, 294, 314, 317, 338, 339, 342, 345, 373, 397, 418, 493, 494, 517, 524, 525, 528, 531, 589, 597, 599, 602–603, 616, 617, 618, 620, 621.
Christopher Park, NYC, 41.
Cincinnati, Ohio, 161, 186, 418, 531, 592, 594, 597, 609.
Claremont, Calif., 600.
Cleveland, Ohio, 182, 186, 328, 338, 507, 592, 597, 615.
College Park, Md., 604.
Colorado, 116, 138, 147, 162, 168, 169, 184, 185, 186, 205, 210, 271, 317, 328, 338, 339, 435, 457, 499, 515, 527, 532, 533, 589, 594, 597, 599, 601, 614, 618.

Columbia, 154.
Columbia, Md., 339, 529, 531, 610.
Columbia, Mo., 590.
Columbus, Ohio, 186, 210, 591, 608.
Concord, N.J., 595.
Connecticut, 176, 185, 186, 192, 210, 271, 296, 314, 321, 338, 339, 500, 502, 510, 515, 526, 531, 589, 594, 595, 602.
Contra Costa, Calif., 406.
Costa Brava, Spain, 156.
Costa Rica, 154.
Coventry, U.K., 154.
Cuba, 288, 493.
Cumberland, R.I., 15–16.
Cupertino, Calif., 210.

Dade County, Fla., 5, 341, 499.
Dallas, Tex., 39, 161, 186, 592, 613, 615.
Dallas-Ft. Worth, Tex., 596.
Davis, Calif., 601.
Davos City, Calif., 98, 339, 531.
Dayton, Ohio, 348, 592.
De Kalb, Ill., 602.
Delaware, 186, 271, 602.
Denmark, 155.
Denver, Colo., 162, 168, 169, 184, 185, 186, 205, 315, 317, 328, 338, 339, 457, 499, 527, 533, 589, 597, 599, 601, 614, 618, 619.
Des Moines, Iowa, 338, 527.
Detroit, Mich., 18, 186, 190, 210, 308, 316, 326, 328, 337, 342, 397, 527, 528, 529, 535, 590, 605.
District of Columbia, 14, 16, 23, 89, 323, 325, 326, 327, 328, 330, 331, 338, 343, 344, 347, 348, 397, 398, 399, 400, 401, 404, 407, 411, 412, 416, 417, 420, 421, 429, 438, 449–454, 498, 502, 504, 505, 506, 507, 514, 515, 517, 589. (see also, Washington, D.C.)
Downsview, Ont. Canada, 611.
Dublin, Ireland, 154.
Dubuque, Iowa, 327.
Duluth, Minn., 316, 525.
Durham, N.H., 605, 608.

Easthampton, Mass., 604.
East Lansing, Mich., 210, 338, 339, 528, 532, 590, 605.

Geographical Index

Geographical Index

Palo Alto, Calif., 210
Paramus, N.J., 339, 533.
Paris, France, 598.
Pasadena, Calif., 600.
Pascoag, R.I., 337, 526.
Pawtucket, R.I., 592.
Pennsylvania, 148, 169, 176, 186,
  210, 253, 271, 286, 290, 291,
  316, 326, 327, 328, 338, 339,
  340, 343, 349, 358, 362, 413,
  502, 512, 530, 531, 534, 535,
  550, 552, 555, 556, 564, 592,
  596, 598, 609, 616, 618, 620.
Philadelphia, Pa., 148, 169, 176, 186,
  210, 286, 290, 316, 328, 343,
  349, 358, 362, 529, 550, 552,
  555, 556, 564, 592, 596, 598,
  610, 614, 616, 618, 620.
Philippines, 154.
Phoenix, Ariz., 314, 343, 397, 569,
  588.
Pima County, Ariz., 45.
Pittsburgh, Pa., 338, 339, 340, 502,
  530, 531, 534, 592, 609.
Poland, 154.
Portland, Me., 604.
Portland, Ore., 22, 176, 210, 592,
  609, 615, 617.
Portugal, 154.
Potomac, Md., 248.
Potsdam, N.Y., 607.
Poughkeepsie, N.Y., 607.
Princeton, N.J., 338, 606.
Princeton Junction, N.J., 591.
Providence, R.I., 338, 530, 610.
Provincetown, Mass., 617.
Pueblo, Colo., 339, 532.
Puerto Rico, 271, 610.
Pullman, Wash., 210, 611.

Quebec, Canada, (P.Q.), 177.
Queens, N.Y., 338. (see also, New
  York, City of)

Racine, Wis., 340, 533.
Raleigh, N.C., 591.
Randallstown, Md., 621.
Randwick, NSW, Australia, 598. (see
  also Australia)
Reno, Nev., 185.
Rhode Island, 15–16, 167, 271, 338,
  526, 530, 592, 610.
Richmond, Va., 23, 316, 317, 326,
  327, 338, 364, 532, 534, 593,
  596, 603, 611.

Riverside, Calif., 186, 588, 600.
Rochester, N.Y., 185, 326, 338, 341,
  499, 516, 532, 591, 596, 608,
  615.
Rohnert Park, Calif., 601.
Rome, Italy, 301, 343, 412.
Roseville, Calif., 594.
Roslyn, N.Y., 595.

Sacramento, Calif., 185, 326, 338,
  457, 526, 588, 601, 614, 617.
St. Augustine, Fla., 321.
St. John's Nfld., Canada, 593.
St. Louis, Mo., 161, 186, 323, 338,
  339, 340, 418, 420, 526, 532,
  534, 590, 597, 599, 605.
St. Patrick's Cathedral, NYC, 546.
St. Paul/Minneapolis, Minn., 186,
  316, 317, 326, 338, 532, 545.
San Antonio, Tex., 186, 593.
San Diego, Calif., 22, 161, 338, 418,
  500, 527, 588, 594, 597, 617,
  619.
San Francisco, Calif., 22, 23, 35, 37,
  39, 51, 52, 53–54, 80, 89, 111,
  120, 131, 148, 154, 159, 161,
  162, 166, 173, 174, 176, 182,
  185, 186, 210, 230, 298, 309,
  316, 317, 323, 326, 339, 343,
  374, 396, 406, 448, 449, 457,
  493, 500, 502, 503, 517, 525,
  531, 532, 533, 588, 597, 599,
  601, 613–614, 615, 617, 621.
San Jose, Calif., 290, 326, 613.
San Juan, P.R., 610.
San Mateo, Calif., 37.
Santa Ana, Calif., 588.
Santa Barbara, Calif., 210, 601.
Santa Clara, Calif., 406.
Santa Fe, N.M., 158.
Santa Monica, Calif., 493, 599.
Santa Monica Mountains, Calif.,
  57.
Sao Paulo, Brazil, 416.
Saskatoon, Sask., Canada, 612.
Scotland, 155.
Seattle, Wash., 39, 52, 169, 186, 293,
  316, 317, 319, 326, 364, 365,
  367, 396, 499, 528, 533, 535,
  593, 599, 611, 615.
Sheep Ranch, Calif., 338, 526.
Sheridan Square, NYC, 41. (see also
  New York, City of; Christopher
  Park, NYC)

Geographical Index

West Patterson, N.J., 339, 530.
Westport, Conn., 515.
West Virginia, 272, 338, 524, 525, 611.
White Plains, N.Y., 515.
Whitewater, Wis., 535.
Wichita, Kan., 148, 326, 526, 589.
Wilkes-Barre, Pa., 592.
Williamsburg, Va., 610.
Williamston, Mass., 604.
Willits, Calif., 97.
Winchester, Va., 610.
Windsor, Ont., Canada, 616.
Winnipeg, Mant., Canada, 338, 593, 594, 611.

Winooski, Vt., 595.
Winter Park, Fla., 418.
Wisconsin, 168, 186, 210, 227, 272, 316, 326, 338, 339, 340, 354, 364, 403, 526, 529, 530, 531, 532, 533, 535, 593, 597, 611, 621.
Woodside, N.Y., 591.
Worcester, Mass., 316, 328, 338, 527, 528.
Wyoming, 338, 272, 593.

Yellow Springs, Ohio, 609.
York, Va., 513.
Youngstown, Ohio, 608.

TOPICAL INDEX

Topical Index

Topical Index

Topical Index

Topical Index

marriage (heterosexual), 91, 116, 233, 256, 265, 266, 302, 303, 306–307, 369, 372, 538, 551, 572–573.
marriage (homosexual), see homosexual marriage.
Marxism, 120–122, 127, 147, 241.
masochism, see sadomasochism.
masturbation, 178–179, 232, 233, 302–303, 542, 556–563.
media, 152, 214, 216, 248.
medical textbooks, see school, textbooks.
Medical World News, 56.
Memorandum Opinion and Order, 24.
mental disorder, see homosexuality as an illness.
military, 14, 23–24, 159, 171, 173, 202, 211, 219, 396, 397, 399, 433.
minority rights, see civil rights; gay rights.
modernism, 300.
Moral Teaching of Paul, The, 253.
morality, see ethics.
moral theology, 21, 335.
motherhood, 81–82.

NAMBLA Bulletin, 177.
NAMBLA Journal, 177, 214.
NAMBLA News, 177.
National Catholic Reporter, 319, 326, 343, 349, 415, 505, 530.
National Convention Project, 190–191, 211, 438, 445, 447.
national defense, 290.
National Gay Task Force, 402.
National Gay Task Force's Newsletter, 247.
National Review, 242.
national security, 218, 219.
natural law, 232, 256, 266, 309, 347, 373, 539–543.
natural order, 172, 198, 199, 224.
Nebraska International Women's Year: see International Women's Year.
networking:
  at the grassroots level, 282–283, 287, 341–342, 404–405, 416, 419.
  national, 150–153.
  use of "front" groups, 151–152, 293.
  liberal organizations, 280–286, 398, 401–419, 434.

with religious organizations, 244, 270–298, 329–332, 334, 336–342, 352, 354, 365, 369, 404, 406–409, 415–419.
New Day, A, 21, 277, 284.
New England Journal of Medicine, 55.
New Left, 130, 319.
New Pioneers: A Program to Expand Sex-Role Expectation in Elementary and Secondary Education, 513.
New Right, 284.
New Testament, 256–258, 260, 303.
New Women New Church, 331.
New York City Gay Teachers Association, 234.
New York Nature, 37, 52, 304.
New York Post, 548.
New York Teacher, The, 163.
New York Times, 25, 26, 223, 249, 374, 414, 415, 546, 547.
New York Times Magazine, 97.
Newsweek, 345.
Nixon Administration, 501.
Non-Sexist Child Development Project, 20.
non-sexist education, see education, non-sexist.
Non-Sexist Education for Young Children, 20.
non-sexist language, see language, inclusive.
Notice of Proposed Rule Making, 24.
Notre Dame Magazine, 335.
novitiate, see Roman Catholic, novitiate.
Now the Volcano: An Anthology of Latin American Gay Literature, 44.
nuclear power, 396, 398, 420.
nuclear weapons, 290, 398, 399.

objective morality, 113–117, 131, 245–246, 302, 307, 314, 542.
objective order, 243, 543.
Old Testament, 253–256, 318, 370.
On Creation Questions Concerning Sexual Ethics, 302.
open marriage, 114, 116, 206.
ordination of lesbians, see homosexuals, ordination of.
ordination of women, 188, 330–332, 347, 508.
original sin, 177–178, 252, 303.
Out, 451.
Out of the Closet, 170.

Topical Index

Roman Catholic (*cont.*)
  prohomosexual organizations, 308, 325, 330–331, 353–369, 524–535.
  religious, 157, 166, 326–328, 337–341, 342–350, 352, 353, 358, 365, 416, 420, 444, 550–570, 579–587.
  support for the homosexual movement, 66–67, 232, 301, 318–324, 326–332, 337–342, 353–369, 524–535, 579–587.
  teachings, 301–307, 309–316, 333, 335–336, 354, 357, 359, 363, 365.
  theologians, 305, 318, 343–344, 526–535.
Roman Catholics, 423–427, 428, 455, 582, 583.
rough trade, 33.

sadomasochism, 33, 35, 56–57, 88–89, 140, 162, 173–176, 187, 370, 502, 503.
St. Louis Globe-Democrat, 323.
San Francisco, 182.
San Francisco Chronicle, 54.
San Francisco Chronicle/Examiner, 53–54.
school:
  counselors, 229–230, 235.
  curricula, see also homosexual studies, 163, 215, 228, 233.
  curriculum development, 202, 501.
  dances, 15–17, 410.
  libraries, 163–164, 230, 236.
  personnel, 162, 163, 229, 233, 620–621.
  prayer, 234, 398.
  teachers, 163, 513.
  textbooks, 19–20, 25, 164, 230, 234, 235, 414.
schools: see also education.
  colleges, 161–162, 164, 291–293, 354, 514.
  elementary, 19–20, 162, 163–164, 227–236, 314, 513, 514.
  law, 191, 517.
  private, 227–236.
  public, 162, 164, 227–236, 514, 518.
  religious, 211, 231, 314, 452.
  secondary, 15–16, 162, 163–164, 227–236, 314, 513, 514.
  universities, 161–162, 242, 354, 452, 502, 503, 504–505, 517.
scientific creationism, 231.

secular humanism, 20, 199, 201, 226, 230–231, 234, 241, 251.
seduction, see child, seduction.
seminarians, 211, 293–294.
seminaries, 211, 354, 505, 562.
Sentinel, The, 37, 52, 148, 159, 343.
sex:
  anal, 50–51, 178–179, 233.
  change operation, 510.
  criminals, 212.
  education, 19–20, 90, 129, 163, 199, 202, 215, 226, 227–236, 398, 513.
  man/boy, see pederasty.
  oral, 50–51, 56, 178–179, 233.
  roles, see gender assigned roles.
  teenage, 232, 453.
  therapy, 18.
"*Sex: Telling it Straight*," 20, 230.
sexism, 120, 125, 138, 202, 215, 229, 278, 398, 513.
Sexism in the Classroom, 513.
Sexual Celibate, The, 334, 556.
sexual identity, see gender identity.
sexual liberation, 174–175, 176, 177, 203, 205, 223, 265, 546.
Sexual Orientation Project, State of California, 448–449.
sexual practices, see also homosexual behavior, 50–56, 116.
sexual revolution, 174–175.
sexually transmitted disease, 37, 49–56, 153, 167–168.
sickness, see illness.
sin, 6, 91, 117, 118, 212, 243, 244, 245, 246, 249, 250, 251, 256–258, 278, 371, 373, 516, 559.
Single Young Adult Sexual Minorities, 308.
sissy, 64.
situation ethics, 245.
social issues, 384, 385, 387, 389, 390, 391, 393, 394, 398, 433.
Society and the Healthy Homosexual, 118.
Sociology and Social Research, 5.
Sodom, 254, 371.
sodomy, 539, 540, 542, 543.
sodomy laws, 202–203, 211, 219, 431–432, 453.
Stonewall riot, 124, 128, 147, 449, 457, 517, 545.
students:
  activity funds, 161, 470.
  college, 135, 161–162, 291–293, 507.